ROGER EMMERSON was born in Edinburgh and attended Leith Academy. He studied architecture under Sir Robert Matthew at the University of Edinburgh and under Professor Isi Metzstein at the Glasgow School of Art, graduating from there in 1982. He has worked in London, Newcastle upon Tyne and, mostly, Edinburgh, running his own practice, ARCHImedia, from 1987 to 1999 while concurrently teaching architectural design at Edinburgh College of Art when he was also visiting lecturer at universities in Venice, Lisbon, Stockholm, Copenhagen and Berkeley. Since 2000 he has worked extensively in the fields of architectural conservation, housing, education and the leisure industries throughout the UK, retiring from architectural practice, although not architecture, in 2016. He is married and lives in Edinburgh close to his four children, their partners and his seven grandchildren. He devotes his free time to writing, painting and playing guitar.

Land of Stone

A journey through modern architecture in Scotland

ROGER EMMERSON

Luath Press Limited
EDINBURGH
www.luath.co.uk

First published 2022
Reprinted 2024, 2025

ISBN 978-1-80425-016-7

The author's right to be identified as author of this book
under the Copyright, Designs and Patents Act 1988 has been asserted.

The paper used in this book is produced using sustainably sourced, natural and renewable material which is 100% recyclable and biodegradable and elementary chlorine free in its pulp and bleaching process.

Printed and bound by
Robertson Printers, Forfar

Typeset in 11 point Sabon LT Pro by
Main Point Books, Edinburgh

All photographs and images © Roger Emmerson unless otherwise stated.
Text © Roger Emmerson, 2022

This book is dedicated to Chris, for supporting with love and patience my several architectural obsessions over the years.

Contents

	Map	9
	Acknowledgements	11
	Foreword	13
	Introduction	15
1	Some regional theory and a little practice	29

Space and light; Terrain, Territory, Patrimony and Polity; the Foreign Gaze; Finnish regional practice, National Romanticism; Czechoslovakian regional practice, *narodní sloh*

2	An architecture of the age: 1753–1887	91

The architectural theories of Allison, Nicholson, Semper; Ruskin, Billings and Thomson; the philosophical theories of Burke, Kant and Hamilton; Artisan housing; the invention of the Baronial; the countervailing architectural works of Thomson and Gowans; Scotland in Union and Empire

3	Hope in honest error: 1887–1919	134

The regional architectural philosophies of MacGibbon and Ross; Berlage, Muthesius, Loos and Worringer; the global planning theory of Geddes; the adaptation of the Baronial; the architectural works of Mackintosh, Burnet, Wright and Hoffman; questions about Mackintosh; the Glasgow Exhibition 1901; Scotland in Union and Empire

4	News from nowhere: 1919–39	184

The regional architectural theories and practice of Wright; Le Corbusier, Gropius and Gray; Dutch Expressionist influence; the architectural works of Burnet, Shearer and Marwick; the legacy of the Baronial; the writings of Gregory Smith, MacDiarmid and Tonge; The Glasgow Empire Exhibition 1938; Scotland in the Union

5   Brave new world: 1939–68   240

Modernist texts in Scotland and England; the Town and Country Planning Act 1947; the Festival of Britain 1951; the Welfare State; the Parker Morris report; tentative Scottish regionalism; Modernism challenged by Collins, Norberg-Schulz and others; the significance of architectural photography; Scotland in the Union

6   A perfect storm: 1968–99   290

The Great Glasgow Storm; the Ronan Point disaster; the recovery of the tenement; post-Modern literary enquiry; the regional architectural philosophies of Bachelard, Derrida, Baudrillard, Harries and Heidegger; reflections on Fascism and regionalism; post-Modern architecture and planning; Frampton's Critical Regionalism; lessons from Japan; Scottish regionalism; the Museum of Scotland; Scotland in devolution and Europe

7   The second-sight: 1999–2022   345

The Scottish Parliament; the rise of Mannerist architecture; more lessons from Japan; regionalism as architectural resistance; Žižek and the continuity of Kant's theory; antinomies in Scottish architecture – wall and frame, montage and joint, the Atlantic edge; Scotland in devolution but out of Europe

Timeline	401
Glossary	410
Bibliography	416
Endnotes	432
Index	459

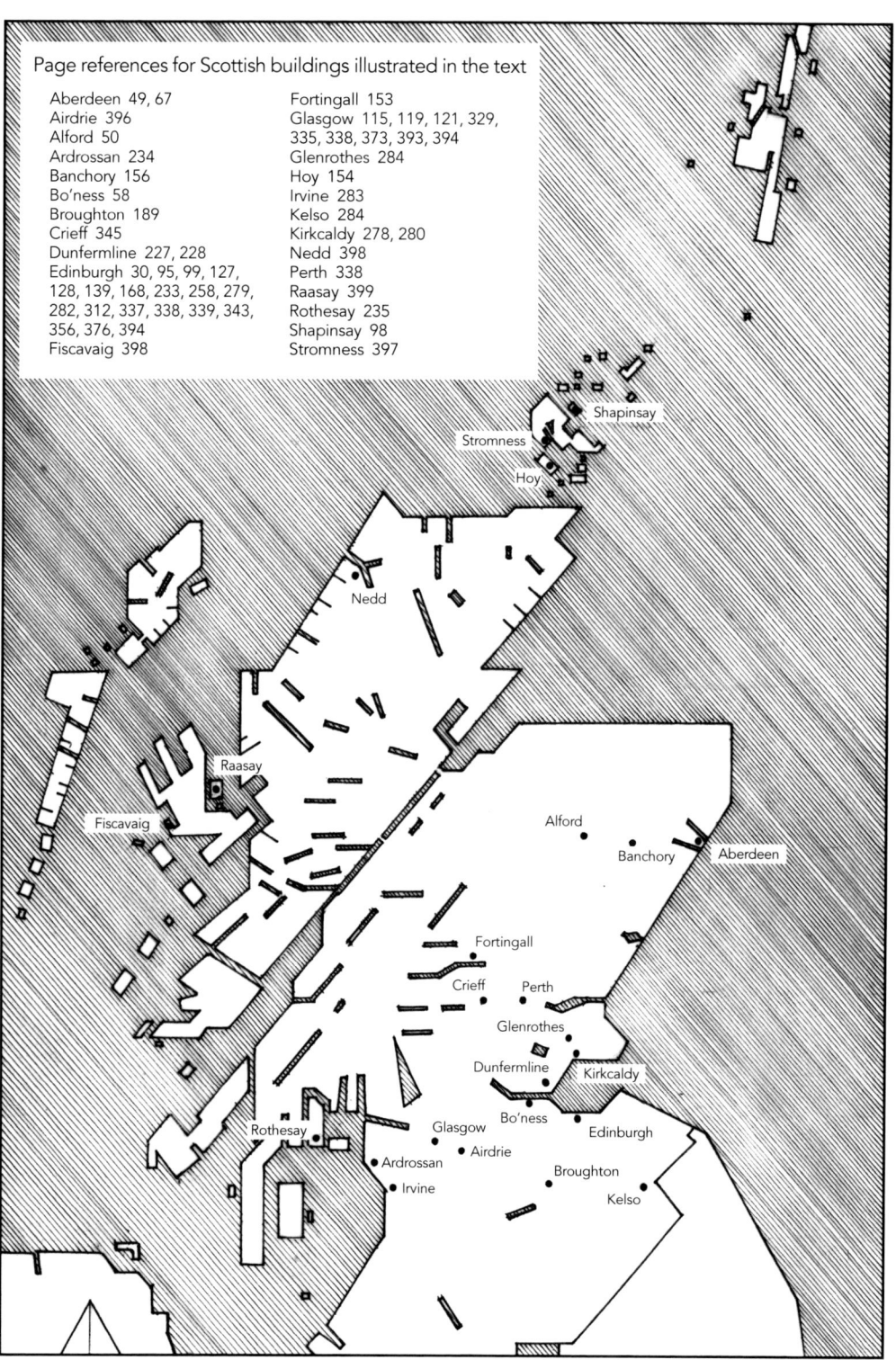

Page references for Scottish buildings illustrated in the text

Aberdeen 49, 67
Airdrie 396
Alford 50
Ardrossan 234
Banchory 156
Bo'ness 58
Broughton 189
Crieff 345
Dunfermline 227, 228
Edinburgh 30, 95, 99, 127, 128, 139, 168, 233, 258, 279, 282, 312, 337, 338, 339, 343, 356, 376, 394
Fiscavaig 398
Fortingall 153
Glasgow 115, 119, 121, 329, 335, 338, 373, 393, 394
Glenrothes 284
Hoy 154
Irvine 283
Kelso 284
Kirkcaldy 278, 280
Nedd 398
Perth 338
Raasay 399
Rothesay 235
Shapinsay 98
Stromness 397

Acknowledgements

THIS WORK WAS long in gestation and many friends, colleagues, teachers and correspondents have been inspirational and helpful along the way. My profound thanks go to John G Archer, Mary Arnold-Forster, Shweta Balasubramoni, Jude Barber, Andrew Brown, Ron Cameron, Ian Campbell, Giancarlo de Carlo, Alan Dickson, Chris Dobson, Gordon Ferrier, Kenneth Frampton, Derek Fraser, Neil Gillespie, Miles Glendinning, Mel Gooding, David Guggenheim, Nicola Hall, Bill Hare, Berty Hornung, Neil Jackson, Alan Johnson, John Kirton, Richard Kronick, David Kroyanker, Manuel da Costa Lobo, James Macaulay, Charles McKean, Kirsten Carter McKee, Laura Maginnis, Joe Masheck, Isi Metzstein, Roy Milne, Richard Murphy, Tom Normand, Marcus O'Hagan, Andrew Patrizio, Andrew Saint, Sari Schulman, Heather Isbell Schumacher, Radomíra Sedláková, Bill Scott, Štephan Šlachta, Peter Smithson, J Craig Stirling, Andy Summers, Timo Tuomi, David M Walker and Peter Wilson. Especial thanks are due to Roy Milne who read the draft texts and prompted me to achieve a better and clearer work. My thanks also to Gavin MacDougall's great publishing team at Luath Press for their kindness, care and professionalism in bringing this work to fruition – in particular to my editor Gwyneth Findlay who gave the work style and accessibility and to my book designer Jennie Renton who marshalled the disparate parts into coherence. Theirs was the inestimable help; mine are the opinions and unconscionable errors.

The title *Land of Stone* comes from Karel Čapek's *Letters from England* written in 1925, in which he eulogises Scotland. Čapek's modernity and the affection I hold for Czechia and Slovakia and the many friends I have made there render his words entirely apposite: 'And now to the north, to the north!... beyond the River Tweed is the land of stone'.

Foreword

THE BOOK YOU have in front of you starts with one of the great opening lines of any book on a Scottish topic. In 15 words you are gently introduced to Scotland as hybrid, ubiquitous, low-brow, high-brow, conflicted and thus deeply plural. The logic, as Roger Emmerson's *Land of Stone* suggests, is that Modernism is equally complex and kaleidoscopic. Note that the book's subtitle is 'A journey through modern architecture in Scotland'. I take this to imply a certain attention to the placed-ness of our understanding, that Scotland provides a particular position from which to look at modern architecture – including the buildings that have been built elsewhere as well as on Scottish ground.

Yet anyone who knows Scotland knows it as a curious place, nested within (and complicit with) constructions of Britishness and colonialism, a part of the United Kingdom (increasingly uneasily), and more comfortable with its historic associations with other parts of Europe and beyond. Where exactly does citizenship reside in such a nested model? Emmerson finds architectural and political inspiration in Finland and Czechoslovakia (now Czechia and Slovakia), in Sweden, Denmark, Latvia, Portugal, Israel and Switzerland. His writing is highly attuned to the seismic shifts in the geo-political landscape, particularly of Europe but also in those more hidden geographies of global transmission – of technologies, people and viruses – that affect our world deeply. What pre-existing architectural models are worth preserving; and what models of democracy too?

Seeking a region on the map where Modernism actually arises, in concrete not to say lithic terms, is another of Emmerson's tasks, and one undertaken lovingly, in acknowledgement of Modernism's presence and influence on him. The importance of Mackintosh is one example, whose austere internationalism, driven by private and interior appetites, is analogic to so many commentators and practitioners of this land, Emmerson included. He is interested not in style, appropriation and quotation but rather the ontologies of Scottish architecture. Thus he sits in the anti-aesthetic camp, against the superficially visual look of architecture, keen to draw out its more communal and philosophical 'pairts'. This is a life task, so inevitably there is reference to 'love', as a term understood to be set against certain forms of rationalism.

I see parallels to the American writer-farmer Wendell Berry who similarly conceived of love as a commitment to the particular, the placed and the tangible; collectively something that can 'turn us from this deserted future, back into the sphere of our being, the great dance that joins us to our home, to each other and to other creatures, to the dead and the unborn...' (Wendell Berry, 'Standing by Words', *The Hudson Review* 33 (4), 1980: 520).

Emmerson is loyal to ideas of place, regionalism, indigeneity and difference represented in architecture by the writings of Kenneth Frampton and others. He insists on the organic connection between contemporary ideas and the ground from which they emerge – and the forms they take in culture. The multiple modes of the modern and contemporary are echoed in the multiple identities of the Scot. There are few better placed to consider these issues as Roger Emmerson, who does so with a wry humour, acute poetics, first-hand experience and deep knowledge of the field. Welcome to a journey of remarkable buildings and remarkable thoughts about these buildings, shaped as they are by deep time, modern ideas and Scottish culture. Readers are sure to see new vistas in the land of stone open before them.

Professor Andrew Patrizio
Chair of Scottish Visual Culture, University of Edinburgh
October 2022

Introduction

EVERYONE FROM IMMANUEL KANT to the Broons[1] has something relevant to say about Scottish architecture. Karel Čapek, the Czech playwright who gave English the word 'robot',[2] called it 'stonily grey and strange of aspect'[3] while the celebrated American architect Louis I Kahn thought of it as 'fairy-tale'. The residents of Gosforth, Newcastle upon Tyne, England were certain it had sprouted in the midst of their English Free-style conservation area in 2006, referring to it as 'the Scottish flats'.[4] They were not to know I was the architect. While these individuals, real or fictional, living or dead, observed something special, even unique, in Scottish architecture, we should also be aware it shares many characteristics with other Western architectures. It is the specifics of place, culture and history which define the individual identity of a regional architecture within that larger context.

On occasion, I have been asked by friends, colleagues or students whether I thought my interest in Scottish architecture might be both limited and limiting. It set me to wondering whether a Japanese architect's interest in Japanese architecture is thought to be limited and limiting. Or an American architect's in American architecture. Or a Danish architect's in Danish architecture. Or

The 'Scottish flats': Elmfield Square, Gosforth, 2004–7, architect Roger Emmerson with Waring & Netts.

any architect in their native architecture. In fact, it's unlikely the question would ever be asked of them, as it imputes considerable disrespect for their cultures. So, why disrespect Scotland's?

My answer is, of course, always 'no'. But more than that, it has always seemed to me that the many nuances of a fuller answer are implicit in the question and need teasing out.

It's a truism that architecture is the art with which we are all obliged to engage, whether that engagement has conscious meaning or is simply the welcome or unwelcome framework of our lives. Ever since the 'granny-tops'[5], rattling and clanking in the wind to draw smoke up the tenemental flues from open coal fires, caught my attention as a three-year-old, architecture and its many parts, purposes, processes and procedures have fascinated me. For me, architecture has always had profound significance. Because we're in Scotland, of necessity, Scottish architecture has significance. It's the purpose of this book to demonstrate that significance and to answer the many-branched question of perceived limitations in architecture in general and Scottish architecture in particular in our modern age and whether they have substance.

To that end, *Land of Stone* examines the issues of Modernism, regionalism and cultural identity which have moulded Scottish architecture in the modern period, roughly since the date of the failed Jacobite Rebellion of 1745, through the contemporaneous ideas and practice of significant theorists and architects and the political context within which they worked. The contribution to that identity of ideas, significant at the time in Scottish philosophy, art and culture, although some are now largely disregarded, is highlighted and the conventional interpretation of the impact of ideas generated furth of Scotland is challenged. The importance of the home and its cultural, ritual and societal meanings and how it has fared over time is presented as a counterpoint to the more purely aesthetic and idealistic narrative of the development and clash of architectural styles. Ultimately, *Land of Stone* seeks to disengage widely-held conceptions of what a Scottish architecture superficially looks like and to focus on the ideas and events, philosophical, political, practical and personal, that inspired architects and their clients to create the cities, towns, villages and buildings we cherish today.

A beginning

One of the earliest commentaries on Scottish architecture was that made by the Anglo-Scot James Fergusson (1808–86) in his *History of Architecture* published in 1867:

> There are few countries in the world in respect to whose architecture it is so difficult to write anything like a connected narrative as it is regarding that of Scotland. The difficulty does not arise from the paucity of examples or their not having been sufficiently examined or edited, but from the circumstance of the art not being indigenous... All these foreign elements, imported into a country where a great mass of the people belonged to an art-hating race, tended to produce an entanglement of history very difficult to unravel. With leisure and space, however, it might be accomplished; and if properly completed, would form a singularly interesting illustration, not only of the ethnography of Scotland but of art in general.[6]

Fergusson questioned the presence of Scottishness, a consistent narrative and the Scots' appreciation of art, seeing only an 'entanglement'. These topics occur frequently later in the discussion of Scottish architecture and are central to this book. Paradoxically, as will become evident, it is that very 'entanglement' which is the key to the understanding of Scottishness, narrative and art appreciation. 'Leisure and space' have been brought to bear in this connection, although whether their products have quite the result anticipated by Fergusson is open to question.

Research for this book began while I was still a lecturer at the School of Architecture, Edinburgh College of Art, in the immediate aftermath of the Scottish Devolution Referendum of 1997. At the time it was felt that some stirrings in Scottish architecture in the 1990s might have matched the political moment. This stemmed from discussions in the 1980s between friends and colleagues centred on the presumed relevance of a contemporary reinterpretation of the distinctive forms of the 15th to 17th century Scottish tower and townhouses epitomised by a negative conclusion I drew in 1986 that

> the facility with which we reel off [the elements of traditional Scottish architecture] convinces us we know whereof we speak but, at root, our seeming inability to effect satisfactory transformations of these elements underlines our transitory interest and suggests that the cultural base for such a conceit as a Scottish architecture may no longer exist.[7]

This was a discussion which continued to lead so many astray in the early 1990s – me included:

> In 1991, Scottish brickmaker Charles Wemyss, after energetically trying to foster a 'Scottish' brick style by commissioning an innovative

The Wemyss Scottish Brick Houses, 1989, architect Roger Emmerson as ARCHImedia.

range of Mackintosh-like house types from Roger Emmerson (1990), ruefully concluded that there seemed no way of throwing off 'the old adages of utilitarian, incompatible and English'.[8]

Wemyss's problem was the appropriateness of the material; mine, at the time, the aesthetic.[9]

Research proceeded steadily throughout the late 1990s and early 2000s, incorporating visits to Finland and Czechoslovakia (subsequently to Czechia and Slovakia) and to Sweden, Denmark, Latvia, Portugal, Israel and Switzerland for comparison and contrast, until I was called back to full-time architectural practice. With the relative freedom of the non-teaching part of the year lost, this book foundered and spent the best part of two decades shuttling from one hard-drive and one cloud to another, adding occasional chapters along the way.

Prompts

The 20-year gap has proved to be a blessing, as what had seemed propitious in the 1990s turned out to be a false dawn; the appearance of the distinct formal characteristics of a national architecture more the result of post-Modernism's ransacking of the historical record for usable motives to cut-and-paste than from any deeper conviction or connection. Devolution and a limited amount of self-government is one thing; the widespread sense of nationhood quite another, and it takes much longer to cohere. Even now it is provisional, and the architecture one might link with such a national project equally provisional. Nevertheless, architectural production in Scotland blossomed at the hands of the many talented architects who either came to prominence or graduated in the few years either side of the millennium; hence it seemed relevant, in 2021, to examine that flowering.

The words of Joanna Frueh (1948–2020) establish the transgressive nature of much of the argumentation of this book:

> 'Love' and 'prophecy' are unacceptable academic and art world vocabulary... Intellectuals and artists reject love and prophecy because they depart from the rationalist thinking that is the cultural establishment's acceptable, respected and appropriate mode of communication and that is the basis of art historiography. To a large degree, art comes from and communicates in nonrationalistic ways, but the mechanisms of art historiography which function, too, in art criticism, inform artists' self-preservation: they know that a certain vocabulary and explanations are approved.[10]

The certainties of the Modern Movement as it metamorphosed into the International Style – providing the conventional 'true' answer to the question, 'what is architecture?' – was the single prescription of many of my tutors at the University of Edinburgh in the late 1960s and contrasted starkly with my enjoyment of much other architecture whose productions they deemed questionable. However, the contemporaneous breaking wave of post-Modern literary debate and practice rehabilitated much of what had been sidelined in their interpretation of Modernism and exposed as relevant the consideration of time, history and cultural difference in architectural discourse. It is important to make a distinction here. The arch-camp whimsy and 'strip-architecture' of much post-Modern architectural practice was of little interest, although the question 'what are the meanings of architecture?' seemed to be as needful and deserving of answer then as had been that of the question 'what is architecture?' previously.

Peter Collins (1920–81) identified early this absence of cultural meaning in the canonic Modernist writings of such as Siegfrid Giedion (1888–1968) and Henry-Russell Hitchcock (1903–87):

Yet works of the type just mentioned inevitably possess one inherent limitation in that they are concerned essentially with the evolution of forms, rather than with the changes in those ideals which produced them, and this tends to minimise one of the most important factors in architectural design, namely the motives which dictate the character of an architect's work.[11]

A generation later, Marshall Berman (1940–2013) observed of 20th-century architectural production and the consequent impact of and resistance to Modernist planning:

All this suggests that modernism contains its own inner contradictions and dialects; that forms of modernist thought and vision may congeal into dogmatic orthodoxies and become archaic; that other modes of modernism may be submerged for generations, without ever being superseded; and that the deepest social and psychic wounds of modernity may be repeatedly sealed, without ever being really healed.[12]

For the undergraduate in the dying days of the conventionally-accepted International Style, 1966 had particular significance with the publication of the Pelican reprint of Nikolaus Pevsner's (1902–83) *Pioneers of Modern Design* of 1936 and of Robert Venturi's (1925–2018) *Complexity and Contradiction* and their inclusion on our university reading lists. Pevsner was too deterministic, conventional and complacent for the 1960s, content that

for this reprint… I have corrected about a dozen small errors and added… a bibliography of new literature. This is all that seemed to me to be necessary.[13]

Nonetheless, I was pleased at his inclusion of a Scot, Charles Rennie Mackintosh (1867–1928). Venturi required a wealth of historical and theoretical knowledge well beyond the capacity of a first-year student to be readily understood, although it hinted that all was not well with Pevsner's notions.

Mackintosh was to reappear within two years in the seminal exhibition, *Charles Rennie Mackintosh*, held at the Royal Museum of Scotland for the Edinburgh International Festival, 1968. Today, in the aftermath of Mockintosh – everything from tea-towels to typefaces – it is difficult to convey the impact of the centenary exhibition, the first major display of the Mackintoshes' joint artistic endeavour since the Memorial Exhibition of 1933 (a smaller exhibition had been mounted by Thomas Howarth [1914–2000] at the 1953

Edinburgh International Festival to coincide with the recent publication of his magisterial Mackintosh biography). Here was a richness and an austerity, a universal meaning and a private language, a future and a past, a triumph and a tragedy, romanticism and rationalism, Scotland and the world that Pevsner only distantly observed because his view was retrospective and normative, having no recourse to the distinct Scottish tradition and philosophical stance that underpinned the Mackintoshes' work. Pevsner's identification of the part-Scottish parentage of Modernism remained a certainty for many, despite his equivocation. An immaculate conception sufficed for the true believer.

A context

At the outset I must record my indebtedness to Kenneth Frampton (b.1930) and his many writings, not only on regionalism, but more generally on architecture, tectonics and architects; to paraphrase FE Towndrow's (1897–1977) acknowledgement of WR Lethaby (1857–1931) on the flyleaf of *Architecture in the Balance:* 'Frampton, the teacher I never met'.[14] In acknowledgement, I also realise that little point is served by the gratuitous rehashing of Frampton's thoughts – although frequent reference is made to them – partly out of respect and partly because my objectives differ from his. Those objectives are: firstly, to trace the course of regionalist and nationalist architectural inclusion or exclusion from the Modernist canon; secondly, to establish a context for a regionalist or nationalist architecture in Modernism; thirdly, to determine the autonomy and relevance of a distinct Scottish architectural culture; fourthly, to ascertain whether regional or national architectural production is in step with political action in Scotland; and fifthly, to identify a contemporary regional or national production in Scotland as the product of fundamental *ideas* about Scotland and its culture and architecture, rather than as the superficial manifestations of *aesthetic* isolates.

My initial difficulty was how to retrieve Scottish culture generally and Scottish architecture particularly from footnote status in the history of a largely English reading of a 'British' cultural and architectural history, and to descend from the isolated peaks of architectural genius – Robert Adam (1728–92), Alexander Thomson (1817–75) and Charles Rennie Mackintosh – to the broad uplands of more general practice, and from 'Scottish castles' to more ordinary buildings. The historiography of Scottish architecture presented a legacy of histories of the typological, aristocratic, antiquarian or simply 'turbulent past' variety. None approached the matter of cultural difference between the nations of these Islands as a territorial and patrimonial consequence of the several distances from the metropolitan centre of a 'British' culture, preferring, perhaps, to understand it as a choice arising from a wilful perversity (see Chapter 1).

At the present time, the situation is changed somewhat for the better, although even so, in the Scottish architectural library, the rooms devoted to Adam, Mackintosh and the Baronial far exceed the narrow shelves allotted to the rest, Thomson included. However, the recent increase in depth and breadth of studies in Scottish architecture permits us to better reflect on its nature, purpose and meanings. This book attempts such a preliminary and ultimately provisional exploration. It is given a larger framework in this through the seismic developments in European politics since 1989; in global information technology post-1999; in world politics post-2001; in world economics post-2009; in the yet-to-concretise British constitutional arrangements post-2019; and in the economic and health fall-out from the Covid-19 pandemic and, at the time of writing, Russia's incursions into Ukraine. These provide 'like-but-not-like' comparisons with the last three periods of the resurgence of European national and regional cultures and nation formation in the 20th century in 1900–18, 1945–8 and 1989–91, when culture, ethnography, politics, economics and constitutional matters in the former great empires were likewise in turmoil.

Horsman and Marshall observed a world reconfigured by the substitution of the supranational for the international, the trading community for a ragbag of one-off trade agreements, the regional for the national, cultural community for geographic proximity, all of which required the discovery or recovery of anchoring precepts, consensual meaning and the defence of local or regional culture. While touching on violent conflict – Bosnia-Herzegovina still live at the time of their writing in 1994 – they noted:

> it is becoming increasingly obvious that the nation-state lacks the autonomous power it once wielded; as a consequence, 'nationalist' agitation in the 1990s [and beyond] is likely to develop a localist aspect that emphasises community over country, cultural and social ties over territory, the nation *tout court* over the specific qualities and advantages of the traditional nation-state and its physical borders.[15]

The issue for Scotland, as it is for all small nations, is participation in union which respects difference in traditions, practice and needs, which facilitates the free movement of people and goods, which taxes enterprise fairly and disburses benefits equitably, which embodies equal participation in union and permits unfiltered access to the wider world. The question for Scotland remains whether the United Kingdom is that union.

The right-wing Scottish-American historian Niall Ferguson (b. 1964) quoted Henry Kissinger (b. 1923), who, in 1973, presciently observed that

> '[t]he structure of the immediate post-war years [WWII]', was based on 'the paradox of growing mutual dependence and burgeoning national and regional identities'.[16]

The contentious nature of this topic since the Bosnian Conflict of 1992–5; the continuing fragility of the Good Friday Agreement between the United Kingdom, Northern Ireland and the Republic of Ireland of 1998, in particular the contesting demands of the Northern Ireland Protocol on the Brexit Agreement of 2019; the inexorable erosion of Palestinian status, occupancy, patrimony and territory in Israel; the Russian invasion of Ukraine and the suppression and transportation of minorities in Myanmar and China, to name but a few, leaves nationalism and its corollary supra-nationalism freighted with prejudice and fraught with misunderstanding. These events do not render nationalism wrong or unworkable in principle; in fact, it is only in the manner of its prosecution in the above cases that nationalism is not merely wrong but evil. Violence and illegality are consistently eschewed in Scotland's version of nationalism.

A caveat

I could do much worse than to quote London-born Michael Fry's (n.d.) concerns at contemporary weighted interpretations and validations of history and his resistance to them. Substituting 'architectural' for 'political' provides both context and caution:

> In the first instance I devoted myself to political history, and so set out against the tide of Whig or Anglo-British historiography, which claimed Scotland had no political history worth the name, as of Marxist or vulgar Marxist historiography, which claimed that such history would always be worthless unless it vindicated the experience of the working class, as of Nationalist historiography, which claimed that such historiography could only be of value if it supported the case for Scottish independence.[17]

Or to quote James Baldwin (1924–87), himself quoting the Afro-Caribbean writer Aimé Césaire (1913–2008):

> The famous inferiority complex one is pleased to observe as a characteristic of the colonised is no accident but something very definitely desired and deliberately inculcated by the coloniser.[18]

While this text was conceived as an act of cultural resistance, it is not a hatchet job on Modernism – others have attempted this and, as they deserve to, have failed[19] – for I am a child of Modernism and value its spirit of change, innovation, autonomy and originality. Rather it is an attempt to excavate, interrogate and celebrate truthfully by means of Frueh's 'love and prophecy' the regional architecture that many Modernist architectural writers omitted, obscured, obfuscated or buried as a problem, a distraction from an otherwise seamless narrative.

Means to an end

TABLE OF CONTENTS: the chapter sub-headings identify themes covered within each chapter.

CHAPTER 1: SOME THEORY AND A LITTLE PRACTICE seeks to establish some basic precepts for the understanding of regional architecture, to address some of the broader issues that surround it and to describe some of the attitudes that colour its appreciation. It employs the experiences of Czechoslovakia and Finland comparatively to understand how particular national architectures were derived, how they related to the national project and how that national project progressed at times of crisis and developed in Modernism.

CHAPTER 2: AN ARCHITECTURE FOR THE AGE discusses the significant international contributions of John Ruskin (1819–1900) and Gottfried Semper (1803–79) when the pressing question for architects and theorists was to find an architecture appropriate to an age when eclecticism and historicism was the norm. Notionally and simplistically, Ruskin may be considered as representative of Romanticism, Semper of Rationalism; the interrelationship of these two poles is one of the principal themes of this book. The future implications for architecture generally of Semper's astylar 'elements' are also considered. The writings of Scottish theorists Archibald Alison (1757–1839), Peter Nicholson (1765–1844) and Alexander Thomson himself on neo-Classicism are examined, as is Robert William Billings' (1813–74) research in what came to be known as Scottish Baronial. The rational/romantic work of Thomson and Sir James Gowans (1821–90) is compared and contrasted. This is set against the political and economic circumstances of Scotland's dichotomous situation in relation to Union and Empire.

INTRODUCTION

CHAPTER 3: HOPE IN HONEST ERROR examines late 20th century translations of seminal pre-Modernist texts by HP Berlage (1856–1934) and Adolf Loos (1870–1933) in respect both of their views generally on architecture and specifically on the vernacular. At home, MacGibbon and Ross's analytical and taxonomic work on largely the same models as selected previously by Billings together with the *Architects' Sketchbooks* are seen as a countervailing local phenomenon. Their continuity into work of Charles Rennie Mackintosh is discussed, as is Herman Muthesius's (1861–1927) promotion of Scottish domestic architecture in the early 1900s. Mackintosh's writings on architecture are considered in context. This chapter also interrogates Mackintosh's relationship with the Wiener Werkstätte and the circumstances of the pivotal moment of his architectural decline and whether he had any significance in the development of European Modernism. The matter of Expressionism in Scottish architecture, raised in passing by Pevsner at this juncture, is elaborated on. Patrick Geddes' (1854–1932) holistic conception of architecture and planning is covered. The lessening of Scotland's Imperial status, the increasing centralisation of British governance and the emergence of Socialist and Nationalist agitation forms a backdrop to the period.

CHAPTER 4: NEWS FROM NOWHERE relates the failure of the European and American Modernism of Le Corbusier (1887–1965), Walter Gropius (1883–1969), Mies van der Rohe (1886–1969), Frank Lloyd Wright (1867–1959) and others to establish a foothold in Britain in the 1920s and '30s and the persistence in Scotland of the pre-WWI stylistic models of the Beaux-Arts Baroque and the Baronial and its derivatives. The artistic and architectural theoretical commentary of the Scots George Gregory Smith (1865–1932), Hugh MacDiarmid (1892–1978) and John Tonge (n.d.) in recording the period in Scotland are compared to the canonic Modernist texts and practice. The philosophical concepts of Immanuel Kant (1724–1804) and, to a lesser degree, Wilhelm Worringer (1881–1965) are noted as significant influences on these Scottish writers. The importance of the *International Style* exhibition at the Museum of Modern Art in New York and Henry-Russell Hitchcock's (1903–87) writings are discussed. The thread of Pevsner's Expressionism is traced through the relevance to Scottish architecture of the architecture of the Netherlands and Germany, in particular the influence of Willem Marinus Dudok (1884–1974) and, to a lesser extent, Erich Mendelsohn (1887–1953) on James Shearer (1881–1962), Thomas Tait (1882–1954) and T Waller Marwick (1903–71), among others. By way of contrast, the persistence of the significance of the work of Billings, MacGibbon and Ross and the *Architects' Sketchbooks* is characterised, as Jacques Derrida (1930–2004) described it, as a 'system of reproduction' which guaranteed the continuity if not the authenticity of the Baronial forms. The period is framed by the consequences of WWI, the difficulties of the Depression and the increasing centralisation of British governance which are set against the tokenism of the appointment of a Secretary of State for Scotland and the saga of St Andrew's House (1913–39). The Glasgow Empire Exhibition 1938 constitutes the period's coda.

CHAPTER 5: BRAVE NEW WORLD is concerned with the brief and belated hegemony of International Style Modernism and its integration with and support of the British Welfare State. The significant public propaganda and policy blitz of the 1940s and '50s promoting Modern architecture is discussed together with the Festival of Britain, which was engineered by several of the more prominent proselytisers and pamphleteers. The consequence of statutory space standards and the claims of the Modernists are set against the experience of the public. A number of texts questioning orthodox Modernism by such as those by Peter Collins (1920–81) and Christian Norberg-Schulz (1926–2000) are used to frame conceptions of architectural regionalism which are further expanded on in a review of a tentative regionalism evident in Scotland at the time. The importance photography in the promulgation of the International Style is considered.

CHAPTER 6: THE GREAT STORM charts the several factors that brought about the demise of doctrinaire Modernism – the post-Modernist literary/critical upheaval, the loosening of cultural orthodoxies, the manifest technical and place-making failings of Modernist buildings and the impact of the computer. Significant texts by Kenneth Frampton, Charles Jencks (1939–2019), Bruno Zevi (1918–2000) and others are reviewed as reflections of the wider turmoil of the period. In Scotland, the emergency of the Great Glasgow Storm of 1968, which seriously damaged over 5,000 tenements, impelled a re-evaluation of the Scottish tenement as a viable and appropriate container of a vibrant urban life. The significance of the Museum of Scotland, Edinburgh, 1991, by Benson + Forsyth is considered from an architectural, regional and political standpoint in the lead up to and creation of the devolved Scottish Parliament in 1997 which began to redress some of the political, economic and identity deficits of the 20th century.

CHAPTER 7: THE SECOND-SIGHT draws together the several themes of Modernism, regionalism and Scotland and develops the philosophical reasoning behind the theoretical conclusions already reached. Continuity from Kant to Smith and beyond is encapsulated and perpetuated in the work of Slavoj Žižek (b. 1949). World-city developments and the supporting architecture and infrastructure are questioned and contrasted with Scottish practice. The significance of the Scottish Parliament, Edinburgh, 1991, by EMBT and RMJM is considered both politically and architecturally. Regret is expressed for the few home-grown attempts at an architecture of empty semiology. The issue of an uncontested official history of Scottish architecture is raised and questioned. Practising architects in Scotland are queried as to the issues of Modernism, regionalism and Scotland. Current work is described and illustrated under three identifiable regionalist constructs derived from the themes previously established under the headings of 'Wall and frame', 'Montage and Joint' and 'The Atlantic Edge'.

Underpinning the text throughout is a search for a specifically Scottish spectrum of ideas, *not* aesthetics, which gives meaning to Scottish architectural production and that might be construed as its inherent Scottishness; perhaps standing in for Fergusson's 'ethnography of art'.

Practicalities

Some clarifications are required in respect to language, emphasis and punctuation. Significantly gendered or racial or otherwise prejudicial, pejorative or *ad hominem* opinions within quotes, acceptable to certain sections of society at the time they were made but not so now nor to me, are retained uncensored but followed by [sic], as are mis-spellings or questionable syntax. The term 'patrimony' is used throughout – despite its unfortunate gendering ('matrimony' is no great help as an alternative) – to encapsulate matters of history, heredity, heritage and tradition, especially where their meanings have been vitiated by over or casual use in the culture and leisure industries, news media and advertising. It also extends to accommodate the products of other activities and their recording not usually included in Modernist historiography, such as women's histories, film, regional culture or song. In particular, it examines where 'heritage signifies the politicisation of culture and the mobilisation of cultural forms for ideological ends'.[20]

Japanese and Hungarian practice in the writing of personal names is preferred, placing family name first and given name last. An attempt is made to avoid essentialisms such as 'working class' or 'upper class', but in dealing with Marxist texts this is virtually impossible. There is no easy answer here when dealing with generalities. Also not easy to define are the multiple and shifting identities and allegiances of the inhabitants of the United Kingdom (England, Northern Ireland, Scotland and Wales). The terms 'Britain', 'Briton' and 'British' are used to identify aspects of its hegemonic cultural and political life. 'Britain' is understood as a loose demographic and collective construct that fails to cohere in the minds and experiences of many of its citizens into an identifiable nation-state while, nonetheless, claiming for itself nation-state hegemony, 'national' values of fair-play and tolerance – despite much evidence to the contrary – and a distant and alien 'heartland'.[21] A 'Briton' is simply a native – either English, Northern Irish, Scottish or Welsh – of that construct who accedes to its authority, although each perceives of their 'Britishness' through the filter of those separate identities to a greater or lesser degree. Being a 'Briton', for some, is but a remote possibility. 'British' is both the collective noun for 'Britons' and the adjectival form of 'Britain', which is largely quantitative and hierarchical in its meaning and by which it extends its self-acquired cultural and political hegemony to appropriate or to unilaterally assign relative value and significance to regional production. Matters of quality are seen generally to reside in the descriptors English, Northern Irish, Scottish or Welsh, each of which carries different weight depending on context and in relation to the other three nations or the whole. These usages should be evident in the text.

Parts of this text were previously published in the journals *292: Essays in Visual Culture, ARCA, Architectural Heritage, Architecture Today, The Book of the Old Edinburgh Club, Building Design, diVersa, Prospect, Reading and Design of the Physical Environment, RIAS Quarterly* and *The Scotsman* and on the *INTBAU* website.

> Roger Emmerson
> Edinburgh
> October 2022

1

Some regional theory and a little practice

Space exploration: what architects talk about

ARCHITECTS, WHEN ENCOURAGED to talk about their craft, might speak about 'space' and 'light'. For architects, 'space' is mostly internal or the relationship between buildings and the landscape, whereas the wider external 'space' is the concern of the urban designer or, sometimes, the architect. In Modernism, 'space' is non-cellular, fluid and aesthetic. It does not form conventional 'rooms', but rather constitutes and links volumes within or between buildings. It is considered aesthetic in itself whereas its framing and orienting surfaces – walls, colonnades, balconies, canopies, ceilings, floors, pavements or parkland – are not necessarily so, although their careful placing enhances 'space'. 'Space' permits differing viewpoints and, through the agency of balconies, mezzanines, stairs, ramps, changes in level and judiciously placed openings, creates 'intervisibility' between those different volumes. Such openings also provide consciously directed natural 'light' which enlivens 'space' and paradoxically substantiates and models it by means of light and shade. Light favours reflective surfaces which might explain architects' preference for white or grey and their frequent hesitancy with colour not intrinsic to the material. 'Space' also entails the relationships of solid and void, thick and thin and heavy and light. In this context, the Main Hall of the Royal Museum of Scotland, Chambers Street, Edinburgh, 1858–61, by Captain Francis Fowke (1823–65), abetted by a 'new' engineering structure, is a 'space', while the nave of St Mary's Episcopal Cathedral, Edinburgh, 1871–2, by Sir George Gilbert Scott (1811–78) is not.

In doctrinaire Modernism, such aesthetic space, shorn of all regional or local cultural information, was deemed autonomously to create 'place'; 'place' being that distinct location where we are at one with ourselves and the world,

Above:
Mass and containment: Nave, St Mary's Episcopal Cathedral, Edinburgh, 1871–2, architect George Gilbert Scott.
(Cornell University)

Left:
Space and light: Main Hall, Royal Scottish Museum, 1864, architect Captain Francis Fowke.

however briefly. Meaningful and aesthetically-pleasing Modernist place occurred infrequently in practice, which suggests that it was wholly dependent on the occasional exercise of rare artistry or that, more often, regional or local cultural information was omitted to its detriment. The availability of 'space' was also paradoxically challenged in doctrinaire Modernism with its substantial reduction to the point that 'place-making' ceased to be possible. While, in due course, I shall discuss in detail such architectural space – and its discontents – my interest for now is an investigation of the properties entailed in the antecedents of place in the region, the haptic responses that transform space to place for us, the measure of the function of place in autonomous culture, the consequent problems with and comparative perceptions of an autonomous Scottish culture and the impact of these issues on Scottish architecture.

Terrain, territory, patrimony, polity: how anywhere becomes somewhere

In the wider context of regional cultures, place is determined by the quartet of terrain, territory, patrimony, polity and their interaction. Terrain is the pre-existent geology, topography, flora, fauna and climate of a defined location on the map of the world. Territory is that part of the terrain over which humankind establishes a domain and claims ownership or stewardship of it, defines the hegemony of the Known and demarcates the edge of the Other. Patrimony actualises, celebrates and perpetuates the Known and characterises, demonises or ignores the Other. To stop, to build a fire pit and rest for the night before moving on the next day, is to delineate territory within the terrain. To return to the fire pit later for the same purpose or to recall it in song or story is to establish patrimony. The boundary between the Known and the Other is where firelight fades and shadows gather.

Polity imposes and regulates that boundary and legitimises territorial extent and defends patrimony.

Topographically and historically, where and how territory is delineated is frequently obvious: a river, a mountain range, a vegetal change, the territorial edge of the Other or, less obviously, the location of a mineral resource or place made sacred in patrimony. While the occupation, demarcation and use of territory for shelter, feeding and breeding is a universal characteristic of the animal kingdom and some animals mark territory and create dwellings of a considerable degree of permanence, sophistication and habitat modification – we refer imprecisely to animal instinct – only the human, as far as we can tell, endows known territory with patrimony. Patrimony is construed as a present lived and a future predicated on the remembrance, celebration and inspiration of the continuity of use and myth of the territory in customary, oral, musical, dance and physical form, whether in nomadic or settled societies. Territory and patrimony modify each other.

Territory is anywhere between a galactic empire and a cosy corner:

> Erasmus, his biographer tells us, was long in finding the nook in his little house in which he could put *his little body* [Bachelard's emphasis] with safety.[1]

wrote Gaston Bachelard (1884–1962). The provision of security is one of the principal requirements of patrimony and polity in territory. Chadwick described

> a world shaped by terms like diffusion, transnationalism, globalisation, hybridity, diaspora, displacement and nomadism... [which] is also a world in which intimate and confessional expressions of sexuality and desire often function geo-politically within broader social constructions of aesthetics, power and sexuality.[2]

Chadwick's territories are both political and personal, especially personal, and require a patrimony of respect, tolerance and understanding.

Today, the determinants of territory and patrimony may be seen as resistance to the negatives of globalism, because what purpose does the polity of the nation-state serve other than to preserve territory and patrimony, their meanings and significance in culture, custom and identity, in the face of existential threat? Moffat and Riach asserted that

> the arts… [are] pre-eminent. Economic, political and social questions need to be asked and answered but without the cultural argument, they are merely the mechanics.[3]

Polity does not necessarily arise 'naturally' but may be enforced on territory and patrimony through the consequences of monarchical or governmental intervention such as the encouragement of the Scottish Protestant settlement of the so-called Plantation of Ulster, then Catholic, in the time of James VI and I, thus, to tip the political, religious and cultural balance in the population and administration of Ireland. Of such imposition the Slovenian Slavoj Žižek commented:

> In a nice case of what Hegel called 'reflexive determination', what Western Europeans observe and condescendingly deplore in the Balkans is what they themselves introduced there: what they fight in the Balkans is their own historical legacy run amok.[4]

Aboriginal territory may be occupied and claimed and its patrimony abrogated through renaming. Owens commented on Lothar Baumgarten's (1944–2018) recovery of the original indigenous place-names of South America from their later Spanish substitutions:

> [Columbus's] is a visual conception of language in which 'words are, and are only, the images of things.' And the New World is simply a series of sites/sights to be named. Not only the new world, but also its inhabitants, were subjected to this visual reductionism… [Columbus] was unable to recognise the Indians [sic] as sign producers. It is not simply that Columbus was *uninterested* [Owens' emphasis] in communicating with the Indians, as Todorov suggests. How could he possibly have communicated with them when, by regarding them primarily as sights, he had already rendered them mute?[5]

He continued:

Thus Foucault and Marin investigate representation not simply as a manifestation or expression of power, but as an integral part of social processes of differentiation, exclusion, incorporation and rule.[6]

The coloniser renames places solely as topographic features of the terrain, which the aborigine previously signified as a record of events and individuals in the narrative of patrimony. In such cases, residual autochthonous patrimony becomes an act of resistance to colonial hegemony whether personal, in dress, in speech, although sumptuary and language laws have effect here too,[7] or more collectively in political or cultural action or in the later recovery of names and implicated legend.

The Known and the Other: belonging or not belonging

Scotland's political boundary with England, established at the Treaty of York, 1237, is the second oldest in Europe,[8] with or without the inclusion of Berwick on Tweed on 13 separate occasions. Arguably its origins are 490 million years older, dating from the collision of the Laurentian plate, incorporating Scotland, with the Avalonian plate, incorporating England; the Southern Uplands being the geologic consequence and obvious topographical origin for the legal boundary. Exceptionally, the national boundary is a wall. Herewith, at random, are eight examples, four in Britain alone: Hadrian's Wall, 122; Antonine's Wall, 142; Offa's Dyke, 757; the Northern Irish 'Peace Lines', 1969; the Limes Germanicus, 83; the Great Wall of China, ca. 650BCE onwards; the Israel-Gaza Strip Barrier, 1994; and the Mexican Border Wall, 2017. While intended to keep the Other out, walls frequently and contrarily trap the Known within, consigning the contained, on the one hand, to morbid introspection or, on the other hand, to an unhealthy fascination with the Other. Anyone who travelled to or between the two Berlins between 1961 and 1989 can attest to this. Scotland, although it was not Scotland then, was accorded beyond-the-pale Other status twice in a generation and the walling-up of the Scots is a useful negative trope for those so inclined:

> It's time Hadrian's wall was refortified
> To pen them [the Scots] in a ghetto on the other side[9]

Today's 'wall' is Deyan Sudjic's (b. 1952) departure gate in an international airport where the 'airport [is] a city square'[10] or Victor Burgin's (b. 1941) firewall in a world where

Today's national borders are largely inconvenient to world capitalism – they have long been routinely ignored by transnational corporations and by a money market become a global computer network, operating at the speed of light. As weak and emergent nations struggle to maintain their faltering identities by drawing their borders more tightly round them, stronger established nations are losing the political will to effectively police their uncertain limits.[11]

Territory as place, time and knowledge: the messages implicit in territory

While the human concepts of terrain, territory, patrimony and polity may be universal, the qualitative understanding and experience of them is not universally the same. For example, for the Australian First People, the terrain – the very trees and rocks and the rock drawings they make thereon – are, in myth and fact, their ancestors, the forms they themselves will become in time. Territory and patrimony are one and the same thing stretching into both past and future wherein time, respect for the ancestors and respect for the environment are interdependent. They constitute an ethos, custom and presence. The First People present themselves in time as looking forward into the past, much as does the James Webb telescope, and backward into the future, since history is open to view and the future closed. Such concepts are further estranged from us in that the First People locate objects and themselves in the terrain, not in the personally-oriented directions of left or right or back or front, but territorially in terms of the cardinal points of a conjectural compass. This understanding of an integrated territory and patrimony is of an unmediated richness, complexity and integration profoundly at odds with the Western Apollonian thinking that John Berger (1926–2017) questioned:

> Many different things can fill the foreground with meaning: personal memories; practical worries about survival – the fate of a crop, the state of a water supply; the hopes, fears, prides, hatreds engendered by property rights; the traces of recent events and crimes... All these, however, occur against a common constant background which I call landscape's address, consisting of the way a landscape's 'character' determines the imagination of those born there.
>
> The address of many jungles is fertile, polytheistic, mortal. The address of deserts is unilinear and severe. The address of western Ireland or Scotland is tidal, recurring, ghost-filled. (This is why it

makes sense to talk of a Celtic landscape.) The address of the Spanish interior is timeless, indifferent, and galactic.[12]

In discussing the opening of Yosemite National Park, California, 1890, Simon Schama (b. 1945) was precise about Western mediation in territory and the purpose of its incorporation in patrimony:

> Nor could the wilderness venerate itself. It needed hallowing visitations from New England preachers like Thomas Starr King, photographers like Leander Weed, Eadwaerd Muybridge and Carleton Watkins, painters in oils like Bierstadt and Thomas Moran, and painters in prose like John Muir to represent it as the holy park of the West; the site of a new birth; a redemption for the national agony [the Civil War 1861–5]; an American re-creation.[13]

Such solitary veneration distances the rest of humankind from nature. Today, it is rare that art mediates landscape for our appreciation of it in quite the same remote and precious way. In drawing our attention to 'wilderness' territory, whether in the detail of Andy Goldsworthy (b.1956) or the civil engineering of Robert Smithson (1938–73), the immediate territory itself is physically altered in the wresting of 'place' from infinite space in the creation of patrimony.

Meanwhile, the wider terrain is threatened by extreme engineering technology which circumvents the otherwise irreconcilable demands of human occupation and those of virgin, marginal or hostile territories while attempting to defray, ever more briefly, the negative environmental, patrimonial and territorial consequences of such intervention. Even so, ancient habitation did not have a simple, symbiotic and Edenic relationship with territory from the time of the earliest cities of the Fertile Crescent and their introduction of the technology which Chant recorded[14] or which Schama questioned:

> Perhaps, say the most severe critics, the entire history of settled (rather than nomadic) society, from the irrigation-mad Chinese to the irrigation-mad Sumerians, is contaminated by the brutal manipulation of nature.[15]

There is no return to an Edenic state of humankind in nature, were it ever so following the mastery of fire; the First People possess that knowledge and use it to control and cultivate the bush. Likewise, recent discoveries in the Amazon basin – in what had been presumed to be virgin rain forest of paleo-biological origin – brought to light by the very resource rapacity objected to by Patrick Geddes, have revealed patterns of prehistoric settlement and arboreal cultivation contributory to the growth and present form of that 'virgin' forest.

The ancient Middle-eastern and historic European models based on the farming or resource community, the city-state, the principality or the nation-state guide my interpretation of territory and patrimony. Geddes' valley section of 1909 is the summation of that model. Welter (n.d.) noted that:

> Geddes's choice of words – nature determines and man reacts – expresses the primary role of nature in the process of 'mutual adaptation… of region and race [sic]'.[16]

Geddes' tacit acceptance of Western understanding of territory as a resource had him concerned with how those resources were to be extracted sparingly, shared equitably and used responsibly so that he can

> get away from the popular social Darwinist notion of society as a permanent struggle for existence, instead foregrounding co-operation as more important for the evolution of all forms of life.[17]

Pierre Francastel (1900–70), in a similar vein, cautioned:

> Man, Nature, and History can only be understood and examined not as essences but as realities within a network of constantly changing relationships. The tendency to consider Art, Nature, Technology, or Man as simple data stems from creation metaphysics, or Bossuetian or Enlightenment philosophy.[18]

Memory loss and knowledge transfer: what remains, is lost from or is gained by patrimony

Historic regional architectures whose origins predate the industrial revolution and which have conventionally been thought of as rejecting it include those that inspired AWN Pugin (1812–52) or that framed John Ruskin's understanding of patrimony:

> It is as the centralisation and protectress of this sacred influence, that

Architecture is to be regarded by us with the most serious thought. We may live without her [sic], and worship without her, but we cannot remember without her. How cold is all history, how lifeless all imagery, compared to that which the living nation writes, and the uncorrupted marble bears![19]

It is the case that, albeit drained of the demands of territory, patrimony, history and aesthetics, a similar 'timelessness' was also a Modernist concern. In this connection it could be argued that the 'third world' second generation recipients of Modernist theory and practice – the nations of South America, the tropical Commonwealth, the Middle East and India – worked more effectively in the accommodation of a reductive Modernism and its spatial concerns with their patrimony. They achieved this, particularly in housing, through the incorporation of culturally appropriate or necessary, socially useful and aesthetically pleasing forms such as balconies, pergolas, brise soliels, *mashrabiyyahs*, *chajjas*, *jalis*, *engawas* and verandahs – the 'boundary layer' – to ameliorate climate, facilitate social interaction and create semi-public space. Second generation 'first-world' Modernist adopters such as Britain did not value the societal benefits of such semi-private spaces and relied on idealistically-derived and naively-predicated behaviours of the intended occupants, the efficacy of contemporary technology and the presumed usefulness of shared public space where, as Berger identified the paradox:

Those who live precariously and are habitually crowded together develop a phobia about open spaces which transforms their frustrating lack of space and privacy into something reassuring.[20]

Proponents of Modernism criticised regionalism as being in permanent stasis in that they claimed regionalism employed, in intent, forms and materials, those of history. It is beyond question that the use of local materials, consequent on terrain, territory and patrimony, according to the then Prince of Wales, had not been possible or, frankly, at issue in Britain since an effective rail network facilitated the widespread distribution throughout the country of brick, corrugated iron from the 1820s and Welsh slate from 1831. The corrugated iron barn and the Welsh slate-roofed farmhouse are as much part of, say, Scottish rural patrimony as their stone and thatched predecessors. Robert Naismith (1916–2004) regarded the use of corrugated iron as an 'established tradition', noting that

crofters have raised corrugated iron to a point of respectability

When non-native materials become indigenous: corrugated iron in the Highlands.

but only after it has rusted... its rich rusty red on ageing is not an inappropriate colour for those northern parts of Scotland where it seems to have settled.[21]

Likewise, form was transplanted. Maudlin recorded:

The neat and regular farmhouses, cottages and planned villages... that transformed the [Scottish Highlands]... through the long 18th century[22]

which replaced the earlier clachans and 'blackhouses'. Likewise, the Chinese 'shophouse', the *tong lau*,[23] was widespread in south-east Asia, Malaysia in particular, brought from its distant origins by Chinese traders in the 19th century. Recent shophouse demolitions in Kuala Lumpur to make way for world-city developments were seen as a threat to a *Malaysian* patrimony.[24]

In Modern regionalist work, Frank Lloyd Wright, Alvar Aalto (1898–1976), Brian Mackay-Lyons (b. 1954), Glenn Murcutt (b. 1936), Peter Zumthor (b. 1943), John (b. 1947) and Patricia (b. 1950) Patkau and others, made connections to territory and patrimony through non-indigenous materials and form in the sympathetic *intent* and *manner* of their use and in the *planning* of the structure rather than through the historic authority of original form and construction. Fromonet noted that

> Murcutt, who began in the 1980s to document the structures of the Aborigines, believes that any resemblance between the form of their bark huts and his own buildings is explained by a similar sensibility to the same territory, not by the deliberate imitation on his part.[25]

In this context, Bell and Rand proposed that

> materiality has now become an instrumental methodology for a clear and bold design statement... [questioning only] [h]ow are materials expressed in a building – are they surface or structural, modern or vernacular? What kind of materials are appropriate?[26]

Meanwhile, Borden believed:

> The matter that we start with now has a sophistication that can no longer be understood by a single designer or craftsman across all material types and requires a new sophisticated synthesis of specific craftsmen with manufacturer with designer.[27]

The implication here for architectural regionalism is that the recovery of relevant territorial and patrimonial determinants are not those physically prescribed by familiar exemplars of form, material and construction from historic time and place, because such resources are exhausted physically, practically and intellectually, but are more usefully the underlying psychic and haptic responses to terrain that brought their use into being in the first place.

The exclusions of patrimony: untold histories, neglected patrimonies

Patrimony is conventionally the stuff of Ordnance Survey maps, official histories, the *Dictionary of National Biography*, Hansard, the Official Report of the Scottish Parliament, obituaries, *Debrett's Peerage*, the National Census, established religion, legal contracts, tombstones, commemorative statuary, the Register of Sasines, law, some gallery art, most architecture and so on. It forms the customary practices, language and manners of a managerial and executive establishment and the precepts, protocols and administration of the unwritten British constitution. Present patrimony was codified by the members of that coterie which conceded the qualified imperfection such that

> we should not delude ourselves into thinking that our historical narratives, as commonly constructed, are anything more than retrofits.[28]

Nonetheless, they undertook that 'retrofit' from what they privately believed, and which, in that retrofit, they construed and confirmed to be the winners' podium. In particular, they wrote out from history even those who had brief contemporary significance but whose personal history, gender or ethnicity disturbed the meta-narrative in which its writers had a vested interest. For example, beyond the handful of female painters which the general thrust of art history has chosen popularly to remember where, perhaps, their biographies meshed with an establishment narrative of helpmeet, muse, victim or survivor, such as Artemisia Gentileschi (1593–1656), Sonia Delaunay (1885–1979), Georgia O'Keefe (1887–1986) or Frida Kahlo (1907–54), there were the very many Fede Galizias (1574–1630), Harriet Powers (1837–1910) or Evelyn Dunbars (1906–60) whose biographies did not and were sidelined.

In a subtly different take on patrimony, Chadwick, writing about Tracy Emin (b. 1963) – who has certainly represented in her work several categories of the pejorative characterisation of the challenging female – observed that

> Emin's 'perfect places' map geographies of intimacy and impersonality, confessional autobiography and social commentary, rootedness and dislocation, trauma and renewal, popular culture, craft and high art through images and artefacts. Her artistic practice… utilises a range of media that have often been historically gendered, including diaries, letters, needlework, family photos and personal objects. These practices draw attention to the ways that personal expressions are mediated rather than transparent, and individual voices reference both the body and the body politic.[29]

Parallax: understanding the inherent dialogue, not dialectic, of Scottish culture

Patrimony is not solely present in its physical representations. How the nation construes patrimony in ideation is as significant a marker of national identity as are architecture and art. TS Eliot (1888–1956), the Anglo-American poet and critic, claimed there was no value in Scottish literature. He believed it lacked coherence and the rootedness of a single literary language, in that its content and treatment varied dramatically across each work. In a rebuttal that might stand for Scottish culture generally, architecture most assuredly, George Gregory Smith challenged Eliot thus:

> The antithesis need not, however, disconcert us. Perhaps in the very combination of opposites – what either of the two Sir Thomases, of Norwich and Cromarty, might have been willing to call 'the Caledonian antisyzygy' – we have a reflection of the contrasts which the Scot shows at every turn, in his [sic] political and ecclesiastical history, in his polemical restlessness, in his adaptability, which is another way of saying that he has made allowance for new conditions, in his practical judgement, which is the admission that two sides of the matter have been considered.[30]

Smith employed the neologism 'antisyzygy' to denote that the 'combination of opposites', as he understood it, was not a 'syzygy', not a 'joining' or 'yoking'[31] or compromise, but that opposites remained identifiable in the Kantian sense of *antinomy*. He recognised the capacity of Scots to encompass opposites together with the space in-between, and celebrated it, in a 50-year anticipation of post-Structuralism, in that

> oxymoron was ever the bravest figure and we must not forget that disorderly order is order after all.[32]

In contemporary philosophical discourse, Žižek reinterpreted Smith – though he did not reference him – in his construct *The Parallax View*:

> philosophy emerges in the interstices between different communities, in the fragmentary space of exchange and circulation between them, a space which lacks any positive identity.[33]

Smith and Žižek were not arguing for a safe middle ground of unsatisfactory compromise but for the insight obtained from the comprehensiveness of a panoptical view *vis-à-vis* thesis and antithesis. In that context, Smith noted that

> though [the Scottish muse] has loved reality, sometimes to maudlin affection for the commonplace, she [sic] has loved not less the airier pleasure to be

found in the confusion of the senses, in the fun of things thrown topsy-turvy, in the horns of elfland and the voices of the mountains.[34]

Parallax, as everyone knows, is what is experienced as we shift our point of view with respect to two or more fixed physical objects as is encountered in a colonnade, or in the *moiré* patterns produced by two overlaid mesh screens. This is profoundly at odds with the finite figure/ground basis of Le Corbusier's claim that 'architecture is the skilful, accurate and magnificent play of masses seen in light'.[35] Žižek asserted that when

> confronted with an antinomic stance in the precise Kantian sense of the term, we should renounce all attempts to reduce one aspect to the other (or, even more so, to enact a kind of 'dialectical synthesis' of opposites); on the contrary, we should assert antinomy as irreducible, and conceive the point of radical critique not as a certain determinate position as opposed to another position, but as the irreducible gap between the positions itself… to face reality that is exposed through difference (parallax).[36]

Kant's antinomy, Smith's antisyzygy or Žižek's parallax, call it what you will, lies at the heart of Scottish cultural production. It is not a concept with which British critics seem to be either familiar or comfortable. It is revealed in the Scots' inclination to respond to a question with a question, seeking to establish the antisyzygy of their interlocutor's position, refusing the empiricism of a simple inquiry and its equally simplistic possible response. Consequently, the Scot is habitually described pejoratively and archetypically as being 'prickly', given to 'pedantry and argumentativeness'[37] or, in the words of Michie's scurrilous doggerel, 'canny, pushy, chippy'. It even arises in the colloquialisms: 'Ah hae ma doots' and 'Ah'm in twa minds'.

Patrimony in the foreign gaze: how others see us

Žižek cautioned:

> This, however, does not in any way entail that one can simply oppose a 'true' identity of a culture to its falsification by a foreign gaze – the next consequence is that this 'true' identity itself, as a rule, forms itself through the identification with a foreign gaze which plays the role of the culture's Ego-Ideal.[38]

Thus, while the French understandably rail at the importance attached by the foreign gaze to Gauloises, berets, baguettes and the Eiffel Tower, or the Germans to knickerbockers, bratwurst, engineering precision and a lack of a sense of humour, or the Japanese to kimonos, tea ceremonies, the Katsura Palace and the bullet-train, these tropes are essential in the construction of being French, German or Japanese and of their nations. There is no requirement that they should harbour more than a modicum of truth.

In finding a place for an independent and confident Scottish patrimony within the hegemonic British cultural construct it is helpful to call upon the validation of the Other. But first, a Scandinavian joke told to me by Swedish architect and academic Anders Johansson: 'A DFDS cruise ship sinks in a violent tropical storm in the Indian Ocean. The search for survivors and wreckage is fruitless and all passengers and crew are presumed lost. Five years later, another DFDS cruise ship, in the vicinity of where the previous ship sank, chances on an uncharted desert island. On sending a party ashore it's found that the island is occupied by six survivors from the sunken ship: two Danes, two Norwegians and two Swedes. The Danes have formed a cooperative, the Norwegians are fighting each other and the Swedes are standing about awkwardly, waiting to be introduced'. As for the fourth Scandinavian partner, Richard Weston (b. 1953) recounted that should you

> [c]onsult any popular book on Finnish design... you will find the same familiar images; a land of lakes and forests adorned by buildings and artefacts designed and made with a special feel for 'natural materials'... Although the romance of it all tends to be played up by foreigners, this is an image which Finns themselves are generally happy to reinforce.[39]

Nonetheless, Finns also suffer from seasonal affective disorder (sad), depression and alcohol-related death rates among the highest in Europe.[40]

The nations of Scandinavia represent enlightened democratic cultures worthy of emulation and have a contemporary architecture of acclaim. Murcutt wrote to his parents in 1964: 'Finland is the house of modern architecture'.[41] Japan, likewise, appeals as a culture of complex completeness and elegance, yet, when reflecting in 1976 on his early career, architect Tange Kenzō (1913–2005) confessed to having

> had these contradictory feelings when I was greatly attracted to Greek and Renaissance arts. I was strongly conscious of the somber [sic] traditional styles of Japanese arts not found in other countries, while,

at the same time, I was strongly attracted to the European style arts...
I may say that my so-called inferiority complex towards things
European was only a reflection of my deep respect of things
Japanese.[42]

The foreign gaze when directed at Scotland is often sympathetic. That gaze, however, is infrequent, mostly historic and is, in some cases, negatively affected by Scotland's selective inclusion in and weighted comparison with the more strident expression of a purely British cultural entity. McCrone quoted the Californian Marinell Ash (1941–88), author of *The Strange Death of Scottish History*, 1980, from her unpublished essay, 'The St Andrew's Myth':

Modern perceptions of Scotland's past are like a foggy landscape; small
peaks and islands of memory rising out of an occluded background.
The names of some of these peaks are Bruce, Wallace, Bannockburn,
Mary Queen of Scots, Bonnie Prince Charlie and the Clearances.[43]

Samuel Johnson's (1709–84) earlier claim that Scots had no sense of their own history was the direct result of his foreign gaze lighting on those and similar isolates and interpreting them solely *as* isolates.[44] McCrone and Beveridge and Turnbull queried how Scots connive in this perception, a perception that plays some part, say, in the mythology of *Brigadoon*, a film musical about a Highland village that appears from the mist for a day and a night once every century.

The accepted story is that the makers of *Brigadoon* (MGM, 1953) concluded, following a location search in Scotland, that the Scotland they visited was not the Scotland they were led to believe it was and retired to Hollywood to construct a Scotland they imagined to be more recognisable to themselves and their potential audience. The flattering implication of this version of the story is that they bought into a Scotland which through repute, rumour or myth, transcended its actuality and simply did not, could not, exist.

Burgin explained the film-makers' difficulty:

Phenomenologically, the field of visual images in everyday
contemporary 'Western' culture (and others, such as Japan) is
heterogeneous and hybrid. The consumer of images 'flips' through
endless magazines, 'channel surfs' on waves of TV shows. The integrity
of the semantic object is rarely, if ever respected... Collecting in
metonymic fragments in memory, we may come to feel familiar with a
film we have not actually seen.[45]

In Hollywood, such fragments might have included LMS railway posters, misty shortbread-tin-lid landscapes, the novels of Sir Walter Scott, calendars featuring Eilean Donan Castle, the sound of the piobaireachd and the vaudeville antics of Sir Harry Lauder, all favourably collaged to produce a constructed version of Scotland with which they became thoroughly familiar and of which they anticipated its physical reality.

The truth was more prosaic. When leading man and choreographer Gene Kelly and producer Arthur Freed scouted out possible Scottish locations in 1953, the cinematically-photogenic 'grannie's heilan hame' of a clachan of 'blackhouses' which they sought was largely superseded by orthogonal 18th-century village and sma burgh improvements,[46] by 19th-century Baronial and Arts & Crafts interventions, by the ubiquity of corrugated iron, or they simply remained as post-Clearance ruins. None were pristine crofting communities. Moreover, the unreliable weather and the inadequate infrastructure of single-track and unmetalled roads, inadequate rail connections and hotels and guest houses with Calvinistic service and opening hours and non-American or poor quality food, prohibited economic shooting schedules, threatened cast and crew comfort and stood to substantially inflate production costs.

To resolve the issues of weather and infrastructure and manage the budget, a possible location in Big Sur, California was considered, but scotched. *Brigadoon* was filmed on MGM sound stages in Hollywood. Set designers and dressers, backdrop and matte painters, make-up and wardrobe did their best but, with the occasional rock formation seeming more at home in Yosemite National Park, a pair of Texas Longhorns substituting for Highland Cattle – their biological progenitors – and the dyeing of cloth a wholly un-Scottish bright red using Californian sumac, 'the integrity of the semantic object [was] not respected'. Cinema audiences, even Scottish cinema audiences, almost certainly did not object. The stagy setting and saturated colour palette (it won a Golden Globe in 1955 for its colour photography) had the beneficial effect of removing a real context and siting the musical in a Caledonian Oz. The foreign gaze, overwhelmed by its preconceptions, conceived Scotland anew. Perhaps in the days of post-war austerity and rationing we were just grateful for Hollywood's interest.

The Czech playwright Karel Čapek,[47] whose words of 1926 contribute the title of this book, was entranced by Scotland, Edinburgh in particular:

> An English friend of mine was almost right when he declared Edinburgh to be the finest city in the world. It is a fine place, stonily grey and strange of aspect.

Implicitly comparing Edinburgh with his home-city of Prague, he observed that:

> Where in other cities a river [the Vltava] flows, there a railway runs; on one side is the old town [Malá Strana], on the other side the new one [Nové Město], with streets wider than anywhere... and in the old town the houses are appallingly high.

He compared Edinburgh with Prague (nostalgically), with Paris (monumentally) and Genoa (topographically) and the people with those of Naples (affectionately). His frequent refrain was either 'and this does not exist in England' or '[s]uch a thing exists nowhere in the world except at Edinburgh'. It was not all sweetness and light, because he saw the slums where 'there are dirty, red-haired children in the streets' and 'the washing is flaunted on clothes-lines above the streets like the flags of all nations'.[48]

Other Czech visitors[49] whom I took to Culross in 1992 found it 'like a little toy town', Sir George Bruce's Palace, constructed 1597–1611, no grander to their *mitteleuropäische* sensibilities than a large farmhouse in Southern Bohemia, although we might reflect that significance is not necessarily a product of scale. Dutch environmental artist and the then curator of the 1990 Leeuwarden Art and Architecture Festival, Dries Wiecherinck, when shown illustrations of 16th and 17th-century Scots urban architecture, exclaimed, 'but they are all Dutch!'[50], while misreading the vertical aesthetic of the bay-windowed four- and five-storey Baronial tenements of Marchmont and Warrender, Edinburgh, as the equivalent of the tall, narrow, single-family houses that front the canals of Amsterdam and Delft.

Perhaps the most widely written-about isolate in Scottish cultural history, on which the foreign gaze rests almost consistently favourably, is the Scottish Enlightenment. Among the many writers asserting its contribution to, even creation of, the Modern world was the American Arthur Herman (b.1956), who explained:

> being Scottish turns out to be more than just a matter of nationality or place of origin or clan or even culture. It is also a state of mind, a way of viewing the world and our place in it. It is a self-consciously modern view, so deeply rooted in the assumptions and institutions that govern our lives today that we often miss its significance, not to mention its origin. From this point of view, a large part of the world turns out to be 'Scottish' without knowing it. It is time to let the world in on the secret Scots have known for a long time: that without

Scotland, to paraphrase Andrew Carnegie, the modern world would be a very poor show.[51]

Although Herman focused on the Enlightenment, his subtitle, 'The Scots' Invention of the Modern World', required him also to consider the substantial later 19th and 20th-century contributions of such as Thomas Carlyle (1795–1881), James Clerk Maxwell (1831–79), William Thomson (Lord Kelvin) (1824–1907), Alexander Fleming (1881–1955), John Logie Baird (1888–1946) or Alasdair McIntyre (b. 1929) while skating rather too lightly over them and ignoring the substantial intellectual, philosophical, scientific and cultural continuity which they represented in Scottish patrimony. He stressed, in the later 19th century, commerce rather than the science, technology and philosophy that were his focus in the late 18th century. This led him to the narrow conclusion that, in the 19th century:

> Scotland's upper and middle classes were losing that hard-driving entrepreneurial edge which had been part of their cultural heritage… [t]he sad truth was that to many educated Scots, their own culture now seemed more provincial than ever.[52]

Herman was seduced by an isolate of Scottish intellectual and practical achievement, sequestering it, as did so many, within the late 18th and early 19th-century ghetto of the Enlightenment. The Checklands observed that parallel loss of identity within commerce, but were more acute as to its cause:

> The Scots were among the most vigorous promoters of British business imperialism. But the benefits to Scotland diminished as the horizons broadened to embrace the world, while at the same time the focus narrowed, drawing so many of the great commercial decisions to London.[53]

Architectural perspectives

The foreign-directed gaze of tourist guides and the foreign gaze of tourists themselves, in neither case entirely the safest authority, comment favourably, say, on the 'architecture of Edinburgh', although Edinburgh has few, if not exactly zero, contemporary world-class buildings. What tourists understand, albeit inchoately, is that the Edinburgh they traverse has significant extant Mediaeval, Georgian and Victorian urban form – with little by way of

20th-century Modernist planning except in the peripheral estates and bungalow-land which they are unlikely to visit. Edinburgh's urban plan subsumes the buildings of which it is composed and discretely frames its monuments – as do the cityscapes of Glasgow, Aberdeen and Dundee.

The Luxembourgeois urbanist Leon Krier (b.1946), who had a very specific urban agenda, was a guest tutor at the Mackintosh School of Architecture in Glasgow in the early 1980s. He was astonished to discover that his idealised new European city of streets, squares, *insulae* (urban blocks) and monuments,[54] based loosely on Roman precedent and which, to his previous knowledge, was only contemporaneously present in fragments, such as the 1737 Friedrichstadt extension of Berlin, existed completely not once, but twice, less than 90 kilometres apart in the Edinburgh New Town and the Glasgow Grid. Should he have travelled more widely he would have encountered similar in Perth, Dundee and Aberdeen and in smaller planned communities such as Thurso and Inverary. What Scots could take from Krier's view was that Scotland's principal cities, at the very least, were shown to have particular international significance in that they represented important essays in the historic development of city-form and demonstrated viable models for a contemporary European urbanism.

Henry-Russell Hitchcock declared Thomson the architect of 'three of the finest Romantic classical churches in the world',[55] and that Moray Place, Glasgow, is 'the finest of all Grecian terraces'.[56] Collins thought,

> Robert Kerr was probably right in claiming, in 1872, that Alexander Thomson was the last of the Greeks.[57]

The Englishman Gavin Stamp (1948–2017)[58] was obliged to note of Thomson that:

> Then, as now, these London-based publications [*Builder*, *Builder News*, *British Architect* and *Architect*] tended to ignore Scotland and very few of even the most important works by Thomson were noticed in their pages.[59]

Hitchcock and Collins' observations, although welcome, lacked the support of adequate published research on Thomson when they were made and were almost of footnote status; a footnote status compounded by the Cinderella condition of much of Thomson's remaining Glasgow works then and now. Likewise, Sixten Ringbom (1935–92) recorded the significance of late 19th-century Scottish masonry construction in general and the work of John Bridgeford Pirie (1848–92) in Aberdeen in particular, both of which were crucial in the development of Swedish and Finnish National Romanticism. The Scandinavian gaze absorbed and valued equally and simultaneously the work of the internationally, even nationally, obscure Pirie and that of the globally celebrated American Henry Hobson Richardson (1838–86).

Herman Muthesius highly rated late 19th and early 20th-century Scottish domestic architecture during Scotland's brief moment in the Modern architectural sun. The wide range of designers he recorded gave credence, not simply to the fact of the individual genius of his friend Mackintosh, but to strength in depth which included, among others, Robert Lorimer (1864–1929), John Marjoribanks MacLaren (1853–90), James Salmon (1873–1924) and George Henry Walton (1867–1933). Both Muthesius and Adolf Loos (1870–1933), for their own purposes, had favourable views of Scotland in the early 20th century. However, it is doubtful whether the detail of their writings had any influence at the time outside the German-speaking nations, and only later as the selectively edited and co-opted support of an orthodox Modernist narrative. Nevertheless, the foreign gaze on Mackintosh fills books.

How inferiorism confers obscurity: 50 Queen's Road, Aberdeen, 1885, architect John Bridgford Pirie.

Less well-known assessments on Scottish architecture and architects include this passage from Vienna-born Rudolph Schindler's (1887–1953) unpublished notes for a series of 1944 lectures on architecture:

> Modern architecture starts with Mackintosh in Scotland, Otto Wagner in Vienna and Louis Sullivan in Chicago.[60]

This view placed Mackintosh, with whom Schindler had no obvious connection,[61] as an equal authority with Schindler's *Wienerschule* training and his subsequent assistantship with Wright, himself Louis Sullivan's (1856–1924) former assistant. The American architect Louis I Kahn (1901–74) reflected on Scottish castles:

'A place to read, a place to sew... Places for the bed. For the stair... Sunlight. Fairytale,' so said Louis I Khan: Craigievar, Alford, Aberdeenshire, 1626.

Thick, thick walls. Little openings to the enemy. Splayed inwardly to the occupant. A place to read, a place to sew... Places for the bed. For the stair... Sunlight. Fairytale.[62]

Kahn, through his acknowledgement and analysis of the importance of the occupied wall developed his organisational principles of 'served and servant spaces' which informed his Esherick, 1959–61, or Korman, 1971–3, houses while facilitating the functional planning of complex buildings such as his Richards Medical Institute, Philadelphia, 1965.

From a different perspective, and one which related to the specifics of Modern architectural development in Britain, Stamp, who was less enthralled than most by the Mackintosh myth, contended that:

> As much of the Mackintosh legend depends upon English indifference to his achievement, there is a certain irony in the fact that while Mackintosh was well aware of the work of advanced English Goths and Arts and Crafts designers, it was Burnet [Sir John James Burnet (1857–1938)], whose sources of inspiration mostly came from Paris, New York and Chicago, who had by far the most important impact on England.[63]

This is not a popular opinion in Scottish architectural circles.

On occasion, a note of overweening desperation creeps in when the foreign gaze is invited. Stamp recorded the 1950 correspondence between the Scottish architect Graham Law (1923–96) and Hitchcock regarding the frequently posited formal similarity between the work of Karl-Friedrich Schinkel (1781–1841), Alexander Thomson and Frank Lloyd Wright, where Thomson is the presumed link in the chain. Hitchcock responded to Law's prompt:

Because of my conditioning, I see considerable resemblance [in Thomson's work] to Wright's handling of structural elements and space. Interpenetrations, or as I would prefer to call it plaiting, or even plaiding is characteristic of Thomson.[64]

In a parallel dimension, Mary Miller (n.d.), *The Scotsman* newspaper's music critic, recounted her interview with the French composer Pierre Boulez (1925–2016):

> He has been fascinated by Japanese *gagaku*… and by the way that traditional Japanese instruments can produce the most subtle grace notes. Tentatively, I say 'like bagpipes?' 'Oh yes,' he says with enthusiasm, 'the bagpipe ornamentation is really fantastic… I really believe that the only untouched music left in the world is Scotland's'.[65]

Miller directed a foreign gaze; Boulez observed what was indicated, obliged with politesse and replied with grace.

An occluded view: Scotland as seen from Westminster Bridge

It is the British gaze which lands most often and not especially beneficially on Scottish patrimony. Muthesius had a shrewd understanding of Scotland's cultural situation. In a footnote to *The English House*, he recorded that

> [MacGibbon and Ross's] study is all the more valuable in that English works generally pass over Scottish architecture, a state of affairs that can be explained by reference to the narrow-mindedness with which artistic questions are habitually treated in England: one generally looks in vain for any parallels or any reference to anything that is not English.[66]

The Scott and Uthwatt Reports of 1943 followed the Barlow Report of 1940 and predicated, in part, the Town and Country Planning Act of 1947, as part of the administration of the nascent British Welfare State. The Uthwatt Report began:

> The Committee quote the words of HG Wells which express their own affections for our [sic] countryside.

This was followed by a long panegyric from Wells (1866–1946), which opened with:

> There is no countryside like the English countryside for those who have learned to love it,

and concluded:

> None changes scenery and character in three miles of walking... as our mother England does.[67]

Jeremy Paxman (b. 1950) located Wells's England:

> [Thomas] called [England] The South Country... he spoke of it as being below the Thames and the Severn and east of Exmoor: It included Kent, Sussex, Surrey, Hampshire, Berkshire, Wiltshire, Dorset and part of Somerset. To all intents and purposes, this is the Essential England. Over time it has expanded to include counties like Oxfordshire... and Shropshire.[68]

As Margaret Drabble (b. 1939) pointed out, Wells was torn between this parochial rural dream and the anticipation of a dystopian future:

> Wells, like Huxley and Evelyn Waugh in different ways show a similar conflict – on the one hand they condemn or question the advance of science, but at the same time they are enthralled by it.[69]

The Committee, however, was not so conflicted. Beyond its Wellsian periphery, its model omitted *every* part of Britain where agriculture was challenged by industry or where the town infiltrated the country. The Committee then excluded Scotland by commission, because:

> In this report, Scotland is outside the terms of reference. Whatever degree of autonomy Scotland may have within the scheme, a national plan must make provision for the whole of Britain. The great problems of Scotland, such as the future of the Highlands, are enormous which ought to be faced by a united nation.[70]

Thus, Scotland was deemed part, but not part, of a nationwide British scheme, was recognised as having great problems but was denied specific solution, which in any case only ever 'ought' to be the responsibility of Britain; a pernicious sophistry that persists in politics and culture to this day.

Beveridge and Turnbull believed that:

> The development of alternative views of the Scottish past is rendered difficult in the face of the social and cultural power within the intelligentsia of English intellectuals who update and embellish the traditional inferiorising view in contemporary works... where the views of the London and Oxbridge reviewers are *sans pariel*.[71]

The issue for Scottish culture and its practitioners is that they are selected for British cultural status not through the totality of their artistic vision and expression but because one significant pole of the framing antinomy is sufficiently concordant with, useful to or fills yawning gaps in the British cultural story. The simple act of validating the few had its corollary in Beveridge and Turnbull's claim of the 'inferiorism' of the many; what came to be known as the 'cultural cringe'.

Hugh MacDiarmid (1892–1978), writing in 1950 but only published posthumously in full in 1984, commented on omission made plain in British ignorance of the autonomy of Scottish art:

> It will be remembered that Sir William Llewellyn, the then President of the Royal Academy, confessed he had had no idea before he saw the Exhibition [The Arts of Scotland, Burlington House, London, 1937] that Scotland had such a rich and distinctive tradition of its own in the art of painting, and a tradition so dissimilar to the English tradition. The Exhibition was, he declared, an eye-opener. Most of the art critics in our leading British newspapers and cultural periodicals wrote in the same strain.[72]

Eric Hobsbawm (1917–2012) could have provided MacDiarmid with an explanation for such oversight when he observed that '[t]he English hardly gave a thought to the preoccupations of the Scots and Welsh'.[73] Moreover,

> there was little dispute about the existence of an English or French nation-people. For, given the identification of nation with state, it was natural for foreigners to assume that the only people in a country were those belonging to the state-people, a habit that still irritates the Scots.[74]

Hobsbawm's comment encapsulated the British Left's accommodation with the Union wherein support of foreign or colonial cultural and nationalist status and claims, provided they met an approved oppressor/oppressed narrative, was readily granted, while closer to home it was not. He had little truck with Scotland's claims of nationhood and, paraphrasing Johnson, stated that it was

> Walter Scott [who] thus built a single Scotland on the territory soaked in the blood of warring Highlanders and Lowlanders, Kings and Covenanters, and he did so by emphasising their ancient divisions.[75]

This notion that 'Scotland' was the recent fabrication of one man, his inspiration gleaned from those isolates of Scottish history evident to the British gaze, rather than the result of a celebrated, progressive and continuous collective history, was repeated by Drabble:

> Dr Johnson found the Scots lacking, precisely, in historical tradition and written history: Scott had achieved a one-man revolution in attitude.[76]

An argument which, as Smith noted, had had no currency since the days of Matthew Arnold (1822–88).[77] A few minutes spent in the National Library of Scotland's history catalogue disproves the lack of the written record, while the near-unbroken list of Scottish monarchs between 858 and 1603 exposes the fiction of a lack of one kind of tradition at least. In Drabble's *A Writer's Britain*, Scotland had far fewer page mentions than Wordsworth alone, and exclusively referenced Walter Scott (1771–1832) and Robert Burns (1759–96). She could not ignore the international Scott; likewise Burns, although he was possibly just too Scottish for her taste and whom she characterised as providing

> some excuse for those who wished to see the Scots nation as a nation of picturesque but feckless drunkards.[78]

Smith observed sardonically that,

> for on all questions as to how the universal appeal of an artist is affected by the parochial and petty, the alien has perhaps the better right to speak.[79]

MacDiarmid, seeking to expand on the philosophical basis of a Scottish literature and Scottish art generally that, at root, seemed to have confused Drabble, reflected:

> In the practice of the arts, the Scot has tended to eschew aesthetic theories, has usually been content to be a traditionalist like Burns, and always at best has been a realist.[80]

but warned,

> This realistic tradition of the Scot is obscured when Scottish art is considered as part of English art.[81]

It is surprising that with his knowledge of Smith's antisyzygy, MacDiarmid did not expand on its relevance here, because in the above examples both Burns and Scott were not wholly traditionalist, modern, romantic or realist but encompassed all these poles.

Where the British foreign gaze cannot penetrate any part of the parallax, the works are rejected as 'philistine', the assessment of the English critic John Pope-Hennessy (n.d.), one of the few who did not care for the Burlington House exhibition. MacDiarmid attempted to finesse the pejorative philistine to the more acceptable realist to explain Scottish art's rejection by a British cultural establishment, but that simply did not work. What Pope-Hennessy and others like him objected to was not realism itself but the fact that such realism was only one aspect of thesis and antithesis present in the works. MacDiarmid identified Scotland's contributory failings:

> Just as the philosophic poverty is reflected in Scottish political thinking, the neglect of aesthetic studies is evident every day in what passes in Scotland for criticism.[82]

This tendentious issue of the parallax of Scottish art and philosophy is underscored by Drabble's almost total avoidance of James Hogg (1770–1835) in *A Writer's Britain*, where he was present but only in passing in a reference to the Brontës. Perhaps the seeming moral ambiguity of his work contrasted too violently with her literature of manners or that she agreed with Eliot or that she was swayed by Wordsworth's precious assessment that Hogg was a genius but of 'rough manners and opinions'. Drabble's '*Britain*' was at root simply a familiar catch-all. Drabble herself was unable to escape the Wellsian English countryside in her realistic urban novel, *The Radiant Way*, which she concluded with an idyllic rural analogy.[83]

You're not my real parents: rejecting patrimony

The most dismaying gaze, by far, is the 'recusing gaze' of those natives who feel the need to distance themselves from Scotland. This is not the gaze of the pragmatic, the sceptic or the inquirer after truth and understanding but the vindictive and comparative glare of the disappointed, the frustrated or the inferiorised seeking other validation, legitimacy and allegiance. It is *not* the gaze of the Orcadian to whom everything furth the Pentland Firth is 'sooth', nor the gaze that recognises the Northern and Western Islands as different to the mainland and to each other, nor is it the occasional thousand-yard stare exchanged between Edinburgh and Glasgow. It is not the embittered gaze of religious sectarianism, which pits a Scottish Protestant supremacy against an Irish Catholic minority, a suppurating sore on the Scottish psyche still shamefully untreated. That these are the gazes of colloquial currency and, other than sectarianism, relatively harmless, does not lessen their mythic properties nor make them less available to the agents of discontent. As McCrone commented:

> The key point is a sociological one, that myth-history is a vital part of the story-telling of any country. Myths do not disappear when they are confronted with facts, because… evidence does not drive out myths for they operate on quite a different plane. In other words, myths validate experience and action independently of their truth status.[84]

The recusing gaze engages in displacement. The English design curator Deyan Sudjic (b. 1952), whose Scottish sojourn included the Directorship of Glasgow's City of Culture 1999 event, claimed Glasgow was

> Scotland's largest city with 600 thousand inhabitants. It is a world city, the closest [Scotland] has to a metropolis. The once bustling city now is shrinking and looking for a new role. It had a peak of 1.2 million people, most of whom I suppose have moved just outside the tax boundary.[85]

Glasgow's elevation to world-city status might have been intended to flatter. There are many factors in the making of a world-city, population being only one. On a population chart Glasgow makes little impact: eighth in Britain behind Brighton, Bristol and Sheffield; 40th in Europe behind Düsseldorf and Riga; ca. 950th in the wider world where the *real* world-cities are located. As for Glasgow's new role, Sudjic was part of it, while the missing 600,000 Glaswegians did not decamp to the suburbs but were simply resident in that part of the city's royalty stripped out by a Tory Government set on weakening the Labour Party's Scottish heartland. Sudjic recused and displaced Glasgow's contemporary reality. His inflated claims were disingenuous, extraordinary and embarrassing, the unfortunate and naive boosterish obverse of the inferiorist coin.

Also engaged in displacement were Scots who actively supported foreign independence struggles, although uncommitted to that at home: Lord Byron (1799–1824) and the Greek struggle for independence in the years 1821–4; Sir Robert Rowand Anderson (1834–1921) and those of Morocco in 1859–80; and RW Seton-Watson (*Scotus Viator*) (1879–1951), first those of Hungary in 1905 – from which he resiled – then Czechoslovakia in 1906–18 and Yugoslavia in 1912–8. Displacement featured in the disproportionate number of Scots, almost a quarter of the British total – many of course Socialists and not nationalists – fighting for the Republicans in the Spanish Civil War (1936–9).

James Gowan (1923–2015) may have had genuine complaint about his architectural training in Glasgow in the 1940s, although such training did not so hinder such as Andy MacMillan (1928–2014) or Isi Metzstein (1928–2012) nor elicit *ad hominem* disparagement of their native or adopted nation and its people:

> In the offices the students were broken on the wheel of practicality and, at the school, were introduced to tired Beaux Arts stereotypes… It was a crushing form of vocational training and it is surprising that the inventiveness of Mackintosh survived and flowered in such a system, but that was a long time ago and the yield since then has been very low indeed. The bias towards this form of training seems to be particularly attractive to the Scots. They excel in producing doctors, engineers and so on; it appears to be a very tartan preoccupation. The appeal has probably got something to do with usefulness and the advantages that are derived from simplifying the educational goals. All the other arguments that come to mind have Calvinist overtones which suggest they are likely explanations.[86]

Nothing transcends on its own account: why confident and engaged cultures matter

Having gazed, as a foreigner himself, on Peter Zumthor's (b. 1943) works at Graubünden, doubt assailed Scottish architect Neil Gillespie (n.d.):

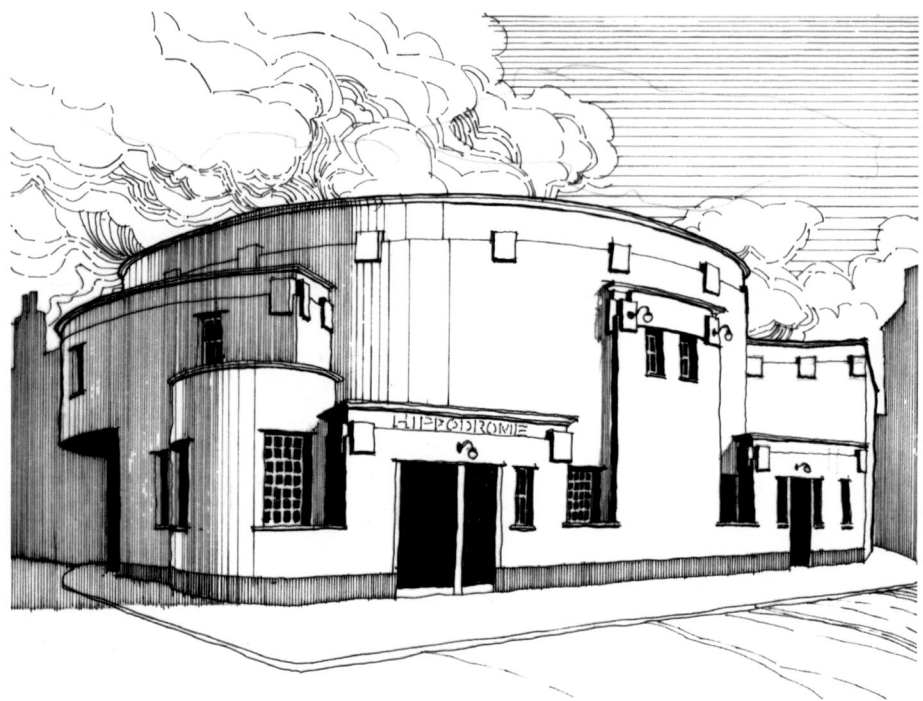

How inferiorism confers obscurity: Hippodrome, Bo'ness, 1912, architect Matt Steele. (Drawing by Roger Emmerson)

> Scotland as a nation struggles to conjure up one building that transcends the local scene to speak on a global stage. Who will produce work that quickens the heart, that causes self-doubt, that touches a chord, that runs deep within us all?[87]

Such works as Zumthor's are accorded global stature for the simple fact that they are produced, recognised and brought to international attention from within a culture self-confident on its own terms. It is necessarily a lack, not of significant Scottish work, but of confidence that consigns it to obscurity.

Nothing transcends on its own account. For example, Matt Steele's (1878–1937) Hippodrome Cinema, Bo'ness, 1912, is presently recognised as important in Scottish architectural history and in the history of British cinema. It should have featured prominently in the account of early 20th-century Scottish architecture, but it did not, for it is an isolate, its proto-Modernist design largely unknown even in Scotland outwith Bo'ness, certainly at the time of its construction and at least until Colin McWilliam's (1928–89) inclusion of it in the *Pevsner Architectural Guide to Lothian* in the 1970s or until 1979 when it was listed.[88] Consequently, its impact on Scottish architectural history and on Modernism in Scotland was nil. Irrespective of its undoubted pioneering qualities, it could not have 'transcended the local scene' without contemporary advocacy.

The causes of this condition are the cultural cringe and the absence of a critical tradition within Scottish architecture and architectural discourse throughout the Modern period. The cultural cringe, if conceded, permits the Scot two courses of inferiorist action: on the one hand, to immediately discount the cultural offering in question without further assessment, assuming it to be from the start worthless, or, on the other hand, to subject it to extraordinary criticism and comparison and subsequently to devalue it; in both cases too ready to employ assessment standards and norms from other cultures as relevant.

The medium is the message

Writing in 1934, though not published in English until 1992, Henri Focillon (1881–1943) was clear that the national project is never actually closed at any stage:

> A nation, too, represents a long drawn-out experiment. It has forever before its eyes the idea of its own self; it is incessantly building itself. A nation may well be regarded as a work of art. Culture is not a reflex, but a progressive appropriation and renewal.[89]

This is especially true now when most peoples and individuals are no longer tied geographically by family, servitude, habit, language or employment to specific locations and customs and where those locations experience continuous radical transformation through material and technological changes undreamt of a century ago. Despite this evident surface fluidity, the ties of territory and patrimony remain significant as:

> Race [sic] and environment are not in suspension beyond and outside of time. Both are time that has been lived and formed, and this is why both are properly historical conditions.[90]

However, the misuse of history as a static measure, or the Modernist interpretation of it, conceives of regional culture as seeking a 'golden age' or sheltering from change as 'in secluded settlements [where] the popular arts cling to their ancient state'[91] or to being perverted to banality such as in totalitarianism. Milena Lamarová (n.d.), writing about *narodní sloh*, the Czechoslovak national style (see more below), typified the orthodox Modernist position thus:

> It was not just cubist architects who went up the blind alley of decorativism; a whole attitude represented by institutions such as Artěl *and the Union of Czechoslovak Artwork* was burdened by the regressive dream of the 'industrial arts', by nationalistic romanticism, and by an inability to embrace the concept of industrial production.[92]

The problem is that machine production, as posited in Modernism, does not predicate lack of decoration. Indeed, the contemporary machine is ideally suited to both repetitive and bespoke reproduction of it. What Lamarová chose to ignore was that the entirely Modern Czechoslovak national project and its initial decorative, romantic and nationalistic semiology was precisely and synchronously mirrored in *narodní sloh*, and it was in the working-out or working through of the national style that the architecture which she so fervently desired came to fruition in the 1920s and 1930s, and by no other means (see more below).

Focillon noted of such developments that

> a sudden shift in the equilibrium of [the artist's] ethnic values may bring him into violent opposition with his environment and hence with the moment, and arouse a nostalgia in him that is highly revolutionary. He [sic] then seeks the world that he needs.[93]

That is, the moment of the eventuation of a politically-conscious regional or national architecture is not that of establishing a fixity of form but the opening of a door to a new reality; 'the world that he needs'. One recalls, in this context, Zumthor's 'the world of my many places'.[94] Fixity of form is the attribute of totalitarianism. Moreover, 'the concept of industrial production' is not what is being sought in either the national project or in the national architecture in the first instance; or at least not unless you are Lenin and believe 'communism is soviet power plus the electrification of the whole country'.[95] In the case of Czechoslovakia or Finland, in the 1920s, after two decades of aesthetic and formal exploration within the context of the adaptation of historic forms, their populations and architects sought and found the Modern world, the architecture they needed and that accorded with the ethos of their young republics.

At the achievement of independence what people want and need are flags, fêtes and fireworks, inspiring songs, dances, falling in love, challenging artworks, inspiring new myths, bright-eyed heroes, simple uproarious fun and an open-ended release which might, in due course, result in relaxed sophistication and intellectual inquiry. Focillon understood this process, ascribed no pejorative values in the definition of the style that might accompany or initiate it and was clear about the evolution of style from *a* style:

> Style is an absolute. A style is a variable. The word 'style' in its generic sense indicates a special and superior quality in a work of art: the quality... that allows it to escape the bondage of time... A style, on the other hand, is a development, a coherent grouping of forms united by a reciprocal fitness, whose essential harmony is nevertheless in many ways testing itself, building itself and annihilating itself.[96]

Modernist critics of national architectures would claim that Modernism is 'style as an absolute' (should they concede the concept of style) which 'allows it to escape the bondage of time', thus conjecturally transcending all other possibilities. Their pretence is that it is astylar, simply contingent upon the material consequences of the instrumentality of the machine, while insinuating that the practitioners of national or regional architectures are locked within the finite.

Contrary to this stance, Michel Foucault (1926–84) generalised:

> the historians of the 19th century were to undertake the creation of a history that could at last be 'true'– in other words, liberated from Classical rationality, from its ordering and theodicity: a history restored to the irruptive violence of time.[97]

While Focillon particularised that

> a work of art is motionless only in appearance. It seems to be set fast – arrested, as are the moments of time gone by. But in reality it is born of change, and it leads to other changes.[98]

Both Foucault and Focillon rejected stasis, predetermination, the vindication of an absolute Divine will and the fictive accepted 'course of history'. The history of regional architecture is more complex than Joseph Masheck's (b. 1947) speculation that '[w]hen the modern falls away, presumably the dismissed classical ideal reappears',[99] which entails 'the matter of the fate of an abstract classical value that modernism... may have preserved'.[100] What is preserved is patrimony, which might or might not include the Classical among many antinomial poles.

Bible class[101]: why what you say matters

Within Protestant enclaves in post-Reformation Europe, the 'national project' was anticipated in the early codification of the regional language, its elevation to literary and legal orthodoxy and its siting in popular use and patrimony initially through the translation of the Bible into the local vernacular: for example, in Lutheran Finland, into Finnish in 1548, *Se Wsi Testamenti Somexi*, and in the Hussite Czech lands into Czech in 1579–93, the *Bible kralická*. In Calvinist Scotland, this process was reversed for the Scots Leid where, although complicated by the entanglement of the Tudor succession with the Reformation, the King James Bible of 1611 promulgated the sole use of English throughout a polyglot Union. In the Gàidhealtachd, the New Testament was not published in Gaelic until 1769, and the entire bible, *Am Bìoball Gàidhlig*, not until 1801. Although, as Dorward cautioned:

> One of the few things that can be said with authority, however, is that Gaelic was never at any time, as is frequently asserted, the language spoken throughout the length and breadth of Scotland.[102]

Not until 1983 was the New Testament translated from Greek into the Scots Leid. In the codification into a language of what, in a British view, was now seen as a collection of dialects, Scotland was required to wait until 1993 for the first English–Scots dictionary with relatively standardised Scots equivalents. Such tardiness may have been of significance.

From interest in vernacular speech and its codification into the formal language of the nation it was but a short step to the investigation of folk-art and architecture in establishing a unique national cultural identity. Many European nations and states undertook such activity throughout the 19th century. It is perhaps of relevance to consider how Scotland fared in comparison with two of these: Finland and Czechoslovakia between 1900 and 1918.

National romanticism: the Finnish experience

Finland, prior to 1918, was never a nation-state as is presently understood. The Finns consequent lack of national consciousness and political sophistication was summed up by President JK Paasikivi (1870–1956)[103]:

These Finns! What have they achieved? Once they inhabited half Russia. But did they found a state? No! As soon as there was trouble they set sail across the sea to Finland, found a suitable birch grove and built a sauna.[104]

Upton commented:

It would be difficult to say when the idea of the Finnish Nation as an identifiable body of people inhabiting a specific geographical location first developed[105]

and Mellor that:

The Finno-Ugrian tribes in the valleys of northern rivers, separated by forest and swamp, were unable to form allegiances against the superior organisation of the invaders, who conquered and absorbed them, or pushed them back into the tundra fringe.[106]

These first-century immigrants, from what is now Estonia and before that Trans-Uralic Russia, remained in isolation until incursions by the Swedes after 1155. Finland was formally established as a province of Sweden in 1362 and political status belatedly confirmed by its elevation to the status of Grand Duchy in 1581.

By the dawn of the 18th century, the adventuring that had benefited Sweden in the 17th, bringing its armies to the gates of Prague, proved foolhardy. The abortive invasion of Russia by the Swedish King Karl XII and his defeat at Poltava in 1709 signalled the reversal of Sweden's fortunes. Consequently, a weakened Sweden and her distracted ally, Great Britain[107], were powerless to prevent the counter-invasion and occupation of Finland and part of Wästerbotten in Sweden by Russia from 1713 to 1721, a period known in Finland as 'The Great Wrath' due to the harshness of its prosecution. A second invasion by Russia gained territory in southern Finland, which was formally ceded by Sweden to Russia in the Treaty of Turku in 1743. The Napoleonic Wars, some 60 years later, provided Russia with the opportunity to annexe Finland entirely, sealing the deed in the Treaty of Hamina in 1809. Recalling the resistance put up by the Finns in 1713 and eager to detach Swedish-speaking bourgeois loyalties from the Swedish crown, the Russians offered the Finns a considerable measure of self-governance. Agreement was reached at the Diet of Porvoo, also in 1809, and the country declared a self-governing province of the Russian Empire.

Gods and heroes: the significance of myth

It is impossible today to appreciate the countervailing romantic impact on European Enlightenment culture at the end of the 18th and beginning of the 19th centuries of James Macpherson's (1736–96) *Poems of Ossian*,[108] published 1761–5. The tales of ancient heroic deeds originating at the periphery of Atlantic Europe provided a northern counterpart to a previously Mediterranean mythic authority. Ossian was rapidly translated into Swedish and Russian, among other languages. Napoleon Bonaparte (1769–1821) carried a copy with him on his conquests; the Prussian architect Karl-Friedrich Schinkel remarked on the 'Ossianic landscape' on his visit to Scotland in 1825; and Ossianic themes inspired 18th and 19th-century art works, such as Alexander Runciman's (1736–85) *The Hall of Ossian*, 1772 (destroyed) or Ingres' (1780–1867) *Dream of Ossian*, 1865, painted for Napoleon III (1808–73). Between the 1890s and 1910s, the Scottish Symbolist John Duncan (1866–1945) employed Ossianic and Celtic themes. Cheape noted:

> Germany and Scandinavia adopted him enthusiastically as part of their own national heritage or mythology which was in the process of being rediscovered at the time.[109]

Smith, name-checking the significant authorities of his day, recounted that:

> When we turn over the minutes of the literary and philosophical societies of the period, we find no subjects so persistent as the Ossianic poetry and the problem of its authenticity... Blair... proclaimed it the equal of Homer. Ossian is the modern Homer, said Madame de Stael. To Klopstock he is the rival of Homer; to Voss 'Ossian of Scotland is greater than Homer of Ionia': and Herder, having at last found his soul's desire, had thoughts of going to Scotland that he might be touched more closely by this inspired writing.[110]

While, in *Suomi*, A MacCallum Scott (1874–1928) wrote:

> The fame of MacPherson's [sic] *Ossian* reached even Finland, and patriotic Finns began to ask what treasures might not exist in their vast forests.[111]

Despite the fact that Macpherson's work was found later to be largely a confabulation which somewhat diminished its significance, its catalytic importance was not in doubt.

Macpherson's Finnish counterpart was Elias Lönnrot (1802–84), a village doctor of humble origins whose purpose and method was the same: collecting stories, sagas and poems in the oral tradition from remote communities in both Finnish and Russian Karelia, and constructing linking elements to provide narrative continuity. The resultant work, the *Kalevala* (the Land of Heroes), was published in 1835, with an expanded version in 1849. In the *Kalevala*, the significance of nature and the sanctity of family life were set within a world where magic touched everything. Sentient nature extended beyond talking animals familiar from other mythologies to talking trees and rocks. Even the heroes and heroines inhabiting this universe of magic material seemed themselves to be part metallic.[112] Žižek provided a present-day perspective on the work:

> This is where modern art meets the ancient epic. Kalevala, the epic poem that put into words the very core of Finnish identity, is composed in so-called 'Kalevala meter': its most characteristic features are unrhymed, nonstrophic, trochaic tetrameters, with the alliteration of lines and 'echo' lines… two singers sat on a bench and held hands; one of them sang a line with eight syllables, then the other took over and sang the same thing, but with different words in his eight syllables… does this strange staging not present parallax at its purest… to encircle/discern the unfathomable gap of the Difference by repeatedly formulating both perspectives?[113]

Ethnographic investigation accompanied such purely folkloric research with Matthias Castrén (1813–52) making an epic journey throughout northern Russia and Siberia in the 1840s to confirm the Finno-Ugric, non-Indo-European origins of his fellow Finns. Likewise, a loose gathering of graduates of the Swedish-speaking Åbo (Turku) University founded, first, The Saturday Club in 1830 as a debating forum and then, in 1831, the Finnish Literature Society, the first national organisation in Finland, whose objectives were

> to propagate more exact notions of the country and its history, to work for the cultivation of the Finnish language… [because] [l]anguage being the foundation of nationality, a national literature is not possible without a national language.[114]

Upton stated:

Through the efforts of these, and numerous lesser men, the intellectuals of the Finnish Literature Society had created the modern Finnish national image.[115]

Architecture was initially untouched by the political, linguistic, folkloric and nationalistic turmoil of the 1870s and '80s when its prime purpose was to reflect the tastes, attitudes and practical dynamism of the new middle classes. It was the artist Akseli Gallen-Kallela (1856–1931) who initiated the investigation of timber folk architecture. On honeymoon in Karelia in 1890, he collected material for what was to become his Kalevala cycle of paintings, exhibiting *The Aino Myth* at the Ateneum, Helsinki in 1891, and which provided much of the graphic imagery infusing the works of the later National Romantic architects. He built a large timber folkloric family hut called *Kalela* at Lake Ruosevi in 1894–5, employing local carpenters, and subsequently designed a National Romantic house and studio with tower at Tarvaspää, Espoo, in 1911–3.[116] Hilding Ekelund noted that:

> This tendency, national romanticism, had as its spiritual originator the artist Axel Gallén-Kalela [the Swedish form of his name], a man of genius, and took on a form here that was, perhaps, more radical and more pronouncedly individualistic than elsewhere; attempts were made to replace the exhausted classic world of design by a new one, founded freely on native or self-created architectural motives.[117]

Scotland, granite and folklore

Finns, in the late 1890s, followed the Swedish architects and engineers who had earlier visited Scotland and the USA beginning in 1871 to learn about granite and masonry construction, largely unused for domestic construction although plentiful in the bedrock of both nations. Geologist and engineer Hugo Blankett (1872–1949) travelled to Aberdeen, Peterhead, Glasgow and Edinburgh in 1896, accompanied in Aberdeen by Alexander Nyström (1869–1926), the architect-brother of Gustav Nyström (1856–1917), for whom he worked. Armas Lindgren (1874–1929) travelled widely in Scotland in 1897 and again, on a diplomatic passport, in 1920.[118] Hugo Lindberg (1863–1932) was in Aberdeen for four months in 1898, while Lars Sonck (1870–1956) may have visited Glasgow in 1901.[119] Eliel Saarinen (1873–1950) was in Edinburgh in 1904.[120] Frequently illustrated in reports presented to their sponsors were St Machar's Cathedral, Aberdeen, and the work of John Bridgford Pirie,

SOME REGIONAL THEORY AND A LITTLE PRACTICE

wherein the response to the hardness of the granite and consequent simplicity of detailing was much admired. The over-working of the stone at Alexander Marshall Mackenzie's (1848–1933), Northern Assurance Building, 1882–5, and Marischal College, 1891 was deplored.

Meanwhile folkloric research proceeded apace at home. Armas Lindgren, sponsored by the Archaeological Bureau and the Antiquarian Society, studied and drew 74 churches up to 1902[121]; Lars Sonck travelled widely in Uusimaa, Satakunta and Häme in 1892, recording 31 churches for the Ancient Monument Society, and in Turku and Porvoo in 1893 on the study and relocation of funeral tablets for the Archaeological Bureau. He only cancelled his proposed Karelian trip in 1894 on learning he had won the architectural competition for St Michael's Church, Turku.[122] Yrjö Blomstedt (1871–1912), Victor Sucksdorf (1866–1952) and Bertel Jung (1872–1946) made several trips in the 1890s to Karelia to study folk-art.[123] Blomstedt and Sucksdorf published the results in the influential *Karjalaisa rakennuskia ja koristemuotoja* in 1894.[124]

The Scottish influence on Finnish National Romanticism: Queen's Road Church, Aberdeen, 1887, architect John Bridgford Pirie.

Even establishment architects such as Josef Stenbäck (1851–1929) and Gustav Nyström were affected by it. Stenbäck made a remarkable swing to National Romanticism after 1904, which may have been due to his contact with the younger Finnish architects of the *fin-de-siècle*. Stenbäck's other significance was in his promotion of 'true materials in church architecture' through the magazine *Suomen Teollisuuslehti*,[125] which he founded in 1883, and in his subsequent espousal of masonry construction and membership of the commission appointed by the Architects Club to investigate its use in general building.[126]

Nyström was uniquely placed to influence an entire generation in running both a successful practice and in teaching at the Helsinki Polytechnic, becoming its Head in 1903 until his death in 1917, although his regular, neo-Classical, 'Germanic' architecture was the very thing that the younger architects rejected. As Saarinen claimed,

Certainly in those days architecture did not inspire one's fancy... It finally became evident that the Classical form after all is not the form to be used for contemporary purpose, but that our time must develop an architectural form of its own.[127]

Nevertheless, Herman Gesellius (1874–1916), Lindgren and Saarinen were employed in Nyström's office in 1898 on the design of the Pohjoismaiden Yhdyspankki to supplement the meagre earnings from their embryonic joint practice. Nyström's Classicism masked structural daring such as the cast iron interior of the National Archives, Rauhankatu, 1890, and technological experimentation such as the first all-native, all-stone façade at the Yhdyspankki, Aleksanterinkatu. His Viennese training obscured a love of his native land as expressed in his Elias Lönnrot Memorial, Sammatti Churchyard, 1886, while his age was belied by his willingness to adopt modern design principles as in his Richardsonesque Turku Art Museum, 1904.

The February Manifesto: the precarity of the rights and responsibilities of freedom

Increasing competition between Germanic and Slavic Europe in the late 19th century had Tsar Nicholas II conclude that 'Russification' of his far-flung and heterogenous empire would bind its constituent peoples more tightly to him and promulgated the February Manifesto in 1899 which abrogated the Finnish Diet, introduced the conscription of Finnish youth into the Russian army and undid much that had been achieved since 1809.

By 1899, contemporary Finnish architecture had claimed the use of granite as an expression of national sentiment; adopted Scottish techniques for how to construct in masonry; studied Scottish and American models for what to construct; and used folkloric research to provide a language of decoration. Nevertheless, Ritva Wäre, quoted by Nikula, cautioned

> that the architects were not consciously striving to create the specifically Finnish style cherished by latter-day National Romantic thought. Their goal was a new style, free from historicist ballast and in harmony with both modern construction techniques and the national heritage.[128]

It was this combination that was to appear in new work in large measure following the promulgation of the February Manifesto. For example, Sonck had won the St Michael's Church, Turku competition in 1894 with a strongly neo-Gothic design, although construction did not start until 1899, during which time he presented at least two variations on his competition entry. He was held to his original design but varied it relatively discreetly. Externally this church was still largely neo-Gothic, though the stilted arched ground floor windows and twin towers flanking the apse were only distantly so, while the interior was a mixture of Secession and folk-art-inspired decoration which resulted in something older and edgier than Gothic. With St Michael's on site, the architectural competition for St John's Church, Tampere was announced, which Sonck duly won in 1900 with a full-blooded National Romantic design.

Sonck claimed of St John's:

> The aim of this entry is therefore to use small dimensions to produce a building with the character of a small church.[129]

However, the building is monumental from the boundary walls of water-rounded river boulders to the prodigious granite columns supporting the interior to the stonework coursing. Kivinen suggested that the masonry was

> laid in a way not invented by Sonck but imported to suit the popular contemporary style,[130]

but it is plain that the coursing he employed did not reflect the tectonic proprieties of either Scottish snecked or American coursed rubble and that Sonck's intent was less constructional than expressionistic. MacCallum Scott commented:

> [St John's] not merely serves its utilitarian purpose, but it expresses in every line and in every stone the creative joy of the

The impact of Scottish and American models on Finnish National Romanticism: St John's Church, Tampere, 1900, architect Lars Sonck.

artist... Not that it is a perfect building! It has the faults of the artist's temperament. There is a freakish element in it; a wanton desire for originality which leads to occasional aberrations from true structural principles.[131]

He went on to say that '[s]ome faint echo of Egypt, or of Assyria, pervades the building' and, in an observation on those boundary walls, commented:

This is the return to nature of the super-civilised. One cannot help feeling a touch of the masquerade in it. Or one may read politics into the structure – a search for the aboriginal Finnish nature, the spirit which is as native to the country as these water-worn boulders or the riven granite.[132]

An architecture of resistance: the political poster in stone

Up to 1899, then, the questions for Finnish architects were of style in general and technique in particular. Other competition wins by Gesellius, Lindgren and Saarinen in this period – the Helsinki Sports Palace and the apartment building at Hämeenkatu, Tampere, both 1898, and even the Turku Library designed between February and May 1899 – were in neo-Renaissance and neo-Gothic styles with nary a hint of the ubiquitous Pirie or Richardson. However, after the promulgation of the February Manifesto that year, both questions were decided: style to be particularised as National Romantic and technique to be generalised as the use of granite. Overnight, architecture became a polemic on national identity when:

Finnish students ski-ed the length and breadth of the land collecting over half a million signatures for a protest to the Tsar. Some eleven hundred eminent Europeans signed a petition, 'Pro Finlandia', and a deputation headed by a French Senator waited on the Tsar in St Petersburg, but was refused an audience.[133]

This transition was concretised in the National Romantic Pohjola Fire Insurance Building, Aleksanterinkatu, Helsinki, 1899–1901, won in competition by Gesellius, Lindgren and Saarinen. Decorative elements were intentionally placed to emphasise tectonic strength in a manner quite unlike that of Classic or Gothic authority. The main entrance off Aleksanterinkatu is of the Boberg[134] type but radically transformed. Masonry is variously massive rock-faced or ashlar soapstone cut as if it were the harder granite. Cyclopean blocks flank the entrance supporting a frontispiece of barbaric splendour representing the flora and fauna of the Finnish forests. The corner tower is framed by four cylindrical pillars and capped by a bullet-shaped, shouldered spire of pitted copper rising from 16 columns of various diameter with scale-like surfaces. In the interior, the architects and the artists engaged by them made the transition from the largely naturalistic form of the elevations to a new symbol language loosely based on folk art.[135] The world was alerted to National Romanticism by their winning entry in the competition for the Finnish Pavilion at the Paris World Fair in the pivotal year of 1900. However, it was a timber building clad in painted canvas pretending to be

Karelian influence on Finnish National Romanticism: Pohjola Insurance, Aleksanderinkatu, Helsinki, 1902, architects Gesellius, Lindgren and Saarinen.

stone and revealed too obviously its many debts to Pirie, Richardson and Boberg to be considered other than transitional. Indeed, its filigree spire, closely related to Pirie's Queen's Cross Church, Aberdeen, 1881, (see page 67) disappeared from their work thereafter.

The Doctor's House at Fabianinkatu, Helsinki, 1900–1, by Gesellius, Lindgren and Saarinen rises on a series of pointed and stilted arches from very low springing points, barely 120 centimetres from pavement level and terminates in a massive tiled roof. Similarly simplified is their competition-winning Olofsborg apartment building, 1902 and Eol apartment building, 1901–3, both Katajanokka, Helsinki, where mass and mushroom or forest-like forms dominate. This format became a standard in

National Romanticism in timber and canvas: Finnish Pavilion, Paris International Exhibition, 1900, architects Gesellius, Lindgren and Saarinen.
(Drawing by Roger Emmerson)

America, Scotland and Karelia in the Olofsberg Apartments, Katanajokka, Helsinki, 1902, architects Gesellius, Lindgren and Saarinen.

The influence of America, Scotland and Karelia in his own house, Hvittrask, 1901–5, architect Henrick Gesellius.

apartment blocks by the likes of Selim Lindqvist (1867–1939), Werner von Essen (1875–1947) and Oiva Kallio (1884–1964) and throughout the districts of Katajanokka and Eira. The Pohjola itself also had its own progeny in works such as the Poli (the former Polytechnic Students Union Building, now a hotel), Lönnrotinkatu, Helsinki, 1903, and the Otava Publishing Company, Uudenmaankatu, Helsinki, 1906, both by Karl Lindahl (1874–1930) and Valter Thomé (1874–1918).

Gesellius, Lindgren and Saarinen hit the high point of folk-based National Romanticism in the four great house designs of 1900–2: K Selim's Villa, Espoo, 1901; Suur-Merijoki Farm, Vipuri, 1900–1; Hvittorp, Kikkonummi, 1901–2; and Hvitträsk, Kikkonummi, 1901– 5. Hvitträsk, their collective home and studio, summed up the trio's philosophy and their individual signatures. Gesellius, relatively over-shadowed by his more distinctive colleagues, slightly distanced and dying young, constructed off to one side of the courtyard a brooding log house on a massive granite base with a little tower at one end. Lindgren, commercial, confident and ultimately Classicising, included a tall timber tower, a variant of the Pohjola, while Saarinen, most original of the three, created a Finno-Ugric chieftain's lodge with wild interiors and a spiralling plan concealed behind a simple Arts & Crafts exterior. The drafting studio provided the link between Lindgren and Saarinen's houses.

Värt museum: a lesson for Scotland

The Finnish National Museum was under discussion throughout the 1890s. Hugo Lindberg produced a conventional palazzo design in 1899, a reworking of an earlier design by Sebastian Gripenberg (1850–1925).[136] The younger architects thought it no better than a warehouse. In an attempt to influence the Finnish Senate who were to meet in 1900 to decide the matter, Gesellius, Lindgren, Saarinen, Sonck, Bertel Jung (1872–1946) and Harald Neovius (1863–1930) published the pamphlet *Värt museum* (our museum) which, while principally aimed at how the museum should be planned, in Nikula's words,

> to change a cultural-historical museum from what was often a tedious collection of objects into a more exciting shrine,[137]

also speculated on its appearance:

> In the great building complex, peaceful yet picturesque in silhouette against the sky, rose a Gothic grey stone church in the style of a massive crown and an antiquated tower like that of a medieval castle. And immediately as one came closer, one could admire the unique and intimate simple decoration of this highly novel building which appeared to consist of styles borrowed from a number of ages and yet produced a remarkable unity and clarity in proportion and

Värt museum: National Museum, Mannheimintie, Helsinki, 1902, architects Gesellius, Lindgren and Saarinen.

line. I could feel my heart bursting with pride as I realised that it was my country, slender in resources, that had fabricated this work of art, that it was the history of my fellow countrymen that had inspired the architect's work and the people's great sacrifices.[138]

Gesellius, Lindgren and Saarinen's competition-winning design of 1902 amply fulfilled these predictions.[139] Moreover, the words of the pamphlet would find an uncanny echo at the end of the century in Scotland (see Chapter 6).

The train now departing from platform... how National Romanticism ended

By 1902, the campaign of civil disobedience prompted by the February Manifesto was flagging in the face of sustained Russian oppression under the hated Governor-General, General Bobrikov, further ennobled in April 1903 with the rank of Dictator. By 1904, around four-fifths of Finnish military conscripts had presented themselves for service. Consequently, folkloric National Romanticism served little purpose in the evaporating atmosphere of national resistance and, in that year, Gesellius, Lindgren and Saarinen were at work on a house design in a loosely Jugendstil format on an as-yet unidentified site for a Count Bobrinsky, a project sponsored by the Russian government. The assassination of Bobrikov by Eugene Schauman on 16 June 1904 and serious reverses in the Russo-Japanese War the following year caused the Tsar to relent. The Finnish Diet was reconvened, albeit in a tighter relationship to the Russian Duma, but, with universal suffrage, was in 1906 the most representative government anywhere in Europe.

National Romantic apotheosis: Helsinki Railway Station, 1904, architect Eliel Saarinen.

It is generally agreed that National Romanticism's brief folkloric existence ended in the controversy surrounding Saarinen's winning of the Helsinki

Railway Station competition in 1904 with a design based, in part, on the National Museum and, in part, on Onni Tarjanne's (1864–1946) National Theatre, 1900–2, with which the station connected. However, this was Saarinen's design alone and not the losing entry he submitted jointly with Gesellius and Lindgren. Saarinen's combination of folkloric National Romanticism and Romanesque met with considerable opposition led by the critic Gustaf Strengell (1878–1937) and architect Sigurd Frosterus (1876–1956), a losing competitor and former assistant of Henri van de Velde (1863–1957). Furthermore,

> [Frosterus's] belief that the new building should reflect rational thinking related to the nature of a railway station and should be less romantic and emotionally nationalistic in tone was expressed by his own project for the railway station, which was rejected by the jury as 'an importation, foreign and not very attractive'.[140]

Notwithstanding the jury's comments on Frosterus's entry, Strengell's and Frosterus's criticism led Saarinen to a redesign which incorporated several features from Frosterus's entry, which he improved upon, aligning it with contemporaneous German work by Peter Behrens (1868–1940) and Hans Poelzig (1869–1936).

International Style: how Finland joined a global family of nations

With Russia preoccupied by the October Revolution, Finland declared independence in December 1917. A brief civil war followed in 1918, mirroring the White and Red tendencies of the Russian civil war and then a short war with Soviet Russia, but by 1920 the matter was resolved. Nordic Classicism became, briefly, the official architecture evident in the new Parliament Building won in competition by Johan Sigrid Sirén (1889–1961) in 1923 and constructed in Mannerheimintie a stone's throw from the National Museum. Saarinen emigrated to the USA in 1923, following his second placing in the Chicago Tribune Tower competition, and constructed a grand 'Germanic' mansion for himself and his family at Cranbrook, Michigan, 1928–9, amongst his other works for the College there.

Ekelund reflected in 1932:

> In general, however, we are, perhaps, too much inclined at the present day to underestimate the importance of national romanticism,

Finnish Modernism: Turun Sanomat, Turku, 1928–30, architect Alvar Aalto. (Derek Fraser)

and to overlook too easily its positive sides, viz., that – at any rate in theory – it proclaimed function to be the deciding factor in architectural creation, that it devoted more interest than before to the solution of problems, that it introduced new materials into architecture and based its effects on the surface influence of the material and not only on the architectural design, whereby the way was cleared for the architecture of the present day.[141]

The 'architecture of the present day' was represented in the Modernism of Alvar Aalto (1898–1976), Pauli Blomstedt (1900–35), Erik Bryggman (1891–1955), Reima Pietilä (1923– 93), Viljo Revell (1910–64) and others. Aalto represented Finland at Hitchcock's and Johnson's International Style Exhibition in New York, 1932, with his *Turun Sanomat* Building, Turku, 1928–30.

Národní sloh: the Czechoslovak experience

The first Czechoslovak Republic[142], comprising the provinces of Bohemia, Moravia (the Czech Lands), Slovakia and, in 1919, Ruthenia, emerged from the collapse of the Austro-Hungarian Empire in 1918 following its defeat in WWI. The Czech lands and Slovakia had been notionally united through the actions of their separate independence movements in the late 19th century, by the formation of Tomáš Masaryk's (1850–1937) Realist Party in 1900, which acknowledged shared culture and related language,[143] and by the post-1914 political agitation of Seton-Watson who represented the Britain of Scotland and England to the Czechs and Slovaks as the model union.[144]

Krajči dated the prelude of statehood to 1891 when

> [t]he General Jubilee Exhibition was the crowning glory of the period of national emancipation, begun in the fields of language and literature and followed by a renaissance in culture, art and science, which peaked with the emancipation of Czech business and industry.[145]

To the usual totems of national achievement, Krajči added 'business and industry' because Czecho-Slovakia, which

Exhibition architecture: Industrial Palace, Prague, 1891, architect Bedřich Münzbeyer.

> despite only encompassing a fifth of the total area and a quarter of the inhabitants of the former Habsburg monarchy... contained much more than half of Austria-Hungary's industrial potential and just under half of the workers who had been employed in the Empire's industry.[146]

Moreover,

> despite the regional socio-economic imbalances inherited from the monarchy, Czechoslovakia numbered among the highly industrialised countries of Europe.[147]

Moderní: an early architectural experiment

While the Czechs and the Slovaks undertook investigations into their own folklore, in particular those of Dušan Jurkovič (1868–1947) in Wallachia, it was not to prove central in the creation of a national architecture at the significant moment and it would be quite wrong to assume that the matter of a Czecho-Slovak national architecture, whether based on folk-art or Art Nouveau, as was the late 19th century pattern, was settled by 1900. The

The influence of Wallachian folk-architecture: private house, Trenčianske Teplice, 1895, architect Dušan Jurkovič.

Bohemian neo-Renaissance, still prevalent since the 1870s, was waning in significance, yet remained a viable, non-political expression of Czecho-Slovak culture. It was the style favoured by Schulz for the Bohemian Museum, hardly surprising, given the building's contents and the Austro-Hungarian sensitivities it stood to offend. Jurkovič continued to work in a folk-based idiom while Art Nouveau in Prague was represented from the rich to the stripped to the monumental.

A stripped Art Nouveau was evident by the Peterka House in Vaclavske naměstí of 1899, where Jan Kotěra (1871–1923) began to develop the principles which governed his subsequent work – sometimes known as *moderní* – namely, function, structure and form, in that order. Kotěra, pivotal in the development of modern architecture in Czechoslovakia, further developed these principles in his own house at Hradešínská ulice, 1908, and in the house for the publisher, Jan Laichter, Chopinova ulice in Vinohrady of the same year, where a mixture of simple forms in brickwork and stucco were volumetrically combined and decoration was composed of banded or modelled brickwork identifying significant elements of structure. Kotěra's student Otakar Novotný (1880–1959) designed the Štenc House, Salvátorská ulice, 1909–10, in a similar manner. Kotěra's Urbánek House,

Jungmannova ulice, 1911, was the clearest expression of the style. Arguably, Kotěra based these principles on a development of his training with Otto Wagner in Vienna and of his understanding of contemporary English and Dutch brick architecture, especially that of HP Berlage, but transformed them into something completely new. There is proto-Cubist detailing in this building in the prismatic investigation of the depth of the façade, the canted copper edges to the dormer windows and the glazing bars to the apartment windows, but one hesitates to make any special claims for this building's transitional importance in that respect. Subsequently, Kotěra was involved in the design of a building which incorporated a number of genuine Cubist details, the General Board of Pensions offices at Rašínovo nábřeží, Prague, 1912–14, assisted by the Czech-German architect Josef Zasche (1871–1957), who later worked with Pavel Janák (1881–1956) in the design of the palác Adria (see more below). Rostislav Švácha commented on Kotěra's tentative relationship with Cubism and how Cubistic aspects were to appear, almost involuntarily, in his work during WWI, including his early designs for the Law and Theology Faculties at Charles University.[148]

Others working in this format included the sculptor František Bílek (1872–1941) in his own house, Mickiewiczova ulice, Prague, 1911; Alojs Balán (1891–1960) at the Budova YMCA, Malinovského ulicí, Bratislava, 1920–3; and even Jurkovič in his later work at the group of houses, Lermontovovej ulicí, Bratislava, 1923–4, which included his own house. Kotěra's vision of a new architecture was codified and monumentalised in his design for the Faculties of Law and Theology, Charles University, 1914, not completed until 1931 under the direction of his pupil Ladislav Machoň (1888–1973), who simplified and regularised Kotěra's original concept.[149] In this revised format, after 1918, Kotěra's architecture was felt to be truly representative of the new Republic, [and] was

Moderní: Štenc Publishing House, Josefov, Prague, 1909–11, architect Otokar Novotný.
(Drawing by Roger Emmerson)

officially adopted. This had a classical feel and made use of a dignified, monumental style of architecture. This direction was taken by many pupils from the Wagner School of architecture in the Vienna Academy, in particular Antonín Engel, František Roith and Bohumíl Hypšman. This style was very successful and, for the duration of the Republic, was used for all government buildings.[150]

Although his *moderní* acted as an intellectual and regulatory framework for subsequent architectural developments in Czechoslovakia, Kotěra's official commissions were limited. *Moderní* was, in part, contributory to Czech Cubism.

Cubism: the art of protest

Two of the principal factors driving the development of Czecho-Slovakian architecture at this time were the authority of Paris and the authority of the avant-garde, the joint expression of which was the phenomenon of Czech Cubism. Within four years of the first meeting of Georges Braque (1882–1963) and Pablo Picasso (1881–1973) in Paris in late 1907, Czech Cubist structures began to appear on the streets of Prague. Given the revolutionary nature of Cubism, its adoption by Czech architects represented a seismic shift in Czecho-Slovak culture, indeed, in architectural culture generally and well-nigh uniquely. Herbert Read (1893–1968) said of Cubism:

Czech cubist architecture: tenement, Neklanova, Vyšehrad, Prague, 1913–4, architect Josef Chochol.

> Cubism was not one more phase in the evolution of art – an evolution corresponding to social and economic trends: it was a decisive break with tradition. For five centuries European art in all its phases had been committed to *representation*; from the advent of Cubism onwards it was committed to quite another aim, that of *substitution*. That is to say, the representation of the phenomenal

image given in visual perception was abandoned as the immediate motif of the artist's activity, and in its place the artist elaborated a symbol, which might still retain reminiscences of, or references to, the phenomenal object, but no longer sought to give a faithful report of the optical image.[151]

Why might Czech architects wish to engage with such an artistic programme? Why is the only concentration of Cubist architecture to be found in Czechoslovakia (there are isolated examples in Wroclaw, Poland)? Why might *substitution* be a more resonant philosophy that *representation*?

Rostislav Švácha commented on the presence of *impression* in Czech architectural thinking:

if it is possible to identify a key term in the unwritten aesthetic of the late historical revival, it would certainly be the term effect or impression – words that appear in the Czech architectural thought from the late 1870s and which were more frequently used around 1900... the word impression may have helped architects express the notion that the building as a whole should hold priority over and above its constituent parts.[152]

Arguably Read's *substitution* is the mechanism, *impression* its effect. It is important to make the distinction that this *impression* is unconnected with Impressionism.

The Habsburg Empire was in stagnation following military defeat at the hands of the Prussians at Hradec Králové in 1866 and from the establishment of the *Ausgliech* of 1867 which divided it into areas of Germanic and Magyar influence – the Austro-Hungarian Empire. German landowners in Bohemia, although declining in numbers, still exerted considerable power within the Bohemian parliament and had influence at the German-speaking imperial court in Vienna, whereas Hungarian cultural and linguistic repression in Slovakia[153] left it without secondary schools and with national societies banned from 1874 to 1918. The Austro-Hungarian parliament was unable or unwilling to make any substantive moves to resolve ethnic tensions within the empire's boundaries or indeed to resolve the paralysing political contradictions brought about by the *Ausgliech*. Arguably, the sheer arbitrariness of life in Czecho-Slovakia under these conditions could have inclined artists towards substitution rather than representation which, by definition, meant more of the same irresolution; more *Ka-Ka*:[154]

the Habsburg concept of dynastic power was inextricably linked with the ideals of stability and the preservation of the existing order; but this cultivation of the status quo brought in its train feelings of futility, a kind of intellectual and moral stagnation which presented a marked contrast to the technological and scientific advances of the day.[155]

Arguably, Cubism in Czechoslovakia was not simply expressing the rejection of representational art but also the rejection of an unrepresentative societal and political construct. One of the first Cubist collectors outside Paris was the Czech Dr Vincenc Kramář (1877–1960), who acquired 20 Picasso paintings, graphics, sketches and sculptures between 1910 and 1913, together with works by Braque and Andre Derain (1880–1954), and who, by 1914, owned the largest private collection of Cubist works in Europe.[156] Guillaume Apollinaire (1880–1918), the poet who coined the term 'Cubism', was in Prague in 1902; sculptors Bohumil Kubišta (1884–1918) and Otto Gutfreund (1889–1927) were in Paris in 1909; Kubišta in Paris again in 1910 and the symbolist poet, Alexandre Mercereau (1884–1945) in Prague in 1913, all four significant Cubist protagonists.[157] Albert Gleizes' (1881–1953) and Jean Metzinger's (1883–1956) article '*du Cubisme*', published in Paris in 1912, had a long extract translated into Czech and was published in Prague only a year later.[158]

Čiháková-Noshiro discussed related influences:

In a way, Cubism became a kind of a modern analogy to the Gothic art which had dominated a significant period in the history of the Czech nation. It represented a spiritualised and logical order of matter, an order which originated in nature and was therefore closely related to the entire cosmic order... But as far as Czech art is concerned, another emotional and dynamical factor enriches the expressivity of our artistic work. Let us trace the strong influence of the Bohemian Baroque style upon Czech Cubist art for it represents another significant link with the traditional, cultural past.[159]

Wittlich recorded that *Umělecký měsíčník* (the Arts Monthly), the journal of the Group of Plastic Artists, whose members included the architects Ludvík Kysela (1883–1960), Josef Gočár (1880–1945), Vlastislav Hofman (1884–1964), Josef Chochol (1880–1956) and Pavel Janák (1882–1956), contained essays on Gothic, Renaissance and Baroque art[160] from 1911 onwards. Šlapeta felt that:

Respect for domestic traditions probably provided a historical context for the architects of this generation, and enabled Cubist architecture and the Gothic and Baroque buildings to co-exist harmoniously in the *genius loci* of the historic centres of Czech towns.[161]

The conundrum of achieving the happy and respectful co-existence of the new with the old greatly troubled Modern architects in Scotland later, as we shall see. However, Čiháková-Noshiro, Wittlich and Šlapeta were careful not to emphasise the national aspects of Czech Cubism because it also responded to German Expressionism and the attempt to escape from the strictures of the *Wagnerschule*. Janák prepared the way for what was to come:

> It is possible to give consideration and compare certain differences in view and development, whereby the present state of architecture has moved away from the beginnings of modern architecture and it can be seen in number and total that these are not the obituary notices of modern architecture nor a proclamation of some new modern architecture, but a diagnosis that recognises the coming revival and transition to a further continuous period in development.[162]

The objectives he stated were at variance with Read's definition of Cubism and reflected the modulatory, transitional function which Cubism played in Czech architecture.

In 1910, Janák was clear about the rejection of Otto Wagner's (1841–1918) 'Modern architecture' and how it would be achieved:

> Here we are of more advanced conviction if we put our own abstract ideas and forms above the individual qualities of the material and if we count with – and not only respect – the firmness and weight-bearing ability of the material which we subject, in view of the idea, to a certain stress and tension.[163]

As we shall see below, these ideas expressed in similar language had already been of significance for 19th century Scottish architecture. It is possible also to hear echoes of Loos's *Ornament and Crime* and *Architecture*, published in 1908 and 1910 respectively, in this statement. Janák went further in his criticism of his professor:

> We have even more definite ideas in view of the poetry of architecture, by which we raise that subordinate poetry in Wagner's motto... the past period of modern architecture has remained a historical one. It conceived and formed for its literary appearance or for qualities derived from

theoretical morale, but it did not understand and did not create form as a plastic shape, as a psychologically active and effective construction of lines, of planes and concrete details, which in their relationship of action and reaction become convincing of the idea with which they were built and are subjected to a common prohibition of affiliation of form, applied equally logically throughout the entire work.[164]

Kubišta conceived architectural styles as having 'empirical' and 'transcendental' forms which were inextricably linked and interdependent. The empirical embodied taxonomically similar forms: the nave of a church and a council chamber or the plant form of a Gothic capital and its replacement by a live plant; while the transcendental form

> contains the characteristic feature that it rouses images that we project into it... an intersection occurs between the symbolic effect and the induced effect existing in our mind, which need not have anything in common with contemporary intellectual views.[165]

He employed this argument to support an emotive plastic art that has 'a good deal in common with movement and rest', which

> can rouse an induced impression definable roughly as strength, longing, pleasure, depression, which is identical only with a general emotion expressed in architecture.[166]

This stance was adopted by the architect Hofman while he pressed for a more expressive architecture:

> To conceive the spiritual principles as something that lies close to man's original disposition, to understand him as a product of pure will leads to academic opinions, which, in the past century, were marked by schematicism, formality and a lack of creativeness.[167]

By entering architecture's forbidden zone of the non-rational, Hofman began to open up the discussion of architectural form to a more inclusive interpretation, one that was capable of acknowledging its historic and regional precedents, the rejection of which was a problem at the heart of Modernism throughout the greater part of the 20th century. He wrote, paraphrasing Ruskin:

> The line leading from the core of a Gothic rib in an abstract internal

form, which changes dead matter into a living form close to nature. Modern architecture longs for a similar expression. It longs for the application of a sense of constructive form.[168]

Although proposing what might have been seen, certainly by its opponents, as a decorative *schema*, Hofman, as did Loos, distanced himself from the Secession:

> Any restless coloured attachment of spotted ornament as found e.g. on modern pseudo-folk crafts would be illogical. The principle of 'space in matter' does not have any need of decorations.[169]

Chochol, though he was soon to abandon Cubism for 'purism',[170] echoed Hofman:

> we have today ceased to be interested in small architectonic detail and we do not believe in it. We are interested in exciting feeling and shape that leaves an impression as a whole, totally, making a total and immediate impression… What we first ask for and need is new excitement of novel intensity artistically, issuing from the stormy and burning matter of contemporary life.
> The disintegrating elements that we have in mind developed primarily in the styles that were born out of the southern psyche, such as the Greek style and that of Antiquity in general, too much based on reason while it lacks the elements of sensibility, fantasy and excitement, closer to our northern character.[171]

Kubišta summed up this attack on the purely rational:

> This shows that the power of reason is at an end here, since it does not in any way regulate the induced impression and does not in any manner determine why… a certain and not a different element was taken as a basis when the alternative might have fulfilled the purpose just as well.[172]

Paris, the centre of Cubism, produced only one design for a Cubist building: that of Raymond Duchamp-Villon (1876–1918), 'Maison Cubiste', which was a model of the front elevation of a small Cubist villa shown at the Salon d'Automne Cubist exhibition of 1912, where he also designed the entrance and rooms. Cubism had developed rapidly from its initial analytic phase to its synthetic phase around 1908, and consequently both were available as sources to architects. Duchamp-Villon's attempt was analytic,[173] as were

Janák's designs such as the Jacubec House, ulice Maršála Koněva, Jičín, 1911, the house at Strachovská ulice, Pelhřimov, 1912 or the reconstruction of Dr Fára's house, Masarykovo náměstí, also Pelhřimov, proving perhaps that the most inspired pamphleteers do not always make the most convincing designers. In the words of Jan Sokol (1936–2021):

> Everything that was new was thought up by Janák, but realised by Gočár.[174]

Gočár's Cubist work, from the start, exhibited a convincing synthetic Cubism; works such as U černé Matky Boží, Celetnákovo ulice, Prague, 1911–2, Spa Bohdaneč, Pardubice or the duplex at Tychonova ulice, Prague, 1912–3. Also synthetic were the group of flats and residences by Chochol beneath the castle at Vyšehrad, Prague: the villa at Libušinkovo ulice, 1911–2; the triplex at Rašinkovo nábřeži, 1912–3; and the apartment block at Neklanova ulice, 1913 (see page 80).

The Czech legions: the nascent state

In WWI, Czechs, Slovaks and Southern Slavs[175] were formed into regiments on the side of the Central Powers of Germany, Austro-Hungary, Italy and Turkey, initially under the command of their fellow-countrymen but later, following mass desertions, under Austrians and Hungarians. As Sheila Grant Duff (1913–2004) (granddaughter of the Scottish imperial administrator Sir Mountstuart Grant Duff) observed:

> [the Czechs] were given little encouragement to fight; for if the Central Powers lost the war, they would be involved in the ruin which those Powers had brought upon themselves. If the Central Powers won, the only outcome would be a strengthening of German Imperialism… Alike in defeat and victory, freedom – even the limited freedom they possessed – would be lost.[176]

Entire Slav regiments deserted to the Russians to be joined by Czech and Slovak prisoners-of-war held in Allied camps. They formed legions which returned to the front as combatants on the Allied side. As Seton-Watson observed:

> Public opinion in Bohemia has always been consistently Francophil and Anglophil, and above all Russophil, emphasising the kinship and blood ties of all the Slav races.[177]

Grant Duff recorded no less than 16 divisions comprising Czechs, Slovaks and Southern Slavs engaged in the Allied war effort, which Seton Watson described in detail in a letter to the Intelligence Bureau of the British government's Department of Information on 6 July 1917:

> Arrangements have now been completed for the definite establishment of a Bohemian army, with its own insignia, flags and organisation, from among the Czech prisoners in Russia, and its despatch to the French front... It is hoped that 30–40,000 troops in all will be sent... Negotiations have been conducted between the Czech Council in Paris and the Italian ambassador in Paris, for permission to secure the Czech prisoners now in Italy – 10–12,000 in number.[178]

The Czech, Slovak and Southern Slav contribution to the war was critical, especially following the Russian Revolution of 1917 which deprived the Allies of substantial military strength. In the summer of 1918, the Czecho-Slovak Legions were formally recognised as a constituent Army in its own right fighting for the Allied cause. Grant Duff noted:

> The justification for their recognition as belligerents was the presence at the front of Czechoslovak Legions. The justification for the recognition of Czechoslovak independence was the course of events in Austria-Hungary.[179]

In the concluding months of the war, Legions fighting in the Russian sector found their westward progress blocked by the Russian Civil War and undertook an epic 9,000-kilometre march across Siberia to the Pacific, thence to return to combat on the Western Front. The march, Legion battle successes at Zborov and Bachač and their gaining of international recognition for Czecho-Slovakia ensured the Legions a special status in the formation of the nation and in the imagination of ordinary Czechs and Slovaks. Contingent upon President Woodrow Wilson's Fourteen Points for peace, independence was declared on 18 October 1918 and the new republic came into existence formally ten days later.

The architecture of nationhood: Rondo-Cubism, *národní sloh*, the national style

This military diversion leads directly to the major work of rondo-Cubist architecture, the Legiobanka, Prague, 1921–3. The transformation of Cubism

Narodní sloh, national style: Legiobanka, Na Poříčí, Prague, 1921–3, architect Josef Gočár.
(Drawing by Roger Emmerson)

National style interior: Legiobanka, Na Poříčí, Prague, 1921–3, architect Josef Gočár.

into rondo-Cubism originated in an unidentified sketch[180] by Janák and in his overlaid amendment to the design for the weir at Předměřice nad Labem,[181] both 1914, where he experimented with circular, semi-circular and rectilinear forms and motives. External colours were those of the Baroque; ochre, cream, pink, rust and grey stucco on brick or in some cases in the use of marble. Folkloric detail was transformed as a substitution not a representation. Cubism was thus reinterpreted in the use of a static Euclidian geometry in architectonic form and detail rather than transcendent planar form-shifting.

The Banka Československých legií was 'established originally as an agency for the financial affairs of the Czechoslovak legions in Siberia' and for 'capital activities particularly in Slovakia and Ukraine'.[182] The Legiobanka also represented the Legions' successes, the founding of the new republic, the foregrounding of finance, industry and commerce in the national project and the further development of rondo-Cubism. Won in competition in 1922 by Gočár, the Legiobanka brought to maturity earlier work such as Janák's Crematorium, Pardubice, 1921, Gočár and Janák's family houses for Josef Zavadil in Štrasnice, Prague, 1919–21, Janák's Hořovský villa, na Lysmách, Prague, 1921–2 and Gočár's temporary Mánes Hall, Vodičkova, Prague 1921. The interior of the Legiobanka has a richness and lyricism that the sober façade masks, especially in the domed Columbarium on the first floor and in the metalwork of the handrails, elevator grilles and gates and the spectacular banking hall with its triple barrel-vault which

> combines the well-known pattern used by Otto Wagner in the Postal Savings Bank in Vienna with Perret's engineering ingenuity.[183]

While the Legiobanka was the zenith of rondo-Cubism, there is no doubt for many that Janák's palác Adria, Jungmannova, Prague, 1923–5, for the Italian financial institution Riunione Adriatica, represented its nadir. Where Gočár's economy, restraint and lightness of touch did much to open up a seemingly restrictive aesthetic, Janák managed to cover

> this truly imposing building with sculptural decoration where overabundance probably did exceed a healthy and tolerable measure, resulting in dull uniformity.[184]

Le Corbusier, on his second visit to Prague in 1925, echoing MacCallum on Sonck, commented on 'the massive building of Assyrian character, which I notice across the street', to which Janák responded, 'What the gentleman is talking about, we have already finished with'.[185] Sedláková suggested rondo-Cubism 'never really gained mass popularity'.[186] Perhaps not, but it is widespread in official and domestic buildings throughout Czechoslovakia.

Veletržní palác: the Modern Movement and the International Style

The demise of *národní sloh* was signalled by the construction of the Veletržní palác, Holešovice, Prague, 1924–8, by Oldřich Tyl (1884–1939) and Bohuslav Fuchs (1894–1979). Its monumental functionalism established the mature shape of a Modernist Czechoslovak architecture as the nation took its place in the world community.

Le Corbusier, at the time working on the design for the Centrosoyuz, Moscow, remarked that:

> Seeing the Trade Fair Palace, I understood how to make large buildings, having so far built only several very small houses on a low budget.[187]

Czech Modernism: Veltržní palác, Prague, 1924–8, architects Bohuslav Fuchs and Oldřich Tyl.

In confirmation of the nation's new international status, the Moravian architect Otto Eisler (1893–1968) represented Czechoslovakia at the International Style Exhibition, New York, 1932, with semi-detached houses for himself and his brother at Lipová ulice, Brno, 1926–7.

In 1994, I wrote:

> each stylistic experiment was aimed at a contemporary expression of what it meant to be Czech. That such an expression of avant-gardism was more than a merely intellectual construct and was directly connected with a national project – the recreation of the Czechoslovak nation-state – is seen in its comprehensiveness. All aspects of life were touched and all men and women could take part: to be Czech was to be avant-garde, to be avant-garde was to be patriotic.[188]

2

An architecture for the age: 1781–1887

A Gothic romance

FERGUSSON EXPLAINED WHY the chronology of an old building was so important to the Victorian because:

> Not only could you fix a date on every part and every detail, but you could read in them the feelings and aspirations that influenced the priest who ordered, or the builder or carver who executed them.[1]

This sense of the building as record of past achievement informed the 'new' architecture of the 19th century where an abiding sense of history-in-the-present affected crucially the stylistic choices of architects and their clients, were they aristocratic, bourgeois or, of increasing importance, mercantile or industrial. They intended, by means of appropriate choice, that their present achievement, as represented in their works, might be favourably regarded by future generations.

Robert MacLeod (1932–2003) described the challenge:

> During a century which was so self-consciously attempting to relate itself to its past, the developing activities of historians were of central importance, not only in explaining that past, but in shaping directions of the future. In architecture this was particularly true.[2]

Whereas Collins got straight to the point: 'The historians would not rest until architects had complied with their demands'.[3]

The matter was further complicated by conflicting calls for an 'architecture of the age'. Collins queried the conundrum and detailed its consequence:

But [Fergusson] found himself, on the one hand, denying that the current architectural expression of his own society could possibly be a true architecture (simply because it was not a new architecture), and on the other hand denying that current architecture was genuinely contemporary, because it gave no indication of the forms which future generations would create.

The result of such paradoxical contradictions was simply to create a sense of acute self-consciousness among architects, who were henceforth unable to design any forms normally because they were watching themselves create.[4]

Such a situation persists today in Tom Dyckhoff's (b. 1971) construct of the 'uneasy architect'.[5] The poles of this dichotomy were most clearly represented in the contrasting positions of John Ruskin (1819–1900) and Gottfried Semper (1803–79). Although Semper was briefly employed by Joseph Paxton (1803–65) and lectured in English as early as 1853,[6] it is highly unlikely, as with Muthesius and Loos later, that he was available to non-German-speakers and consequently that his direct practical influence in Scotland was limited at the time.

Semper anticus: a pun, ever forward

Semper's *The Four Elements of Architecture* of 1851 established a series of astylar ur-principles in a far-reaching – in that it remains relevant today – and wholly original examination of how things, not just buildings, are made, how the parts come together and the manner in which those junctions are celebrated decoratively and/or constructively. It is possibly helpful to describe in *very* brief outline the elements of Semper's system: 'Textiles, ceramics, tectonics (carpentry) [and] stereotomy (masonry, and so on).' He defined 'textiles' as 'pliable, tough, lightly resistant to tearing, of great absolute strength', that is, it is two-dimensional and membranous; 'ceramics' as 'soft, malleable, capable of being hardened, easily shaped and formed, and retaining a given form when hardened', three-dimensional and plastic; 'tectonics' as 'stick-shaped, elastic, principally of *relative* strength, that is, resistant to forces working vertically along the length', slender and tensile; and 'stereotomy' as 'strong, *densely-aggregated*, resistant to crushing and compression thus of significant *reactive* strength', massive and compressive.[7]

He further reordered his elements to reflect the sequence of construction from 'hearth' – foundation, plinth and lower floor; to 'framing' – upper floors and roof; to 'weaving or cladding' – boarding, sheeting or cladding on walls, thatching, slating or sheeting on roofs; to 'berm or mass walling' – outer walling, mass masonry construction, civil engineering. The non-specificity of the material referred to in Semper's 'divisions' permits equal validation of materials and constructions available in the 1850s and of any materials or constructions that might subsequently be invented and used, from the Modern Movement's so-called 'new' materials of glass, steel and concrete through to present-day alloys, resins, modified timbers and so on.[8] Semper explained:

> It is essential for what follows to clarify this classification by adding every division is to be taken in its broadest sense.[9]

Semper conceived of these constructional processes as the 'husk' which contained the 'kernel' which is the use or idea. This is the merest headline précis of Semper's dense and extensive text, but will serve to elucidate some of its several fundamental astylar principles and how they continued to guide architectural production in the Modern period.

Semper acknowledged that objects so designed and fabricated might reveal symbolic or representative content either in conventional formal decoration or in the abstract signification of the inhering stresses at the joints and junctions of the object. In a lecture given at the Zurich Rathaus in 1869, berating the purveyors of a contemporary aesthetic eclecticism which ignored more fundamental architectural verities, he noted:

> there is, as we said, the chorus of private style innovators, who shine their cheap inventive spirit on every large and small residence, railway station, and everywhere. In most cases they start from the erroneous assumption that the question of style is chiefly a constructive question and do not acknowledge the inherited traditions of artistic symbolism.[10]

Semper identified these practitioners as

> 'architectural materialists', those swept away by new constructional possibilities… 'historicists'… those eager to take as models certain works of art from times long past… and the 'purists, schematicists, and futurists' led by the abstract formulas of contemporary aesthetics.[11]

In a sly reference, possibly to Ruskin, he admonished that:

Finally, we should mention those who seek in a return to the medieval or the so-called Gothic style the future of the national architecture and their own future – and they are hardly ever mistaken regarding the latter.[12]

Despite the acuity of his analysis, Semper, to his own considerable dismay, was unable to synthesise the 'style of his age' that he deemed relevant. He settled instead for a competent Baroque through which he demonstrated his 'elements' but with nothing like the authority inherent in their astylar conceptualising.

The lamplighter: Ruskin's gothic

Ruskin's meticulous, conservative, rigorously academic, passionately committed and seminal research, published in *The Stones of Venice* in 1851 and 1853,[13] considered the ancient works *in situ* and set the template for subsequent historic and architectural investigations and conservation in the second half of the 19th century. His insistence on the significance of the building or artwork in its time, in its present milieu and its preservation in its present state, not its conjectural restoration, focussed attention on the specific cultural and personal relevance and resonance of these objects within their historic places as they then stood. He sought to stay the 'improving' hand, his artistic vision encompassing decay, incompletion and irregularity because

> it so happens that, in architecture, the superinduced and accidental beauty is most commonly inconsistent with the preservation of original character, and the picturesque is therefore sought in ruin, and supposed to consist in decay… so far as it can be rendered consistent with the inherent character, the picturesque or extraneous sublimity of architecture has just this of nobler function in it than that of any other object whatsoever, that it is an exponent of age, of that in which, as has been said, the greatest glory of the building consists… so essential to my mind that I think a building cannot be considered as in its prime until four or five centuries have passed over it.[14]

The ashlar-clad 14th-century Cathedral of St Giles on Edinburgh's High Street is evidence of the 19th-century 'improver' at work, simultaneously destroying much of both the historic fabric and character of the building.[15] Fergusson concurred with Ruskin:

AN ARCHITECTURE FOR THE AGE: 1781–1887

The conflict of history and the 'improving' hand: St Giles Cathedral, Edinburgh, 1829–38, architect William Burn.
(Bewahrerderwerte, own work, Creative Commons)

Neither can I look without extreme sorrow on the obliteration of everything that is truthful or worthy of study in our noble cathedrals or beautiful parish churches: nor do I care to refrain from expressing my dissent from the system which is producing these deplorable results.[16]

The second half of the 19th century was, in large measure, a period of eclecticism and differentiation in architectural styles when Ruskin's monism presented as possibly just too demanding in terms of taste, skill and budget for the average client, architect and artisan. To meet client demand for novelty, architects sought out ever-more arcane corners of the near-forgotten past as resource, although, by the 1850s, such manifestations at home were now less the display of the plunder of ancient artefacts, as in the days of the 'Grand Tour', than the reproduction in new construction of the simpler, less doctrinaire styles of previous centuries such as the early non-Italian Renaissance and regional French, German or Flemish Gothic styles repurposed from the obscure non-metropolitan corners of Europe or, indeed, to a limited extent and later, from those at home.

95

Beyond Ruskin's international influence as a writer in Europe and North America or AWN Pugin's (1812–52) Gothicising reaching as far as Budapest,[17] these studies by architects were for domestic consumption, presented as papers at local philosophical, antiquarian or architectural societies or in the journals of the day[18], or, in practice, they became part of the architect's stock-in-trade. However, differentiation was not so simple or discrete, because clients' catholicity of choice was such that, as Curl puts it:

> architects were obliged to be *acquainted* [Curl's emphasis] with all styles, but that, while architects of talent could produce respectable and scholarly essays in Classical or Gothic styles, their less competent brethren were likely to be uneasy with some styles, cautious with others and hamfisted with the rest.[19]

Respect for the past was widespread and conservative and depended on careful method far more than on radical concept, whereas contemporaneous formation of the future was infrequent and progressive and required radicalism in means, method and concept, which clashed with the fact that

> the evocative or associational value of certain styles for certain uses was a dominant element in Victorian architecture.[20]

Those 'values' only rarely implicated nationalist sentiment while proponents of an 'architecture of our age' left the message for posterity unresolved. Architecture was further challenged by the acquisition of technology, materials and constructions previously the province of the engineer and of engineering structures such as mills, bridges and railway sheds. Francastel commented:

> The economic and mechanical consequences of the discovery of new technologies had obvious practical repercussions: every day, the application of new procedures made it possible to produce new devices and materials; it offered the evident industrial potential of mass production. In contrast, the intellectual, social and aesthetic consequences of new technology were not clear. Theorists were divided, and artists were not producing works that seemed to bear out a new style.[21]

Ruskin latterly abandoned his earlier interest in Gothic stereotomy – his 'science of inner construction' – for the surface effects of Venetian polychromy. This dislocation, possibly arising from the sheer proliferation of the new and unincorporable technologies, at least, unincorporable for Ruskin, was evidently not what he envisaged when he began his work. As he surveyed the late Victorian city, Ruskin felt his efforts had been lacking:

> I perceived that this new portion of my strength had also been spent in vain; and from amidst streets of iron, and palaces of crystal, shrank back at last to the carving of the mountain and the colour of the flower.[22]

Greek tyranny

Ruskin did not like the New Town in Edinburgh. He instructed his audience at the Philosophical Society of Edinburgh to:

> [w]alk round your Edinburgh, and look at the height of your eye, what you will get from them [sic]. Nothing but square-cut stone – square-cut stone – a wilderness of square-cut stone for ever and for ever; so that your houses look like prisons, and truly are so; for the worst feature of Greek architecture is, indeed, not its costliness, but its tyranny.[23]

His walk to the Queen Street lecture hall from his lodgings in Albyn Place was a sore trial for him:

> How many windows precisely of this form [Fig.1] do you suppose there are in the New Town of Edinburgh? I have not counted them all through the town, but I counted them this morning along this very Queen Street, in which your Hall is; and on the one side of that street [Queen Street has a garden on the north side], there are of these windows, absolutely similar to this example, and altogether devoid of any relief by decoration, six hundred and seventy-eight.[24]

Ruskin's was less a lecture on architecture in general than a promotion of the Gothic and denigration of the Greek and, in consequence, of Classical Edinburgh, a point which he further expanded on in the published Addenda to the lectures. Ruskin possibly did not know what Robert Billings (1813–74) knew contemporaneously about the Baronial[25] nor what Macleod, Campbell and Fawcett later ascertained in respect of the persistence of Classical form and Scottish divergence from the architecture of England (see more below). It would seem that he may have had sight of Billings' illustrations, commenting favourably on Craig Millar [sic], Holyrood, Crichtoun [sic], Roslin Chapel and Melrose Abbey among others, but, beyond their irregular profiles and the associational qualities they shared with a more universal Gothicism, their Scottish national significance did not register with him.

When Ruskin raised a matter of moment – square-cut stone – it was dismissive and he was on to another topic in an instant; the contrasting aesthetic and haptic merits of a six-hundred-year-old English ogival window. However, Scotland's masons now working on the asymmetric Baronial designs of William Burn (1789–1870), David Bryce (1803–76) and others were those self-same masons who most recently had shaped the square-cut stone Ruskin so reviled. Moreover, in the age of eclecticism, masons, as Curl confirmed, turned their hands to construct details in Greek, Roman, Renaissance, Gothic and even Egyptian styles or, indeed, any denomination or combination of them which the client chose and the architect contrived. The new Baronial structures, such as Balfour Castle, Shapinsay, Orkney, 1846, by Bryce, then in construction were not decaying or ruinous. They inevitably featured not the lime renders and lime washes, distressed ashlar and random rubble walling and the weathered embellishments of Billings' originals, of which Ruskin would have approved, but the precision of sharp arrises, machine-cut or regularly chiselled, droved or broached facing stones, regular coursed or snecked rubble, repetitive mouldings and plate glass throughout; exactly what Ruskin's contemporary Gothic revival – which he came to question – entailed. The Baronial was an interpretation, not a reconstruction

Scots Baronial in ashlar and plate glass: Balfour Castle, Shapinsay, Orkney, 1846, architect David Bryce.

(Purplebaron, own work, Creative Commons)

or replication of an original. The choice of a 'noble' material – ashlar masonry – immediately set it apart from the 'humble' lime-harled[26] or lime-washed appearance of some of its models.

The question of appropriate material in national style construction – of ashlar and its jointing, of various rubble coursings and their jointing, of lime harling or wash, of their presence or absence, their colour or whiteness or the timber jettying, framing and panelling such as is still visible at John Knox's House, Edinburgh – returned from time to time over the following 170 years. It dogged the heels of the proponents of a Scottish architecture based on reproductions or reinterpretations of Billings' 15th to 17th-century models in their search for an appropriate materiality. These adherents also repeated, as if a mantra, variations on his claim that

The formally and materially expressive late mediaeval house: John Knox's House, Edinburgh, 1490 onwards.

> [w]e say, without fear of contradiction, that there is no mistaking a Scotch house of the period named, for that of any other nation.[27]

Although that could not help them in their quest for either authenticity or an expression of contemporaneous identity.

Reports of Ruskin's lectures recorded that his delivery veered between the humorous and the preachiness of a minister,[28] the latter something of which the good burghers of Edinburgh had a sufficiency on Sunday. For all his conviction and Gothic religiosity, Ruskin was no prophet. The iron and glass architecture he decried came to dominate city centres worldwide, even in Scotland. The sprig of ash he satirically redrew in a geometricised 'Greek' style to press home his point about the inferiority of Greek architectural decoration[29] was, in 40 years' time, to be matched and surpassed by the use of equivalent geometricised arboreal and horticultural abstractions in the designs of Louis Sullivan, Frank Lloyd Wright, Charles Rennie Mackintosh and Josef Hoffmann (1870–1956). Despite this early dislike, Ruskin later favoured the red-black Greek pottery designs of the 5th to the 3rd centuries BCE. Ruskin's position was refused half a century later in Wilhelm Worringer's (1881–1965) *Abstraction and Empathy* of 1908, in which he noted,

> the basic purpose of my essay is to show that this modern aesthetics, which proceeds from the concept of empathy, is inapplicable to wide tracts of art history.[30]

By 'modern', Worringer meant the aesthetic theories of the 19th century, including Ruskin's. He continued in Kantian fashion:

> Its Archimedean point is situated at one pole of human artistic feeling alone. It will only assume the shape of a comprehensive aesthetic system when it has united with the lines that lead from the opposite pole.
> We regard as this counter-pole an aesthetics which proceeds not from man's urge to empathy, but from his urge to abstraction.[31]

The fitness of proportion: why things look 'right'

The *Edinburgh Guardian*'s polite, if mildly censorious criticism – of Ruskin's style rather than substance – was not the stance adopted by Alexander Thomson in Glasgow. While he appreciated Ruskin's industry and the integrity and authenticity of his theory he believed, in its application, to

> know no one who has done more to mislead the public mind in matters of Art than he.[32]

By the mid-19th century, the antithetical thread of Classicism was not simply the matter of a particular Scottish taste and history as proposed by MacLeod,[33] but was given theoretical bases in the writings of the Irish philosopher Edmund Burke (1729–97), of the Scottish Episcopalian priest Archibald Alison (1757–1839)[34], of the Glasgow architect and mathematician Peter Nicholson (1765–1844)[35], of the Anglo-Scot historian James Fergusson, and, indeed, of Thomson himself.

In 1757, Burke published a treatise on aesthetics entitled *A Philosophical Enquiry into the Origin of Our Ideas of the Sublime and Beautiful*, which interested Immanuel Kant. Kant, who 'claimed that Hume's skepticism awoke him from his dogmatic slumber',[36] took the view that Burke did not probe deeply enough into what drives human responses to the sublime and the beautiful and that it was for Kant to pick up where he left off. Kant proposed that

> reason is divided against itself, a state at which the sceptic rejoices, but which must make the philosopher pause and feel ill at ease... Thus they reveal by the use of these principles, the dialectical illusion of pure reason, which would otherwise forever remain concealed.[37]

He added:

> I would be pleased to have the critical reader to devote to this antimony of pure reason his chief attention, because nature itself seems to have established it with a view to stagger reason in its daring pretensions and to force it to self-examination.[38]

It is in the Kantian tension of thesis and antithesis that we may reconfigure those orthodox oppositions of Scottish architecture – rational/romantic, classical/gothic, traditional/modern, or Worringer's abstract/empathetic – as *antinomial*. Hare has observed in some contemporary Scottish art a similar antinomy which he has characterised more Classically as *Thanatos* and *Eros*.[39] Moreover, the art that concerned Alison and Burke, rather than the art that concerns us today, was *not* one

> whose forms have become autonomous from the dominion of the metaphysical assumptions and orientations of Christian faith.[40]

Nor were they autonomous from any other metaphysical assumptions. Alison, in 1815, broached issues of Modernity:

> That this Quality in Forms [fitness or function] is productive of the Emotion of Beauty, every one [sic] must probably have perceived... [e]ven the most common and disregarded articles of convenience, are felt as beautiful, when we forget their familiarity, and consider them only in relation to the purposes they serve.[41]

Sullivan's later aphorism that 'form follows function' and, later still, Le Corbusier's everyday *'objets types'* are here in embryo. Alison then treated with that which is not thought beautiful:

if the admirable Fitness of... [the] construction [of the head of the Swine], for the necessities of the animal, are explained, there is no person who will not feel, from this view of it, an Emotion of Beauty.[42]

In architecture, Alison maintained:

The Propriety or Fitness of any Building, intended for the habitation of Man, (as seen from without), consists chiefly in two things. 1stly, In its Stability; and 2dly, In its being sufficient for the support of the Roof.[43]

He clarified further:

A common wall is intended to support a roof, and derives its proportions in a great measure from this destination. To [a classical] order, the consideration of the roof is unnecessary. It is complete without any roof, and where a roof is necessary, it is generally so contrived as not to appear. The weight which is supported, or which appears to be supported in an order, is the Entablature.[44]

This separation into two classes of support and load had considerable impact on how Thomson later developed his architecture into the same two classes: wall/roof and column/entablature. Alison set considerable store in what he called 'Proportion', which he construed as the visual appropriateness, the relative slenderness or girth, of the support to its load, that is, of wall to roof or of columns to entablature. He wrote:

If it appears firm, it has all the proportions we desire or demand, and its form may be varied in a thousand ways, without interfering with our sense of its Proportion.[45]

While not claiming an absolute condition for Proportion in walls and roof and column and entablature, he recognised an inhering rightness and pleasing appearance which he construed as beauty. This source of beauty was quite separate from the decorative outer trappings of Doric, Ionic or Corinthian Orders and consequently had more general application in its essence. Thus:

The Proportions of these orders, it is to be remembered, are distinct subjects of Beauty from the Ornaments with which they are embellished, from the Magnificence with which they are executed, from the purposes of Elegance they are intended to serve, or the scenes of Grandeur they are destined to adorn.[46]

Alison considered then the imposition of one form on top of another and its consequences for the proportions of the forms thus superimposed:

> A plain stone, for instance, set upon its end, has no proportion further than for the purpose of stability. If it appears firm, it has all the proportions we desire or demand, and its form may be varied in a thousand ways, without interfering with our sense of its Proportion. Place a Column, or any other weight upon this stone; immediately another Proportion is demanded, viz. its Proportion to the support of this weight.[47]

This could be interpreted simply as a description of the parallel of the orders whereby the sturdy Doric supports the decorative Ionic which in turn supports the fecund Corinthian in increasing slenderness over three storeys or, later, over five storeys, with the introduction of the Tuscan between the Doric and the Ionic, and the Composite order surmounting the Corinthian – although Alison rejected them both as capricious Roman inventions. Given Alison's isolation of the decorative significance of the Orders, his notion related universally to any structure that showed progressive diminution in Proportion relative to the imposed load as the elevation rises. Anticipating Semper, although by different means, Alison sought an 'architecture of the age' where

> it ought to be the increasing study of the Artist to disengage his mind from the accidental Associations of his age, as well as the common prejudices of his Art; to labor to distinguish his productions by that pure and permanent expression, which may be felt in every age; and to disdain to borrow a transitory fame by yielding to the temporary caprices of his time, or by exhibiting only the display of his own dexterity or skill.[48]

Finally, and as a priest must, Alison related the matter of Fitness, Proportion and Beauty to the presence of a deity:

> There is yet, however, a greater expression which the appearances of the Material World are fitted to convey, and a more important influence which, in the design of nature, they are destined to produce upon us; their influence I mean in leading us directly to RELIGIOUS [Alison's emphasis] Sentiment.[49]

Alison is relevant for four reasons: firstly, because he posited his antinomial thought to include the rational and the numinous, the actual and the abstract, decoration and construction; secondly, he opened up a more considered understanding of the nature of the wall and column and of the subordination of the roof to the entablature in columnar construction; thirdly, for his very direct effect on Thomson's thoughts on architecture and in his practice; and fourthly for his elucidation of how an astylar 'architecture of the age' was achievable.

Romancing the stone: the romantic and rational attributes of the Baronial

Sir Walter Scott constructed the first house of an approximate Scottish revival character at Abbotsford, near Melrose, in three phases: 1811–2, 1816–9 and 1822–4. He employed two English architects, William Atkinson (1774–1839) and subsequently Edward Blore (1787–1879), although Blore was more of an illustrator whose *The Provincial Antiquities and Picturesque Scenery of Scotland* of 1819–22 probably caught Scott's attention. Everyone from Scott to his architects to his tradesmen had a hand in the design of this rambling confection of Gothic, Jacobethan, Baronial and Adam Castellated styles.

The Englishman Robert William Billings, with support from William Burn, brought some order to the topic with *The Baronial and Ecclesiastical Antiquities of Scotland*, published in four volumes between 1846 and 1852.[50] He suggested that:

> Scotland has been variously described as a poverty-stricken field as regards architectural illustration; and the writer, when he commenced his labours as a stranger to the country, of course shared in that general opinion.[51]

He corrected this initial negative reaction with his 240 plates, proving the depth of Scotland's historic architectural resource. His unexceptional aim was to encourage the preservation of their patrimony, fixing the characters, lives and times of the buildings' creators and makers. And he, like Ruskin, admonished that:

> Many edifices, of both historical and architectural interest, are silently disappearing from the land, without even the existence of a drawing to recall their features in times to come, when it will become, not

a mere fashion, but a matter of deep interest and pride, to preserve
the only tangible objects which as visibly connect men with their
predecessors while living, as the kirkyard does invisibly when they
mingle in death.[52]

Billings was not shy:

It has, perhaps, never before occurred that the Antiquities of a country
have been so carefully collated, as those of Scotland have now been,
by one individual.[53]

He claimed to downplay the use of shadow compared to others in this field
with quite a Modern comment that:

Light upon all features requiring delineation has been the rule; for it would
have been inconsistent with the object of affording an accurate representation of interesting details, to present them in the obscurity of shade.[54]

There is no question, however, that many illustrations, while revealing
sufficient architectural detail for the determined copyist, were romantic and
picturesque. Glendinning et al commented that:

Although based on accurate drawings, the finished illustrations
presented dramatically shaded (and sometimes imaginatively
embellished) perspectives of castles and churches. As with Adam the
subjects, even if symmetrical on plan, were presented in an irregular
and asymmetrical manner.[55]

This seems a testy assessment in that one of the specific attributes of the
architecture of the 16th and early 17th centuries was its volumetric
composition, best shown obliquely and sciagraphically. Moreover, Billings'
subscribers did not expect the illustrations to be orthogonal measured
drawings but to reveal associational and narrative content and the buildings'
present decay, albeit romanticised and elaborated.

Billings inveighed gently on the gentry to save their patrimony from
present ruin and use as convenient quarries for contemporary work. He
hoped to spread his message widely, more, one suspects, to prevent similar
thievery of masonry by the poor, than for their education:

He considers that were a respect for Antiquities once created among the labouring population, it would do more, by tenfold, for their preservation than any means which could be devised short of actual restoration.[56]

The Baronial was not simply about romantic association. It had become clear by the early years of the 19th century that the symmetrically-planned Classical or Gothic house, with its offices and kitchens located in wings distant from the main building attached by long corridors such as at Hopetoun House, 1699–1702, or Floors Castle, 1721–6, was inconvenient to manage and regulate. This was especially the case where establishments were reduced – meals cooling rapidly by the time they were brought from distant kitchens to the dining room or to the pantry to be reheated, servants requiring to be summoned from remote servants' halls or distant work, delays in answering the front door, and so on – and that a more convenient arrangement between master and servant, while still retaining class, sex and physical distance, was necessary. The historic architecture of Scotland and its asymmetric accretive nature and functional rather than formal arrangement of stairs and corridors enabled Burn to provide the efficient planning now demanded, to maintain the master/servant separation, to clearly identify, assign and celebrate the public and private parts of the house and to segregate male and female zones while satisfying a taste for narrative. His kitchens were still at some, if not too great a distance from the dining room. Muthesius commented later:

> Herein lies the 19th century's true cultural contribution to the English house. This is the work of science and hence a true child of a scientific century. Developed initially at large country-houses, it was fostered in the main by a group of Scottish architects headed by William Burn, who was a genuine pioneer in the science of planning.[57]

While the Baronial presented romantically, the logic of its planning was antinomially rational.

His support of Billings' project enabled Burn to develop further his mastery of the 'new' style through the acquisition of a multiplicity of useable models; to inculcate a supportive taste for the Baronial amongst an actual and putative British clientele – much as had Robert Adam for the Roman Diocletian amongst his – through subscription to the publications; and to secure authority and authenticity from well-researched originals. Burn, Billings and Blackwood's, the publishers, each put up a substantial sum. Burn's prestige as a significant country house architect for the Tory aristocracy and Billings' reputation as an architectural illustrator encouraged subscribers. Burn's contacts were such that he 'was sure of the Queen, Prince Albert and lots of Grandees' as subscribers; a confidence not misplaced. Among the grandees listed were several architects of repute: his partner David Bryce (1803–76), later to enjoy a substantial solo career as *the* architect of the Scottish Baronial; William Henry Playfair (1790–1857), Burn's competitor and rival and occasional essayist in the Baronial; (Sir) William Tite (1798–1873), establishment architect, architectural administrator and MP; (Sir) Charles Barry (1795–1860), joint architect with Pugin of the Houses of Parliament and infrequent Baronialist; George Aitchison (1825–1910), designer of the neo-Classical Leighton House, London, 1866–96, for the academic painter Frederick, Lord Leighton (1830–96); David Rhind (1808–83), pupil of Pugin, colleague of Barry and designer of the Baronial Selkirk Courthouse, 1865; Arthur Ashpitel (1807–69), prolific architectural writer and companion of the Scottish topographical painter David Roberts (1796–1864) on his Roman sojourn in 1853; Henry Ashton (1801–72), who may have known Burn, following him some years later into the office of Sir Robert Smirke (1780–1867) as an apprentice; and John Baird Premier (1798–1859) – no connection to Alexander Thomson's partner of the same name – designer of the innovative cast iron Gardner's Warehouse, Jamaica Street, Glasgow, 1855. It is not clear whether Philip Webb (1831–1915), William Morris's architect, had sight of Billings' volumes, but nonetheless he made a study tour of Scotland in 1857 and subsequently produced an Anglicised Baronial at Arisaig House in 1864.

Union and Empire: a context for the Baronial

The political circumstances into which the Baronial was pitched were, as Lynch noted, such that:

> The concentric loyalties of Victorian Scotland – a new Scottishness, a new Britishness and a revised sense of local pride – were held together by a phenomenon bigger than all of them – a Greater Britain whose prosperity and stability rested on the Empire.[58]

Ferguson noted that the Empire benefitted Scotland disproportionately to England due to 'the greater readiness of Scotsmen to try their luck abroad',[59] although he did not make clear whether that was as a consequence of limited opportunity at home. Lynch continued that the 1850s

> was also the decade which saw the first concerted 'nationalist' protest,

in the shape of the Association for the Vindication of Scottish Rights, formed in 1853... Scotland wanted not less union but more – in parliamentary representation and government expenditure – and on a fairer basis... The Association fizzled out in 1855, but it left an agenda which Scottish nationalism has drawn on ever since.[60]

Unlike its Czech and Finnish comparators, the Baronial had no discernible nationalist political content in the sense of its being a flag-bearer for separatism. Indeed, middle-class Scots in the main did very well from both Union and Empire and the slave-based colonial industries of tobacco, sugar and cotton in the 18th and early 19th centuries while Burn's clients and families like them did extraordinarily well from mining and agriculture at home. Rural and working class lives and their catastrophes – the Clearances and the famines in the Highlands or the weavers' strikes and revolts in the Lowlands in the 1820s to '40s – affected the commissioners of Baronial structures only insofar as they were inconvenienced in their functions as laird, landlord, plantation or factory owner. The visit of George IV to Edinburgh in 1822 and the acquisition and Baronialising of Balmoral by Prince Albert for Queen Victoria in 1852 put a monarchical stamp of approval on what Lynch tentatively offered as 'A new Caledonia?'.[61] The question mark is significant in that

> [a] new, sanitised vision of Scottishness emerged – in the minds, at least, of Lowlanders and tourists,[62]

the Royal Family presumably occupying that latter role. For the former, such was the fervour aroused by the Baronial that on winning the Pugin Travelling Studentship in 1877, (Sir) George Washington Brown (1853–1939), best-known for his later adaptation of the Francois I style at the Edinburgh Central Library, 1887, was tempted to travel at home since

> patriotism suggested I should avail myself of such an opportunity of becoming familiar with the architecture of my own country.[63]

He went in due course, as the promoters of the award intended, to France and Belgium to study the Gothic.

Such an architectural revival as the Baronial was not a novelty in Scotland. Campbell noted that earlier:

> The rejection of English influence in [14th century] architecture and the adoption of Romanesque revival elements is part of a wider

movement in Scottish society concerned with defining national identity… Three possible reasons present themselves: first, that it evoked associations of the very remote past, i.e., Scotland's Greek ancestors; second, that the Romanesque style was associated with the beginnings of the Scottish church; and third, that it refers to the period when the high Romanesque style was actually current.[64]

Campbell referred to a Scottish origin-legend told in a poem by Maelmura of Othain (d. 884) who 'assigns a Grecian origin to the Gaels', whereby ancient peoples from the Mediterranean basin were called on to authenticate longevity and continuity in patrimony and to present 'a riposte to the Brutus myth of the Britons'.[65] An alternative origin-myth had Pharaoh's equally-fictional daughter Scota – contemporaneous with Moses – as the begetter of the Irish Scotti,[66] who later migrated to Argyll and became the Scots.

Those factors which Campbell deemed significant in the revival of Romanesque were also present in the Baronial. He raised a fourth as to what a revival might *do* in that

> Brunelleschi's revival of Romanesque idioms paved the way for the full-blown classical revival of his successors in Italy. The Scottish Romanesque revival may have performed a similar function.[67]

Campbell's thoughts were echoed to an extent by Fawcett on the Renaissance who, while conceding that 'it is always debatable how far "national" qualities can be identifiable in any art form', took the view that there is an

> increased openness to *direct* [Fawcett's emphasis] inspiration by Continental architecture although any imported ideas were usually modified to attune them to Scottish usages; it may be mentioned that these usages seem also to have involved some renewed interest in earlier architectural solutions that had been current within Scotland itself.[68]

In search of the infinite: the rational and romantic attributes of the neo-Classical

Alexander 'Greek' Thomson's architecture has been the subject of considerable study, in particular Mark Baines' (1967–2020) investigation of his volumetric and symmetrical composition and use of columnar and wall motives.⁶⁹ However, Baines' account did not encompass Thomson's sources, Alison and Fergusson, of whom Craig noted that

> Fergusson insists on knowing a building from the inside outwards before he will judge it. In nothing is he more Scotch, Victorian, moralistic, and indeed modern, than this. And surely he is right.⁷⁰

With Alison's theories and Fergusson's models in mind, perhaps, Thomson had developed the core of his architectural thinking by the time of his first lecture, 'The Sources and Elements of Art Considered in Connexion with Architectural Design', delivered to the Architectural Institute of Scotland in St Mary's Hall, Renfield Street, Glasgow on 24 March 1853.⁷¹ This found concrete expression in his mature works from 1856 onwards.

One strand was the architecture of Egypt. He described idealistically a temple which could be that of Horus at Edfu, 237BCE and which Fergusson had illustrated, although Thomson never experienced it first-hand⁷²:

Thomson's model for wall and window: Temple at Edfu, Egypt, 237BCE.
(Library of Congress, Creative Commons)

First, all the intercolumniations except the centre are filled to a certain height with slabs of a plain character, giving an effect of solidity and breadth to the lower portion of the centre. Then the side piers and architrave enclose the design in, as it were, a continuous frame, and to complete the whole, the edifice is crowned with a cornice remarkable for its simplicity and dignity, consisting of a single curve of large proportions terminating in a narrow fillet. But while the attention is kept lingering about the centre half, chained by the fascination of its beauties half confined by the power of the surroundings and superincumbent mass, the management of the lines of contour awaken feelings which cannot be embodied.

The external lines of the side piers inclining towards each other as they ascend not only give an appearance of stability and suggest duration, but indicate a point of junction at an indefinite altitude; and the sharp clear horizontal line of the fillet of the cornice – hung, as it were, in air over the shadow of the curve and projecting considerably over the walls – points laterally into unlimited distance. In this composition we see variety in unity, a complex system controlled and governed by a presiding principle, thus realising in some measure that idea of order and harmony which every human soul thirsts after.[73]

The other strand was Greece. Thomson described:

This monument [the Choragic Monument of Thrasyllos, Athens, Greece, 320–19 BCE] has three columns of a square form, an arrangement which has been denounced by critics as intolerable in ordinary circumstances but, in this case, the balance is maintained by the centre column being narrower than those at the sides, and also the skilful management of the superincumbent structure.[74]

Thomson's model for the door and window: Choragic Monument of Thrasyllos, Athens, Greece, 320–19BCE.
(Creative Commons)

These were not simply archaeological descriptions but interpretations of the abstract architectural possibilities embodied in their forms and motives which Thomson used subsequently: the colonnade and framing entablature; the intercolumnar partial infill; the pronounced cornice; the incorporation of part wall and column; and the conjectural extension of forms infinitely vertically and horizontally. Alison's 'proportion' was present in the 'power of the surroundings and superincumbent mass' and 'the skilful management of the superincumbent structure'. Moreover, Thomson saw the inherent beauty of the Thrasyllos form exactly as Alison did in that 'if it appears firm, it has all the proportions we desire or demand'. He noted,

> [i]t is relative proportion, not actual magnitude that produces greatness, and this the Greeks understood thoroughly.[75]

He disdained the decorative excess of Roman architecture, as did Alison, where 'in short the Decorator took the place of the Architect'.[76]

Thomson's comments on the planar aspects of Edfu and the 'proportion' of the Choragic Monument of Thrasyllos and their use in both his wall and columnar designs anticipated Worringer's observation that

> the artistic volition of the ancient cultural peoples impelled them to approximate the artistic representation to a plane, because in the plane the tactile nexus was most strictly preserved and because, for this reason, the sought after depiction of external things in their closed materiality was most readily given expression in the plane.[77]

Thomson's flexibility in his combinatory use of these archaic models permitted him the freedom of abstraction, although it was unlikely that he would have so understood it, rather that it represented an 'eternalisation'[78], as Worringer put it, or the 'indefinite and incomprehensible', as did Thomson himself when he posed the antinomial question:

> What is more real than Deity, Space, Duration and Life, and at the same time what is more indefinite and incomprehensible?[79]

He considered the analogy of space-travel and relativity where

> [p]hilosophers, in explaining the nature of light and endeavouring to give us some idea of the rate at which it travels, tell us that some stars are so distant that, although they may have been created thousands of years ago, their light may not have reached us yet; or, that if it were

possible for us to fly off into space, we might, as we retire, survey backwards, as it were, all the events that have happened on our planet – that we might, by going to a sufficient distance, witness the very first act of its creation.[80]

Thomson placed himself in relative motion to other bodies in motion, which allowed him conjecturally to move both forwards and backwards in space and time, linking the transience of this life and the infinitude of his religious belief. He included 'duration' as one of his realities, which suggests he considered time from the variable subjective experience of a continuum rather than time as an absolute. There were perhaps echoes of both Kant's thoughts on time and space and his First Proposition in Thomson's observations. This might seem entirely contradictory to the fixed verities of his Protestantism or, possibly, simply reflected Thomson's antinomial stance, that is:

> *Thesis* The world has, as to time and space, a beginning (limit).
> *Antithesis* The world is, as to time and space, infinite.[81]

It is this notion of the existence of an antinomy that we might suggest Thomson investigated, possibly unknowingly, in an architecture which contrasted and combined the infinitude of the horizontal repetition of the regular, implacable and permeable columniated bay with the progressive dematerialisation of the massive eroded and 'ruined' solid wall to reveal that locus and the implicated relationships of the definite and the indefinite, the comprehensible and the incomprehensible, the commensurate and the incommensurate.

Widely available in *The Edinburgh Review*, and posthumously in *Lectures of Metaphysics and Logic*,[82] was the work of Scots philosopher William Stirling Hamilton (1788–1856). Hamilton proposed that an object can only be known as a consequence of its relationships to other objects which brings us close to Kant's 'thing in itself' and indeed to that strand of Scottish philosophy where, as Beveridge and Turnbull recount, there was

> the inclination to question the claims of science, the concern with the threat posed to ethics by the spread of positivist modes of thought, and the refusal to ignore or disesteem the dimensions of experience, knowledge and reality which are beyond the scope of scientific reasoning.[83]

Hamilton asserted that, although in purely scientific understanding space and time are mathematically commensurable to the rational mind, infinite space and absolute time are concepts rationally inconceivable to the rational mind and create the realm of religious faith such as might have appealed to the devout Thomson, or indeed to a vaguer sense of the numinous in those not so obviously religious.

Thomson's stints on two library committees – of the Glasgow Architects' Society from 1863 and the Royal Philosophical Society of Glasgow from 1869 – where he made suggestions for book acquisition[84] indicate he was not averse to book learning, only rote learning. It is well-known that he donated his personal copy of Karl-Friedrich Schinkel's *Sammlung Architektonischer Entwürfe* of 1858 to the Glasgow Architectural Society library in 1863, the library being subsequently subsumed into the library of the Philosophical Society following the reorganisation and amalgamation of Glasgow's learned societies in the late 1860s. Less well-known are some of those other titles from the Architects' Society collection held in the Philosophical Society's library[85] to which Thomson had access. In addition to Alison and Fergusson, there were works by Stuart and Revett, the Adams, the Pugins, Owen Jones, Sir John Soane, Joseph Gwilt and the Glasgow architect Peter Nicholson.

Of particular interest are the several books by Nicholson, grandfather of Thomson's wife,[86] illustrated by himself and by his son Michael Angelo Nicholson (1796–1841), Thomson's late father-in-law. The elder Nicholson, a noted geometrician, mathematician and publisher, produced the text and the more complex geometric and mathematical constructions, and the reproductions of the orders, amongst which was shown the square column and capital of the Choragic Monument of Thrasyllos,[87] while his son contributed the illustrations of idealised building designs.[88] This Nicholson, in echo of Alison, advised that:

> He, therefore, who wishes thoroughly to understand what the ancients have done, or to do any thing [sic] yet unattempted, must not content himself with merely drawing from their works, and then superadding the inventions of his own imagination; he must continually recur to the ground on which they trod, and make that the criterion of all his attempts.[89]

It is difficult to imagine that the contents of the Nicholsons' books and articles were not occasional dinner-table topics in the Thomson and Baird households, their authors so recently active and present in memory.

Fergusson's *History of the Modern Styles of Architecture*, while featuring Leo von Klenze's (1784–1864) Ruhmeshalle, Munich, 1850, on the title page, was equivocal about developments in Germany. Nonetheless, his broad coverage of the works of von Klenze, Schinkel and Semper was likely to interest

Thomson.⁹⁰ Fergusson's peculiar addendum of the section entitled 'Ethnology from an Architectural Point of View', which claimed that 'the ruling passion in the mind of the Celt is war', conventionally perpetuated the caricature of the unruly Scot.⁹¹ The Philosophical Society collection also contained Leo von Klenze's *Sammlung Architektonischer Entwürfe* of 1830, Franz Christian Gau's (1790–1853) *Antiquités de Nubie* of 1822, Charles Lenormant's (1802–59) *Antiquités Egyptiennes* of 1841 and Sir Austen Henry Layard's (1817–94) *A Popular Account of Discoveries at Nineveh* of 1851. This last alternated detailed accounts of archaeological finds with dramatic travellers' tales of Layard's exploits among the Ottoman Turks, Kurds and Arabs.

No one can know for certain what Thomson did or did not read, but, as a noted non-traveller, he must have obtained his understanding of Egyptian, Assyrian and Greek motives from books, and the works by Gau, Lenormant and Layard seem likely suspects. Friedrich Gilly (1772–1800), von Klenze and Schinkel were the obvious German neo-Classical sources, although they were generally more archaeologically exact in their use of the detail of their models, although inventive in formal composition. Thomson observed:

Egyptian and Greek models combined: 47–49 Oakfield Avenue, Glasgow, 1856, architect Alexander Thomson.

(Argymeg, own work, Creative Commons)

> The [Greek] revival was hailed by the learned and thinking classes throughout Europe with the greatest enthusiasm. It struck its roots deeply in many parts of Germany.⁹²

Schinkel included the Thrasyllos motif in the entrance to the Altes Museum, 1825–30. Thomson used a simpler version for the paired porches at the terrace in Oakfield Avenue, Glasgow, 1862–4. Schinkel further included a version of the Thrasyllos motif at the attic level of the Schauspielhaus in the Gendarmenmarkt, Berlin, 1818–21, creating an entirely new form which merges solid and void in a tight reciprocal formal arrangement. In the main gable attic at the Gardener's House at Potsdam, 1829–33, he disengaged the windows from the columns and, under the adjoining roof slope, alternated a window with blank panels, although he never pursued this motif with Thomson's rigour and inventiveness.

The Schinkel link: Gardener's House, Potsdam, 1829–35, architect Karl Friedrich Schinkel.

Similar expressiveness in neo-Classical form and detail was found in Scotland in the 1820s, '30s and '40s, for example, in Thomas Hamilton's (1784–1858) Falcon Hall, ca.1830 (destroyed ca.1909), and Arthur Lodge, 1830, both Edinburgh⁹³, or in his superimposition of different assemblies and creation of long colonnades at the Royal High School, Edinburgh, 1825⁹⁴ and, in particular, at his unbuilt proposal for the Scottish Academy and National Gallery of Scotland at the Mound, Edinburgh of 1847–9,⁹⁵ which reappeared generically in Thomson's unbuilt design for the South Kensington Museum, London, 1864. Moreover, Thomson had the paintings of John Martin (1789–1854) and David Roberts (who also provided perspective illustrations for Hamilton) as possible models. Roberts, in works such as *Aaron Delivering*

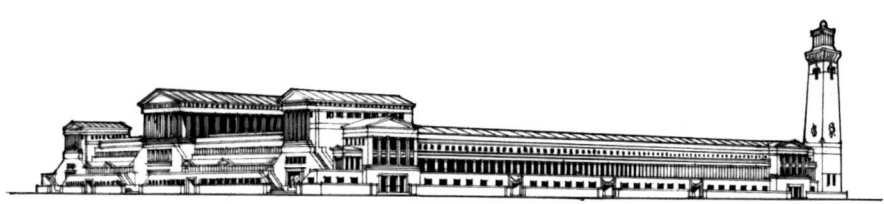

The sublime monumentality of the neo-Classical project: Kensington Competition, London, 1864, architect Alexander Thomson.
(Drawing by Roger Emmerson)

the Message to the Elders of Israel of 1827 or *The Israelites Leaving Egypt* of 1829, produced more academically accurate delineations of the architecture than did the wildly apocalyptic Martin.[96]

In a lecture given to the Glasgow Architectural Society in 1864, Thomson rejected Ruskin's stereotomy of the arch:

> We are all aware of the power of the wedge as a mechanical agent. The arch is composed of a number of wedges driven in by the pressure of the superincumbent parts of the wall. What are we to think of the soundness of the mode of construction which is based upon an essentially active principle of destruction?[97]

Thomson made an exception of the Islamic arch and dome, on which he commented favourably.[98] The Islamic dome, derived from the Byzantine, where outward thrust is mitigated by the system of pendentives and the load is contained within the substantial wall depth, met his stereotomic objections to the artifice of buttresses, flying buttresses, relieving arches and counterweight pinnacles required of the Gothic vault, while it is possibly the regular repetition of the columns of the colonnade and hypostyle hall beneath which absolved the Islamic arch of his disapproval. Thomson particularly rejected the Gothic treatment of the wall where

> the wall is lost sight of altogether: the buttresses and parapets are over-run with elaborate panelling – the use of the plain wall as a means of contrast being entirely thrown away or, if small portions do here and there occur, they serve the purpose that ornament does in the simpler styles by giving relief to the general fritter of detail and the order of design is reversed.[99]

Trabeated structure was what mattered:

> By cultivation [the architect] makes what is good better, and in the many instances changes what is positively bad into something that is most excellent and useful.[100]

One of the simplest and most dramatic representations of this was shown in Gilly's stripped down preliminary sketches for his design for the Pfielerhalle (pillar hall) of 1797. In pressing his case, Thomson stated, 'Stonehenge is more scientifically constructed than York Minster'.[101] This may simply have been intended to turn Ruskin's argument on its head, or it may be from Alison:

> A plain stone, for instance, set upon its end, has no proportion further than for the purpose of stability... The laws of architecture do not consist of a series of arbitrary contrivances. They were not invented by man, but were discovered by them [sic].[102]

'On Masonry, and How it might be Improved',[103] Thomson's presidential address to the Glasgow Architectural Society at the Scottish Exhibition Rooms, Bath Street, Glasgow on 22 February 1859, while seemingly a plea for better practice and economy in stone quarrying, cutting and installing, can also be read as a proposal for how contemporary masonry construction might be reconfigured, refined and modernised to assist in his investigation of the wall depth, the lightening of its 'proportion' as one rises through the elevation and the maintenance of stability through more economic variations on traditional construction such as a cavity brick back-up wall.[104] It would be another 50 years before cavity-wall construction became widely-used, while the traditional ashlar outer face, stone-chippings and mortar-filled cavity and inner face of random rubble or brick walling with occasional bonders persisted into the first half of the 20th century.

As Baines observed, Thomson challenged the accepted status of the wall and the framed and glazed window. A progressive 'excavation' or 'paring back' of the depth of the wall or a reduction in columnar and intervening entablature 'proportion' until either roof or the final entablature is reached was crucial to Thomson's architecture, whether in the seemingly simple two-storey version of the domestic terrace at Moray Place, 1858–9, or in the Egyptian Halls, 1871, both Glasgow. Trabeation, repetition, horizontal extension, paring back of the wall depth, alternating solid and void panels and disengagement of the fenestration from the frame are variously present. Enrichment was found within the masonry depth and not generally to any

Alison's proportion and Worringer's plane: Egyptian Halls, Union Street Glasgow, 1874, architect Alexander Thomson.
(Maccoinich-commonswiki, own work, Creative Commons)

great extent imposed upon it except when consistent with an identifiable and discrete formal Classical composition, both in incised decoration and in the formation of secondary attached columns, pilasters, lintels and panels successively stepped back from the masonry face with selective incorporation of projecting cornice and more regular classical capitals. The wall plane itself was never static but nor was it modulated by the gratuitous addition of columns or enrichment.

Thomson's use of constructional parts related to Semper's four elements of plinth, framing, weaving or cladding and berm or mass walling. The difference was that whereas Semper's approach to construction was sequential and additive, Thomson's was subtractive, an act almost archaeological, even to the extent that his columns appear often to have been likewise disinterred from the wall rather than formed at the stone-yard to be installed subsequently. We might question what is wall and what is column. Thus, while Thomson followed Alison's injunctions on the wall/roof and column/entablature ensembles, he approached the wall as an ur-element that may remain as wall or may be successively excavated to reveal within the wall plane incised decoration, mullions, square stub columns, recessed pilasters and panels, fully-formed columns and finally an order, leaving until the last moment the decision of termination in roof or entablature depending on whether the final range is wall or colonnade. Thomson's colonnades played out successively over the floors of the building. On one rare occasion, such as the Buck's Head Building, 1863, where he used cast iron columns and transoms, the 'non-proportional' heavy masonry of the top floors diminished the effect. It could be argued that, in Alison's sense of it, proportion had failed at the Buck's Head due to the perceived mismatch between load and support. Thomson never returned to this arrangement.

Dematerialisation occurred in the principal elevations of Holmwood, 1857–8, one of his largest domestic commissions. At the ground floor level the dining room and parlour windows are ranged behind the columns, 600mm back in the case of the square columns in the dining room and roughly the same behind the circular columns of the partially engaged or disengaged rotunda fronting the parlour, loosely interpreted from the discrete formal Classical composition of the Choragic Monument of Lysicrates. At the first floor drawing room above the rotunda, the window screen is set back behind a tetrastyle. Even the butler's pantry and the kitchen windows on the east elevation, seen obliquely on arrival, are given significance and set back roughly 400mm behind distyle and tetrastyle ranges of square columns. Thomson mentioned the roof in his writings, only once commenting favourably on Swiss examples with shallow pitches and wide projecting eaves,[105] precisely the roof form used at Holmwood and in many of his villa commissions and the Chalmers Memorial Free Church, Govan Street, Glasgow, 1859 (demolished 1971).

The timber or lead-framed and glazed window presented a problem for neo-Classicists because their antique models had none. Presentation drawings of the 18th and early 19th centuries showed cross-hatched voids absent astragals and representations of glass. Robertson quoted the conditions for entries to the Alexander Thomson Memorial Prize competition, one of which was that 'the windows or other openings in elevations are [to be] tinted in sepia or ink'.[106] The windowless building, that is, a building with openings but apparently without glass, was later to intrigue architects such as Wright and Kahn. In Wright's Storer House, Los Angeles, 1923, for example, the pre-cast concrete blocks have intaglio decoration and the openings are set up in trabeated rows separated by square columns with the glazed windows set approximately 600mm back from the face. Frampton commented: 'with

AN ARCHITECTURE FOR THE AGE: 1781–1887

Wall-depth and neo-Classical vignette: Holmwood, Cathcart, Glasgow, 1857, architect Alexander Thomson.

such devices, masonry walls could be partially dematerialised'.[107] Thomson's use of opaque cast glass at Holmwood in rooflights and clerestories to light the stairwell and over the sideboard recess in the dining room[108] hinted at a future development of his already novel approach to the window and to the natural lighting of the interior.

Repetition, which was Ruskin's principal objection to Edinburgh's New Town, was actively sought in Thomson's symmetrical work as an entirely Modern means of using window ranges to front repetitive cellular or open space effectively and democratically and to present the same to the urban street. The contrast between Thomson's rigour in this matter and the more widespread Victorian eclectic offerings is most clearly shown in Gordon Street, Glasgow, where his 1861 design acquired a Baroque addition of 1902 by JH Craigie (1870–1930) who, as the 1894 Alexander Thomson Travelling Scholarship winner, should have known better. Like Burn with the Baronial, Thomson incorporated the asymmetric assembly of symmetric parts, since it facilitated the functional domestic planning then in demand or, in the churches, the housing of different liturgical elements. Thomson's domestic planning has a generic similarity to that of Burn's smaller houses such as Milton Lockhart, 1829–36,[109] although even there Burn still located the kitchen in the basement or in a somewhat distanced service wing.

Blackie's *Villa and Cottage Architecture*[110] of 1868 was a significant platform for the promulgation of Thomson's work, which outclassed aesthetically and intellectually the designs by other architects illustrated therein. Among Scottish architects whose work was illustrated were John Gordon (1835–1912), who submitted a Thomsonesque Oakleigh Villa, Loch Long, 1863, and whose son, John Graham Gordon (fl. 1903–11), with his partner, David Bennett Dobson (fl. 1903–7), designed one of the few full-blown Art Nouveau houses in Edinburgh at 53 Pentland Terrace, 1904; James C Walker (1821–88), pupil of Bryce, architect of the Franco-Scottish chateau-style Dunfermline Municipal Buildings, 1875, Carnegie Library, Dunfermline, 1880, and Hawick Town Hall, 1888 and contributed a Sir James Gowans-influenced villa at Trinity, Edinburgh; John T Rochead (1814–78), another pupil of Bryce, who introduced commercial Scots Baronial at the City of Glasgow Bank, 1855, and in the National Wallace Monument, Stirling, 1859; and John Baird (1816–93), Thomson's brother-in-law and erstwhile partner, with a Thomsonesque villa at Crosshill.

Thomson's work was continued by several reincarnations of his practice and by others after his death in 1875, although his methodology was often used purely aesthetically. Nevertheless, James Sellars's (1843–88) powerful St Andrews Halls, Glasgow, 1873–7 (part destroyed and incorporated into the Mitchell Library), within an overall planar elevation comprising end pavilions and a receding central section under a continuous entablature over columns in antis, owed much to Thomson. To a much lesser extent, debt was also due at Sellars's Milton School, Glasgow, 1877–8, while at his New Club, Glasgow, 1878. Thomson was but a distant memory in the overall order of the elevation and in the ranges of windows and square columns in antis at first, third and fourth floors and the partial investigation of wall depth at the second floor. In 1895, Thomson's former assistant, Alexander Skirving (1849–1919) built the Langside Free Church, Glasgow in a distinctly Thomsonian manner. The discrete composition of the Ionic portico is raised on a base of banded masonry which incorporates a distyle entrance in antis flanked by plain drums with square columns between the windows. Thomson details crop up in the most unlikely locations, for example, in Edinburgh at tenements in Gillespie Crescent, 1880–5, or at 5–9 South St Andrew Street, 1883, by the obscure Knox and Hutton. It is found in the work of John Bridgeford Pirie in Aberdeen, last encountered influencing Finnish National Romanticism, in his 1880s domestic work and in his, albeit Gothic, Queens Cross Church, 1881, where the hardness of granite invites a simplification of form and decoration which brought the work close to that of Thomson in intent and detail. Thomson influence turns up in Dundee and Perth in the work of John Murray Robertson (1844–1901), at India Buildings, 1874, and Victoria Buildings, 1872, respectively and in Alloa at 41–45 Mill Street,

1874–5, by Adam Frame (1837–1901). There is also a clone of Holmwood, although more conventionally detailed, in Adelaide, Australia, 1885. Even today, the English architect Eric Parry (b. 1952) has acknowledged Thomson's influence on his practice[111] in works such as 23 Savile Row, 2009, and One Eagle Place, 2013, both London.

Go west, young man! Thomson and the Manhattan skyline

The Thomson style crossed the Atlantic via London and Liverpool, in the work of the peripatetic Elgin-born architect and author brothers, William James Audsley (1833–1910) and George Ashdown Audsley (1838–1925), neither of whom seems to have had any evident connection with Thomson. Indeed, one of their many published works, *Cottage, Lodge and Villa Architecture*[112] of 1862 contained substantial pro-Gothic commentary from John Ruskin and Sir George Gilbert Scott (1811–78) (Thomson's anathema at Glasgow University) and a highly negative paragraph on Harvey Lonsdale Elmes's (1814–47) neo-Classical masterwork, St George's Hall, Liverpool, 1854. The Audsleys' early work in England, particularly at the Prince's Road Synagogue, Liverpool, 1874, and the New West End Synagogue, London, 1877–9, showed the influence of Schinkel's brick-built Gothic work in the rigour of their exteriors while some interior detailing, in form and colour, owed a little to Thomson's Glasgow church interiors. Their use of a version of Thomson's more expressive neo-Classicism may have been both cover for their earlier Gothicism and their *entrée* to neo-Classical Liverpool, such as at their Racquet Club, 1874, destroyed in the Toxteth riots of 1981, remaining as a re-sited doorcase at 102 Upper Parliament Street; the Liverpool Union Bank, 43–47 Bold Street, 1870, a remodelling of an 1840 building; the Scottish Equitable Chambers, 19 Castle Street, 1878; the shop at 92 Bold Street, 1890; and possibly the Thomsonesque warehouse at 17 Seel Street, 1888.[113]

The Audsleys' first American work, the Layton Art Gallery, Milwaukee, Wisconsin, 1888 (demolished 1958), was a highly mannered version of Thomson. In 1892 they set up in practice in New York with a commission from the Broadway Realty Company for the 17-storey Bowling Green Offices, New York City, 1895–8, then briefly the tallest building in New York – subsequently raised in 1919 to 22 storeys. This is a sophisticated, fire-proofed, steel-framed building on the base, shaft and capital model clad in white marble, brick and terracotta, with a complete electrical installation, eight lifts and a novel pumped sprinkler system rather than the more usual New York rooftop gravity-feed storage tank. The Landmarks Preservation Commission citation states that:

Thomson in New York: Bowling Green Office Building, New York, 1895–8, architects W&G Audsley.
(Library of Congress, Creative Commons)

Thomson in Liverpool: Bold Street, Liverpool, 1890, architects W&G Audsley
(Rodhullandemu, own work Creative Commons)

in its effective use of continuous piers and concentrated ornament, [it] is analogous to Louis H Sullivan's Wainwright Building (1890–1) in St Louis, and other buildings of the Chicago School.[114]

The Bowling Green Offices are a clear, though sadly solitary, demonstration of how effectively Thomson's adaptation of the neo-Classical could match Sullivan's formal skyscraper model (see page 179) and satisfy the Semperian logic of decoration integral to the construction common to both.

The Audsleys produced one other American design of significance with an un-premiated entry for the New York City Hall architectural competition, 1893, won by the neo-Classicist John Hemenway Duncan (1854–1929).[115] The competition was possibly predicated on the remodelling of an earlier building designed by Mangin and McComb, 1810–2. The Audsleys' entry had a pronounced generic similarity to the composition of William Young's (1843–1900) Glasgow Municipal Chambers, 1888, while the detail was thoroughly Thomsonian, which they surmounted with a tower based on those of Thomson's St Vincent Street and Queen's Park United Protestant Churches, respectively 1857 and 1867. Although none of the Audsleys' three American works was more than superficially Thomsonian, they hinted at the representative buildings which were not to come Thomson's way.[116]

The yearning for a Schinkel/Thomson/Sullivan/Wright connection arising from the formal similarities of the Gardener's House, Holmwood and the Prairie House is explicit in texts by MacMillan, Law, Hitchcock and McFadzean, despite much fruitless searching for hard evidence. It represents a similar plea for access to the orthodox history of Modern Architecture – in which British architects played little part – to that of the, albeit equivocal, architectural endorsement of Mackintosh by Pevsner. Even Stamp, usually careful about over-simplification and special pleading, was thus taken:

> For all the subtleties of detail and optical corrections which Thomson employed in his urban façades, they manifest a rationality and a quality of abstraction that can make them seem very modern. There can be no doubt that Thomson can be placed on that direst line from the cubic austerity of Karl Friedrich Schinkel's Classicism to the rectilinear structural grids of Mies van der Rohe.[117]

Well, there is doubt. All that can be said with confidence is that Schinkel, Thomson, Wright and Mies shared the practice, if not necessarily the knowledge of the trabeation of Gilly and Semper. However, their approaches to the wall were fundamentally different: cryptically described, Schinkel accepted the wall as a given, Thomson eroded it, Wright removed the corners while Mies dematerialised it into discrete planes.

Thomson's validation is in the facts of his theory, in the extant work and in the brief, if often less than expertly managed, reappearance of the aesthetic, in Aberdeen, Alloa, Dundee, Edinburgh, Liverpool, London, Adelaide, Helsinki, Milwaukee and New York. Thomson's architecture was called 'utopian' by Glendinning et al and, in the sense of its stylistic rigour, completeness and consistency across building types, it represented a utopianism that is unusual, Sullivan excepted, in the second half of the 19th century and is more usually thought of as a phenomenon of 20th-century monist Modernism. It was also the search for the eternal where:

> All those who have studied works of art must have been struck by the mysterious power of the horizontal element in carrying the mind away into space, and into speculations upon infinity.[118]

Whether Thomson treated his architecture intellectually in the manner inferred above or pursued it more intuitively or whether he read closely all the authors mentioned or studied all the architecture illustrated is beside the point. His architecture thus subjected to present-day inquiry still leaves ample room for further interrogation and alerts us to the fact that he perpetuated a particularly Scottish late 18th and mid-19th-century intellectual understanding of the Scottish characteristics of an expressive neo-Classicism, its history, its materiality and its spirituality. Expounded by Alison and Nicolson, it was evident in the practice of the likes of Playfair and Hamilton, which allied it to an equivalent German intellectual and architectural tradition. Thomson categorically rejected an overt timebound 'Scottishness':

> In the very old parts of the city where the houses are tall and narrow, a new erection in Gothic or old Scotch style is at least in keeping with the general aspect of things; but when we discover that it is new, we regard it as an attempt to deceive, and turn away with a feeling of anger and disgust at the miserable forgery that has vitiated to our imagination the integrity of the whole locality.[119]

A daisy-chain: romance and rationality in construction

If Thomson was the rational-romantic in the West then, contemporaneously, (Sir) James Gowans (1821–90) was the romantic-rationalist of the East. In this connection and in the title of his biography, McAra provided an intriguing antinomy, although it is not so described, and, frustratingly, is accompanied by the briefest of descriptions of its realisation. McAra observed that

> Scottish architect and engineer Sir James Gowans… in his own idiosyncratic way… had an expressive and complex vocabulary.

He continued:

> The essential importance of Sir James Gowans is this: that in the relative isolation of Edinburgh during the 1850s and '60s he designed buildings, based on consistent theory, which were a signpost in one of the several directions architectural theory was later to take. This is best shown by his romantic, polychromatic, but basically rational buildings which display Gowans's rigorous adherence to a 2ft module and fixed angles [of 22.5°, 45° and 67.5°] to facilitate standardisation and economic mass-production of stone building-components.[120]

AN ARCHITECTURE FOR THE AGE: 1781–1887

The achievement of James Gowans reveals itself in his attempt by the middle of the 19th century to create modular architecture which was economically realistic, and visually satisfying and imaginative.[121]

Gowans' use of the module and the standard angles simplified and standardised stone production at the quarry and cutting in the yard. On site, the bounding frame of the masonry module contains an infill of lightly-dressed polygonal stones laid not on the natural bed but on cant, to present their face.[122] Although this practice courts the risk of delamination of the individual infill stones, Gowans' quarries seemed to produce stone hard enough to resist it. The framing masonry, of stones a manageable 45 or 60 centimetres long by 15 centimetres wide and deep,[123] is conventionally laid parallel or perpendicular to the bed course. Gowans, like Thomson, wrote about contemporary masonry practice and how it might be improved in a paper given at Edinburgh in 1883 entitled 'On the Uses of Building Stones', although he was less driven by material quality, other than requiring sufficient hardness, than Thomson, whose aim was to circumvent the difficulties posed by the noted softness of the Giffnock sandstone he used. Gowans' expressive use of geometry and module is made evident at Lammerburn, Napier Road, Edinburgh, 1859, while subsumed within the wall at Castle Terrace, Edinburgh, 1866–70. McAra linked Gowans' practice aesthetically with the American Stick Style, although clearly it relates neither mechanically nor structurally to it. Gowans' masonry frame is structurally dependent on the mass wall and on the levelling and limited adhesive effects of lime mortar for structural integrity rather than load transfer through the joints of a mechanically fixed structural frame.

While accepting the significant differences in Thomson's and Gowan' theories and practices, there remains the sense in the work of both men of a search for the virtues of a system of 'frame and infill' in the surface appearance of their mass masonry work. Gowans' approach is the more literal in the very direct representation of a simple frame, while Thomson's emerges more in his mass walling or blank colonnades, as the consequence of his paring back of the masonry depth to reveal its implicated column

Modular geometry expressed: Lammerburn, Napier Road, Edinburgh, 1859, architect Sir James Gowans.

Modular geometry implied: Castle Terrace, Edinburgh, 1866, architect Sir James Gowans.

and entablature form. In both cases, it is the deep theoretical and physical structure simultaneously revealed which is of significance rather than the immediate outward appearance of either Gowans' 'Orientalised Gothicism' or Thomson's Greco-Egyptian modes. Plainly, Thomson's use of framing in his cast iron columnar structures had a contemporary engineering practicality, whereas Gowans' use of it in mass masonry was one of modular planning, material economy and constructional efficiency. In this context, both architects' concerns were entirely Modern and sat comfortably alongside other Modern architectural theoreticians and practitioners of the mid-19th century, such as Semper or Viollet-le Duc in the search for 'an architecture of the age'.

McAra recorded that the British reaction to Gowans's Rockville, Edinburgh, 1858 (demolished 1966) the earliest and most complete representation of his theory and practice – in effect, 'manifesto-architecture' of the highest order – 'was uncertain about so unorthodox a design'.[124] Moreover, Gowans was as antinomial in his professional life as he was in his design work in that he encompassed the vocations of architect, engineer, quarry-master, railway-builder, developer, entrepreneur and social-housing pioneer which, perhaps, freed him from a rigorous Victorian academism or fixed societal construct or position that would require his adoption of a discrete persona, distinct profession or niche practice to secure a clientèle.

As Modern men not averse to publicity, both 'signed' their buildings graphically: Thomson employed a version of the Greek key motif which reads as a repeating 'T' while Gowans included carved and stylised wild daisy blossoms, in Scots the *gowan*.

Approaching the 1890s, then, one might be inclined, on the face of it, to define a Scottish national architecture as a series of linked dualities: East, Traditional/Baronial/rational-romantic; West, Experimental/Classical/romantic-rational. However, one would be wrong because nothing is ever so neat, nor, in respect of a national architecture in Scotland, is it especially desirable for it to be so split into two distinct houses. As always, events beyond architecture are to impinge and

> [w]hile ethnonationalisms are plainly rooted in the past, they also highlight continuing societal transformation and discontinuity.[125]

The appearance of 'new' materials were less injurious to Thomson's neo-Classicism, Gowans' Rationalism or even to Bryce's Baronial than to Ruskin's Venetian Gothic. They were accompanied by more reliable structural calculation methodology permitting beams to be longer, columns and piers less massive, whereas plate glass came in larger sheets and concrete was quick and cheap to construct and easily covered by 'noble' materials, as both Thomson and Gowans anticipated. Alison's concept of proportion, based on masonry construction, was challenged in the engineering of cast iron and steel structures. The lighter framed and engineered iron and steel structures in architecture were problematic, as Thomson discovered at the Buck's Head Building, and remained so almost universally in the 19th century, obscured by the masonry of more palatable eclectic styles. Meanwhile, several of the next generation of Glasgow architects opted to take part or all of their training at the École de Beaux-Arts in Paris, where they were schooled in the compositional responses required of the larger representational and commercial constructions that would soon be asked of them – among them JJ Burnett, JA Campbell (1859–1909), AN Paterson (1862–1947), Henbest Capper (1860–1925) and John Keppie (1862–1945) who, as principals, passed on that knowledge to their assistants.[126]

Going to the country: mythology and vernacular architecture

In the closing decades of the 19th century, European architects investigated their own patrimony as discussed above. Contemporaneous Pre-Raphaelite[127] art, a British phenomenon, found its subject matter in the magic and mysticism of regional legends, including imagery from Celtic mythology, Nordic sagas, Germanic folk-tales, the Arabian Nights and Indian cosmology. Arts & Crafts interest in traditional hand-crafts widened to incorporate local traditional building methods, materials, forms and, ultimately, types. In Britain, these were not the versions of the vernacular timber cottages and farmhouses of Central and Northern Europe with colourfully-painted, folkloric carved detail, for none such existed. It was the dwellings of the squire and laird that were studied: in England the mediaeval 'hall-house' – with its distinctive 'screens' dividing the hall, its first floor musicians' gallery and solar – or the late 17th-century British 'vernacular' of the reign of Queen Anne; and in Scotland, the 15th–17th-century town and tower-house with their 'inhabited wall' and compact corridor-less L, E or Z plans centred on one or more spiral stairs – 'the building's vertical corridors'.[128]

Frank Walker described

> a fashion which in England took the form of the half-timbered manor-house historicism of the Tudor squirearchy and in Scotland bubbled above bleak castle walls in the frothy exuberance of Baronialism.[129]

Queen Anne – largely the reinvention of the Anglo-Scot Richard Norman Shaw (1831–1912) – had British significance, for its eclectic bridging of 'native' styles which, in Collins's quotation of the Rev. JL Petit's 1861 lecture at the Architectural Exhibition, was

> expressive, or capable of being made expressive of the spirit of the age; and sufficiently comprehensive to embrace both vernacular and monumental works, and that class which partakes of both characters.[130]

As his former student Annemarie Adams noted of Collins, the

> notion of the Vernacular was particularly thorny... [because, in his view]... in addition to the lack of a clear program... it had no clear relationship to precedent.[131]

Vernacular building is an activity that is not instinctive nor is it a re-enactment; it has volition and is adaptive, however inchoate. Rudolph Schindler (1887–1953) noted that

> [t]he peasant who is trying to build his house exactly like his father's modernises it unconsciously.[132]

To that extent it embodied the ideas, programme and precedent Collins reckoned was missing. However, Collins was partly correct when he added:

> [m]ost of the [19th-century] theorists thought in terms of regional domestic architecture, little realizing that regional architecture was being killed by the impact of the industrial revolution... James Fergusson... perceived that the modern equivalent of mediaeval vernacular construction was to be found in the latest works of the civil engineers.[133]

Herewith Collins attempted to support an underlying Modernist theme of a 'vernacular of engineering' to which, in reaction, the historicist suspended judgement on the evident changes wrought in territory and patrimony and drew such conclusions as Frank Walker described fancifully and erroneously:

> So, too, out of a sublime darkness wrapping its mysterious quasi-medieval world around rock-perched castle, ruinous folly, rustic retreat, or rambling vicarage [surely he meant manse], there emerged from the shadows a humble rough-hewn cottage, the folk-house, its rude but vital vernacular spoken in stone, wood and thatch with a robust simplicity increasingly valued less for any sentimentalised picturesqueness it lent to poetic vision than for its unaffected direct response to the contingent needs of time and place.[134]

Walker idealistically attempted to remove the 'folk-house' from the mid-19th century romantic brew of Baronialism, forgetting that he could not remove it from its own history which included its earlier and substantial physical removal from territory and patrimony as part of 18th and 19th-century rural improvement.

Eclectic, dialectic or antinomial? Regional architectural authority

Although a book such as *Scotch Baronial* is unlikely to be much concerned with Classicism, Glendinning and MacKechnie made the observation that:

> Alongside [the Baronial], of course, a richly eclectic classical architecture still flourished in Scotland's cities, as exemplified in the work of Glasgow's Alexander 'Greek' Thomson.[135]

The use of 'eclectic' seems designed to distance non-indigenous Classicism from an idealised Scottish architecture, although, together with Fergusson, MacLeod, Campbell and Fawcett, they acknowledged the several equally non-indigenous, eclectic sources of Baronialism and the Scottish adaptation of them. Rather, the issue is: what constituted a Scottish architecture in the second half of the 19th century? Did it encompass Bryce's Baronial and Thomson's neo-Greek equally, or did it privilege one at the expense of the other and, if so, on what basis? The descriptor Scottish may be simply geographic, that is, that anything built in Scotland qualifies; it may be mimetic in that it adopts the architecture of an earlier 'golden age' such as the continuity of Romanesque, the persistence of the Classical or the periodic reversion to the model of the 'tower-house'; or, it may be ideational in that it responds to and records in patrimony ideas implicit in the Scottish psyche and its ahistoric response to the climate, topography, resources and epoch of the territory. From the geographic to the mimetic to the ideational is a progression of increasing idealistic complexity which contrasts with a decreasing aesthetic obviousness or, rather, requires more acute interrogation of the expressed aesthetic.

The Baronial was mimetic and presented recognisable historic signs removed from a specific social and epochal context although not freed from their implicit meanings of hierarchy and privilege. It did not share Gothicism's concern with the signal contribution of the humble artisan. Likewise, the widespread use of the Baronial in representative, public and domestic buildings in the 19th century was not evidence of its democratisation or representative of a commonly-held view of Scottish identity. Rather, it was the assertion of the status of the Scottish landed, managerial, administrative and academic classes within the British Empire/Union duality. The Royal imprimatur of Balmoral was a *noblesse oblige* recognition of that status which placed no formal obligation on Britain's rulers to treat with Scotland other than as a holiday retreat, curio or Other. There was no intellectual or philosophic basis for Baronial because, as Collins retold Fergusson's complaint: 'current architecture… gave no indication of the forms which future generations would create'. The mimetic and free application of aesthetic motives such as crow-steps, corbelling, turrets or cap-houses did not have even the theoretical rigour of Classicism's orders, proportioning and optical correction. The Baronial was Ruritanian fancy-dress, not a demonstration of national identity.

The starting point for Alison, Nicholson, Thomson and Fergusson was equally an architecture of mimesis but which they subjected to an exegesis lacking in Billings' and Burn's Baronial beyond an account of its historic stylistic development which might have been taxonomically useful although hardly a theory. While none of the Scottish theorists quoted referenced Kant, and only Alison had any particular connection with his thought via Burke, all evinced variations on Kant's thesis/antithesis proposition which enabled them to encompass the philosophic and the aesthetic rather than the aesthetic alone. Thus, Fergusson would not have needed to know the 'forms which future generations would create', because the philosophic would permit of an architecture wherein he would have been content to understand the consistent means by which they would come about, rather than the aesthetic which would constrain those future generations to permanent compliance with 'the historians' demands'.

3

Hope in honest error: 1887–1919

A modest monumentalism: early Modern architecture in its setting

LATE 20TH-CENTURY ENGLISH translations of the works of pre-Modern writers originally published in German and Dutch between 1890 and 1920 by the German Herman Muthesius, the Netherlander HP Berlage (1856–1934) and the Moravian Adolf Loos, permitted these authors' views wide circulation for the first time in the English-speaking world. They paralleled the historically accessible contemporaneous English texts of Louis Sullivan (1856–1924), WR Lethaby (1857–1931), Charles Rennie Mackintosh and Frank Lloyd Wright although, patently, the dissemination of German and Dutch texts in British architectural circles at the time was limited and their influence almost non-existent. However, inasmuch as their writings and practice were enlisted by others in a largely retrospectively constructed 20th-century orthodox Modernist dogma, through which the regionalist productions of the *fin-de-siècle* and later were filtered to conform to a Modernist narrative, it is helpful to have the site cleared back to formation level and to see what kind of different and non-determinist edifice might now begin to arise from those writings.

Berlage was pivotal in the development of early Modern architecture in Europe, in his own work and writings from the late 1880s, through his promotion of Wright post-1910, to his participation in the first meeting of CIAM (Congrès Internationaux d'Architecture Moderne) at La Sarraz in 1928, although he was never a member. Indeed, he disagreed in principle with some of the more hard-line Modernist delegates present – Le Corbusier, Hannes Meyer (1889–1954) and André Lurçat (1894–1970). In a series of papers published between 1886 and 1909, Berlage advanced a programme of architecture which touched on many of the themes that were to become problematic a generation later, although he did so in a more open, self-effacing and consistent format than did the later Modernists in either writings or works. Berlage, in the words of Hans van Dijk,

> strove for a communal, non-individualistic architecture that in his opinion could be based only on the material and social development of the day. The modelling of space he found more important than the outlining of facades. He laid stress on the role of the wall as element [sic] for defining space, and referred to geometric proportional systems such as those developed by JH de Groot, whose acquaintance he had made at Cuypers' office.[1]

He recognised the drive to make conscious design ideas based on national culture while cautioning against reversion to the vernacular:

> For the same reason stylistically deliberate clothing – the national costume, even military uniform – also accords with nature, for once again it represents beauty of a higher order. Our culture forces us to work deliberately. The return to the peasant cottage would mean a return to a lower culture, ultimately to a nonculture.[2]

Berlage understood that, as Burgin later put it,

> it is the mission of high culture to guarantee the stability of the social order, a mission it can only fulfil through the continuity of its traditions.[3]

In the pre-Modern age, 'beauty' was still an accepted concept and artistic objective, if somewhat fugitive in definition and of declining importance. In *Architecture's Place in Modern Aesthetics* of 1886, unconsciously echoing Alison, Semper and Thomson, in particular Alison's 'fitness' and 'proportion', Berlage asserted that:

> Beauty in the artistic sense exists only in the visible expression of the purely aesthetic functionality of the components, so that they can contribute to the whole and give a sensory representation of the tension between load and support... During the design process one should never think of the building's nonaesthetic purpose, but only of the distribution of masses in response to gravity.[4]

Community was exemplified by the anonymous craftsperson whose unattributed work thereby presented as a unified societal expression of ethos and practice which, in Berlage's lukewarm Marxism,[5] created the condition for the Modern architect where

> true individualism is aimed at this common cause, and its work emanates from self-sacrifice, its personal expression can make the artist's nature grow to brilliant proportions and make him [sic], through his ethical work so mature, so strong, and so satisfied that a great personality reveals itself through it... [adding]... [t]his is not the case with subjectivism, which is to individualism as idiosyncrasy is to will. And haven't we known such idiosyncrasies as, for example, Jugendstil?[6]

In this he was at one with Loos and Hofman. Further drawing together these several strands, he explained,

> Architecture will then reassume the first position among the arts, precisely because it is the true art of the people, not the art of the individual but the art of all, the art of the community in which the spirit of the time is reflected.[7]

However, such concepts insensitively and doctrinally applied by others were later to cause much grief.

Unlike Semper, whom he greatly admired[8] and quoted frequently, Berlage *was* able to develop an architecture of its time from Semperian first principles. It resulted in the masterful stereotomic form of the brick-built neo-Renaissance Amsterdam Stock Exchange, 1898, which 30 years later blossomed into the modest monumentalism of the Gemeentesmuseum, Den Haag, 1927–9, completed in 1935. Here the several themes inhering in Berlage's production were brought together and effortlessly incorporated: Semper and Gilly's trabeation; Jan Hessel de Groot's (1865–1932) triangular proportioning system from the Stock Exchange; De Stijl's volumetric composition; Loos's paratactical fenestration; and Wright's extended occupation of the site and relation to water as he demonstrated at the Imperial Hotel, Tokyo, 1922.

German cultural perception: Scotland' affinity with Hanseatic Europe

Uniquely among non-Scottish architectural writers, Muthesius devoted considerable attention to developments in Scotland, and not just to the work of his friend Mackintosh.⁹ While claiming England as the 'birthplace of Romanticism', he paradoxically noted that:

> The most powerful Romantic influence came from Scotland, passing not only England but the whole of the civilised world.¹⁰

The influence on mainland Europe of the Ossian legend and Scott's novels remained unabated. Muthesius's search for a more primal sensibility led him to contrast matters in Britain where:

> If Scottish Romanticism sprang from the innermost recesses of the nation's soul, making it less of a new phenomenon than a visible manifestation of a national characteristic, its beginnings were more superficial in England. Here the awakening interest in the Middle Ages was less the product of a period of national self-communing than of a need for distraction.¹¹

Collins later observed in this context that

> the great weakness of the English architects' claim to be resurrecting an indigenous style was their disinclination to base their designs on national prototypes.¹²

Muthesius reported:

> London, and in fact England as a whole, remained stationary at the point to which Morris had taken it.¹³

At the same time, he recognised a cultural connection where:

> In this self-sufficient island kingdom, the Germanic culture [as opposed to the Latin] has not allowed itself to be overrun to the same extent as in the rest of Northern Europe.¹⁴

    Muthesius was, of course, untroubled by a Modernist outcome – for it was unknown to him and he did not speculate to any great extent – whereas that outcome and his implicated part in it has been consistently post-rationalised by Modernist apologists. Absent its Scottish content, beyond the inescapable Mackintosh, British Modernists were desperate to fix the 'English' – and here I mean English – house as a significant vector in the approved trajectory of the Modern Movement. In contrast, Muthesius appreciated and valued the modern 'English' house in his own time, in its several discrete regional and national manifestations. This permitted him, although it still troubles some Scots writers today, to grant commensurate status to the Edinburgh-based Robert Lorimer as that presently accorded the Glaswegian Mackintosh. He recognised the normative qualities of Lorimer's production as complementary to Mackintosh's invention, because, as he said:

> Scotland will not achieve what England has already achieved – a completely national style of house-building based on the old vernacular architecture – until it follows the lead given by Lorimer.[15]

The Brno-born, Viennese-domiciled, German-speaking Moravian architect and cultural commentator, Adolf Loos, left several occasionally enigmatic, sometimes ironic but always acute texts in addition to a questioning oeuvre. In *Culture,* written in 1910 but not published till 1930 in the collection *Trotzdem* ('Nevertheless' or 'Despite'), Loos noted, in an echo of Muthesius, that:

> In the island empire, too, there was room for two cultures to exist side by side through the centuries, the English and the Scottish. The Scottish culture proved to be the stronger one, as it conforms more to the Germanic cultural perception. The English have become Scots.[16]

Although Loos adopted the integrated and self-effacing view of life, dress, manners and architecture which he perceived as 'English', did he pine for something less self-consciously self-deprecating, less comfortably bourgeois? In Loos's scheme of things, the 'Englishman' took his pleasures – hunting, fishing, shooting – in a wilder Scotland and adopted Scottish clothing – 'Scottish socks'[17] – for this purpose, becoming briefly Scottish, subtle with earth-knowledge yet artless; artless in the sense of not being knowingly or showily contrived, artless in the manner Loos sought in his architecture.

Masheck recorded Loos's own situation, firstly in Brno, then in New York, then in Vienna, finally in Paris where

> with Czechness problematically dissolved (since 1867) into Austro-Hungarian imperiality, and that subsumed into a gnomic German 'other,' in late 19th-century New York, Loos would likely have felt some ethnic ambiguity.[18]

Such dualities and estrangements would have had cultural resonance with

Plain exterior, complex interior: Muller House, Stresovice, Prague, 1931, architect Adolf Loos.

the contemporary Scot implicated within the contrasts of Union and Empire. In claiming Scotland's conformity with the 'Germanic cultural perception', Loos was, no doubt, aware that this included shared traditions in philosophy, law, religion and trade which placed Scotland within the orbit of a Calvinist/Lutheran, Hanseatic, Baltic and North German Europe in marked contrast to England's more readily-accessible Latin connections and compromised Reformation. It may be possible to refine Loos's notion of a 'German cultural perception' with which he associated Scottish cultural practice by referring to T Lux Feininger's (1910–2011) discussion of the Bauhaus *gestalt* as

> a feeling for the close proximity of pure thought and concrete substance [which is] typically German.[19]

The architecture of a Hanseatic Scotland: Lamb's House, Leith, Edinburgh, early 17th century. Restoration and additions, 2010, architects Kristen Hannesdottir and Nick Groves-Raines.

Such an antinomy of the abstract and the concrete, the romantic and the rational, was part of Scottish intellectual and practical enquiry since at least the Enlightenment and can be summed up in the archetypical figure of the poet/engineer; rather less the panicky Scotty Scott of Star Trek fame and rather more James Watt (1736–1819) of whom Herman noted that, at

> twenty-seven years old, Watt was largely a self-taught man, but what he knew impressed everyone who came into his shop. Even the university professors were impressed. 'I saw a workman, and expected no more,' said one, 'but was surprised to find a philosopher'.[20]

In *Cultural Degeneration* of 1908, Loos acknowledged the signal contribution of Muthesius, 'to whom we are indebted for a series of instructive books on English [sic] life and culture', although he recognised Muthesius's attempt to formally codify 'vernacularism' through institutional structures as inimical to Loos's own interests and expectations of architectural development because:

> [Muthesius] has presented the aims of the German Werkbund and has attempted to justify its existence. The aims are good. But it is precisely the German Werkbund that will never achieve them.[21]

Loos the outsider – *das Andere*[22] – was suspicious of the cosy mutuality of interest embodied in such organisations, especially their propensity for 'groupthink' which shuts down intellectual discussion and the dissenting voice.

Although his writings treated sympathetically with the vernacular/architectural interface, he seemed at first, in *Vernacular Art* of 1914, to take an entirely negative stance where he was of the opinion that:

> Architects have been shipwrecked with the reproduction of old styles, and now having failed to find the style of our time, they are once again running aground. The catch phrase 'vernacular art' is now coming in very handy as the last lifeline. I hope that this is the last we hear of it. I hope that the arsenal of evil has at last been exhausted. I hope that people will finally become conscious of themselves.[23]

But then he went on to say that 'the cultivation of the vernacular manner of building is a legitimate demand'.[24] He shared with Berlage a view of the vernacular as being, in Berlage's terminology, 'lower culture', although not devalued for being so. It was the Secession misuse of the vernacular, as he saw it, to which he objected. He understood that the proponents of such a self-consciously derived vernacular, even 'vernacularised', art, had attempted to patent the term Modern for their sole use. Architecture for Loos had its discrete place and time but in this was not to be thought either Modern or traditional. Thus the vernacular and its cultivation had validity in its setting and in its own time and as a source. Loos's objection was to its modish and transformed importation into the city by those whom he believed should have known better. Using a typical Loosian tailoring trope, he satirised in *Cultural Degeneration* those who

> were dressed in frock coats of Scottish plaid and velvet lapels, a piece of cardboard stuck in their turned down collars – trade-mark 'Ver Sacrum' – was covered with black silk and gave the illusion of a tie which had been wound around their necks three times.[25]

I am unfortunately reminded of the Annan photographs of the roughly contemporaneous Mackintosh and McNair.

In representing to Loos – and the world at large – the self-conscious personification of the art-architect and art-architecture, Josef Hoffmann's fleeting adoption of the vernacular and his predilection for gratuitous ornament amounted to everything that Loos thought irrelevant. As Masheck commented:

> The trouble with the Vienna Secession [for Loos] was that *ornament reformed* was still *ornament as usual* [Masheck's emphasis].[26]

It was not that Loos was attempting the unique creation of the architecture of the age for, as Dietmar Steiner noted:

> In the last analysis, for Loos the sole justification of the origin of architecture itself rested once again in antiquity.[27]

Loos's response to Hoffmann's 'para-vernacular' was that,

> if one could in the end return to the one truth, which I have always proclaimed: tradition. One should become accustomed to building like our fathers, and should not be afraid of being unmodern.

In concert with Kubištá, he believed that

> [w]e work as well as we can without even thinking for a second about the form,

and with Berlage, in doing so, that

> one will have served one's time, oneself and one's people and humanity well. And by that, one's native country.[28]

Loos, Kubištá and Berlage raised here the question of that which was usable from within tradition and that which was susceptible to being invented anew. They did not accept the authority of any novel architectural style that might have dispensed with everything that preceded it and begun again from a clean slate. Form was not merely comprised of the novelty of its surface appearance but of its programme, its materials and its construction systems and processes; Semper's 'husk' and 'kernel'. Loos accepted and was content, as was Berlage before him, that his method would not gain him prestige such as publication

> in the magazine *Deutscher Kunst und Dekoration* and one would not be appointed professor at the arts and crafts college.[29]

Moreover,

> [t]he architect, however, cannot work in this way [like the farmer]. He works according to a fixed plan. And if he wanted to copy the naivety of the farmer, he would get on the nerves of cultivated people as much as young girls of Ischl or the stockbrokers when putting on an upper Austrian accent.[30]

Loos appealed to tradition, continuity, conformity, even modesty, for he claimed his mode to be building, not architecture. In a paraphrase of Berlage's,

> architecture is an art only when it builds dwellings for the deity... architecture is totally devoid of dignity when it is used solely for the decoration of houses.[31]

Loos, in *Architecture* of 1910, reserved the status of 'architecture' to the monument and the tomb,[32] whereby his buildings and others like them formed the background to that architecture.

The locus of contention for Loos was not simply the art-architecture or building-vernacularism nexus, but also the social consequences of the business of building and the impending monumentalism of working-class housing. He was briefly City Architect for Vienna between 1921 and 1924, resigning when hard-line socialists managed to have Karl Ehn's (1884–1957) vast and monolithic Karl Marx Hof approved for construction and social housing in Vienna took a heroic proto-socialist-realist turn in unprecedented form. But Loos was equally concerned with the potential benefits that the virtues of aesthetic simplification and standardisation might bring as a social, cultural and moral gain throughout all strata of society without differentiation: consumers to benefit from reduced construction costs and the adaptability of the elegant reductivist aesthetic and the producers from reduced working hours due to the abandonment of ornament. He wrote:

> And if there existed no ornament at all, a condition which might arise in millennia, man would only need to work four instead of eight hours, as the time spent on ornament represents half of today's working day. Ornament is wasted manpower and therefore wasted health. It has always been like this. But today it also means wasted material, and both mean wasted capital.[33]

Loos's hopes for a better life/work balance in capitalist society were well put, although historically misplaced, and his thoughts on waste were pertinent. There are some superficial similarities to Ruskin's search for liberation of workers in their labours through the relatively free exercise and individual expression of their art and craft, although Loos reserved to himself the pursuit of the craft of architecture – he denies it is an art – and only sought to liberate workers from tedium through the apparent simplification of the builder's task. The problem for both was that neither the carving of metres of Ruskin's ogee moulding interspersed with the occasional personalised gargoyle or mask nor the accurate fitting of book-matched sheets of Loos's cipollino marble was especially liberating or especially moral other than in the sense of good work well done. Despite such qualification, Ruskin on waste was prescient. Loos would almost have certainly agreed that:

> The idea of self-denial for posterity, of practising present economy for the sake of debtors yet unborn, of planting forests that our descendants may live under their shade, or of raising cities for future nations to inhabit, never, I suppose, efficiently takes place among publicly recognised motives of exertion. Yet these are not the less our duties; nor is our part fitly sustained upon the earth unless the range of our intended and deliberate usefulness include, not only the companions but the successors of our pilgrimage.[34]

Berlage, Muthesius and Loos evinced far more inclusive views of regional and national culture than was credited to them in subsequent Modernist histories which focussed on a more orthodox and normative narrative and selectively played up their contribution to it. Muthesius and Loos, in particular, had a clear understanding of Scotland's contemporary cultural predicament; possibly clearer than that of many Scots then and later. For the moment, I leave Loos with a final word on Scotland and a prophecy of a future world in *Culture*:

> But the new Werther [Loos's fictional German avatar] continues to astonish the world, in his lace-up shoes and Scottish socks, knickerbockers and jacket of coarse cloth [the tweedy Englishman], until the day in a hundred years when the German professor pays a visit to the minister [of state] in this dress [meaning it is now unremarkable]. However, then a man will stand opposite Lotte [the fictional Werther's wife] wearing a wide pair of trousers up to the armpits, held in place with shoulder straps. The American worker had conquered the world. The man in overalls.[35]

In the island nation: the fabrication of a 'national' mythology

It is moot whether Loos's view of Scotland extended to his sharing Muthesius's perception of its 'unspoilt, imaginative and almost dreamily Gaelic folk-like character'.[36] Its origin may have been Muthesius's knowledge of Mackintosh's Celtic and early Symbolist leanings, or his German misreading of Scotland's peasantry, largely supplanted by mechanisation and sheep following the agricultural reforms of the 18th century and the Clearances of the early 19th. Such romanticism, alien to Loos, was entailed in the Victorian adoption of the culturally repurposed, Anglicised and historically and geographically re-sited Arthurian Legend which gripped the nation. Adam Ardrey's carefully charted and consistent match of the Scottish locations of Arthur-named sites to known and dated events of 6th-century history and the related significance of Celtic customs,[37] if accurate, revealed the comprehensiveness of that repurposing. Nevertheless, much cultural production, aesthetic sensibility and moral authority was devoted to the Anglicised version such as was made plain in: Alfred, Lord Tennyson's (1809–92) poems *Lady of Shallot*, 1832, and *Idylls of the King*, 1859–85; the Pre-Raphaelites' many Arthurian subjects (although it was a Scot, the painter William Dyce [1806–64], who introduced the Pre-Raphaelites to Ruskin); the paintings of William Morris (1834–96), *Queen Guenevere (La Belle Iseult)*, 1858, his poetry, *The Defence of Guenevere*, 1858, and his vaguely erotic, quasi-Arthurian novels such as

The Well at the World's End, 1896; and in the architecture of the High Victorians such as William Burges (1827–81) and the Scot Robert Rowand Anderson (1834–1921) for their shared aristocratic Scottish client the 3rd Marquess of Bute (1847–1900).

EM Forster (1879–1970) asked in 1910, '[w]hy has not England a great mythology?'[38] The Arthurian tales, representing the missing 'British' legend and cosmogony appropriated from the Celtic fringes, adventitiously emphasised chivalric values as being indigenous 'British' attributes at the zenith of a rapacious Empire. Hobsbawm claimed that:

> In the 19th century the English were quite exceptional in boasting of their mongrel origins (Britons, Anglo-Saxons, Scandinavians, Scots, Irish, etc.) and glorying in the philological mixture of their language.[39]

However, he failed to acknowledge the implicit corollary whereby the Scandinavians, Scots and Irish were themselves homogenised and identified as 'English' in that process and for whom Arthur, the 'once and future king', was the intended all-embracing Imperial British myth. In mirror image, at the Imperial nadir, JRR Tolkien (1892–1973), perhaps the 'great poet' of Forster's desiring, attempted something similar[40] from much the same source material, although now with a philological representation of Elvish, based in part on Finnish phonemes, as the language of the heroes and the civilised, and Orkish, based in part on Magyar, as that of the villains and the barbaric. Finnish and Magyar share the same non-Indo-European Ugric roots, which Tolkien would have known.

Let's do the time warp again: the persistence of the Baronial

A considerable volume of perspectives, plans and elevations of both new work and of surveys and restorations of existing buildings was published in the Edinburgh Architectural Association's *Sketchbooks* of 1876, 1879, 1882, 1886 and 1894 and in those of the Glasgow Institute of Architects of 1886, 1887, 1888, 1894 and 1904. Inspiration was provided by the built work of Burn, Bryce and others, by Billings' illustrations and commentary, in the efficacy of asymmetric Baronial planning for both large and small domestic and commercial commissions, in the widespread use of its turrets, bays, crowsteps and oriels to provide townscape interest and significance and in

Ruskin's exhortations for irregularity of building profile and for preservation. Such was the interest of Scottish architects in historic Scottish architecture that David MacGibbon (1831–1902) and Thomas Ross (1839–1930) had the confidence, within 30 years of Billings, and while going over some of the same ground, to publish another large compendium in two volumes, *The Castellated and Domestic Architecture of Scotland from the Twelfth to the Eighteenth Centuries* in 1887.[41] They noted that:

> A number of the sketches and plans which form the illustrations in the following pages were exhibited a few years ago in connection with papers on 'Scottish Castles and Houses,' read before the Edinburgh Architectural Association, when the attention they received suggested the idea of the present book.[42]

MacGibbon and Ross acknowledged the contributions to the book from two generations of Scottish architects: David Bryce and his nephew John Bryce (1805–51), Hew Maitland Wardrop (1856–87), (Sir) Robert Rowand Anderson, Hippolyte J Blanc and James Lorimer LLD (n.d.), father of Robert Lorimer. They also gave due regard to Billings' efforts while explicitly responding to Fergusson's criticisms of Billings' lack of plans and system, noting that

> the absence of plans [in Billings] is a serious drawback, and the descriptions of the buildings, although full of interesting matter, do not deal in a systematic manner with the history of our Architecture, especially with the domestic portion of it.[43]

However, they took Fergusson to task, who they claimed

> has also touched slightly, in his *History of Architecture*, on the subject of Scottish Domestic Architecture, but so slightly that it is evident he has not regarded it as an important element in the general history of art.[44]

That is not exactly what Fergusson had said in his plea for a more detailed study (see Introduction) which, in part, MacGibbon and Ross achieved through the addition of a taxonomical history and measured plans and sections. The more in-depth analysis proposed by Fergusson was beyond their scope, as it has been for every subsequent writer on the Baronial. They concluded that:

> One important result of the present inquiry is to bring into prominence the fact that Scotland, like every other country in Europe

during the period from the 13th to the 16th century, possessed a Castellated or Domestic Architecture of its own, and that even in the 17th century, when almost everywhere else the Renaissance style reigned supreme, the native style still flourished.[45]

They made the inevitable plea for preservation.[46]

These houses and castles demonstrated distinctive architectural devices. Those illustrated by Billings and by MacGibbon and Ross were not 'in-the-ground' or 'of-the-ground', they were unequivocally 'on-the-ground', often on an eminence, at odds with man, nature and the climate, three, four, five or six storeys tall in the main apartments, sometimes more in the secondary spaces, on tight floor plans. The authors' inclusion of floor plans revealed the sophistication and economy of Scottish 14th to 17th-century domestic planning of, initially, a series of single stacked spaces and a connecting stair over several storeys which evolved into two or more main spaces pinwheeling round the principal stair, sometimes a turnpike throughout, sometimes a grander dogleg between the main floors. In duplication, in the later houses, this facilitated the more complex 'L', 'T', 'U', 'Z', 'E' or 'H' plans comprised of rectangular and circular elements.

The walls, external and internal, found space within their depth and at their junctions – *poché* space – for ancillary functions such as embrasures, closets, entresols, carrels, bible-closets, ingle-neuks, private chapels, privies, subsidiary stairs, flues and corridors. These occasionally 'grew' 'organically' out from the external wall in more or less defined form, sometimes on clearly delineated and moulded corbelling, sometimes not (see page 50). Windows increased in size from the small, militarily defensible openings of the lower floors of service accommodation, through the climatically defensible openings of the upper stories, to the generous openings in the less accessible – to assailants – upper floors containing the principal apartments. In the earlier examples, window location was dependant entirely on the demands of the room behind, while in the later they were consciously architecturally grouped either symmetrically, sometimes as part of Renaissance interventions, or more often, paratactically. The complex split-level section brought together all these apartments, ancillary spaces and differing floor levels within the tall tower. Such features were shared with many European castle cultures. Their significance in Scotland was in their longevity, being constructed well beyond the time when the cannon rendered the masonry curtain wall ineffective and palaces were the norm elsewhere.

Four of the many castles and houses illustrated by MacGibbon and Ross in volume one should suffice to explain these features: Elphinstone Tower,

Complex interior revealed: Craigievar, Alford, Aberdeenshire, 1596.

Ormiston[47]; Camlongan Castle, Dumfriesshire[48]; Cardoness Castle, Kirkcudbrightshire[49]; and Borthwick Castle, Midlothian with, unusually, a near symmetrical plan and paired turnpike stairs.[50] MacGibbon and Ross also noted the growing domestication of the fortified dwelling where:

> The keeps were also sometimes enlarged by additions made to the keep itself as to convert it into an enlarged mansion.[51]

These examples prefaced, in a sense, volume two and the great Perthshire and Aberdeenshire Scots 'chateaux', from the relatively modest Craigievar, Alford to Crathes Castle, Banchory; Castle Blair, Blair Athol, Pitlochry; Muchalls Castle, Kincardineshire; Castle Menzies, Aberfeldy or Castle Fraser, Inverurie where, other than the earlier Italian Renaissance interventions at, say, Caerlaverock Castle, Dumfriesshire, Linlithgow Palace or Crichton Castle, Midlothian (though even that last is asymmetric), elevations were for the first time aesthetically and stylistically designed in a conscious way.

The Hill House model: Crathes, Banchory Aberdeenshire, 1626.

Not one of the above observations is new or news and they, and the buildings in which they appear, have been comprehensively described in any of the legion of texts on the Baronial. However, they bear repeating here *in précis* in order to establish the very particular aesthetic of a mimetic Scottish national architecture based on recovered 14th to 17th-century models and motives which were deemed to have relevance to the architecture of the closing decades of the 19th century and to a more general perception of a regional Scottish architecture even today. These models were not of a kind with the Gothic manor house and cottage survivals in lost corners of rural England which inspired Philip Webb (1831–1915) or with the early 18th-century Queen Anne reinventions of the Anglo-Scot Richard Norman Shaw (1831–1912), both of which underpinned English Arts & Crafts; nor were they the kind of folkloric dwellings studied by the Czechs, Slovaks, Russians and Finns in the same years. They were, with few exceptions, the castles, forts and houses of the clan chieftain, the baron, the laird or the land-owner, or the townhouse or *hôtel* of the merchant or solicitor. Equally, due to the relative intractability of the construction material, in the earliest models, they were obliged to eschew external decoration of even a formal simplicity such as was derived from folk pottery or needlework and relatively easily reproduced in timber components by any reasonably competent woodworker in timber cultures. Only in later models where economic and military pressures were alleviated was there extensive intricacy and delicacy of decoration and which followed the more sophisticated patterns of Classic or Gothic authority.

Practitioners' and historians' interpretation of the constructions illustrated in Billings' *Baronial* or MacGibbon and Ross's *Castellated and Domestic* or in the architects' *Sketchbooks* has been limited by their interest in stylistic development and an engagement with building forms which arose from the timebound cultural response of a Scottish elite to territory, their patrimony and polity. The bases of such a response came to an effective end long before the eventuation of the Modern age, should we so define it by the emergence of the Scottish Enlightenment around 1745, despite its perpetuation by the elite and manifestation subsequently through its agency in 19th-century rural improvement or planned village and sma burgh schemes.

Having proposed a Baronial and Castellated aesthetic as *the* representation of a Scottish regional or national architecture, indeed, as a representation of Scottishness, the historicist argument leaves no ground in the conventional history of Scottish architecture for other responses to territory and patrimony at other times by other groups which have equally justifiable claims to Scottishness such as can made for Thomson. Territory and patrimony in the 19th century are not the same as those of, say, the 15th, for both are irrevocably altered by the processes of time, nature and culture. The architecture which arose in the interim between the 15th century and the late 19th century was fundamentally different because it must, of necessity, have incorporated the architectural consequences of the changed territory and patrimony. It, too, in turn changed territory and patrimony. This does not simply mean better plumbing or electric lighting. Mackintosh was alive to this when he took to task

> the men of our profession… who imagine they are helping on the cause of our art whereas they are retarding it by feebly imating [sic] some of the visible and superficial features of beautiful old works and neglecting the spirit the intention the soul that lies beneath.[52]

However, while acknowledging these factors, he too shied away from the 'product of learning and accumulated knowledge', preferring to address 'the etherial [sic] the indefinable side of art'.[53]

Artisan housing: an interlude and precursor

Besides showpiece individual demonstration cottages, such as the Prince Consort's artisan dwellings at the Great Exhibition, 1851, the Model Cottage designed by (Sir) James Gowans at the 1886 Edinburgh Exhibition or the Port Sunlight-influenced cottages by James Miller at the Glasgow Exhibition, 1901, artisan housing has not generally featured in the conventional account of Scottish architecture to any great extent – at least not until post-WWII Welfare State ubiquity and an associated Modernist orthodoxy prevailed. Housing for the most deprived sectors in the 19th century was confined to 'model' lodging houses of questionable virtue. Social housing was at issue, as it is today, and its funding, space standards and availability contentious.

Contemporary analysis was thorough and aims were high, if paternalistic. Promoters were concerned equally with the domestic security and felicity of better-off neighbourhoods immediately adjacent to those areas from where the poor were to be liberated or in which they were to be rehoused, as with actually housing the self-same poor:

> Society is not only disfigured but endangered by the Poverty and Ignorance and Vice of a multitude of its members; and its *security* and *happiness* [Allen's emphasis] demand nothing so much as that this wretched mass should be enlightened, elevated and redeemed.[54]

Moral improvement was as much at issue as was domestic improvement. Construction, drainage and ventilation methods, some more experimental and questionable than others, were all given close consideration. Nicholson hit the nail on the head, however,

> as mistakes with regard to space tend to create imaginary difficulties, and either impede sanitary reform, or cause a serious unnecessary expenditure.[55]

There seems to be more information on experimental working-class housing in Edinburgh than there is elsewhere in Scotland. Early developments included the Pilrig Model Dwellings, 1847, and Chalmers Buildings, Fountainbridge, 1853, both by Patrick Wilson (1798–1871); the brick-built Rosemount Buildings, Fountainbridge, 1858, and Patriot Hall, Stockbridge, 1871, both by William Lambie Moffat (1807–82), a pupil of Burn's who practised between 1836 and 1855 in Doncaster, which may have accounted for his material choice. By far the largest of the developments were those of the Edinburgh Cooperative Building Company (ECBC), formed by stonemasons locked out in 1861 following a strike in protest at the employers' refusal nationally to reduce the working day from ten to nine hours. The first of these developments, which are known throughout Edinburgh as 'Colonies', was the 15 streets at Stockbridge constructed between 1861 and 1875 with a further small extension in 1911. Shareholding in the company and house purchase was encouraged, which tended to favour single women with a small private income, clerks, artisans or the skilled working class, or those renting to them, rather than the labouring classes. Subsequently, a further ten sites were developed between 1863 and 1934. Post-1914, the company was resistant to new construction methods and materials and persisted with mass masonry construction and, with only limited and sporadic development subsequently, finally liquidated in 1954.[56] By 1907, the company had built 2,300 houses which, with an average household of around four, was equivalent to the population of a town the size of Haddington, East Lothian, today.

Architecturally the houses are plain with minimal decoration, and the earlier types gained urban significance from their external stairs while later terraces acquired arched lintels and the ubiquitous Edinburgh bay window, with the benefit of useful private external space for all dwellings. Socially they worked largely as did the tenement by requiring owner or tenant cooperation in the maintenance of the four-in-a-block sub-divisions of the longer terraces. In discussing the planning of the houses, Rodger noted of their space standards:

Furthermore, the parlour or best room in the Colonies permitted a degree of privacy and ceremony which was impossible in the undifferentiated space of even a two-roomed tenement flat. In this sense, the ECBC properties were indeed 'colonising,' that is, not unlike English style working class housing which differed fundamentally from Scottish tenement flats by creating private in place of public or communal space. However, unlike English terraced houses where the scullery, wash-house and kitchen extension became closely identified with women's space, the gendered nature of space, or 'separate spheres', was by the very design of the earlier ECBC houses less likely to develop.[57]

Making an exhibition of oneself: the international exposition as design showcase

The period of the late 19th and early 20th centuries was the age of international exhibitions. Their purposes were varied as nations and empires jostled for position. In some senses, the parade of exhibitions provided a peaceful simulacrum of the clash of empires. At their most basic they were showcases for current achievements in science, industry and art – most usually for the luxury market – as at Paris 1900; or were limited to single nations and the promotion of their colonies and empires such as the exhibitions of 1895, 1899 and 1911 in London. They embellished the signing of trade or military treaties such as the Franco-British Exhibition, London, 1908, celebrating the 'entente cordiale' of the Triple Entente between the empires of Britain, France and Russia of 1904, or the Japan-British Exhibition, London, 1910, in anticipation of the Japanese Empire's joining the 'entente' in 1914 (Japan was already party to a 1902 treaty which helped ensure the security of British Far East colonies). By way of contrast, the Imperial Austrian Exhibition, London, 1906, seemed a doomed attempt to ease relationships with one of the empires signatory to the Triple Alliance of 1882 which conjoined Germany, Italy and Austro-Hungary up to and, briefly, beyond 1914.

Scotland made efforts at Edinburgh, 1886, and Glasgow, 1888, although, as the Kinchin sisters observed, the arena of contest, in the eyes of Glaswegians at least, was parochial: 'Manchester and Edinburgh may *try* it, but Glasgow can *do* it'.[58] Perhaps Glasgow did, because the profit from the hugely successful 1888 Exhibition paid for what became the Kelvingrove Art Gallery and Museum. It was won in competition in 1892 by John William Simpson (1858–1933) and Edmund Milner Allen (1860–1912) with a safe, eclectic Spanish Baroque design in red Locharbriggs sandstone, shorn in early planning of the intended School of Art component with significant later consequence. An exhibition was planned to celebrate the opening of the completed Art Gallery and Museum in 1901, inevitably inviting comparison with other international exhibitions which bracketed the centennial: the World's Columbian Exposition, Chicago, 1893; the Exposition Universelle, Paris, 1900; the Esposizione Internazionale d'Arte Decorativa Moderna, Turin, 1902; or the Esposizione Internazionale del Sempione, Milan, 1906.

An 'architecture of the age' was belatedly represented by Louis Sullivan's Transportation Museum at Chicago, and Gesellius, Lindgren and Saarinen's Finnish pavilion at the strongly Art Nouveau Paris Exposition of 1900 – where it sat comfortably amongst contributions by Hector Guimard (1867–1942) and Otto Wagner and alongside Boberg's remarkable red and yellow proto-Constructivist Swedish pavilion. Turin 1902 was a wholly consistent tour-de-force in an opulent Italian Liberty designed by Raimondo d'Aronco (1857–1932), then architect to the Ottoman Sultan Abdulhamid II. A room within d'Aronco's main pavilion was devoted to Scotland (see overleaf), master-planned and designed by the Mackintoshes. Also exhibiting were Frances MacDonald McNair (1873–1921) and James Herbert MacNair (1868–1955), Jessie M King (1875–1949), Talwin Morris (1865–1911) and

Italian Liberty excess: Turin International Exhibition, 1902, architect Raimundo d'Aronco.
(Drawing by Roger Emmerson)

Glasgow School restraint: Turin International Exhibition, 1902, architects and designers the Mackintoshes, the MacNairs et al.
(Drawing by Roger Emmerson)

others. The combination of an overall Germanic regularity in planning was enlivened by isolates of intense Symbolist and Celtic-influenced jewel-like decoration in both room decoration and the objects exhibited and was a profound corrective to the uncontrolled floridity and licence that was on show at Paris and Turin and more generally in European Art Nouveau, Liberty, Secession or Jugendstil styles. Josef Hoffmann, Mackintosh's correspondent, for example, was still contemporaneously influenced by such as the Jugendstil exponent Josef Maria Olbrich (1867–1908) in that, as Borsi and Godoli remarked, Olbrich's style could be felt in Hoffmann's entry for the 1900 Paris World's Fair at the Grand Palais in Paris...

[although] [b]y the time of the following [Secession] exhibition in 1902, Hoffmann had exhausted what he could draw from Olbrich's curvilinear style and he embarked on a personal interpretation of *Japonisme* that, alongside the influence of Klimt and Byzantine artists, became a component of his geometric idiom.[59]

The influence of Mackintosh, of course, was also of significance.

However, at Glasgow in 1901, the Glasgow School was confined to the margins of James Miller's (1860–1947) 'white city' 16th-century Spanish Renaissance confection – thought, at the time, to be 'Oriental' – which deferred too readily to the role of whimsical counterpart to the stolid Spanish Baroque of the building it was intended to celebrate. Mackintosh designed four small stands – for the Glasgow School of Art, for Pettigrew and Stephens, for Francis Smith and for the Rae Brothers. George Walton (1867–1933) designed a photographic studio for T&R Annan. David Gow (n.d.) produced the Wylie and Lochhead stand with interiors by John Ednie (1876–1934), EA Taylor (1874–1951) (husband of Jessie M King) and George Logan (1867–1939), which transferred to the Budapest Arts & Crafts Exhibition the following year. Paintings by the 'Glasgow Boys' were on show, as were works by Jessie M King, Ann MacBeth (1875–1948), Phoebe Traquair (1852–1936) and the Wilson Sisters (n.d.) (The Glasgow Girls). However, this was small beer compared to the insistent and ubiquitous new architecture and design content at Paris and Turin. The only substantial contribution from the cutting edge of contemporary design thinking at Glasgow was the Russian Village designed by Fyodor Shekhtel (1859–1926).

For all its asserted bustling, go-getting American comparison, Glasgow remained resolutely part of a British culture drifting ever further from the high point of Imperial entrepreneurship of the mid-19th century, because now 'British attitudes towards their Empire flipped over from arrogance to anxiety'[60]. The Empire, moreover, that was no longer guarantor of Scotland's fragile economic and political status. Here then was the conundrum of Glasgow, so frequently compared in Scottish accounts to the then great cities of the world such as Chicago, Barcelona or Milan, contrarily having missed the moment and finding itself out of sync with the *zeitgeist* in 1901. Hobsbawm commented that:

> By and large – Vienna and the planned global show of the 1900 Exposition in Paris are the big exceptions – art nouveau is not characteristic of national metropoles, but of the self-conscious and self-evident bourgeoisies of provincial or regional ones.[61]

Despite historians' frequent use of a loose Art Nouveau catch-all to include works by the Mackintoshes, the MacNairs, Salmon, Son and Gillespie, Gordon and Dobson and Walton, Glasgow's contribution in such international company was woefully thin and isolated. It did not have the entire streets and quarters of Art Nouveau such as one finds in, say, Prague, Helsinki or Riga, cities which had a similar scale of resource and industry hinterland and historic population size and trend, albeit the extent of such Art Nouveau urban development was determined by contemporaneous economic growth. There is a more general point here in such cultural and architectural comparisons, in that hard fact gives way to a Scottish exceptionalism based on the very few, although exemplary, works. They are awarded 'what-if' or 'if-only' status to promote the notion of a Scotland 'punching above its weight' in whatever division it finds itself. At best, as the Kinchins conceded, Glasgow in 1901 'had too little that was new'.[62]

Spring: Baronialism's progeny

Glendinning et al identified several separate variants of a Scottish national architecture in addition to the Baronial, which arose both from architects' own practice in the 1870s and '80s and from MacGibbon and Ross's publication in 1887.[63] Robert Rowand Anderson was the leading light of a Traditional variant, partly through his architecture, especially the exemplar of his own house, Allermuir, Edinburgh, 1879–92; partly through the work of his pupils Robert Lorimer, Sydney Mitchell (1856–1930) and John Kinross (1855–1931) and others such as James Jerdan (1839–1913); and partly through his involvement in the founding of the Edinburgh School of Applied Arts, 1892, and the National Art Survey, 1895 and ultimately in the creation of the Incorporation of Architects in Scotland in 1916. Anderson followed Pugin, Ruskin and Morris in his use of local craftsmen, such as Scott Morton and Whytock & Reid, in the design of the interiors. In a claim reminiscent of Morris's, he proposed that one should only have 'some good big things... not much on the walls'.[64]

Glendinning et al deemed the Traditional as largely an East Coast phenomenon while its West Coast counterpart was identified as 'Monumental Traditionalism'. Again, the materials of construction had some bearing on their stylistic denominations, the latter featuring harling or render prominently in some examples in contrast to exposed masonry construction. In the traditional Scottish dwelling, whether hovel or castle, large areas of walling tended to be constructed of cheaper random rubble which was harled if the stone was especially poor or irregular and lime-washed otherwise, saving the expensive cut-stone for door cases, window architraves, mouldings, decorative or armorial panels and copes. It might be thought perverse that a 'humble' material was used in monumental construction. However, it permitted some expressive complexity

The sma burgh interpretation: Kirkton Cottages, Fortingall, 1890, architect James Marjoribanks McLaren.

The English Arts & Crafts interpretation: Melsetter House, Hoy, Orkney, 1898, architect WR Lethaby.

and contrast in elevational treatment where harling had a part to play. It avoided Baronial excess and retained the appearance of traditional materials and methods such as in the work of MacLaren at Glen Lyon, 1889–91, or WR Lethaby at Melsetter, Hoy, including a very English Arts & Crafts triple gable, 1898, or Mackintosh at the door case and lintel at Windyhill, Kilmacolm, 1901.

At Hill House, Helensburgh, 1902, Mackintosh regrettably specified Portland cement and dispensed with copes which caused dampness to be retained within the wall rather than using lime harling which would have drawn it out. Moreover, harling was also used to cover a truly cheap method of construction, such as the growing use of common brick solid and cavity walls, allowing savings to be made and redistributed to more expensive and elaborate masonry detailing elsewhere. Another material formerly regarded as 'humble', rock-faced rubble, was employed to give dynamism to wall-face and profile. It appeared in McLaren's Stirling High School extension, 1887–8, in some of Lorimer's castles of 1900 to 1914, such as the partially reinforced-concrete-constructed Formakin, 1912–4, in Mackintosh's Mossyde, Kilmacolm, 1908, and in William Leiper's (1839–1916) domestic work. Glendinning et al also identified ecclesiastical designs which employed those Romanesque revival forms reported by Campbell and Fawcett such as the First Church of Christ Scientist, Ramsay Traquair (1874–1952), Edinburgh, 1910–1.

Frank Walker, in charting the considerable spread of these commercial, domestic and ecclesiastical Baronial, Traditional and Monumental styles – although he tended to describe them all as Baronial – throughout Scottish cities in the late 19th century, noted that in Glasgow, the 'Baronial was slow to appear'.[65] This is corroborated, perhaps, by the later appearance, by ten years, of the Glasgow Institute of Architects Sketchbooks (see above) or in the persistence of neo-Classicism. McWilliam thought that:

> For all their bad reputation, Glasgow's tenements were and are finer than those of the capital. Edinburgh's long affair with the bay window may have been influenced by what Ruskin had said there.[66]

He noted, with approval, Glasgow's preference for a more vernacular form, though did so in contradiction to his relative negativism about similar work by Anderson in Edinburgh. The slapstick Glasgow/Edinburgh antipathy often leads to inconsistent opinions. What can be said is that Glasgow evinced a preference for simpler decoration in tenemental construction. Bryce's busy turrets, intricate stepped mouldings, corbelled gables, polygonal bays and pentangular mullions were often avoided, although not universally, and were replaced by plainer profiles and shallow quarter-round, or even shallower, bays, square mullions and narrower strictly horizontal square mouldings which gave tenemental terraces an altogether sharper, tighter appearance and in which one seems to see the ghost of Thomson.

The issue here is that these several divisions of a Traditionalist position were no more historically or architecturally 'Scottish' and 'correct' than that of the Baronialists, and their conflict was bogus in that both, by using the same models, responded anachronistically and of necessity to the territorial, patrimonial and hegemonic cultural and aesthetic demands of the tastes of the 14th to 17th centuries. Mackintosh reminded us that:

> The props of art are… the slavish imitations of old work no matter what date or from what country… and the absurd and false idea – that there can be any living emotion expressed in work scientifically proportioned according to antient principals [sic] – but clothed in the thin fantasy of the authors [sic] own fancy.[67]

He excoriated the rampant eclecticism and revivalism of the age, and his words recalled Semper's censure of the 'architectural materialists, historicists, purists, schematicists and futurists' of 30 years previously.

The real confrontation was between the shared origin of the Traditionalist and Baronialist positions and that of the contemporary seeker after an 'architecture of the age'. It was a confrontation based on the thesis/antithesis of truth/logic; simplicity/complexity; honesty/elaboration; spiritual/religious; secular/faith; community/individual. The Traditionalist/Baronialist proposition never quite incorporated the 'truth/simplicity/honesty/spiritual/community' pole of the antinomy because, in preterition, it closed off the argument at the outset by confining it to the superficiality of a discussion about specific aesthetics and simply asserted moral and historic inevitability through the invocation of the vintage of that specific aesthetic and possibly the patrimony and polity of its originators.

Summer: the Mackintoshes and the European avant-garde

Absent the discovery of fresh material, there seems little to add to the voluminous library on the work of the Mackintoshes,[68] although perhaps some key episodes should be read differently. I write 'Mackintoshes' because Mackintosh was quite clear on this matter. In correspondence with his wife, he wrote:

> You must remember that in all my architectural efforts you have been half if not threequarters in them.[69]

The works are well-known, his writings less so. Largely lifted by Mackintosh from those of Billings, Fergusson, MacGibbon and Ross, Lethaby and MacLaren,[70] they were comprehensively and effectively reviewed by Robertson and others in *The Architectural Papers*. There is possibly a handful of marginal points which I might raise in connection with this collection. Frank Walker queried what Mackintosh meant in saying 'the style [a Scottish national architecture] is coming to life again', although, plainly, Mackintosh was engaged in a contemporaneous transformation of that which Bryce, Burns, Anderson and others in that century had already merely reinterpreted. From a Glasgow viewpoint, Frank Walker denied that Mackintosh included his Edinburgh contemporaries as participants in this venture,[71] despite Mackintosh's evident approval of Lorimer:

> We hope Mr Lorimer will come and see us sometimes. We consider him the best domestic architect in Scotland and admire his work very much.[72]

James Macaulay wondered at the anachronistic use of 'our country' in Mackintosh's essay on Elizabethan architecture,[73] although Scotland's singular situation in the late 19th century was to play a distant second-fiddle in the Union while accorded significant status and autonomy within the Empire where the notion of 'our country' – Scotland or Britain – was flexible in that context and was not as contrary to Scotland's interests of identity and autonomy as it later became. These peccadillos aside, David Walker observed:

> The sources from which his ideas were drawn, particularly in the first lecture, must sometimes have seemed to his listeners strangely old-fashioned.[74]

And that surely was the point.

David Walker's observation notwithstanding, Mackintosh created the richest, most promising and most innovative development of a Scottish national architecture inspired by the Traditional/Baronial antecedents seen then or at any time since. Mackintosh averred:

> I will admit an architects [sic] art is apt to represent a good deal more survival than revival… [but] here we have design that is not survival but that is alive with individuality and revolutionary motive.[75]

He said so because he believed that:

> Surely the architecture which grew up among men so nearly allied to us has a preeminent claim upon our attention.[76]

In pursuit of that 'individuality and revolutionary motive', Mackintosh transcended the superficial timebound limitations of the Traditional/Baronial aesthetic and, in the elevations of the Willow Tea Rooms, Sauchiehall Street, 1904, Scotland Street School, 1904–6, and the Art School West Wing, 1907–9, left behind or subsumed his earlier more overt stylistic influences. This transformation was rapid.

MacLeod described Hill House, Helensburgh, 1902, as being 'less urbane, and more overtly Scottish'[77] while Frampton reckoned it 'somewhat chaotic and unresolved'[78], although he was not to know that Mackintosh interpreted MacGibbon and Ross, in that 'additions [were] made to the keep itself as to convert it into an enlarged mansion'. At Hill House, dining room, kitchen, offices, children's rooms and servants' quarters are located in a notional 16th-century keep with the living room and the parents' domain in an abstracted 18th-century addition, such as is found at Crathes Castle, Banchory (see page 148). The way ahead in Frampton's view was the disqualified competition design for *Das Haus Eines Kunstsfreundes*, 1901, but such opportunities did not present themselves subsequently and the differences between the situation of, say, Hoffmann in Vienna and Mackintosh in Glasgow became cruelly apparent.

Although Hill House briefly post-dated *Das Haus Eines Kunstsfreundes*, it is the latter which had the more sophisticated and Modern plan of the two. Two long parallel ranges were arranged at either side of a circulation zone with, generally speaking, the principal apartments in the more regular range to the south, and the entrance and ancillary spaces – *not* 'servant' spaces in the Kahnian sense – in the more fragmented range to the north. This was a composition with which Mackintosh had tentatively experimented at Windy

The one that got away: Haus Eines Kunstfreundes, 1900, architect Charles Rennie Mackintosh; constructed at Bellahouston Park, Glasgow, 1990, executive architect Andrew MacMillan.
(Jean-Pierre Dalbéra, own work, Creative Commons)

room, music room and breakfast room almost *en enfilade* with bedrooms above and facilitated the regular, very nearly symmetrical, south elevation. The north range created a series of zones and a freer elevation: the gable of the gentlemen's room and the dressing room above framing one side of the modestly-scaled entrance court; the stair tower; the honorific windows to the *diele* behind; and the more domestic section containing the dining room and children's apartment above framing the other. By permitting the two ranges to minimally 'slip and slide' against one another, Mackintosh released the potential of the end gables to create dynamic asymmetry. The horizontal and vertical elements and windows are organised paratactically to sit in montage and planar harmony in a manner that tower-houses, on which they are presumed to be based, never present.

The Mackintoshes' entry emphasised the datedness of the silver-medal-winner in the same competition, that of the Anglo-Scot Mackay Hugh Baillie-Scott (1865–1945). Today, a direct comparison can be made between the Mackintoshes' *Haus Eines Kunstsfreundes,* as erected in 1996 by Graham Roxburgh in Bellahouston Park, Glasgow, with Andrew MacMillan as executive architect, and Baillie-Scott's roughly contemporaneous design, Blackwell, Bowness, Cumbria of 1898–1900, restored 2000–1; both are open to the public. Despite the decorative tour-de-force of the surfaces, Baillie-Scott complicated his plan with randomly-distributed ingle-neuks, bay windows, screens, an unmemorable stair – located largely to facilitate access to the isolated and stagey minstrels' gallery – and scattered circulation, which MacLeod described as his 'calculated inconsistencies'.[79] Baillie-Scott, nonetheless, had a highly successful career in domestic architecture throughout Northern Europe, completing around 130 houses up to his retirement in 1935.

Robert Lorimer, who could be as irascible as Mackintosh was moody, had in spades, like Baillie-Scott, what Mackintosh lacked at the fin-de-siècle and into the first decades of the 20th century. His training was with the Scots Renaissance and Baronial architects, Anderson, Wardrop and Browne, and with the English Gothicist, George Frederick Bodley (1827–1907), himself mentor to the young Giles Gilbert Scott (1880–1960) at Liverpool Anglican Cathedral (1904–78). Lorimer was also briefly with John Marjoribanks McLaren. Although based in Edinburgh, he was active and had contacts in several British art and architecture movements at the close of the century. These included Arts & Crafts practitioners, the High Victorians and the Pre-Raphaelites. He employed the workshops of Morris & Co. and Watts & Co. in England and Scott Morton, Whytock & Reid and the artists Thomas Hadden (1871–1940) and Phoebe Traquair in Scotland. He maintained friendships with the influential Anglo-Scots Richard Norman Shaw and John James Stevenson (1831–1908), had membership of the Architectural Association and the Art Workers' Guild and belonged to an extended family which provided access to the many social circles from which his clients were drawn almost equally from Scotland and England. By way of contrast, notwithstanding the Mackintoshes' significant but brief European presence in Vienna, Munich, Dresden, Berlin, Moscow and Turin between 1900 and 1904, they were unable, at home, to generate a sufficiently broad clientele, even in Glasgow, beyond the Davidsons, the Blackies and Miss Cranston or through the influence of Fra Newbery.

Autumn: taxing times

Dubbed the 'People's Budget', David Lloyd George's Finance Act 1909 raised taxes to finance welfare programmes, in part to contain working class agitation for something more radical, and to construct battleships to counter Germany's growing naval strength. A 20 per cent tax was levied on the unearned increase in land value arising from its development and a tax of $^1/_2$d in the pound on underdeveloped land and minerals. One of the unforeseen consequences of the Act was its impact on the architectural profession in Britain, as land-owners abandoned developments to avoid the tax. Celebrated practices ceased to trade and others shrank, Keppie and Mackintosh amongst them. Their partnership, agreed in 1901, was for a ten-year duration. Reviewing the practice finances in 1911, Keppie found Mackintosh's client base had contributed less than a third of the practice income over the period while, on the basis of their prior agreed division of profits, Mackintosh had earned £500 more than he had brought in. Moreover, Mackintosh was proving late with competition entries, losing some clients and being reprimanded by others such as the Glasgow School Board and the Glasgow School of Art. The partnership was finally dissolved in 1914[80] on the eve of WWI.

For over eighty years since he made it, and despite many nuanced studies of the period since, Pevsner's less-than-complete, less-than-accurate, dictum that

> [Mackintosh's] synthesis of [Voysey's, Beardsley's and Toorop's] style was the legacy of Britain to the coming Modern Movement[81]

still holds water for many. The Modernism that most believed Pevsner had referred to, because that was what had become orthodox, was that branch that led directly to the Bauhaus, to Ludwig Mies van der Rohe and to Le Corbusier. In this conception it was the origin of the subsequent spurious and oft-repeated 'Craigievar/Mackintosh/Corbusier-Bauhaus' trajectory, deemed plausible largely because of their shared whiteness, volumetric composition, functional fenestration and, of course, the misreading of Pevsner.

What Pevsner wrote was:

> From here [the West Wing of the School of Art] a direct way leads to that peculiar and short-lived Expressionism in Continental and especially Dutch architecture which for a while *held up the progress* [Pevsner's emphasis] of the main stream of modern architecture about 1920.[82]

Pevsner was dismissive of Expressionist tendencies in Modernism, in which he included Mackintosh, because, in his view, it hindered Modernism's 'true' path. Nevertheless, a sentence later, he fudged the authority of his claim: 'Whether the Dutch architects had actually taken notice of Mackintosh's later buildings is not certain'. On the one hand, Pevsner denied Mackintosh's significance in an orthodox and normative Modernism while, on the other hand, seeming to lack confidence in his contrasting claim that Mackintosh's work could indeed be associated with or corresponded to the Amsterdam School's brick-built Expressionism such as Het Schip, Amsterdam, 1917,

Pevsner's Dutch expressionism: 'De Dageraad', Amsterdam, 1919, architects Michel de Klerk and Piet Kramer.

by Michel de Klerk (1884–1923), Burgemeester Teelegenstraat, Amsterdam Suid, 1920–3, by Piet Kramer (1881–1961) or De Dageraad, Amsterdam, 1919–22, by de Klerk and Kramer. However, what Pevsner clearly identified was a shared Expressionist component of Scottish architecture – arguably the Expressionism of the tower-house via the Glasgow School of Art West Wing – which received little or no attention then or subsequently (see pages 50 and 148), the theoretical drive in Scotland being always to prove and establish as fact the part-French origin of the upper stories of the later castles and the conjectured Craigievar/Mackintosh/Corbusier Bauhaus and Schinkel/Thomson/Sullivan/Wright Modernist connections.

Pevsner's mis-read assertion remains an article of faith for some Scottish and British Modernists, despite MacLeod's cautionary note of 1968, repeated in 1983, that it

> is increasingly apparent that Mackintosh and his works sit very uneasily in any campaign which numbered among its goals the rejection of tradition, the glorification of new technology, the rejection of ornament and the substitution of cool generalisation for intense individuality... If he ever intended to be modern it was never in that way.[83]

Not merely misreading Pevsner, the British Modernist is required also to misinterpret the entire Mackintosh oeuvre in the manner described by MacLeod to fit the accepted narrative.[84] Together with Stamp, MacLeod is one of the few writers to have presented a candid reassessment of Mackintosh's final years:

> In Britain, his architectural eclipse was total. He can scarcely, therefore, be considered a pioneer of modern architecture in the usual sense of having contributed to a developing collective ideology, or

even to a developing vocabulary of form... he was one of the last and one of the greatest Victorians.[85]

The rancorous split in the membership of the Secession in 1904 between the *Klimt-gruppe* – which included the painters Gustav Klimt (1862–1918) and Carl Moll (1861–1945) and the designer/architects Otto Wagner, Josef Hoffmann and Koloman 'Kolo' Moser (1868–1918) – and the *Nur-Maler*, essentially the easel painters, with the resignation en masse of the *Klimt-gruppe*, meant that

> the halls of their own exhibition buildings were now closed to the artists of Klimt's circle, who had, by their manoeuvrings, deprived themselves of an essential focus for their activity.[86]

This loss equally reduced Mackintosh's *mitteleuropäische* opportunities before the completion of the West Wing of the Glasgow School of Art could demonstrate that, if he ever was the synthesis of 'Voysey, Beardsley and Toorop', he was definitely not so now. Yet, despite his undoubted genius, there is the very real sense that Mackintosh was as much an end as he was a beginning. Indeed, at the *Internationale Kunstschau Wien*, 1909, the Mackintoshes and Charles Robert Ashbee (1863–1942), promoted by a consortium of London-based Arts & Crafts businesses, were confined to one of the three smaller spaces devoted to the Arts & Crafts (*In Den Schränken Englisches Kunst Gewerbe*), adjacent to the Hoffmann-designed *Grosser Hof*.[87] Charles had four exhibits, Margaret three and Ashbee two; none were described. There was no 'room' for the Mackintoshes at Wien. Oskar Kokoschka's (1886–1980) poster for the 1908 *Kunstschau* and Bertold Löffler's (1874–1960) for that of 1909 signalled new stylistic directions. Vergo noted:

> The financial disappointments that accompanied the two Kunstschau exhibitions left no resources available for further experiments of this kind. No other major exhibitions of avant-garde painting took place in Vienna after 1909; strictly speaking, it is impossible not to regard the period between the closure of the second Kunstschau and the outbreak of the First World War as a culturally barren epoch.[88]

The sense of an end understandably transfers from the works to Mackintosh's mental and physical retreat from architecture post-1915, and it may seem grossly unfair now to unpack and unpick the content of his twilight years. However, in tracking the presence and course of a Scottish national architecture it is relevant to turn the spotlight back on Mackintosh's few late projects, despite their being the products of that retreat. Modernist architectural historians are ever quick to establish a new beginning, eager to identify a heyday, diffident about continuity and forgetful of ends; practising architects live daily with the consequences of all such leaps.

Winter: the consequences of honest error[89]

Hoffmann moved on architecturally at the Purkersdorf Sanatorium, Lower Austria, 1904, the Palais Stoclet, Brussels, 1907–11, and in his later Classicised houses where, as Kallir recorded, he was not immune to

> a somewhat modernised variant of historicism [which] had already emerged in the work of Olbrich and Behrens in Germany [and which] after 1906 began sweeping all of Europe.[90]

This is evident in the Hochstetter House, 1906–7, the Villa Ast, 1909–11, and the Villa Skywa-Primavesi, 1913–6, all Vienna. By way of contrast, Mackintosh's brief Austrian sojourn as expressed in his furniture was not an unalloyed success. Bilcliffe observed,

A parting of the ways: Palais Stoclet, Brussels, 1906, architect Josef Hoffmann.
(PtrQs, own work, Creative Commons)

for what made Mackintosh different from an Ashbee, and even a Hoffmann, was his concern not with material, craftsmanship, nor construction, but only with final appearance... This meant that many of his pieces have not stood the test of time and that, in Glasgow at least, his furniture acquired a reputation for shoddy construction as well as providing an inhuman lack of comfort.[91]

This was echoed by Vergo, who added that 'Hoffmann, Moser and their contemporaries advocated a return to "genuine" craftsmanship'.[92] The educated, wealthy, and demanding patrons who supported the Wiener Werkstätte had numerous furniture options in the well-made productions of Hoffmann, Josef Maria Olbrich, Kolo Moser and Otto Wagner or in the bentwood furniture of the Brothers Thonet and Brothers Kohn.[93]

Mackintosh's 1906 proposal to his partner Keppie that he spend part of each year in Austria to deal with or to develop European business was declined. Meanwhile, there was no Glaswegian Secession of artists, architects and designers of sufficient number and means to have afforded their own permanent exhibition premises and, although there was a loose 'Glasgow School', there was no equivalent Glasgow Werkstätte to regulate and promote production. There was no Strathclyde Wärndorfer to fund the operation – although he, too, was bankrupted by the Wiener Werkstätte in 1913 and left for America – nor was there a local artists' colony such as that in Vienna where Hoffmann designed eight villas for Kolo Moser, Carl Moll and other artists and patrons of the Werkstätte at the Hohe Warte between 1901 and 1911. And there was no Palais Stoclet for Mackintosh.

The matter of the Mackintoshes' influence on the European avant-garde beyond 1904 was lost in the accumulation of a wider cultural exchange where the product design of British designers such as Ashbee and the Anglo-Scot Dr Christopher Dresser (1834–1904) had a longer-lasting impact in mainland Europe at the Wiener Werkstätte and the Bauhaus. In contrast, only isolated Mackintosh motives featured in Hoffmann's and Moser's contemporaneous work such as Hoffmann's brief adoption of the Mackintosh 'grid' in his furniture, metal work and silverware designs in its decorative application on buildings such the Henneberg House, Vienna, 1900-2 (to which Mackintosh contributed furniture designs), the several early houses at Hohe Warte, Vienna, 1901-4, the Purkersdorf itself or the second Moll House, Hohe Warte, Vienna, 1906-7, disappearing soon after. The Mackintosh 'bullet' stair and the oval Ladies Room from *Das Haus Eines Kunstsfreundes* appeared in Hoffmann's Ast Villa, Vienna, 1910 and there is a generic elevational similarity, although not in the detail, between Mackintosh's unbuilt Artist's Cottage, 1900,

Waving or drowning? Derngate, Northampton, 1915–9, architect Charles Rennie Mackintosh.
(Tony Hisgett, Creative Commons)

Hoffmann's unbuilt Artist's House, 1906, and, as Masheck highlighted, in Adolf Loos's likewise unbuilt 'Project for a Settlement with Seven-Metre Long Gardens', Vienna, 1921.⁹⁴ There is also a coincidental similarity between the gridded canted glazed bays of the first floor of Loos's Goldman and Salatsch building, Michaelerplatz, Vienna, 1910 and the library windows at Mackintosh's Glasgow School of Art, 1907–11. These may be no more than simultaneous invention, for Loos made no reference to Mackintosh in his writings, perhaps lumping him with Hoffmann, whose work he detested.

Within the wider context of Muthesius' English House legacy is Ludwig Mies van der Rohe's earliest independent house design, the Rhiel House, Potsdam of 1906 which has an entrance, hall, stair and ground floor sequence nearly identical to CFA Voysey's (1857–1941) The Orchard of 1900. In his account of Loos's Khuner Country Villa, Kreuzberg of 1929–30, August Sarnitz noted that 'the spatial nucleus is the great hall according to the 'English' model',⁹⁵ while Masheck came to a similar conclusion on Loos's Spanner House, Grumpoldskirchen, 1924.

Mackintosh's works for Wenham Bassett-Lowke at 78 Derngate, Northampton, 1915–9), are often promoted by historians as a proto-Art Deco link to Modernism, although with little conviction given that Art Deco, in the orthodox Modernist narrative, is Modernism's commercialised sibling-from-hell, while to postulate yet another undocumented link to an event a decade in the future entails a clairvoyance which does not become the professional historian. Indeed, Derngate shared as much decoratively with the Expressionistic interiors of Wright's Imperial Hotel, Tokyo, 1919–23, or the Sommerfeld House, Berlin, 1920–22, by Walter Gropius (1883–1969) and Adolf Meyer (1881–1929) as it did with a putative Art Deco. There is so much going on in Derngate that it seems like a last glorious throw of the design dice because it is not repeated in Mackintosh's few subsequent architectural works.

Perhaps there is another interpretation. While some of the stacked, interpenetrating rectilinear, diagonal and gridded forms were plainly derived from those of West Wing, Mackintosh's formal decorative language acquired an angularity – charted diagrammatically by Kimura[96] – at Derngate and in the Dug Out at the Willow Tea Rooms, 1917, not seen before in his work. It had much in common with the graphic, furniture and architectural work of Hoffmann, Moser and Hoffmann's students Otto Prutscher (1880–1949), Carl Witzmann (1883–1952) and Emmanuel Josef Margold (1888–1962) and in the graphic work of Hilde Exner (1880–1922) in the two to three years following their resignation from the Secession in 1904. Indeed, Kallir illustrated a poster design by Exner of 1903–4[97] which was comprised entirely of the geometric forms which Mackintosh employed at Derngate more than a decade later. Moreover, during the period 1900–10, in painting, product design and graphic work, Secession and Wiener Werkstätte artists and designers exhibited strong Egypto-Greek influences which Mackintosh, despite his physical and intellectual proximity to Thomson, did not.

Bilcliffe noted the Prutscher connection in that he

> produced in about 1907–10 much the same kind of designs as Mackintosh turned to in 1916–17[98]

but missed entirely how Prutscher's work developed subsequent to 1910 in a radically different direction to that pursued contemporaneously by Mackintosh. In 1910–1, Prutscher designed a Woman's Drawing Room for the Museum of Art and Industry

> that marked a clear step away from his previous geometrical orientation... [and] was the first appearance of the Neo-Rococo 'feminine' [sic] style.[99]

Thereafter, Secession artists, designers and architects incorporated a Klimt and Prutscher-inspired ellipse and curving line in their work – not an Art Nouveau 'whiplash' – which was evident in the graphics of Löffler, Peche, Leopold Förstner (1878–1936) and Carl Otto Czeschka (1878–1960) and, in concert with its Classicising tendencies, in the architecture, fabrics and room settings of Hoffmann, Moser and Alfred Roller (1864–1935). Similar curving forms only appeared almost a decade later in Mackintosh's abstracted flower paintings post-WWI such as a *Basket of Flowers*, 1918–20, and in the later fabric designs.

Was Derngate, in part, a signal to his former colleagues of the Secession that he was still active, but couched in their 1904 or 1909 aesthetic – when last he had direct personal contact – and that they had replaced by that of the coming generation of designers? While formal connections can be made between Mackintosh's *Haus Eines Kunstsfreundes* and Hoffmann's Purkersdorf – although not remotely as many as between its south elevation and Hoffmann's unexecuted design[100] – there are manifestly none to be made between Derngate and Hoffmann's Primavesi Country House, Winkelsdorf, (now Kouty, Czechia), 1913–4, Witzman's Kosmak House, Vienna, 1912–3 or Prutscher's Women's Room in the Café Heinrich-Hof, Vienna, 1910.

HS Goodhart-Rendell (1887–1959), who admittedly had a Modernist axe to grind, observed of Mackintosh's 1920 Chelsea Studios project exhibited at the RIBA in 1922 that:

> Two exhibits sent by Mr CR Mackintosh looked curiously old-fashioned and recalled to mind the illustrations which one finds in turning over the pages of the early volumes of 'The Studio'.[101]

The Chelsea designs were an awkward, scaleless, anti-urban clash of styles, rhythms, steeply-pitched roofs, plain and artless facades and motives from Mackintosh's earlier career. Salmon, a decade earlier, had managed the contemporary multi-storey urban building so much more convincingly at Lion Chambers, Glasgow, 1904–7. Likewise, Mackintosh's unbuilt theatre for Margaret Morris, also from 1920, could have been substituted for Lethaby's title page illustration in his *Architecture, Mysticism and Myth*, 1891, especially when compared to Gropius's Total Theatre project of 1926.

It could be said that Mackintosh's career as an architect ended in a perfect storm of the profound loss of the support of a shared intellectual and artistic community, the consequences of damaging legislation, the dissolution of his partnership with Keppie, desultory commissions post-1917 and the privations of a war economy, besides whatever personal flaws and illnesses dogged him and Margaret. Bassett-Lowke lost touch with (or declined to re-engage) Mackintosh following the works at Derngate and commissioned Peter Behrens in his stead in 1924 to design a new house, New Ways in Northampton.[102] Unlike Sullivan, whose career had a similar decline, Mackintosh left no assistants imbued with his method which they might have perpetuated and developed, nor wrote explication of his intents and processes which might have educated others. The work remains an isolate of a unique artistic expression which, at the same time, contemporaneously isolated him. It could be that subsequently he had chosen fully to redirect his energies and become the fine artist that Margaret MacDonald Mackintosh always recognised in him.

The valley section, cultural institutes and *Stadtkronen*

In 1915, Patrick Geddes briefly supported Mackintosh, lodged at King's College, London,[103] to contribute two designs, perhaps only illustrative graphics, to his Indian planning work which was to be presented in exhibition at Madras (Chennai), Calcutta (Kolkata), Nagpur and Lucknow between January 1915 and March 1916.[104] Mackintosh's contribution was possibly part of the replacement exhibition assembled by Geddes' friends in London following the loss of the original exhibition in September 1914, when the SS *Clan Grant* in which it was being transported was sunk off the southern tip of the sub-continent by the buccaneering German warship SMS *Emden*.[105] Mackintosh provided a generic design of a warehouse and a row of shops and offices, of which the latter revealed a small debt to Loos at Goldman and Salatsch, Vienna, 1910, and a rather larger one to Thomson – its arched windows at second floor notwithstanding – with its 'Egyptian' enneastyle in antis shopfront and paired columns and detached glazing at the fourth floor. Mackintosh's remuneration was uncertain for, as Boardman related, Geddes

> confessed that he must do his best for this cause [town-planning in India] 'by extorting work (not I hope to be all unpaid!) from friends'.[106]

Geddes recognised the numinous in Mackintosh's work, that brand of romantic or metaphysical rationalism which he himself harboured. For the War, as Welter confirmed,

> reemphasised what he had believed and argued since the 1890s: that rational-scientific principles on which the order of modern societies rested would only be beneficial to mankind if they were complemented by a metaphysical and spiritual orientation.[107]

Geddes was of considerable significance to architecture and planning in Scotland and the wider world from his selective interventions and demolitions in Edinburgh Old Town from 1887 onwards, to the creation of the Outlook Tower, Edinburgh, 1896, as a permanent demonstration of his thinking to his *City Development: A Study of Parks, Gardens and Culture-Institutes* of 1903 for the Carnegie Dunfermline Trust, to his 'valley section'. Geddes employed those architects conversant, as Glendinning et al observed, with 'the Andersonian language of golden-age harmony'[108] for his Edinburgh projects: Henbest Capper (1860–1925) at James Court, 1892; Sydney Mitchell and Henbest Capper at Ramsay Garden, 1892–93; George Shaw Aitken

(1836–1921) at Lady Stair's House, 1895 and Robert Wilson (1834–1901) at Outlook Tower, 1896. Subsequently, architect (Sir) Frank Mears (1880–1953), Robert Weir Schulz's (1860–1951)[109] assistant, became both Geddes' architect in 1913 and son-in-law in 1915 and, in many ways, a surrogate for Geddes' own son, Alastair, who had been intended to carry forward Geddes' ideas but was killed in action in WWI. Through association, Mears' career suffered the same fate as Geddes', because, while enjoying considerable contemporary renown and exerting considerable influence as a teacher, architect, interpreter and promulgator of Geddes' vision, Mears subsequently joined him in relative oblivion only partially recovered in the 1990s.

Unlike Mackintosh, whose oeuvre was cherry-picked by many to fit pre-conceived narratives, Geddes's science-based work challenged and defied easy categorisation while his considerable and effective global status and influence stood in stark opposition to the one-way traffic and short-lived internationalism of Mackintosh's *mitteleuropäische* connections. Consequently, the diversity of Geddes' thought and ambition and frequent absence from these shores rendered him diffuse, sometimes to the point of invisibility. Geddes' inclusiveness, which was evident in Alison, Thomson, Gowans and Mackintosh, was the very thing that Modernism's monistic programme resisted. While Geddes and Modernists were agreed on the city as the highest human expression as the container of a cooperative and communal life, Modernists' rejection of the 'ambivalence' of human action required that they should create 'borders against... common sense, beliefs, superstitions, and ignorance',[110] whereas Geddes' looser framework, by not standing in stark opposition to territory and patrimony, encompassed and assimilated. Geddes proposed a 'neo-technic age'[111] which would culminate in

> the Rehabilitation of Beauty... in the ordering of nature, and the creation and conservation of art.[112]

Welter commented:

> The rehabilitation of beauty is the return to the balance and harmony between input and output in nature accomplished by returning to nature an order that will help to create permanent wealth in the form of super-necessary art and architecture.

He continued that Geddes' concept of the 'supernecessary' was that 'necessaries like food or clothing, although of essential importance, are transitory, whereas supernecessaries... are permanent'.[113] Welter relates that architects through 'their power of resource and practical organisation' and artists 'through their social idealism and often collective pattern of work' would be the agents; 'the natural and eternal leaders'.[114] In anticipation of Baudrillard, Geddes observed that the drive of capitalism was that volume production of the short-lived necessary should increase exponentially to the detriment of more permanent formation, in the process of which such exaggerated production would squander material and energy resources. Geddes hoped to rebalance the scales in favour of the production of the supernecessary, for, as Welter observed,

> whether newly produced or already accumulated in the past, [they] constitute the real wealth of a society and, ultimately, of mankind.[115]

In effect, the supernecessary is part of the nation's physical patrimony. Like the Modernists, however, Geddes expected too much competence, perhaps, from architects and artists in their presumptive role as leaders, though he did not fall into the Modernist trap of substituting art for the metaphysical, besides whatever metaphysical content inheres in an individual artwork.

He conceived the *Jahrhundertwerk* of the *Stadtkrone* as the significant supernecessary in his city formation, and, indeed, commissioned several: the Temple of Geography, Edinburgh, 1902; the Culture-Institutes of the Dunfermline Plan, 1903; the University of Central India at Indore, 1918; or the Hebrew University, Mount Scopus, Jerusalem, 1919, although only one, the Hebrew University, was built, and, shorn of its great domed Hall, not as completely as was planned. Today, the world-city is crammed with a menagerie of *Stadtkronen*, though few are the Culture-Institutes which Geddes envisaged and all have substituted cheap semiology for the metaphysical content he anticipated.

The 20th century: entrepreneurial failure

'By 1900 the Scottish economy had reached maturity'[116] and, as the Checklands recorded, achieved much in industry, agriculture and finance, while:

> Against these real achievements must be placed negative aspects. Even the progressive industries and firms could not generate enough employment to keep Scots at home... [and] [t]hough there were promising beginnings in automobile production... these failed to come to real fruition. Scottish engineering, in spite of its great achievements (perhaps because of them) could not gain a secure foothold in the

revolutionary new developments of the internal combustion engine
and the vehicles it was to power.[117]

Aside from the contribution of individuals like Thomas Lipton or RW Forsyth:

> The second of the new developments of the later 19th century to
> which Scotland found it difficult to respond was the growth of new
> consumer industries, beginning to become important as the age of
> mass consumption began to dawn.[118]

Employment practices were equally resistant to change and '[t]rade unions were resisted, and where possible excluded'.[119] Michael Fry noted that in terms of Scotland's capital investment:

> The export of her own funds, coupled with sustained demand from
> overseas, especially the Empire, reinforced technological conservatism.
> This ensemble posed by 1914 a formidable barrier to change.[120]

Insofar as architecture is a mirror of its times, that which was driving a largely backward-looking Scottish national architecture – with a few notable exceptions – was the exact same

> nostalgia for an old way [that] results in mutually reinforcing cults of
> the classically educated gentlemanly generalist on the one hand and
> the unintellectually handy practitioner on the other.[121]

Lynch observed that '[f]or many, the war restored a much-needed sense of unity to the nation',[122] although this had little to do with countering such nascent political nationalism as existed and more with the steady although not dramatic increase in Socialist party success in eating away at the sclerotic and hegemonic Liberal Party support. Indeed, it was Socialist rather than nationalist agitation on Clydeside which occurred during and at the end of the war: two industrial strikes and a rent strike in 1915, a strike in 1916 and the 'Forty Hours' Strike' in

> the *annus mirabilis* of 1919, when the Red Flag was brandished during
> a demonstration of more than 100,000 in George Square in Glasgow,
> and the government sent in troops and tanks to quash what the Scottish
> Secretary Robert Munro described as a 'Bolshevist uprising'.[123]

The Red Flag, mind you, not the Saltire.

I got you under my skin: modernity as structure not surface

Modernity made its constrained appearance in Britain in the years either side of WWI, not through the philosophic innovations of Thomson or the aesthetics of Mackintosh but in the works of the Baroque eclectics and Beaux-Arts scholars of whom Mackintosh cautioned in 1892 that '[t]here is hope in honest error, none in the icy perfections of the mere stylist' and of whom Thomson wrote in 1853,

> let him have his library in his mind but use no man's thought till he has made it his own.[124]

Theoretical positions were not so clearly delineated, because the late 19th and early 20th-century eclectics' Modernity was a cutting-edge steel or concrete frame buried within a conventional masonry skin. (Sir) John James Burnet (1857–1938) was representative of this trend. Stamp noted:

> As much of the Mackintosh legend depends upon [contemporary] English indifference to his achievement, there is a certain irony in the fact that while Mackintosh was well aware of the work of advanced English Goths and Arts and Crafts designers, it was Burnet, whose sources of inspiration mostly came from Paris, New York and Chicago, who had by far the most impact on England. But, of course, while Mackintosh's style was self-consciously and distinctly Scottish, Burnet strove for a more anonymous international character.[125]

Returning to Glasgow from the École des Beaux-Arts in Paris, Burnet joined his father's practice and, in 1882, became a partner. Burnet Sr retired in 1889 or 1890, and in 1891, Burnet and his then partner and contemporary John Archibald Campbell (1859–1909) undertook the first project in which Burnet Sr was not involved, the Athenaeum Theatre in Buchanan Street, Glasgow. Gomme and Walker, respected chroniclers of Glasgow architecture, observed,

> the Athenaeum is well worthy of comparison with contemporary American work… The detail in this extraordinary design comes from all over the place – some still Renaissance, some faintly Flemish, some distinctly Scottish and the frieze Greek.[126]

A narrow townhouse site was occupied by a young man's fancy; a building more than twice the height of its neighbours split vertically into the two elements which Burnet would continue to develop over the next 15 years: a Baroque and Scots Renaissance gable and canted bay to the left with a proto-Secessionist tower[127] to the right. This last feature, in its representation in masonry fins and aedicule of the mechanism of the Otis elevator, clearly identified in mimesis one of the defining signs of modernity at a time when architects struggled to find an architectural representation of their age when, as MacLeod commented, 'the single most dominant characteristic of Victorian architecture was its diversity'.[128]

In 1896, Burnet visited the USA where he befriended the Beaux-Arts-trained Charles Follen McKim (1847–1909), one of the partners in McKim, Mead and White. McKim's architectural influence on Burnet may have been to encourage him to take the vertically composed Athenaeum single-bay gable, adopt a simplified American Beaux-Arts approach and regularise and repeat the bay in a longer elevation such as he achieved at Waterloo Chambers, Glasgow, 1899. Burnet also regularised the vertical pattern of two or three lower floors of shopfronts and offices, surmounted by a grand order rising through two or more stories to an attic which might, post-1903, incorporate a balcony and a prominent entablature proud of end or corner towers or pylons, reversing the conventional Classical composition.

Burnet's Glasgow development of his commercial style between the Athenaeum of 1891 and Waterloo Chambers of 1899 was marked by the consecutive introduction of those features which ultimately defined it: a giant order at the Glasgow Stock Exchange extension, 1894; regularised bays, a strong terminating entablature and balconied attic storey at Albany Chambers, 1896; the corner tower at Blacks Warehouse (RW Forsyth's), 1896; the organisation of the elevation into horizontal bands of windows, the regularisation of repetitive canted bays and a prominent attic at Atlantic Chambers, 1899; and a growing response in elevational treatment to the orthogonal demands of the structural steel frame. Burnet's stylistic innovations became widely known as Burnetian Baroque and were much copied by his fellow-architects and competitors.

In 1903, Burnet began work on the Civil Service and Professional Association's department store in George Street, Edinburgh (now Hollister), where the model was the central three bays and flanking half-bay towers of Waterloo Chambers. In 1906, at RW Forsyth's on Princes Street, the first steel-framed building in Scotland, he extended the idiom in four bays on Princes Street and three on South St Andrew's Street, but dispensed with the flanking towers to acquire a corner tower loosely based on that of the Athenaeum. Gomme and Walker made the Athenaeum's embryonic American comparison in Glasgow;

The steel frame disguised: RW Forsyth's, Edinburgh, 1906, architect John James Burnet.

in Edinburgh, at RW Forsyth's, Main Street USA was fully realised. Further works in Glasgow, each successively and increasingly stripped of Baroque elaboration, such as McGeoch's, 1905 (demolished), underline this American modernity. Not that Burnet in his time was averse to a bit of the Baronial or, as developed by Rowand Anderson, a Scots 'Renaissance', as at the Public Library and Museum, Campbelltown, 1896–8.

In 1903, Burnet was selected by HM Office of Works for the development of the British Museum site – for which design he was knighted in 1914 – and opened a London office at Montague Place, later to become the head office in 1918 of the enlarged practice. Burnet completed the thoroughly modern, thoroughly American, steel-framed Kodak Building, Kingsway, London in 1911. He followed it up in 1913 with the Wallace Scott Tailoring Institute for RW Forsyth at Cathcart, a resolutely functional factory based on equally contemporary brick-clad, reinforced concrete American models, with astonishing corner pavilions, recessed from the colonnades in the manner of the British Museum, but with almost Thomsonesque detailing, and coloured brick spandrels in the colonnade which recall the frieze of William Leiper's (1839–1919) Templeton's carpet factory, Glasgow, 1889 (cf. E-Z Polish Factory, Chicago, Illinois by Frank Lloyd Wright, 1905). The design of both these buildings was possibly the result of his 1908 visit to the USA. Following the death of Daniel Burnham (1846–1912),[129] Harry Gordon Selfridge's American architect, Burnet was engaged in 1919 to oversee the second and third phases of the store on Oxford Street, London, including a remarkable unbuilt 300-ft (30.5m) tower.

Burnet's celebrity was not confined to Britain. Largely forgotten now were his jury memberships, judging the significant international architectural competitions of the day: in the company of Otto Wagner and Louis Sullivan for the Australian Parliament, 1914; and with Victor Horta (1861–1947), HP Berlage, Koloman Moser, Josef Hoffmann and Nordic Classicist Ivar Tengbom (1878–1968) for the League of Nations Building. Stamp summed up the conundrum of this pivotal period somewhat gloomily because he patently did not expect much support for his views:

> Unfortunately, many historians cannot see the form for the style. Seeking 'free-style' or non-stylar buildings as pointers towards the future, they fail to appreciate that a design expressed in a conventional historical language may still be innovative in terms of planning, spatial organisation and construction – which was conspicuously the case with John James Burnet.[130]

It was the design of memorial chapels, shrines, monuments and cemeteries for the war dead, for the most part in various historic styles both at home and in Northern France and Belgium, which, in the 1920s, occupied those architects who mercifully did not die for King and Empire between 1914 and 1918.

They've all come to look for America: the Sullivan aesthetic

The romanticism of Sullivan did not arise from the ur-architecture of Native American or settler culture or their legends because there were none which satisfied the programme of his designs, nor was he in any doubt about the art of architecture. His visionary, poetic, Emersonian and Ruskinian philosophy more nearly equated to that of Frueh in that:

> I have sought with all due insistence to impress upon you, as a maxim, the simple truth that the heart is greater, worthier, nobler, finer than the head: that the heart is the sanctuary of the Temple of Man, the head its portal.[131]

Specifically, he observed the connection of architecture and the progress of the nation.

> Whichever way our architecture goes, so will our country go; or, if you prefer, whichever way our country goes, so will our architecture; it is the same proposition in different ways. We are at that dramatic moment in our national life wherein we tremble evenly between decay and evolution, and our architecture, with strange fidelity, reflects this equipoise. That the forces of decadence predominate in quantity there can be no doubt; that the recreative forces now balance them by virtue of quality; and may eventually overpower them is a matter of conjecture.[132]

Sullivan's Ledoux-inflected, Semper *Bekleidungsprinzip*-decorated and wholly original Transportation Museum at the Columbian World's Exhibition, Chicago, 1893, stood out from the dated Beaux-Arts Baroque of Burnham and Root and others as precise metaphor and physical embodiment of his observation. While the public revelled in Sullivan's novel forms and rich complex polychromatic decoration, it would be the staid Beaux-Arts Baroque of the so-called 'White City'[133] which was favoured by federal and state institutions and corporate America for the next half-century. Sullivan rejected the historicism and maintained that

> [o]ur architecture reflects us as truly as a mirror, even if we consider it apart from ourselves.[134]

He presented the dilemma of the experimentalist in national architecture:

> While we may compromise for a time, through a process of local adaptation, no architectural style can become a finality, that runs counter to popular feeling. The desire at once to follow and lead the public should be the initial attitude of our profession towards the formation of a national style.[135]

The steel frame expressed: Wainwright Building, St Louis, Missouri, 1890, architect Louis Sullivan.
(Missouri History Museum, Creative Commons)

The last sentence reveals the conundrum of Sullivan's work because ultimately it did 'run counter to popular feeling' or, at least, counter to the sensibilities of those who, prior to the Colombian World's Exhibition, were his clients and thereafter declined in large measure to commission him.

Lacking or avoiding indigenous American models, Sullivan adopted the parts of an archaic architecture and stripped them of all recognisable details and embellishment, substituting his own motives. Thus treated, the architrave and the arch appeared as the whole of the composition at the Carrie Eliza Getty Tomb, Graceland Cemetery, Chicago, 1890, and in the small-town Mid-West banks such as the National Farmers' Bank, Owatonna, Minnesota, 1908 or as elements in larger compositions such as the Auditorium Building, Chicago, 1889, or the Transportation Museum. The column and its parts were abstracted into the multi-storey Wainwright Building, St Louis, Missouri, 1890, Guaranty Building, Buffalo, New York, 1894 and the Carson Pirie Scott Building, Chicago, 1899–1904. Post-1910, his philosophy and practice were left to his fellow-Celt pupils, the Scot George Grant Elmslie (1869–1952) to perpetuate and the Welsh-blooded Frank Lloyd Wright to transform.

Elmslie is the parallel and documented footnote to the speculated Schinkel/Thomson/Sullivan/Wright connection. Huntly-born, he emigrated to Chicago in 1884 at age 15, met Wright in the architectural office of Joseph Silsbee (1848–1913) in 1887, and subsequently joined him at Adler and Sullivan, on Wright's recommendation, in 1888. 'George wasn't a minister's son but ought to have been', Wright observed.[136] Following Wright's dismissal by Sullivan in 1893 for moonlighting, Elmslie became Sullivan's chief draftsman and decorative designer responsible for the ornamentation on the Wainwright Building. There is a considerable body of present-day American research (by such as David and Patricia Gebhard, Richard L Kronick and Robert Winder) which is inclined to attribute the post-1895 Sullivan decorative works largely to Elmslie.[137] In 1909, as Sullivan's practice imploded and his employment terminated, Elmslie declined a proposal from Wright, then intending to travel to Europe to oversee the *Wasmuth Edition*, that he might buy into Wright's Oak Park Studio. It is unclear whether Wright intended partnership, although, given Wright's propensities, it seems unlikely. However, in 1910, Elmslie declined the offer and commenced in partnership with William Gray Purcell (1880–1965). Purcell, on a European trip in 1906, had met the proto-Modernists Boberg and Berlage, with whom he corresponded regularly throughout the 1910s and '20s. Subsequently, Purcell and Elmslie became the premier second-generation Prairie School architects with such works as their Sullivan-influenced Merchant Bank, Winona, Minnesota, 1911 and Old Second National Bank, Aurora, Illinois, 1924. For posterity's record, Wright, immodest as ever, observed:

> When Louis Sullivan had eliminated background in his system of ornament in favor of an integral sense of the whole he had implied this larger sense of the thing. I now began to achieve it.[138]

The Wright vernacular: the invention of an American architecture

Wright's design of houses from the 1890s to the mid-1930s can be seen as the pursuit of regional vernaculars, albeit vernaculars which he invented or adapted for a second- or third-generation, almost exclusively white, suburban settler population. In a young country, young, that is, to the settlers, and where the status and various cultures of Native Americans were still largely ignored or worse,[139] this cultural and temporal expropriation is perhaps unsurprising and its lack of self-consciousness in Wright's work commonplace at the time. Viewing Wright's oeuvre as vernacular in the broadest sense contradicts much received wisdom about and post-rationalised achievement of the architect as Patrick Pinnell had observed, much as had MacLeod on Mackintosh:

> Once a long-standing editorial agenda, the one wanting to see in Wright's early work only that which anticipates what he and others would do in the 20th century is removed, another thread of argument concerning his formation becomes available.[140]

In this vernacular light, the actions of two of those editors, Philip Johnson and Henry-Russell Hitchcock, in their equivocal admittance of Wright to their 1932 exhibition (see Chapter 4) was obvious and inevitable.

From 1890–1910, Wright developed the Prairie style, inspiring a small school of followers. His writings on the matter related to the nature of the home, home-life and to the openness and horizontality of the Mid-West.[141] Wright's publication of his projects in *The Woman's Home Journal* is well-known. While one might attribute his un-Victorian response to conventional domesticity to the influence in his upbringing among strong, confident, nurturing women – his mother and his aunts – there is no doubt that he also considered significant the contribution of women to the new bourgeois house with no live-in servants, even no servants at all. The opportunist in him recognised that such publicity might result in further work. The house designs were promulgated in continental Europe, partly through the publication of the *Ausgeführte Bauten und Entwürfe* – the Wasmuth Edition, 1910 – and partly through the support of Berlage, although their contemporary effect in mono-lingual Britain was negligible.

These houses were notable for several ever-present formal elements: over-sailing roofs; ranges of floor-to-ceiling French doors contrasted with lightweight fretted screens and clerestories and solid panels of brick, timber, stucco or pargetted plaster; concrete, stone or brick hearths and chimneys; plinths, podia, panels and planters of Roman brick; decks, balconies and portes cochères – in fact, the full gamut of Semper's Four Elements[142]. These, of course, were not the forms nor the materials which were employed in the impromptu and expedient vernaculars of 19th-century first-generation settlers of the Mid-West; neither the crude ground-hugging log cabins of Indiana nor the sod houses of the Dakotas.[143] They were not even the relative 18th-century sophistication of the New England salt-box,[144] nor that of the utopian Lutheran settlement at New Harmony, Indiana, 1814, nor the widespread mid-century Carpenter Gothic illustrated in builders' manuals. The only unmediated vernacular element Wright's houses shared with those pioneer vernaculars, where warmth in the brutal winters was paramount, was the large open fire:

> So the *integral* [Wright's emphasis] fireplace became an important part of the building itself in the houses I was allowed to build out there on the prairie.[145]

Nor was an urban extension, as is Oak Park, Chicago, the setting of Wright's pioneer homes, truly in and of the prairie.[146] Nonetheless, he said with a measure of truth of the prairie house in the rolling landscape of Wisconsin at Taliesin, 1911–59, that it is

> A house of the North! The whole, low, wide and snug, broad shelter seeking fellowship with its surroundings.[147]

In a brief sojourn in California and Japan following the tragedy of the murders and fire at Taliesin in 1914, Wright experimented with pre-Columbian architecture, although he referred to the Hollyhock House, Hollywood for Aline Barnsdall, 1919, as a 'California Romanza'.[148]

This American excursion has significance for Scottish architecture in three ways. Firstly, it illustrates the futility of speculating an active Scottish connection to the approved pantheon of Modernist architecture solely on the basis of superficial formal similarity of Schinkel/Thomson/Sullivan/Wright. Thus, for all his genius, Thomson's potential international legacy is inhibited by its largely Scottish context and the few dead-ends of its further international expression. It seems more profitable to track his influence through his assistants and their pupils, although, of course, that is an entirely Scottish venture. Equally, the pursuit of the Craigievar/Mackintosh/Corbusier-Bauhaus axis must founder for similar reasons.

Secondly, both such procedures require substantial revision of the intent and consequence of Thomson's and Mackintosh's works to effect the

Modernist connection. By way of contrast, the architecture of Czechoslovakia and Finland, through a combination of the achievement and recognition of statehood and an identifiably local accommodation with Modernism, achieved international recognition and ratification without subsequent historic amendment.

Thirdly, the discussion of Scottish Modernity is proscribed by the preterition which limits which architectures are admissible. It is not receptive to the claims of historic regional architectures which, at the time, had failed to break free of the shackles of historicism or architectures which embodied new technologies within historic skins. Consequently, in resistance, Scottish commentators insist on the presence of canonic aesthetic identifiers implicit in the historic patrimony of Scottish societal elites as being the signifiers of a Scottish architecture and make the Mackintosh connection. They do not seek a deeper impulse, and fail to rescue from isolate status and promote those other works of significance that do not correspond to the approved aesthetic, thereby failing to gain admission even to an enlarged and more inclusive 21st-century international pantheon.

4

News from nowhere: 1919–39

The anxiety of empire

THE BRITISH EMPIRE EXHIBITION proposed by the British government in 1902 and again in 1913, intended to bolster the engagement of its subjects in the Imperial project in the face of growing international competition from the USA and, particularly, Germany, was finally confirmed in 1920 and held in 1924 at Wembley, London. By then, Germany was, for the moment, not a threat, while the USA was well on its way to becoming the 20th-century superpower. The Exhibition took place in the reduced Imperial circumstances of a post-war economic slump, the commitment of 1917 to grant India independence – much-delayed and only messily ratified in 1947 – the independence of the Protectorate of Egypt in 1920 and the Anglo-Irish Act of 1922 which partitioned Ireland. The *Daily Express* reported the opening address of King George V, who hoped that

> the exhibition may bring lasting benefit not to the Empire only, but to mankind in general.

The *Express* continued:

> A few minutes later, a messenger boy handed him a large, white envelope – a telegram, announcing the opening, which had gone round the world in 80 seconds.[1]

This was less a fact of present Imperial innovation than the recollection of past vigour. The 'All-Red Line' of telegraph cables connecting the Empire was two decades old. Moreover, the Empire was patently no longer 'first among equals' when the first global standard time signal was transmitted at 10.00am on 1 July 1913, in the decade of greatest Imperial territorial extent, not from Greenwich, but from the Eiffel Tower,[2] possibly a more fitting symbol of modernity than Sir Christopher Wren's (1632–1723) Royal Observatory, 1675. The telegram was, in any case, in relative decline by the early 1920s due to the increasing cheapness and frequency of letter-post and the efficiencies obtained by the amalgamation and monopolisation by the GPO (General Post Office) of the several local telephone companies.[3]

The Exhibition was another expression of the 'anxiety of Empire' through which, as Ferguson observed, '[i]mperceptibly, even the arch-imperialist was mutating into a Little Englander'.[4] In Scotland, Lynch cautioned that:

If the war was a crucible, producing a heightened working-class consciousness, a new involvement of women in the national effort and a new relationship between organised labour and the state, it also reproduced some of the old moulds which had distinguished pre-1914 society.[5]

Resisting those 'old moulds', British working-class politicisation began with the relatively ineffectual Labour Representation League founded by the Irishman Patrick Lloyd Jones (1811–86) in 1865, followed in 1888 in Scotland by the Scottish Labour Party led by Keir Hardie (1856–1915) who then, in a peripatetic career on the Left, created the Independent Labour Party (ILP) in 1893 which, among other policies, promoted Scottish Independence. Ramsay MacDonald (1886–1937), the third Celtic Socialist in this brief account, became secretary of the Labour Representation Committee in 1900, which merged with the ILP in 1906 to become the Labour Party. The ILP caucus remained a significant force in the Labour Party in the early decades of the 20th century and ensured that 'The Self-Determination of the Scottish People' and 'The Complete Restoration of the Land of Scotland to the Scottish People' were planks in the 1918 election platform. Whether self-determination was taken to mean outright independence or Home Rule is moot, although both were still seen in the context of the Empire. That same year, suffrage was extended nationally to more sections of society, more than doubling the number of male electors, and including those women over the age of 30 who met certain property-owning qualifications. Suffrage was not universal until 1928 and compared poorly with that, say, of pre-war Finland.

The sheer weight of numbers of English members in the Labour Party resulted in the ILP commitment to Scottish self-determination being dropped, the Scots finding themselves, as they did so often in the 20th century, an inconvenient adjunct to a larger entity. In the fluctuating political climate, a

Government of Scotland Bill was talked out that same year. McKean recounted it as 'the 21st such rejection since 1889'.[6] The General Strike of May 1926 and the allegedly widespread appearance of the middle-class undergraduate strike-breaker reaffirmed Labour in its British class-struggle objectives and Marxist-Leninist internationalism. Scotland as a distinct entity and the need for its singular problems to have an appropriate solution did not feature in centralist British politics, either Right or Left, then or later. Almost an act of desperation,

> Hugh MacDiarmid's [1892–1978] unfortunate call for a 'Scottish Fascism' as early as 1923, following Mussolini's march on Rome,[7]

providentially failed because

> Mosley's Scottish legion… was already torn by peculiarly Scottish contradictions. Religious sectarianism and the question of the union coalesced to divide and weaken Scottish fascism.[8]

Both remain at issue today. The confirmation of the Scottish Secretary to full cabinet status in 1926 was tokenist.

Of the 573,000 British war dead, between an eighth and a fifth were Scottish, markedly disproportionate to the respective national populations, Scotland's being roughly one-eleventh of that of Britain. In Glasgow, the death toll accounted for ten per cent of all adult males, and in some districts it was twice that.[9] While 12 out of every 13 fatalities were working-class infantry privates aged between 20 and 40, there was also a *pro rata* number of officer-class deaths, the loss of whom contributed to what Lynch identified as the

> failure of Scottish industry in the 1920s and early 1930s [which] has been interpreted as largely the product of a weakness of management.[10]

The war economy briefly benefitted Scottish heavy industry but turned into the slump of 1921 which dominated the inter-war years until the government-subsidised completion of No. 534, subsequently-named the Queen Mary, on Clydeside in 1936. The Crash of 1929 and the Depression which followed merely steepened the slope of decline. In 1913, unemployment in Scotland was 1.8 per cent; in London it was 8.7 per cent. By 1923, with unemployment a more general problem, Scotland's had increased 800 per cent to 14.3 per cent, while London's by 30 per cent to 11.6 per cent. Lynch contended:

The theme of a rich south and a poor north, which dominates much of Britain's social history for the rest of the 20th century, was a product of the First World War.[11]

Whether or not 'Alexander McArthur (of Glasgow)' was a real inhabitant of the 1930s Gorbals as portrayed in *No Mean City*, the events he and his co-author related convince in their account of multiple-deprivation:

> The Authors wish to state that their novel deals only with one seam in the crowded life of the Empire's Second City. In their view, unemployment and overcrowding are primarily responsible for conditions which may be paralleled in all great cities, but which are, perhaps, more conspicuous in Glasgow than in any other. It is only fair to add that no other city is making a more determined effort to re-house and help its poorer citizens. Nor should it ever be forgotten that Glasgow, with less than a sixth of London's population, carries an equal burden of workless men and women.[12]

The statistics of deprivation in the Appendix were supplemented by the observation that

> Extracts of the same kind could be quoted *ad nauseam* from the Glasgow and the national newspapers of recent years.[13]

In 1943, and revelatory of British insensitivity to Glasgow's (and Scotland's) plight, (Sir) Arthur Bliss (1891–1975) composed music for the one-act ballet *Miracle in the Gorbals*, story by Michael Benthall, choreography by Robert Helpmann and set design by Edward Burra (1905–76). Burra is best-known for his voyeuristic and quasi-surrealist interpretations of the urban underworld, Black culture, 1930s Harlem, which he visited in 1933–4, and his 'sardonic'[14] painting, *Gorbals, Glasgow*, 1944. It is difficult to see Burra's paintings as other than knowingly titillating encapsulations of the Other. The ballet, loosely based on scenes from the life of Christ, featured Moira Shearer (1926–2006), niece of architect James Shearer, in a lead role. It was part of the Royal Ballet's repertoire in their extended British tour between 1944 and 1950. It was *not* performed when the company visited Glasgow in 1945.

Scotland's 19th century context, in union with England but with relative autonomy within the Empire, ended abruptly. Lynch recorded

> the increasing intrusion made by the British state into the ordinary

lives of those who lived in Scotland... [It was] Scotland's culture rather than the new 'Scottish' institutions of government which maintained a distinct national identity. And low culture played a greater role than high in keeping it so.[15]

Moreover, the great driver of the economy and architectural opportunity in the 19th century, the Scottish city, was in stasis. Whereas,

> in 1911, a fraction under 40 per cent of Scots lived in towns of 50,000 inhabitants or more; in 1951 the figure was just over 42 per cent. Glasgow's 'growth' over the same period, from 784,000 to 1,089,000, stemmed largely from the inclusion of Govan and Partick [previously separate burghs] within the city after 1912... This was the age of emigration and de-urbanisation. Its symbol was the new-style tenement or cottage in 'garden suburbs', such as Hamiltonhill or Possil.[16]

Edinburgh likewise 'grew' through incorporation, absorbing the burgh of Leith, population ca. 80,000, in 1920, enlarging by one sixth to 467,000 inhabitants.

The new architecture: Netherland, France, Germany, the USA

Polano noted that Theo van Doesburg's (1883–1931) creation, De Stijl, aimed at the 'aestheticisation of the environment and the transformation of metropolitan life into art',[17] but that

> the attempt to translate this theoretical process, the monumental integration of the arts, into a style... led, in fact, to a breakdown in the relationship between the members [of De Stijl] and to thoroughly inconclusive results.[18]

De Stijl today is represented largely by interior design, furniture, painting and graphic art, while van Doesburg's solitary construction, the house he built for himself and his wife at Meudon-Val-Fleury, Paris, 1929, is 'more Corbusian than De Stijl in its final resolution'.[19] Gerrit Rietveld (1888–1964) and Truss Schröder-Schräder's (1889–1985) Rietveld-Schröder House, Utrecht, 1924, is De Stijl's definitive architectural statement.

Van Doesburg did not acknowledge his sources, although they were

The aestheticisation of the environment: Rietveld-Schröder House, Utrecht, 1923, architect and designer Gerrit Rietveld and Truus Schröder-Schräder.

manifold, such as were embodied, say, in the design of Robert van t'Hoff's (1887–1979) Henny House, Utrecht, 1916,[20] which was itself loosely based on Wright's Gale House of 1909.[21] Van t'Hoff, a former Wright assistant then van Doesburg's De Stijl associate, subsequently essayed the *Stepped Column*, 1918,[22] possibly inspired by Wright's Dana House newel, 1902, and which was mirrored in the Suprematist 'architectons' *Alpha*, *Zeta* and *Gota 2a*, 1923, by Kazimir Malevich (1879–1935),[23] with whom van t'Hoff was in contact that same year. The similar accretive, volumetric and rectilinear forms of De Stijl and of Malevich's 'architectons' had significant impact on architectural composition and detailing throughout the 20th century, whereas some of Rietveld's furniture designs – the Child's' Chair, 1918,[24] and the sideboard, 1919[25] – retroactively referenced Mackintosh and Ashbee respectively.

Van Doesburg sought the corroboration of Modernity rather than its influence and contacted the Russian Constructivist El Lissitzky (1890–1941) in 1921.[26] The following year he had an essay, 'The State of Contemporary Art', published in *Object*, the Constructivist periodical.[27] Continuing with his corroborative rather than collaborative approach, in the article 'A young culture striving for innovation', published in *Het Bouwbedrijf* of August 1926, van Doesburg wrote:

> The ability of younger nations, which can not [sic] yet offer a well-rounded, unified culture, to absorb new ideas and new construction possibilities with greater alacrity than do nations having an age-old tradition... finds its explanation in profound cultural causes. The former have a great deal to gain by this kind of absorption, and they have but little to lose; the latter, on the other hand, can lose much and gain relatively little.[28]

It is impossible to ascertain whether he ascribed a jejune naivety or need for novelty to 'younger nations' – which briefly included the youthful Constructivist Soviet Russia – in their urge to adopt 'new ideas'. His reservations on their ability to 'offer a well-rounded, unified culture' were simply his unrealistic attempted imposition of his universalist De Stijl objectives, given that 'unified culture' is, in any event, only ever a totalitarian or utopian construct. A younger nation does not necessarily entail a new culture but may evince new practices within a regional culture of considerable pedigree, which is an altogether different proposition. He expanded on innovation:

> I am of the opinion that an attempt at innovation is only justifiable when it originates from the living impulse of an individual or of a nation. This is what I have always taken as a standard for all attempts at innovation which I could detect in various countries; so it is in Czechoslovakia.[29]

Van Doesburg understood the positive links of cultural innovation from an original source which others negatively argued was the moribund and reactionary vernacular origin of regional or national architectures.

Despite Czechoslovakia's success in engaging with innovation, van Doesburg perceived a

> gradually widening gap between architectonic construction and esthetic [sic] imagery... [The] attempt to unite these two in equal balance (in an anti-decorative manner) has failed in Czechoslovakia as well as in other countries.[30]

He identified

> Gočár and Janák... [as] the first ones who tried to innovate architecture on the basis of cubist principles. Of course, such an

'innovation', which was not dictated by new dwelling requirements, was bound to lead to an ornamental, merely externally modified, monumentality.[31]

Van Doesburg was alive to the subtleties of architectural development in cultures not his own, although it is worth remarking on the importance which he attached to 'new dwelling requirements' as central to the aesthetic response, as they would come prominence as the century advanced. Such conditions were *imposed* intellectually – by van Doesburg and other manifesto-Modernists – from without, in contrast to what *arose* naturally from within society, from a vernacular, however that vernacular might have been construed, which was the stance of Berlage and Loos earlier. Moreover, the 'ornamentality' of such a vernacular as transformed by, say, the Czechs, Slovaks or Finns, was inevitably not abstract, hegemonic and universal as van Doesburg intended for De Stijl but specific, anti-hegemonic and regional to meet pressing local conditions.

Domestic machinery: Le Corbusier's 'contraptions'

In 1923, Le Corbusier declaimed 'A house is a machine for living in!', continuing,

> baths, sun, hot-water, cold-water, warmth at will, conservation of food, hygiene, beauty in the sense of good proportion,

were entirely the purview of those 'men – intelligent, cold and calm' who were 'needed to build the house and lay out the town'. This programme also required substantial societal change:

> If we eliminate from our hearts and minds all dead concepts in regard to the houses and look at the questions from a critical and objective point of view, we shall arrive at the 'House-Machine', the mass-production house, healthy (and morally so too) and beautiful in the same way that the working tools and instruments which accompany our existence are beautiful. Beautiful also with all the animation that the artist's sensibility can add to severe and pure functioning elements.[32]

Houses were later redefined: collectively as 'housing'; scientifically as *existenzminimum*; pejoratively as *panely dům*.[33] What individuals understood as the characteristics of home in general and their own culturally-imbricated home in particular were jettisoned by those same 'men – intelligent, cold and calm':

> We must create the mass-production spirit.
> The spirit of constructing mass-production houses.
> The spirit of living in mass-production houses.[34]

With little more than the architect's self-appointed status as artist/scientist and non-legally-binding exhortation for reassurance, many dwellers were expected to make the change to the new modes of living in spaces which were but stunted versions of the ascetic double-storey-height and galleried studio-houses occupied by Le Corbusier, Amédée Ozenfant (1886–1966), Tristan Tzara (1896–1963), Raoul La Roche (1889–1965), William (1881–1959) and Jeanne Cook (Jeanne Moallic, n.d.), Rob Mallet-Stevens (1886–1945), Antonin Planeix (n.d.) and other intellectual aesthetes in and around 1920s Paris. In their universalist manifestations, such dwellings lacked both double-height space and gallery while retaining substantial amounts of asceticism.

Mindful of potential private clients with rather more than an *existenzminimum* budget, Le Corbusier had an alternative, more sumptuous, set of principles for house design in *The Manual of the Dwelling*, which he hoped 'the temperance societies and anti-Malthusians [family planners]' would distribute to 'mothers of families' – such a catalogue of rage, repression and misogyny in those few words. He insisted *inter alia*:

> Demand a bathroom looking south, one of the largest rooms in the house or flat, the old drawing room for instance… An adjoining room to be a dressing room… Never undress in your bedroom. It is not a clean thing to do and makes the room horribly untidy… Demand one really large living room instead of a number of small ones… If you can, put the kitchen at the top of the house to avoid smells… Demand that the maid's room should not be an attic… Take a flat which is one size smaller than what your parents accustomed you to.[35]

Le Corbusier was concerned that houses should express and intersect with his idealised life and not, as he saw it, become the mere repository of furniture. He convinced Pierre and Eugénie Savoye, his clients at Villa Savoye, Poissy, 1928–31), to dispense with the three-piece suite they intended to install in the living room.[36] Of all his houses, Villa Savoye is the one from which even a minimalist kind of domesticity has been drained: more art than life, more machine than art. In a 1934 piece for the *Dune Forum*, Rudolph Schindler noted,

The machine for living: Villa Savoye, Paris, 1928–31, architect Le Corbusier
(Derek Fraser)

> Most of the buildings which Corbusier and his followers offer us as 'machines to live in', equipped with various 'machines to sit and sleep on', have not even reached the state of development of our present machines. They are crude 'contraptions' to serve a purpose.[37]

Schindler went on to assert:

> The reaction to the sterile repetition of historical styles took the path of least resistance by eliminating architectural consideration altogether... *Functionalism* [Schindler's emphasis]... Art and real architecture is of necessity individual and local and has to have deep roots in soil and national character.[38]

Le Corbusier's personal manifesto, as expressed in his platonic designs of the 1920s, found ready and widespread acceptance with architects throughout the 20th century and later as a basis to promulgate mass-production houses, because there existed already a persistent line of minimalistic architectural thinking which endorsed a bohemian asceticism, associated the simple with the moral with the beautiful and excluded all other meaning, the ethical, the individual, the local, the regional and the national. What the followers of Le Corbusier clearly demonstrated was that the benefits of the new thinking, seemingly democratic in intent, were not to be equally shared throughout society and, instead, created a language and programme of *rigorous aesthetic similarity* across all building types to camouflage actual, substantial difference and the loss of a *vigorous ethical sensibility* in how people were to dwell.

The not-so-primitive hut for part-time peasants

Le Corbusier's 1911 tour of Istanbul, Mount Athos, Athens, Pompeii and Rome – described in his less frequently read *The Journey to the East*[39] – alerted him to the architectural possibilities of the Classical and the archaic; the former underpinning the canonic white villas and houses of the 1920s, the latter contributing to the unbuilt projects for the Villa Errázuriz, Chile, 1930, and the Maison de Mandrot, near Toulon, 1931. Weber observed that Le Corbusier's client, the heiress Eugenia Errázuriz (1860–1951), 'had Le Corbusier's sensibility before she even knew his name',[40] quoting John Richardson, in that she became known for her 'minimalist version of the decorative arts' and her taste for what was

> very fine and very simple – above all, things made of linen, cotton, deal or stone, whose quality improved with laundering or fading, scrubbing or polishing.[41]

I imagine very little laundering, scrubbing or polishing (or, indeed, fading) was to be done by Mme Errázuriz. It all smacks of a latter-day Marie Antoinette posing as a milkmaid at L'Hameau de la Reine with Le Corbusier on hand to produce *une cottage ornée de nos jours*. Gaston Bachelard (1884–1962) wrote that

> [w]hen we live in a manor house we dream of a cottage, and when we live in a cottage we dream of a palace.[42]

For the Villa Errázuriz, Le Corbusier specified field-stone flags for the floors, masonry walling in irregularly-shaped blocks, rough-cut tree trunks for columns and a shallow butterfly roof clad in terracotta Roman tiles, the forms and materials derived from an archetypical rural dwelling. Weber thought it 'a significant shift to what was local and biomorphic'.[43] The Villa l'Artaude (Maison de Mandrot) followed in similar manner with masonry walling on a reinforced concrete frame. Both houses contrasted the massive with the lightweight, the rough with the smooth. Yet the forms and materials were entirely generic and experimental rather than vernacular and it is not coincidental that, in the same year, Le Corbusier designed an equally experimental Surrealist apartment in Paris for Charles de Beistegui (1895–1970). Norberg-Schulz later commented on Le Corbusier's Maison Errázuriz and Villa de Mandrot:

> The two houses, however, represent only a very general kind of rootedness; they relate to the landscape and they employ natural (and local) materials, but they do not embody any regional *character* [Norberg-Schulz's emphasis].[44]

There was so little regionally identifiable character present, in fact, that Antonin Raymond (1888–1976) built for himself a copy of the Villa Errázuriz at Karuizawa, Japan, 1933, exchanging timber or board-marked concrete for Le Corbusier's stone facing on the internal ramp.[45]

Le Corbusier's client for the Cité de Refuge, Paris, 1933, Albin Peyron (1870–1944), had him design a holiday home, Le Sextant, 1934–5, at Les Mathes, near Royan. Peyron produced early guide sketches for the master in a simulacrum of Le Corbusier's platonic style but which Le Corbusier transmuted into the quasi-vernacular of his two current 'regional' essays, identified by the use of rough-hewn and coarsely-worked 'natural' materials rather than from any reference to a specific local constructional tradition. They were more romantic than 'biomorphic' and, possibly, were intended to suggest a rural lack of sophistication or to romanticise the facts of a harsher existence – although these houses had contemporary conveniences – rather than afford any intimate engagement with the *genius loci*. As Tim Benton made plain:

> The avant-garde could recuperate the vernacular only if it was stripped of its nationalist and traditional associations and rediscovered as a fragment of 'nature'... Their approach was a staunchly modernist one. Natural materials had to be used in a 'pure' form, even if this meant ignoring much local wisdom about sound construction.[46]

In the light of his later work in *béton brut*, such as at Maison Jaoul, Neuilly-sur-Seine, 1954–6, Le Corbusier's interest in the vernacular was confirmed as being rather more about an aesthetic appreciation of the contrast of roughness and smoothness in form and texture than it was about any deeper meanings implicit in local or regional vernacular construction.

Weber noted that Le Corbusier

> had developed a theory that Neuchâtel mountain farmhouses had not been designed to withstand heavy snows but had instead been imported from Armagnac in 1350 when the Albigeois were exiled to the Alps, proving that domestic architecture reveals that origin has greater cultural importance than the requisites of climate or other external conditions and that style is derived from reasons other than efficacity.[47]

Whether or not Le Corbusier's view is provable is hardly germane, because buried in it is the idea of the house as a repository of memory which is represented in the comfort and familiarity of known domestic forms. Moreover, it suggests that regional architectural development does not necessarily have an unbroken, shared and congruent lineage of form, patrimony and territory, although this is not to approve of Le Corbusier's use elsewhere of deracinated motives.

An ethic of care: a more relevant intervention

Eileen Gray's (1878–1976) more sympathetic, particularised and local understanding and engagement with the vernacular such as she revealed at the Zervos House, La Goulotte, 1926–31 (assisting Jean Badovici [1893–1956]), Tempe a Pailla, Castellar, 1932–4, and Lou Perou, Chapelle-Ste-Anne, 1954–61, stand in direct contrast to Le Corbusier's aesthetic approach. Peter Adam quoted Gray's somewhat gnomic regionalist observations in her *Notes on Colour and Materials*, which may relate to the Zervos House:

> There is something embarrassing about regional architecture which does not always suit the variety of the building. I would like to see a rigorous discipline in the application of colour, for instance, in a region of white rocks. I like to paint houses in brown and build from natural stone; they should have a square tower painted to the colour in bleu outre mer [ultramarine blue].[48]

This suggests that through the use of discrete form and colour Gray thought regional buildings could be equably combined with new work to the benefit of both. Constant recalled that on Gray's seeing the existing building which was to form the shell of her last house, Lou Perou,

An accommodation with the vernacular: Villa Tempe a Pailla, Menton, 1932, designer Eileen Gray. (Drawing by Roger Emmerson)

[She] was delighted by the simple vaulted space enclosed by crumbling stone walls and a tiled roof... She detailed the highly visible northern and eastern facades in an anonymous vernacular manner.[49]

Wilkinson remarked that Gray and Badovici's Modernist E.1027, Roquebrune-Cap Martin, 1926–9,

is certainly a fitting monument to the moment when women finally won the power to build.[50]

Gray was not alone, nor the first, though it is a small company. Early exponents included Sophy Gray (1814–71) in South Africa; Louise Blanchard Bethune (1856–1913), who set up a joint practice with her husband in 1881 in Buffalo, New York; Julia Morgan (1872–1957), California, with works for the Hearst family and the University of California beginning in 1902; Marion Mahoney (1871–1961) with a house for her brother at Elkhart, Indiana, 1907, and subsequent works in partnership with her husband,

Burley Griffin (1876–1937); Wivi Lon (1872–1966) in Finland; Amaza Lee Meredith (1895–1984), doubly refused entry to the profession as a woman of colour in Virginia; Hana Kučerová-Záveská (1904–44) in Czechoslovakia; or Margaret Brodie (1907–97) in Scotland. Wilkinson's singling-out of Gray had possibly rather more to do with the presence of Le Corbusier in the narrative than the achievement – against the odds – of women architects *per se*. The 'winning of power' was premature in Gray's case, given that Le Corbusier's later intervention in E.1027[51] is crudely evident in the brutal over-painting of many of the interiors and one exterior[52] in 1938.[53]

Davidson commented:

> If I were in the business of making trouble, I would suggest the thought-experiment 'for Classical read Modernist'. For Napoleon, as it were, read that far less liberal dictator le Corbusier [sic]. There is no orthodoxy like unto an orthodoxy that doesn't realise it is one, and that it is behaving like one.[54]

Or as Karen Franck observed:

> In provocative works, Carol Gilligan… finds that women and girls draw upon a 'reflective understanding of care' requiring that no-one be hurt and that one responds to the needs of others, whereas men and boys are concerned that everyone be treated fairly. Gilligan calls the first, women's 'ethic of care' and the second, men's 'ethic of justice'.[55]

With justice, of course, comes judgement, and much of what was given by Le Corbusier was judgement. The subtlety of Gray's plan at E.1027 and its original decoration, obscured by him, while patently not within a work of regional architecture, was of significance for her later regional work. Gray showed care. Le Corbusier judged and, perforce, condemned.

Wohnberge: communal living and the dissolution of the family

Gropius's design of the Sommerfeld House – based on his client's timber building system – owed a tectonic debt to the Wright designs published in the Wasmuth edition and Expressionist features to the explorations of the *Gläserne Kette* (1919–20)[56] and had an ersatz Schwarzwald regional character. Gropius's brief foray into Expressionism and regionalism had several manifestations: his *Mountains for Living (Wohnberge)*, 1919; the illustration of the Sommerfeld House on the topping-out ceremony programme; Lyonel Feininger's (1871–1956) woodcut cover illustration, *The Cathedral of Socialism*, for the 1919 Bauhaus programme; the design for the *Monument to the March Dead (Denkmal für die Märzgefallenen)*, 1920-2, commemorating the Kapp Putsch of 1920, erected in the Weimar central cemetery (subsequently destroyed by the Nazis as *entartete kunst*); and his entry for the Chicago Tribune Tower, 1922. He did not engage with either Expressionism or regionalism after 1922.

Isaacs quoted the prospectus for the unbuilt *wohnberge*, where:

> Gropius, visualising a change in social order, wrote that in these Mountains for Living the individual woman or man is the social unit of a more perfect society rather than the state or family. Family duties as such would not exist; elimination of all housework would provide equal leisure time for both sexes. Women of equal capabilities would have the same earning power as men.[57]

Already, three essentials had been established as necessary for Modernist living: a change in the social order, the dissolution of the family and the abolition of housework. Gropius eulogised:

> Past development thus shows steadily progressing socialisation of former family functions of legal, pedagogic and domestic nature, and thus we perceive the first beginnings of a communal era which might someday displace the era of individual rights.[58]

Such housing with communal kitchen, dining room or canteen, lounge, toilet facilities and support staff, was built: for example, at Narkomfin, Moscow, 1928-32, by Moisei Ginzburg (1892–1946) and Ignati Milinis (1899–1974) at Zlín in Czechoslovakia for the Baťa Shoe Company in the 1920s by Vladimír Karfík and František Gahura (1891–1958), or closer to home at the 'child-free' Isokon Flats, Lawn Road, Hampstead, 1928–34, by Welles Coates (1895–1958) – which was where Gropius came to live following his flight from Germany in 1934 – but rarely for the working family as conceived by Gropius. The Baťa housing was for single men and women employed in Tomáš Baťa's shoe-factories and is hostel-like, while the serviced Isokon Flats were for an elite left-of-centre ascetic artistic and intellectual urban commune. In both cases some commonality of outlook might be supposed amongst the occupants: shoes in Zlín and a cosy English Marxism

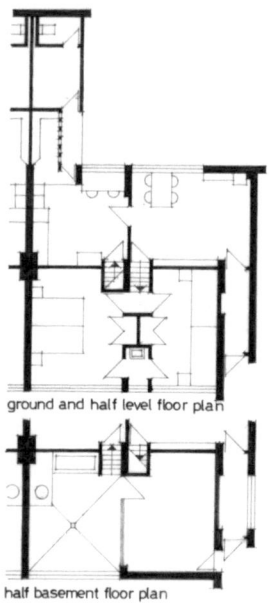

ground and half level floor plan

half basement floor plan

A life of some richness: floor plans, row house, Torten Siedlung, Dachau, 1926, architect Walter Gropius.
(Drawing by Roger Emmerson)

at the Lawn Road where the fissiparous community was widely believed to be a nest of Soviet Russian spies.

However, in his row-houses at the Törten Siedlung, Dessau, 1926, Gropius included those spaces which he proposed were to be communally provided in the *Wohnberge* and which later he 'scientifically' expunged from the *existenzminimum* flat, such as utility room, family room/workshop, adequate storage and a wet-room/laundry/bathroom. The Törten plan locates two storeys of accommodation to the front – the large family work room and the wet room in the half-basement and two bedrooms above – while to the rear and at an intermediate level, the one-and-a-half storey height of a dayroom and kitchen linked to a secluded outdoor space and larder, storeroom and toilet. He dispensed with a corridor, other than the entrance hall, so that the split level and half-flight provide seclusion for the bedrooms. A life of some complexity and richness could be housed in such a dwelling. However, as the decade progressed, such generosity was to be wrecked on the reef of the contradictory 'science/*zeitgeist*' premiss and was subjected to a *reductio ad absurdum* in space standards.

Total architecture: science and art in the design of dwellings

His merited Bauhaus celebrity notwithstanding, Gropius's positivist and contradictory *The Scope of Total Architecture* does not read well today. It provided much of the justification and exculpation required by architects subsequently engaged in poorly-funded and, as it proved, poorly-researched and negligibly-evaluated experimental housing programmes. This manifesto, published in the early 1950s, summed up his architectural thinking since the mid-1920s. It included a section entitled 'What is regional expression?'

Bauhaus regionalism: Gropius House, Lincoln, Massachusetts, 1938, architect Walter Gropius. (Daderot, own work, Creative Commons)

Gropius misread regional architecture, crediting it with insubstantiality both ontologically and epistemologically, which he contrasted unfavourably with the presumed rigour of his scientific method and vigour of his aesthetic sensibility. This recent émigré (he arrived in the USA in February 1937) blithely claimed of the house he built at Lincoln, Massachusetts, 1937–8, that:

> As to my practice, when I built my first house in the USA – which was my own – I made it a point to absorb into my own conception those features of the New England architectural tradition that I found still alive and adequate.[59]

Beyond the use of painted timber siding, a brick flue and fieldstone retaining walls amongst the far more prominent flat roof, steel, plate glass and glass brick, Gropius seemed to have concluded that very little indeed was 'alive and adequate' in the New England tradition. Even his biographer was constrained to observe that

> the house at Lincoln... immediately struck us as a European House or, to be more precise, a Bauhaus house in its coolness and confidence.[60]

Gropius extrapolated from his New England experience, declaring,

> The regional character cannot be found through sentimental or imitative approach by incorporating either old emblems or the newest. If you take, for instance, the basic difference imposed on the climatic conditions of California, say, as against Massachusetts, you will realise what diversity of expression can result from this fact alone if the architect will use the utterly contrasting indoor-outdoor relations of those two regions as focus for his design conception.[61]

In support of his scientific design principles Gropius promoted the simplistic statistical results of behavioural psychology as representing a complete haptic programme, while his visual theory was little more than an expiation on the mechanics of optics and the physiology of the eye together with reference to mood-associative colour. His biology required only the satisfaction of the basic requirements of shelter, nourishment and procreation and his sociology the measure of what the masses might endure. His empathetic artist purported to bridge the chasm between the individual's innate sense of home and the geometric limitations of Gropius's arithmetic sciences. There was no sense that he contemplated anything as substantial as, say, George Peter Murdock's (1897–1985) 75 'cross-cultural essentials', as quoted by Kate Fox in *Watching the English*.[62] The few early built examples aside, Gropius paid little attention to the 'habits of people', at least not to the habits of those destined for his *existenzminimum* dwellings where, as Hall noted, he, as did Le Corbusier,

> missed the real criticism [of the dwellings he inspired], which was of design solutions laid down on people without regard to their preferences, ways of life, or plain idiosyncrasies.[63]

Bachelard observed,

> A geometrical object of this kind ought to resist metaphors that welcome the human body and the human soul. But transposition to the human plane takes place immediately whenever a house is considered as space for cheer and intimacy, space that is supposed to condense intimacy. Independent of all rationality, the dream world beckons.[64]

'Cheer and intimacy' featured little in Gropius's prospectus, which contained nothing about the homeliness of home-life nor how homeliness might be derived other than through the spurious guarantee of the artists' aesthetic contributions to make it possible, liveable and pleasurable; artists who failed in large measure to materialise, as likewise had the scientists before them. Gropius told the reader how he or she should look at and appreciate the dwellings he and his colleagues designed, about which even Gropius was obliged to concede: *'every adult shall have his own room, small though it may be!* [Gropius's emphasis and exclamation]'.[65] Even Bachelard, despite rejecting Gropius's reductive aims for the single-family house, had no interest in the spaces allocated to the flat-dweller:

> In Paris there are no houses, and the inhabitants of the big city live in superimposed boxes... *Home* [Bachelard's emphasis] has become mere horizontality. The different rooms that compose living quarters jammed into one floor all lack one of the fundamental principles [verticality] for distinguishing and classifying the values of intimacy.[66]

In theory, space was to 'flow' artistically in these designed Cartesian interiors, presenting multiple perspectives and intervisibility, provided that space was in sufficient supply to allow mobility and afford multifarious points-of-view. However, virtually the Modernists' first act was to deny it to those they claimed to serve, in that their designs demarcated and sequestrated space. Loss of space was not simply the neat, economic – in its several senses – and scientific aggregation of those square metres occupied by discrete physical activities which fortuitously occurred at different times in the day – the 'shared activity space' as we now know it – but the profound loss of particular space for 'cheer and intimacy' which had no explicit quantifiably-measurable use-value in Gropius's reckoning but which impacted crucially on the individual's sense of the implicit value of home or work. Burgin quoted Henri Lefebvre's (1901–91) thoughts on space, that it is

> not a container without content... Not an abstract mathematical/ geometrical continuum, independent of human subjectivity and agency.[67]

Burgin went further to note:

> In the modern period, space was predominantly space traversed (by this token we judge that the prisoner has little of it),[68]

thus inviting the reader to reflect on the incarceration of the occupant of the *existenzminimum* dwelling, or, as Collins put the converse, that Victor Baltard's (1805–74) critique of the panopticon

> could hardly have expressed more clearly the idea of a prison as a 'machine for living in'.[69]

Gropius attempted later to distance himself from the very thing he had promoted – Modern architecture – while insinuating it under the cover of another label, a 'tendency' – to reassure and convince people that what they were to receive was familiar territorially and patrimonially to them:

> And how deceiving a precipitate terminology can be! Let us analyse, for instance, that most unfortunate designation, 'The International Style'. It is not a style because it is still in flux, nor is it international because its tendency is the opposite – namely, to find regional, indigenous expression derived from the environment, the landscape, the habits of the people.⁷⁰

By declaring Modern architecture generally 'in flux', Gropius awarded it the status of an ongoing scientific or sociological experiment whereby the reporting of its inconclusive results could be indefinitely postponed and, providentially, its critique likewise deferred and judgement suspended; a preteritive argument still in use today by doctrinaire Modernist apologists. Levin was clear about the requirements of the scientific method:

> Among scientists, it is practically criminal to be wrong. Verifiability is substratal to any scientific endeavour. There is nothing to be gained and everything to be lost with false claims of an experiment that rings for you if the apparatus can only return dead silence for the rest of the world.⁷¹

Finding Usonia: an American vernacular

Wright's first pre-Columbian essay, Hollyhock House, Los Angeles, 1919–21, for Aline Barnsdall, was followed by La Miniatura, Pasadena, California, 1923, for Alice Millard, the earliest of the 'Text-Tile' concrete block houses – the Storer, 1923, Ennis-Brown, 1924, and Freeman, 1926, Houses, all Los Angeles – where the combination of the novel construction technique – a quite literal interpretation in concrete block and steel rods of Semper's *Bekleidungsprinzip* – and Wright's fascination with Mayan architecture acquired an almost ur-character. McCarter observed that:

> It is interesting to note that the two architectures Wright admired most, the heavy, earthbound Maya and the light, articulately framed Japanese, share the characteristic of being without glass; in both,

'Text-tile' construction and a drama of Sophocles: Ennis House, Los Angeles, 1923, architect Frank Lloyd Wright.
(Kyle Magnuson, own work, Creative Commons)

space is continuous from exterior to interior, palpably present in the shadow of the masonry lintel and frame roof.[72]

Chris Hawthorne claimed in his film *That Far Corner: Frank Lloyd Wright in Los Angeles*, 2018, that 'these houses are shadowed by violence and death… and seem a precursor to "LA noir"'. Wright was quoted by Hawthorne as calling them a 'drama of Sophocles'.[73] Hawthorne speculated on the cathartic effect on Wright, following the murders and fire at Taliesin East in 1914, of the implicit Mayan death-cult aspects of the houses. Present in the first three houses are narrow, low-ceilinged corridors, tall sepulchral rooms, ubiquitous hard surfaces and mastaba-like construction. Such is the seeming strangeness of Wright's Text-Tile architecture that, since its first appearance in a film of contemporary sexual mores, *Female*[74] of 1933, the Ennis-Brown House – or sets based on it – have featured as an unsettling cinematic location in the horror *House on Haunted Hill*,[75] in the psycho-drama *The Day of the Locust*[76], in the science-fiction *Blade Runner*[77] and influenced the design of the interior of the Great Pyramid of Mereen in the fantasy world of *Game of Thrones*[78].

For Wright, the ten years between 1925 and 1935 were those largely of retrenchment and consolidation in the design of Taliesin II, 1925, the Ocatillo

Desert Camp, 1928–9, and the Richard L Jones House, Tulsa, Oklahoma, 1929. Only the Chandler Block House project, Arizona, 1928, and the Willey House, Minneapolis, Minnesota, 1934 – the first true 'Usonian' house – represented any continuity with the earlier Prairie houses, leading Wright to a distillation of these several vernaculars into an architecture of closed masonry elements contrasting with open lightweight frames and glazing, bedded on a concrete or masonry base and supporting a floating cantilevered roof. As Frampton observed:

> It is but a short step from Wright's timber architecture of the turn of the century to this work [the Usonian house] and the fact that this move comes with Wright's literal return to the Midwest should remind one of the regional inflection that was always latent as a creative impulse within Wright's work.[79]

Following the monolithic nature of the Text-Tile block houses, where the later Freeman House represented a clear transition in the treatment of solid and void, Wright returned, in the design of the Chandler House, to the open and closed forms of the Prairie houses and their quasi-vernacular antecedents. Now the work presented in a yet more fundamental Semperian aspect and was influenced by his knowledge of the graphic conventions and visual content of the *ukiyo-e* print and from his several projects in Japan. In the plan of the Willey House, Wright broke down 19th-century domestic hierarchies even further beyond his freer planning of the previous decade by integrating the kitchen – which he now described as the 'workspace' – into the living and dining spaces and predicated how the Usonian House would develop in use.

The Usonian house: the first Jacobs House, Madison, Wisconsin, 1936, architect Frank Lloyd Wright.
(James Steakley, own work, Creative Commons)

The 'workspace' had yet to find its precise pivotal location and role in the house, as it did finally and conclusively in the first Herbert and Katherine Jacobs' House, Madison, Wisconsin, 1936.

A Hitchcock plot: the International Style

Whether because Wright simply did not build enough or whether the little that was built was thought by Henry-Russell Hitchcock (1903–87) and Philip Johnson (1906–2005) to be decorative and irrelevant to the several contemporary strands of stripped European aesthetics and practice they promoted, he was sidelined in their influential 1932 exhibition, *Modern Architecture*, held at the Museum of Modern Art, New York. Even Rudolph Schindler's more stripped-down, experimental and prescient work in, for example, the 'Slabtilt' Schindler-Chase House, Los Angeles, 1921–2, was not featured despite Schindler's request to Johnson for inclusion. A testy correspondence followed in which Schindler set out his stall:

> It seems to me that instead of showing late attempts of creative architecture, [the exhibition] tends to concentrating on the so-called 'International Style'. If this is the case my work has no place in it. I am not a stylist, not a functionalist, nor any other sloganist... The question of whether a house is really a house is more important to me, than the fact that it is made of steel, glass, putty, or hot air.[80]

Schindler's writings on Modern architecture and Modern life were widely and popularly published in the USA, although such non-doctrinaire and inclusive views from within the Modernist camp were rare and easily lost in the appeal of a simplistic stylism. The work of Schindler's Austrian compatriot, brief partner and fellow Loos and Wright alumnus, Richard

'Slab-tilt' construction for the Californian lifestyle: Schindler-Chase House, West Hollywood, California, 1922, architect Rudolph Schindler.
(Julius Schulman, Creative Commons)

Neutra (1892–1970), proved acceptable to Hitchcock and Johnson as more obviously 'European' and non-vernacular or regionalist. Moreover, Wright's and Schindler's regional investigations encompassed in their aesthetic that which Chambers characterised as 'historical dwellings [which] are missives of time, destined for decay',[81] whereas Hitchcock and Johnson were those

> others [who] have chosen to submerge and repress such inscriptions of transition in the anonymous transcendence afforded by the flat surfaces and direct lines of an ever-new and ever-white modernism.[82]

The *Modern Architecture* exhibition had three parts. The first was devoted to the 'exhibiting architects' which, contrary to much received opinion, included Wright, although he was confined to an essay in the catalogue and was there because he was simply unavoidable, whereas those others exhibited were seen as the prophets.[83] A second section concentrated on housing and the work of Otto Haesler (1880–1969) in Celle, Rathenow, Karlsruhe and Kassel, Germany, between 1928 and 1932. In an accompanying essay, Hitchcock presented a familiar 'scientific' prescription:

> The modern house is a biological institution. It is a shelter devoted primarily to the functions of reproduction, nutrition and recreation… Add to these primarily physiological requirements, the provisions of space for social companionship and play and study and the definition of the house is complete.[84]

A final section entitled 'Photographs in the Exhibition Illustrating the Extent of Modern Architecture' featured a subaltern group displaying a catholicity of styles absent from Hitchcock and Johnson's subsequent publication, *The International Style*.[85] Its easy polemic and assimilable prescriptions of what constituted the new architecture granted to society an understanding of an approved style and, to architects of varying ability, access to a reliable pattern-book. This, plainly, was *not* the authors' intention:

> 'The principles are few and broad' [H-R H from the 1st ed]. Too few and narrow, I would say in 1951 of the principles that were enunciated so firmly in 1932.[86]

They wrote further:

> The mistake made by many readers of *The International Style* was… to assume that what the authors offered as a diagnosis and prognosis

was intended to be used as an academic rulebook.[87]

Their architectural audience was one of variable taste and talent, for many of whom a pattern-book was precisely what was wanted and needed.

Getting one's excuses in early

Following the creation of the CIAM at Sarraz in 1929, largely at Le Corbusier's prompting, the tenor of mid-20th-century architectural historiography was established internationally by, of course, Gropius and Le Corbusier and, to a lesser degree, Wright, but also Hitchcock, Johnson, Pevsner and Siegfrid Giedion (1888–1968), locally by Reyner Banham (1922–88) and, equivocally, by JM Richards (1907–92), with Peter Collins (1920–81) and Colin Rowe (1920–99) as correctives.

In simple terms: Hitchcock and Johnson collated and curated their selection of the Modern Movement, derived the canonic form and codified the International Style – centred on the work of the Bauhaus and Le Corbusier and their followers – and proscribed the rest; Pevsner unearthed the Modern Movement's antecedents and delineated the 'true' path to the International Style; Giedion defined its ethos – space creation – and attempted to predict its future; Banham sought to connect a limited British Modernist practice to international Modernism; while Richards contrived an accommodation between Modernism and a peculiarly English view of an architect-derived vernacular and the appeal of suburbia. Collins conducted a rather more rigorous theoretical and historical search for the origins and authority of Modern Movement ideas, and Rowe questioned its intellectual bases. All seven adopted a universalist position from which to press their various cases, a position which left little room for any detailed consideration of regional architecture in their construct. Such was the force of their arguments, underscored by the adoption of the Athens Charter on urbanism at the 1933 CIAM Conference and as it was subsequently interpreted, that promotion of regionalism, where it occurred, was seen, within the context of the Modern Movement, as a protest[88] rather than as a viable position in its own right.

Nevertheless, Hitchcock retrospectively confirmed in 1966 that the ship had sailed almost immediately:

> Since then [1932] in our different ways, [Johnson] most strikingly in his buildings... I in various writings... have offered the conclusion that the International Style is over.[89]

Unease followed hard on the heels of this apology and Hitchcock's triumphant claim of 1932 that:

> This contemporary style, which exists throughout the world, is unified and inclusive, not fragmentary and contradictory like so much of the production of the first generation of modern architects[90]

was amended to read:

> To refuse a comparable liberty of choice [to other styles] today, merely because 25 years ago the development of modern architecture began to be notably convergent, is certainly a form of academism. This is already only too evident in just the places one would expect to find it, that is, in prominent architectural schools and in large, highly institutionalised offices.[91]

Hitchcock qualified his *apologia* by locating such narrow-minded academism in 'prominent schools' and 'institutionalised offices', which were patently not then in Hitchcock's view, if indeed they ever had been, at the cutting-edge. One senses that Hitchcock realised he had overstated the universality, vitality and durability of the International Style's present artistic invention and, by manufacturing a 'convergence', had circumscribed its future.

By way of contrast, in his earlier *Modern Architecture* of 1929,[92] Hitchcock had defined a 'new tradition' as a Modern development of the moribund past. Indeed, it was central to his argument in *Modern Architecture* that connections be made to the plurality of earlier periods of architecture so that bases could be identified from which the new tradition would spring. Within the growth of the new tradition he recognised each flowering on its own merits rather than judging such blooms against the cultivar of the later International Style. Hitchcock defined some of their regional or national characteristics:

> For it was generally known that [Sir Walter Scott] lived in a castellated house... with markedly Scotch character,[93]

but he cautioned,

> the ornament of the New Tradition [ca. 1900–10]... rapidly became subject to a formula, or rather a set of national formulas.[94]

He touched lightly and briefly on a core issue, although he drew no conclusion or resolution from it, that:

> The continued existence of Romantic individualism is not a question of architecture alone. There is a dichotomy of the spirit more profound than any mere style can ever resolve.[95]

Hence Hitchcock's brief note of approval for non-overtly Modernist buildings, but from which he later resiled, such as:

> Lallerstedt's Technical High School, Tengbom's Hogalid's Church, and above all Ostberg's City Hall finished in 1923, all in Stockholm, display a wide dependence on the architecture of the past and magnificent traditional execution integrated into a definitive national style.[96]

Hitchcock wrapped up this more inclusive, yet still compromised, view of architecture in the early 20th century:

> Yet in retrospect there is very little difference in the dependence on the past of those who early announced themselves as the creators of a new architecture and those who remained respectful... toward some principle of single or multiple revivalism.[97]

A kitchen-sink drama: the Frankfurt kitchen

Housework greatly troubled male architects. Their proposed solutions in the Modernist single-family house still revealed their 19th and early 20th-century origins with distant kitchens, intervening pantries or relegation to a servant part of the plan, as was made plain by Gropius at the Masters' Houses, Bauhaus, Dessau, 1926; Le Corbusier at the Wiessenhofsiedlung, Stuttgart, 1927; or Erich Mendelsohn (1887–1953) in his own house at Rupenhorn, Berlin, 1930. In mass housing, Gropius first denied housework its existence through the agency of an unseen servant class of Morlocks in the *wohnberge*, then admitted it in the 'emancipation' of the housewife through the availability, for some, of 'white goods'. Wright, despite eventually locating it centrally, reduced the Usonian kitchen to a tight, often windowless, clerestory or rooflit 'workspace'. Later, Bachelard, in conformity with the gender mores of the 1950s, referred patronisingly to housework as the '"wax" civilisation' and offered predictable and equivocal praise to the contribution of women in the 'building' of the home, even questioning whether home design was a task for the male:

> In the intimate harmony of walls and furniture, it may be said that we

become conscious of a house that is built by women, since men only know how to build a house from the outside, and they know little or nothing of the 'wax' civilisation.[98]

It was a woman, Margarete Schütte-Lihotzky (1897–2000), who produced the definitive design, the Frankfurt kitchen, 1926), which, she claimed, she 'designs as an architect, not a woman'. Perhaps her male counterparts' failure was that they tried to design the kitchen *for a woman* rather than *as an architect*. The long-lived, life-long communist and peripatetic Schütte-Lihotzky was the first female architecture student at the Kunstgewerbeschule in Vienna, 1915–9, where she was taught by Oskar Strnad (1879–1935). She worked on public housing projects with Adolf Loos in Vienna, 1922–4; with Ernst May (1886–1970) in Frankfurt-am-Main, where she designed the kitchen for which she is best-known; and subsequently in Magnitogorsk in the USSR, Paris, Sofia, Cuba, China and the German Democratic Republic. The Frankfurt kitchen, and variants of it, was one of the few parts of the *existenzminimum* dwelling designed in a reliably scientific and functional way.

In brief, at 3.1 metres by 1.9 metres, it was compactly organised and featured natural woods adopted for their bacterial, meal-worm and damage-resistant qualities. Spices, herbs, loose grains and pulses were stored in zinc drawers, and the wooden units were painted blue, to which house-flies, seemingly, are averse. It came with a cooker, double sink and draining board, fold-down ironing board and a low workbench against the window wall at which one could sit to prepare food, take a snack or do the household accounts. The white goods much favoured by (male) architects were conspicuous by their absence. The Frankfurt Kitchen was, in part, a functional compensation for the 'secularising' of the home whereby the ritualistic and celebratory spaces such as those provided by a vernacular 'farmhouse' kitchen-cum-family room or a parlour were removed from the traditional house[99] and the area of the remainder reduced to

The emancipation from housework: the 'Frankfurt kitchen', 1926, architect Margarete Schütte-Lihotzky.
(Christos Vittoratos - own work, Creative Commons)

bare 'biological' function. In size, although lacking its sophisticated design and ingenious and costly cabinetry, the Frankfurt kitchen became the model for subsequent *existenzminimum* dwellings.[100]

Late arrivals: Modernism in Britain

Hobsbawm said of certain sections of British society that

> the avant-garde became, as it were, part of established culture; it became at least partly absorbed into the fabric of everyday life… Except for a somewhat larger minority than before 1914, it was not what most people actually and consciously enjoyed.[101]

He described its wider application, where:

> The impact of the avant garde [German Expressionism, Art Deco, Futurism, Wright's Text-Tile] on the commercial Cinema already suggests that 'modernism' began to make its mark on everyday life. It did so obliquely, through productions which the broad public did not consider to be 'art'.[102]

Lynch concurred that '[m]ore immediate in its impact was a new popular culture [of the cinema]', but set Modernism in the context of a Scottish resistance arising from its cultural predicament. This was explicit in the founding of the Scottish National League, 1928, the Scottish (Self-Government) Party, 1932 and the amalgamation of all nationalist political groups into the Scottish National Party (SNP) in 1934; in the literary phenomenon of the Scottish Renaissance 1922–60; and in the formation of the Saltire Society in 1935. However, Lynch thought that

> By 1936 the Scottish Renaissance, an astonishing outburst of creative talent, self-propagandising, emotion and vituperation, was all but over. Its effects are still reverberating over half a century later.[103]

The Modernist architectural ideas of the 1920s belatedly reached Britain and Scotland from Europe and the USA in the canonic texts and in periodicals of the early 1930s. As Hitchcock observed in 1932:

> In Italy, Spain, England [sic] and Japan really modern Architecture has only begun to appear… Emberton, Etchells, Connell and *Tait* [my emphasis]

have done the most thoroughgoing modern work in England.[104]

In the light of the appearance of the significant texts referred to above and of subsequent architectural developments in Scotland, not least in Tait's career, it is interesting to note that Langmead recorded for Britain a mere four books and articles on contemporary Dutch architecture published between 1922 and 1926, whereas, between 1926 and 1939, there were published no fewer than 27 books and articles on Willem Dudok (1884–1974) alone.[105]

At home, articles on Modernism were published by the likes of Ninian Johnston (1912–90),[106] editor of the Glasgow School of Architecture magazine *Vista*, who was one of those whose careers blossomed post-WWII, and by the young (Sir) John Summerson (1904–92), who taught architecture between 1929 and 1930 at Edinburgh College of Art. Under the direction of lecturer EAA Rowse (1896–1982) – later Assistant Director at the Architectural Association in London – the School of Architecture at Edinburgh College of Art between 1928 and 1933 was part of a Modernist clique in Edinburgh where (Sir) Herbert Read (1893–1968), Professor of History of Art at the University of Edinburgh 1931-3, tried unsuccessfully in 1931 to raise interest in and funds to establish a 'centre of modern art in Edinburgh modelled on the Bauhaus'.[107] MacDiarmid noted that:

> I may refer gratefully to the period in the 20s [sic] during which Dr. Read occupied the Chair of Fine Arts in Edinburgh University and stirred up the dovecots there with his lively modernistic doctrines and impatience with pompous humbugs.[108]

International travel was hugely significant for architects in exposing them to the concrete reality of Modernist practice unavailable to them at home.[109]

More populist routes of Modernist dissemination were such as the 1934 publication edited by John Gloag (1896–1981) based on a series of radio talks broadcast by the BBC in 1933 entitled *Design in Modern Life*. Gloag began with the question, 'Who knows what the public wants?' and then answered it, none too subtly, that it was he and the design luminaries of the day – Maxwell Fry (1899–1987), Elizabeth Denby (1894–1965), Frank Pick (1878–1941) and Gordon Russell (1892–1980) – who knew because only they were *not* duped by reproduction. He wrote:

> Please do not imagine that this book is a piece of high-brow carping at what exists… It is written by people who know their own subjects thoroughly, and who know how well we can plan and design in

England [sic] when we are allowed to... And it is at this point that a great secret may be revealed: the public doesn't know itself what it wants.[110]

Is your furniture by any chance pretending to be Chippendale, or Sheraton, or Jacobean, and if so, why?... Why are you, or perhaps your neighbours, living in an imitation Tudor house with stained wooden slats shoved on to the front of it to make it look like what is called a half-timbered house?[111]

By way of contrast, FRS Yorke's (1906–62) *The Modern House*, also 1934, was aimed at the architect and perhaps some of Gloag's wireless-listening public. He headed the chapter entitled 'Twentieth Century Architecture' with an illustration of labourers' cottages from Gandy's *Cottages and Lodges* of 1805 and opened with the statement that '[t]he art of building has its roots in contemporary economic, producing and social conditions',[112] thereby removing territory, patrimony, polity and aesthetics as relevant factors in architectural production, while implicitly alerting the reader to the 'fact' that the-old-is-the-new-is-the-old by the inclusion of Gandy's cottages. Yorke made comparisons, his benchmark of approval being the English builders' Georgian, also much-admired by Classicists and staunch opponents of Modernism such as Geoffrey Scott (1885–1929) and Roger Scruton (1944–2020), and by Traditionalists generally. No wonder the public was confused north *and* south of the Border. By the sixth edition of 1948, due to the passage of time, these largely white houses had acquired perforce both the history and aestheticism that Yorke initially denied them.

A more accessible text was Randal Phillips' *Houses for Moderate Means*, published by *Country Life* in 1936, which acted less as a doctrinaire espousal of the benefits of the Modern house and more as record of it in its several recent British varieties and was a companion piece to his earlier *The £1000 House* of 1928. This latter was comprised entirely of neo-Georgian and Arts & Crafts *manqué* designs and was cast as a riposte to a perennial truism because:

There is here abundant proof that architect-designed houses can be achieved at a cost no greater than that of speculative builders' houses.[113]

In *Houses for Moderate Means* Phillips made '[n]o attempt to sponsor any particular style' but believed 'that they are examples of honest building, with no sham features and make-believe about them'.[114] He queried the proliferation of 'modern materials' in new houses and doubted that '[o]ne might think that the whole house was being made anew'.[115]

Modernism was also promoted in the popular press, such as Summerson's article 'Modernity in architecture: an appeal for the New Style' in *The Scotsman*, 21 February 1930, or Robins Miller's review of Gropius's *The New Architecture and the Bauhaus* in the *Glasgow Evening Times* entitled 'Why not a City of Leafy Housetops' of 12 July 1935. However, if McKean, Hobsbawm and Lynch were correct, Scots preferred the cinema to Cubism and that their Modernism be safely framed by the proscenium arch and not a manifesto.

Can't, cant or Kant: the lack of architectural philosophy in Scotland

McKean's quantitative survey of Scottish architecture of the 1930s[116] had the unintended merit of exposing an architectural confusion at the heart of the period which arose from the loss of both architectural opportunity and theoretical clarity. He wrote:

> Trying to define Thirties architecture is like chasing a chimera: the closer you get, the further out of reach it seems.[117]

In response to the new continental domestic models, dated domestic construction methods such as mass masonry, rendered brick cavity walling, floor and roof spans dictated by economic timber joist lengths and an absence of central heating – still at issue in the 1960s – predicated discrete rooms, while flat roofs disguised merely irregular, not 'open', plans, and white render and functionally distributed windows invoked the hugely speculative Craigievar/Mackintosh/Corbusier-Bauhaus aesthetic link. McKean, avoiding any qualitative assessment of actual production, included every new house which met his determinants of being

> usually pink or white geometrical sculptures in space, plonked firmly in the ground, windows are holes punched through a white skin... [and] were entirely appropriately highjacked by Hurd, Reiach, Spence, Lindsay, Forbes and Mears, as representing not a Continental import wished upon Scotland as recommended by John Summerson, but a reawakening of an indigenous native tradition brought up-to-date.[118]

McKean's 'hijackers' were a disparate gang of Modernist (Reiach, Spence,

Forbes) and Traditionalist (Hurd, Lindsay, Mears) architects, although even these distinctions were not exclusive, for whom the Craigievar/Mackintosh/ Corbusier-Bauhaus link was equally appealing, although for quite different reasons and purposes: for the Traditionalists because it validated a Scottish architecture and promised a potential compromise with Modernism; for the Modernists because it confirmed Scotland's putative formative role in Modernism and postulated how new work could be inserted alongside the old.

Glendinning et al, in partial echo of McKean, claimed that

> the luxuriantly diverse traditions of 1880–1914 began to coalesce into two formulae: Traditional and Modern. These seemed in many ways to be opposed, but had in common a new ideological and moral intensity, focussed on the reconstruction of [Scotland] as a whole.[119]

They continued:

> It is more difficult to pin down any exact relationship between the economic and political difficulties of those years and Scottish architectural *ideas* [Glendinning et al's emphasis] of the time.[120]

This is because there were *no* 'Scottish architectural *ideas* of the time' that were any more than stunted versions of notions current in Scotland before WWI or were acquired second- or third-hand from continental Europe. Or, at least, there were none that seem to have been recognised by later historians as such. Normand commented:

> Scottish art was so rooted in a narrative tradition that the embryonic elements of a conceptual modernism was allowed no space for growth.[121]

More specifically, he observed that:

> There was a kind of conservatism to this modernism, for it consistently remained within the boundaries of established taste... In fact the very foundation of radical avant-garde activity was absent. This absence was shaped by a temperamental disinclination for Scottish artists to engage in theory, and the all-encompassing dominance of art institutions in Scottish cultural life.[122]

The asserted 'reconstruction of the nation' is a retrospective fabulation arising from the authors' post-WWII Welfare State managerialist construct (see more below), for there was too much to reconstruct. The causes were structural, and there was neither the intent nor instrumentality to effect change. Butt noted:

> Effort by government has not been continuous nor has it been consistent; rarely has the examination of the structure of employment gone beyond the shallows; solutions have been sought in special agencies, some of them national, in regional economic measures, and – by some – in political independence.[123]

Moreover, it was not in the gift of Scottish architecture by itself to reverse decline, notwithstanding the actual although limited construction of cinemas, Homes Fit for Heroes, slum replacement council housing, bungalow speculation and military cemeteries. Such work may have been considered idealistic by its practitioners, but it was sporadic and theoretically incoherent. There *was* an 'economic and political' relationship, for it was the very precariousness of Scotland's economic and political condition and the centralisation of the British state that impacted on and impoverished architectural opportunity absolutely. This was the Scotland in which Modernism and the new architectures struggled to find a place.

Glendinning et al inferred an intellectual ferment in Scottish architecture comparable to that of MacDiarmid's literary Scottish Renaissance and which McKean also claimed, somewhat parochially, was conducted in the pages of the *RIAS Quarterly*; a publication of limited circulation to chartered members of the professional institute. Architectural discussion in such quarters, whether Traditional or Modern, was not about what was Scottish or Modern in Scottish architecture, for that was agreed;[124] rather it was how, on the one hand, Traditionalism might *accommodate* Modernism and, on the other hand, how Modernism might *accommodate* Tradition. To be clear, this was a compromise, *not* an antimony. It was significant in Normand's survey of Whyte's influential journal, *The Modern Scot*, which was published between 1931 and 1936, that he could identify only Hurd – a very occasional Modernist, more frequent Traditionalist – as the sole architectural contributor to it, thus suggesting considerable limits to the reach and intensity of the architectural ferment.[125]

Beyond the purely architectural community, John Tonge (n.d.), in *The Arts of Scotland*, published in 1938 to coincide with the Burlington House exhibition, proposed a more fundamental view of architecture than these subsequently inferred aesthetic niceties. In discussing Scottish spatial practice, Tonge noted of Celtic art:

it was one of the art-forms that conceive of space as, in Henri
Focillon's terms, *espace-milieu*, as opposed to *espace-limite* – that is, it
was constructed with reference to space, and was not framed off from
it, like the Pyramids or the Parthenon.

And, in a footnote, elaborated:

> The filigree technique so common in Celtic art presents a very obvious
> example of an art in which it is difficult to say whether the tangible
> forms or the immaterial intervals are the more important.[126]

Tonge seemed to refer to polar opposites such as were posited by Kant
and Smith or were evident in Thomson's architecture. In a more nuanced
interpretation of neo-Classicism in Scotland than MacLeod later managed,
Tonge, referring to the architecture of Edinburgh's New Town, observed that

> Celtic Art comes within Worringer's category of Nordic Arts, and
> from his viewpoint Scotland in the neo-Greek movement, could be
> regarded as indulging in something like the German *sachlichkeit*,
> a merely temporary reaction from the characteristic Nordic
> *Expressionismus*.[127]

Tonge thereby clearly identified Expressionism as a significant pole in Scottish
architecture.

MacDiarmid took exception to Tonge's Worringer reference, deeming
Nordic art doom-laden[128] and, in contrast, foregrounded the exuberance and
exoticism of the alleged Eastern ethnographic origins of the Celt as the true
impulse of Celtic art, although he did not refuse its Expressionist component.
Tonge sought agreement:

> Scottish art as a whole… is much more involved and restless and
> dynamic than English art, and these characteristics we find in the
> asymmetrical, intricate, organic Celtic art. This, I think, is what 'Hugh
> MacDiarmid'[129] has in mind when he speaks of the Scottish genius
> as 'in general brilliantly improvisatory'. Scottish architecture… at
> its most characteristic evolves like a cellular structure, not from the
> piecing together of elements in classical fashion.[130]

MacDiarmid's 'brilliantly improvisatory' categorisation of the Scottish
genius was matched in Tonge's thoughts on Robert Adam in that

one has only to compare his Edinburgh buildings with the heavy neo-classicism of Berlin to see how remarkable an achievement his re-creation of old forms was.[131]

Moreover, in a more strictly biological version of the theory of 'organic' architecture, when speaking of the Glasgow School of Art, Tonge noted:

we see the old Scottish feeling for three-dimensional design conditioned by the disposition of the rooms, the same impression of cellular growth, the most important of the old Celtic characteristics brought up to date.[132]

MacDiarmid's objection notwithstanding, Worringer, too, was favourably inclined to Kant's concept of antinomy – 'no pole exists that does not have its counter-pole'[133] – as the means of understanding the aesthetic object through the immediate experience of it. He claimed that:

The feeling of the 'thing in itself', which man lost in the pride of his spiritual evolution and which has come to life again in our philosophy only as the ultimate result of scientific analysis, stands not only at the end, but also at the beginning of our spiritual culture... the end point, which for us is Kant.[134]

These were plainly 'ideas' *about* architecture generated in Scotland, although seemingly not *in* architecture, which were made evident in the first half of the 20th century. The question remains whether they were 'ideas' prevalent *in* architecture. Certainly, they were not the very limited empiric 'ideas' identified by McKean, Frew, Walker or Glendinning et al as being current and relevant. MacDiarmid noted of such a pragmatic approach:

Seen in the light of the progress of transcendental philosophy since Kant and of the more modern discoveries in the field of psychology, the common-sense aesthetics of the 17th and 18th centuries appear rather faded and only distinguished by the grace and urbanity of their presentation.[135]

MacDiarmid recognised, in respect of the totality of Scottish art, including architecture, that

[Scottish philosophers] were fortunate in lighting on the old conception of unity in multiplicity as a condition of beauty. But it was not until the influence of German [Kantian] philosophy began to be felt that an attempt was made to exhibit any rational connection between this condition and its effect.[136]

Nonetheless, although he was relaxed and confident in discussing the challenging work and writings of contemporaneous Scottish Modernist painters and writers, MacDiarmid had regrettably nothing whatsoever to say about the Scottish architecture of his own time.

In a more general survey of Scottish philosophy, Beveridge and Turnbull noted that much Kantian philosophy emerged from Scottish theological colleges in the 19th and 20th centuries, quoting the American philosopher Lewis White Beck's (1913–97) observation that Scotland was 'over the last hundred years a "world centre" of Kant studies'.[137] They also acknowledged Scottish-Australian John Anderson's (1893–1962) rejection of the normative, reductive and scientific, in effect, Marxist/Leninist analysis:

> In his later philosophy Anderson expressed a deep distrust of all progressive, reformist and meliorist discourse, attacking the cheap optimism of those who envisaged a New Jerusalem organised by the planners and experts on the basis of the judicious application of science and technology. Progressivists, he argued, overlook 'qualitative distinctions and oppositions', neglect the incompatibility of different values and traditions, different moralities and forms of life, and collapse ethics to questions of distribution.[138]

They called upon the Scottish-American Alasdair MacIntyre in questioning the positivist, universalist argument and its presumption of a universalist everyone that was to prove so troublesome later:

> If in other words, capitalist society is composed of individuals who are acquisitive, self-seeking and morally deficient in other respects, where are the human resources for the creation of a good society? 'It is not surprising,' comments MacIntyre, 'that at this point Marxism tends to produce its own Übermensch: Lukac's ideal proletarian, Leninism's ideal revolutionary.'[139]

The landscape of Scottish manors: 'manifesto-houses' in Scotland

Mark Wigley (b. 1956) quoted Jacques Derrida (1930–2004):

> Contrary to what we might believe, the experience of ghosts is not tied to a bygone historical period, like the landscape of Scottish manors... When the very first perception of an image is linked to a structure of reproduction, then we are dealing with the realm of phantoms.[140]

The works of Billings, MacGibbon and Ross and the *Architects' Sketchbooks* were, in Derridian terms, a 'structure of reproduction'. They dominated the second half of the 19th century and the first half of the 20th whereby the 'Scottish manor' was serially replicated and which facilitated Glendinning's et al concept of pre-1919 'luxuriantly diverse traditions' and their subsequent Traditionalist-Modernist simplification in the 1930s. Nevertheless, such architecture exhausted itself in serial repetition, in increasing distance from the model and in decreasing relevance. Muthesius's proto-Modernist 'class of 1906' was largely *hors de combat* by 1920. Anderson's Traditionalists contributed, although with decreasing frequency, to the design of housing projects arising from the several housing acts – the Housing and Town Planning (Scotland) Act 1919; the Housing (Financial Provisions) Act 1924; the Housing (Scotland) Acts 1930 and 1933; 'Homes Fit for Heroes' developments in Garden City planning arising from the 1919 Act[141] – and in MacRae's urban work in Edinburgh, 1925–1946.[142] Scots Gothic ecclesiastical stylists merged with the Traditionalists to produce the Scottish National War Memorial at Edinburgh Castle, 1919–23, by Robert Lorimer, the Reid Memorial Church, Blackford, Edinburgh, 1929, by Lorimer's pupil Leslie Grahame Thomson (1896–1974) or the Carnegie Birthplace Memorial, Dunfermline, 1925, by James Shearer, a Lorimer afficionado. Monumental Traditionalists seemed to have continued only sporadically beyond 1914, although MacRae's work at Piershill, Edinburgh, 1935–8, could be classed as such.

Insofar as the 'manifesto house'[143] was emblematic of the 1920s and '30s, it was significant that, of all the houses recorded by McKean, only the Lane House, Dick Place, Edinburgh, 1933, by Kininmonth, and Lismhor, Easter Belmont, Edinburgh, 1935, by Kininmonth and Spence, sported relatively free Modernist ground floor plans. They seemed to reference the Frederick Vanderbilt Field House, New Hartford, Connecticut, 1930–1, by the Swiss-American William Lescaze (1896–1969) contemporaneously at work in

England. The 'L'-shaped living spaces of Lismhor and the Lane House were divided by a curtain to form dining room and living room which, in Lismhor, opened onto the entrance hall by means of wide sliding doors. In the Lane House, the construction of the great south-facing curved bay was simplified and made economically and structurally possible by the polygonal plan, vertical mullions and narrow floor-to-ceiling windows and afforded views to the broom-covered Blackford Hill. In the dining room, the window had the same view, except the sill was at table-top height and the lintel roughly 75 centimetres above it; low when one is standing but ideal and intimate in framing the view when sat at the table. The stair to the first floor bedrooms and roof terrace had a two-storey shallow triangular-bay window, which may account for Glendinning's et al dismissive description of the Lane House as 'boxy Art Deco',[144] thereby missing the point entirely.

McKean compared Kininmonth's Lane House to Sven Markelius's own house, the Villa Nockeby, Stockholm, 1930.[145] Besides a semi-circular bay attached to a cubic block of other accommodation there was little else in plan, form or material to relate the severe board-marked reinforced concrete box of the Villa Nockeby[146] to the Lane House. In any case, the Lane House originally had exterior walls of

The un-manifesto house: The Lane House, Edinburgh, 1933, architect William Kininmonth.

stock bricks lime-washed, quality being obtained by flushing the vertical joints and raking out the horizontal joints.[147]

The walls were later harled to improve weathering. In its original form, however, with the horizontal emphasis of the raked brick coursing and the concrete framing of the windows, the Lane House had much in common with the Expressionist work of Mendelsohn, particularly his houses at Karolingerplatz and Heerstrasse, Charlottenburg, Berlin, 1922–4, which he further developed in the later 'pragmatic Expressionism'[148] of his London houses.

Other than Lismohr and the Lane House, only Lamburn, Old Edinburgh

Road, Inverness, 1935, by Robert Carruthers-Ballantyne (1891–1981) passed muster as a reasonably competent Modernist exercise, although it seemed to have been a direct lift from a house at Hornchurch, Essex, 1933, by Stewart Thomson (n.d.).[149] This left McKean with a large number of less-than-scintillating Modern houses, factories, cinemas, roadhouses, pavilions, hotels, etc where fun, in most cases, very quickly became dumb, became glum became grim. Mies' glass curtain-wall had to wait till 1937, and David Harvey and Philip McManus's St Cuthbert's Cooperative Society Showroom, Bread Street, Edinburgh, or the Daily Express Building, Glasgow, 1936, by Sir E Owen Williams (1890–1969).

Meanwhile, McKean

> looks in vain, at Broughton, for any hint of Mackintosh influence ex Hill House; or even a baronialising of modern attitudes towards indoors/outdoors.[150]

He was right to have felt thwarted. Broughton Place, Broughton, 1936 by Kininmonth and Spence was not the first, nor would it be the last, only one of the more convincing, in a seemingly inexhaustible supply of throwbacks and clones. While the 16th and 17th-century Scottish tower-house may appear to have presented in the 1920s and '30s as an enduring Scottish architecture, amenable to whatever age in which it is situated, even to some minds *the* Scottish architecture *sans pariel*, it ceased to be so in this period for its architects. Traditionalist and Modernist alike, in their separate compromises, were unable to attain either the timelessness or the Modernity – let alone the sublimity – that Mackintosh had achieved for it. Mackintosh was Baronialism's apotheosis. Baronialism had a past, but not a future. It was a ghost. It continues to haunt Scottish architecture. Derrida, for once, was not wrong.

Going Dutch, part 1: Pevsner's link

The relative lack of architectural opportunity for all architects in the constrained 1920s was absolute in the 1930s up to ca. 1935, which led to a hiatus in the careers of many older architects[151] and the almost complete absence of opportunity for those few educated in the precepts of the Modern Movement in the early 1930s, only for that brief post-1935 window to be slammed shut in 1939 with the onset of WWII. Glendinning's et al Traditionalist/Modernist divide reached an antinomial conclusion, not in their post-rationalised social project, but in buildings of simple worth. Pevsner, in his uncorroborated claim that Mackintosh influenced the Dutch Expressionists of the Amsterdam School of the late 1910s and early 1920s, quite providentially hit on the sensibility, nascent in Mackintosh's oeuvre – and manifested in 1930s architecture – of an *accommodation* with the Expressionism of Dutch architecture and subsequently with the work of Willem Marinus Dudok (1884–1974), the city architect of Hilversum, 1928–54. Nevertheless, Langmead cautioned,

A more convincing Baronial clone: Broughton Place, Broughton, 1934, architects Kininmonth and Spence.

that there is absolutely no evidence to support the idea, first offered in 1935 [by former De Stijl member JJP Oud] and repeated *ad nauseum* that Dudok's individual manner was an amalgam of Amsterdam School fantasy and De Stijl's version of cubism.[152]

Berlage and Wright seem the more likely influences.

Though less-well-known than that of his contemporaries, the work of James Shearer, conditioned through his assistantship with Burnet, exemplified how Modernism in Scotland was represented as much, perhaps more so, in implicit technological innovation as it was in explicit Modernist aesthetic conformity. In 1912 he travelled briefly to Germany,[153] possibly in connection with the 1913 project to extend Campbell Walker's Carnegie Library, Dunfermline, 1880. The writer in *The Architects' Journal* commented favourably on

> the floors throughout the building, and the barrel vault and roof over the new lending department (which are of reinforced concrete)... [where] the arches and sub-divisions and coffers of the barrel vault (35ft. clear span) [10.67m], all are indispensable elements in the structure, and nothing superfluous has been added... the method of approach is one our contributor would like to see more fully explored, for it seems that in this direction a more architectural use of reinforced concrete than is usually practised might be reasonably sought.[154]

Alastair Service recorded the paucity of architect-designed reinforced concrete buildings constructed in Britain prior to 1914.[155] At the date of its design, Shearer's vault, on the Mouchel system, was the largest reinforced concrete structure of its type in Scotland, yet it was contained within a modified Traditionalist aesthetic.

Shearer's Traditionalist design for the Carnegie Birthplace Memorial, Dunfermline, 1926–8, for the Carnegie Dunfermline Trust (CDT) was preceded, in 1925, by a week in the company of Mrs Carnegie and Clive Barrow, her secretary, at the Carnegie Foundation offices in New York and Pittsburgh. Travelling by train through the Pennsylvania landscape, Shearer found parallels at home, for when

> we came to Johnstown – a large manufacturing town – two storey wood houses: factory chimneys: tanks: sheds etc. etc. and the whole place grimy and rain-sodden… Cowdenbeath at its worst could look no worse.[156]

The Memorial is an exercise in Traditional Scots architecture, constructed in a grey Swallowdrum sandstone with gauged Scotch slate roofs. It exhibits features that Shearer employed throughout his career: subtle planning; symmetry of the parts within an asymmetric composition; overlap or montage which he got from Burnet; the skewing of some aspect of the plan or detail; shallow projecting bays; coursed rubble contrasted with ashlar where all decoration, carvings, and lettering are intaglio, based on that of Abbot Pitcairn's (1520–84) tombstone in Dunfermline Abbey.[157] Viewed from Priory Lane, a Scots streetscape is maintained between the old and the new while from Moodie Street, the Carnegie cottage is privileged. The view of the south elevation from Rolland Street across the public garden, part of Geddes' aborted 1904 plan, takes on an American small town urban quality while the massing and the robustness of the detailing recalls the work of Henry Hobson Richardson. One of the eight Pittsburgh Carnegie Libraries available to Shearer in 1925 was at Allegheny, 1886–90, designed by the German-American architects John L Smithmeyer (1832–1908) and Paul J Pelz (1841–1918)[158] in Richardson's rugged Romanesque Revival manner.[159] There is much more in the *accommodation* of the Modern by the Traditional in this building than Gifford's assessment that it 'nannies the cottage'.[160]

Work was sparse in the succeeding five years and the Carnegie United Kingdom Trust (CUKT) appointed Shearer as consultant to the Cambridgeshire county surveyor and architect, HH Dunn (1865–1935), on the design of Sawston Village College, 1930. The village colleges[161] were the brainchild of Henry Morris, the County Education Officer, who, in Andrew Saint's (b. 1945) words,

American urbanism, Scots tradition: Carnegie Birthplace Memorial, Dunfermline, 1928, architect James Shearer.

> became an inveterate and unapologetic cadger to make up for the meanness of his county councillors.[162]

Saint, when I confirmed Shearer as the designer, agreed that 'its planning is rather more sophisticated than some people have given it credit for' and added,

> it would not surprise me if I were told that someone emanating from the Burnet office had improved the arrangements and perhaps the detailing of a rather stodgy county architect.[163]

The reviewer in *The Architect and Building News* (ABN), reflecting the theoretical confusions of the age, noted that:

> It would be a mistake as well as a disappointment to search for particular originality in the design, for the object was to co-ordinate traditional, and particularly 18th-century forms into a modern unity and, in effect, a new style has been evolved to meet a new idea.[164]

The Dunfermline Fire Station for Dunfermline Town Council of 1934, then, had no obvious aesthetic precedent in Shearer's earlier works, although it embodied many of his design principles. Perhaps the Council's insistence on a flat roof [165] predicated the more Modern form derived from Dudok's Hilversum Town Hall, 1930. Marcus Johnston (n.d.), former Shearer assistant and subsequently principal in Shearer & Annand, recalled the parapet being designed to disguise the presence of the flues from the firemen's apartments below and to maintain the Modern appearance.[166] The turbulence and downdraft thus engendered caused constant blowbacks in the open fires in those rooms.[167] William Dey (1911–97), who later worked with Shearer on the Clackmannan County Plan, claimed that Shearer, in the Fire Station, 'was making an explicit attempt to introduce Scottish feeling into the modern movement'.[168] The review in the ABN – thought to be by John Summerson – reported that

> this new building at Dunfermline recalls the work of Scotland's pioneer modernist Charles Mackintosh [sic]. Continental influence is not lacking, but it is pleasantly blended with a suggestion of Scottish vernacular tradition, and the picturesque grouping arises from a logically asymmetrical plan... [It] represents an interesting development from the same architect's Beautiful Carnegie Museum [sic].[169]

The ABN refers to Mackintosh at a time when his reputation was in reappraisal, most recently in Pevsner's *Pioneers of Modern Design*. The means by which Mackintosh allowed the planar elements of the end elevations in his great houses to slip past each other, providing sculptural significance to the ensemble of entrance/window/chimney, is replicated generically on the

Dudok in Dunfermline: Fire Station, Carnegie Drive, Dunfermline, 1935, architect James Shearer.

A modest monumentality: Hilversum Town Hall, 1930, architect Willem Marinus Dudok.
(GVR -own work, Creative Commons)

west elevation of Shearer's Fire Station. There is no evidence, however, that Shearer ever used Mackintosh as a model. He was known to admire the work of Lorimer and to own a copy of Lorimer's detail book.[170] References to 'continental influence' were on surer ground. Dutch and German work of the 1920s appears to be the inspiration. Dudok is evident in the overlapping planes of the front and side and in the treatment of the hose tower while, to the rear, the architecture becomes almost Germanically Expressionist such as in the Berlin work of Mendelsohn[171] in the dynamic tension of the asymmetric composition. 'Scottish vernacular tradition' is represented by the dynamism and asymmetry of the volumetric composition and in the detail of the masonry cartouche above the front door within the blue brick base and the little attached Scots Renaissance pylon/finials of similar overall form, performing the same framing function as those at the Carnegie Library; an accommodation of the Traditional with the Modern. The Fire Station is the first sighting of Shearer's mature style and one of the more striking and convincing examples in Scotland's rather thin catalogue of quality pre-WWII Modernist architecture.

On his visit to Holland to meet Dudok in 1952, Shearer observed that,

> we had no difficulty in finding Mr. Dudok's house... a quiet
> welcoming house, of moderate size; simple but infallible massing,

horizontal lines, deep shadows, a characteristic use of narrow brick; its authorship visible at a glance.[172]

Shearer recorded that, on studying some of his host's drawings, he

> asked [Dudok] about the tall, slender columns of the portico. 'Are those of concrete?' I asked. He replied 'No, they are of steel. I do not like exposed concrete. It is a good structural material, but I do not like the colour'.[173]

Shearer's work for the North of Scotland Hydro-Electric Board (the Hydro) between 1946 and 1963 gave evidence of his mastery of the Dudok idiom and its appropriateness to the Scottish landscape. To select just one, the stone-clad Fasnakyle Generating Station was opened in 1952 by the Duke of Edinburgh with the words:

> I am entirely relieved of all anxiety [that the Board was wantonly wrecking the Highlands]. To suggest that this power-house alone destroys the beauty of Glen Affric is being as fastidious as the fairy-tale princess who could feel a pea under 15 mattresses.[174]

Going Dutch, part 2: from Baroque to Dudok

The commercial Baroque of Burnet and others had aesthetic continuity within the neo-Classical family, but disconnect due to its temporal and societal distance from the origin of Classicism. It accommodated the Modernism of steel-framed American Beaux-Arts Baroque post-1891, Art Deco post-1925, and Dudok's more palatable and modest monumentalism post-1930, where he

> early achieved symbiosis between architecture and the decorative arts which would help save his mature work from the dead letter of Modernism.[175]

It had no need for fabulation in how it perceived itself or in how it was perceived by others because it was self-confident and attached no deep significance to its adoption of those various aesthetic approaches.

Adelaide House, London, 1919–25, by Burnet and Tait, was transitional and has significance in that it was the work of wholly Scottish architects who were part of an ideological thread that originated with Alison. As Glendinning et al noted,

We should bear in mind that, although Burnet's main office was located in the British capital, his practice was chiefly concerned with carrying forwards the developing Scottish Beaux-Arts world-outlook.[176]

But it is more than that. Burnet and Tait's choice of a version of Thomson's Greco-Egyptian at Adelaide House seems fortuitous. Tutankhamun's tomb, which galvanised the 1920s Egyptian craze, was not discovered until November 1922, post-dating by a year the publication of Tait's perspective of Adelaide House in *Academy Architecture* and by three years the date of Burnet's commission. Although Tait was dispatched to Egypt by Burnet both to supervise the construction of the war cemetery at Heliopolis (Port Tewfik) and to study Egyptian architecture, influences just as significant in the design may have been Tait's apprenticeship to a former Thomson assistant (James Donald [ca.1854–1917]) or the Audsleys' Bowling Green Office Building, New York, which he must have known from his time there.

Adelaide House, approached from London Bridge, takes the basic Burnet elevational mode, in limestone, of the colonnade, now transformed into mullions, sitting proud of the side pavilions and attic, and terminates it, over a tetrastyle in antis gallery with deeply recessed windows, in an imposing Egyptian cavetto entablature. The attic above this ends in a flat, unembellished cope. In the original design this was to be completed by a further terraced storey under an almost Wrightian overhanging canopy. This elevation treatment is repeated, almost, on King William Street. The central ground floor in contrasting grey granite has the overall form of the Bowling Green House entrances without the Thomsonian anthemion detailing. However, the symmetrically placed corner pavilion that might be expected where the

Thomson to Tait via Audsley: Adelaide House, London, 1925, architects John James Burnet and Thomas Tait.

(Stephen Richards - own work, Creative Commons)

building turns into Lower Thames Street is omitted and Adelaide House negotiates the corner in the same plane, although subtly different in detail, which then stretches across the Lower Thames Street elevation with minimal end pylons to contain the vertical piers between the windows as if in antis. The gallery and attic are as before. Grey granite bands emphasise the termination of the piers or pylons just below the gallery. Masonry in the piers or pylons is laid in alternating shallow and deep courses; not quite Thomson's pseudo-isodomic coursing, but appropriately neo-Greek nonetheless. Adelaide House also demonstrates the increasing sophistication of building technology and Burnet's willingness to use it: it is steel-framed and the first office building in Britain to have mechanical air-handling and telephone and electrical systems on each floor.

A more developed Expressionism is seen in Tait's house designs at Silver End, Braintree, Essex, 1926–32, Frank Crittal's (1860–1935) model village for the workers at his window manufacturing plant where some Amsterdam School single-family houses and Wright's Hollyhock House are the likely models. Burnet and Tait's Expressionist synthesis did not immediately find a home in Scotland, nor indeed in England, and their Art Deco design for the Daily Telegraph Building, Fleet Street of 1927–9, while retaining the overall *parti* of a colonnade proud of the end pavilions and attic, reverted, almost, to a stripped-down version of the Civil Service and Professional Association, Edinburgh. The Civil Service distyle in antis with attached columns is extended at the Daily Telegraph to a tetrastyle with attached columns in antis and from two floors to four, the fluted columns becoming quasi-Egyptian with lotus capitals, while an honorific balcony is interposed at second-floor level and some Expressionistic display cases with stilted jambs appear at ground floor.

Spanning most of the period, its politics, economics and architectural struggles was the saga of St Andrew's House (1912–39), which is comprehensively covered in David Walker's *An Edinburgh Controversy*.[177] Walker quoted author and MP John Buchan, who, having viewed HM Office of Works' proposals, warned the House of Commons in 1932 that:

> We are in danger very soon of reaching the point where Scotland will have nothing distinctive to show the world.[178]

Tait was appointed architect in 1933. Walker pinpointed the pivotal moment of his use of a symmetricised Dudok at the Royal Masonic Hospital, London, 1929, which is

> the radical shift in architectural direction for which Tait had been preparing... [and] never wavered from the path of modernity again.[179]

St Andrew's House draws the several American, Dutch and even Egyptian themes in Burnet and Tait's oeuvre together with the frontispiece of Paul Nénot's (1853–1934) Palace of Nations, Geneva, 1931–7, while transcending antinomially the seemingly eclectic consequences of its influences. The great south elevation is wholly Expressionistic. Walker quoted FA Warners's (Philip Anne Warners, [1888–1952]) Atlanta Building, Stadhouderskade, Amsterdam, 1927 as the Dutch influence. Arguably, this link accords with Pevsner's signposting of a route from Mackintosh to the Amsterdam School and Dutch Expressionism via, say, the stair towers at the Scotland Street School.

McKean, whose 1930s thesis was questioned by McMillan and Metzstein

The antinomy of St Andrew's House, Edinburgh, 1933–9, architect Thomas Tait.

in papers given at the 1990 Playfair Lectures at the Royal Society of Edinburgh, returned with a modified prospectus in 1991 entitled 'The Nordic Virus' wherein he promoted Dutch and, in particular, Dudok's architecture as significant. However, in summation, he did no better than to state:

> So much for the Dutch virus: modern, efficient, provides light, good views and air, and is characterised by clean lines and a marked absence of fuss.

He seemed unable to understand in depth what is Dutch about Dutch architecture and, disappointed again, concluded that there is '[n]ot much with which to ignite the world'[180] in it. He was even less convincing on Scandinavian and German influence, partly because it was sporadic and

233

partly because such influence is most clearly seen in the 1950s and beyond. Little wonder that his grasp of these architectures was so tenuous, given that his understanding of what is Scottish about Scottish architecture remained entirely formal, aesthetic and historic – 'c.1600... "our most national period"'.[181]

Amsterdam School Expressionist influence is apparent in Jack Coia's (1898–1981) brick frontispiece at St Patrick's, Greenock, 1934–5, in the ensemble of pointed brick arch, exaggerated voussoirs, concrete keystone, vertical fin and flat console at pediment level and mannered and mobile frontispiece at St Peter in Chains, Ardrossan, 1938, and in the triangular geometry of St Lawrence's RC Church, Greenock,

The influence of the Amsterdam School: St Peter-in-Chains RC Church, Ardrossan, 1938, architects Gillespie, Kidd & Coia.
(WF Millar, Creative Commons)

1951. Rodger saw in it 'clear influence from the continental work of Dudok and other contemporaries', and which, in a 20th-century recall of Campbell's comment on the 14th, he maintained anachronistically entailed 'an embrace

The expressionism of pleasure: Rothesay Pavilion, 1938, architects J & JA Carrick.

of the neo-Romanesque style'.[182] Dudok turned up at Hawkhead Hospital, Paisley, 1932–4, by Burnet, Tait and Lorne; and at Cardowan Pithead Baths, Lanarkshire, 1933, by JA Dempster (1892–1956). His influence was also apparent in leisure buildings such as Cragburn Pavilion, Gourock, 1935, combined with a bit of Mendelsohn and Serge Chermayeff (1900–96) lifted from the De La Warr Pavilion, Bexhill-on-Sea, 1935, at Rothesay Pavilion, 1936, both by James Carrick (1880–1940); and at the Cosmo Cinema, Glasgow, 1938, by James McKissack (1875–1940). Gropius's Expressionist entry for the Chicago Tribune Tower competition, 1922, by way of Mallet Stephens' Tourist Pavilion at the Paris Art Deco exhibition, 1925, and Dudok's De Bijenkorf Department Store, Rotterdam, 1930, was present in Tait's Tower at the Glasgow Empire Exhibition, Bellahouston, 1938.

A refined production in the Dudok mode was T Waller Marwick's (1903–71) stone-clad temporary headquarters for the National Bank of Scotland, George Street, Edinburgh, 1935 (demolished ca.1974). McKean quoted Hurd's 1938 claim that it was 'a direct descendant of Mackintosh's Glasgow School of Art Library',[183] although, again, this statement seems to have been driven more by the fervour of the contemporaneous resurrection of Mackintosh's reputation

From Gropius to Dudok to Tait: Tait's Tower and panorama, Glasgow Empire Exhibition, 1938, architect Thomas Tait.
(Wikimedia Commons)

and Hurd's Traditionalist/Modernist equivocation than with motives inherent in the design. Marwick's Modernity, which was subsequently to result in the loss or committee mutilation of his later designs and his desultory post-WWII practice, arrived at something rather more subtle than a Mackintosh interpretation.

At the National Bank of Scotland, Dudok was represented by its modest monumentality and the grouping of five stacked vertical windows incorporating an honorific keystone or decoration at the topmost window, in this case, a stylised allegorical figure and deep slot in the balcony front above. The range of horizontally-astragalled vertical windows began in a half-basement, with, successively, a 12-paned ground floor, under a narrow canopy/cornice linking to adjacent windows, a ten-paned first and an eight-paned second, separated by shallow-angled intermediate panels of an almost Czech cubist subtlety such as at Chochol's Neklanově ulice, Prague (see page 80). The heights of the ascending window were subtly mirrored in the heights of the descending spandrel panels. The windows could be read as a tetrastyle in antis, separated by flat mullions at ground floor and angled mullions above, although the angled intermediate panels, in montage, overlapped the bounding frame of the antis. This ensemble itself projected slightly from the plane of the elevation that contained the entrance door which was otherwise unpunctured and unmodulated. This in turn projected beyond the final plane of the building facade which terminated in an attic of a near Thomson character and which, due to the cumulative effect of the successive recessing of the planes, included the narrow balcony noted above. The attic, a hexastyle in antis, occupied very nearly the full width of the final plane and was topped by a narrow canopy/cornice, echoing that at the ground floor, and a deep parapet. The location of the door and the inverted 'L' of its side screen and canopy simply but effectively undermined the symmetry of the elevation.

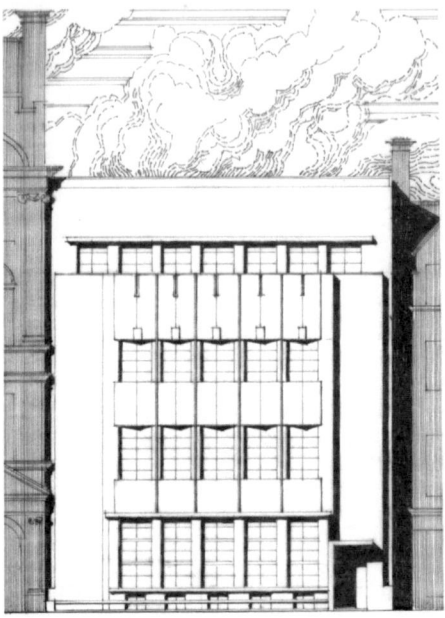

National Bank of Scotland, George Street, Edinburgh, 1937 (demolished), architect TW Marwick.
(Drawing by Roger Emmerson)

Marwick pared away his elevation, not as did Thomson from the centre out, but from the edges inwards. Such was the shallowness of the successive planes that the effect was similar, that is, that a planar structure was eroded to release the elevational form embedded within. This operation also recalled, in a way, Burnet's revealing of his principal colonnades or elevation ranges through the setting-back of the corner pavilions from the bulk of the façade such as at the King Edward VII wing at the British Museum, London, 1904. In this sense, and in this sense alone, does Hurd's Mackintosh observation have much meaning in that the shallow canted bays of the west and particularly the south elevations of the Glasgow School of Art West Wing could be read less as features applied to the elevation as, say, might be comparable elements in the work of Norman Shaw, rather more the paring away of the façade, from the edges in, even to the depth of exposing the random rubble side wall of the studios. Such adventitious paring away at the harled south elevation was presumably to meet property boundary conditions.

There are several reasons for choosing to devote space to a lost building by an architect little known outside architectural historical circles. Firstly, this small work drew together some of the issues of the preceding century thrown up by the work of pioneering Scottish architects and confirmed the continuity of certain significant forms both implicit and explicit in the work of Thomson, Gowans, Mackintosh, Burnet and Shearer. Secondly, it provided, in that continuity, a more reliable place for Mackintosh in the history of Modern architecture in recognising both his Scottish and international antecedents and influence, supporting and expanding on Pevsner's cryptic Expressionist assessment and rejecting the nonsense of the Craigievar/Mackintosh/Corbusier-Bauhaus fabulation. Thirdly, the National Bank of Scotland and buildings like it constituted, until very recent time, the last appearance of a thread of contemporary Scottish architecture that was both Modern and drawn from Scottish resources. Finally, both Marwick and the architecture he represented effectively disappeared during WWII. The thread was broken and the debate in Scottish architecture fractured along a divide represented, on the one hand, by the adherents of the International Style architecture of the Welfare State, governmental and corporate patronage and, on the other hand, of the now much smaller contingent promoting a 'golden age' Baronialism. The break was exemplified in Rodger's comment on the work of Gillespie, Kidd and Coia pre- and post-WWII:

> But if that achievement [of 1956 to 1987] 'arose from the launching pad of the reputation established by the practice before the 1939–45 war' then any real comparison of those two bodies of work separated in time reveals them to be something very different in terms of

historical, technological, architectonic and programmatic aims and influences.[184]

And therein lies one of the problems of Scottish architecture. The insufficiently critical assessment of the architecture of the 1920s and '30s, *pace* McKean, has skewed other subsequent interpretation of both pre- and post-WWII production.

Classical convention: the architecture of government and institutions

The rather more conventional use of neo-Classical and neo-Renaissance styles in representative buildings and the Baroque in large commercial buildings was maintained, although that virtually came to a stop in 1929 following the Crash and subsequent Depression, with only those buildings substantially underway at the time completing post-1930. The kick-start given to the economy in the late 1930s resulted in such as HM Office of Works' grimly squared-off Sherriff Court (now High Court), Lawnmarket, Edinburgh, 1934–7 (initially part of the St Andrew's House project). Professor T Harold Hughes's (1887–1947) trabeated brick-built stripped Roman Classical Glasgow University Reading Room, 1939, with its dated panopticon plan, perhaps perfectly illustrates the architectural philosophical conundrum of the 1920s and '30s. In Hughes's Reading Room, the continuity of the rather more overtly classically-derived forms begins to register as disconnect and fabulation. By way of contrast, his Chemistry Building for Glasgow University, 1939–54, is an elegantly symmetricised version of HP Berlage's Museum voor Moderne Kunst (Haags Gemeentemuseum), Den Haag, 1931–5, in which the continuity of the ordering tradition of Gilly's and, indeed, Alison's, stripped trabeation, volumetric composition and symmetry is maintained, but comes to an accommodation with Berlage's continuous development of a Modern monumental brick-built Dutch architecture and the spatiality of De Stijl, and is absolutely not, as McKean claimed it to be, 'Mendelsohnian'.[185]

Back to the future: the Glasgow Empire Exhibition

> Above the distracting noises of a confused world there rings out from this Exhibition a clarion call to the scattered family of the British Commonwealth of Nations to come together and talk as a family over

the old days and ways, and see the achievements in science, art and industry and in other spheres of two decades of peace.[186]

Thus, in 1938, did the Empire, now a cosy 'family' and a 'commonwealth', announce its aims, the first of which was predictably to look backwards. It ran from 3 May to 29 October 29, bracketing Neville Chamberlain's (1869–1940) 'peace in our time' moment.

Tait was commissioned for the masterplan and assembled a talented cast of Scottish designers: T Waller Marwick, Margaret Brodie, Launcelot Ross (1885–1956), Esme Gordon (1910–93), Gordon Tait (1912–99), Jack Coia, J Taylor Thomson (1887–1953), AD Bryce (1890–1940) and Basil Spence. The Exhibition introduced Scots to Modern architecture *en masse* for the first time, although, with very few exceptions – Coia's Scandinavian Palace of Industry North, Marwick's Lescaze-influenced Garden Club and Lucullus Restaurant, Brodie's Women of Empire Pavilion and Ross's sophisticated Palace of Art (the only extant pavilion) – the pavilions would not have been out of place at the Paris Art-Deco Exhibition 13 years before.

This was not a failing of Scotland's architects alone; pavilions by English designers were equally backward-looking: Joseph Emberton (1889–1956), who had exhibited at the MOMA exhibition in 1932, designed the vaguely Expressionist and pedestrian British Railways pavilion; Herbert Rowse (1887–1963), the United Kingdom Pavilion, an overblown version of his rather better Amsterdam School-inflected Liverpool Concert Hall, 1936; and R Furneaux Jordan (1905–78), best known as a teacher, writer and the author of a 1938 proposal to rebuild Princes Street, Edinburgh as a series of vast glazed blocks with a walkway at first floor level, paradoxically contributed the Timber Pavilion. Perhaps to meet the objective of directing 'attention to Scotland's historical and scenic attractions', the Exhibition also had its *fabulation* of Highland life, 'An Clachan', designed by the antiquarian architect Dr Colin Sinclair, where the curious visitor could find 'real Gaels, mending nets, making creels and spinning yarn',[187] much as they had done at Gowans's 'Old Edinburgh' in 1865 and at the 1911 Glasgow Exhibition. The Known were reframed as the Others and became strangers in their own land; the "sites/sights" of which Owens wrote (see Chapter 1).

5

Brave new world: 1939–68

A benevolent autocracy: Scotland in wartime

ON THE EVE of and throughout WWII, Scotland benefitted from two independently-minded Secretaries of State: the Conservative and Unionist MP Walter Elliot (1888–1958), 1936–8, who set up the Scottish Special Housing Association (SSHA) in 1937, and the Labour MP Tom Johnston (1881–1965), 1941–5. Johnston had an acute understanding of Scotland's economic woes and how he believed they must be addressed. Among several special entities he established were, in 1941, the Scottish Council of Industry to counteract the concentration of industry in the English Midlands which managed to return, he claimed, 700 businesses and 90,000 jobs to Scotland, although the temporary evacuation of essential industries from bomb-targeted English cities may have contributed to this total. In 1943, he created the North of Scotland Hydro-Electric Board, which had the subsidiary task of rescuing the moribund Highland stone-quarrying and stonemasonry industries. He expanded the Emergency Hospital Service, formed in 1939 to build new hospitals to cope with large numbers of civilian casualties from German bombing raids which never quite materialised, and went on to become a precursor of the National Health Service (NHS) provision by alleviating waiting lists for general hospital admissions. All involved areas – jobs, housing, health and infrastructure – which partial and inconsistent attention from previous Westminster governments had allowed to fester. Johnston was a supporter of Home Rule within the context of the Union and used his position and achievements to forestall the rise of outright separation.

Lynch cautioned that

[Johnston] wrote his own headlines, both before and after his period in office. His claim that 'we had to get Scotland's wishes and opinions respected and listened to as they had not been respected or listened to since the Union' has not yet been seriously disputed. It was centralisation without tears, devolution without anxieties. The intricate mechanisms of the new Union were a solution for a collectivist age.[1]

In the chaos of war, Johnston had a measure of autonomy, much of which was to initiate processes that were of direct benefit to architects and architecture in the decade subsequent to 1945. Nevertheless, from a British point of view, despite such a propitious start, post-1945 it was back to business as usual in the Secretary of State's office and, as Howarth noted, 'Scotland... remained in many respects an intractable problem'.[2] No one at Westminster seemed overly troubled to do anything about it and the problem was compartmentalised as a purely Scottish problem with random, ill-considered, top-down, sporadically-funded, short-term forays in economic planning and industrial intervention from London, later poignantly encapsulated in the words of the Proclaimers' 1987 song *Letter from America*. Over-optimistic market research, poor product concept and design, insufficient retraining of the workforce, inadequate infrastructure, distant and over-stretched supply chains and markets and grudging budgets did not amount to a recipe for success. The presentation of these projects and their funding as isolated headline-grabbing announcements underscored Scotland's post-Imperial supplicant status. The issue of local solutions not being funded consistently by a more equitable distribution of tax revenue remained unaddressed.

Under Britain's opaque fiscal system it is impossible to get at the truth of whether there is parity between the tax raised on total Scottish endeavour and the funds subsequently returned to Scotland for regional expenditure.[3] An Imperial economy is essentially extractive in practice based on the import of cheap raw materials from the colony and their subsequent export to the colony as value-added finished goods coupled with the centralisation of taxation and foreign trade in the Imperial capital; a state of affairs which, even in the Empire's shrunken condition, persisted in the Commonwealth until 1965, and yet remains in Britain. However, an extractive economy in Britain was not accompanied by an extractive political system as Acemoglu and Robinson have so defined it.[4] What was more clearly identifiable was an extractive cultural system where the self-appointed jury of achievement, principal marketplace and, consequently, point of origin for fiscal purposes of the regional artefact or product was deemed to be London and Oxbridge and not the region which had profound regional economic and cultural consequences.

By way of resistance, economic and cultural, the Scottish Covenant Association, formed in 1949, presented Westminster with a Home Rule petition containing 2 million signatures (out of a population of 5.1 million) in 1951. The Association's respectful plea concluded:

> With this end in view we solemnly enter into this Covenant whereby we pledge ourselves, in all loyalty to the Crown and within the framework of the United Kingdom, to do everything in our power to secure for Scotland a Parliament with adequate legislative authority in Scottish affairs.[5]

The Association had little political clout. The Tories proposed a Royal Commission, while Labour simply dismissed the petition out of hand. Centralisation, collectivism and consensus politics, with minor shifts left or right, were the mark of the period.

There were larger issues which concerned the British government because, in Ferguson's words, 'Britain was bust – and the Empire mortgaged to the hilt'.[6] Despite the familial sentimentality for Empire that had characterised the Exhibition in Glasgow not seven years earlier, now:

> The break-up of the British Empire happened with astonishing – and in some cases excessive – speed. Once the British had made up their minds to get out, they aimed to catch the first boat home, regardless of the consequences in their former colonies.[7]

Howarth noted graphically

> that the resources simply did not exist which would enable the British to remain sufficiently long in their former dependencies to avoid the bloodstained consequences of their departure.[8]

The accepted Imperial end date is 1956: when the lingering daily costs, although not the debt,[9] of WWII at home were at last reduced somewhat with the end of rationing; when Britain's gunboat-diplomacy was finally sunk in the Suez Canal; when the autonomous spheres of influence of the leading states of East and West were consolidated; when many British Marxists came to the delayed realisation that the Soviet Union was not the ideal communist model following its invasion of Hungary; and when the significance of the USA in these events as Western power-broker, strategic planner and International Monetary Fund (IMF) guarantor was confirmed. There was now no effective

Empire. The Commonwealth was a ceremonial substitute largely of benefit to the House of Windsor and to off-shore funds, Britain was the junior partner in the questionable 'special' relationship with the USA and Scotland's historic Imperial role was finally abrogated.

Whiteout: the blizzard of Modernist propaganda and policies

The Welfare State, through statute and ubiquity, substituted for the Modernist moral purpose embodied in the socially and 'scientifically' based programmes emanating in the 1920s and '30s from Europe which failed to take root in Britain in those years. The use of 'new' materials and new construction methods, the promotion, adoption or imposition of new modes of living and the new aesthetics of function came to define and underpin the architecture of the Welfare State and were, in part, predicated by it.

It was a time of pamphlets to reassure, squibs to encourage, conferences and reports to prepare the way, and policies to enact the framework of post-war development and its architectural production. The Town and Country Planning Association's Oxford Conference entitled *Replanning Britain*, 1941,[10] subtended from the conclusions of the Barlow Report on Industrial Planning, 1940.

The Conference Report is a fugitive document, its conclusions inevitably general, although determinedly centralist in authority and decentralist in purpose. The ghost of Ebenezer Howard (1850–1928) haunted the conference with many Garden City adherents present and Barry Parker (1867–1947) being presented with the Ebenezer Howard Memorial Medal for his significant contribution to Garden City planning. Ravetz identified the core issue precisely:

> As a practical discipline, [planning] was not too concerned with theoretical issues but tended to stick to the ideas formed during its evolution, or to borrow from other fields. Its practitioners justified this by the intrinsic and lasting value of the dictates of Howard and other founders; but if no equivalent ideas were put forward for 20th-century patterns, in particular for all that developed around economic growth and the 'end' of growth, the risk was obvious.[11]

Councillor Mrs Jean Mann (1881–1964) from Glasgow was a vocal Scottish delegate and, although not a platform speaker, took a prominent pro-Garden City part in post-talk discussions citing a 1934 survey of tenants in Kingswood, Glasgow who – 434 out of 500 – indicated a preference for 'cottages' over the tenements which she actively disliked.[12] She recounted a visit with fellow-councillors to Parker and Unwin's Letchworth and Welwyn, where

> their eyes were opened to a better life. The common people [sic] wanted a house and garden, but they could not pay the cost of travel to the suburbs.

She noted how Glaswegians went readily to Corby for employment opportunities in the steelworks there, although like many Garden City enthusiasts and, indeed, conference attendees generally, she seemed not to grasp that the larger effects of such centrally-directed urban depopulation and loss or redistribution of industry were among the long-term structural issues that dogged the Scottish economy. She continued:

> The drive for a more spacious environment must come from the people themselves; but the planners must stir their imaginations... one of the best methods would be some good films of Letchworth and Welwyn.[13]

Neither Letchworth nor Welwyn were centres of the kinds of industry prevalent in the West of Scotland – although Corby was – and consequently they were hardly the appropriate urban solution.

The conference's 'Nine Points' were, in brief, the need for: one, urgent action; two, a central planning authority; three, the central authority to be supra-governmental; four, redevelopment or decentralisation of urban centres and the diversification and balance of industry nationally; five, action to halt the drift of industrial population to London and the Home Counties as a structural, economic and strategic issue; six, the detail of the planning systems required by point four; seven, the central authority to have monitoring powers over all planning proposals; eight, the facilities for research and forward planning for changing economic circumstances; nine, ancillary activities pursuant to point two and in the exercise of the other stated aims.

Discussion of regionalism foundered on what actually constituted a region. The Geddesian territorial and patrimonial method was contrasted with the culturally incoherent but militarily appropriate and administratively aggregated wartime Civil Defence Regions. Professor (Sir) Patrick Abercrombie (1879–1957) was reported as proposing two ways of approach towards regionalism: one was the grouping of local authorities, the other was devolution from Westminster.[14]

Devolved regions defined territorially and patrimonially were problematic because, although it was what happened with Scotland, while the region was so defined, its administration, due to the Conference's centralising of authority, was not devolved. Prevention of the 'Home Counties' drift was never addressed, because that would be to confront the bastions of privilege dependent on the extractive nature of the British economy.

Abercrombie understood that it was the proposed centralist managerial aspects of planning, its organisation and implementation that would ultimately grant planners authority rather than (Sir) Frederick J Osborn's (1885–1978) more localised laissez-faire Garden City aesthetic. Towndrow quoted Abercrombie's hopes, still couched in the 1930s' abstractions of science and art, that:

> No matter what we did, no matter how we perfected our legislation and administration, we would still need ideals and imagination, and a living school of trained and enthusiastic designers to direct and carry out the work. Control was not enough; the mere prevention of muddle and ugliness does not by itself produce great art.[15]

Arguably, it was that foregrounding of 'art' and 'control', and the concomitant and immediate validation by its producers of the resultant production as having the status of architecture, although that accreditation was more correctly in the subsequent gift of others, which was part of the cause of later trouble. Absent entirely from the Conference's deliberations was any discussion of architectural patrimony, which left MacRae's meticulous *The Heritage of Greater Edinburgh*[16] of 1947 as a prescient exemplar of the kind of conservation studies which became widespread in the 1970s. The emphasis, for the moment, was all on the new and its polity.

Building Scotland: Past and Future[17], ca. 1944, by architects Alan Reiach, the Modernist, and Robert Hurd, the Traditionalist, was both pamphlet and squib, both reassurance and encouragement. In a process of selective, oranges and apples comparison, the authors chose those familiar douce and largely white examples of Scottish 16th and 17th-century churches, halls, houses and terraces and 18th-century sma burgh townscapes with which they contrasted the incommensurate products of the soot-stained 19th-century industrial city.[18] They also placed, within adjacent pages of the book, examples of the best of 1930s European practice alongside the most dismal contemporaneous Scottish

The old-is-the-new-is-the-old: *Building Scotland* by Alan Reiach and Robert Hurd, ca. 1944.

versions, thereby to insinuate by physical proximity and the association of a shared whiteness and paratactical fenestration of the examples of European Modernism and sma burgh Scotland that a theoretic, aesthetic and practical connection existed between the best recent European practice and that of a pre-19th century Scotland; 'the-old-is-the-new-is-the-old'. The clue, of course, is in the book's title. In their penultimate statement, of a typical Scottish inferiorism, a conspicuous and celebrated isolate was employed to cement that putative connection and to diminish all else. Their recusing gaze asserted that:

Not we, but those in other countries profited by the pioneer work of Charles Rennie Mackintosh in Scotland, and it is mainly to other countries that we must look for the flowering of good 20th century architecture.

Reiach and Hurd provided an early Scottish slant on a more widespread drive to educate the British public in matters of Modern design and the consequent behaviours required by it.

Penguin produced the populist series *The Things We See*, the first volume being the Canadian Alan Jarvis's (1915–72)[19] *Indoors and Outdoors*[20]. A discussion of 'good taste' was initiated and then hurriedly resiled from,[21] although 'good taste' and the obligatory acquisition of a commensurate 'discernment' were implicit throughout the text and images. The suggestion was that for British society – or at least, for some suitably informed and influential part of it – the choice of the better product and better environment was immediate, available and within each individual's orbit rather than at the discretion of a distant and distanced authority. However, it *was* a distant and distanced authority which, on the pretext of engaging in open discussion, dictated standards from the safety of the printed page, because, as the publisher conceded, this series 'was undertaken as a result of suggestions made to [them] by the Council [of Industrial Design (COID)]'. Other titles in print or in preparation at this time were *Furniture, Pottery and Glass,*

Public Transport, Ships and *Gardens*,²² which was a substantial reduction from the almost manic comprehensiveness of the original prospectus and which included *Radios, Textiles, Lettering and Printing, Advertising, Shop Windows, Private Cars, Aircraft, Domestic Equipment, Shops and Cinemas, The Things We Wear* and, incredibly, *Toys*.²³ As Aristotle said, 'give me a child until he [sic] is 7 and I will show you the man'.

Lionel Brett (Lord Esher) (1911–90) contributed the second volume, *Houses*. Brett wrote, allegedly,

> not for the architect, but for the man and woman who pay the piper, and have every right to call the tune.²⁴

Although such choice remained – as it always had and as Brett knew and confirmed by his examples that it did – the preserve of the client with resources for bespoke design. Brett privileged Baudrillard's 'model', not his 'series' (see more below), excluding from his consideration 'flats, shacks, maisonettes and mansions', although his intent was clearly to insinuate the 'series'. He employed domestic stooges and named them. 'Clarence' was a nondescript speculative house-builder's neo-Tudor villa, which he deplored. 'Fred' was a neat local authority bungalow designed by those skilled regional residential architects of the 1940s to the early 1970s, the Scottish-Dutch Herbert Tayler (1912–2000) and David Green (1912–98), which he quite liked.²⁵ Brett talked of 'the return of the prodigal son'²⁶ (Georgian vernacular) and 'the return to a friendlier texture'²⁷ (brick, stone and timber) and required that 'the cactus must learn to flower',²⁸ whereby he confirmed the historicity and dated aesthetic of Yorke's only very recently Modern houses. However, Brett's brief discussion of contemporary domestic planning and novel construction techniques referred exclusively and specifically to those required to construct the high-rise and mass housing projects which were to come for the many, while he illustrated *only* the individual house or the polite terrace which was for the few.

Ralph Tubbs (1912–96), designer of the Dome of Discovery at the Festival of Britain, 1951, took a Marxist historical approach in his *The Englishman Builds*. In 'Scene Four: The Age of Classical Convention', headed by a portrait of that well-known Englishman, Robert Adam, he noted that

> the pure classicism of the upper classes never succeeded in divesting itself of a certain artificiality and unreality,²⁹

thus implying an unexplained authenticity and reality inhering in the 'architecture of the people'. All this was by way of introducing the reading public to the 'scientific' new architecture while contrarily noting its dependence of the *zeitgeist,* because its

> fate... lies in our own hands. It will achieve a place amongst the great architectures, only if we have a set of values which are not entirely materialistic, if we have faith in the Spirit of Mankind, if we have eyes that have learnt the power of discrimination.[30]

Taste, discernment and discrimination; the watchwords of a design elite.

Max Fry in *Fine Building*, meanwhile, jumped to the other extreme and replanned London *au Corbusier*.[31] When he engaged with the planning of the flat, he indulged in familiar associative reasoning. He invited favourable comparison between the axonometric of the 'work unit' (kitchen and bathroom) at Kensal House, London, 1937 – designed by himself and Elizabeth Denby and based, in part, on the Frankfurt kitchen (see above) – illustrated in Fig. 4[32] with the rather more luxurious kitchen and bathroom illustrated in Plates 19 and 20. Fry wrote:

> Now remember, if you can, the swaggerest kitchen you ever saw in the Ideal Home exhibition at Olympia, with lots of cupboards and a double sink in shining metal with swivel taps, and a gleaming white refrigerator that lights up when the door is opened, a plate rack over the sink, a cooker with a hood over it, and all manner of other things to comfort the heart of a housewife and bring joy to her work.[33]

Setting aside yet another attempt at the materialist seduction of women as proxy in the promotion of the *existenzminimum* flat, *none* of the culinary blandishments which Fry listed was visible in the Kensal House 'work unit'. In passing, Fry's 'giant hand from the sky' illustration[34] was hardly a sage comparison of the competing strengths and weaknesses of Modernist or Traditionalist construction options, as it ripped either the reinforced concrete-framed or mass masonry house off their foundations, the framed building more or less intact apart from some loose plumbing, the masonry building shedding bricks, stones and timbers in quantity. An image which was barely relevant even in Tornado Alley: 'Toto, I've a feeling we're not in Kansas anymore'.[35]

Fry summed up his position:

> The history of 19th-century architecture is a chart of the winds that blew there and has little or no bearing upon present development. The bases of the art were lost and we are seeking them today. That is all.[36]

Except the bases were not lost. Simply, Fry and his pals – deliberately or not – mislaid them. It is difficult to know for whom Fry wrote. There was a deal of practical explanation of the facts of the new architecture, but also a great amount of rarefied architectural theorising in the final chapter. Perhaps the key message came early in the text:

> If I consider honestly the course of architecture and town planning after this interruption of war, not forgetting the impetus to new works that peace will bring, I am bound to admit that development will rest, as it must always rest, upon the capacity of the common people [sic] to understand and to appreciate the quality of good things, and doing so to place their confidence in those who can best help them to it.[37]

Other than Penguin Books' COID-inspired *Things We See* series, there was no sense of an overarching organisation behind these contemporary publications from Penguin, Pilot Press, Faber & Faber or the Saltire Society. However, there was plainly a widely shared and interlocking agenda amongst design pundits north and south of the Border about how things *must* be post-War and how society at large *should* 'understand and appreciate' the pundits' efforts. Jarvis's fabrics were to embellish Brett's and Reiach's homes that sat in Richards's suburbia, though more likely in Fry's slab blocks.

There was resistance of a sort. Looking back over the first half of the 20th century in 1946, Richards claimed prejudicially of the suburban house that:

> It is each individual Englishman's [sic] idea of his own house, except for the cosmopolitan rich, a minority of freaks and intellectuals and the very poor.[38]

He echoed Brett and anticipated Bachelard, who were both likewise unable to encompass the fact that the choice of the new flatted accommodation in England was preferred by the few (the cosmopolitan rich), necessitated for some (the freaks and the intellectuals) and obligated for most (the very poor). Scottish cultural attitudes to the ubiquitous and classless four or five, occasionally 6-storey flatted tenement, were markedly different. Richards' suburbia was a petit bourgeois redoubt against

> the general world, where problems are largely those created by the transitional stage through which it is passing... [whereas] the suburban style shall continue to contain an element of fantasy and make-believe.[39]

The specificity, poetry and fantasy with which Richards imbued the Englishman and his suburban retreat was less relevant for Scots culturally than was the fact that through the centralising agency of several 1930s housing acts, cheap mortgages and the activity of the speculative builder, suburbia, as Lynch pointed out, became part of Scotland's urban reality too. MacTaggart and Mickel's Broom Estate brochure, lavishly produced, unusually for the 1930s, with colour reproductions, eulogised:

> For natural beauty this Estate cannot be equalled by any other in Scotland, or for that matter, in Britain. Here, in the quiet calm that Nature demands for her own, we find magnificent old oaks, stately young pines, firs, and trees of every description; in summer months, flowering shrubs and bushes give a veritable blaze of colour, and in the dark days of winter a large variety of evergreen bushes softly shade the tone of an already magnificent landscape. To further increase its charm, picturesque streams, which have their source somewhere in the moorlands of Renfrewshire, wind gaily through the Estate, suddenly widening out into a delightful miniature lake [sic], to mirror this picture of a perfect painting. This lake has a background of rhododendron bushes which flower in a multitude of colours, the beauty of which must be seen to be appreciated.[40]

Tools of the trade: a Modernist education for architects

As with society at large, not all architects were on board with the new architecture; certainly not with the theory or the technical skills. Texts were made available to those who otherwise were inclined to consult such authorities as the incredibly dated *Mackay's Building Construction*, published only as recently as 1938.[41] In the first, edition of his *New Ways of Building*, 1948, editor Eric de Maré (1910–2002) was concerned that:

> In the gigantic job of building which faces this country, in spite of present restrictions [of building permits and materials] architects will eventually be presented with greater opportunities than they have ever had before. But there is a danger that many of those opportunities, both aesthetic and practical, will be missed through lack of time to study and assimilate new ideas and techniques.[42]

For de Maré, as for Yorke, Reiach, Jarvis, Tubbs, Brett and Fry, it was not only the matter of architects' acquisition of current technical and material knowledge and technique that was at issue, but also their engagement with a new society, because:

> The work of both planner and architect, and of the specialised technician too, depends in its turn on something even wider and more difficult to define than the physical framework – the cultural *milieu* itself.[43]

The 'cultural milieu' was that already set out in those authors' 'brave new world' texts, based on little more than their personal opinion and that of their cohort.

De Maré's 'milieu', for some, was one of radical and enforced change and adaptation and, according to John Madge,[44] insecurity:

> In view of the rapid – and increasing – mobility of the population, it is already the exception for any one family to go on living in the same house for more than a decade. This mobility makes nonsense of the suggestion that security of tenure is the basic element in promoting the stability of family life.[45]

In the construction of the modern house, Madge preferred the economies of scale, the benefits of standardisation and prefabrication, and the use of 'new' materials and techniques. He claimed of brick construction that

> it would be a mistake to encourage further capital investment in those branches of the building materials industry which are generally agreed to have passed their heyday... [and that] the perpetuation of an obsolescent craft by the strength of vested interest cannot be tolerated... The centre of gravity of the building process... is shifting from the craftsman to the drawing board and to the machine shop.[46]

Madge seemed to have no real understanding of the practical production processes and end-product differences between the precision engineering required of the frequently comparatively referenced automotive industry and the crudity and approximation of the off-site of casting steel-reinforced concrete panels. Unfortunately, as a denizen of Madge's brave new world, it was the poorly-trained, poorly-paid, unmotivated, inadequately-supervised, unskilled labourer, now lacking even domestic security, who was expediently placed in a key role in both the manufacture and assembly of the pre-fabricated buildings that were to be its brave new patrimony.

As a design and management handbook, *The Information Book of Sir John Burnet, Tait and Lorne*[47] became, by the 1940s, the *Architect's Journal*'s (AJ) 'Handbook' featuring contemporary architectural detailing each week. *The Architect and Building News* (ABN), likewise, had a weekly 'Architects' Portfolio' from 1949 onwards, and matched the AJ with *Architects' Detail Sheets*,[48] which it published in book form in 1952. Neither contained the millennialist preaching of the texts quoted above – perhaps the assumption was that task was done – and were concerned solely that architects working in these new media should get it right. The AJ's details were initially derived from the work of Burnet, Tait and Lorne, while the ABN incorporated work from around the world: Le Corbusier's balcony detail from l'Unité d'habitation, Marseille; fireplaces by Born and Chermayeff and Marcel Breuer; an external staircase by Marcel Breuer; prefabricated window surround by Belgioiosi, Peressutti and Rogers; the rooflight at St Peter's College by Gillespie, Kidd and Coia, and so on.

The final wave of this flood of information and opinion was that which became government policy such as the technical studies produced by the Ministry of Works (MOW) and the Scottish Housing Advisory Committee (unfortunately acronymised as SHAC). The MOW's *Post-War Building Studies No. 1: House Construction*, published in 1944, was a review of experiments in non-traditionally constructed houses conducted in the 1920s and '30s, their performance in use and their applicability in assisting to procure the projected 4.5 million units required within ten years of the war's end. Axonometric projections of the experimental types clearly conveyed the essence and detail of their construction. There was a cautious welcome that a number of these systems only required unskilled labour, for example:

> As with other types of poured concrete a large percentage of unskilled men can be employed.[49]

> Local authorities and builders stated that both types [of concrete house] can be built more rapidly than normal brick houses and with a high proportion of unskilled labour.[50]

> Unskilled labour was used to erect the wall slabs; but some experience seems to be advisable, for it was noted that the Boot houses built on the Castelnau estate for the LCC, where skilled operatives were available, had been much more free from trouble than similar houses elsewhere.[51] Semi-skilled engineering labour was employed in the erection of the cast-iron plates.[52]

In the 'Summary of Report and Conclusions', the authors remarked:

> Many concrete walling systems, either as precast or poured in situ, are good alternatives. They give scope for the employment of unspecialised labour, with the possibility of some increase in the speed of erection of that part of the building. It must be realised that the success of concrete construction depends on the careful control of materials and workmanship... Further systems suitable for labour untrained in the building industry are being encouraged.[53]

They called for

> a high degree of organisation on site... if the full benefits offered by standardisation are to be obtained.[54]

Unskilled labour was now transferred from the enclosed and theoretically tightly-monitored production-line of Madge's pre-casting factory to the weather-dependent and scattered environs of the building site – or was present at both locations – while the caveats about control and supervision, seemingly more feasible in the factory than on the building site, came to haunt the prefabrication industry later due to their relative absence. Moreover, there was unexamined irony in that the provision of social housing and infrastructure was to be obtained cheaply and speedily, based, in part, on the deskilling and de-waging of the industry whose workers, in some measure, were to be the users of those self-same houses, health centres, schools and hospitals.

At this time, the non-traditional systems under consideration were almost exclusively for two-storey semi-detached houses or four-in-a-block flats. While many later proved to have defects, they were not, perhaps, in quite the same order of magnitude of fault as what was actually built in pursuit of the standardisation and prefabrication of high-rise slab and point-blocks, although defects in both low- and high-rise experiments were especially challenging for owners and, subsequently, purchasers under 1980 Right-to-Buy legislation and their tenants. In this context, undue reliance was placed on manufacturers' and contractors' claims for the suitability in use of systems based on those originating in the 1930s and earlier in France, Netherland, Germany and Denmark within more clement climates and familiarity in the historic use of these systems and building industry regimes and practices where there were not the same culturally-imbricated, hierarchical, patronising and negative attitudes to unskilled labour; all markedly different to what pertained in Scotland.

Also enthusiastic about standardisation and prefabrication was *Planning Our New Homes* of 1944,[55] which included considerable study of house planning and a positivist statistical analysis of a questionnaire of preference[56] and illustrated this with plans thus derived. It hazarded how these houses might look, offering options of conventional types of vertical proportions and pitched roofs and Modernist versions of those having flat roofs and horizontally-oriented windows. Significantly, little shown was over four storeys in height. The conventional types were very much in line with various model dwelling types produced in the 1930s. There were also pages devoted to the same visual comparisons presented in *Building Scotland* – no surprise given that Reiach was Secretary to the Advisory Committee's Sub-committee on Housing Design. Everything shown was of a cosy sma burgh or Garden City cast, and the only building over four storeys illustrated and accorded approval was Kensal House, London. However, lurking in paragraph 22, spotted and objected to by the keen-eyed Jean Mann, was this:

> If lifts are provided, the number of storeys clearly depends on the particular conditions of locality and we do not altogether exclude the possibility that in some districts, particularly in the large cities, blocks of flats of six to ten storeys may be appropriate, provided the overall density of the development is not excessive and ample provision is made for open space, recreational facilities, etc.[57]

Of the 24 plans shown in the book's Appendix 1 there were four designs for flats, only one of which had provision for a lift for a building over four storeys in height and which was illustrated neither in elevation nor in context, although plainly the provision of multi-storey accommodation formed a significant part of the intended housing programme. Furthermore, Mann cared little for the committee's conclusions on kitchen design, noting that

> most women prefer the square kitchen of about 130 square feet [12 sq.m, twice the area of the Frankfurt kitchen] and want the intimate planning of this to be left to themselves.

Mann concluded:

> My chief criticism is that in these smaller matters [kitchen planning] the Committee have overplanned, and that in the larger vital issues [high-rise development] they have not recognised the need for planning.[58]

Reiach's colleague Robert Matthew (1906–75) had already interested the Department of Health for Scotland, and was employed by them, with a proposal based on Bauhaus *zielenbau*.[59] In such a context, *Planning Our New Homes* was the Trojan Horse. It was dressed up in *Building Scotland*'s tendentious the-old-is-the-new-is-the-old argumentation, implied a generous allocation of green space to each family in Garden City layouts, split the model plans into 'short-term' and 'long-term', implying the former were to resolve pressing immediate housing need and the latter the preferred permanent solution. Only the latter had decent and flexible accommodation and the former became the norm in that inexorable process whereby the minimum becomes, at best, the optimum, at worst, the maximum. Soon paragraph 22, and its sub-section, out of 392 paragraphs, came to define a sizeable portion of Scotland's urban housing programme in the 1960s.

Young, Willmott and Stacey's study of populations in Bethnal Green and Essex, published as *Family and Kinship in East London* in 1957,[60] challenged the positivist and statistical basis on which much contemporary Modernist housing theory was based. It described the way of life, community and support systems of those who inhabited the urban slums and who were, arguably, shortly to become either the dwellers in that brave new world or were required to make way for it. By the time *Family and Kinship* appeared in print, the edifice of the Welfare State consisting of the 1947 Town and Country Planning Act, the housing, schools, hospital and university construction programmes arising thereby and their approved ethos and aesthetic, was firmly in place and not susceptible to subsequent amendment by evidence of actual scientific study to any great degree.

It is essential to stress that the academics, administrators, architects and their amanuenses pursuing these Modernist objectives were not bad actors of ill-intent – the housing and infrastructure needs were self-evident – simply that they were constrained by their patent need to belatedly join the Modern Movement. They were liberated – 'ecstatic' in Rowe's terminology – in that the practice of canonic Modernism, denied them in the 1930s and '40s, was now to be made available through the corporatist structures of the state, industry and commerce. They were limited by the social conventions of their class, having little understanding of communities not their own. They were supported in this by the Modern Movement's notion of an acculturated, democratised and universalised individual such as was characterised by McIntyre which alleviated the need for further detailed sociological and cultural investigation or familiarisation. Unquestionably, those rehoused enjoyed a honeymoon where the amenities provided and their initial maintenance, both within the dwelling and beyond it, exceeded tenants' previous experience by some margin. Films made between 1961 and 1968, held in the National Library of Scotland's Moving Image Archive, record public satisfaction and optimism. The sense of some of the rehoused, in those early years, as being initially willing participants in a great social enterprise is palpable.

When and what: the appearance of Modernism

For a brief moment, Modernism in Scotland might have looked like Furneaux-Jordan's glass and steel Princes Street, Edinburgh or like the 1945 Bruce Report for Glasgow.[61] Robert Bruce (1900?–56), City Engineer and Master of Works for the City of Glasgow, in his central Glasgow plan, conflated mid-rise versions of Bauhaus *zielenbau* and Le Corbusier's *ville radieuse* blocks in an axial processional plan comparable to Albert Speer's grand avenue at Germania. All of central Glasgow was to be razed to the ground in a manner Reichsmarschall Goering could only have dreamt of a few years previously and a new city was to rise from the *tabula rasa*. A massive central boulevard and park bridged the Clyde, connected huge north and south railway stations of a bloated 1938 Empire Exhibition aesthetic, and encompassed all the major representational and administrative buildings. The whole was contained within a motorway box of which only two sides were subsequently constructed as the M8. Bruce's vision remained council policy until it was overtaken by Abercrombie and Matthew's Clyde Valley Regional Plan of 1949 and the proposal to resolve Glasgow's urban malaise through decentralising industry and population to 'overspill' housing as far distant as Haddington, East Lothian, or encouraging their transfer to the Mark I New Towns of East Kilbride, designated 1947, and Glenrothes, designated 1948. The tussle between the transfer of population away from the city and Glasgow's bent to rehouse those displaced by bomb damage and slum clearance in point and slab-blocks within its royalty was as much about the retention of local tax revenue as it was about rehousing. A softer approach was the Inch Housing Scheme, Edinburgh, 1946–52, won in competition by the Garden City-influenced English architect David Stratton Davis (1919–2000), which more nearly equated to the preferred sma burgh aesthetic of the several Scottish housing documents, receiving a Saltire Award for the best-designed local authority housing in Scotland, 1953. It has been suggested that a multi-storey alternative was under serious consideration in 1952 just prior to construction.

The Festival of Britain, 1951, in contrast to the stolid and portentous 1938 Glasgow Empire Exhibition, looked febrile and whimsical: febrile in that it seemed to perpetuate an 'imperial anxiety' and the overweening boosterism of

Sma burgh urbanity: Inch Housing Estate, Edinburgh, 1951–3, architect David Stratton Davis.

the *Britain Can Make It* exhibition of 1946; and whimsical in the sense that the implicit and complacent superiority of a 'we-can-still-laugh-at-ourselves' attitude yet had currency in post-Imperial British life. It was lightness of surface not depth of substance that was addressed. Terence Cuneo's (1907–96) illustration for the special Festival edition of the *Illustrated London News* had an anxious-looking Britannia staring to her right out of the frame – certainly not to the future, and definitely not to the future represented by the exhibition on her left, perhaps there was another future to her right that unnerved her – while the delicate fingers of her right hand lightly brushed an indistinct globe covered in unrecognisable brown and green splodges with not the slightest hint of Imperial pink to be seen. Behind her, the 'Englishman-who-builds' looked out towards Tubbs's Dome of Discovery over an unfamiliar low-rise London – the tallest building visible being Ralph Knott's (1878–1929) County Hall, 1911.[62]

Reyner Banham observed that

> it is difficult to find a better collective noun [than *establishment*] for all the salaried spokespersons of the Council of Industrial Design, the editorial 'We' of the *Architectural Review*, and other former officers and gentlemen whose common triumph 'the Festival Style' undoubtedly was – and who later and almost unwittingly became the guardians of the myth.[63]

The 'establishment' included those responsible for much of the Modernist propagandising of the 1940s. Banham questioned both the 'Englishry' and the novelty of the festival's architecture and design and identified the origins of the Festival Style in the Triennali di Milano of 1930 and 1948 and, respectively, their de Chirico colonnades and lightly-framed tension structures. CIAM 8 took place concurrently at Hoddesdon, Hertfordshire, attended by the likes of Le Corbusier, Tange Kenzō, Jaap Bakema (1914–81), Sigfried Giedion, Josef Lluìs Sert (1902–83), Ernesto Rogers (1909–69) and others. Banham remarked:

> The lack of any raving enthusiasm on the part of the guardian spirits of modern architecture may well have been due to a sense that there was nothing very new about what could be seen at the Festival – though the British deserved a bit of a pat on the back for finally having caught up.[64]

The Festival's design legacy seemed to have been primarily of benefit to the illustrators of popular science fiction, although Frank Hampson's (1918–85) illustration of Mekonta in the *Eagle* comic, issue 15, 21 July 1950, suggested some graphic cross-fertilisation.[65] Reina Mary Bull's (1923–2000) cover illustration for *New Worlds: Fiction of the Future*, Autumn 1951, incorporated the Festival Hall, the Dome of Discovery and the Skylon,[66] while James Stark's (pseudonym for American history-writer and graphic artist Robert Conroy Goldston [1927–82]) late 1950s illustrations for the short-lived (1956–9) Scottish science fiction magazine *Nebula* showed Festival-like structures,[67] as did those of Brian Lewis (1929–78)[68] who later worked on the Beatles' animation *Yellow Submarine*, 1968.

The more robust architectural detailing of Lansbury Estate, Poplar, London, by Frederick Gibberd (1908–84) constructed as the Festival demonstration project in 1951–2, had greater success. Its Scandinavian-influenced[69] repertoire of verticality, concrete-tiled or copper-clad pitched roofs, flat roofs with narrow projecting eaves, patterned and projecting brickwork, narrow columns, projecting concrete canopies and balconies, gridded balcony fronts and narrow concrete window surrounds was ubiquitous. In Scotland its progeny can be found, modestly, in Sir Frank Mears's Housing and Coronation Clock Tower, John Street, Penicuik, 1953; in Basil Spence's housing at Dunbar, 1951; in Robert Gardner-Medwin's (1908–95) Sighthill Health Centre, Edinburgh, 1951; in Rowand Anderson, Kininmonth and Paul's Pollock Halls of Residence, Edinburgh, 1959, among many others.

The period was characterised by pragmatists and idealists. This is not to imply that the pragmatists lacked ideals, simply that they were not slaves to those ideals and were prepared to make compromises. The idealists were represented by individuals as various as FRS Yorke (initially), Robert Bruce, Alan Reiach and Max Fry while the pragmatists were the likes of JM Richards, Lionel Brett, Jean Mann, Robert Matthew and Patrick Abercrombie, although it should not be assumed there was unanimity in these loose groupings. The idealists found themselves on the wrong side of history because they got it hopelessly wrong (Bruce) or because they hoped for a last epiphany (Fry with Le Corbusier at Chandigarh, India) or were stuck in time for a while (Yorke) or with little work (Reiach). The pragmatists had the ear of government (Matthew and Abercrombie) or became international and corporatist (Yorke, making an effective switch, at Yorke, Rosenberg and Mardell [YRM], or Matthew with Robert Matthew, Johnson Marshall and Partners [RMJM]) or accepted employment in the rapidly expanding architects' departments in Local Authority and the New Town Development Corporations.[70] The pattern for the next 20 years was set by the pragmatists through their involvement in government policy, in the architecture of corporatism, in architectural education and through the waning impact of the first generation of Modernists. CIAM split in 1955 and imploded in 1959. In 1956, Team Ten was created, comprised of the younger CIAM members – Aldo van Eyck (1918–99), Alison (1928–93) and Peter Smithson (1923–2003), Giancarlo de Carlo (1919–2005), Ralph Erskine (1914–2005), Oswald Mathias Ungers (1926–2007) – all of whom were to be of significance in the architecture of the latter half of the 20th century.

The idealism of the 1940s very soon clashed with the constraints of budget, vision and context. Berthold Lubetkin's (1901–90) Expressionist Modernist urbanism of high-rise town-centre development, which he pioneered at Spa Green Estate, Finsbury, London, 1946, had no place in the low-rise solution demanded at Peterlee New Town by the perversity and economic necessity of continued coal extraction from seams directly beneath the new works which adversely affected ground bearing capacities. Meanwhile, his individualistic elevational treatments were at odds with the positivist expectations of his paymasters. He resigned the commission in 1950. However, even Richards, brought face-to-face with the physical representation of the new suburbia of his imagining, found a lack of urbanity in the low-density, low-rise planning of the Mark I New Towns:

> It should hardly be necessary to emphasise that a town is, by definition, a built-up area, whose role is to provide for a particular mode of living. It is a sociable place, for people who want to live close together, and expresses itself as such through the compactness of layout, through the sense of enclosure experienced within it and through being composed of streets. The new towns, by and large, have none of these attributes.[71]

He was incapable of coming to any conclusion on Glenrothes and East Kilbride because, as he claimed, they were

> predominantly miners' towns [and] depend upon the special circumstances of the coal industry and are therefore not typical.[72]

Nonetheless, they shared the same economic *raison d'être* as Peterlee; perhaps they were just too Scottish and 'therefore not typical'.

However, what *really* troubled him was the patent failure of his hoped-for new vernacular of the suburb, postulated in *Castles on the Ground*, which he seemed to have imagined was implicit and realisable in the new town concept and which, very nearly, had him double back on his suburban argument:

> The battle against the disintegration of the town is not a new one… with garden-city enthusiasts taking one side and the modern architects the other… the former quite unjustifiably identified the idea of a garden city with low density building… and the latter allowed themselves to be side-tracked into a different and unreal battle of cottages versus flats, thereby making the garden city fanatics a present of the allegiance of that majority of Englishmen [sic] who are wedded to the idea of the one-family house with its bit of garden.[73]

Meanwhile, Brett was constrained by a particular English preciousness which had him splitting hairs with Richards. For Brett, urbanism 'is intimacy, enclosure, floorscape, immediacy, all the pleasures of the small cathedral town',[74] none of which made much sense to the inhabitants of the Scottish Central belt, South Wales or the industrial towns of the North and Midlands of England. With the larger battle lost, as Richards conceded, the idealists fought amongst themselves over who, in defeat, yet nobly retained the purer Modernist urban credentials. Anarchist-architect Colin Ward (1924–2010), for whom the social aspect of social housing was paramount, recalled in a rancorous article from 1993 that in late 1953:

> a party of Italian architects came to London, and it was my task to show them the schemes on our drawing boards… They were full of envy for their British counterparts, not for the quality of their architecture, but for the opportunity to be useful in society.[75]

Science or the zeitgeist: the sequestration of space and the homogenisation of use

Homes for Today and Tomorrow – otherwise known as the Parker Morris Report – published in 1961, has almost Biblical authority. Its provisions were not mandatory until 1967 for housing in New Towns and not until 1969 for local authority housing generally. Despite its being replaced with quite miserable housing standards by the then Conservative Government in 1983, mention of it today still brings a metaphoric tear to the eye of the older architect.

The committee, chaired by Sir Parker Morris (1891–1972), Town Clerk of Westminster Council, was

> appointed by the Central Housing Advisory Committee 'to consider the standards of design and equipment applicable to family dwellings and other form of residential accommodation, whether provided by public authorities or by private enterprise, and to make recommendations.'[76]

The committee rounded this out in its conclusion:

> Our work has been to take stock of accumulated experience; to evaluate the social and economic trends which are reshaping our lives; and to formulate recommendations, which, while ensuring sound and well-designed homes, will also encourage among architects and all concerned a creative response to the requirements of our age.[77]

These were entirely admirable aims and there was much that was admirable in the document. However, despite the report's publication within four years of *Family and Kinship*, there was no sense that the authors of the Parker Morris Report grasped 'social trends' beyond those implicit in an ascetic version of a consumer society, nor rose above the purely numeric, both ergonomic and financial, because its subjects were variously the *zeitgeist* or 'science', and how they benefited Modernism's acculturated everyone. The study on which the Report's conclusions were based consisted of visits to some 600 houses in England and Wales in 1959 and 1960, with one brief visit to Cumbernauld in Scotland. It also subsumed earlier space standards.

The report presented a fragmented *zeitgeist*, compromised science and a dated consumer society. The European experience of Modernism in domestic planning included the use of individually controllable district or central heating systems since at least the early 20th century, which facilitated the Modernist open plan and freed up the multi-use of spaces within the home, signally absent from Scotland's 'Modern' housing of the 1930s. Yet, for the two-storey single-family dwelling, the four-in-a-block flat or the three or four-storey tenement, the Parker Morris Report established the open coal fire with back boiler in the living room and indirect heating of the bedrooms through adventitious convection as a viable option amongst the several other heating systems which were examined.[78] Such a system predicated cellular accommodation despite the assertion that '[b]etter heating is the key to the design of the home, and the demand for it is strong'.[79] The Report's authors then worried that:

> To judge by the evidence we received on open planning, it has been disliked so far in local authority housing, mainly on the grounds that it provides little privacy from view, from noise, or from distraction... it would be easy to attach too much weight to these views... for [the open plan] gives a sense of space, and it can certainly help in producing a very attractive home.[80]

The committee were caught between a rock – or a lump of coal – and a hard place. The old-may-be-the-new-may-be-the-old but habituated living patterns and a customary cheap energy source requiring limited capital investment and known and relatively uncomplicated construction in installation were strong countervailing arguments. From a peak annual extraction of 292M tonnes in 1913, it took almost 50 years for coal production to drop by a third to 192M tonnes annually in 1961 at the date of the publication of the Parker Morris Report. This reduction included a substantial decline in industrial use and its total abandonment by the Royal Navy. Domestic use was largely unaffected, which may have been influential in the continued promotion by the coal industry advisers to the Parker Morris committee of the coal fire as a viable heating system. However, despite this support, continued decline in the short quarter-century to the date of the cancellation of the Report saw coal extraction dropping by almost a further third to 119M tonnes in 1983.[81] The coal industry never subsequently recovered from the results of the Conservative government's economically and politically, although not climatically, driven depredations of the coal industry and the Miners' Strike the following year while steadily being supplanted by natural gas. Assumptions about domestic heating in low-rise construction in the Parker Morris Report were amplified by cultural inertia which proved ultimately both unsustainable in every sense and, in their impact on domestic planning at the time, unscientific in the Modernist sense.

Space standards in the Report were derived from the activities to be accommodated[82] and not the minimum areas of rooms, as shown in previous documents which the Report's authors claimed produced house designs which were now 'too small to hold the possessions in which so much of the new affluence is expressed'.[83] By concentrating on activities, the Report hoped designers would find and maximise potential spatial trade-offs between activity and area within the house through the use of the 'shared activity space'. The activities which the report envisaged being contained within these plans were remarkably culturally exclusive in scope, delineated solely on ergonomic studies in which the explanatory diagrams showed uses that were either sedentary, static or of limited radius, such as movement within the triangle of sink/cooker/fridge in the kitchen or between facilities in the bathroom. Moreover, the equipment deemed necessary for these uses was minimal even for the late 1950s and especially for the early 1970s, by which time the majority of houses based on the provisions of the Report were either in construction or available for occupation.

The living room, 'even when bedrooms come to be put to wider... use' – although how that was to come about with dated heating systems is moot – was expected to facilitate

> children's play, homework, watching television, sewing and mending, hobbies, entertaining friends, and dealing with casual callers, often with two or more of these activities going on at once.

The equipment required to support this was to be

> two or three easy chairs, a settee, a television set, small tables, and places suitable for a reasonable quantity of other possessions such as a sewing box, toy box, radiogram and bookcase... [which] will often be pushed back against the walls to give a clear space, and this should be allowed for.[84]

Any hobby more complex or messier than knitting or stamp-collecting was a non-starter. Given that the living room walls also accommodated at least one door, a window and possibly a fireplace, perhaps a radiator, design options were limited.

Baudrillard identified the core issue in the provision of mass (serial) housing:

> There are always too many objects in serial interiors. And too many objects mean too little space. Promiscuity or saturation occur as

reactions to scarcity. Loss of quality must be made up for by the sheer number of objects.[85]

The *existenzminimum* dwelling was so much less heroic when described thus, and the omission of the parlour from the house plan, initiated in the Tudor-Walters Report of 1919 and perpetuated in the Dudley Report of 1940, was all the more to be regretted. Young, in his pre-publication article announcing the imminent *Family and Kinship*, observed:

> The nearest thing to a shrine in many houses is the sideboard in the parlour covered with its handsomely mounted photographs of dead and departed relatives.[86]

Doubts emerged at clause 28:

> It is thus not to be wondered at that the adaptable house – the house which could easily be altered as circumstances changed – is a recurring theme in the evidence we received and in our thoughts. At the present stage of development, such a dwelling is some way from practical reality, because of the high cost and other difficulties… We see the investigation of the practical possibilities of doing it easily and at reasonable cost as one of the most important lines of future research into the development of design and structure. The sooner it is started the better.[87]

Only to be compounded at clause 106 in that there was no factual basis for one of the basic premises of the Report: that the accommodation, designed according to its prescribed activities, was to be supported by equipment of necessarily occasional use which could be adequately accommodated, when not in use, within the stipulated area of built-in storage:

> In considering our recommendations on the subject of storage, we have been conscious of the lack of accurate information about the possessions which the average family in various income groups chooses to keep, with the result that designers are short of facts on which to base their work. We think it would be very helpful if a factual investigation were made.[88]

Innovative planning of houses and housing, the implied new ways of living required to go with them and the use of unfamiliar materials and new and relatively untried construction systems were not the only factors in play in the production of state corporatist architecture. The Housing Act of 1956 offered subsidies to local authorities for every floor constructed above the fifth which, for the developer, potentially reduced land purchase, site set-up and foundation costs and the unit cost component of the lifts while affording savings, through quantity and repetition, the taller the construction. Taken with politicians' escalating claims of numbers of new houses to be constructed, the incentives to build high were there and the material required to do so, cement, was still stockpiled at pre-war prices. Contemporaries observed:

> The recent orgy of nostalgia over the outbreak of WW2 reminded a chemist friend of the great clinker mountains of the war years. Pre-war propaganda greatly exaggerated the destructive potential of the German bombers and large scale devastation was expected. Convinced the Luftwaffe would have Britain's cement works high on its list of targets, the authorities built up vast stockpiles of clinker, the easiest way to store cement. At the end of the war the reserves were virtually untouched and even the post-war reconstruction boom failed to level the mountains. Cement industry folklore has it that the pre-war clinker was still being used in cement manufacture until the late 1970s.[89]

A 'managerial semirevolution': the architect as design manager

The climate of the times was such that

> [f]or Peter Shore (1924–2001) [Labour Secretary of State for Economic Affairs 1967–9]... 'the peaceful revolution of post-war Britain turns out to be no more than a managerial semirevolution'.[90]

The official architecture arising from the 'semirevolution' was likewise managerial and, while many of its structures were formalised in the organs of architectural governance in Scotland, its instrumentality originated in Oxford. A coterie of public authority Modernists within the Royal Institute of British Architects (RIBA), led by (Sir) Leslie Martin (1908–2000), (Sir) Robert Matthew[91] and (Sir) Richard Sheppard (1910–82), responding to government favour – statutory through the protection of the title 'architect' confirmed by the 1931 Architects' Registration Acts and active through the award of commissions to effect delivery of the infrastructure of the Welfare State – sought to reframe the architect's role. At their instigation, the Oxford

Conference was convened in 1958 to review the training of architects. Crinson and Lubbock, admittedly with a Traditionalist agenda, observed:

> By 1955 a new breed of younger, public authority modernists had come to dominate the Board of Architectural Education and the RIBA Council. By 1958 a rigged conference at Oxford set out the necessary framework and by the early 1960s the RIBA had been made into a kind of crypto-government department to carry [a nationalised architectural production] into effect.[92]

They elaborated that

> preparatory papers [were] circulated, and attendance restricted to fifty-three invited guests and speakers... Save for one or two traditionalists like Raymond Erith, almost all of the participants were modernist reformers, including the key figures: Leslie Martin, Richard Llewellyn-Davies, Percy Johnson-Marshall, William Allen, Richard Sheppard and Robert Matthew. In the absence of surviving minutes we are largely dependent on Leslie Martin's official report for an account of what actually happened.[93]

Anticipating the Conference conclusions, a complementary architecture course, which was managerial in tone, the School of the Built Environment – ostensibly modelled on Gropius's Graduate School of Design at Harvard – was instigated by Matthew together with planner Percy Johnson-Marshall (1915–93) within the Faculty of Social Science at the University of Edinburgh in the mid-1950s. Matthew's teaching staff appointments to the School were made from within his former architects' department at the London County Council (LCC) and from within his own practice, RMJM.[94] The training of the architect was now purposed for a career in central or local government or New Town Development Corporation employ or in the large practices, such as Matthew's, Martin's and Sheppard's, commissioned by these agencies. The architect's implicated societal sanction – the professional duty – and the 'scientific' moralist social service ideals of Modernism were elided under the umbrella of public service and the implementation of government policy. Crinson and Lubbock were in no doubt as to the operational principles of the profession at the time of the 1958 Conference:

> RIBA has regarded [architectural education] as one of the three pillars of the profession, the other two being public sector housing and the post-war British planning system.[95]

The ship that sailed: the dissolution of the International Style

Even as the promoters of a managerial Modernism corralled the Oxford Conference, news from Modernism's heartlands suggested their moment had passed. Questions as to Modernism's historicity, cultural relevance and aesthetic validity had arisen, which prompted a reconsideration of regionalism. The 1930s construct of Hitchcock, Johnson and Pevsner of a single, simple Bauhaus/Corbusian/Miesian stylistic representation of the age – the International Style – where issues of agreed – and consequently assumed – shared taste might determine the individual worth of its productions was countered by such as Siegfried Giedion, who proposed that there were several such representations. Firstly, the aesthetic of these differing styles did not have quite so serious an impact on Modernism's monism as their appearance alone might have implied; secondly, there were deeper significances in architecture; thirdly, insistence on conformity with stylistic norms blinded the commentator as to where real cultural development was taking place; and four, there was an imminent danger of the entire discussion descending into a bathetic, style not substance row where continued Modernist rejection of aesthetics and history stood to unmoor its own project. Giedion observed:

> With no clear perception of the relation in which it stands to the past or of the route by which it must advance into the future, the life of any period will be lived on an aimless, day-to-day basis.[96]

Giedion was less constrained than either Hitchcock or Pevsner in the matter of appropriate architectural stylistic response to the challenges and demands of building for the age in conformity with the *zeitgeist*. He was still clear, however, that he lived in his own time where: '[t]he historian, the historian of architecture especially, must be in close contact with contemporary conceptions'.[97] However, living in the present should not have so coloured judgement as to render the past a disservice, because:

> Absolute points of reference are no more open to the historian than they are to the physicist; both produce descriptions relative to a particular situation.[98]

He also reflected on the content of historiographical orthodoxy as it became established in the 1930s and early 1940s and the doubts that were then being raised in that:

It is being recognised in all quarters that the ideas which we have taken over from the past are both too complex and too crude.⁹⁹

He did not enlarge on the complex/crude dichotomy to any great extent, but with reference to the general trend of his argument it could be inferred that the complexity issue was concerned with an over-emphasis on matters of detail and stylistic nuance for their own sake whilst ignoring a larger haptic picture, and the crudity issue with the universalist argument promoted by Gropius, Hitchcock and Pevsner and its consequent architectural production. Superficial aesthetics mattered less to Giedion than more profound, essentially spatial, architectural considerations:

> If it is the general line of evolution which interests us – the development which runs through different periods, social orders and races [sic] – then the formal and stylistic variations which mark the separate stages will lose some of their importance.¹⁰⁰

Giedion went much further than any Modernist before in an appreciation of regional or national architectures. He approached with equanimity the fact that:

> A universal civilisation is in the making but it is by no means developing in every country at the same pace.¹⁰¹

This notion allowed him to retain his universalist Modern Movement credentials whilst opening up a rather larger arena of potential enquiry into 20th century architecture. He developed this argument in a quite surprising and inclusive manner, anticipating much of the discourse that would be engaged in by others a decade later. Giedion contended that there was

> another factor... which lies at the base of the best contemporary architecture. Its emanating force is generated by the respect it has given to the eternal cosmic and terrestrial conditions of a particular region. Instead of being regarded as hindrances, these have served as springboards for the artistic imagination... This penetrating into the cosmic and terrestrial elements of a region I have elsewhere called the 'new regionalism'. The contemporary space conception and contemporary means of expression can re-open a dialogue with these unchanging elements.¹⁰²

Where Giedion advanced the Modernist argument was in his concession of a 'dialogue'. Nevertheless, the 'new regionalism' sounds very much like the old regionalism, narrowly focused on the 'unchanging' matters of climate, topography and resources or, in other words, territory without patrimony.

Pierre Francastel reckoned, in 1959, that

> the true problems of 1930–1950 involved not the as-yet-undemonstrated revelation of an inspired, supra-material architecture but, rather, the possible transcendence of cubism by a new principle of inspiration.[103]

The anti-historical Modernism of Gropius, Hitchcock, Pevsner and others was informed by the artistic licence of Cubism which, by 1950, was itself part of 40 years of art history and had pedigree from which, constrained by that continuous artistic practice, it could not escape. Meanwhile, a 'supra-material architecture' was hampered by social, material and constructional experimentation which was compromised, on the one hand, in that it was not especially scientifically-determined or technologically advanced and, on the other hand, in that over-optimistic conclusions were drawn far too early from patchy results and mass promulgation initiated too soon. While these were the physical and aesthetic results of manifesto-Modernism, they were evidently not what the manifesto writers anticipated in the improvement of the human condition arising from the socialistically-driven vision and machine instrumentality of their texts.

Within a year of the completion of Robert Venturi's (1925–2018) Vanna Venturi House, Philadelphia, 1962–4, which signalled the coming post-Modern project, Christian Norberg-Schulz (1926–2000) identified Modernism's problems from which post-Modernism was briefly to divert attention. While excusing Modernism in that:

> So far [it] has had the character of a 'belief', rather than a worked-out method based on a clear analysis of functional, sociological, and cultural problems,[104]

Norberg-Schulz yet sought his answers from within the very dogma which he critiqued. He was convinced that despite the 30-plus years of inconclusive inquiry, which Gropius also conceded had not provided an authoritative answer,[105] a solution still lurked within the orthodox Modernist corpus which was amenable to a new interpretation of its present methodology. Norberg-Schulz wrote:

> Two basic creeds dominate the situation: the 'organic', represented by architects as different as Wright and Aalto, and the 'technological',

The post-Modern manifesto: Vanna Venturi House, Philadelphia, Pennsylvania, 1962–4, architect Robert Venturi.
(Smallbones - own work, Creative Commons)

represented by Mies van der Rohe... The problem, thus, is to unify the 'organic' and 'technological' tendencies... because... historical continuity does not mean borrowed motives and ideals, but human values which have to be conquered in always *new* [Norberg-Schulz's emphasis] ways.[106]

By engineering an 'organic/technological' duality as explanation, he contrived a compromise solution in their union as a third way wherein the question of symbol is foresworn and the seeming dichotomy of technology and organicism resolved.

The modern forms... have never been ordered, they have never become a real formal *language* [Norberg-Schulz's emphasis]. This is the basic problem that the present generation of architects face, and it can only be solved through the formation of types.[107]

It is entirely possible Norberg-Schulz did not entertain the thought that the variations he observed were not between technologists and organicists but rather those of available architectural talent and that his proposed 'types' were little better than an 18th-century builder's pattern book. Collins observed, as Norberg-Schulz did not, that in any art which really flourishes, the only values recognised are those concerned with degrees of excellence, and the decline in architecture occurred when architects forgot this, and started worrying about whether they were being 'contemporary' or 'reactionary' instead of whether their work was good or bad.[108]

Or that, as Hall commented,

> their ingenuity might avoid this through a truly insidious innovation: a consensus of mutually enforced mediocrity, designed to protect each individual bourgeois from the risks of competition, and bourgeois society as a whole from the risks of change.[109]

Ultimately, Norberg-Schulz's was a qualified remorse at the Modern Movement's failures because he, too, offered the Gropian excuse that

> criticism in most cases has a certain narrowness of view. Generally the client will criticise on the basis of personal needs without recognising that his project in many ways forms part of a larger whole. He is therefore not conscious of and amenable to the new possibilities the architect can offer him, possibilities which may only become manifest after a long period of getting accustomed to the finished product.[110]

More pertinently, Norberg-Schulz did not recognise the antinomy of his two 'creeds' or that their two poles were rather more intimately connected in a Kantian sense than he credited them with being.[111]

In his search for a valid architecture, for all that Norberg-Schulz proposed respect for the *genius loci* in its response to territory, he excluded the contribution of patrimony because:

> A new aesthetic orientation transcending the arbitrary play with forms is surely needed, although it is not claimed the result should resemble the styles of the past. But so far we have not found any answer to the question whether... [it] should also acquire a symbolizing aspect... with the purpose of 'representing' a cultural structure.[112]

Falteringly, he interrogated Le Corbusier's efforts at Villa de Mandrot and Maison Errázuriz, but could not address regional architecture in other than an equivalent abstraction of material and forms. In 2000, in *Principles of Modern Architecture*, a post-post-Modern *apologia* for Modernism, in a chapter specifically entitled 'The New Regionalism', he observed:

> Regional character is a necessary property of any authentic architecture... it implies a coming to terms with the *genius loci* [Norberg-Schulz's emphasis], and must be understood in terms of space and form. The problem evidently also comprises the embodiment of the new conception of space.[113]

Finally, he lamely wondered whether '[i]t might seem that the idea of a new regionalism is pure nostalgia'.[114]

Collins in a more general critique was caught in equivocation over regionalism. He formulated an expedient archaic architecture to finesse Modernism's widespread failure to produce monumental forms appropriate to existing environments of strong and sustained character. He established the conundrum thus:

> architects should feel no shame at adopting archaic forms and techniques in order to harmonise new buildings with an existing architectural environment, *provided they do not betray the contemporary principles of stylistic unity* [Collins' emphasis]; a unity which, in the 20th century, is best defined by what John Summerson calls 'obedience to the programme' (or, as we usually say – Functionalism) but which is also to be defined, to my mind, as the notion of the honest expression of the structural means employed.[115]

There was no real discussion by Collins of what an archaic architecture might consist of because he was principally concerned with precedent, convention and evolution. Collins' archaic architecture had, and equally was, no precedent, for it was time-bound and its origins unrecorded. It had no contemporary convention because its conventions were equally tied to its unknown historical period and to a narrow societal milieu and materiality. In seeking a necessary accommodation of the new with the old in existing environments, Collins struggled. He was forced to ensnare the unwitting architect who attempted to place the new in amongst the old by the use of value-laden terms such as 'shame', 'betray', 'obedience' and 'honest', and through the invocation of Sir John Summerson, who himself subsequently and famously recanted his Modernist stance in a paper given at Edinburgh College of Art in 1984.[116] Within the straitjacket of Collins' prescription, the architect had virtually no room for manoeuvre, common sense was turned on its head, the old must accord with the new, programme took precedence over monumentality, function obscured symbol.

Both Norberg-Schulz and Collins, despite the sincerity of their attempted critiques, were obliged to call upon avatars – the technologic/organic duality and an archaic architecture respectively – to finesse their argumentation within the orthodox Modernist construct. Less constrained by doctrinaire Modernist baggage, Berman, Rowe and Vidler proffered contrasting explanations of the orthodox Modernist difficulties with the past and permitted understanding of why regional architectures posed a challenge to it. Berman noted:

> the primacy of dialogue in the ongoing life of modernism means that modernists can never be done with the past: they must go on forever haunted by it, digging up its ghosts, recreating it even as they remake the world and themselves.[117]

Rowe asked:

> Technology as arbiter? The time-spirit as arbiter? Why was it that the incompatibility of these two doctrines remained for so long invisible?[118]

To which he gave answer that it was

> the intellectual laziness (and, ironically, the conservatism) of those who subscribe to its parti pris. With its accessory (and equally antique) fantasy as to the obligatory avant-garde role of the architect, this body of ideas is the psychological equivalent of a lavish insurance policy. By citing this body of ideas all failures may be extenuated. They will become either the simple products of 'science' or the inevitable results of the 'spirit of the age'.[119]

Vidler described the rhetorical devices used by the apologists of orthodox Modernism to forestall its criticism:

> For no matter what the future imagined by the modernists, the figure of proleptic projection determined their efforts, a double figure including that of prolepsis, or the representation of something in the future as already done, and projection, in which objecting arguments are anticipated in order to preclude their use.[120]

Doubts also surfaced at home, although these had rather more to do with perceptions of the validity of Britain's Modern Movement credentials than questions about Modern architecture itself. Reyner Banham, referring in 1960 to a passage in the *Architectural Review* of July 1905 by 'a source close to Lethaby' who called for an unchallenged acceptance of 'modern materials and modern conditions', commented:

> This... shows how close to the mainstream of development [of Modern architecture] the English Free architecture could have been. The dramatic reduction of that Free architecture to a mere provincial vernacular, in competition with a provincial version of Beaux-Arts Classicism, is a singular example of failure of nerve and collapse of creative energy. To some extent this may be due to muddled thinking and squeamishness – the failure to identify the Glasgow School as an ally, or to accept machine production, are examples of the squeamishness.[121]

The Glasgow School's association with the decorative tradition of the Wagnerschule, the Secession, the Wiener Werkstätte and Josef Hoffmann, and from which, by 1915, it seemed unable to escape, distanced it from that strand of Modernism, that of Gropius, Le Corbusier and machine production – to which Banham so desired there to be a fundamental British contribution. Moreover, it is clear that neither Banham nor his historic Lethabite authority recognised the Glasgow School in one of its several guises – a national design tradition – except, perhaps, at some subliminal level where the incompatibility of an English Free Style and a Scottish national architecture was inescapable and 'squeamishness' was the result. We observe the equanimity with which an English Modernist indulged in an attempted cultural expropriation in order to support the proposition of a near-miss by English Free-style architects in the leadership stakes of the Modern Movement.

Psychogeography: a brief prophetic interlude

In 1960, Kevin Lynch (1918–84) provided a methodology and language for the understanding of contemporary (American) urban form and of way-finding while exposing the downside of comprehensive redevelopment and urban motorway construction.[122] In 1961, Jane Jacobs (1916–2006) tackled the consequent matter of the loss of community brought about by first, zoning, and second, the characterising, even stigmatising, of areas as slums and their blanket clearance:

> The [planning] method fails. At best, it merely shifts slums from here

to there, adding its own tincture of extra hardship and disruption.[123]

Much closer to home, MRG Conzen's (1907–2000)[124] copiously-illustrated Alnwick study[125] of 1960–9 gave research-based substance to the evolution and sophistication of the planning of the previously romantically characterised mediaeval town or sma burgh and its consequent impact on the promoters of a historic British urban form. In particular, Conzen formulated the concepts of 'burgage plot' and 'burgage cycle', and identified their uses and dimensioning systems in the determining of plot depths and bay widths in street-fronting development, in the historic aggregation of plots and in the development of the back-land 'rigg'.

A decade would pass before these three texts found vindication and use in the re-examination of historic and Modernist urban planning strategies.

Official history: a quarter century of International Style Modernism

Meanwhile, through the agencies of national policy and state and industry corporatism, a delayed Modern architecture became the fact of contemporary British life. It was facilitated in Scotland, as Lynch described, in that:

> For more than 20 years after 1945, Scotland was a virtual two-party state... broadly line in line with the pattern set by British politics... [and it was] marked by a benign neglect of all such constitutional questions, by both Conservatives and Labour... [acquiring the character of] a semi-Union... [and] a state within a state.[126]

Overall policy strategy was decided on a British basis, which was then adjusted to what the unelected Scottish Office administration construed would, with least effort politically, socially and especially financially, facilitate an accommodation of the Scottish situation as perceived in Scotland to that of the Union or to the whims of their current political masters in London. Unquestionably, large numbers of Scots – architects included – benefitted from the Welfare State, the New Towns, education, health and slum clearance programmes. However, this was merely to ameliorate the symptoms and not cure the underlying political and structural deficits in Scotland's governance and economy.

Architectural issues in the 1950s and '60s in Scotland, insofar as they were represented by the working-out of the Traditionalist and Modernist positions of the 1930s, are possibly epitomised by two campaigns pursued, during its brief existence, by the Architectural and Artistic Advisory Committee (AAAC) of the National Trust for Scotland (NTS). Architects invited by Lord Wemyss in December 1952 to join the newly-formed agency were almost evenly split by generation and, by implication, into either the Traditionalist or Modernist camps: Graham Henderson, Sir Frank Mears, Leslie Grahame-Thomson, Alexander Mackenzie and James Shearer born between 1879 and 1882; Ian Lindsay, Robert Hurd and Basil Spence born between 1905 and 1907. In terms of allegiance, however, Henderson, Mackenzie, Shearer, Hurd and Spence were in both camps, while Lindsay was conservationist and Traditionalist. The inaugural meeting was held on 28 April 1953 with Shearer elected to the Chair. The committee was soon expanded to include the Modernists Robert Matthew and Alan Reiach. Lord Wemyss's letter of invitation set the scene for the AAAC's activities:

> The Trust is to an increasing extent being consulted on architectural matters... Instances of threats to old houses come to us from all over the Country. The only hope of trying to help in these matters is to cast our net of experienced and qualified advisers much wider than at present.[127]

The first issue attended to by the AAAC was whether to harl or, more accurately, re-harl the masonry of existing buildings. Historic pre-18th-century structures revealed, when harl was removed or became detached, the presence of much poor quality random rubble, never intended for exposure. When consciously exposed – a then current aesthetic preference for stone masonry – the pointing nightmare of friable and multiply-jointed stonework and the loss of the hygroscopic lime coating, whether wash or harl, stood to retain moisture and resulted in deteriorating facades. An extended discussion on harling of the exposed masonry of Sailors' Walk, the oldest extant building in Kirkcaldy, characterised this debate and was only resolved in 1959 by Wheeler and Sproson's restoration, a year after Shearer's resignation from the Committee.[128]

The other matter was the AAAC's attempts to find out what the University of Edinburgh intended with George Square, planned in 1766 by James Brown (1729–1807). In late October 1955, Robert Hurd had got sight of Basil Spence's development plan for the square, which allowed for the preservation of the west side only. The AAAC, without the voice of Alan Reiach, for reasons which soon became apparent, were of the opinion that the entire square was worth preserving and that the University should be asked to clarify its intentions.[129] The AAAC resolved at the meeting of 23 April 1956

> that the Trust should make known publicly its desire for a Public

Mid-century interest in tradition: Sailors' Walk, Kirkcaldy, 17th century on 15th century base.

Enquiry into the University plans for the development of George Square, Edinburgh.[130]

On 9 January 1958, the AAAC recorded that a joint letter from the NTS, the Saltire Society and the Cockburn Association had met with no response from the Secretary of State.[131] At the following meeting, 15 July 1958, Basil Spence tendered his resignation.[132] Within five years, Colin McWilliam (1928–89), Secretary to the AAAC, wrote his winding-up report on its work while several former committee members were busily engaged designing university projects on the north, south and east sides of George Square: Robert Matthew at the David Hume Tower (renamed 40 George Square in 2020),[133] 1963 – which bears a generic likeness to Josep Lluis Sert's Law and Administration Building, Boston University, 1960–4 – and the William Robertson and Adam Ferguson Buildings; Basil Spence, the University Library and Lecture Hall, 1965–7, which may be based on Tange's Kurashiki Town Hall, 1958–60; and Alan Reiach, the Appleton Tower, 1963–6. Significantly, even then in the fullness of the Modernist opportunity, the models were imported.

Such architecture arising from the rationale behind the persuasion, policies and administration of the late 1940s was represented effectively, if

Mid-century Modernism: Edinburgh University Library, 1966, architect Basil Spence.

anachronistically, in the later 1993 Scottish selections for inclusion in the DOCOMOMO (International Committee for the Documentation and Conservation of Buildings, Sites and Neighbourhoods of the Modern Movement) record. Beginning its survey in 1945 and concluding it in 1970, DOCOMOMO Scotland included only two buildings dating from the 1930s: David Carr's (1905–86) Kirkcaldy Town House, won in competition in 1937; and Fairlie's National Library of Scotland, 1934, largely since they completed in the mid-1950s. The omission of the nearly one-third-century of prior building seems wilful. By way of contrast, Latvia's equivalent DOCOMOMO survey begins in 1912,[134] Denmark's in 1921, Finland's in 1917, Iceland's in 1930, Norway's in 1927 and Sweden's in 1924.[135]

There are three reasons one might deduce for the Scottish DOCOMOMO response. Firstly, while the list rightly did not include Mackintosh's proto-Modern pioneer work – or the work of others identified by Muthesius – it avoided challenging the difficulties raised by the apparent lack of a verifiable and documented post-1919 Modernist influence and consistent connected Modernist narrative in Scotland. Secondly and concomitantly, it avoided the handful of exploratory, if hesitant, works from the 1910s, '20s and '30s such as the Lion Chambers, Glasgow, 1908, by James Salmon; the Hippodrome, Bo'ness, 1911, by Matt Steele; Burnet's Wallace Scott Tailoring Institute, 1913, and Adelaide House, London, 1919; Kininmonth's Lane House, 1932; Shearer's Dunfermline Fire Station, 1934; Joseph Gleave's (1907–64) remarkable Columbus Memorial Lighthouse, San Domingo Este, Dominican Republic, 1931–92, which addressed Giedion, Sert and Leger's *Nine Points of Monumentality* head-on; Sir E Owen Williams' *Scottish Daily Express* Building, Glasgow, 1936–39; Marwick's St Cuthbert's Cooperative Store, 1937; or Neil and Hurd's Ravelston Flats, Edinburgh, 1937, although these omissions are perverse. Thirdly, by aligning architectural production alongside and in the delivery of governmental Welfare State policy post-1945,

A 1930s survivor: Kirkcaldy Town House, 1937–56, architect David Carr.

indeed, contingent upon it, DOCOMOMO Scotland seems to have sought to repurpose and resynchronise a Modernist narrative to replace its more usual interpretation of the period which was only partial in Scotland.

Arguably, with Scotland's having missed the Modern Movement's heroic 'golden age' of the second quarter of the 20th century, a strained attempt was hazarded retrospectively to consolidate a specifically Scottish 'golden age' in the third quarter; a consolidation which requires that we do not recall or reflect upon those faltering steps leading up to it or the failures appearing in quantity post-1968 which signalled its rapid subsequent decline, nor question unchallenged assertions about the history of 20th century architecture in Scotland, its theory and productions. MacDiarmid, speaking of Scottish art generally, put his finger on it:

> Worst of all is the continued absence of competent modern philosophising in Scotland, and above all the absence of esthetic [sic] thought of any such value as might align Scotland with other eastern European countries and induce aesthetic developments on Scottish roots and yet able to withstand comparison with the contemporary aesthetic thought of other countries.[136]

As the several critiques of the International Style showed, loss of cultural meaning and connection to territory and patrimony were compensated by their subsequent tentative re-investigation. Scotland was no different, although a

Scottish regional or national architecture went largely underground in these years, because the post-WWII break, which Barley identified for Gillespie, Kidd and Coia, was profound and widespread. While Traditionalism and Modernism remained relatively fluid in character up to 1939, very nearly antinomial in their relationship, by 1945, the organisational, managerial, statutory and architectural procedures either in place or nascent drove both into antagonistic monisms. Traditionalism was framed by its reaction to the loss, actual or potential, of historic buildings, townscapes and communities due to the perceived depredations of a positivist Modernism. Neither now proposed that the-old-is-the-new-is-the-old, because Modernists were convinced the argument was won and the sophistry unnecessary while Traditionalists simply turned the clock back and became or joined with the Conservationists.

Conservation had historic institutional, cultural and customary, although not contemporary statutory, support in Scotland where a constant from the late 19th century onwards was the influence of the conservation societies. The oldest in Britain is the Edinburgh-based Cockburn Association founded by Lord Cockburn in 1875 to protest the proposed removal of trees from Bruntsfield Links. The oldest in England is the Society for the Protection of Ancient Buildings (SPAB), founded in 1877 by William Morris. It did not have a Scottish branch until 1995, formed then to recognise Scotland's specific building traditions, corroborating a growing Scottish awareness in the late 20th century of the value of a distinct Scottish culture. The struggles of the NTS over George Square were taken up by the Edinburgh Georgian Society founded in 1956, to become the Scottish Georgian Society in 1959 and, in 1984, the Architectural Heritage Society of Scotland (AHSS) whose remit is to cover all historic periods. The Victorian Society was founded in 1958 and, later, the Charles Rennie Mackintosh Society in 1973, the Twentieth Century Society (C20) in 1979, and the Alexander Thomson Society not until 1991. This brief list ignores the very many single-issue conservation groups.

A cautious regionalism

Tentative essays in a contemporary Scottishness were marked by new or adapted motives such as the mono-pitch roof – avoiding recourse to the *passé* double-pitch or to the challenging flat roof – in grey Annandale concrete tiles aping the costly and relatively unavailable Ballachulish slate – most often now appearing in slate-hung panels – which was used to break up the urban skyline. It was present in the SSHA's ubiquitous three-storey link-blocks, in Cocker's Link Housing Association (LHA) work throughout East

BRAVE NEW WORLD: 1939-68

The regionalism of mimesis: Canongate, Edinburgh, 1966-8, architect Basil Spence, Glover & Ferguson.

Central Scotland, in Eric Hall and Partners' Danish-influenced Gracemount Road, Edinburgh, 1963, clad in roofing felt in Sir Basil Spence, Glover and Ferguson's 79-121 Canongate, Edinburgh, 1966-8 or in many New Town housing areas well into the 1970s, such as at Girdle Toll, Irvine. Broad cement or precast concrete window surrounds, mostly painted black, were featured around isolated windows in Wheeler and Sproson's white rendered Dysart flat blocks, 1958, or at Seafar, Cumbernauld, 1962, and, again, in much LHA and SSHA work or in white on the blue render of Gillespie, Kidd and Coia's Round Riding Sheltered Housing, Dumbarton, 1967. Volumetric composition and the framing of the infinite were encapsulated in the Scottish Provident Association, Edinburgh, 1961 (demolished 2014) by William Leslie (1930–2005) and Richard Ewing (n.d.) of Rowand, Anderson, Kininmonth and Paul. Robust black-stained timber porches, balconies, handrails, fascias, infill panels and window frames, reminiscent of Mackintosh's heftier joinery, initiated at Gillespie, Kidd and Coia's St Paul's, Glenrothes, 1956, also contrasted with white render or blockwork as at Clapperfield, Edinburgh, 1959, by Stuart Renton (1929–2006) of Reiach and Hall, or at Burgess Terrace, Edinburgh, 1966, by Ian Marshall (1933–2016). Drawing these reinterpreted historic signs together in an elegant and efficient plan reminiscent of the work of Louis Kahn was the antinomial Edenside Group Practice Surgery, Kelso, 1965,

The regionalism of invention: St Paul's RC Church, Glenrothes, 1956, architects Gillespie, Kidd and Coia.

The regionalism of invention: Edenside Medical Practice, Kelso, 1967, architect Peter Womersley.

The regionalism of mimesis: Girdle Toll Housing, Irvine, 1960, architects Irvine Development Corporation.

by the émigré Englishman Peter Womersley (1923–93). Glendinning et al recorded it as 'a precursor of the Vernacular forms of the 1970s',[137] although it was never bettered and, indeed, was an altogether more sophisticated and subtle design than merely and pejoratively 'vernacular'.

'Vernacular' was in frequent use as a late 20th century, depoliticised, non-patrimonial and anodyne descriptor of an architecture, which paradoxically embodied an aesthetic patrimony of resistance to a Modernist cultural hegemony, attempting thereby to diminish such architecture by positing it in the non-historical and unthreatening space previously the sole preserve of the expedient astylar works of the untutored builder (see Chapter 6).

Meanwhile, in Japan...: comparative uses of traditional forms in Modern expression

Mirroring what Scottish architects had been interpreting from their patrimony, Tange Kenzō characterised in 1964 what he and his colleagues had been doing in the waning years of the International Style. He wrote:

> we Japanese architects have considered Japanese tradition from almost every possible angle. The conclusion I have reached is that tradition is like a *catalyst* [Tange's emphasis] – it can stimulate or hasten creativity, but not a trace of it should remain in the finished product.[138]

Kurokawa, Tange's colleague and fellow-Metabolist, recorded four streams of influence in Japanese architecture:

1. Academic architecture – pseudo-functionalism behind a superficial mask of modern architecture;
2. Architecture strongly influenced by the expressionism of Le Corbusier;
3. Architecture influenced by Frank Lloyd Wright;
4. Traditional architecture – aiming to continue the expressionism of traditional Japanese architecture

He then noted

> that young Japanese architects and critics are reacting against the ideas of these groups, emphasizing the importance of re-establishing tradition to create a new philosophy.[139]

These were thoughtful interpretations of regional architecture and a methodology which seemed to have entirely escaped Western thought and production, or at least was never expressed.

Nevertheless, Tange's intention that traditional forms might wholly disappear was not entirely borne out in contemporary Japanese architecture where traditional form often remained subtly explicit. For example, Tange's own Kurashiki Town Hall, 1958–60, employed reinforced concrete in simulacra of traditional timber post and beam construction with paired beams and an implied *torii* gate. His National Gymnasia, 1961–4, for the 1964 Tokyo Olympics had plan forms which can be read as *mon* – heraldic devices – while the concave curves of the cable-suspended roofs mimicked the traditional sweeping Buddhist temple roof forms or the design of samurai armour, the end elevations resembling helmets. Kikutake Kiyonori's (1928–2011) design for the Izumotaishi-Chonoya, 1963, incorporated paired beams, reinforced concrete *amado* (storm shutters) and an implied *torii* gate, while Kurokawa Noriaki (Kisho)'s (1934–2007) pavilions at Kodomo-No-Kuni 1963–5 featured interpretations of *engawa* (verandas) and *shinbashira* (central columns) and the traditional concave-curved Buddhist temple roof. It was more than a little odd that some of these recovered and adapted Japanese motives should appear in Scottish Modernist work, although they seem to emphasise those Scottish architects' desire for an 'anywhere-but-Scotland' aesthetic.

Altered images: photographic propaganda

Photography perhaps seduced as many into the fold of the International Style as were enjoined through their own appreciation of its polemic. Indeed, for not a few architects, their sole contact with the signal building which, by proxy, constituted the totality of the inspiration and justification for their own architectural practice and philosophy was effected through the fixed and unchanging glare of the aesthetically composed, craftily developed, artfully cropped and seductively printed image drawn from a rotating and misleading peep-show of similar images. In a sense, these images were architectural pornography, and, inasmuch as no one ever learned anything useful about meaningful relationships from 'adult' movies or how to dress themselves appropriately and elegantly from catwalks, their architectural equivalent was likewise no guide to sound architectural practice.

There are several well-known Modern Movement propagandist photographic deceits. Le Corbusier used photography[140] artistically in his collages and misleadingly in the doctoring of the concrete grain elevators illustrated in *Vers une Architecture* to remove the Classical pediments which originally adorned their roofline, the more forcefully to press home his functionalist argument. A selective viewpoint or blanking out of the adjacent traditional detached houses allowed Mies van der Rohe's Tugendhat House, Brno, 1928–30, to be read, when viewed across the rising lawn, as a topographically isolated canonic villa in an archetypical Modernist figure/ground presentation. Conversely, the very conscious foregrounding of the traditional terrace to which was added the Rietveld-Schröder house in Utrecht, 1924, was used to emphasise the house's De Stijl purity, colour, openness and extension, in contrast to its closed, bricky neighbours. Jackson has observed how Tange edited, cropped and disembodied Ishimoto Yasuhiro's caption-less photographs of Katsura in their joint production *Tradition and Creation in Japanese Architecture*, by

> often reducing exterior and interior views alike to Mondrianesque patterns, playing up the grid or emphasising the perspective.[141]

The International Style cemented its near 40-year hegemony as an art-world monochromatic monism almost uniquely through the seductive and largely black-and-white sun-drenched photography of such as Ezra Stoller (1915–2004), Julius Shulman (1910–2009) and Richard Einzig (1932–80). As Rowe said, 'an ideal July – the favourite light of the architecture of good intentions'.[142] Gössel asserted that:

> The photographer, therefore, assumes a role of tremendous responsibility in reporting, literally as a communicator. The mind, the dexterity, and the ability of the person with the camera can become

the vehicle by which the image of architecture is transferred to the publications of the people of the world,[143]

while Shulman confirmed:

> As evidenced by my own experiences over many decades, photographs become part of history and, therefore, the documentation of a structure must be such that the viewer of the photograph is first attracted to the graphic impact of the photograph. And then, in turn, the quality of the design becomes much more evident; it has an impact on the mind and eyes of the viewer, who can then form an estimation of it.[144]

Beatriz Colomina reflected:

> Modern architecture becomes 'modern' not simply by using glass, steel or reinforced concrete, as it is usually understood, but by engaging with the media.[145]

Richard Murphy (b. 1955) contrasted the resistance of a regional architecture to the prevalence of global architectural photography to observe that

> we do not subscribe to the world of international 'starchitects' depositing iconic... buildings in different cultures round the world, which whilst having some superficial photo-journalistic value, rarely in my opinion repay close inspection.[146]

Photography has long since passed from merely being the recorder of objects, events or people to having fine-art status in its own right with its own set of principles, techniques and objectives in the manipulation of light and image. Thus, in Shulman's work, for example, the high-art values of the art-photograph were interposed between the architecture and the viewer, obfuscating what the viewer was meant to see, although it is undeniable that the photographic image was very nearly *sui generis*. The photograph is a framing device to the architecture in exactly the same way that the picture frame or gallery wall is to the contemporary art work. All privilege the frame, conferring on the object thus framed or encapsulated a secondary representational authority, constraining the object's own inherent authority as an object in its own right, thereby distancing the viewer from the object represented. O'Doherty stated the matter exactly:

The cultivation of the picture frame resulted in an entity with length and breadth but no thickness, a membrane which, in a metaphor usually organic, could generate its own self-sufficient laws. The primary law, of course, was that this surface, pressed between huge historical forces, could not be violated.[147]

For most architects working in the heyday of the International Style's canonic built models, most such models were out of reach other than to those fortunate souls in locations boasting a precious few examples, to the recipients of travelling scholarships or to the wealthy. Even for architects, extensive foreign travel in the days before cheap flights was not a given. Consequently, the only available contact with the buildings for many was by means of the photograph in the architectural magazine. Collins observed:

> Similarly [to earlier wood and steel engraved reproductions], one can hardly over-emphasise the importance of the introduction in 1856 of photographic reproduction into architectural periodicals, since not only did this obviate the need for periodicals to rely on architects providing them with their own perspectives, but it encouraged their editors to show a preference for photogenic buildings and a corresponding lack of enthusiasm for buildings, however excellent, that did not provide flattering points of view for the camera.[148]

Richards echoed Collins's view and confirmed that what was illustrated was selective:

> In the [*Architectural*] *Review* [of which he was editor], as in other architectural periodicals, criticism of buildings was implied rather than direct. It was expressed in the choice of the buildings editors took seriously enough to think worth illustrating, rather than in adverse comment on the buildings they did not. Throughout the 1930s the *Review* paid increasing attention to buildings of the modern school in Britain and abroad.[149]

Richards went on to note that:

> At the same time, historic and vernacular buildings were being studied by the modern architects and their apologists with a critical instead of an antiquarian eye, making them, too, play their part in the reformation of principles towards which the energies of the new

generation of architectural writers were directed.[150]

However, welcome although it was, such critical appreciation of traditional and vernacular examples was undertaken essentially in the context of how they might function as a formal, material or associative resource to inform the investigations of the Modern Movement. The undeviating use of elevated contrast in black and white photographic image-making was not kind to older buildings or to the effects of the north-west European temperate climate, where a softer light revealed the detail which makes sense of the architecture. Stark contrast favoured the abstract and simple geometries of most Modernist structures. Moreover, the hard-edged photograph – no matter how sun-suffused, perhaps because it was sun-suffused – like the hard edge of the orthographic measured drawing or the Modernist use of the mechanistic axonometric projection, differed radically from the indeterminacy of the conventional means of representing traditional and regional architectures in the sketch, watercolour or hand-drawn perspective illustration. Rowe described how photographic representation privileged the new in contrast to the old in that 'the light preferred is hard, brilliant, white and the effects of chiaroscuro are not admired'.[151]

The end of an era

It is almost certain that none of the Scottish architects named above progressed their architectural thinking either in resistance to Modernism or in the theoretical manner described; their objectives and methodology were almost certainly conventionally couched in the formal and functional language of Modernism. However, even Glendinning, Matthew's biographer and apologist for the architecture that resulted, was obliged to concede that it was all over in less than 15 years:

> But finally, from the mid and late 1960s onwards, all of these contextual frameworks were swept aside by the beginnings of a completely new set of relationships and mentalités – the start of a new phase of 'disembedding' that would tear apart and discard the painfully constructed structures of collective cohesion, including the dominance of the state, the pursuit of the new, and the insistence on planning.[152]

The sense that a period in international architectural history and production had ended and a new one had begun in the 1960s was possibly confirmed by Vincent Scully's reflection on Louis Kahn's oeuvre:

> They are thus the single wholly satisfactory achievement of the late modernist aim in architecture: to reinvent reality to make all new.
> They are more than that though. They begin something. They effectively bring the International Style to a close and open the way to a much solider modernism, one in which the revival of the vernacular and classical traditions of architecture, and the corollary mass movement for historic preservation, would eventually come to play a central role.[153]

Many of the issues raised by Hobsbawm at the start of this chapter were not merely impending, but now present. Post-industrialisation was signalled in Scotland by Labour Secretary of State William Ross's (1911–88) *National Plan for Scotland*, which resulted in the creation of the Scottish Development Department (SDD) in 1965. All of Scotland, with the exception of Edinburgh which rode out the worst effects of the 1930s Depression, WWII and the decline of Empire, was declared a development area. Within a decade this led to the creation of the Scottish Development Agency (SDA) in 1975 (subsequently Scottish Enterprise in 1991), which early on eased – in comparison to the rest of the UK[154] – the structural economic shift from the moribund heavy industry model to a largely light to medium industry, service, electronic and arts entrepreneurial mode. The activity of the SDA offset, in part, the occasional doomed attempts to transform that self-same heavy industry through the belated and fateful Scottish entry into a crowded small car market through the agency of the struggling and under-capitalised Rootes Group at Linwood in 1960, into the trucks market at Bathgate through the inefficient and incompetently-managed British Leyland in 1961 or in the creation of the Ravenscraig steel-strip mill, 1954, operational in 1964 (peremptorily closed in 1992 due to a temporary slump in British Steel profits, emphasising Scotland's branch economy status). In politics in Scotland, the 'two-party state' ceased to exist by 1965 as initially Conservatives began to haemorrhage support to the SNP, thus bequeathing the Nationalists the soubriquet of the 'Tartan Tories', still occasionally affixed *ad hominem* to the party by Scottish Labour, although its fallout must wait on the devolution referendum 30 years hence.

6

A perfect storm: 1968–99

The times they are a-changin'

ARGUABLY, 1968 WAS the climacteric of both the latter half of the 20th century and of Modernism. A very brief selection of pivotal moments includes: when the Blues became Rock at Led Zeppelin's first live performance at Surrey University; when the Prague Spring and the Summer of Love had their brief moments; when the USA came off the Gold Standard; when the 'Troubles' began in Northern Ireland; and when hypertext and the computer mouse were first shown at the ACM/IEEE Computer Society's conference in San Francisco, still known in IT circles as 'The Mother [sic] of All Demos'.

Architecture in this period was characterised by five new pre-occupations. First was the weakening of Modernism's anti-historical and anti-aesthetic stranglehold and the emergence of nuanced reflections on the historiography of earlier periods, partly through the publication in the 1970s of many studies of the Modernist period, its participants and their works and writings, and partly through the recovery of 'lost' European architectures from Totalitarian imposition post-1945 and from behind the Iron Curtain post-1989. Second was an engagement with post-Structuralist philosophic and linguistic enquiry as a challenge to Modernism's orthodoxy. Third was its corollary in the use of the now historic architectures of Modernism as aesthetic and conceptual, even vernacular, resources *pace* the New York Five's[1] New England clapboard versions of Le Corbusier's platonic houses of the 1920s; Richard Meier's (b. 1934) render and metal panel interpretation of the same thing in large representative, official and cultural buildings; Mario Botta's (b.1943) domestic and representative versions, in the *arte povera* material of concrete blockwork, of Le Corbusier and Louis Kahn models; Aldo Rossi's (1931–97) interpretation of Terragni and de Chirico; or Co-op Himmelb(l)au and others' take on the

Constructivism of Iakov Chernikhov (1889–1951) and Konstantin Melnikov (1890–1974), often known as Deconstructivism, to name but a few. Fourth was the emergence of equality, ethical and environmental themes, often highly politicised, representing more subtle interrogations of Modernism's crudely bundled together and unexamined 'science' and 'social' mission. Fifth were the opportunity and economic consequences for architects of globalisation and neo-liberalism.

First principles, second thoughts, Third Reich: spurious totalitarian comparisons

Hitchcock returned to the earlier inclusivity of his *Modern Architecture* in *Architecture: Nineteenth and Twentieth Centuries* in 1969, but could not reconcile an International Style revisionism with his integrity and consistency as a historian, and he faltered. He might have been wiser to recant. He applied to Modernism the trope of 'the hero's quest' and recast his earlier 'magnificent traditional execution' of the non-conforming architectures into the character of 'the dutiful servant' whom he construed as dull, unimaginative and hidebound. He wrote:

> The historian *must* [Hitchcock's emphasis] attempt to give some sort of account of things like the Stockholm City Hall and the Woolworth Building. But the story is not an easy one to tell because it seems – at least to most scholars today – to lack plot[2]... The rise of modern architecture, on the other hand, offers material for a dramatic narrative, for it follows the pattern of the 'success-story', just as does that of the Gothic in 12th-century France or the beginnings of the Renaissance in 15th-century Italy.[3]

He employed familiar argumentation in his International Style assessment of regional architecture:

> Despite prolific production and the quite remarkable things that were occasionally achieved when historicism came to uneasy terms with new technical means... the traditional architecture of the 20th century is primarily an instance of survival; and cultural survivals are among the most difficult problems with which history has to deal. Their sluggish life, sunk in inertia and conservatism, is very different from the vitality of new developments. Yet survivals are tough and resilient,

tending always to maintain themselves by their very uneventfulness. Static, not to say smug, assurance is their greatest strength; their greatest danger is that boredom resulting from excessive familiarity which they eventually induce even among their most accomplished exponents.[4]

His interpretation of the Nordic achievement, about which he had been consistently equivocal, was that, somehow, it was the exception that proved the rule, whereupon he claimed that:

In the Scandinavian development from 1890 to 1930 there is therefore a sort of 'plot' or recognisable sequence of phases despite their overlappings.[5]

He still felt no compulsion, contrary to his earlier assertions of obligation, to investigate and elucidate fully what that plot might constitute:

To pursue the subject of traditional architecture further would be merely to explore what can now be seen to have been not so much a cul-de-sac as a road without a goal... However the future may evaluate the achievements of the traditional architects of the early 20th century, this chapter is now closed.[6]

But, of course, it was not.

Also having second thoughts was Pevsner, who revisited the fulcrum of Art Nouveau in an equivocal introduction to *The Anti-Rationalists*[7] of 1973, where he characterised his interest in the style as now 'the product of the historian's curiosity, not the *aficionado's* [Pevsner's emphasis] passion',[8] belatedly accepting its wider significance and engagement with regional and national architectures. Even in revision he harboured doubt:

Hoffmann brings up the most fascinating historian's problem of Art Nouveau and anti-Art Nouveau – the role of Mackintosh, whose group was invited by the Secession to show in its eighth exhibition in the autumn and early winter 1900. Mackintosh is for Art Nouveau in the north what Gaudí is in the south – the man of genius and an enigma.[9]

In his canonisation of Mackintosh, Pevsner expanded almost to *sui generis* status the rather more cautious significance which he had awarded him earlier without seemingly gaining much insight into Mackintosh's practice along the way.

William Curtis (b.1948) eschewed the later Modernist constructs placed upon Art Nouveau, siting it, in its own terms, chronologically, stylistically and spatially at a critical juncture in the history of architecture, reconnecting the link denied by Pevsner:

> But if Art Nouveau artists rejected historicism, they could not altogether reject tradition, for even the creator intent on producing new forms will rely, in some degree, on old ones. Indeed, what is often meant when the claim is made that such and such a movement was 'new' is that it switched its allegiances from recent and nearby traditions to ones more remote in space and time.[10]

Art Nouveau, for Curtis, replenished itself from deep and ancient wells of culture that were allied to a social programme which might be regional or national. This returns us very firmly to the pre-Modern analysis of Berlage and Loos, despite their shared dislike of Jugendstil, and touches on Jeremy Howard's thesis that

> overtones of nationalism, or at least an attempt to construct something of a National Style, are frequently present in Art Nouveau.[11]

Colin Rowe clarified what had puzzled Modernists because

> [the architect] stood as heir and critic to the 19th century... [whereby] one could begin to understand the pictorial rebellion of the early 20th century. It was a rebellion against anecdote which it often confused with symbolic meaning.[12]

With the Modernist model returning always to a cyclical discourse with and about itself and entering prolonged entropic decline, regional architectures were freed to occupy an, as yet, poorly defined position within the historiography of late 20th-century architecture. David Crowley observed:

> The history of the Cracow School suggests that interest in vernacular concerns were not closed by the intellectual wave of Modernism that washed over Europe in the 1920s nor by the neo-classicism of the 1930s, and might prompt the reader to consider to what degree the Polish experience of vernacularism was unique. 'Heroic' modernism has dominated the recording of the history of design, yet many other histories are still to be written.[13]

Jacques Gubler wrote, in contrasting reflection,

> Art Nouveau could be dismissed as non-Swiss or even dangerous in its 'cosmopolitan' or international circulatory aspects. In other words, the very ideological motivation which served Art Nouveau in Scotland, Catalonia or Piedmont, i.e. the quest for an autonomous national identity, in fact worked to its detriment in Switzerland.[14]

The post-Constructivist and post-Bauhaus countervailing architectural histories of Germany, Russia and, to a lesser extent, Italy of the second quarter of the 20th century emerging piecemeal post-WWII, and from behind the Iron Curtain post-1989, were given critical revisionist attention by a younger generation of writers not constrained by the need to privilege an orthodox Modernist narrative. Spiro Kostof (1936–91) said of his *A History of Architecture: Settings and Rituals*, published posthumously in 1995, that

> [he] would not be at all unhappy if [it] were to be seen as an offering of cultural history.[15]

Its sub-title promised an investigation of meaning in regional architectures. In this connection, Kostof foregrounded the totalitarian link while acknowledging its more conventional stylistic parallelisms in the continuity of Classicism:

> This public architecture of America, uneasy as the thought might be for those who believe that what we build is what we are, looks very much like the public architecture of the 1930s in Hitler's Germany, Mussolini's Italy, and Stalin's Russia.[16]

In the Western non-totalitarian world, such stripped- or not-so-stripped-Classicism was largely confined to official or representative buildings such as HM Office of Works' High Court, Lawnmarket, Edinburgh, 1934–7; E Vincent Harris's (1876–1971) Ministry of Defence Building, Whitehall, London, 1939–59 (designed 1915); Paul Philippe Cret's (1876–1945) Federal Reserve Building, Washington, DC, 1937; or Sir Edwin Lutyens' (1869–1944) Viceroy's House, New Delhi, 1912–30. However, any more thorough exploration by Kostof of this wider manifestation seems to have been obscured by the long shadows cast by the swastika, the red star and the fasces. Meanwhile, Frampton considered the use of the vernacular as it was represented in totalitarian architecture:

> An associate of Heinrich Tessenow in the creation of a whitewashed,

pitched roof Heimatstil manner, Schultze-Naumberg[17] sought as early as the mid-1920s to resist the internationalist and mechanistic tendencies of modern life... For Schultze-Naumberg, however, the issue of form had political connotations, and in opposing the Neue Sachlichkeit architecture of the Weimar Republic he soon adopted right-wing, racist attitudes that were readily assimilable to the reactionary ideology of the [Nazi] party.[18]

In addition to these Classical and archaic excursions, Charles Jencks (1939–2019) observed of the period's Modernist architects that

> the common historical opinion is that the architects of the Heroic Period were utterly opposed to Fascism; a closer look at their pragmatic statements and emphasis on 'the State' and other authoritarian means should have suggested otherwise.[19]

Pragmatic Modernists chasing work in Fascist Germany and Soviet Russia included Mies van der Rohe, Walter Gropius, Wassili Luckhardt, Herbert Bayer (1900–85), Hugo Häring (1882–1958), Frank Lloyd Wright, Philip Johnson and, of course, Le Corbusier, who claimed, with an insouciant opportunism masquerading as benign apoliticism, that:

> I crystallise round such ideas certain groupings that seek prominence. And on the left as on the right I am incorporated: here by communists, there by fascists, here by royalists, there by international organisations. Thought spreads like a drop of oil, touching many realms.[20]

Curtis, while validating neither the politics nor architectural production of totalitarianism, recognised the limitations of Modernism in dealing with monumental and representative architecture against which the Classical tradition and totalitarian architecture in particular pressed so hard in the 1930s:

> A persistent theme in all three countries was the reinforcement of nationalist sentiments by appeal to earlier national architectural traditions[21]... One does note, however, a preponderance of the racist style of argument combined with a fairly sound general assessment that modern architectural imagery would not be suitable to grand civic monumentality or to regionalist, *volkish* expression.[22]

He discussed the unbuilt *Danteum* by Italian architect Giuseppe Terragni (1904–43), best-known for his fascist-Modern Casa del Fascio, Como, 1932–6, and how it combined in one programme the three aspects of architectural authority – the archaic, the Classical, the Modern – whereby

> [Terragni's] intellectual strategy was a demonstration of one possible way of fusing the ancient and the modern without ending in a betrayal of both.[23]

The *Danteum* is one of several, mostly unbuilt, monumental projects of the first half of the 20th century – the so-called *Jahrhundertwerken* – such as HP Berlage's *Beethovenhuis*, Rotterdam, 1907–8; Hans Poelzig's (1869–1936) *Haus der Freundschaft*, Istanbul, 1916; Josef Hoffmann's *Weltfriedenshaus*, Vienna, 1917; Eliel Saarinen's *Kalevala House*, Helsinki, 1919; Jože Plečnik's (1872–1957) designs for the *Slovenska akropola* and the *Katedrala svobode*, Ljubljana, 1947; Patrick Geddes and Frank Mears' Hebrew University, Mount Scopus, Jerusalem, 1919–25; Joseph Gleave's Columbus Memorial Lighthouse, Dominican Republic 1939–92, or Frank Mears and Charles Carus-Wilson's (1886-1962?) Scottish Office on Calton Hill, Edinburgh, 1933. These projects were aspirational, combining both universal and national meanings and symbols. They contrasted markedly with the stolid totalitarian constructions built to provide the stages on which fascism's static ideological, moral and cultural rituals were re-enacted, of which Curtis noted:

> [Hitler's] patronage was ideally suited for the production of a bathetic, banal, instant culture of little lasting depth: and that is what most Nazi architecture usually became,[24]

and of which Gombrich observed,

> where ritual is concerned there is no demand for novelty. Ritualistic art rests on the strong desire for re-enactment and preservation rather than for fresh stimulation.[25]

Where totalitarian ritual in the 1930s – and indeed today in such nations as North Korea – depended at all on Modernism it was, as Peter Blundell Jones remarked, that in order to bring them to fruition they required 'the effects of mass transport and mass communication'.[26]

Totalitarianism seeks the hyper-conscious consolidation and continuity of Known culture and the vilification of the Other. This aids the state in its promulgation of an ersatz mythology, the creation of propaganda based on it and, ultimately, control of the populace through contingent privilege, co-option, coercion or terror. It is a utopian project which closes off future development by establishing *now* the full range of opportunities, rights, responsibilities and duties of the broad citizenry while permitting licence in the conduct of the ruling elites. It is inseparable from such as 'Hitler, whose rigid, inflexible psychology extended into the ideology of a rigid and inflexible state',[27] and where:

> Isolated stands the leader, Robespierre or Hitler to whom [the masses] give themselves body and soul in order to escape the fearful loneliness of an uprooted social system and who fills the void left by the disappearance of God.[28]

The purpose in discussing an architecture of the 1930s as described in the historiography of the late 20th century is to expose a prevalent contemporary argument which associated regionalism and nationalism with racism and totalitarian absolutely and as a consequence denigrated and devalued from the outset regionalism's architectural products. In their examination of this period, Kostof, Jencks, Frampton and Curtis contested the presumption that a national architecture is *de jure* and *de facto* totalitarian and found a space for those architects and their works with whom and with which Hitchcock and Pevsner had but toyed: the likes of Peter Jensen-Klint (1853–1930) and Kaare Klint's (1888–1954) Grundtvig's Church, Copenhagen, 1920–41, Gunnar Asplund's (1885–1940) Stockholm Public Library, 1924–28,[29] Erik Julius Lallerstedt's (1864–1955) Royal Institute of Technology, Stockholm, 1914–7, Ivar Tengbom's (1878–1968) Högalidskyrkan, Stockholm, 1923, and Ragnar Ostberg's (1866–1945) Stadshuset, Stockholm, 1923. Even the Marxist Hobsbawm noted that:

Inventive continuity: Grundtvig's Church, Copenhagen, 1920–41, architects Peter Klint and Kaare Klint.

> Some exceptions apart, the bulk of public building, including public housing projects by municipalities of the Left, which might have been expected to sympathise with the socially-conscious

new architecture, showed little sign of its influence except an apparent dislike for decoration.[30]

The non-architect Joachim Fest (1926–2006) summed up:

> Hitler's architectural ideology essentially consisted of hugeness, of what the world had never seen before... Contrary to widespread belief, his predilection was not even for classicism, which is unjustly described as the epitome of the 'totalitarian' style... That chimerical architectural vision of his, which he proclaimed as his guiding idea and the 'style of eternity', was essentially just a hotchpotch of his emotions translated into stone: his desire for theatrical backdrops, his insatiable hunger for stunning symbolism, and his desire to intimidate.[31]

Dissentient memoranda: theory

Martin Heidegger (1889–1976) is contentious because of his membership of the Nazi Party, 1933–45, and of the seeming obscurantism of his thought. However, as one of the few philosophers to engage with architecture as architecture rather than as philosophical analogy, his *Building Dwelling Thinking* has status in architectural discourse. The absence of commas in the title makes clear that his text is not intended as expiation on three separate activities but rather as an understanding of one comprehensive antinomial action. First published in German in 1954, it received wide attention following its English translation in 1971. However, even Heidegger's editor, David Farrell Krell, voicing a positivist Modernism, was perplexed:

> For here Heidegger sees the thing as the concrescence of what he calls the fourfold (*das Geviert*) of earth, sky, mortals and divinities. No introductory word of ours can explain what Heidegger means by this fourfold.[32]

What Heidegger said is this:

> the human being consists in dwelling and, indeed, dwelling in the sense of the stay of mortals on the earth.
> But 'on the earth' already means 'under the sky'. Both of these also mean 'remaining before the divinities' and include a 'belonging to men's being with one another'. By a *primal* [Heidegger's emphasis] oneness the four – earth, sky, divinities and mortals – belong together in one.

He elaborated on the fructifying earth 'spreading out into rock and water, rising up into plant and animal' and the changing sky and its seasons and climes and its diurnal course while the 'divinities are the messengers of the godhead' in which one assumes, if not a specific religiosity, then at least, in a challenge to rationalist or positivist thought, a general spirituality and an awareness of the infinitude of cosmic processes, wherein:

> The mortals are human beings. They are called mortals because they can die. To die means to be capable of death *as* death.

That is, human beings are mortal because they have certain knowledge of both their transience and own death. Heidegger also observed that when we think of each of the fourfold we are perforce thinking of the other three.[33] The First Peoples of Australia, say, would have no difficulty in understanding him; nor, in Scotland today, should we.

Heidegger posited the human response to the fourfold as 'dwelling', dwelling being both a constructive and agricultural act and a state of being. He employed the verb *bleiben*, 'to stay' or 'to keep', not *wohnen*, 'to live', as a synonym for 'to dwell'. Scots do not ask someone where they *live*, which merely imputes a geographic location; they ask 'whaur d'ye stey?',[34] because that encompasses the fourfold, *das Geviert*. Heidegger's *das Geviert* challenged absolutely the hard positivism and scientism of canonic Modernism and its concomitant elevation of a redemptive and autonomous 'space' because:

> When we speak of man and space, it sounds as though man stood on one side, space on the other. Yet space is not something that faces man. It is neither an external object nor an inner experience. It is not that there are men and over and above them space; for when I say 'a man' and in saying this word think of a being who exists in a human manner – that is, who dwells – then by the name 'man', I already name the stay within the fourfold among things.[35]

Karsten Harries (b.1937), using the home as the universal model of occupation – because in Bachelard's words, 'all really inhabited space bears the essence of the notion of home'[36] – further challenged Modernist claims about the nature and content of the dwelling:

> Many children, to be sure, continue to be raised in similarly stable environments, but the evolution of the modern life-world seems to point in a very different direction: how does a much more unstable

lifestyle – in which families move, disintegrate, and reform; in which often there is no family at all, but a single parent struggling to maintain a house – affect our dreams of houses? Of what houses do the inhabitants of our ghettos dream?[37]

Harries' concerns in architecture were to attempt a rapprochement between the reductive functionalism of the Moderns and those potent, primal and existential acts of dwelling, posited by Heidegger, and to query what 'home' might mean to the 'forgotten' or excluded.

In this connection, in *The System of Objects*, Jean Baudrillard queried the authority of Modernist orthodoxy in domestic design in two observations; firstly, on what he termed simply the 'Traditional environment', thus:

What gives the house of our childhood such depth and resonance in memory is clearly this complex structure of interiority, and the objects within it serve for us as boundary markers of the symbolic configuration known as home.[38]

Secondly, he questioned the revolutionary nature of Modernist design emancipation in what he called 'The modern object liberated in its function' where:

The organisation of space changes, too, as beds become day-beds and sideboards and wardrobes give way to built in storage. Things fold and unfold, are concealed, appear only when needed. Naturally such innovations are not due to free experiment: for the most part the greater mobility, flexibility and convenience they afford are the result of an involuntary adaptation to a shortage of space.[39]

Baudrillard was not seduced by Modernism's aesthetic justification of minimisation but recognised the managerial, financial and availability demands on space and the concomitant compromise of its functionality of which, for the most part, its aesthetic treatment as 'space' by Modernism is no more than a secondary and expedient characteristic.

Collins observed, '[a] great deal of cant is talked nowadays about space in architecture',[40] while Bernstein recorded a matching loss of substance:

The path from Van Gogh traces the disappearance of substance from art, while the development of abstraction (into the aptly named 'minimalism' that, at worst, conflates materiality with sensuousness, and at best uses materiality as a reminder of a loss of sensuousness) traces an increasing loss of sensuousness.[41]

For the fortunate, who were more than adequately housed, Gilson celebrated:

> Not only our memories, but the things we have forgotten are 'housed'. Our soul is an abode. And by remembering 'houses' and 'rooms', we learn to abide within ourselves. Now everything becomes clear, the house images move in both directions: they are in us as much as we are in them, and the play is so varied.[42]

While Bachelard asked,

> [d]oes there exist a single dreamer of words who does not respond to the word wardrobe?[43]

Harries, Bachelard, Baudrillard, Bernstein and Gilson all refused the reductivist Modernist house or workplace in its representation as an aesthetic stage-set for a superficial consumerist monasticism where the equipment of its ethical or ritual functions seem to be missing but which are confined to cupboards or to Bachelard's attic and cellar. Those storage spaces are crammed with the instruments of daily life which leave the arena of actual human occupation, action and imagination bare, literally and figuratively or, as is presently described, to be 'curated' with significant and approved pieces of Modernist art, décor and furnishings.

In contrast to the aridity of Modernism's value-free asceticism and self-denying Functionalism, Japanese arts appeared to represent a softer model, anchored in its region, redolent with the earth-magic of natural materials, the subtlety of Japanese carpentry and the philosophies of Buddhism and Shinto. Jackson, quoting Christopher Dresser, clarified that we are looking at not one but two models because:

> The two religions are as distinct as their architecture is different:...
> [Buddhism] is recognised by its richly carved colourful buildings, while [Shinto], indigenous to Japan, is characterised by its simplicity and fine workmanship... the first which promoted a love of nature and the second which encouraged the most careful and meticulous workmanship.[44]

Moreover, the movable nature of Japanese partitions and furnishing was part of the powerful image of an exquisite adaptable multi-purpose minimal space. Modernists were seduced by their tacit but overweening need for the very aesthetic and historic corroboration and validation they had initially refused in the European tradition and which the Japanese house conveniently, and conveniently distantly, provided. Such cultural, temporal and geographic distance facilitated Modernists' denial of the dual Korean and patrician patrimony of the Japanese house in order that they could impose a deracinated Rousseauian naturalism on it.

Kawazoe, in the corollary, identified

> The bare rooms in both houses [the Farnsworth House, Plano, 1950, by Mies van der Rohe and the Glass House, New Canaan, 1949, Philip Johnson], with their so-called universal space, no doubt immediately reminded Japanese architects of the ancient *shinden-zukuri* ('palace-style') architecture, which was intended to be used only as a shelter with nothing in the spacious room but a sleeping area in the north corner.[45]

The key dwelling concepts are 'palace' and 'shelter'.

In contrast, Jackson described

> *minka* or people's houses... in which rooms frequently had no designated functions but would change their usage throughout the day, or even, by the removal of all the external walls, dematerialise.

He continued:

> The clearest analysis of the Japanese house was made by Christopher Dresser when he said that 'the Japanese may be said almost to live an out-of-door life, the house being rather a floor raised above the ground with a substantial roof than a series of rooms properly enclosed by substantial side walls'... less than a century later, [it] had become a trope in Modern architecture.[46]

This was most clearly expressed in Schindler's and Wright's inward-focussed domestic work which sought an accommodation between the habits and practices of Western living and those of Japan, and most abstractly in the glass-and-steel houses of Mies van der Rohe and Johnson which permanently exposed the temporarily open Japanese house and substituted extensive private parkland for a shoji screen to ensure privacy.

In *The New Japanese House*, Chris Fawcett considered the bases of that trope:

> But these stereotypes are in fact a bunch of isolates wilfully grabbed from the authentic Japanese environment… What has made it possible for us to mistake this hotch-potch of figments of our Western imagination for the real thing is the deep-rooted misconceptions by which we surround the 'exotic'.[47]

The emptiness of the 'exoticised' Japanese house which impels this trope and, by extension, bedevils *existenzminimum* mass housing by its impossibility, is facilitated by the little-documented *kura*. Jackson commented:

> It was the sanctuary of the *kura* [a free-standing storage facility, separate from the house] which allowed the Japanese house, always prone to burning, to appear so free of clutter and bric-à-brac. The *kura* was in almost every way the opposite of the house: it was solid and robust.[48]

In the chapters 'House/Home' and 'House/Ritual', Fawcett confronted an altogether messier picture of Japanese family life and the occasional tackiness of some of its representations. The house as museum: storing objects, recording histories, representing change, hoarding and recovering memory. The house as temple: celebrating or commemorating births, adulthood, marriages, successes, deaths. The house as retreat: sanctioning repose, consoling loss or failure. All of which are Heidegger's divinities and mortals and all of which the *existenzminimum* dwelling should have been required to accommodate but did not, through the minimisation of those empty spaces and surfaces, support them. Loos the cultural critic, writing, with tongue in cheek, in the *Neues Wiener Tagblatt* in 1900, saw the imminent Modernist tyranny for what it would become:

> We can't hide the fact however, that he tried to be home as little as possible. Now and then one needs a break from so much art. Could you live in an art gallery?… He had expected something different. But art requires sacrifice.[49]

Fawcett categorised dwellings as 'ritual-affirming' or 'ritual-disaffirming' and threw down a challenge:

> One is entitled to ask that a house should be something other than

a fine intellect, which makes us forget. There are tasks more urgent, more pressing, more deserving of our attention than the manipulation of forms in harmonic constellations... But real genius is rarer than the architect fancies, and hangs on a judgement that his age is not qualified to give.[50]

Harries echoed Fawcett:

It is therefore not surprising that... architectural modernists should have found domestic architecture an especially challenging problem: houses are more than complicated machines. Dwelling does not just mean being sheltered.[51]

Doctrinaire Modernist architects, in this light, may simply have misconstrued their 'dreams of houses', and their alienation from the populace at large, which has been their unthinking complaint, may be the result of that misconstruing.

Dissentient memoranda: how sound analysis...

Jencks set out the moment immediately preceding post-Modernism's architectural critique in his *Modern Movements in Architecture* thus:

Dazzled by this display of a consistent [Modernist] plot and inexorable development, the reader forgets to ask about all the missing actors and their various feats – all that which ends up on the scrap heap of the historian's rejection pile. In part this selection and omission of data is desirable, since it creates some conceptual order. But unfortunately it often serves to reinforce one ideology – one tradition of development – at the expense of a live plurality.[52]

Kurokawa echoed the contradictions and raised the issues which Modernism's monistic, ascetic and anti-historical project had abrogated and against which post-Modernism attempted to push back:

[semantics and ontology] do not assume a single, ideal image of architecture that exists as a truth transcending time, history and the differences among cultures. Rather it is the very differences that arise in the unfolding of time and history that produce meaning. From the epistemological standpoint of Modernism, which asked 'What is architecture?' the truth is given *a priori*, and the problem was how to attain that truth through the power of reason.⁵³

... became bad alternate theory

The English crime writer Dorothy L Sayers (1893–1957), who had an early career as an advertising copywriter, made this prophecy in 1936 of commodification and, possibly, its architectural expression:

> He had never realised the enormous commercial importance of the comparatively poor. Not on the wealthy, who buy what they want when they want it, was the vast superstructure of industry founded and built up, but on those who, aching for a luxury beyond their reach and for a leisure forever denied them, could be bullied or wheedled into spending their hardly won shillings on whatever might give them, if only for a moment, a leisured and luxurious illusion. Phantasmagoria – a city of dreaded day, of crude shapes and colours piled Babel-like in a heaven of cobalt and rocking over a void of bankruptcy – a Cloud Cuckooland, peopled by pitiful ghosts.⁵⁴

Denise Scott-Brown's (b. 1931) eerie 1973 echo ignored the considerable negatives identified by Sayers and acquiesced in the parallel commodification of architecture:

> Think of the many products which are sold 'just like grandma used to make', or 'finger-licking good', which are reminders of days back on the farm. Now Madison Avenue can handle that need very well. Why shouldn't architects be able to?
> I would say that we are talking about a very broadly based thing, which is the popular culture... and we're trying to make it acceptable to an elitist sub-culture, namely, the architects and [those] who hire architects. It becomes high culture rather than low culture.⁵⁵

Berman recognised the same trend in literature where:

> There is an important body of modern writing, often by the most serious writers, that sounds like advertising copy.⁵⁶

Scott-Brown, using a version of Berlage's notion of high and low culture, although not at all as he intended it, and substituting possession for expression, made a fundamental shift between actual lived popular culture and how the media, commerce and advertising mythologised rural and small town American experience, replaying it for a world audience and where, in turn, those other nations likewise mistreated their own culture. Despite her populist claims, Scott-Brown was unable let 'low culture' alone but must transmute it to 'high culture' so that it presented acceptably to her kind. Advertisers were not slow to appreciate the fatuity of this device and to put a cynical, self-deprecatory spin on it. In an attempt to imply that it might have the pedigree, quality and taste of butter, while recognising that to many it did not, an advertisement for a margarine popular in late 1990s' Britain – with voice-over by a well-known Scots actor – put it exactly:

> It took me back, back to a golden childhood, a carefree time living among honest country folk. A golden childhood indeed. But was it mine though? I grew up in a council flat in Greenock.[57]

That Scott-Brown sought to ground an architecture on these flimsiest of foundations and to establish a cultural superstructure from such fragile materials merely follows a neoliberal monetarist *zeitgeist*. Implicit in her philosophy was what Peter Dormer (1949–96), referring to the design of the Boeing 747, described as 'above the line' and 'below the line' meanings in design, where above the line was 'what it is thought the consumer wants to see and understand'[58] – post-Modern gaiety, say – and below the line was 'too complicated, too numerous and frequently too arcane to interest the lay consumer'[59] – opportunity deficits, discrimination and personal debt. However, as with Boeing's 737 Max or the London Borough of Kensington's Grenfell Court, it was often what was below the line that impacted most crucially, even fatally, on the consumer. Consumerism was all, and in Richard Demarco's words, '[w]e have lost the sense of the ridiculous'.[60]

The first substantial revision of Modern architectural history post-1965 was Charles Jencks's (1939–2019) *Modern Movements in Architecture* of 1973,[61] although it was greatly overshadowed by his later work on post-Modernism to which it now seems something of a scene-setting. Jencks took a taxonomical approach to the architecture and architects. He included a section on regionalism – although he used the term but twice – entitled 'The Contribution of Locale'. He observed of the criticism made by Norberg-Schulz – himself influenced by Heidegger – of regionalism that

> those solutions which were too overtly historicist or provincial were

condemned, where those works which answered a specific need were praised,

because Norberg-Schulz's 'too overtly historicist and provincial' were relative. They created an entirely subjective scale of achievement where architectures were to a greater or lesser degree successful depending on an assessment of whether or not they embodied narrative or symbol to a greater or lesser degree or confused either with the other. Attempting to put some flesh on the bare bones of 'locale', Jencks went on to say:

> Thus Scandinavian modern was generally nature-oriented and socially responsible, German was tough and ordered, Swiss was bourgeois and clean, Italian vigorously modelled, sophisticated and slick to the point of decadence, Indian was strong and impoverished, Israeli full of hexagons and six-pointed stars, Japanese was constructivist, black on white, full of slight curves and so on.[62]

One could interpret Jencks's characterisations as brief and un-nuanced national stereotypes of the kind discussed in Chapter 1. However, Jencks's broader revisionist architectural philosophy allowed him an acceptance of regionalism and its archetypes consistently rejected up to this point and created agreement with McCrone:

> Of course all this national identity was continually eschewed or, where found, explained away and condemned. But this embarrassment did not make it any less of a fact. The point was that an architect would as inevitably use a traditional set of forms as he would speak a local language with regional inflection and certain built-in assumptions. Besides, the justification might continue, to avoid a solution just because it was traditional was as silly as accepting it just because it was traditional.[63]

Jencks rounded off with the intriguing *post facto* observation that:

> The forms, as opposed to being historicist, do not recall their previous use until *after* [Jencks's emphasis] they are seen to work in their present context.[64]

In such contrast is revealed, on the one hand, the contemporary relevance of a forbidden symbolism to which the Modernist had imputed historicism and aestheticism and, on the other hand, that the notion of 'the-old-is-the-new-is-the-old' had not facilitated the successful insinuation of doctrinaire Modernism into extant cultures and subsequent judgement of the Modernist work still ignored its historic context. Post-Modernism did not merit a single mention in Jencks's text, although, within three years, it was to be the whole of his philosophy.

Post-Modernism very nearly eclipsed Bruno Zevi's *The Modern Language of Architecture* – published in Italian in 1973 and English in 1978 – in which Zevi defensively demoted Jencks's book to the status of 'a most amusing essay'.[65] Zevi sought the apotheosis of Modernism in the complete dissolution of perspectival space, three-dimensionality, symmetry, proportion, regularity, repetition, assonance and the façade.[66] His thesis was demanding intellectually, aesthetically and practically and the architect was not encouraged to learn that:

> The modern language is a precise and almost ruthless instrument of criticism, a kind of litmus paper that scientifically determines whether and to what degree an architect is modern.[67]

So much easier to follow the loose prescriptions of Jencks.

Zevi had nothing to say about regionalism, though he regarded Rudofsky's 'architecture without architects' with some favour:

> Sociologists have found that slums, *bidonvilles*, *favelas*, and *barriadas* have an intensely vital sense of community that is unknown in 'planned' lower-class housing developments. Why is that? Because adventure, the pioneering spirit, and neighbourliness are missing in planned settlements, together with that spontaneous kitsch which, despite its negative features, can be extremely stimulating.[68]

Zevi seemed unknowing of or untroubled by the fact that the asserted vitality of communities at the margins is bought at the cost of abject poverty, disease, police brutality, random evictions and demolition, drugs and crime. He seemed more concerned with the aesthetic demerits of kitsch. One is reminded of the arch-Classicist Roger Scruton's equally questionable 'glory of the Victorian slums'.[69] Zevi was on safer ground with his predictions about the use of the computer,[70] although he was not to know how 'classicised' that use would become in the 21st century.

Carry on camping: the wit and wisdom of post-Modernism

Modernism's anti-historical project became ahistorical in post-Modernism and Late Modernism in that the historicity of historic motives was ironicised and sampled. There was no place for regional architecture in post-Modernism, since regionalism's values predated and transcended post-Modernism's brief, borrowed and helicoptered intellectual hegemony which was merely required to be, in Jencks's usage of 1974, 'camp', by which it

> tries to outflank all the other stereotyped views of failure which are moribund or moralistic and substitute a sort of cheerful openmindedness. It starts from failure and then asks what is left to enjoy, to salvage. It is realistic, because it accepts monotony, cliché and the habitual gestures of mass-production society as the norm without trying to change them... Thus the epitome 'it's so bad that it's good', which accepts the classifications of traditional culture but reverses the verdict.[71]

Meanwhile, Kurokawa's special pleading told us that post-Modernism's aesthetic and historicity remained no more substantial than its philosophy:

> Eco's *The Name of the Rose* is rich with quotations, metaphors and signs. But who would say of this best-selling novel that it is nothing more than a hybrid *pastiche*, lacking in creativity? For Eco, medieval Europe served as a pretexte to transcend Modernism... His method is similar to my own, as I have chosen Japan's Edo period as my own *pretexte* from which I have extracted my own quotations, metaphors and signs.[72]

There was no discussion by Kurokawa of a comprehensive cultural resource, nor of a cultural continuity, on which such transformations might have been effected. Rather, his choice of historic or regional or national authority was one of personal volition and autonomy, in other words, entirely random, and in which intellectual or aesthetic authority from elsewhere – from everywhere – was invoked simply because it was *not* Modern. At least Kurokawa, and others like him, had the wit to confine this choice to their personal practice and, unlike the proselytisers of the 1930s and '40s, not to a presumed universal societal good. The issues were strictly aestheticised and intellectualised and any lingering social and cultural concerns were presumed to be competently satisfied by the actions of the market and the productions of consumerism. The uses to which such authority were put were similarly individual, idiosyncratic and autonomous. The key issue was the rejection by post-Modernists of the validity of transformable architectural motives arising from within a cultural continuum where the general characteristics were a shared experience, as was proposed by, say, Curtis and their contrasting adoption of the ephemerality of a transcendent architectural imagery from within a highly personal imagistic constellation as offered by Kurokawa. Such a constellation could as easily derive from myth, legend and fantasy as from the facts of architectural history. Kurokawa's contribution was all the more disappointing insofar as his analysis of Modernism's problems seemed so clear.

Jencks developed an ambivalence to matters of cultural specificity in between his 1973 and 1977 publications, from a general camp irony to a subsequent recovery of the neo-Platonic and syncretic language of symbol last culturally current pre-1919,[73] which were subsequently made evident in his own designs such as the Thematic House, Holland Park, London, 1983, and the cosmogonic gardens in Scotland: Landform at the Scottish National Gallery of Modern Art, Edinburgh, 2002; The Garden of Cosmic Speculation, Dumfriesshire, 2003; Cells of Life, Jupiter Artland, Edinburgh, 2003–10; and, with Cecil Balmond (b.1943), the as yet unbuilt Star of Caledonia, Gretna, 2019. In the search for architectural authority, Jencks undertook a

Mimetic continuity: Scandic Crown Hotel, Edinburgh, 1988, architect Ian Begg.

post-Modern parallel of Curtis's Modernist analysis of Terragni with his own thoughts on the work of Mario Botta.[74]

Post-Modernism also provided a vehicle by which those, following long careers in relative architectural obscurity because they were too individual or anachronistic or their work too idiosyncratic to fit anywhere, and to which they were soon to return, briefly found a voice. One thinks, for example, of Quinlan Terry (b.1937) and his English Palladianism; or Mackovecz Imre (1935–2011) and his interpretation of an Art Nouveau-influenced Hungarian timber folk-architecture; or Ian Begg (1925–2017) and his 16th-century Scottish tower-house model (see previous page); or Amancio d'Alpoim Guedes (1925–2015) and his Guadí-inflected, aboriginal-influenced work in Mozambique; or Herb Greene's (b.1929) Midwest Expressionism; or Paolo Soleri's (1919–2013) ad hoc adobe (later concrete) in Arcosanti, Arizona. However, it was the very recognisable and time-bound specificity of the historicist architectural signs they, and others like them, employed that anchored their work in the permanent static recreation of a part-known, part-imagined past.

Regionalism's emancipation: Frampton's 'critical regionalism'

The single most significant and influential revisionist text of late 20th-century architectural historiography was Frampton's *Modern Architecture: A Critical History* of 1980. Especially rewarding was the Second Edition of 1985 with its chapter on 'Critical Regionalism', based on his essay of 1983. Frampton crucially separated nationalism from fascism and began cautiously to shift towards a more sympathetic definition of regional and national architectures:

> This disturbingly regressive tendency [the architecture of the Third Reich] no doubt accounts for our mutual efforts to qualify the term *regional* with the adjective *critical*, [Frampton's emphasis] although what this might mean in specific terms is admittedly more difficult to define… I wished to employ the term to allude to a hypothetical and real condition in which a local culture of architecture is consciously evolved in express opposition to the domination of hegemonic power.[75]

If regional or national architectures are about anything at all, it is the 'express opposition to the domination of hegemonic power' (see Chapter 1). In

Frampton's terminology, regional or national architecture *is* a form of 'critical regionalism'.⁷⁶ His 'Six Points for an Architecture of Resistance' are: 'Culture and Civilisation'; 'The rise and fall of the avant-garde'; 'Critical Regionalism and world culture'; 'The resistance of place-form'; 'Culture versus nature'; 'The visual versus the tactile'⁷⁷. Beyond *Critical Regionalism*, Frampton developed his thinking in many discursive introductions or *apologias* to the work of architects whom one would have expected to encounter in a regionalist pantheon, such as Alvaro Siza, John and Patricia Patkau and Brian MacKay-Lyons.

Edinburgh College of Art alumnus Alan Colquhoun (1921–2012), partly in agreement, partly in contra-distinction to Frampton, observed that:

> the promotion of a 'critical regionalism' in which what is celebrated would seem to be more the *loss* [Colquhoun's emphasis] of authenticity than its recovery... Rather it manifests itself in the form of nuances... Needless to say, the kind of regionalism I refer to had nothing to do with the old 'regions of culture' attributed to ethnic characteristics, climate, language and so on.⁷⁸

While Colquhoun, from his orthodox Modernist position, undermined and, in part, refused critical regionalism, there remained much of value in his claim of a 'loss of authenticity' because it directed attention to the Modernist understanding that conventional regional authenticity was represented by the superficial constructional and aesthetic responses to territory, patrimony and polity which had been made at a particular and usually distant juncture in the region's history. It warned that, were this debate to have been centred on aesthetic representation alone, orthodox Modernism would have prevailed in that it had made plain its anti-historic and non-aesthetic credentials from the outset and removed such topics from the discussion. It required Colquhoun to jettison the territorial and patrimonial significance in regional architecture, that is, its 'ethnic characteristics, climate, language and so on', while he questioned their use by regionalists as 'inauthentic' due to that temporal distance. However, I am not so thirled to aesthetic representation and the reproduction or transformation of historic motives because it is the ideational processes driving each separate regionalism that interests me.

Peter Zumthor posed the question as to where local and regional architectures, and indeed individuals, sat within the post-Modern vortex:

> 'Anything goes', say the doers. 'Mainstreet is almost all right', says Venturi, the architect. 'Nothing works any more', say those who suffer from the

hostility of our day and age... Everything merges into everything else, and mass communication creates an artificial world of signs. Arbitrariness prevails... The real thing remains hidden. No-one ever gets to see it.[79]

Pallasmaa described the poles of contemporary architectural experience:

> By rejecting the wisdom and resistance of tradition, architecture also drifts towards a deadening uniformity on the one hand [Late Modernism], and towards a rootless anarchy of expression [post-Modernism] on the other.[80]

Craig Owens offered a comparison:

> in 'Fantasia of the Library' Foucault discusses Manet's art as 'museum painting' – painting as 'a manifestation of the existence of museums and the particular reality and interdependence that paintings acquire in museums'.[81]

Consumerism and globalism are post- and Late Modernist architecture's 'particular reality' and with which they are 'interdependent'.

Britpop: the British reception of post-Modernism

Sutherland Lyall (n.d.), writing in 1980, dated the end of the International Style in Britain to the late 1950s. Given the circumstances discussed in Chapter 5, it could hardly have been said to have got going in any real sense until then. Lyall's cuspidal moment was the passing of the major architectural figures of the Modernist period, Wright (1959), Le Corbusier (1965), Mies van der Rohe (1969) and Walter Gropius (1969), when '[f]reed from their physical presence, historians and critics began to move in'.[82] Other than Giedion, who died in 1968, the other principal Modernist historians and apologists were to live on into the 1980s – Collins (1981), Pevsner (1983), Hitchcock (1987) and Banham (1988) – although revision of the canonical texts was already well underway. Zevi had acknowledged the passing of this architectural generation, decrying that 'some of them stopped nourishing their children long before they actually died'.[83] In this seeming authoritative vacuum, Lyall ascertained that

> If there is any major theme among the contemporary *avant garde* it is probably that of ambiguity and the deliberate juxtaposition of half-familiar images from the architectural past.[84]

He enumerated various sub-themes as discrete manifestations: 'brutalism', 'vernacularism', 'system-build', 'western primitivism', 'community architecture', 'hi-tech' and so on – terminology with meaning at the time although for the most part recondite in practice today. He, too, even at this late date, did not mention post-Modernism.

Lyall was greatly taken with a 'contemporary vernacular' which he inherited, consciously or unconsciously, from Richards. He recharacterised it as the 'neovernacular'[85] encapsulated in documents such as the *Essex Design Guide* or in Gordon Cullen's (1914–94) drawings for *Architectural Review* or in *Townscape*[86], which had considerable impact in the 1970s and '80s on developments such as at Eaglestone, Milton Keynes, 1975, by a pre-Byker Ralph Erskine; or at Hillingdon, 1978, by Shankland Cox; or inflated to Civic Centre scale by RMJM, also at Hillingdon in 1978. Lyall was inclined to be casual with his categories and snared the rather less than neovernacular productions of John Darbourne (1935–91) and Geoffrey Darke (1929–2011) such as Lillington Gardens, Pimlico, 1961–72, and Marquess Road, Islington, 1966–7. The neovernacular as promoted by Lyall exhibited a preference for recognisable historic motives which, when later clumsily constructed, of necessity, to the Lego-brick proportions of a standard machine-made concrete block or common brick together with standard window frames and roof trusses, achieved neither a subtlety of composition, detail or dimension nor the timelessness of a vibrant regionalism and dated them absolutely to the 1990s. The apotheosis of such vernacularism and historicism was the Leon Krier master-planned Poundbury, Dorsetshire, 1993, which, due to its extensive use of bespoke components, largely avoided such crudity of execution, although not such anachronism.

A Baronial clone: Aberdeenshire, late 20th century.

Only two years after Lyall's 1980 review, Andreas Papadakis (1938–2008) collected, in *British Architecture*, some of the themes expressed by Lyall and Jencks in a definitive precursor to the next 20 years' of post-Modern architectural practice,[87] such as Richard Reid (b.1948) and Ralph Lerner's (1949–2011) exposition of their Arts & Crafts elevational reinterpretations[88] in the design for the Vasone Villa in São Paulo, Brazil.[89] Reid admonished that

> the elements of Englishness [in those elevations] are not
> copies of those belonging to a vernacular tradition, but instead
> are comments on the interpretation of such elements as developed
> by Shaw, Voysey and Lutyens.[90]

Such distancing by the architects from their vernacular sources provided the simulacrum of validation and intellectual underwriting of the project, while finessing post-Modernism's need to reframe, rather than reject, history and, perversely, a Modernist urge to initiate novel form. There was no evidence in Reid and Lerner's project that the Englishness of their twice-distilled Home Counties and Queen Anne regionalisms had any relevance to the Vasone Villa's 'mountain top site', since there was no site or location plan attached to the text. A separately published perspective was gnomic and entirely lacking in detail, as was a tiny and well-nigh unreadable plan of the house. Moreover, in the last glorious days of the hand-drawn image prior to the hegemony of the computer,[91] the villa was illustrated in that graphic concatenation, current at the time, of a hard-edged mechanical representation of the toy-building-block post-Modern simplifications of vernacular motives within an orthogonal axonometry which presented the 'compromise' of the 'vernacular' with the Modern with the ironic.

Looking backwards and outwards for guidance, Peter Davey (1940–2018) wrote comparatively in the August 1997 issue of the *Architectural Review*:

> Talk about an Architecture Parlante: turn-of-the-century Milanese Liberty
> architecture scarcely stopped chattering… the genial, witty, curiously
> revealing masks form a charivari: a metaphor and embodiment of
> prosperous bourgeois flaneur life in the Milanese bella epoca… No
> wonder that… Le Corbusier and his contemporaries wanted to restrict
> the causerie to the interplay of abstract forms. Yet… we have lost a great
> deal of value to humanity in the pursuit of mute abstraction. It cannot be
> refound in the piffling inanities of PoMo [post-Modernism], or any other
> attempt to re-invent ornament in the late 20th century. Is it gone forever?
> Perhaps we could find it again if only we could define it.[92]

The architecture spoke to him, Davey found it mellifluous, but he was no linguist. Its meaning, the implicit nationalism of Milan Liberty's predominantly

Italian Liberty: Tre Oci, Venice, 1910–3, architect Mario De Maria.

Venetian Gothic, Classical and Baroque bases, in contrast to the regionalist folkloric bases of much Northern European Art Nouveau, entirely eluded him. Italy, unified in 1871, was a nation-state less than a generation at the time of the Liberty style, while its architectural corollary, the bloated Classical monument to Vittorio Emanuele II, the Altare della Patria, Rome, by Giuseppe Sacconi (1854–1905), begun in 1885, was not completed until 1935, well into Fascism's brief hegemony.

In this context, Tobia quoted Camillo Boito (1836–1914)[93] from 1880, who stated,

> nations are already searching for a style: the Germans return to their ogival style, the English to their Tudor, the Russians hold on to their Byzantine, the French are undecided between their Gothic and their Renaissance style. For Italy, the marvellous richness of its past constitutes its greatest obstacle.[94]

This quest was

> the same problem confronted by the first Italian Artists' Congress of 1872, which had complained of the paradox in Italy where, before political unity, a stylistic unity had existed (neoclassicism) which, after unification, had broken up into regional schools.

Milanese Liberty was one product of that diversity. Tobia went further to posit the specifics of this quest by Italian architects:

> The close dialectic between *tradition* and *modernity* [Tobia's emphases] is the first characteristic to be noted in examining the process of nationalisation of the masses which took place in Italy in the second half of the 19th century through the new urban structures and use of monuments.[95]

Learning nothing from what he had seen, Davey had no way to achieve what he plainly desired – an architecture of the 20th century that was neither post-Modern nor mute.

In Scotland, Glendinning produced the squib *The Cumbernauld Conservation Society* in the early 1980s in an attempt to encourage his then employer, the Royal Commission for the Architectural and Historic Monuments of Scotland (RCAHMS), to give due regard to the architectural production of the Welfare State. Initially it landed Glendinning in hot water, although his subsequent success has had far-reaching consequences in determining how Scottish architecture of the 20th century, in particular that of the third quarter, has been viewed, written about, approved of and supported officially from the 1990s onwards.

At the close of the 20th century, Jonathan Glancey (b.1954) produced a popular, well-illustrated, catholic, deceptively simple and concise gazetteer of Modern architecture, *C20th Architecture*,[96] with no less than eight thematic chapters, each continuous throughout the century. For example, 'Arts and Crafts' began with CFA Voysey's The Orchard of 1900 and ended with the Klints' Grundtvig's Church, 1940, while 'Classicism' began with Peter Behrens's AEG Turbine Factory, Berlin, 1909 and ended with Robert AM Stern's Celebration, Florida, 1996. While we might have objections to some of his categories and entries, there is no gainsaying that Glancey's inclusive taxonomy more nearly reflected a real history of architecture of the 20th century than many other compendia. Regrettably, he still felt constrained to issue the standard unqualified Modern Movement *apologia* in the Foreword that it was others and the *zeitgeist* which were to blame when things went wrong:

> In fact, architects – Le Corbusier first among them – have been accused of trying to destroy civilisation in the 20th century with designs for towers of concrete and steel and ambitions that witnessed the unprecedented demolition of historic buildings, streets and squares. This is unfair, although the architect was, on the whole, a willing collaborator with governments, property developers and the moving spirit of the times.[97]

Glancey had no category for regional and national architectures nor, significantly, did he give much indication of what was to come in his 'Futures' section beyond the Petronas Towers, Kuala Lumpur, 1997, by Cesar Pelli (1926–2019) or the exponential growth of Shenzhen city in China, thus signalling how sudden and rapid was the eventuation of Mannerist Modern in the opening two decades of the 21st century (see Chapter 7).

The Great Glasgow Storm: the rehabilitation of the tenement

Appropriately, perhaps, it was the weather and a fuel source and not theory that in part facilitated Scotland's re-examination of Modernist orthodoxy. In January 1968 the Great Glasgow Storm left nine dead, 54 collapsed or dangerous buildings and 5,000 damaged tenements. Four months later, a small gas explosion at the 22-storey pre-fabricated concrete panel Ronan Point tower in Newham, Canning Town, London, opened in March, caused the near complete collapse of an entire corner of the block, killing six inhabitants and injuring 17. Superficially, there may seem little to connect these events but, in principle, they were intimately bound together as opposite poles and framed the debate around mass housing and urban form for the remainder of the 20th century.

By the late 1960s a little of the gloss had come off post-war rehousing and urban planning programmes, although nothing quite like it did in the 1970s and 1980s. Alison Ravetz's *Model Estate*[98] of 1974, Adam Curtis's (b.1955) 1984 film *The Great British Housing Disaster*[99] and Sam Webb's (b.1932) supervision, recording and report of the 1986 forensic demolition of Ronan Point and numerous other writings provided detail that does not need repetition here. However, these were the failures so casually dismissed by Cooper et al as biased press coverage[100] (see Chapter 7) and which continued to emerge throughout the next 20 years.[101]

While there were clear benefits in slum clearance – although one could argue about the quality of some of the replacements – there were consequences, as outlined by Pacione.[102] Glasgow's large population losses were contrived through the centrally-enforced transfer of former slum-dwellers to overspill communities and the New Towns – a process that also, but to a much lesser extent, impacted the other cities – although Aberdeen was buoyed, late on, by the nascent oil industry. Edinburgh suffered commuter drift to East Lothian, Midlothian and Fife as did Dundee to Broughty Ferry and Tayport and Aberdeen to Deeside, but all such urban losses were exacerbated by the structural factor of the continued shrinkage in Scotland's traditional industrial base and the less than commensurate rise, at the time, of the service sector coupled with the consequent loss of the fiscal base in the flight or transfer of ratepayers beyond city royalties. Glasgow's situation was further compounded by the great extent of council ownership of the housing stock which, while it simplified slum clearance and the transfer of tenants to peripheral estates, brought with it huge pressing responsibility and unanticipated costs in the wake of the Great Storm, the effect of which may be compared relatively to that of a tornado or tsunami.

The 'new' materials: stone, lead, slate, cast iron and lime

The immediate consequence of the Great Glasgow Storm was the re-evaluation of the affected tenements not, as they had been regarded previously, as impediments to the construction of a new Glasgow but as valuable housing stock and urban fabric in their own right requiring immediate emergency repair. This had the incidental benefit of reviving traditional trades such as stone masonry, lime mortaring and harling, cast iron drainage and leadwork. Architects, so recently trained in modern construction techniques, needed to quickly learn or relearn the constructional and environmental peculiarities of the traditional tenement: the strapped-and-lined 35–60 centimetre thick masonry wall and its particular vapour permeable needs; the significance of the fireplace flue in providing ventilation to rooms; the subtle balance required between heating, humidity and ventilation of the dwelling; the fire-resisting and acoustic properties of the timber floor construction and the importance of ensuring the integrity of the ash deafening between the joists, the lathe and plaster beneath and the 25mm boarding above.

Engagement with these basic practical considerations prompted wider recognition of what made the tenement work: in urban formation; in the urban streetscape; in the nature and use of the street; in community-generation or community-retention; in the self-policing 'close' or 'stair' with its minimum of eight and maximum of ca. 20 flats; in the self-maintained communal access with its stair-cleaning rotas; in the security provision of the main door latch (soon to be upgraded to electronic stair-entry systems); in the amenity and drying area potential of the formerly neglected 'back courts' or 'greens'; in the degree of 'ownership'; and in the tenement's relative technological simplicity in operation and fabric access and maintenance requirements. Once past the immediate challenge of making the buildings weathertight, it became apparent there was substantial utility in upgrading the 'room-and-kitchen' or in combining one and two apartment flats to increase usable space and numbers of rooms, to add or extend kitchen and bathroom facilities and general amenities while reducing overcrowding but

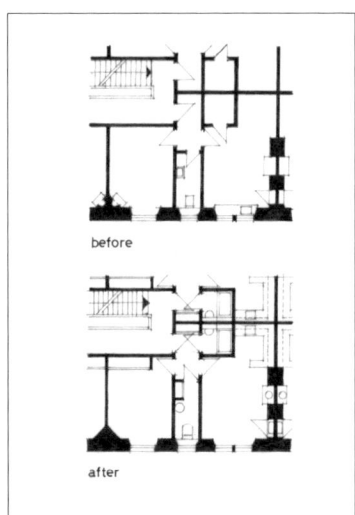

After the storm: a generic 'room-and-kitchen'.
(Drawn by Roger Emmerson)

still maintaining a sufficient density of urban population to support viable community facilities, shops and services.

It was the relative structural flexibility of mass masonry construction, derided by Fry, which made the internal alterations possible. The use of the 'loop-vent', later the air-admittance valve (AAV), freed up the bed recess at the back of the 'kitchen', distant from the nearest downpipe, for conversion into a regular fitted kitchen, while the adjacent 'coal cellar' became a shower-room. It was not hard for public and private landlords, astute property developers acquiring semi-derelict tenements for a song, pioneering first-time buyers and long-time owner-occupiers and their architects to see that, in simple terms, the traditional tenement answered many of the tendentious cultural, societal and responsibility questions posed by much of the housing erected not merely since the end of WWII, but since 1919. To be clear, what entailed in the renovation of the tenement was not architectural conservation *per se* as it was more commonly understood, although, as the attention of the listing bodies belatedly turned to streetscape and the creation of Conservation Areas following the Civic Amenities Act, 1967, an element of conservation was included.

Reclaiming the streets: life in urban Scotland

The recovery of the tenement, whether from omission in the 19th-century Scottish novel – 'a sorry failure of nerve'[103] – or from the titillation of *No Mean City*, or from the romanticisation of *Miracle in the Gorbals* or from the condemnation of Medical Officers of Health,[104] was the recovery of significant territory and patrimony, subsequently supported by a revised polity, brought about through the ingenuity of architects in the provision, initially, of emergency housing. For the first time, Modern architects met those formerly destined to occupy the Modern Movement's mass housing programmes as the present clients of their soon-to-be rehabilitated homes, largely without the intervention and filter of the political, class, aesthetic, ethical or moral agendas of housing committees, public health departments or other welfare organisations. The signal importance of the involvement of the 'end-user' in this process of design and creation had them characterised, with typical Glasgow bombast, as 'the Medicis of Maryhill'. Glendinning et al acknowledged this implicit assault on Modernism's verities, although not necessarily with favour:

> The strength of this reaction was epitomised in the way in which the

central Modernist socio-psychological ideal, Community, was turned on its head. It was seen no longer as something created for users by design of new buildings, but as something to be protected against new development by the action of residents or users.[105]

Mongold was more succinct, stating

> that participation is a better process than anticipation with regard to the users and their environmental needs.[106]

In the light of these developments, the Skeffington Report, *Planning and People*, published in 1969, was ostensibly aimed at engaging the wider public in the debate over planning processes. However, the report was still hung up on the top-down governmental philosophy of the time and focused on the planners rather than the public; polity not patrimony. Ravetz noted that

> an influence on planning policies in the 1970s… in the first place… was not so much the pressure from below, as the sheer burden of casework involved in planning appeals, that prompted a government reform of the mechanisms for participation.[107]

Glass endorsed Ravetz's view, in that

> [t]hrough the [Skeffington] report the authors argue that the role of the public is to understand and support the planning authority through feed back [sic] and comment, rather than the planning authority providing plans that reflect community needs.[108]

Of more immediate help to beleaguered owners and tenants in urban tenements the Housing (Scotland) Act 1969 incorporated, for the first time, a statement of Tolerable Standards. At a stroke, the *real* issues in the tenement of actual structural damage, sub-division of accommodation, overcrowding and unhygienic shared water supplies, sinks and toilets were identified and opportunity for improvement presented and legitimised. No longer could apocryphal Council building control officers, alerted by building owners or their agents, declare the building uninhabitable and a candidate for demolition on the strength of a pavement-level observation that a length of rhone four floors up was missing, in finessing the qualifying requirements of a hoped-for Comprehensive Development Area classification and compulsory purchase on favourable terms.

The recovery of the tenement through, initially, emergency repair, was significant in the patrimony of a national urban architecture and popular culture in Scotland. Since their introduction in 1936, Scotland's favourite cartoon characters, the timeless Broons and Oor Wullie – albeit drawn initially by an Englishman, Dudley D Watkins (1907–69) – lived respectively in a tenement in a typologically consistent big toon (Dundee?) and a simple two-storey house in a typologically consistent sma burgh (Coupar Angus?).[109] Scotland's popular literature was urban and gritty and rural and gritty.[110] It was the perversity of Modernism in Scotland to have ignored the significance of the humble tenement in the formation of custom, language, aesthetics, socialisation, community, tactility, psycho-geography and other behavioural or haptic faculty possessed by the urban Scot. An entire non-architectural vocabulary concerned the tenement, its parts, social distinctions and customs: the 'stair', 'close', 'pend', 'vennel', 'back green', 'back court', 'granny-top', 'rhones', 'cludgie', 'siver', 'main door', 'room and kitchen', 'single end', 'double-upper', 'press', 'finger-latch', 'stair turn', 'washing day', 'lobby dosser', 'stair-heid rammy' and so on.

By way of contrast to Glasgow, treatment of disrepair in Edinburgh Old Town had been sporadically ongoing since David Cousin's (1809–78) work in the middle decades of the 19th century and was particularly extensive in the 1950s. Comparable decay in the New Town resulted in the belated formation of the Edinburgh New Town Conservation Committee in 1971 following interest raised by John Paterson's (1931–89) 1966 Edinburgh International Festival Exhibition 'Two Hundred Summers in the City'. It also resulted in the attempted visual homogenisation of Princes Street by the Princes Street Panel with its inexplicable, inaccessible and narrow first-floor shopping gallery, insufficiently raised to bridge omnibus or pantechnicon use of the cross-streets. Disrepair was particularly acute at St James Square at the east end and at Jamaica Street towards the north west and for which some disastrous projects were proposed: the St James Centre by Ian Burke (1915–99) and Hugh Martin (1922–81), constructed 1964–9, demolished 2014, and the eight-storey residential megastructure over two floors of car parking in Jamaica Street by Philip Cocker and Partners, in planning 1972–8, and ultimately refused. However, these were not quite the disconnected interventions into Edinburgh's urban fabric they might superficially appear to have been.

The occasional virtue of prevarication: how Edinburgh avoided an urban motorway

The City of Edinburgh Planning and Transport Study, initiated in 1965 by Freeman Fox with planning consultants Colin Buchanan and Partners appointed in 1968, was published as *Edinburgh: The Recommended Plan* in 1972. Conscious that they trod a narrow path with the forces of conservation on one side and those of Modernism on the other, the authors alleged the pragmatism of their proposals with perhaps a nod to Glasgow's urban motorways and use of the 'bad press' argument:

> the lesson of these examples round the world has been wrongly interpreted. The lesson is not that all new road construction is bad and that savage measures of traffic restraint must be adopted instead. The true lesson, we would suggest, is that the amount and scale of road provision should be kept to the lowest practical limit, and that the works entailed should be undertaken with far greater sensitivity than has characterised urban road construction in the last few decades.[111]

The core aim of the document was to facilitate easy vehicular access to the city centre, although it presumed there would be no rise in city centre employment over time beyond the one-for-one replacement of jobs in declining industries by clerical or administrative positions.[112] Any major employment growth was to be decentralised to Livingston New Town or the Esk Valley.[113] This had consequences. It actively militated against increased employment and population growth within the city's royalty to a real extent. Decentralisation was still the core tenet of regional and urban and, arguably, political planning in Scotland and prevented the major cities becoming what they needed to be in population size, employment opportunity, entrepreneurial interaction and regional and national influence. Indeed, as noted above, Glasgow was significantly reduced in size through the redrawing of its royalty. Edinburgh and Glasgow were simply too small and were consciously maintained as such.

The *Recommended Plan*'s 'greater sensitivity' was strictly relative, and its 'regard to communities and aesthetics' was partial because only the First New Town was sacrosanct.[114] Two and three-lane dual carriageways were to be tunnelled under parts of the Queen's Park and the South Side, emerging as a bridge over Waverley Station before being tunnelled again beneath Calton Hill leading to a large interchange at Elm Row. A two-lane dual carriageway was to be carried on stilts through the Meadows to a huge interchange at Tollcross.[115] A motorway-scaled tunnel was to be dug from behind Charlotte Square to where the Western Approach presently terminates, connecting to an incoming dual carriageway from the West. The suburban railway looping South and East was to become a two-lane dual carriageway and the M8 extended as a three-lane dual carriageway roughly along the route currently taken by the tram as far as Haymarket. Street widening was proposed at Buccleuch Street, Dundee Street and Fountainbridge with the loss of settled urban communities, and so on. For the better part of the 1970s, planning blight hung over the South Side, an otherwise vibrant, multicultural, multi-generational and relatively classless residential, educational, cultural and commercial centre.[116]

Lofty account was made of the circumstances of those potentially to be dispossessed:

> Of course, it is very difficult for people who stand personally to lose their homes to take an objective view of the matter and to balance up gains and losses for the community as a whole; but experience suggests that not a little of the anxiety is connected with fears of inadequate compensation and unsatisfactory resettlement, and that if these fears could be removed, more dispassionate attitudes might prevail.[117]

Here was writ large all of doctrinaire Modernism's inherent contradictions and blindspots. It was 'scientific', which is why it was important to have an 'objective' view and be 'dispassionate'. It reflected the *zeitgeist* because that is what its authors claimed. It was 'top-down', for it was what the authors' 'experience', in their distanced understanding of a universalised and normalised urban solution, 'suggested' was correct. It was not the particular, personal and psychogeographical experience of the resident. It was judgemental, for the expert had an especially low opinion of those affected in that they might be bought off by 'adequate compensation'. It was altogether too certain of its successes where the aim that 'fears could be removed' seemed to be the principal objective rather than the guarantee that 'satisfactory resettlement' would be found. It was coercive and disruptive in that such satisfactory resettlement accommodation was certain to be in a peripheral estate or in a New Town.

Edinburgh dithered, recorded a near miss and, in 1979, the incoming Labour administration abandoned the proposals and future transport flexibility and urban vitality was assured.

Oil-rigged: the fossil fuel of independence

Oil was discovered in the West Sole Field in 1965 and natural gas in the Viking, Leman and Indefatigable Fields in 1966. Early interest was patchy and only ramped up with the tapping of the massive Forties Field in 1970. The oil crises of 1973 and 1979 and the tripling of oil prices by OPEC (the Organisation of Petroleum Exporting Countries) rendered the hazardous and costly North Sea operations viable, even necessary. At a stroke, Scotland appeared to have a resource to offset the dying coal mining industry, although in practice it was considered a British asset, was taxed and squandered in London, never featured in the Scottish accounts and never created a sovereign wealth fund in either Scotland or Britain as, say, did Norway's oil. However, it gave the Scottish National Party (SNP) a slogan and a sense of purpose lacking post-1951: 'It's Scotland's Oil'. Winifred Ewing's (b. 1929) brief Hamilton breakthrough at the 1966 by-election was backed with success in the 1970 General Election. The equally brief success of Margo MacDonald (1943–2014) in Glasgow Govan in the 1973 by-election heralded SNP gains at the first General Election of 1974 of seven seats at Westminster, and at the second, of 11. The jerrymandered 1979 Devolution Referendum[118] was lost and in the General Election that year SNP representation at Westminster dropped to two seats, rising to three in 1987 and fluctuating around six in the several elections of the 1990s, although recording several important second places on which it built subsequent electoral success. It may have been Scotland's oil, but no one in Scotland, for the moment, seemed to be able to take advantage of it.

Britain joined the European Economic Community (EEC), subsequently the European Union (EU), in 1973. Virtually all of Scotland, routinely ignored by Westminster, immediately qualified for the European Regional Development Fund (ERDF). Here was a political and economic structure with which Scotland was last familiar in the 19th century, the EU a more equable and reasoned substitute for the Empire, its additional funding awarded on a strategic basis, that is, as a Europe-wide social and economic policy disbursing funds according to need, rather than a tactical basis, that is, as a Westminster-framed politically-motivated expediency. Despite a substantial reduction in qualifying areas and in sums available following the redirection of the ERDF to the 'accession states' post 1989 – Bulgaria, Romania, Hungary, Czechoslovakia, Poland, East Germany, Estonia, Latvia and Lithuania – there was a palpable kick-start to Scottish confidence and self-image in those years.

In the early 1990s, politics in Scotland settled into a three-way fight between Labour, Conservative and the SNP, with the Liberals trailing some way behind. There was still no great nationalist upsurge, with the SNP vote in the local and general elections of 1990 and 1992 fluctuating between 21.5 per cent and 24.3 per cent. The significant changes were Unionist allegiance flitting between Labour and Conservatives: Labour on a high in 1990 of 44 per cent falling to 34 per cent in 1992; the Conservatives increasing from a low of 19.2 per cent in 1990 to 25.6 per cent in 1992. The Campaign for a Scottish Assembly (CSA), formed in the aftermath of the failed devolution referendum of 1979, became the Scottish Constitutional Convention in 1989. The SNP initially took part in the Convention but withdrew when they realised independence was not a constitutional option under consideration. In 1991, in the run-up to the 1992 general election, a design for the original Parliament site of the Royal High School, Calton Hill, Edinburgh was commissioned by the CSA from me as architect and Sandy Stoddart as sculptor, funded by the National Union of Civil and Public Servants. It was exhibited in Glasgow and Edinburgh with an accompanying talk, but refused in what was then the Conservative stronghold of Perth.[119] The *RIAS Review 1992* recorded that:

> In February, the hypothetical and imaginatively designed *Designs for the Scottish Parliament*, mounted by the Campaign for a Scottish Assembly, raised more than a few eyebrows.[120]

Art in the park: a cool diversion

Briefly hinting at new architectural directions were the entries to the architectural competition for the Burrell Gallery, Pollok Park, Glasgow, 1971:

> The changing architectural philosophies of the time, in the vacuum left by the collapse of the International Style were illustrated by a number of entries. [Paffard Keatinge-Clay] played what must be one of the earliest post-modern jokes in British architecture with a design based on the diagram of the 'golden section' and which clearly caught the assessors' attention. Also catching the assessors' and the public's attention was the entry of Ray Bryant and Peter Mason which consisted of three giant linked cows in a last echo of Pop Art. The young John Outram had a group of traditional-looking buildings arranged around a series of courts anticipating, perhaps, post-modern classical assembly.[121]

The winning entry by Gasson, Meunier and Andreson, from the Cambridge School of Architecture, was an outlier of the Cambridge School's interpretation of Norberg-Schulz's *genius loci*. Meunier and Andreson departed early on, and the project was brought to fruition by Barry Gasson (b.1935) alone. Despite its considerable initial fanfare, its long gestation and the actuality of post-Modernism dated it immediately on its opening in 1984 and it exerted no

Nordic cool: Burrell Collection, Pollok, Glasgow, 1971–84, architect Barry Gasson.
(Finlay McWalter, own work, Creative Commons)

measurable influence on Scottish architecture, other than to display a restraint frequently missing from the architectural production of the 1980s and '90s. It had endnote status in Glendinning's et al *History* and did not appear in the DOCOMOMO list. It may have lived on through Gasson's students, Dalibor Vesely (1934–2015) and Eric Parry (*q.v.*), themselves subsequently tutors at the Cambridge School, and their influence on Mary Arnold-Forster's design philosophy which she brought first to Dualchas and then to her own practice after 2000.[122]

In the mainstream: Scottish architecture in time and in tune with the zeitgeist

From the late 1970s onwards, Scottish architecture was in step theoretically, practically and temporally with larger global movements for the first time since 1900–10. It was so precisely from within the precepts of its own architectural and urban history and philosophy. It was given popular, though not critical, impetus by the Glasgow Garden Festival of 1988 and Glasgow European City of Culture 1991. The amusement park architecture of the Garden Festival did not move the British architectural press, who complained, not unfairly in the main, of 'a desire' at Glasgow to accommodate the mediocre design ambitions of a good proportion of the Scottish landscape architecture profession, assisted by some of their architectural brothers [sic].[123]

The *RIAS Review* of 1992 revealed the pervasiveness of the contemporary ethos in that the completed buildings illustrated were overwhelmingly post-Modern. The majority of these buildings had been initiated sometime in the mid- to late-1980s, indicating widespread familiarity with post-Modernism at that time among Scottish architects. The *Review* did not exercise editorial control and entries were paid for by the submitting practices, thus the predominance of post-Modern design in its pages was representative of a cross-section of actual practice rather than the consequence of partisan editorship.

Scots architects operated within a Scottish philosophical tradition which favoured Kant and Smith – although one suspects the architects were largely ignorant of it – and within which post-Modernism sat easily. The recovery of oxymoron was inherently if inchoately acceptable to Scots. Certainly there was assurance, authority and mastery of the aesthetic in many of the better productions of the period while the revival of the tenement and traditional Scottish urban form coincided with the work and theory of European post-Modern urbanists such as the Italian Aldo Rossi, who reinterpreted the city of Giorgio de Chirico and the works of Giuseppe Terragni and Adolf Loos;[124] the Greek Demetri Porphyrios (b.1949), who sought an astylar Classicism derived from his structuralist analysis of and affinity with the Nordic Classicism of the 1910s and '20s;[125] the German Oswald Mathias Ungers, who proposed an investigation of visual metaphors[126] and the Luxembourgeois Leon Krier and his Roman city. The writings of all four were of significance contemporaneously in the teaching at the Mackintosh School of Architecture, where Krier was a guest lecturer. Moreover, the early and largely hand-drawn design drawings for the forthcoming *Internationale Bauaustellung* Berlin of 1987 (IBA), which addressed identical themes to those being investigated contemporaneously in Scotland, were widely published in architectural magazines from 1980 onwards and where, among others, Scots architects Doug Clelland (b.1945) and Peter Wilson (b. 1956) contributed proposals for the Centre for the Deaf, Friedrichstrasse, 1984.

A mid-period snapshot of architectural interests and illustrative styles was revealed in the entries to the competition for St Peter's and St Paul's RC Church, Rosyth of 1984; one of the several RIAS competitions where the client did not proceed to erect the winning, or indeed any, design. (A reduced version of the winning entry by James F Stephen was later constructed as St Anthony of Padua at Kirriemuir in 1987.) Architectural competitions have interest in that they provide a snapshot of prevailing architectural preoccupations among the potential clients, competition judges, architects and the public.[127] The St Peter's and St Paul's competition entries were recorded in a book published in 1985 and tended to three types: the post-Modern; the aspirational timber roof; and the unclassifiable. The winning entry and the three joint second premiated entries by the Appleton Partnership, Patience and Highmore and James Watson Associates, all had prominent roof structure, as did the commended entries by Andy Bow and Graeme Robertson, Design Detail Group and Jonathan Douglas. Bow and Robertson's entry straddled categories as being also one of the many essays in post-Modernism. Among the unclassifiable were France Smoor's Arts & Crafts, Robin Webster's industrial shed, Cochrane McGregor Partnership's truncated version of the Bagsværd Church, Copenhagen (Jørn Utzon, 1968–76) and Michael Brackenbury's broch.

What was also of interest was the early appearance in the *Record of Entries* of several architects who gained later significance. Andy Bow, still a student at the Mackintosh School of Architect, graduated in 1988 to work with post-Modern illuminati Jeremy Dixon and Ed Jones, Terry Farrell and finally as Director with Norman Foster Associates from 1996. It was plain from his Germanic entry why he was of interest to Dixon, Jones and Farrell. Doug Clelland anticipated the motives of his Berlin work while Richard Murphy investigated the section and *poché* space that came to represent one of the features of his subsequent oeuvre and which was more fully developed in his winning entry at the similarly aborted Inverewe Gardens Tea Room competition. Neil Gillespie contributed a cool interpretation of Aldo Rossi's Il Teatro del Mundo, Venice, 1979, signalling his intellectual approach. A Thomsonesque post-Modern classicism by Ken MacRae prefigured some of the motives he was to use at Stratford Street (see further below), whereas the awkward geometries of Barry Gasson, Gillespie, Kidd and Coia or Ewen and Fiona MacLachlan's entries disappointed and gave little hint of their work elsewhere.[128]

Out and about with Toshie and the Greek

Refocussing on the European city meshed with the major reappraisals of the works and writings of Alexander Thomson following the outrage of the gutting by fire of the Caledonia Road UP Church in 1963 and its being left in ruinous condition. McFadzean's Thomson biography was published in 1979 and the several publications with which Stamp was subsequently involved initiated a virtual Thomson-industry. Stamp also co-founded the Alexander Thomson Society in 1991. Thomson's 'rediscovery' and reappraisal were near simultaneous, nuanced and largely free from the over-riding extraneous Modernist architectural agenda which had bedevilled contemporary interpretation of the work of Mackintosh since the 1930s.

These Modernist agendas were evident at a major conference held in Glasgow in August 1983, the proceedings of which were published in 1988 as *Mackintosh and His Contemporaries*. Mackintosh's reappraisal tended frequently towards the hagiographic, unsupported and unbelievable. Nuttgens asserted that

> what everyone [the contributors to the conference] was clear about was the importance of colour – probably colour intrinsic to materials rather than applied colour.[129]

Nuttgens and his Modernist cohort had somehow been blind to every multi-coloured stencilled interior, every lacquered or painted item of furniture, the tilework on the Daily Record Building, Renfield Lane, 1900, on the Scotland Street School, 1903, or inside the Glasgow School of Art, 1897–1909. Such wilful lack of observation was no better than P Morton Shand's myopia of 1933 where, as Stamp noted,

> Shand could only make Mackintosh seem to fit his defining of 'being modern' by tampering with the evidence, for he could not bear the decorative element in his architecture.[130]

Andy MacMillan, professor at the Mackintosh School of Architecture, claimed that

> [Mackintosh's] vision supported the institutions and approach of the early European pioneers and prepared the way for the later influences of Wright and Le Corbusier. Their work confirmed Mackintosh's revelations, displaying similar characteristics and a further extension of the architectural possibilities inherent in the abstraction of the building and in the employment of the machine in the building process... which not only made him a fore-runner of the Expressionist approach on the one hand and the Constructivist on the other.[131]

In MacMillan's assertion, Mackintosh singlehandedly initiated or sign-posted *every* Modernist architectural philosophy, *every* -ism, of the first half of the 20th century. Lacking any coherent philosophy of Mackintosh's work on which to base it, MacMillan made a claim that came across as simplistic and contradictory, even preposterous, and, in his overstatement of the case, undermined any pioneering authority Mackintosh might have possessed. Wright, Corbusier, Expressionism and Constructivism had little in common with each other or with Mackintosh. It is not that Mackintosh is a 'forerunner', only that through the retrospective lens of the work of those others was the full extent of the architectural and philosophical antinomial space he occupied made evident. That does not mean he was precursor or 'pioneer' of those other design philosophies.

David M Walker was more circumspect, remarking simply that:

> It would be overstating the case to suggest the cubist domestic style of the 1920s and 1930s would not have developed exactly as it did [but for Mackintosh]... Nevertheless, I think it can be fairly said that Mackintosh was in the forefront of those whose work anticipated and helped create that style in the years before 1914.[132]

More practical, less fanciful intimations of Thomson and Mackintosh turned up early in the 1970s' *architectural* work of Andy MacMillan and his partner Isi Metzstein of Gillespie, Kidd and Coia (GKC). Despite Baines' significant interrogative work on the interpretation of the wall separately in both Thomson's and GKC's work, he did not make the Thomson connection in his essay[133] on the latter and simply identified their preference for 'long established structural techniques and traditional materials' where

> [p]hysical mass and depth is predominantly favoured over or contrasted with the slender and the lightweight.[134]

In GKC's use of the load-bearing wall, Baines reported that:

> They favoured its physical plasticity, linear continuity and its capacity to induce a pronounced sense of enclosure.[135]

Baines' notion of 'linear continuity' approached Thomson's search for the infinite. Benson echoed this in stating that they were '[s]triving all the time for a "culture transcending sense of timelessness"'.[136]

We see also the Mackintosh influence and that of Pevsner's Dutch Expressionists where GKC's

> [l]oad bearing walls are expressly modelled and their sense of mass often accentuated through the aesthetic exploitation of their inherent

qualities of thickness, weight and structural buttressing. The wall surfaces are elaborated by brick patterning or, in other instances, rendered externally.[137]

The constructional detail of Mackintosh's walling was often obscured by ubiquitous harling, although the glazed brick at the Daily Record building reveals how a brick building by him might have looked. Jack Coia's Dutch-influenced churches of the 1930s were also implicated, while

> [h]igh level set back clerestories are also used in conjunction with profiled light shelves positioned over a continuous band of windows,[138]

which recalled Thomson's attic storeys. These architectural moves were

> accommodated within a physical construct in which entry, threshold and domain are clearly defined within a perceptibly closed or finite architectural composition.[139]

Out and about with Toshie and the Greek: Robinson College, Cambridge, 1974–8, architects Gillespie, Kidd and Coia.
(Vysotsky, own work, Creative Commons)

The Mackintosh influence, from St Paul's, Glenrothes, 1956, onwards, was fully realised in their brick-built Robinson College, Cambridge, 1974–8. Here the more overt moves are such as the entirely Scottish 'inhabited wall', *poché* space, the gridded windows, the post-Modern stepped sill and the Scarpaesque serially set-back architraves. Indeed, the ensemble of door to the chapel, the stair to the communicating bridge and the John Piper (1903–92) stained glass window behind the altar visible from the entry court are a superb antinomial encapsulation of these influences whereby the overall composition transcends the discrete parts. The framing of the door incorporates Thomson's paring back of the wall together with Scarpa's serially set-back architraves within brickwork detailing as expressive as anything attempted by the Amsterdam School. The stained glass windows in subtly gridded framing and with stepped sills are set in a bay that is freed from the principal external wall much as were Mackintosh's at the West Wing of the Glasgow School of Art or, less obviously, in Thomson's expressed portals at either end of the nave at the St Vincent Street Church. The overall composition, in the relationship of its parts, is Corbusian in the looseness of Ronchamp, 1954, or Firminy, 1964-9.

Motives borrowed from Robinson College, which saw much use in the 1980s, were the square-gridded Mackintosh windows and stepped sills, blocky timberwork, lattice-work timber roof structure redolent of Scandinavian work and the Scarpaesque architraves together with the late 1970s use of concrete blockwork or brickwork as alternatives to stone masonry construction. Roughly contemporaneous and employing some of these motives is the Church of St John Ogilvie, Irvine, 1979, by Clunie Rowell (1916–2001), Douglas Niven (n.d.) and Gerard Connolly (n.d.), the latter pair design studio tutors at the Mackintosh School of Architecture in the 1970s and '80s. Its grandest although least resolved manifestation in Scotland is the National Library of Scotland Extension, 1987, on a corner site at Salisbury Place and Causewayside, Edinburgh, by Andrew Merrylees Associates. An awkward and gestural 45° perimeter planning geometry implying an 'inhabited wall' – it does not continue much beyond a partial and hesitant two metres into the depth of the rectilinear building – is combined with metal-gridded glazed and masonry towers, masonry walling and gridded-metal banding.

In a much more subtle essay, Thomson and Mackintosh appear conjoined in the winning entry by Ken MacRae (n.d.) with McGurn, Logan, Duncan and Opfer in the 21st Century Tenement competition for Stratford Street, Maryhill, 1984-8. The close entry and common stair

At home with Toshie and the Greek: 21st century tenement, Stafford Street, Maryhill, Glasgow, 1984, architects Ken MacRae with McGurn, Logan, Duncan and Opfer.

window have flattened echoes of the stair towers at the Scotland Street School, with a simulacrum of its top floor glazing allowed to segue neatly into that of the adjacent flatted accommodation in a manner reminiscent of the first floor at Thomson's Moray Terrace. Coloured tile inserts recall similar at the Scotland Street School or in the contemporaneous Dutch work of Herman Herzberger. The split level section of four floors to the front and six to the rear provides higher ceiling heights to the living rooms and recalls the complex section of the tower house while permitting a balconied *piano nobile* on the street frontage.

Remaking the Scottish city: the contemporary tenement

A major test of the traditional urban form, the tenement, in conjunction with the post-Modern aesthetic was encapsulated in the 1990 Crown Street masterplan by the 'English Extremists', CZWG.[140] Crown Street was the community-led development to replace the Hutchesontown E development of deck access slab and multi-storey tower blocks, locally known as the 'Dampies' due to the consequences of cold-bridging, built 1970–80 using the French Tracoba prefabricated system and demolished block-by-block between 1986 and 2013.[141] Within the masterplan, perimeter tenements were designed by Elder and Cannon, Page \ Park and Hypostyle Architects, all of whom were to prove influential subsequently. The authors of the Scottish Government's advice note, PAN83, implicitly identifying some of the failures of the mass housing programmes that had preceded it, had this to say, in 2008, of the near-completed development:

> The strengths of the Crown Street masterplan are illustrated by how closely the actual development conforms to it. The scheme has succeeded in its aim of creating a place where people want to be... The form of development, based on Glasgow's tenement tradition, has provided a clear distinction between public space, defined by the front facades, and the semi-private space in the courtyards. This makes responsibility for management clear.[142]

In Edinburgh, by way of contrast, the tenement revival stemmed initially from isolated infill developments within the context of larger conservation efforts in the Old Town from the 1950s onwards. Moncrieff Terrace, 1978–82, by Nick Groves-Raines (b.1950) and Michael Spens (1939–2014), in the

Learning from IBA 1: Moncrieff Terrace, Edinburgh, 1978–82, architects Nick Groves-Raines and Michael Spens.

Sciennes district is a six-storey infill in a traditional tenemental street which reveals knowledge of the contemporaneous work of Vittorio Gregotti (1927–2020). The City Architect contributed a Baronial pastiche blockwork infill in Blackfriars Street, 1981. Calthrop and Mars' Thomson's Court, Grassmarket, 1984, sought a sma burgh Victorian urbanity in brown harling and green-stained timber while, further out, just beyond Dundee Street, they experimented with pink blockwork and gable piends at Angle Park Terrace, Edinburgh, 1979. Nearby, Reiach and Hall designed the IBA-influenced high and wide Yeaman Place infill, 1988. Charles McKean, although not a designer, pursued a Baronial/Mackintosh/Corbusier-Bauhaus 'manifesto' extension to his own house at Hill Park Road, Edinburgh, 1989–91, through the agency of my design company ARCHImedia, which he subsequently dubbed as 'curved Scots Cubism'.[143] The issue of a contemporary interpretation of the Baronial was still live at this time (see Introduction).

Wann McLaren's 'Holyrood 2000' charette, 1986, for the Scottish Brewers' site between the Canongate and Holyrood Road, now part-occupied by the Parliament, anticipated the subsequent 1992 masterplan by John C Hope which now includes work by Ewen and Fiona McLachlan, Ungless and Latimer, Richard Murphy and Malcolm Fraser. While fitting the urban tenement pattern, these designs, with the exception of Murphy at 112 Canongate, 1999, are considerably less overtly Scottish in origin and motives.

Above: Sma burgh urbanism: Commercial Road, Perth, 1974, architects James Parr & Partners.
(Lis Burke, geograph.org.uk, Creative Commons)

Left: 'Curved Scots Cubism': McKean House extension, Hillpark, Edinburgh, 1989–91, architect Roger Emmerson as ARCHImedia.

Elsewhere, the sma burgh model resurfaced in James Parr and Partners' pink concrete blockwork gable-piended and Scotch-slated Commercial Street, Perth, 1978, and in Baxter Clark and Paul's several housing projects in Peterhead and Fraserburgh in the mid-1970s to early '80s.

In the early 1980s, the professional institutes – the RIBA and the RIAS – amended their byelaws to permit architects to act as developers. Among the first to take advantage of this freedom was Kantel, the Edinburgh practice of Andrew Doolan (1951–2004) and Andrew Burrell (b.1950) with a flatted development on the site of the former Tudor Cinema, St Bernards Row, Edinburgh, 1982, followed by flat conversions on the reprieved Edinburgh South Side at Forest Hill and East Crosscauseway. They are probably best known for commissioning work in the former warehouse and commercial quarter at Ingram Square, Glasgow, 1984 in what came to be known as the highly-desirable upwardly-mobile 'Merchant City'. In time Kantel was spun off into the Burrell Company and, in partnership with the City of Edinburgh Council, as Buredi, both involved in substantial urban developments, new-build and conversions of flats, offices and hotels.

Learning from IBA 2: Ingram Square, Glasgow, 1984, architects Elder and Cannon.

Our museum: the Scottish counterpart to a Finnish original

The antinomy of Scotland 1: Museum of Scotland, Edinburgh, 1991, architects Benson + Forsyth.

Despite some non-constitutional and thwarted Princely meddling prior to the announcement of the result, Gordon Benson and Alan Forsyth won the Museum of Scotland competition in 1991. It opened to considerable acclaim on St Andrew's Day, 30 November 1998. Peter Davey in the *Architectural Review* recognised

> the quotations from medieval buildings from Scarpa, Corbusier, Aalto and the rest are incorporated in an unobtrusive way, so that the different layers of the building resonate with the collections they hold... Walking along the street to the north, and turning round for a moment, you realise that the whole building both inside and out, is a contemporary example of a quality that has been remarkably out of fashion for a long time: the picturesque.[144]

Perhaps his wishes of a year previously had been answered (see above).

Architecture Today celebrated its 100th edition and tenth year of publication with an issue substantially given over to a consideration of the Museum of Scotland with a brief account by Jim Hutcheson of Benson +

Forsyth and critiques by John Allen (also of Benson + Forsyth), Patrick Hodgkinson, Paul Clarke and Neave Brown. John Allen (n.d.) observed,

> the past is apprehended not through sampling but through metaphor... devising a response that is, *sui generis*, undeniably contemporary, Scottish in spirit yet with a reach far beyond its obvious local significance to touch on matters of universal validity.[145]

In his reflection on the Museum, Patrick Hodgkinson (1930–2016), designer of the Brunswick Centre, London, 1967–72, attempted, if not a recantation, then a minor *mea culpa* on the 'frailty of the doctrinaire modern movement... which many of my generation took on too glibly' and 'how many of us also eschewed those once-strong British notions [of masonry construction for] a relatively soulless functionalism'. Of the building he claimed that

> the architecture [is] thinking its way towards something we haven't arrived at yet but provoking an answer from others yet to come.[146]

Artist Paul Clarke (n.d.) recalled:

> For the 1991 competition Benson and Forsyth presented a diagram of the cross-section of their proposal. The elements of this drawing sit like symbols of a Pictish stone, distinct and absolute. A bull-horned roof of flora rises from within a labyrinth box. A head-shaped frame looks back across the city. A great winged bird lifts to the sky. After our cultural wanderings, our search for meaning, we find ourselves at home, standing on the roof, open to the world, sensing the edges of the island.[147]

While Neave Brown (1929–2018), architect of the Alexandra Road Estate, London, 1978, summed up:

> an internal apsidal block; almost a nave; and aisles... The tower is porch and entry... As climax the museum is surmounted and crowned by a roof garden... Building, display, and the history of Scotland become one.[148]

The writing veered sharply towards Joanna Frueh's 'love and prophecy', the views of Davey, Allen, Hodgkinson, Clarke and Brown mirroring not merely the hopes of the authors of *Vårt museum* (see Chapter 1) but the actual vocabulary employed: 'picturesque', 'medieval', 'tower', 'crown', 'timeless', 'church/nave', 'styles become one/are absorbed' and so on. Although there is no over-arching formal or aesthetic connection between these buildings, there is intent in shared meaning. Does this mean simply that conventional modes of art/architectural criticism are to be abandoned temporarily in the face of what is undeniably a highly significant and complex work, or is there something lurking at the heart of the Museum of Scotland, beyond architecture, that begs a question our critics were not quite able to answer but yet felt, in some way, constrained to respond to? That in addition to their evident joy did they experience that 'grief' of which Bernstein spoke or the 'guilt' which troubled Lyotard? Bernstein observed:

> In modernity beauty is not only alienated from truth, but grieves its loss; modernity is the site of beauty bereaved – bereaved of truth.[149]

In his low-key book on the museum, concerned more with the historical, administrative and museological frameworks behind the collection and building, McKean sounded disappointed:

> People had aspirations for it – aspirations of national identity far beyond a mere collection of antiquities. When the competition-winning architects came to encapsulate such notions in a building, they had as an aim that it should be 'a benchmark for the quality of Scottish cultural endeavour at the end of the 20th century'.[150]

However, despite winning the Edinburgh Architectural Association's (EAA) Gold Medal in 1999, no other awards were forthcoming from the architectural profession in Scotland. More mature counsel prevailed in London and a special category was devised within the context of the RIBA awards to recognise an outstanding building. The Museum achieved everything and more that McKean hesitantly wished for and British commentators fulsomely and perceptibly recognised. It was, perhaps, just too hot to handle in Scotland, where the 'tall poppy syndrome' was at work yet again amongst Scotland's architects. The best that McKean could manage was the tired and largely unexamined, by him, trope that the building had 'a Scottishness of abstract geometries in the tradition of Charles Rennie Mackintosh'.[151]

It is crucial to identify – as McKean and others in Scotland did not – those aspects of the Museum which, at the fin-de-siècle, characterised and summarised a Scottish regional or national architecture. Returning to the abstract characteristics ascribed to the 15th to 17th-century tower-house in

Chapter 3, we find that the Museum of Scotland satisfies any number of them without resorting to a Baronial aesthetic. Although it has its own 'boundary layer' of porch, basement area and overhangs, it sits resolutely 'on-the-ground'. As it rises, Benson + Forsyth's achievement was to adopt the tower-house's three-dimensional spatial devices of the split-level section, 'inhabited wall', secret stairs and poché space, and to combine them seamlessly by means of the two main stairs into a plan of a Corbusian promenade architecturale. Intervisibility and surprise is constant.

Spaces are shaped and formed appropriate to their task: the crypt-like chambered-tomb of the basement exhibiting pre-historical archaeology; the honorific great hall; the monitor-lit and steel-gantry accessed workshop of industrial exhibits and the many discreet rooms of humbler, small-scale or precious display. Stairs, grand or servant, and secret rooms are hidden away in *poché* spaces, and great Piranesian shafts reach from basement to roof framed by inner walls that have the appearance of having been external walls in some previous time. The opening mechanism of the great glazed door onto Chambers Street is equally Piranesian in its forms and engineering. Screens, balustrades and balconies are treated like complex furniture, part industrial, part architectural-historical, part ceremonial. Kahn's 'places to sit' are formed from partitions, pulpits and alcoves and every wall, inside and out, is pared away in a manner Thomson would recognise. Openings, inside and out, are celebrated with Scarpaesque serially-receding regular square architraves or jambs, or Expressionist pin-wheel cut outs or Thomsonian blank panels or are combined in complex vertical ensembles redolent of the frontispiece of an Aberdeenshire 'chateau'. Basal masonry has coursing of the order of James Playfair at Cairness House or Thomas Hamilton at the Royal High School. Black-stained timber screens of almost agricultural robustness recall GKC's at St Paul's, Glenrothes, Womersley's at Edenside or Mackintosh's more massive work at the School of Art. Everywhere, mass is contrasted with lightness, thickness with thinness, dark with light, curved with straight. It is all of these things and yet none of them, for their origins are in the antinomy which it encapsulates. This is a building to get lost in, to be immersed in, philosophically, figuratively and literally.

Escaping post-Modernism: other traditions

Were that all there was to go on architecturally at the close of the 20th century, we would be obliged to recognise yet another isolate. However, Weston commented:

There is already talk of a 'School of Murphy' in Edinburgh, and his office spawned several younger practices who are beginning to do interesting work on their own.[152]

This was only partly true. Nevertheless, it is important to understand the lasting significance for Murphy of his lifetime's study of the work of Carlo Scarpa[153] and how that had fed, via Murphy's work and influence, into Scottish architecture by the year 2000. Those issues of the overlapping of flat planes, the juxtaposition of contrasting materials, the celebration of junctions, the creation of incident, the incorporation of the precious, the separation from existing construction and the importance of the ruin, the occupied wall and the incomplete construction that Scarpa handled sublimely at, say, the Museo Castelvecchio, Verona, 1956–64, the Fondazione Querini Stampalia, Venice, 1961–3 or the Brion Tomb and Sanctuary at San Vito d'Altivole, 1969–78, all resurfaced, transformed, in Murphy's work and in the work of those formerly his assistants.

Scarpa via Murphy, however, was not the only source of this more intricate, almost jewel-box, method of designing and, especially, detailing

Montage and joint: Tomba Brion, San Vito d'Altivole, Italy, 1969–78, architect Carlo Scarpa.

Montage and joint: St Andrew's House, Edinburgh, 1933–9, detail, architect Thomas Tait.

buildings. Arguably it is evident in the late 1930s works of Tait. Many of Murphy's assistants – and those of Malcolm Fraser, Lee Boyd and others – of the mid to late-1990s were trained at the School of Architecture, Edinburgh College of Art during Trevor Denton's (b. 1937) professorship there between 1991 and 1994. Denton was a member of a community of architects whose Milton Keynes Development Corporation (MKDC) and private practice work shared an architectural vocabulary.[154] It consisted of overlapping planes, cut-outs, separation of parts, juxtaposition of different materials, floating roofs, expressed framing in timber and metal, and an outer assembly of balconies, screens, verandahs and colonnades as apparent at Stantonbury Campus, Milton Keynes, 1974–8; Neath Hill Housing and Health Centre, Milton Keynes, 1977; Cippenham Medical Centre, Slough, 1992 or Headington Baptist Church, Oxford, 2002.[155] The School of Architecture at Edinburgh College of Art was serendipitously producing a stream of graduates at that time with precisely the design skills and ethos that matched Murphy's and others' intent and which acted as a countervailing force to that of a doctrinaire post-Modernism.

In Glasgow, post-Modernism had a stronger and longer-lasting influence in the work of Page \ Park, Elder and Cannon, Simister Monaghan and others. In time, the early Hans Hollein-influenced (1934–2014) exuberance of Elder and Cannon's National Bank of Pakistan, Sauchiehall Street, 1982 or Ingram Square or the Church of the Holy Name, Mansewood, 1984, became the regular grid and frame that forms and contains building, balconies, porches and colonnades in a tight urban block in works such as St Aloysius College Junior School, Glasgow, 1999. Speaking to journalist Penny Lewis in 2005, Dick Cannon (b.1943) described his work thus:

> When we use embellishment it's to support the main idea. When you look at some architects in the 1980s, like Venturi, often the main idea was obscured by the embellishment. I don't think our work was like that; it was about clearly organised spaces with decoration that was appropriate.

Lewis went on to write:

> When you ask Cannon what the influences have been in his work, he admits that the practice's tastes are catholic (he mentions both Foster and Moneo as the two ends of the spectrum), and says that the practice absorbs influences from people and buildings in 'their own city'.[156]

While most Scottish architects are reluctant to examine closely what drives them, or perhaps to express it more openly, uninformative generality of this sort is the norm. It invites speculation but provides so few clues that any meaningful dialogue is impossible and the conventional historian has recourse only to retro-fitting the work under consideration to an orthodox history of architecture, that is, to another, not Scottish, history of architecture. For sure, Norman Foster (b.1935) and Raphael Moneo (b.1937) could well be construed as the 'ends of the spectrum' although, equally, they can be thought of as the antinomy that frames the work, but then one could be accused of putting thoughts into Cannon's head, never mind words into his mouth.

The response of the Nicoll Russell Studio in Dundee was grittier while still operating within this multivalent aesthetic. The blocky Dundee Rep, 1979, and the finely modelled housing at Palace Green, Berwick-on-Tweed, 1980 gave little hint of the Grianan Building in the Dundee Technology Park, 1986, which incorporates a lively, almost Wrightian, use of random rubble in contrast to the lightness of the steel columns and roof structure. In a similar post-Modern ethos to Elder and Cannon's National Bank of Pakistan, Nicoll Russell's TSB, St Andrews, 1988, sports a greatly enlarged Mackintosh mantel clock and side screens. However, eschewing the more obvious antecedents in their earlier work, their Scrymgeour's Corner, Crieff, 1990, is one of the more

Inventive regionalism: Scrymgeour's Corner, Crieff, 1990, architects Nicoll Russell Studio.

convincing contemporary interpretations of the Scotticisms of Mackintosh. The White Top youth day-care centre, Dundee, 1992, further develops the motives originated in the Grianan and at Scrymgeour's Corner.

Devolution: a measure of cultural, political and economic autonomy

The incoming Labour government in 1997 had devolution of parts of Scotland's governance as a policy plank, although there was much speculation whether it was seen rather as a means of containing and managing more comprehensive nationalist aims rather than providing genuine regional control over government. The use of proportional representation on the alternative member system to elect members of the Scottish Parliament seemed intended to prevent any party, especially the SNP, achieving a clear majority, a situation that little troubled the unionists of Labour, Conservative or Liberal persuasion whose attention was centred on Westminster and what they construed as the real seat of power in Britain. However, devolution proved popular. In 1997 the Devolution and Tax-varying Referendum was resoundingly won on a 60 per cent turnout: for devolution, 74.29 per cent Yes; for tax-varying powers the vote was 63.48 per cent Yes, possibly the first time an electorate had voted *for* a tax. Subsequently, in 1998, Enric Miralles (1955–2000) and Benedetta Tagliabue (b.1963) (EMBT) with RMJM won the competition for the new Scottish Parliament on the former Scottish Brewers site at the bottom of Holyrood Road with a wildly Expressionistic design. Construction began in 1999.

7

The second-sight: 1999–2022

Of certain memory and from hidden causes

> The 'Second-Sight' (Da-radharc, Da-shealladh, Taibhsearachd – the three Gaelic words have been used in this connection) is popularly believed to be a faculty of prophetic vision long supposed in the Scottish Highlands and elsewhere to belong in particular persons. As known in the Highlands of Scotland it has one feature in common with the oracular responses of old, that of being uttered by the subject of it when in a state of mental exaltation or even delirium. The Second-Sight is in every case regarded as troublesome to the possessor of it. It differs, however, from the class of divine prophecies or of heathen oracles, according to Bacon, and belongs rather to prophecies that have been, to use his words, 'of certain memory and from hidden causes'. This definition excludes from it the prophecies of St Columba, for example, and of other saints ancient and modern.[1]

LAND OF STONE is concerned precisely with a 'certain memory' – mine – or rather, my interpretation of generally accepted, although largely uncontested 'facts' of Scottish architectural history, theory and practice, and with 'hidden causes' arising from rarely interrogated texts and works.

Recent events are raw and episodic, their future significance uncertain, each one tumbling over the previous, demanding our immediate attention, yet to be reinterpreted or even included as part of the nation's preferred historical narrative. In our understanding of the history of Modern architecture we are often misled by its tendency to the flippancies of aphorism as aide memoire:

Form follows function, Louis Sullivan, 1896;
Doing more with less, Buckminster Fuller, 1938;

Less is more, Ludwig Mies van der Rohe, 1946;
Much ado about next to nothing, Frank Lloyd Wright, 1947;
Almost nothing is too much, Reyner Banham, 1962;
Less is a bore, Robert Venturi, 1966;
I'm a whore, Philip Johnson, 1982;
Form follows finance, Carol Willis, 1995
Too much is never enough, Morris Lapidus, 1996;
More and more, more is more, Rem Koolhaas, 2002;
Yes is more, Bjarke Ingels, 2009;

to which I am inclined to add, 'enough, already!' By way of contrast, I have sought to interrogate these aphorisms' implicit assumptions and to establish some principles which may govern the architectural choices made today by architects and their clients. I have queried how they see those choices, and whether there is any discernible connection between, and realisation of, them in contemporary Scottish architectural production and in the working through of late Modernism and present nationalism.

The millennial Scot

Despite the brief gaiety of fireworks, the abiding emotion bracketing the eventuation of the second millennium was anxiety. Would the Y2K software glitch delete swathes of information and crash the world economy on the stroke of midnight as it rang out sequentially over a 24 hour period? Then: nothing happened.[2] But perhaps people were right to feel anxious, for looming over all subsequent financial, political and ethical catastrophes were the inescapable facts of global heating, territorial depredation, resource depletion and nuclear holocaust, and the patent inability of major governments and international capitalism at present to understand that existential threats of this magnitude required a unified response which entailed sacrifice, for that was to challenge their raison d'être.

Further consideration at home concerned the less apocalyptic although no-less-pressing understanding and expression of Scottish patrimony and polity. Prior to 1997, the Church of Scotland, and in particular its annual General Assembly, represented the only home-based nationwide quasi-authoritative body whose pronouncements and enactments had some presence in and effect on Scottish life, albeit marginal for the most part. Nonetheless, the archetypical Calvinist Scot – whether a religious observant or not – was linked anecdotally to the official Protestant church and represented by it in official society, both within and beyond Scotland, while, at its margins, Catholicism derived its identity from Rome and Protestantism shaded to sectarianism. Arguably, the General Assembly in its heyday, supported by a compliant press and a thankful Westminster, sustained, beyond viable independent existence, the polity of those consoling establishment traditions of Scotland in Empire and Scotland in Union. These traditions were shown to be politically and economically bankrupt through sustained governmental centralisation in 20th-century Unionism and unrepresentative of the nation authoritatively, politically and culturally by the fact of the Scottish parliament in the 21st. The General Assembly of the Church of Scotland at the close of the 20th century was even less of a proxy government than was Glasgow a proxy capital at the end of the 19th, and its limited notional authority was eroded completely due to the precipitous early 21st-century drop in Scottish churchgoing.[3]

In the world of real politics, the long decline in the Scottish Conservative and Unionist vote share from a high of 50 per cent in 1955 was arrested and, in the new Scottish parliament, allowing for a blip in 2011, improved from the 15.5 per cent low in 1999 to nearly 22 per cent in 2021. Scottish Labour's 'machine' politics, nurtured in the West in the latter half of the 20th century and promulgated in its attempted management of expectation and containment of nationalism in the Parliament's early years, backfired and vote share dropped from 36.3 per cent in 1999, the largest in that parliament, to 21.6 per cent in 2021. The Liberal Democrat vote halved. The SNP vote, however, beginning in 1999 with a respectable 28.1 per cent rose to 44.1 per cent vote share in 2016, to 47.7 per cent in 2021 and, in 2007, counter to the mathematics of a seemingly insurmountable electoral system, achieved largest party status to form a minority government. Four years later, it did what the alternate member voting system was specifically designed to prevent and formed a majority government. It fell back from that position in 2016 while the Greens doubled their vote share in 2021, but raised the aggregate percentage vote of parties with an independence platform to 55.8 per cent. One seat short of a majority, the SNP made a 'co-operation agreement' with the Greens. In effect, while the number of MSPs espousing independence doubled in a little over two decades, the traditional 'big three' unionist parties – Conservative, Labour and Liberal – shrank to trade the remaining 44.2 per cent of the votes between them.

This nationalist impetus resulted in the convening of the Independence Referendum in 2014, which was lost roughly 55/45 per cent. Adding little to the debate at the time, 'Architects for Independence', a short-lived ginger group, met belatedly in the RIAS Council Room in Rutland Square, Edinburgh, a few weeks prior to the Referendum vote. There was no structure to the organisation, no names of attendees taken, no programme tabled, no resolutions proposed for vote and none of the transactions were recorded. There was no vision and discussion centred parochially on job opportunities for architects post-Independence.

Following the 'NO' result of the Referendum the SNP lost direction, although not support. The fallout of the rancorous Salmond Enquiry in early 2021 was only just offset by the gain obtained by the SNP government's apparent command of the Covid-19 pandemic. Support for independence presently fluctuates between 40 and 50 per cent. For many Scots, an enhanced Scottish identity more than adequately compensates for the continuing absence of the full governmental powers of home-rule or outright independence. Departure from the European Union in 2016, formally concluded in 2019, put Scotland's devolved constitutional settlement within the Union in a potentially retrograde situation.

Many icons, few gods, little faith: the mannerist architecture of the world-city

With the Dancing House, Prague, 1996, by Frank Gehry and Vlado Milunić (b.1941); the Guggenheim Art Museum, Bilbao, 1997, by Frank Gehry; Bergisel Ski Jump, Innsbruck 1999–2002, by Zaha Hadid (1950–2016); and the Jewish Museum, Berlin, 1989–2001, by Daniel Libeskind (b.1947), Late Modernism entered public consciousness in its Mannerist phase. Perhaps it was evident to all as early in the appearance of 'that distant precursor'[4] the Sydney Opera House, 1957–73, by Jørn Utzon (1918–2008) and Ove Arup & Partners of which and of similar designs Collins wrote presciently in 1965:

> There is no doubt that both the Guggenheim Museum [Frank Lloyd Wright, 1959] and Toronto City Hall [Viljo Revell, 1965] will be regarded by future historians as great works of art, because historians tend to see buildings as abstract sculpture, requiring neither antecedence nor succession for their justification. It will be a mark of excellence that no-one has ever designed anything like them before, and that no-one will ever design anything like them again.[5]

Late Modernist and post-Modernist modes, based on shared, though differently interpreted, post-Modern philosophical premises simply 'fell into' each other in the 1990s. On the one hand, post-Modernism's catholicity, even profligacy, in its selection of formal models and motives gave licence to a variety of architectural choices absent from the normative architectural forms

Late-Modern mannerism: the Dancing House, Prague, 1996, architects Frank Gehry and Vlado Milunič.
(Pedro Szekely, own work, Creative Commons)

of International Style Modernism. On the other hand, Late Modernism's lately-acquired familiarity with and increasing mastery of the sophisticated and innovative structural, engineering, constructional and, for the first time, 'green' environmental systems required of large and complex Modernist constructions coupled with the contemporaneous advances in materials production and in computer software and imaging provided the real constructional substance for the wildest post-Modern imagining; a state of affairs acknowledged in Jencks's *The New Paradigm in Architecture*.[6]

The choice of 1999 as the start date of Mannerist Modernism is not unconnected with the comparable exponential growth in the use of computing by architects. In the mid-1980s, few outside the very largest or most innovative architectural practices were more than partially equipped with computers. By the end of the 1990s it was *de rigeur* even although some still retained drawing boards well into the 2000s, a terrain whose poles Mitchell characterised in 1996 as those where:

> From the side-lines, no doubt, technoromantic theoreticians will egg [architects] on to Gibsonian[7] gestures of dematerialisation and radical renunciation of traditional architectural means, while materiality

chauvinists will provide ringing denunciations of a world that they see going to hell in a handheld device.[8]

Mitchell's predictions met with agreement 20 years later in the work of Rid[9], Taplin[10] and others where, to his observation that

> [the bitsphere] will overlay and eventually succeed the agricultural and industrial landscapes that humankind has inhabited for so long,[11]

were added the landscapes of fun, gossip, finance, shopping, sex, war, crime, art and politics.

Available now to a competent keyboard operator was that which previously had been the graphic province of only the most talented of three-dimensional conceptualists and two-dimensional draughtspersons such as Eisenman, Libeskind and Hadid and which was the constructional domain of those engineering companies such as Arup's, who wrote the computer programmes. This resolved into the procedures of evidence-based design, computer-aided structural design programmes such as AutoCAD, design tools such as Revit, comprehensive whole-building modelling such as BIM (Building Information Modelling), component manufacture, assembly techniques such as MMC (Modern Methods of Construction) and performance-in-use assessment by QR labelling of components such as the Twinview system, whereby designs were programmatically, technically, constructionally, financially and risk-reductively verified in virtual three dimensions prior to construction and validated subsequently: in effect, Zevi's 'classicised' computing. Likewise, computer-aided laser-cutting, 3D-printing, precision jointing, costing, product tracing and performance monitoring of materials, components and assemblies, permitted the more economic creation of both serial and bespoke products from within the same production run in production, installation and use.

The resultant aesthetic content of such form and the expression of its exterior and interior spaces was thus freed – by means of the agency and 'heavy-lifting' capability of the computer whereby conventional architecture/engineering design conflicts were resolved – to become a thing apart. For example, the creation of abstract form in, say, moulded modelling clay, *pace* Gehry, was 3D computer-scanned in a simulacrum of the sculptor's method to provide the quantifiable and locatable three-dimensional spatial information of the surface.[12] Zevi, whose thesis was an unacknowledged source for Mannerist architects, predictively illustrated this process in 1973[13] and claimed with precision that '[m]annerism neither popularizes nor democratizes. It is a highly intellectual operation and almost untransmutable'.[14]

THE SECOND SIGHT: 1999–2022

The construction of late-Modern mannerism: Riverside, Glasgow, 2001, architect Zaha Hadid.
(Irid Escent, own work, Creative Commons)

Foster commented on such a design process:

> Hadid tends to collapse her representation into her objects. Indeed, she seems to use digital technology to minimise material constraints and structural concerns as much as possible, and so jump from drawing to building as directly as she can.[15]

The structures of Hadid's buildings sit within an amorphous zone where attention is distracted from their scale and muteness by the perfecting of the bounding surfaces of their containment while the intermediate zone is expanded or shrunk at will to meet the engineers' call upon it. For example, the roof of her Riverside Museum, Glasgow, 2011,[16] presents at the gables as a folded plate. However, to accommodate the considerable steel structure between inner and outer skins to facilitate unsupported ridges and valleys and transfer load to available support requires a zone approximately 2 metres deep packed with steelwork and the single discordant column. There is an element of structural perversity in assembling a folded plate from steel beams, which is essentially 'stick' construction in Semperian terms. As Pallasmaa observed:

351

'[t]hese products of instrumentalised technology conceal their processes of construction, appearing as ghostlike apparitions'.[17] Foster expanded on this thought, interrogating a Modernist trope:

> Again, it might be that modernist transparency mystifies more than it demystifies, that it cannot reveal the technological basis of a contemporary building (or anything else) in contemporary society. But is this pretext enough to produce an architecture of obfuscation, one that tends to reinforce a subjectivity and society given over to a fetishism of image and information? In our present of ever-greater financial, corporate and governmental black boxes, transparency might be a value to recover.[18]

Collins in 1965 had some conception of what was to come where,

> [w]ith the abandonment of 'composition', the notion rapidly gained credence that planning is essentially a technique for situating partitions within an all-embracing pre-conceived container... But it is clear that this type of planning favours an arbitrary external wrapping even more insistently than the techniques used by the 19th century Revivalists.[19]

In these constructions, surface is what presents externally and has no materiality or depth while the interior has no immediately usable volume, being simply that which is left, not formed, within the outer shell. Surface is modulated by the inherent scale and jointing of the materials of which it is composed or it may wholly ignore such constructionally predetermined jointing and impose its own paralogism of jointed construction, such as the Central China Television Building, Beijing (unfortunately acronymised as CCTV), 2004–8, by OMA and Arups, but it is pure surface, nonetheless.

The nature and form of the consequent interior space is predicated on the residue of the spatial consequences of the engineering and constructional systems required to support the form and its surface. Mannerist Modernism manipulates exterior and interior space and form independently of each other, where structure and container are wholly divorced from content, where content seems an afterthought or entails great size or height, or incorporates exaggerated emblematic symbolism or simply overstates its formal characteristics. Exterior space, not place, is simply that part of the XYZ Cartesian frame of the site plot remaining after the object has expanded to the fullness of its projected three-dimensional form. Its ideal setting is the infinite space of the prairie, parkland or the desert, but such are its infrastructural, rental and use demands that, usually – there are a few exceptions, such as the proposed Line City of Neom, Saudi Arabia – it only exists in fully-serviced central urban locations within world-cities.

We're all going to the zoo, tomorrow

Early post-Modern projects, in contrast to their Mannerist counterparts, were medium-sized, not much larger, say, than Michael Graves' 15-storey Portland Building, Oregon, 1982[20]; soon to be modestly trumped by his 26-storey Humana Building, Louisville, 1985, or Philip Johnson's 37-storey AT&T Building, New York, 1984. However, all showed signs of the privileging of surface, incipient gigantism, gratuitous and deracinated symbolism and opacity of meaning, despite or because of the use of that self-same symbolism and opacity of use where form was no guide. As Mike Davis observed:

> Philip Johnson's Chippendale ATT Building (or the 'pink pay phone' as it is sometimes called) is one of the most popularly notorious examples of the comedic or bathetic triumph of the familiar object over abstract, functionalised structure. In the hands of post-modernist architecture the skyscraper passes from monumental machine to massive collectible.[21]

Vidler records the operation of such an approach where

> [t]he surrealist transposition, the formalist shock, the metaphysical 'heightening of experience', the materialist deidealisation, all these maneuvers and many more have their place in the repertoire of contemporary effects, whether commercially useful or culturally disjunctive.[22]

Commercial, luxury apartment, leisure and representative buildings became grossly magnified and abstracted versions of small-scaled domestic objects – 'massive collectibles' – and acquired cosy soubriquets, such as the 'Pink Pay Phone', the 'Walkie-talkie', the 'Gherkin', the 'Razor', the 'Cheesegrater' or the 'Shard', as if to reduce their scale to that of the kitchen worktop and, through the agency of everyday language, to re-humanise them. Such constructions are disconcertingly contorted: smooth, flat-sided, inclined or angular spires; smooth and rounded or twisted tubes; gravity-defying angled and bent ideograms; amorphous and homogenous amoebas; galleried and stretched pagodas; fretted and pierced mashrabiyyahs; skeins of fibres;

diatoms. These forms and their surfaces, however, are not employed to carry other than the most banal of meanings, if any meaning at all. They elide, randomise or elaborate volumes; they conceal or misdirect the nature of their construction; they obscure structure and inflate their envelopes to sandwich and conceal the staggering engineering facts of their existence. They are supranational, ubiquitous, eroticised, and strain average human comprehension, experience and psyche.

The architecture of soubriquet: W Hotel, St James Quarter, Edinburgh, 2021, architects Jestico and Whiles.

In Scotland, Glasgow has the modest 'Armadillo' at the SECC, 1997, by Norman Foster (b. 1935) and Dundee the overblown entrance lobby that is the V&A, 2010–8, by Kengo Kuma (b. 1954) with its perfunctory Scottish Design exhibit. Even eight-storey Edinburgh has acquired its own version of the 'icon', the W Hotel, St James Quarter, 2021, by Jestico + Whiles which bears more than a passing resemblance to the Ribbon Chapel, Hiroshima, 2013 by Nakamura Hiroshi (b. 1932) and NAP. The bronze-coloured ribbon apparently '[evokes] the festive spirit of Edinburgh'[23] although why it should need to remains moot. It is known locally, depending on how it appeals, as either the 'walnut whip', recalling a favourite confection produced by the sadly missed Duncan's of Edinburgh, or the 'dog turd', for obvious reasons.

Bread and circuses; but mostly circuses

Architects are seduced by the apparently unlimited aesthetic possibilities of 'parametric design' – it has its own descriptor – and its frequent electronic reproduction captures the attention of the idle moment and infers a universality of application. Reiner de Graaf commented:

> In the name of creativity, architecture sides with the masterpiece and the cliché, with the unique against the common, with the specific against the generic. Creativity prioritizes the exception over the rule

and chooses the margins over the mainstream. In doing so, it leaves a vast territory unaddressed.[24]

Meanwhile, Gehry, in a conversation that Dyckhoff recounted, seems to have shared few of de Graaf's doubts while exculpating himself:

> The world is about spectacle. So what do you do about it? I can't change it. I'd like to be able to change it, but I can't. So you pick your fights. I'm an architect. I do buildings.[25]

Vidler reflected further on these constructions and, more specifically, on the anti-urban pathology of the spaces they create, contain or invade. He recognised how they stand in total and complete contra-distinction to regional architectures and that they challenge stridently for society's attention:

> Even as we experienced a severe nostalgia for time and history at the beginning of the modern period, a nostalgia resurrected from time to time throughout the century in order to counter the uncertainties of spatial modernism, we are now in the throes of an equally strong nostalgia for space, in both theory and practice.[26]

Moreover, he singled out part of the operative strategy required of the regional architect or the architect of resistance in these times in that

> the business of the architect would not be to arrest the tempo of history, nor to return to a better time, but to deploy space in a historical way that recognises its own temporality at the same time as it provides a momentary fusing of the two, a temporary respite for reflection and experience, and thus a momentary point of reference for the modern psyche: a 'post-spatial void' so to speak.[27]

Vidler's 'post-spatial void' confirms a more general societal sense of a lack of space, lack of modesty, lack of modest space, a lack of place. His use of 'void' does not imply emptiness, vacuity, but rather he seems to envisage a place in architecture and planning that refuses the flawed physical manifestations of a non-territorial, non-patrimonial space and its associated crudely mimetic historic or symbolic models.

Vidler employed the productions of the contributors to the Vienna Architecture Conference of 1992 – Wolf Prix (b. 1942) and Helmut Swiczinsky (b. 1942) of Coop Himmelblau, Zaha Hadid, Steven Holl (b. 1947), Thom

Mayne (b. 1944), Eric Owen Moss (b. 1943), Carme Pinós (b. 1954) and Lebbeus Woods (1940–2012) – as psychoanalytical case studies of the new neurotic spatial formation. In 1992, Prix et al were full of revolutionary zeal and youthful brio, although many later became the in-house architects of conventional spectacle and, in large measure, now design Vidler's 'architecture of anxiety' to be constructed as Burgin's 'in/different spaces' in the packed and soaring centres of Sudjic's 'hundred-mile city'. Moss, in a paraphrase of Zevi from 20 years earlier, claimed that:

> Most architects have lost sight of the mega-urban environment – the ghettoes, crumbling walls, back alleys, makeshift residences under expressway overpasses, subway catacombs. Neither the nomadic nature of our industrial and leisure society, nor war, commerce, phallocracy, or general all consuming chaos, have served as an impetus to discover new spatial organisms, new dimensions of space – to find a fitting architectural expression.[28]
>
> What these people want is the same thing as the magus-musician wants: mobility, fluidity, poise, agility, the ability to draw strength from the turbulence of existence itself.[29]

One hoped for the promise of care to arise from such analysis, but the attitudes and solutions were unchanged from those of doctrinaire Modernism, because the dispossessed, like the International Style's universalised working class before them, were a generality, an essentialism, on which the 'magus-musician' could predicate 'new dimensions of space'. This was, in Moss's words, '[a]rchitecture as an axe (and maybe a stiletto too)',[30] or in Zevi's, 'a revolutionary weapon, one that is actually explosive by virtue of architecture'.[31]

Žižek observed comparatively of the professional trajectory of Prix et al:

> Nothing is more conducive to proper integration into the hegemonic ideologico-political community than a 'radical' past in which one lived out one's wildest dreams.[32]

Confirming Žižek's observation, Moss, in an echo of Le Corbusier, Johnson and Gehry, later recanted, because now he did not

> mean to sound like a Berkeley subversive… [t]hat was adolescent. I think I got over it, although I get a certain amount of energy out of contesting the world, as if it were purposeful and homogeneous.

Attacking the banks? The clients? The mayor of Vienna? Whoever is diabolical that week? But these are all external, extroverted. A deeper architecture starts with the introverted.³³

An architecture of anxiety and disconcertion was appropriate at Libeskind's Jewish Museum, but degenerated to the level of a theme-park attraction in Moss and others' conception. Glass floors hundreds of metres above ground level, towers linked by glass-sided and glass-bottomed swimming pools,³⁴ glass slides attached to the sides of skyscrapers and prodigious cantilevers concomitantly devalued the disconcertion Libeskind intended us to feel when faced with his building and its recognisably insubstantial and compromised representation of the Holocaust. One preferred the sober, unvarnished, and raw telling of a similar story in the Riga Ghetto and Latvian Holocaust Museum (formerly the Occupation Museum), 1969, by Dzintars Driba (1928–93) and Gūnars Lūsis-Grīnbergs (1932–2015).

The *zeitgeist* is the exponential acceleration of inequality at every level in society. It should be no surprise that current architecture in its most egregious manifestations reflects it, as in Carol Willis's 1995 epigram that 'form follows finance'.³⁵ It does so, on the one hand, in set-piece constructions occupying their limited and delimiting Cartesian space like so many over-sized pieces on a chess board or, on the other hand, in the increasing miniaturisation or unavailability of a home for those of moderate means and less. Vidler attempted to explain, although he sounded less than convinced, indeed hopeless and helpless, and had no real solution to the

> [e]strangement and unhomeliness [that] have emerged as the intellectual watchwords of our century, given periodic material and political force by the resurgence of homelessness itself, a homelessness generated sometimes by war, sometimes by the unequal distribution of wealth.³⁶

There is no place for regional or national culture in Mannerist Modernism. Patrimony is ransacked, on the one hand, for historic symbol to attach to and imbue with meaning otherwise empty form or, on the other hand, abstractly derived form is explained through a superficial similarity with a cultural artefact. Randomly chosen examples of recent Mannerist work (at the time of writing) demonstrate how this is effected. Firstly, it is overblown and multifarious, such as the entire section in their Wikipedia entry given over to the overt and clumsy symbolism of Taipei 100, 2004, by CY Lee & Partners,³⁷ or in Bjarke Ingels Group's (BIG) claim of their National Library, Astana, Kazakhstan, 2009, that it combines four universal archetypes across space and time into a new national symbol: the circle, the rotunda, the arch and the yurt are merged into the form of a Moebius strip.[38]

Secondly, it is inadvertently revelatory of its exclusivity, as in the China Olympic Stadium, Beijing, 2008, by Herzog and De Meuron, based on their alleged study of Chinese ceramics. Their lead architect, Li Xinggang (b. 1969), reflecting on its non-ceramic nickname of the Bird's Nest, observed that 'in China, a bird's nest is very expensive, something you eat on special occasions'.[39] Thirdly, it presents as plainly vacuous as in the King Abdulaziz Centre for World Culture, Dharan,[40] 2017, by the usually more self-aware Snøhetta, a shopfront for and funded by Aramco, which is claimed to be a

> landmark on a regional, national and global horizon...[since] without culture no country or company can create a future.

The building, some leaning globular forms that look like a toppled metallic *ferocactus pilosus*, is described, Tardislike, as 'both past and future embraced in the present',[41] a claim redolent of the selective cultural acquisitiveness and stasis of 21st-century oil-wealth capitalism. Foster noted:

> Yet what is most characteristic of global style is its 'banal cosmopolitanism': even as its signal buildings respond to local conditions and global demands at once, they often do in a manner that produces an image of the local for circulation to the global.[42]

Berman put his finger on it:

> When contemporary modernists lose touch with or deny their own modernity, they can only echo the ruling-class self-delusion that it has conquered the troubles and perils of the past, and meanwhile they cut themselves off, and cut us off, from a primary source of their own strength.[43]

Ascetics as aesthetics: the Japanese house, again

At the level of detail and in seeming resistance to such gigantism, the perennial Modernist misreading and exoticising of the place and content of Japanese architecture (see Chapter 6) was repeated in 2006 by Alain de Botton.[44] He asserted:

in reality, no country ever either owns a style or is locked into it through precedent.⁴⁵

However, he expended several pages establishing a very specific case for Japanese ownership of Japanese architecture despite its being culturally transferable since the late 19th century.⁴⁶ Likewise, he remarked that

[a]t issue, therefore, is not so much what a national style is as what it could be made to be,⁴⁷

which returned the discussion to one which again avoided recognition and acceptance of both the Korean and aristocratic origins of Japanese architecture – or at least the Japanese architecture which he and others chose to reference – and its misinterpreted evolution in Modernism.

He described Japanese domestic architecture as having 'simplicity, efficiency, modesty and elegance',⁴⁸ which he categorised as 'essences' while discounting every other attribute it might embody, such as custom, habit, memory or significant cultural form, which he categorised as 'phenomena'. However, de Botton's asceticism, as did that of others before him, ignored the sheer complexity and intricacy of form and the colour and richness of pattern and detail of much else in both Japanese arts and architecture that had appealed to Western designers over the previous 150 years. De Botton employed the implicated ascetic content of Western Modernism, validated, in part, through the Western cherry-picking of traditional Japanese arts, to return – in concentric illogic – to the minimalism of the contemporary Modernist Japanese house, which is itself the historic product of the engagement of Japanese architects, post-imperium, with Western Modernism in the 1950s. Thereby he declared the present achievement of Japanese architecture a consequent corroboration and reaffirmation of the authority of the ascetism of Western minimalist Modernist architecture. He noted these houses as 'echoing the long-standing pull of Japanese aesthetics towards emptiness and austerity'.⁴⁹ But this is a Western fabrication based on the transposition onto Japan of Western values where the adoption of a superficial materialist denial is deemed to resist the Siren call of an otherwise materialist society, although its realisation is perversely costly and the very materialism it purports to refuse has long since become part of contemporary Japanese culture. Not addressed by de Botton are the implicated and questionable moral values – virtue-signalling – of such a public demonstration of seeming frugality and modesty in the 'architecture of happiness'.

Minimising and minimalising are very specific, personal life-style choices for those so resourced and equipped to make them, much as were those embedded in those single-family 'manifesto' houses that predicated the *existenzminimum* flat in the 1920s. Neither of these, being Baudrillard's 'model' for the few, is an appropriate base for the 'series', the universalised dwelling for the many. However, this is not to deny the quite exquisite, although heavily circumscribed, spaces that are illustrated in books such as *living large in small spaces*, in which the author quoted Bachelard in support of the 'hermit's hut'.[50] Ruth Slavid, in *Micro: Very Small Architecture*, recalled the 'Ideal Hut Show' at Glasgow City of Architecture in 1999 as a marker in this connection,

> so successful that it migrated to… Quebec in 2002… [and] London's Victoria & Albert Museum… in 2005.[51]

This idealised perception of the small is unequivocally contradicted in the images of contemporary tiny Japanese dwellings, where, in effect, the *kura* is the home, made by photographers Araki Nobuyoshi (b. 1940), Moriyama Daido (b.1938), Kawauchi Rinko (b.1972) and, particularly relevant to Fawcett's rejection of the West's attempted reification of 'traditional' Japanese culture and home-life, Daifu Motoyuki (b.1985).

Ruskin's return: a computational and fractal comparison

Lars Spuybroek (b. 1959), in 2016, re-presented for the contemporary age a reflection on Ruskin's understanding of Gothic rib and tracery systems and Semper's *Bekleidungsprinzip* in stone which, although patently not woven fabric, may have pattern inscribed in or superimposed on it.[52] However, Spuybroek had little truck with the rest of Semper's elements other than as an argument for ornament. There is much to be challenged in Spuybroek's contentions, although this book is not the place for it. The intent is merely to understand where he sits within a Mannerist canon and where regional and national architectures might figure in his philosophy.

Spuybroek opposed 20th-century Modernism in that,

> if there is one thing we can learn from John Ruskin, it is that each age must find its own way to beauty, and in our case, this means finding our way *back* [Spuybroek's emphasis], since we have lost sight of it completely. One cannot hope to survive a hundred-year obsession

with fracture and fragment by accident.⁵³

'Beauty' was never satisfactorily explained by him, as it can *never* be satisfactorily explained, being simply a self-justifying manifestation of the tendentiously defined qualities and characteristics of a work of art or architecture the writer personally finds especially pleasing. Apart from brief negative mentions of Frampton, Renzo Piano (b.1937) and Gehry, Spuybroek had little, in fact, to say in the matter of Modernism. In contrast, he expanded on the 'digital' nature of the Gothic, citing formal or graphic similarities between diatoms, biological structures and body plans, contemporary computer-generated fractal structures and the fractal-like plan generation of the multi-columnar and rib-based structure of Gothic piers, as illustrated in *The Stones of Venice*⁵⁴ to support both the asserted universality and contemporaneity of his formal and aesthetic arguments.

Spuybroek saw realisation of his aesthetic through the agency of the computer where, as

> in Gothic, *work, activity and craft were taking place at the design stage* [Spuybroek's emphasis], rather than only appearing on the scene at the execution stage.⁵⁵

By this intellectual sleight of hand, and by ignoring Ruskin's view of the importance of the individuality of Gothic craftsmanship and the supposed artistic or craft 'freedom' permitted the mediaeval mason, Spuybroek attempted to equate the solitary immediate precise and virtual processes of the computer work-station with the communal protracted approximating and physical processes of the Gothic building site. He concluded ecstatically:

> The Internet is not particularly modern or in any way related to space; on the contrary, it is a Gothic project… because *it interrelates work and aesthetics* [Spuybroek's emphasis]… There will be no desires, no opinions, no critics, no designers, just pure flourishing.⁵⁶

All of which was but a confection of van Doesburg's 'aestheticisation of the environment and the transformation of metropolitan life into art', a paraphrase of Focillon's 1948 observation that 'Gothic architecture is guesswork and reasoning, empirical research and inner logic all at once',⁵⁷ with the addition of the John Lennon paraphrase⁵⁸ at the end.

In his own work with his practice NOX – his entry to the World Trade Centre Competition, New York, 2001, or the Son-O-House, Son en Breugel,

Netherland, 2018 – Spuybroek's designs were aesthetically, sensationally and constructionally indistinguishable from the many Mannerist constructions referenced above which patently do not observe any of Spuybroek's niceties about 'form and force', decoration and structure, art and handcraft, Ruskin or Gothic. Indeed, it could be argued Spuybroek's theory was simply a strained justification of yet more of the same, this time emanating from his hard-drive where the 'accidental' was as consciously contrived as were Baillie-Scott's 'calculated inconsistencies'.

Taking the Mickey: Walt Disney design

Peter Zumthor wrote:

> I believe that architecture today needs to reflect on the tasks and possibilities which are inherently its own. Architecture is not a vehicle or a symbol for things that do not belong to its essence. In a society that celebrates the inessential, architecture can put up a resistance, counteract the waste of forms and meanings and speak its own language.[59]

By way of contrast, Sudjic, in a distant echo of Scott-Brown, approved of the inessential:

> In Disney's hands the amusement park has moved on from the unselfconscious level of popular entertainment to what aspires to high culture by employing academically respectable architects. You don't have to swallow Disney's world view to see that what he is doing is astonishing, the urban equivalent of NASA. Most ideal worlds stay on paper, Disney has built his.[60]

While we cannot talk about finality in such constructions –

> [f]or a house that was final, one that stood in symmetrical relation to the house we were born in, would lead to thoughts – serious, sad thoughts – and not to dreams[61]

– we surely expect architecture of an optimally useful duration, especially now where the illogic of waste has planetary consequence. It is difficult to see amusement parks, their ten-year, or less, commercial cycles and their fleeting attractions, or rather the fleeting attention-span of their customers, as more than temporary, notwithstanding the academic qualifications of their designers. Indeed, it is rather to put the architectural cart before the horse to assert that by the academic qualification of its practitioners alone the fairground is elevated to high art, for that is a judgement of an altogether different sort and of another time. Disney's 'ideal world' for the Eloi is in any event serviced (yet again) by a vast troglodytic work crew of Morlocks.[62] Moreover, the Disney empire simply shuts down and leaves to rot, in a simulacrum of the society of waste for which it provides amusement, those parts of its ideal world that do not meet financial expectations; within the past 20 years, Discovery Island (formerly Treasure Island), River Country, Pop Century, Lake Buena Vista Airport (to service Orlando), all Florida and, as the result of a failed licencing deal, Nara Dreamland, Japan.

The essences of which Zumthor wrote are those primal resources which Ruskin acknowledged and of which, in a world threatened by humankind, safeguarding and modest and appropriate use is the overriding concern. Gablik updated the instrumentality behind Ruskin's ecological concerns:

> Most of us work within a system of categories provided by society. Patriarchal structures are especially strong in the art world. Becoming aware of how much they enslave us is the first step towards breaking the cultural trance. So far… this awareness is still confined primarily to women, and now needs to spread to men. Many men will be receptive… especially if they perceive that a change in beliefs is essential for saving our ecosystem and society… whether to stick with the 'old mind' conditioned by our culture, or to move into the very different consciousness of the ecological self.[63]

Such hopes are set against the ever taller, larger, more frequent and more extravagant constructions located expediently according to availability of land and its commensurate dollar-value where every four years yet another overblown Olympic Park teeters on the brink of falling into disuse, or where the 'Bilbao effect' does not translate to glitzy urban regeneration in your city, or where the 'Palm Islands' are reclaimed by the Gulf, or where yet another ghost-town is created in China to join those of Chenggong, Lanzhou, Nanhui, Pudong and Yingkou. Foster observed that,

> in architecture no less than in art, the putative extrapolation of a scheme from its site has become a familiar operation; first embraced as a way to avoid the arbitrary, it has become arbitrary in its own way.[64]

The world-city is comprised of arbitrary sites where such cultural continuity as exists is facilitated by the technology of ever-more rapid land and air transit systems. There can be nothing arbitrary about a regional architecture and its intimate relationship to its site, physical and ideational, in territory and patrimony.

The world of my many places: global regionalisms

Within his personal conception, Zumthor understood experiential resonance in architecture:

> And although I cannot trace any special forms, there is a hint of fullness and of richness which makes me think: this I have seen before. Yet, at the same time, I know that it is all new and different, and that there is no direct reference to a former work of architecture which might divulge the secret of the memory-laden mood.[65]

He extended this to a consideration of historical resonance, not as stylistically contrived by Scott and Scruton in Classical guise or by Spuybroek in the Gothic, but qualitatively in essence:

> Every new work of architecture intervenes in a specific historical situation. It is essential to the quality of the intervention that the new building should embrace qualities which can enter into a meaningful dialogue with the existing situation. For if the intervention is to find its place, it must make us see what already exists in a new light.[66]

This parallels Jencks's observation that existing forms

> do not recall their previous use until *after* they are seen to work in their present context[67]

and is the exact opposite of Collins's 'the old must conform to the new'. It requires the reciprocity of equals rather than the hegemony of one as the operative function in the incorporation of the new with the old. Said Zumthor:

> So I immerse myself in the place... and try to inhabit it in my imagination and at the same time I look beyond it at the world of my many places.[68]

Essy Baniassad wrote of Brian MacKay-Lyons's Nova Scotian work:

> It is at the same time conventional in the context of what we would call 'low-brow' buildings in the vernacular tradition. Yet the work is quite consciously that of architecture as it embodies the history of architecture.[69]

The extension of the ideistic content of regionalism to enable it to share in the history of 20th century Modernism returns us to the proto-Modern concerns of Berlage and Loos. It also brings with it the concomitant extension of geographic content to consider more closely and learn from other regionalisms throughout the world. This takes us to cultures far different from a local Scottishness, say, where the qualitative essence of earlier regional knowledge which has been misplaced here – to be supplanted by that of the tower-house – is still understood, used and nurtured elsewhere. '[MacKay-Lyons's] plain modern[70] is not a style but a philosophical attitude', said Quantrill, expanding on Baniassad's thoughts, and it 'resists the counter-culture of tourism and its insidious companion, popular magazine imagery'[71]

Such engagement needs to expand spatial concerns beyond both the purely sublime, abstract, aesthetic and framing functions Modernists have required of them and decorative significance of the bounding surfaces as prescribed in historic regionalism. Zumthor said:

> I do not think of [architecture] primarily as either a message or a symbol, but as an envelope and background for life which goes on in and around it, a sensitive container for the rhythm of footsteps on the floor, for the concentration of work, for the silence of sleep.[72]

What regional and national architectures display in the early 21st century are not fireside images of a former golden age of national history, architecture or vernacular achievement but precisely what current conditions – personal, accessible, social, communitarian, ecological, climatic, political – require of it and within a constellation of forms and motives that are recognisably particular to place.

Crisis? What crisis? Scotland's architecture at the turn of the century

> This book was originally envisaged as a publication about the new works and thoughts of contemporary Scottish architects' practices. In the course of our discussions with these firms, we became convinced that before a book of that kind could properly be written, a more urgent initial task was to challenge the global commodification which constrains all Scottish designers. The result was the present volume, a polemical and generalised rather than descriptive and specific book.[73]

These are the opening lines of *Clone City: Crisis and Renewal in Scottish Architecture*, published 1999, by architectural historian Miles Glendinning (n.d.) and architect David Page (n.d.), both highly regarded in their fields. 'Crisis and renewal' sounded promising as an opener for the new millennium; it made me wonder why I experienced contemporaneously so much doubt about virtually the same topic.[74] *Clone City* was of interest: first, because there is so little theoretical writing on Scottish architecture, even for that reason alone; and second, because it purported to be a significant intellectual analysis of the state of *Scottish* architecture at the *fin-de-siècle* and a prediction of what was to come. However, Glendinning and Page's focus shifted abruptly within a sentence to a macro-scale investigation of the condition of and for architecture in the context of a proposed positivist town and regional planning project for the Central Belt between and including Edinburgh and Glasgow. It claimed that for architecture to flourish or express itself what was required was a more benign, ordered and administratively-centralised dispersed economic, political and planning setting, ignoring that, as Johnson had confirmed, architects are opportunistic and promiscuous and their works, accepting of the current milieu, are often brilliantly pragmatic and expedient.

Glendinning and Page thus progressed from buildings to a polemic on the aesthetics of Scottish urban and regional planning over time.[75] Of course, polemic is so much easier than analysis. However, few of my architectural generation would recognise a situation where:

> For young architects coming into practice in the 1970s and early 1980s, the possibilities of architecture seemed to be limited to new tenement doors and back-court railings. More often than not, people just tiptoed between broken glass.[76]

Whereas, at the same time, inhabitants of Glasgow and Edinburgh might question, yet again, their lazy appellation by the authors as 'the expansive, modernising west and the romantic, reflective east', and wonder why

> [t]hat contrast is specially important because, in it, we begin to encounter for the first time a reaction against the architecture of progress and the very tentative beginnings of the concept of inclusive or cumulative modernity – the concept which forms the main theme of this book[77]

because they were never told.

Glendinning and Page presented, without reason other than their difference, various examples of Scottish city-formation since the 17th century as clashing and incomplete Utopias seeking hegemony, claiming each to be in denial, rejection or denigration of its predecessors. There is an abiding sense of the need for tidiness and conclusion in *Clone City*. However, the 'city of perpetual incompleteness'[78] is where

> the edges are rough and chafe against each other. Here sparks fly, here ideas catch fire, here experience burns.[79]

For Glendinning and Page, the city of incompleteness and difference was invariably a zone of aesthetic contention as static as trench warfare. City-dwellers' urban mental mapping is a deal more sophisticated and accommodating than Glendinning and Page allowed, and what is perceived, understood, enjoyed and relished is the 'city of difference' and not a 'city of conflict'. Kevin Lynch (see Chapter 6), more generous and less precious than Glendinning and Page, described a 'visual plan' for the city where:

> The final objective of such a plan is not the physical shape itself but the quality of an image in the mind.[80]

Moreover:

> It is clear that the form of the city or of a metropolis will not exhibit some gigantic stratified order. It will be a complicated pattern, continuous and whole, yet intricate and mobile. It must be plastic to the perceptual habits of thousands of citizens, open-ended to change of function and meaning, receptive to the formation of new imagery. It must invite its viewers to explore the world.[81]

One can take little exception to such a programme. However, in contrast, Glendinning and Page framed the city plan in doctrinaire Modernism as aesthetic, which is the 'physical shape' rather than 'haptic', which is the 'image in the mind'.

Glendinning and Page's target was the 'fundamentalists' who, they claimed, proposed

> the myth of the dense tenement community, the cult of Tenementopia, [which] has virtually monopolised architectural debate over Scottish urban housing.[82]

Contrary to such a claim, it was the proliferation of tight and unsanitary mediaeval cores of Scottish cities – as Geddes recognised – the decay and over-scaled back courts of *some* Scottish tenements, the barren figure/ground planning of Modernist point- and slab-blocks and the consequent loss of the variety of usable human-scaled urban place that was at question. The tenement was merely one component of this critique. Their comparative model of the historic over-development of the originally open courts of the 18th-century German *Mietkasernen*,[83] to call the Scottish tenement into question, was not well chosen, since the present condition of the *Mietkasernen* is the result of that creeping occupation of back-courts over the centuries. One of the IBA objectives, which impacted crucially on late 20th-century Scottish urban planning, was the investigation of models that would resolve the several challenges listed above, including that of the over-developed *Mietkasernen*.

Glendinning and Page's concept implied substantial state intervention and a return to the planned Central Belt decentralisation of the 1960s. There was far too little examination of the societal and rather too much of the administrative drivers behind this, which took no account of the structural, economic, demographic and employment factors that, in their construct, might perhaps necessitate such planning reforms. Too much polity, not remotely enough patrimony. Such revisionism extended to this re-interpretation of the mass housing programmes of the 1960s and 1970s:

> Robert Matthew argued in 1952 that the only worthy comparison was Periclean Athens: 'for the first time since the fifth century BC, public architecture has become popular architecture – in the strict sense, by the people, for the people!'[84]

The authors offered as model for a non-elitist, universalist architecture of our times that of an exclusive, male, Athenian society based on the subjugation of women and facilitated by slavery. It was insufficient for them later, in *apologia*, to question whether Matthew's vision 'of authority-led democracy proved unsustainable in the face of societal change'[85] might possibly have been 'unsustainable' in part, for it manifestly was at every level of patriarchy that one could imagine.

They restated Gropius, Hitchcock and others' outdated prescriptions of the 'breakdown of rigid class divisions'[86] whereby

> we cannot pretend that the iron bonds of family, industrial class community or unitary nation still remain, when they have so obviously been ripped apart.[87]

Class divisions are not broken down; it is simply that the definition of the middle class is extended from a British one of birth, education and connections to an American one of achievement, purchasing-power and mobility – whether one welcomes that or not – while the 'bonds' of community and nation, as *Land of Stone* attempts to describe, similarly undergo redefinition, as do the definitions of family. Family is variable and is not, as conventionally defined two parents and 2.4 children. Rather, it is multi-generational, or comprised of parents of either complementary or the same gender or ethnicity, or of only one parent, or where children share biological and non-biological parentage, or the parentage of more than one household, or of a multiplicity of parents or, indeed, that the family is a group of close friends of discrete parentage. Nevertheless, familial bonds remain intact and the family-unit, however constructed, occupies a familiar place in society. The poor remain. Their definition, too, expands to include the 'working poor' who are in steady but inadequately-paid employment or in any paid employment and who have been enticed into taking on over-extended credit or are in endemic debt; the 'information poor' who, lacking internet connection, are increasingly ostracised from a web-based society; the 'access poor' barred from many locations due to disability; the 'travel poor' whose horizons, lacking a car, are limited by the presumption of the availability of private transport and the fact of its lack of investment, even disinvestment in public transport; and the 'opportunity poor' who through location, health, gender or ethnicity are denied it in dwelling, companionship, employment or leisure.

None of this features in *Crisis and Renewal*. Indeed, Glendinning and Page's prescriptions on family, class and nation returned us to where:

> Gropius, visualising a change in social order, wrote that in these

Mountains for Living the individual woman or man is the social unit of a more perfect society rather than the state or family. Family duties as such would not exist; elimination of all housework would provide equal leisure time for both sexes. Women of equal capabilities would have the same earning power as men.[88]

Mitchell's earlier *City of Bits* raised these issues, but yet again in electronic rather than physical exclusion:

Today, as telepresence augments and sometimes substitutes for physical presence, and as more and more business and social interactions shift into cyberspace, we are finding that accessibility depends even less on proquintity, and community has become increasingly unglued from geography. Our network connections are becoming as important to us as our bodily locations.[89]

Glendinning and Page seemed as distanced from their subject as was their photographer in the helicopter as they took the views of urban formation that interleave the text. The flattened perspective of the aerial photographs gave no sense, for one, of urban topography, whether Glasgow's dunlins[90] or Edinburgh's Old Town crag-and-tail and New Town ridge[91], so significant a feature of the urban-dweller's psychogeographical, haptic and physical engagement with the city. The image of the 'monument to the future' of youthful Scottish Episcopalian choristers in St Mary's Choir School set against Phoebe Traquair's murals, 1888–92,[92] was simply perverse or possibly a private joke. Kerevan summed up:

The root of Glendinning and Page's non solution is defined in passing, 'There is, today, no simple definition of the essence of place in the Scottish city'. Absolutely true. The joy of the 21st century will be the multitude of spaces we can inhabit. The agenda requires an architecture of quality control not quantity control. But the role of aesthetics is one thing this book pointedly dismisses as a post modernist [sic] conceit.[93]

Summer in the city: a contemporary urbanism

While Glendinning and Page were theoretically conjoining Edinburgh and Glasgow in one urban enterprise, those two cities vied for the City of

The contemporary tenement: Lanark Street, Glasgow, 2001, various architects.

Architecture, 1999, accolade and the architectural jamboree it entailed. Glasgow won. Neither the Garden Festival of 1988 nor the City of Culture of 1991 had resulted in much of lasting significance; the City of Architecture was different. Homes for the Future, now called Lanark Street, near Glasgow Green, master-planned by Page \ Park, demonstrated novel site-planning, perhaps a version of the Modernist/post-Modernist hybrid Page and Glendinning had skirted around in *Clone City*. There were blocks designed by Ushida Finlay, RMJM, Ian Ritchie, Elder and Cannon, McKeown Alexander (subsequently jm architects), Wren Rutherford ASL (subsequently Austin, Smith-Lord) and Rick Mather. With the exception of the temporarily-Edinburgh-based Japanese-Scottish Ushida Findlay, the Scottish architects all won Saltire Awards or Commendations in 2000 and 2001. Demonstration projects such as this are fraught with contradictions, the most significant and most usual in this case being the presumption that the future can be reliably extrapolated from the present or the series from the model. Welch wondered, 'is this a model for the future or a zoo for preening architects?'[94]

The generic urban form of the masterplan, though not in the subsequent varied aesthetic of the constructed dwellings, confirmed that Page \ Park had knowledge of the IBA work of Herman Hertzberger at Lindenstrasse and Markgrafenstrasse, 1987,[95] Ungers at Lützowplatz 1983[96] or Moore, Ruble and Yudell's masterplan at Tegeler Hafen, 1980,[97] not to mention the experience they and Elder and Cannon brought with them and refined from Crown Street. IBA 1979–87 was a regular and easily accessible port of call for Scottish architects, academics, students and developers throughout the mid to late 1980s to the early 2000s. Derek Fraser, author of *Berlin*, recalled a conversation with Mike Galloway, then Project Leader of the Crown Street Regeneration Project, Glasgow, on the completion of Phase 1 in 1996:

> Galloway's desire for a more integrated, practical and recognisable urban form at Crown Street was met with some resistance by the developer/contractors. Galloway remembers their saying that 'we are interested in building the flats but don't do shops'. He organised a visit to Berlin for them to study the completed IBA projects, in particular, those consisting of perimeter blocks with shops at street level which convinced them of the viability of the mixed-use urban form.[98]

As a viable architectural response to late 20th-century inner urban Glasgow life rather than to an undefinable domestic situation 20 years hence, the urban blocks of Elder and Cannon, Rick Mather and Ian Ritchie showed the greatest promise. They provided a perimeter frontage and contained the inner court of terrace and stand-alone blocks. Elder and Cannon and Mather created a link block signifying entrance to the site. At the level of practical detail, Ritchie incorporated a genuine outside room which had the twin benefits of providing dedicated usable external space to each flat in a six-storey tenement, much better than a balcony, while resolving the means of escape issues generated by the internal accessing of one of the bedrooms off the free-flowing open living room and kitchen. Ritchie, Elder and Cannon and Mather all reinterpreted Hertzberger's investigation of public, private and semi-public/semi-private space and the thresholds between them – the 'boundary layer' – as constructed at his IBA work and at the earlier Haarlemmer Houtuinen, Amsterdam, 1978. The stand-alone blocks within the landscaped court defined their own private/public relationship to the public space of the court through decks, bridges, stoops and courtyards and derived their form in part from the 'urban villa' apartment block, initiated by Ungers, that made its appearance at IBA, particularly at Tegeler Hafen by Paolo Portoghesi, Antoine Grumbach, Stanley Tigerman, John Hejduk and Robert Stern,[99] and at the Tiergarten by Hans Hollein, Aldo Rossi and Giorgio Grassi.[100]

Nevertheless, the publicly-accessible shared garden court at Lanark Street was still required to perform the Modernist role of the ground whereby the figure of the buildings were established and framed. The 'boundary layers' notwithstanding, the very limited amount of useable dedicated private and shared semi-private external space was compensated only horticulturally and aesthetically by the garden court. With the few exceptions noted above, these flatted blocks were normative in that they defined from the outset that very specific sort of aestheticised urban living questioned at length earlier in this text. It is difficult to imagine children, youths or old people in a setting such as

Learning from IBA 3: Urban Villa, Tegel, Berlin, 1988, architect Robert Stern.

Lanark Street, for they present the opposite of a normative aestheticised lifestyle: they are anarchic, messy, non-aesthetic, unimpressed and largely unimpressible.

The loss by Edinburgh of its bid to host the City of Architecture event had a silver lining. Peter Wilson, who led the bid, founded, in its wake, the Manifesto Foundation for Architecture and published *ARCA*, Scotland's interrogative architectural journal. In its brief life (1999–2003), *ARCA* dealt with major issues in Scottish architecture within a larger world context. It never really established itself in Scotland's architectural community, which seemed habituated to the London-centric *Architect's Journal*, or at ease with the undemanding local gossip and publicity pap content of *Urban Realm* and the *RIAS Quarterly*. Perhaps all that *ARCA* did, could do, in an inferiorist, non-intellectual architectural culture, was to point up what was missing.

Zevi's riposte: the exquisite contrariness of the Scottish Parliament

When finally opened for business on 7 September 2004, the Scottish Parliament, Holyrood, Edinburgh, designed by highly individual, perfectionist and Catalan architects Enric Miralles (1955–2000) and Benedetta Tagliabue

The antinomy of Scotland 2: Scottish Parliament, Edinburgh, 1999–2004, architects EMBT and RMJM.

(b.1963) (EMBT), with RMJM as local executant architects, located on an awkward site, to a constantly revised and enlarged brief, was late, hugely over budget and aesthetically challenging, all of which did much initially to damage its reputation with the Scottish architectural commentariat. As with the Museum of Scotland, English opinion was much more positive. Glendinning recorded enthusiastic reactions from Hugh Pearman, Deyan Sudjic and Marcus Binney.[101] In the *Times*, Pearman focused on the detail:

> [It is] insanely bespoke, positively wilful, but potentially glorious…
> I had expected the building to make a big statement in today's
> fashionable 'signature' style, but to be let down by its details, to wilt
> under close scrutiny. But the opposite is true… the quality of the
> finished work, the level of detailing, is prodigious. It is remarkable to
> find such a level of individual craftsmanship in a building of this size.[102]

In Scotland, one view which began to get at some of the philosophical ideas in Scottish architecture that the foreign gaze of the Parliament's architects addressed was that of Neil Gillespie, who raised potently its aspect of a *Nordic Expressionismus*:

> [It] is a building which we should know and understand. It evokes a
> landscape, a hyperborean landscape, a FINN land, a White land. It is
> about the glacier, in the crush and folding of space and form. It is about
> the birch tree, the girl of the forest, given architectural form in the

delicate timber screens to MSP offices. The concrete Canongate throws fragments of stone and drawing to its surface like some glacial moraine.

It eschews passing beauty for something more profound and grounded in this territory. It is about a place beyond the restrictive parochial boundaries of Scotland, it is located firmly in a northern territory. This is not an easy landscape, it is the chaos of the moraine, the anxiety of the gorge, the horror of the void, the silence of Munch's scream.[103]

The Scottish Parliament is not the kind of building that suggests it would have appealed to Gillespie, whose architecture is cool, controlled and, on occasion, of an almost German *sachlichkeit*, but it was a measure of the building's catholicity and Gillespie's perceptiveness and generosity of spirit that it did.

It was through the generality and the detail and in what they believed to be the Parliament's equivocal stance *vis-à-vis* 'iconic' architecture that Glendinning and MacKechnie were vexed. In their account of the building, which served as a puzzling and somewhat redundant coda to their *Scotch Baronial*, they remarked:

> Yet it was unclear, to say the least, whether Miralles's own design was any less rhetorical and image-driven, than mainstream classicism or modernism – especially as the design as executed (1999–2004) became more dense and even monumental, while trumping the most elaborately ornate of the stately parliament buildings of the 19th century in its prodigious architectural excess, heaping detail upon detail, leaving no space or surface untouched by motifs and metaphoric references.[104]

Arguably, Glendinning and MacKechnie's preferences and knowledge bases – the Renaissance, the Baronial and the Modernism of the third quarter of the 20th century – blinded them to Miralles and Tagliabue's sophistication in manipulating the tropes of Mannerist Modernism, as recognised by Pearman and Gillespie, while obliging Glendinning and MacKechnie to consider the restoration of Queensberry House, which also disappointed, as the 'focus of the complex'. Surely the Debating Chamber occupies that position. The Parliament's Scottish significance is not in the fictionalised 'skater' motif of Raeburn's painting cladding the building, nor in the diagrammatic Saltires cast in the concrete vault of the entrance lobby, nor in the poetry inscribed on or the Scottish rocks embedded in the Canongate façade but in the implicated and looser astylar psychological principles that bring such an architecture into being in the first place.

In time and in the way of things, furore was overtaken by favour. Unfairly, Glendinning and MacKechnie attempted to deny the widespread public appreciation and enjoyment of the building by ghettoising its support, decrying its relatively limited accessibility while ignoring the regular guided tours and access to the public gallery. They asserted that,

> [a]lthough widely acclaimed by the Scottish architectural and cultural elite, the completed building remained as closed to the public as any traditional monumental parliament, owing to its fortress-like plan as built.[105]

Thereby, they ignored the considerable access-limiting consequences of the addition of the post-2001, 9/11, and post-2007, Glasgow Airport, anti-terrorist protection measures. If any choice is to be made about any parliament, openness of governmental process is infinitely preferable to universal access to its container.

When in doubt, make a list: distinction and explanation by numerical ranking

Rather than engage in serious debate, the Scottish architectural establishment seemed to prefer the list. The list has all the intellectual content and historic permanence of the weekly Scottish Professional Football League (SPFL) table, which fails to explain why Scottish Cup success does not translate to Champions League achievement. To enter the lists is to take part in a joust. In 2005, *Prospect* magazine listed the 100 best Scottish buildings of the previous 50 years. This list shared some entries with the esoteric DOCOMOMO list (see Chapter 6), although it almost entirely removed those where engineering constituted the principal content and most of the several mass housing and New Town projects favoured by DOCOMOMO. Neither list, by design, included anything earlier than 1945, and both lists contained different long-demolished colliery buildings by the relatively obscure Egon Riss (1901–64).[106] Nonetheless, the *Prospect* list hinted at the work that came to define Scotland's regional architecture in the following decade with entries by such as Richard Murphy, Page\Park, Elder and Cannon, Munkenbeck and Marshall, Reiach and Hall and NORD, although it made no such regional connection, overt or covert, treating each as an isolate.

Whereas the DOCOMOMO list was for adherents of the Modern Movement and the Prospect 2005 list was for architects, the RIAS list of 2016, in its centenary year, on which the public was invited to vote, had a populist slant in that overwhelmingly the buildings illustrated were accessible to the public or featured in societal memory as once accessible. It included only one engineering structure and no buildings previously demolished. It was based on Sinclair's earlier 1984 outing, *Scotstyle: 150 Years of Scottish Architecture*,[107] although authorship was expanded. (Surprisingly, given its bold appellation of *Scotstyle*, the 1984 list included 24 works by non-Scottish architects out of a total of 144, whereas, in perverse non-reciprocity, it contained no works by Scottish architects furth of Scotland.) The 100 buildings of the 2016 list were whittled down to ten, with one to be selected as winner by public vote.[108] Other than the hokey inclusion of the Hermit's Castle, Achmelvich, 1955,[109] in the final ten, there was nothing listed in the 'top ten' built between 1938 and 1978 (the span of the DOCOMOMO list), tending to confirm a more general public – even professional – avoidance of the period. To the disbelief of architects throughout Scotland, Princes Square Shopping Mall, Buchanan Street, Glasgow, 1985, by Hugh Martin and Partners, won. The RIAS attempted justification of both the process and the choice.

Although they cover different periods of the 20th century, *Scotstyle* 1 (Q1- Q3), DOCOMOMO (Q3), Prospect (Q3 and Q4) and *Scotstyle* 2 (Q2–Q4 and Q1, 2000) shared only seven entries from the 30 or so jointly available. A poll of polls revealed an approved mid-20th-century magnificent seven of: St Peter's Seminary, Cardross, 1967, by Gillespie, Kidd and Coia; the Bernat Klein Studio, near Galashiels, 1972, by Peter Womersley; the Royal Commonwealth Pool, Edinburgh, 1970, by Robert Matthew, Johnson-Marshall and Partners; St Paul's Church, Glenrothes, 1957, by Gillespie, Kidd and Coia; Avisfield, Cramond, Edinburgh, 1957, by Morris and Steedman; the Pathfoot Building, University of Stirling, Bridge of Allan, 1967, by Robert Matthew, Johnson-Marshall and Partners; and the Stow College of Building and Printing, Glasgow, 1964, by Wylie Shanks and Underwood. It is of interest, perhaps, but no more reliable or permanent than any Top Ten and proof of the futility of exercises based solely on the subjectivity of taste, the arbitrariness of date and the futility of geography as the only constant. They are seven isolates.

(Groucho) Marxism: the challenges of club membership

Peter Wilson identified some commonality in certain Scottish architects' approach, claiming that

[n]o area of the British Isles is better able to demonstrate regional distinctiveness in its modern architecture than the Isle of Skye.[110]

Nevertheless, such a view may not necessarily be that of those so conveniently bundled together nor the association more than aesthetic. Alan Dickson of Rural Design, Skye, one of those so identified by Wilson, when queried whether he saw himself as part of such a distinct group of architects, observed:

> No, but others may not share that view. Many see [Rural Design] as part of an overall approach shared with Dualchas or Mary Arnold-Forster – I believe our work is very different.

He qualified this in that '[a]lthough not a group, I believe we are all pursuing variations of a regional approach'.[111] This sense of belonging but not belonging, wanting to but not wanting to belong, was also expressed by Andrew Brown of Brown and Brown based in Aberdeenshire:

> We would actually like to view ourselves as part of a defined group in a way, but unfortunately we don't feel this way.

Brown shared Wilson's 'outsider' assessment:

> [I am] aware of a 'critical regionalist' group (if that's the correct phrase), which seems to exist, including practices producing work of a high calibre such as Dualchas or Rural Design, but whilst they have undoubtedly influenced our work, we don't identify ourselves as belonging with them.[112]

Mary Arnold-Forster, who had worked with Dualchas and currently works on her own account, tended to support Wilson's and Brown's opinion, although her regionalism was of a more general global sort where there existed

> a generation of architects described by Richard Gibson in Shetland as 'on the edge' but clearly aware of developments in other peripheral coast or mountainous regions of the world.[113]

This accorded with Dickson's 'Atlantic Edge'.

A similar point of belonging to such a wider community was made by Neil Gillespie of Reiach and Hall in that, although he did not see himself as part of an identifiable group, he, like others, posited himself in loose comparison or association with the ostensibly like-minded, although he described his objectives in orthodox Modernist terminology:

> I think Reiach and Hall Architects sits within a fairly identifiable group of architects possibly Bennetts Associates, John McAslan, Elder and Cannon. Pretty straight modernist practices that care about professionalism and the making of a good product. Interested in material and detail resolution, daylight, generosity and simplicity of space as opposed to form-making.[114]

An equivocal longing persisted within other less geographically identifiable groups. Nicola Hall of Lee Boyd, Edinburgh, felt she was

> [n]ot specifically [part of a group] in name but there are several different practices whose work I admire, and I believe share a similar approach.[115]

Those practices were, in the main, that cohort of Edinburgh College of Art graduates of the mid- to late 1990s and the offices of Richard Murphy, Malcolm Fraser, Lee Boyd and, briefly, Ungless and Latimer and Ewen and Fiona MacLachlan.

Academic Andy Summers and the English-born, Scottish-domiciled Chris Dobson of 3DReid likewise took the broader Scottish/internationalist view through their work with the agit-prop group Architecture Fringe while many architects, like Jude Barber of Collective Architecture, favoured a more specific local creative community including painters, photographers and craftspeople such as that which, as Barber asserted, 'has its roots in actions that are frank, challenging, collaborative and supportive'. Barber experienced this in Glasgow

> where there is a long history of activism and social justice (which is geographical but also political and cultural).[116]

Community was rarely mentioned as being represented by the functions and organs of the professional institutes. It was even contradicted, as was made clear in Roy Milne's comparative experiences of working in New Zealand and Scotland in the 1970s, where

> there was a lot of friendship and interaction amongst architects in New Zealand. They seemed to be willing to share their knowledge and experience and took delight in doing so... Back in Scotland after some years, I found the opposite and, although I developed lots of contacts

and friends in the profession, there seemed to be a general tendency to keep business affairs and skills closely guarded.[117]

This atomistic architectural community, where particularised belonging was seen as something others did and where the individual reported an anomalous 'part-of-but-not-part-of' membership, thus described anecdotally, was further compounded by dichotomous expressions of Scottishness. Nonetheless, there were more complex and nuanced ideas present, such as those of Summers:

> For example, I never say Scottish architecture, but also [sic] architecture in Scotland. I'm averse to saying Scottish architects, more architects in Scotland. I am averse to flags. What I try and do in my work is anchor it in Scotland, so it is of Scotland. If that's seen as Scottish, well so be it but that is not my intent. I am interested in producing high quality, internationally-oriented work which comes from a deep acknowledgement and connection to a place, in this case a place called Scotland. So I do not see it as tenuous or irrelevant.[118]

Brown said, 'I feel our work is undeniably Scottish and draws inspiration from here'. On the face of it these comments are encouraging, but one might legitimately ask two further questions, that is: what is it that 'anchors' Summers's architecture in Scotland rather than, say, Finland, or that makes Brown's architecture 'undeniably Scottish'? What is the 'international orientation' of which Summers spoke? Chris Dobson, 'as an outsider', referred to Scotland's 'contrasting cities and staggering rural environment'[119] as an influence, though this was equally non-specific and could likewise have been applied, say, to Yorkshire.

These statements are linked and crucial. By seeking a priori an international orientation, Summers put the architectural cart before the horse because, as the comparative examples of Czechoslovakia and Finland revealed, what is first required of the nascent nation before it joins the global family is a distinct and confident regional or national architectural culture. Brown and Summers' unexplained and unqualified assertions of Scottishness suggested that the absence of debate about a recognisable contemporary construct of Scottish architecture has had the result that the concept and language of a distinct Scottishness in architecture simply does not exist at present in Scotland and that other languages and modes of expression, say, those of International Modernism, have been enlisted to fill the critical gap. Some architects attempted a degree of specificity: Gordon Ferrier hazarded the view that Scottishness entailed 'an innate practicality and frugality';[120] Mary Arnold-Forster proposed an 'architecture of restraint';[121] Neil Gillespie recorded 'particularly a sense of a northern hardness or a brittle aesthetic';[122] Nicola Hall understood it in a specific materiality in construction and raised the relevance of the 'boundary layer' in 'bespoke benches on the metalwork bridges' at Pitt Street, Edinburgh;[123] Richard Murphy spoke of the 'occupied wall' and 'poché space' as being of significance.[124] Arnold-Forster and Gillespie discussed an 'architecture of melancholy'. One of the non-clinical dictionary meanings of melancholy is 'indulgence in thoughts of pleasing sadness'[125], which implicates the antinomy of pleasure and pain. Melancholy is not an isolated architectural phenomenon and is present in Scotland's many national songs: *Scots Wha Hae*, *Scotland the Brave*, *O Flower of Scotland* or *Caledonia*.

Certainly, there was no overt politicisation in these architects' nebulous expressions of Scottishness, although there was a general understanding of the cultural significance of the Scottish Parliament since 1999 as model and custodian, function and building. Barber said:

> I do think there is a degree of confidence in our studio's work, and my own approach, that came from the opportunities, ideas and optimism generated post-1997.[126]

Gillespie took a similar view, although he focused on the apparent disconnect between political and architectural culture in Scotland:

> I am hugely supportive of the political intentions embodied in a Scotland post-1997. I think it is absolutely relevant to architecture. However, I am not convinced that the rhetoric of a fair, democratic, open society which is the stated ambition of the Scottish Government is in any way reflected in a new architectural culture.[127]

A nuanced version of such a view was that of Hall, who

> [did] not see any Scottish intent in my work relating specifically to the wider political and cultural events in Scotland, but undoubtedly Scotland has changed considerably since the devolved Scottish Parliament was created and has grown bolder and more assured.

She went on to suggest equivocally 'that Architecture in Scotland is equally bolder and more progressive', but wondered 'whether it is cause and effect'.[128] Dobson made an interesting note. There was nothing comparable to the surge in contemporary architecture of distinction, in Ireland, of the late 90s/2000s [sic]. Although whether this can be attributed to politics or policy is probably up for debate.[129]

One wonders whether his downbeat assessment was in fact premature.

As a young practice, formed in 2010, Brown and Brown could know of nothing other than working in a devolved Scotland.[130] It is interesting to speculate whether their considered Miesian approach would have been likely or feasible prior to 1997. Consistent with his 'Atlantic Edge' stance, Dickson claimed,

> the stimulus for rural architecture in the west highlands [sic] has more to do with the construction of the Skye Bridge [completed 1992] and the availability of internet connections [than Scottish devolution].[131]

Both Gillespie and Arnold-Forster[132] also saw relevance in the Scottish Parliament building's architectural significance in that it resolved into popular culture through rapid and widespread public approval.

Given these architects were established in their art and practice, the imprecision, even vagueness, of their understanding of the very specific nature of the business of practising in Scotland was matched by an inevitable randomness of early inspiration. Some, following the precepts of Bachelard, referred to the family home: Hall's grandfather's quirky house in Jordan Lane, Edinburgh; Arnold-Forster's grandmother's house, Carradale, one of the smaller David Bryce houses built 1844; Milne's uncle's house and surgery at Ormiston, designed by Basil Spence in 1952. Others identified as influence a wide range of canonic Modernist building. Some were from within Scotland, such as Barber's preferences for the Dollan Baths, East Kilbride or Royal Commonwealth Pool, Edinburgh; Gillespie's for Gillespie, Kidd and Coia's St Bride's Church, East Kilbride; Dickson's for the Burrell Gallery, Glasgow; all recognisable from the several lists discussed at the start of this chapter. Others were from without Scotland such as Dobson's liking for Roche Dinkeloo's Cummins Engine Factory, Darlington; Brown's for the Therme Vals by Zumthor; Summers' for works by Herman Herzberger; Ferrier's for Wright's Falling Water; and Hall's for the 1920s and '30s Berlin Housing of Bruno Taut.

The question to be asked perhaps is not 'would I really want to belong to a club that would have me for a member?' but rather 'where's the club?'

Uncontested history: the pressure of polity

With a straw poll of Scottish architects disinclined to draw any conclusions from their work beyond describing it in the conventional language of the Modernist project, the sense that analysis of Scottish architecture lags far behind its World comparators is palpable. Architecture as Scottish patrimony has been dependent on the official custodianship of and interpretation by Historic Environment Scotland (HES) since the days of the Royal Commission for Historic and Architectural Monuments in Scotland's (RCAHMS) photographic reconnaissance of potentially bomb-threated historic structures in WWII. HES's duty is to protect works of merit of 30 years-of-age or older while, as a government agency, it is beholden to deliver relevant parts of current government policy, all of which requires a consistent and emollient historical and cultural narrative. The writing of architectural history in Scotland is largely the purview of those employed by or closely associated with HES because, at the very least, it has the largest extant publicly-accessible archive of Scottish architectural drawings, texts and records. This, of course, raises the issue of what is the prime responsibility of HES – patrimony or polity – and how might that effect the reporting of architectural history?

An example of one consequence of this process is the 2017 listing citation for the *zielenbau* Cables Wynd House, Leith, Edinburgh, 1966, by Alison and Hutchison. The unusually extended 'Statement of Special Interest' reads as *apologia* for the *type* and not a detailed analysis of the actual building¹³³. Where it does venture into such discussion it claims the concrete crosswalls and inset balconies to be 'innovative', although these two features are sources of the cold-bridging that bedevils this and slab blocks like it. 'Innovation' here has privileged compliance with a Modernist type over the demonstration of actual technical proficiency. Judgement by HES is largely aesthetic and historical and quite unrelated to actual dwelling experience despite the crucial importance of the *existenzminimum* flat in driving these

Modernist apotheosis: Cables Wynd House, Leith, 1963–5, architects Alison & Hutchison.

determinedly non-aesthetic and anti-historical constructions:

> The treatment of the interior communal spaces is typically sparse and functional with in situ concrete flooring, ceramic tiling to lift areas for example. Individual flat interiors were not seen and have not been taken into account as part of this assessment.[134]

Listing adds immeasurably to the complications and costs of resolving the insulation, condensation and heating challenges posed by the construction of the building to owners of such flats by restricting choice in corrective measures to those that do not affect the building's external appearance.[135] That these constructions, in the main, are occupied by low-income groups in society, either as tenants or as owners under Right-to-Buy legislation or as low profit-margin landlords, further compounds the issues and highlights a problem of the clash between architectural conservation, global heating and energy costs, still unresolved after 40 years' debate.

Glendinning maintained that in Scotland, the rise of Modernism

> paralleled the wider movement of the state, and the increasing emphasis on the unified nation as the main source of social and economic initiative.[136]

This claim, which I dispute, was underscored in other retrospective publications of the 1990s and later such as *Rebuilding Scotland: The Post-war Vision 1945–1975* again by Glendinning[137] and, expanded with other contributions, in 2010, in *Scotland: Building for the Future: Essays on the Architecture of the Post-war Era* by Cooper et al.[138] The latter included the old-is-the-new-is-the-old argument to justify its claims for the 'post-war vision'. The authors maintained that

> Scotland specialised in new towns and a 'rational' approach to development and improvement, and there is a strong echo of the work of Robert Adam and the Edinburgh New Town in the 'age of improvement' of the post-war period.[139]

The authors were tone-deaf to the dissonance of that 'echo' and made no explanation of what connected Robert Adam, Edinburgh New Town and the productions of the 'post-war vision'.

They went on to claim:

> It is generally recognised that Scotland had architects of world renown in the Georgian and Victorian periods including Robert Adam, William

Playfair and Alexander 'Greek' Thomson. The international importance of Scotland's early 20th century architects is increasingly being acknowledged. It seems reasonable therefore to believe that this internationally important architectural tradition continued into the post-war period.[140]

It was not *reasonable* to make such an assumption because no reasons – verifiable or comparative – were offered by the authors that could result in such a conclusion, nor was it stated who 'generally' recognised and verified this 'achievement'. The 'acknowledged' architects of the early 20th century – which must include Mackintosh, Salmon, Lorimer, Shearer, Burnet, Tait, Coia, Brodie and Marwick – were, unlike their 19th-century predecessors, un-named in Cooper's et al account and the authority for their 'international importance' unstated. Such argument as was presented sheltered under the assertive *post facto* rationalising umbrellas of 'the post-war vision' and 'the age of improvement'. This anachronistic millennial doctrinaire Modernist orthodoxy perversely mirrors the institutional orthodoxies which Tonge identified in the 1930s as being then inimical to the acceptance of that self-same Modernism in painting. There needs to be a more considered and authoritative method of establishing, both at home and abroad, Scotland's late 20th and early 21st-century architectural credentials other than relying on sweeping *ex cathedra* pronouncements from HES.

In mitigation, these publications have suffered from the missing component of the architecture of the 1920s and '30s due possibly to McKean's encyclopaedic although uncritical reading of it. McKean's subsequent retreat to the comfort of the romanticist 'Scottish chateaux', where architectural worth was neither in question nor unsupported, suggested that he had in fact no basis on which to assess the production of the 1930s or later. Glendinning's positivism found events post-1975 troublesome and McKean's romanticism those post-1800. Moreover, by mooring themselves to opposite poles, McKean and Glendinning avoided the subtleties of the antinomy of rationalism and romanticism for over-simplified concepts of Scottish culture – the engineer and the poet – rather than the engineer/poet.

Nonetheless, Scottish architectural historiography is all the better for Glendinning, MacInnes and MacKechnie's *A History of Scottish Architecture*, to which frequent reference is made in this text, and to Glendinning's and McKean's several independent works, for they present the arguments, previously lacking, against which one might test other interpretations. Indeed, had these texts been available to him at the time, Gowan might have resisted making the disputatious claim about Scottish architecture that 'the yield since [Mackintosh] has been very low indeed'.

The Scottishness of Scottish architecture: the pitfall of aestheticism

Scottish architecture shares with regional architectures globally three attributes: the geographic, the mimetic and the ideational. The geographic is patently any building constructed within the territory of Scotland and consequently encompasses the mimetic and ideational. However, there is a very specific geographic architecture which consciously, in mimesis and ideation, borrows its principles and aesthetics from beyond Scotland and does not respond culturally to the climate, topography, resources and epoch of the Scottish territory, patrimony and psyche but contrives an accommodation with them, or not. Within the period 1846–2021 are three such architectures: the archaic, the Classical and the Modern, all of which provide authority of a sort. The archaic is taken to be largely that, in the West, which predates the architecture of Ionian Greece or is represented in more recent cultures as the local vernacular. The Classical is that architecture which in its several guises – Romanesque, Palladian, Greek Revival, Adam, neo-Classicism, neo-Greek, Renaissance revival, Baroque or stripped – is present as a consistent thread in Scottish architecture in a way that the Gothic is not. The Modern is that architecture arising from the manifestos and models of the first half of the 20th century.

The Scottish mimetic is the Baronial which seemingly meets every demand except that of epoch, because its epoch is that of a historic societal elite and their sectional needs and interests. Its relevance to a hierarchical and status-ridden Victorian society, which staggered on post-WWI, has no moment for most today. Nevertheless, there remains a body of opinion that seeks to ensure that it does, for largely the same elitist reasons.[141] Brennan-Inglis inquires rhetorically:

> Is there any other building type that has the same power to attract fascination, interest and even devotion in people of all ages, cultures and classes, and the same symbolic representation of power and romance?[142]

She answers her own question that, in the second half of the 20th century, castle restoration is impelled by

> a romantic yearning for an ideal age, bourgeois pretension, nationalistic pride and scholarly interest, in particular,[143]

most of which aims have little to do with national identity in the Modern period and, in fact, largely dispense with 'all cultures and classes'. *Scotland's Castles* has a substantial contemporary castellated bibliography running to three pages.[144]

In *Scotland's Castle Culture*, 2011, in a chapter entitled 'Castles in the Modern Age', Ian Begg opined:

> What I am getting at here is the dichotomy that occurs when people want an architecture of our time, and want to be modern, whatever it produces; and others, like me, who want sympathetic implants to keep the scale and character of an area like Old Edinburgh. Anyway, what has our time got to offer that is so fine as we see here?[145]

This desire to be out of time and, indeed, out of place, that is, to be removed from the situations, locations and behaviours of contemporary Scotland, seeks resolution in an 'ideal age' or from 'sympathetic implants', inferiorist sentiments echoed by Johnny Rodger writing about commemorative monuments, national and personal, although mostly Baronial:

> The study of this history can, however, help prevent our being confined to our own particular intellectual province of time, and open up a wider panorama of the infinite possibilities in the historical relations between the nation, the state, the land, identity and literary and material culture.[146]

As to be expected, Glendinning and MacKechnie's *Scotch Baronial* is based on sound, confident and authoritative scholarship. However, confidence and authority falter in 'Chapter 10: 1914 Onwards: Scottish Architectural Identity in the Age of Modernism', where their brief and compromised account of the architectural subtleties of the 20th century also stands as a summation and long delayed *ave atque vale* of the Baronial architecture of a previous and, for most Scots, departed sectional Scottish sensibility. Referring to the Scottish Parliament, Glendinning and MacKechnie concluded regretfully and erroneously, misjudging or misunderstanding the contemporary connection between politics and image:

> That in contrast to the strong integration between imagery and political-economic reality in both the First and Second Castle Ages, the story of 'national identity' in contemporary Scottish architecture – so far – ends on an uncertain rather than a triumphal one.[147]

The uncertainty is of Glendinning and MacKechnie's making.

The Scottishness of Scottish architecture: the scope of ideation

To recap, Scots express several dualities in daily life with greater or lesser seriousness, commitment and force, and it could be argued that engagement with and, mostly, acceptance of duality is the Scottish psychical norm, encapsulated in the Scots equivocal colloquialisms 'Ah hae ma doots' or 'Ah'm in twa minds'. Such seeming oppositions are those of: Scotland/Empire; Scotland/Union; Britain/European Union, Glasgow/Edinburgh; Dundee/Scotland; Glasgow/Scotland; Highland/Lowland; island/mainland; teuchter/townie; Celtic/Nordic; Catholic/Protestant; Scots/Gaelic; Scots/English; Lallans/Doric; Modernist/Traditionalist; ploughman/poet; engineer/poet; romantic/rationalist; romantic/classicist; empiricist/analyst; pensive/reckless; reserved/sociable, and so on. While the locational, belief and personal examples are typical of Known/Other dualities common to local rivalries the world over, those centring on the romantic/rational duality seem unique to Scotland. However, these are dualities, not dialectics.

Kant cautioned in the matter of the understanding of the dialectic:

> A dialectical doctrine of pure reason must therefore have this following characteristic to distinguish it from all purely sophistical propositions; firstly, it must not refer to gratuitous questions such as may be raised only for an arbitrary purpose, but to one which human reason in its natural progress must necessarily encounter; and, secondly, such a doctrine, as well as its opposite, carries within itself not merely an artificial illusion which disappears once we have insight into it, but a natural and inevitable illusion which, even when it deceives us no longer, still continues to delude us, and which can be rendered harmless, but can never be annihilated.[148]

Kant was concerned with the existential thesis/antithesis dualities as set out in brief in the *Prolegomena*[149] and, in such a context, terrain, territory, patrimony and polity are neither 'gratuitous' nor 'arbitrary'. Kant here seems to be referring to what Žižek later enlarged upon as 'parallax' whereby what we see or understand changes as we alter our viewpoint to it yet remains in our consciousness as something already acknowledged. Now, however, it has become illusory and remains with us in memory – an after-image – even when we understand the truth of it. Much as it lingered in the doubt and melancholy so clearly expressed above by contemporary Scottish architects.

Antinomy is a problem for Marxist, British Empiricist and Scottish

Common-Sense cultural criticism alike and, as the consequence of the pre-eminence of those empiric philosophies in the interpretation of British cultural history, is a problem for the interpretation, status and wider representation of Scottish culture now. Glendinning et al dismissed Gregory Smith's Kantian critical practice, believing that

> [t]he concept of 'antisyzygy' popularised by G. Gregory Smith and Hugh MacDiarmid in the 1920s Scottish (literary) Renaissance allowed almost anything to be embraced within the unique Scottish 'essence'.[150]

Well, not 'anything'; only those productions so identified by their thetical/antithetical engagement as I have attempted, in this book, in making plain the historical interpretation of Scottish architecture and the larger ideas that drive it.

In finer detail, Heidegger's *Geviert* of an inter-related earth, sky, man [sic] and the gods relates directly to the climate, topography, resources and epoch of the Scottish territory and to the Scottish psyche and patrimony, while his 'building dwelling thinking' is the primal act of being in the world for humankind and which subsumes the essentially biological needs of nourishment, shelter and reproduction. The *Geviert* (the fourfold) has four poles of reference; to understand any one pole, Heidegger requires we understand them all. Similarly, 'building dwelling thinking' is a compound action whereby each component part requires the other two to make sense of both the parts and the whole and to locate it as the founding principle – not principles – of the *Geviert*. Heidegger provides an intellectual, ideational and operational structure which has the potential to fill out inchoate descriptions of territory and patrimony such as Dobson's 'contrasting cities and staggering rural environment' or which 'anchor' Summers' architecture in Scotland.

At an even finer grain, Bachelard described the action of 'building thinking dwelling' as it is realised with respect to an idealised childhood home – what Harries referred to as the 'oneiric Black Forest farmhouse' – or as is experienced by Arnold-Forster, Milne or Hall. Hall recounts her own antinomy and *Poetics of Space* where the

> house is one of contrasts; a maze of nooks and crannies, winding stairs, dark cellars, and heavy walls set against the lightest of industrial glazing and slender steel rafter ties [of the conservatory].[151]

Despite Bachelard's rejection of the tenement as lacking in poetry, even the simple room and kitchen, such as was my childhood experience, is poetic for those who care to look: the central significance of the coal-fired range for cooking and heating; the bed recess my parents refused to use as such since living and sleeping in the same place was unacceptable to them and which became a play-space and the location of the sideboard; the 'room' split by wardrobes into a half for my parents and half for myself and my brother; the cramped, cold and unlit lobby which was a fearful void to be traversed as quickly as possible; the equally cold toilet; or the proximity and immediacy of street-life visible from the kitchen and room windows. Neither Heidegger nor Bachelard has unique relevance to a Scottish regional or national architecture quite in the way that Kant, Smith or Žižek do, although they provide authority and modes of expression for those concrete facts that carry a psychic as well as a physical charge. Ultimately, it is the poles of rationalism and romanticism that govern Scottish architectural production.

Contemporary expressions in Scottish architecture: wall and frame

Alexander Thomson's Neo-classicism is not simply new (neo) but qualitatively different from that which preceded it in that it is an Expressionistic treatment of Classicism which is supported by his transcendent philosophical and religious beliefs. Indeed, we may see within it a physical manifestation of the antinomy of Tonge's 'German *sachlichkeit*' which we might perhaps, in gross oversimplification, characterise as the frame and 'Nordic *Expressionismus*' which we might likewise characterise as the wall.

Elder and Cannon, following their significant post-Modern excursion, can be thought to sit within that tradition. Pivotal in their recent work is Shettleston Housing Association Offices, Glasgow, 2008–10. Donald Shearer, the project architect, was quoted as seeking to create a 'strong public building' that 'accentuated the civic nature of the space'[152] While on the face of it this is achieved by adopting the overall three-storey five-bay neo-Classical format of the red sandstone former Shettleston Co-op to which it is linked, there is rather more in evidence in this building's modest monumentalism.

The choice of a contrasting material, white pre-cast concrete casing framing glazed panels, is respectful of the colour and solidity of the original structure and establishes a dialectic with it. Leaving the second floor vacant for future expansion allowed Elder and Cannon to form usable outdoor space behind the continued frame of the colonnade. It is this colonnade and its partial infill that returns us to Thomson's observations on the Temple at Edfu and the use he made of it in the investigation of the wall and the frame. To

Wall and frame: Shettleston Housing Association, Glasgow, 2005, architects Elder and Cannon.

install a second-floor extension at the Shettleston HA Offices, say, to respond to client instruction, would be to deprive this building in some measure of its architectural significance and authority. The Shettleston *parti* is repeated at the Glasgow City Mission, 2009, over five storeys and on a corner site of five and six bays with fourth-floor construction omitted to create a roof garden. Greater expressiveness is evident in the free alternation of solid and glazed panels within the intercolumniation, although the prominence of the columns at ground and fourth floors allows them to be read notionally as continuous from pavement to cornice. Elder and Cannon commented on the importance of the staggered and recessed window details in contributing weight and depth to the elevation.[153]

The Tollcross HA offices, Glasgow, 2019, in a blue engineering brick, contrasts a frame on the front and side elevations with a wall to the rear, where the depth of elevation and its exposure for both programmatic and aesthetic purposes is a defining characteristic. Also in blue engineering brick, Sandiefield, Glasgow, 2019, for the New Gorbals HA expressionistically resolves several three-dimensional geometric constraints on an important obtuse-angle corner. Elder and Cannon noted:

> The decision to rise to six storeys was itself a response to the existing asymmetric grouping of four and five storey existing buildings on the opposite corner and was intended to balance out this quartet of corner elements.[154]

The colonnade partly frames the flats and their balconies and is partly disengaged to respect the geometry of the extant adjoining structure. Both these motives further reveal the importance of this treatment of the wall/colonnade-depth in expressively establishing the antinomy of an 'Expressionist classicism'. The repetitive window openings, taller on the top floor as if to recall the Shettleston *parti*, permit reflection on Thomson's investigation of the infinite. In contrast to Shettleston and the Glasgow Mission, the colonnade is terminated in a deep entablature. In all cases, Alison's prescriptions on 'proportion' are faithfully adhered to.

Reiach and Hall's Community Health Centre, East Kilbride, 2016, also incorporates a Thomsonian investigation of the wall depth, although in a more complex plan form that any of the Elder and Cannon examples. Four blocks of varying five and six storeys flank a core, all in a warm red brick. A classical grid of 'q'-shaped windows of square fixed light and screened ventilator terminate in the six-storey block in a recessed and patterned brick panel, inverting the Thomson motif.

Wall and frame: Sandiefield, New Gorbals, Glasgow, 2010, architects Elder and Cannon.

The exposed walls of the central core, likewise employing the Semperian *Bekleidungsprinzip*, are set back from the flanking blocks in patterned brickwork. A simpler version without the recessed panel is the Community Health Centre at Wishaw, also 2016. A different investigation of the wall is undertaken at Saltire Square, Granton, Edinburgh, 2008). Within an awkward figure/ground urban plan lacking containment, the terraces in white brick and precast concrete panels to the public side are regular and closed with small gardens fronted by precast boundary walls with impressed floral designs while the private side is comprised of a complex boundary layer of outhouses and screens. Breaking free of any rigidly classical interpretation is the wholly Expressionistic eight- and 11-storey corner block.

Wall and frame: Saltire Square, Granton, Edinburgh, 2009, architects Reiach and Hall.

The investigation of wall depth and its paring away is even evident recently in the commercial work of

Allan Murray Architects (AMA Studio, since 2020) where previous 'thin-skin' elevations such at Lochside View, Edinburgh Park, 1999–2002, and Calton Square, Edinburgh, 2002, are replaced by a Thomsonian depth at St James Quarter, Edinburgh, 2021.

Contemporary expressions in Scottish architecture: montage and joint[155]

The work of Richard Murphy is widely regarded to consist in the inventive use of the building section, the use of *poché* space to incorporate ancillary functions or contemplative space, and the 'occupied wall' for much the same purpose. He also investigates the relation of the new work to existing structure or ruin. In particular, in the concealment and revelation of its parts and construction, he also features prominently the concept of 'montage and joint', derived from a lifetime study of the work of Carlo Scarpa. Murphy commented:

> To heavy stone bases we have added light thin-walled tectonic constructions and flying, floating roofs above expressed structures.[156]

Of all art processes that might be described as antinomial, montage, in its materials and practice, must be its epitome. Murphy's Dunfermline Library and Galleries extension, 2017 (won in competition in 2007), encapsulates these several interests, influences and practices and stands as archetype for this kind of approach. The extension conjoins and consolidates the several parts of the library: Campbell Walker's 1883 original, Shearer's 1915 extension, Dunfermline Council's post-Modern extension of 1993 and Wardrop and Reid's separate 5 and 7 Abbot Street of 1882–3. Use of the section, concealment and revelation are captured in the entry hall, light shaft, bridges and stair element and the adjacent spaces. However, it is the west elevation that best demonstrates the subtlety of Murphy's use of montage and joint.

Parts such as window assemblies are allowed to exist as discrete elements or to elide with other construction. The former are definitively framed and separated from adjacent construction (such as the projecting second floor bay at the southwest corner), which recalls the corner rooflights at Scarpa's Gipsoteca Canoviana, Possagno, 1955–7. The latter elide with other construction as occurs where the first-floor windows meet the oak panelling, where, at the southwest corner, the vertical oak slats are a mediating detail, such as used by Aalto at Säynätsalo Town Hall, Finland, 1949–52. Materials

Montage and joint: Dunfermline Library Extension, 2017, architects Richard Murphy Architects. (Chris Humphreys)

are treated as distinct layers. In particular, masonry walling is either pasted over to conceal or pared back in Thomsonian fashion, or as at Scarpa's Banca Popolare di Verona, 1973–80, to reveal other construction beneath. Thus, the continuous clerestory and the one large and one small cut-out in the masonry below can be read as only those parts of a larger window which Murphy chooses to expose.

Towards the north end, the elevation is successively pared back from masonry to glass to corten steel panelling before the elevation is dematerialised to fully expose the heart of the extension. The roof partially oversails this assembly and is echoed by the projecting roof line string course and gable of the Wardrop and Reid building. Here, the benefits of montage and joint reveal themselves in the marriage of old and new. By cutting out the existing gable from under the gable string course, thence down the side of the projecting flue to the first-floor string and then somewhat arbitrarily to the ground, it is possible to work back out from the corten panelling to glazing to stone in a simulacrum of sequence, materials and forms previously established in the new work. Murphy notes that 'on most occasions the original buildings have been deliberately "ruined"' with 'new superstructures growing out of the wreckage'.[157] Furthermore, part cladding in aluminium panelling, the masonry 'cut' in the existing gable accentuates its character of a 'cut-end' related to similar 'cut ends' in the new work. Fine detail is found in the boundary layer

Montage and joint: Maggie's, Lanarkshire, 2018, architects Reiach and Hall.
(Jim Stephenson)

of balconies, canopies, handrails, gates and Scarpaesque double columns and in the interiors.

The antinomies of regularity and irregularity, the open and the closed, symmetry and asymmetry, consistency and inconsistency, the unique and the repetitive, the old and the new masterfully validate Smith in that 'disorderly order is a form of order, after all'.

There is a hybridity in Reiach and Hall's work which has them straddling several of these new directions. The ultimate paring away, even dissolution, of the brick wall is seen in their Maggie's Centre, Lanarkshire, 2015 which aligns them with their 'wall and frame' work. However, they refer to Crichton Castle as central to their concept of an outer shell concealing an inner treasure and to the 'textile' effect of Sigurd Lewerentz's (1885–1975) 'wild coursing', which is perhaps simply to again call upon Semper,[158] while the random omission of pale buff hand-made Danish bricks in both court and building recalls the visual permeability of Wright's Text-Tile walling system. Reiach and Hall also utilise montage and joint where the structurally necessary dwangs between timber roof joists are used decoratively.

While Murphy consistently developed his design methodology and material palette throughout his work, other architects, from time to time, worked in a similar vein, including Malcolm Fraser at the Scottish Storytelling Centre, Edinburgh, 2006; Reiach and Hall at the plainer, more classical 10

George Street, Edinburgh, although much fine Scarpaesque detail apart from the masonry coursing of the west gable has been lost in recent alterations; Page \ Park at the Lighthouse, Glasgow, 1991, and The Spens Building, Fettes College, Edinburgh, 2015, although their oeuvre is generally of a more orthodox Modernist slant.

Contemporary expressions in Scottish architecture: the Atlantic Edge

'Atlantic Edge': NEDD, Nedd, Highland, 2019, architect Mary Arnold-Forster.
(David Barbour)

The 'Atlantic Edge' is less a place than an attitude of mind to rural and coastal development. In form it initially adopts the model of the archetypical agricultural or coastal shed with steeply-pitched tightly-gabled roofs – Scotland's version of Laugier's Primitive Hut or Semper's Caribbean Hut – or that of the Hebridean 'blackhouse'. These models are compact in plan form and sit squarely on the ground, being respectively neither in nor of the ground, as is the sprawling kit-house with its apologetic shallow-pitched roof or the 'organic' Modernist house of Womersley or Morris and Steedman, and present a climatically considered site location, adventitiously functional planning and clarity and significance

'Atlantic Edge': Pier Arts, Stromness, Orkney, 2007, architects Reiach and Hall.
(Gavin Fraser FOTO-MA)

of structure. The materials of the Atlantic Edge are various – timber cladding, metal sheeting, glass, steelwork, stone, rendered brick, concrete, slate, sedum – although with a preference for the sustainable; sometimes only the one material, sometimes collaged or montaged out of several. The resultant structure embodies both the originating masonry or harled form and the new material, both without compromise. The Atlantic Edge has its counterparts in the contemporary regional architectures of Canada, although not always coastal, and Norway and extends to encompass the continental regional architectures of Australia and Switzerland. The Atlantic Edge engages with the antinomy of its archaic models, the Modernity of its planning and the sophistication of its construction. On the face of it, the Atlantic Edge presents as the most obvious regional architecture given its recognisable hut model. However, it is the implicit philosophy that guides its development, not its superficial form. Wilson noted:

> The R House [by Rural Design, 2011, various sites, Isle of Skye]… offers a contemporaneous response to the paradox posited by Kenneth Frampton

in the 1980s: the R House convincingly demonstrates that it is possible simultaneously to become modern and to return to sources.[159]

That is, it is antinomial where one would favour 'parallax' as a descriptor rather than 'paradox'.

Such a design philosophy is represented in a range of excellently crafted private houses on Skye, such as Rural Design's Hen House, Fiscavaig, 2010 and Turf House, Kendram, Skye, 2012; Dualchas's Boreraig, Skye, 2011, and the house at Colbost, Waternish, Skye, 2012. It is, however, a much wider rural phenomenon. With houses such as The Mill, Southside Steading, Scottish Borders, 2014, by WT Architects; Tigh Beag, Nethybridge, Cairngorm National Park, 2015, by SHS Burridge or Little Lindisfarne, Hawick, Scottish Borders, 2015 by Brian Robertson. However, the interrelatedness of contemporary Scottish regional architecture is revealed in the montage and joint of Rural Design's Bogbain Mill, Dingwall, 2011, and their substitution of marine-grade stainless steel for corrugated iron at the Invisible House, Colbost, Isle of Skye, 2018 or in Mary Arnold-Forster's Expressionistic NEDD, Nedd, Highland, 2019.

Atlantic Edge is also evident in Reiach and Hall's Pier Art Centre, Stromness, 2007, in NORR Architect's Dalmunach Distillery, Carron, Morayshire, 2014, in Dualchas's Raasay Community Hall, 2010 and in their remarkable unbuilt Ionad Hiort Visitor Centre, Uig. HRI Architects' stalled projects at Fort William Biomass Centre 2009 and at Brachla Harbour, Loch Ness, 2010, also exhibit montage and joint, but significantly also design features that can be considered Atlantic Edge. All five projects clearly demonstrate that the Atlantic Edge in Scotland is not merely a residential type.

'Atlantic Edge': Raasay Hall, 2010, architect Mary Arnold-Forster with Dualchas. (Andrew Lee)

In the end

In the end, this book is not an exhaustive catalogue of a contemporary Scottish regional architecture and its three interlinked variants of a Nordic *Expressionismus* and a German *sachlichkeit* – Wall and Frame, Montage and Joint and Atlantic Edge – although it identifies exemplars. Rather it is an attempt to consider another way of looking at Scottish architecture from a wider and deeper perspective than is the norm; one not constrained by the specificity of a particular historic architectural form. In doing so it reveals the philosophical connective tissues of Scottish architectural and cultural practice that fill gaps between the celebrated isolates of that same history. The book will have succeeded if it has you look at Scottish architecture from a different point of view. From a parallax view, perhaps.

Timeline

Significant philosophical, political or economic ideas and events
Contemporaneous buildings in Scotland or by Scottish architects illustrated in this book

1460	*Sailors' Walk, Kirkcaldy.*
1490	*John Knox's House, Edinburgh.*
1596	*Crathes Castle, Banchory, Aberdeenshire.*
ca. 1600	*Lamb's House, Leith, Edinburgh, restoration and addition, 2010-5, by Kristin Hannesdottir and Nick Groves-Raines.*
1626	*Craigievar Castle, Alford, Aberdeenshire.*
ca. 1745–89	The Scottish Enlightenment, rationalism and the Modern age.
1757	The romantic alternative of the *Philosophical Enquiry into the Origin of Our Ideas of the Sublime and Beautiful*, Edmund Burke.
1760	Origin myth and cosmogony and the *Fragments of Ancient Poetry*, James Macpherson (*The Tales of Ossian*).
1781	The philosophic challenge to the Scottish Common-sense of Hume: the *Critique of Pure Reason* by Immanuel Kant (first English translation 1881).
1792	French revolutionary wars restrict European travel and Grand Tours to the Classical world.
1809	*The Principles of Architecture*, Peter Nicholson, Alexander Thomson's grandfather-in-law.
1811–24	*Abbotsford House, near Melrose, Sir Walter Scott et al.*
1815	The Napoleonic wars end and Europe, the Classical world and the near East again become accessible to architects, archaeologists, artists and antiquarians.
	Essays on the Nature and Principles of Taste by Archibald Alison is influential in the development of Alexander Thomson's later theory and practice.
	The Provincial Antiquities and Picturesque Scenery of Scotland, William Blore. Scott employed Blore as architect at *Abbotsford*.
1818–22	King George IV visits Scotland; the first visit by a British monarch since 1650.
1829–38	*'Improvements' to St Giles Cathedral, Edinburgh, William Burn.*
1846–52	*The Baronial and Ecclesiastical Antiquities of Scotland* (4 vols), Robert William Billings establishes the canonic form of a

	distinctive Scottish architecture.
1846	*The Baronial-style Balfour Castle, Shapinsay, Orkney*, David Bryce.
1848	*An historical enquiry into the true principles of beauty in art, more especially with reference to architecture,* James Fergusson.
	The Stones of Venice by John Ruskin is a founding text of the Gothic Revival.
	Socialist uprisings throughout Europe.
1851	The Great Exhibition, London, showcases the contemporary – Modern – products of the arts, sciences, industry and commerce.
1852–6	Prince Albert buys Balmoral for Queen Victoria and rebuilds it in the Baronial style to designs by William Smith.
1853	*The Sources and Elements of Art Considered in Connexion with Architectural Design,* Alexander Thomson's first lecture to the Architectural Institute of Scotland.
	The Edinburgh Lectures by John Ruskin publicises his views on Gothic architecture and its revival.
	The Four Elements of Architecture by Gottfried Semper (English translation 1988) presents an astylar way of looking at designed objects.
	Growing nationalist sentiment leads to the Association for the Vindication of Scottish Rights being formed.
1857	*Holmwood, Cathcart, Glasgow,* Alexander Thomson.
1859	*Lammerburn, Edinburgh,* Sir James Gowans.
1859–60	*History of Architecture in all countries from the Earliest Times to the Present Day* (2 vols), James Fergusson.
1861	Builders' strike in Edinburgh and the formation of the Edinburgh Cooperative Building Company by the striking builders which goes on to build 2,500 artisan homes.
1862	*Cottage, Lodge and Villa Architecture,* WJ and GA Audsley, is a typical pattern book for the untutored builder and/or designer.
	History of the Modern Styles of Architecture, James Fergusson and Robert Kerr.
1864	*Royal Scottish Museum, Edinburgh,* Captain Francis Fowke.
	Kensington Competition, London, Alexander Thomson.
1865	*47–49 Oakfield Avenue, Glasgow,* Alexander Thomson.
1866	*Castle Terrace, Edinburgh,* Sir James Gowans.
1868	Blackie's *Villa and Cottage Architecture* extensively features Thomson's domestic work.

1871–2	*St Mary's Episcopal Cathedral, Edinburgh, Sir Giles Gilbert Scott.*
1874	*Egyptian Halls, Glasgow, Alexander Thomson.*
1875	Cockburn Association formed in Edinburgh; the oldest conservation organisation in Britain.
1883	Sir James Gowans' Edinburgh lecture *On the Uses of Building Stones.*
1883	*50 Queen's Road, Aberdeen, John Bridgford Pirie.*
1886	Edinburgh International Exhibition master-planned by Sir James Gowans.
1886–1909	*Thoughts on Style,* Hendrik Petrus Berlage (English translation 1996); proto-Modernist writings.
1887	*The Castellated and Domestic Architecture of Scotland from the Twelfth to the Eighteenth Centuries* (2 vols), David MacGibbon and Thomas Ross; the history and taxonomy of historic Scottish architecture.
1887	*Queen's Road Church, Aberdeen, John Bridgford Pirie.*
1888	Glasgow International Exhibition.
	Keir Hardie forms the Scottish Labour Party.
1890–1920	Finnish architects in Scotland to study granite construction.
1890	*92 Bold Street, Liverpool, WJ and GA Audsley.*
	Kirkton Cottages, Fortingall, John Marjoribanks McLaren.
1891	*Architecture, Mysticism and Myth,* WR Lethaby, has influence on Charles Rennie Mackintosh's architectural philosophy.
1893	World's Columbian Exhibition, Chicago, features Sullivan's Modernism and a more conventional Baroque Classicism.
1895	*Bowling Green Offices, New York, WJ and GA Audsley.*
1898	*Melsetter House, Hoy, Orkney, WR Lethaby.*
1900	Paris International Exhibition.
1901	Glasgow International Exhibition.
1901	*Haus Eines Kunstfreundes (realised 1990, Bellahouston, Glasgow) Charles Rennie Mackintosh.*
1903	*City Development: A Study of Parks, Gardens and Culture Institutes* by Sir Patrick Geddes; an internationally significant approach to town planning based on Dunfermline.
1904	Turin International Exhibition at which the Mackintoshes, the MacNairs and others exhibit in the Scottish Room.
	The Viennese Secession splits into the *Klimt-gruppe* and the *Nur-maler* with profound consequences for Mackintosh.
1906	*Das Englische Haus,* Herman Muthesius (English translation 2007); a survey of British domestic design with substantial

	Scottish input which influenced design in Europe over the following two decades.
	British Labour Party formed.
1906	RW Forsyth's, Princes Street, Edinburgh, John James Burnet.
1908	*Abstraktion und Einfühlung*, Wilhelm Worringer (*Abstraction and Empathy*, English translation 1997).
1909	9th Kunstschau, Vienna. The Mackintoshes exhibit *In der Schränken Kunst Gewerbe*, one of the smaller rooms.
	David Lloyd George's Finance Act negatively affects the construction industry.
1910	*Ornament and Crime*, Adolf Loos; one of the defining texts of Modernism.
1911	*Journey to the East* by Le Corbusier in which he recounts his exposure to the Classical and archaic architectures of Europe and the near East.
1912	*Hippodrome Cinema, Dunfermline, Matt Steele.*
1913	The British Empire commands its greatest territorial area.
1914	Keppie and Mackintosh partnership dissolved.
1914–8	The Great War (WWI).
1915–18	Sir Patrick Geddes' Indian Planning Exhibition, Madras (Chennai), Calcutta (Kolkata), Nagpur and Lucknow for which Mackintosh produces some designs.
1915–9	*Basset-Lowke house, Derngate, Northampton, Charles Rennie Mackintosh.*
1919	*Wohnberge*, Walter Gropius's concept of multi-individual serviced dwellings.
	Scottish Literature: Character and Influences; George Gregory Smith's Kantian riposte to TS Eliot.
1920–45	Approximate dates for the literary and cultural phenomenon of the 'Scottish Renaissance'.
1921	Post-WWI economic slump.
1922	Anglo-Irish Act partitions Ireland.
1922–5	*Adelaide House, London, Sir JJ Burnet and Thomas Tait.*
1923	*Vers une Architecture*, Le Corbusier; one of the defining texts of Modernism.
1923	Mussolini and supporters march on Rome and create the fascist dictatorship.
	The failed Munich beer hall *putsch*. Adolf Hitler and supporters jailed.
	Hugh MacDiarmid flirts with fascism.
1924	Empire Exhibition, Wembley, London.

1924–31	*On European Architecture: Essays from* Het Bouwbedrijf
1924–1931	Theo van Doesburg (English translation 1990)(essentially the De Stijl manifesto).
1926	The General Strike.
	The British Empire is redefined as the British Commonwealth of Nations.
1928	Universal suffrage in Britain for those over 21 years of age.
1928	*Carnegie Birthplace Memorial, Dunfermline, James Shearer.*
1929	Wall Street Crash.
1932	Modern Architecture Exhibition at the Museum of Modern Art, New York; the defining moment of Modern architecture.
	The International Style, Henry-Russell Hitchcock and Philip Johnson; the book that followed the exhibition written by the exhibition organisers.
1933	*The Lane House, Edinburgh, William Kininmonth.*
1933–9	*St Andrew's House, Edinburgh, Thomas Tait.*
1934	*Broughton Place, Broughton, Basil Spence and William Kininmonth.*
1934	Scottish National Party formed.
1935	*Dunfermline Fire Station, James Shearer.*
1936	*Pioneers of Modern Design,* Nikolaus Pevsner, which equivocally links Mackintosh to the early years of Modernism.
1937–56	*Kirkcaldy Town House, David Carr.*
1937	*National Bank of Scotland, Edinburgh, T Waller Marwick.*
1938	Glasgow Empire Exhibition.
	The Arts of Scotland, John Tonge's attempt to formulate cultural identifiers in the Scottish arts.
1938	*Glasgow Empire Exhibition Plan and Tower, Thomas Tait.*
	St Peter-in-Chains, Ardrossan, Gillespie, Kidd & Coia.
	Rothesay Pavilion, J & JA Carrick.
1939–45	World War II.
ca 1944	*Building Scotland: past and future,* Alan Reiach and Robert Hurd's populist pamphlet.
1947	*Space, Time and Architecture,* Siegfrid Giedion; a nuanced development of Modernist thinking.
	Partition of India sets the seal on the imperial project.
1951	*Building Dwelling Thinking,* Martin Heidegger (English translation 1971) is an integrated and spiritual understanding of the purpose of architecture.
	The Festival of Britain.

1951–3	Inch Housing Estate, Edinburgh, David Stratton Davis.
1953	Queen Elizabeth I & II crowned: the 'new Elizabethan age'.
	The Scope of Total Architecture, Walter Gropius. A summation and codification of his life's work.
1956	Scottish Georgian Society formed (ultimately the Architectural Heritage Society of Scotland).
	The Suez Crisis.
	Wartime rationing ends 11 years after VE Day.
	USSR invades Hungary.
1956	*St Paul's RC Church, Glenrothes, Gillespie, Kidd and Coia.*
1958	*The Poetics of Space*, Gaston Bachelard (English translation 1964); a literary, poetic and experiential exposition of the home.
1960	*Girdle Toll Housing, Irvine, Irvine Development Corporation*
1963	*Intentions in Architecture*, Christian Norberg-Schulz; a reappraisal of Modernism and the search for a new understanding.
1963–5	*Cables Wynd House, Leith, Edinburgh, Alison and Hutchison.*
1965	*Changing Ideals in Modern Architecture*, Peter Collins; an exploration of ideas rather than aesthetics.
1966	*Complexity and Contradiction*, Robert Venturi; the post-Modern architectural manifesto.
1966	*Edinburgh University Library, Basil Spence, Glover and Ferguson.*
1966–68	*79–121 Canongate, Edinburgh, Basil Spence, Glover and Ferguson.*
1967	*Edenside Medical Practice, Kelso, Peter Womersley.*
1968	*The System of Objects*, Jean Baudrillard (English translation 1996); an investigation of the relative status of the original model and its subsequent copies.
	The 'Troubles' begin in Northern Ireland; sectarian strife between the then Protestant majority and Catholic minority and the civil rights exclusions imposed on the latter.
	The Great Glasgow Storm and the rehabilitation of the tenement.
	Charles Rennie Mackintosh Centenary Exhibition, Edinburgh International Festival.
	The 'Prague Spring'. USSR invades Czechoslovakia.
	The 'Summer of Love'.
1969	*Housing (Scotland) Act*, mandates tolerable domestic living standards for the first time.

	Planning and People (the Skeffington Report); a first attempt at legislating public participation.
1970	Forties Oil Field opened up; the SNP acquires a slogan and a theoretical economic rather than cultural argument for independence.
	Edinburgh New Town Conservation Committee formed.
1971–84	*Burrell Collection, Pollok, Glasgow, Barry Gasson.*
1973	*Modern Movements in Architecture*, Charles Jencks; a critical taxonomic analysis of Modernism.
	Britain joins the European Economic Community (EEC), subsequently the European Union (EU).
	OPEC Oil Embargo and '3-day-week'.
1973–84	All Scotland, barring Edinburgh, eligible for the European Regional Development Fund (ERDF).
1974	*Model Estate*, Alison Ravetz; early analysis of a lived-in experience of Modernist housing.
1974	*Commercial Road, Perth, James Parr & Partners.*
1974–8	*Robinson College, Cambridge, Gillespie, Kidd and Coia.*
1975	Scottish Development Agency formed (ultimately Scottish Enterprise), early on, providing support for post-industrial employment.
1976	Pound devalued and British government obtains loan from the International Monetary Fund.
1977	*The Language of Post-Modern Architecture*, Charles Jencks; becomes a post-Modern pattern-book.
1978	*The Modern Language of Architecture*, Bruno Zevi (1973 in Italian); a late attempt to codify Modernism.
	'Winter of Discontent'; widespread strikes.
	Second 'Oil Crisis'.
1979	Failed first Devolution Referendum.
	Campaign for a Scottish Assembly formed.
	Internationale Bauausstellung (IBA), Berlin inaugurated; proves a significant conceptual and aesthetic resource for Scottish architects.
1980	*Modern Architecture: A Critical History*, Kenneth Frampton; a major reappraisal of Modernism.
1983	*Critical Regionalism* by Kenneth Frampton addresses the matter of local cultural responses to Modernism.
1984	*Aesthetics in Scotland*, Hugh MacDiarmid (written in 1952). An important contribution to the subject but with nothing about architecture since Mackintosh.

1984	*Stratford Street, Maryhill, Glasgow, Ken MacRae with McGurn, Logan, Duncan and Opfer.*
	Ingram Square, Glasgow, Elder and Cannon.
1987	'Black Monday', 19 October, Stock Market Crash.
1988	Glasgow Garden Festival.
1988	*Scandic Crown Hotel, Edinburgh, Ian Begg.*
1989	*The Wemyss Brick Scottish Brick Houses, Roger Emmerson as ARCHImedia.*
1989–91	*McKean House Extension, Blackhall, Edinburgh, Roger Emmerson as ARCHImedia.*
1990	*Scrymgeour's Corner, Crieff, Nicoll Russell Studio.*
1991	Glasgow European City of Culture.
	Gulf War.
1991–9	*The Museum of Scotland, Edinburgh, Benson + Forsyth.*
1992	'Black Wednesday' 16 September 1992, UK forced out of the European Exchange Rate Mechanism (ERM) due to falling value of the pound sterling.
1992–5	Bosnian War.
1997	Second successful Devolution Referendum.
1999–2004	*Scottish Parliament, Edinburgh, EMBT and RMJM.*
1998	Good Friday Agreement' ends 30 years political strife in Northern Ireland.
1999	Glasgow City of Architecture.
2001	'9-11' atrocity in USA.
	Afghan War (ends in defeat for Western powers, 2021).
2001	*Riverside, Glasgow, Zaha Hadid.*
	Lanark Street Glasgow, various architects.
2004–6	*Elmfield Square, Gosforth, Newcastle upon Tyne, Roger Emmerson with Waring & Netts.*
2005	*Shettleston Housing Association Offices, Glasgow, Elder and Cannon.*
2006	*The Parallax View,* Slavoj Žižek; Kantian reflections on contemporary society.
2007	*Pier Arts Extension, Stromness, Orkney, Reiach and Hall.*
2008	The Lehman Brothers initiated banking crash.
2009	*Saltire Square, Granton, Edinburgh, Reiach and Hall.*
2010	*Sandiefield, New Gorbals, Glasgow, Elder and Cannon.*
	Hen House, Fiscavaig, Isle of Skye, Rural Design.
	Raasay Hall, Raasay, Mary Arnold-Foster with Dualchas.
2013	Voting age in Scotland reduced to 16; matching

	representational rights with legal and taxation responsibilities.
2014	First unsuccessful Independence Referendum.
	ISIS in Iraq and Syria until 2019.
2016	Britain (not Scotland) votes to leave the European Union.
	Architecture Fringe a loose research, project and ginger group founded.
2017	*Dunfermline Library Extension, Richard Murphy Architects.*
2018	*Maggie's (Cancer Hospice) Lanarkshire, Airdrie, Reiach and Hall.*
2019	*NEDD, Nedd, Sutherland, Mary Arnold-Foster.*
2019	Britain leaves the European Union.
	The covid pandemic.
2021	*W Hotel, St James Quarter, Edinburgh, Jestico and Whiles.*
2022	Russia invades Ukraine.
	Queen Elizabeth I and II dies. Charles III proclaimed King. Government led by an unprecedented three separate Prime Ministers within the space of three months.

Glossary

antinomy	Kant's philosophical concept which embraces both thesis and antithesis in the understanding of any proposition.
antisyzygy	A similar concept coined by the Scots literary critic George Gregory Smith.
arcuation	Structure that employs arches to span openings.
Art Deco	Art, architecture and product design derived from the style exhibited at the exhibition, *Exposition international des arts décoratifs et industriels moderne*, Paris, 1925.
Arte povera	An Italian art movement of the 1960s and '70s which utilised everyday 'humble' materials.
Art Nouveau	Specifically and simply a French aesthetic style of the late 1800s which employed a sinuous line and jewel-like decoration. Generally employed as a catch-all to cover several radical aesthetic styles and movements extant in Europe at the time: Art Nouveau, Jugendstil, **Secession**, National Romanticism, Stile Liberty, Glasgow School, Modernisme català and so forth.
Bauhaus	School of Design, 1919–33, Weimar then Dessau, Germany.
Bekleidungsprinzip	Semper's concept of wall-cladding.
cold-bridging	Where external construction connects directly with internal construction without intervening thermal insulation, creating thermal paths resulting in cold walls, floors and/or ceilings within rooms with concomitant running condensation and black mould. Prevalent in 1960s and '70s concrete construction.
Constructivism	An art and architecture movement of the 1920s in the USSR which placed emphasis on the physical representation of the technological means of assembly or reproduction. Frequently known as Russian Constructivism.
Critical Regionalism	A theoretical means of understanding regional architecture within the context of **Modernism** derived by Kenneth Frampton.
cross-wall	A structural system that provides structural support

	to floors and roofs from walls that span front to back from one long elevation to the other of a construction.
Das Geviert	An integrated philosophical construct of Martin Heidegger which draws together humankind, the earth, the sky and the 'gods' in one.
Deconstructivism	Generally, a branch of post-Modern literary and linguistic criticism popularly associated with Jacques Derrida. Architecturally, a design philosophy of the 1980s and '90s that sought to merge the interrogative approach of literary deconstruction with a Mannerist interpretation of the architecture of Russian Constructivism. Known among students at the time as 'plane-crash-architecture'.
De Stijl	Aesthetic movement in 1920s Netherlands created and curated by Theo van Doesburg.
dwang	(Scots) A bracing timber located between the joists in floor and flat roof construction.
English Free-style	A loose catch-all descriptor to cover the architectural styles Arts & Crafts, Queen Anne, **Art Nouveau** and the work of Voysey and his imitators. Essentially, the 'modern' styles between 1890 and 1910.
EPDM tape	EPDM rubber (ethylene propylene diene monomer rubber) is a type of synthetic rubber used in many building applications. Adhesive-backed, it is used to seal sheets of weatherproof membrane together and to adjacent or penetrating construction to maintain a continuous weathertight envelope.
existenzminimum	The **Functionalist** reduction of space within the dwelling to its bare ergonomic minimum.
Expressionism	A movement in art and architecture which exaggerated a work's formal characteristics to convey in the artwork or induce in the viewer a strong emotional or visceral charge.
figure/ground	An artistic device whereby the object of interest, the figure, is clearly delineated as separate from its surroundings, the ground, which constitutes a subordinate frame or backdrop.
Functionalism	A movement in architecture that concentrated on the satisfaction of purely functional or biological needs – shelter, nourishment and procreation – in the dwelling.

Futurism	An Italian art and architecture philosophy of the 1910s and early '20s that placed emphasis on speed, movement and war.
genius loci	The spirit, character or essence of a place or locality. A term originally brought to prominence in architectural theory by Christian Norberg-Schulz.
Gothic	Any of the pre-Renaissance architectures of the 12th to the 15th centuries in Europe subsequently revived in the 19th.
in antis	A colonnade contained by projecting side walls or *antae*. Found in more ancient Greek and Egyptian construction rather than the more familiar continuous colonnade wrapping around a building such as at the Parthenon.
inhabited wall	Originally any massive masonry wall which incorporated embrasures, privies or other ancillary function. Later appropriated and expanded to describe the typical Scottish tenemental street as such.
International Style	Those **Functionalist** architectures encapsulated and codified by Hitchcock and Johnson in the 1932 Exhibition in the Museum of Modern Art (MOMA), New York.
intervisibility	A property of **Modernist** space whereby different perspectives from various viewpoints at various levels are made available to the inhabitants of the space and which provide visual although not tactile proximity.
Jahrhundertwerk	A monumental building celebrating a centennial or other significant event.
Klimt-gruppe	Those artists, designers and architects who split from the **Viennese Secession** under the leadership of Gustav Klimt.
Mannerist Modernism	The architecture of the 21st century in which its inherent **Modernist** characteristics, form or scale are hugely exaggerated.
megastructure	An architectural complex comprising shops, community facilities and housing within an overtly expressed and infinitely extendable structural system. Cumbernauld Town Centre, 1966, is one such. See **Metabolism**.
Metabolism	Japanese architectural and urban planning movement of the 1950s and '60s predicated on **megastructural** organisation.

Mietkasernen	German rental apartment blocks.
Modernism	Generally, the over-arching progression of ideas and practice arising largely from the (Scottish) Enlightenment.
	Architecturally, a blanket term to cover the several different styles or types of non-aesthetic, anti-historical, **functionalist** architecture that arose in Europe and the USA in the first half of the 20th century.
Modern Movement	Another term to describe those architectures.
Moderne	A popular, non-doctrinaire form of **Modernism** with its roots in **Art Deco**.
Neo-Classicism	Any development of the Classical canon which, while observing its general rules and employing its motives, is not necessarily based on Classical building models from Greece.
Neue sachlichkeit	The new objectivity. A realist/**functionalist** art and architecture movement in 1920s and '30s Germany.
Organic architecture	A softer, more nature-oriented **Modernist** style emanating from the practice of Frank Lloyd Wright. Also implicated in the works of second-generation Modernists such as Alvar Aalto.
parallax	A Kantian concept of the Slovenian philosopher Slavoj Žižek. See **antinomy** and **antisyzygy**.
parametric	Non-symmetrical, non-regular architectural composition.
paratactical	Irregularly organised, non-symmetrical, but balanced detail.
parti	The overall intrinsic or generic form and composition of an architectural design omitting all stylistic identifiers.
poché space	The space left between or within larger structure or structures which can be utilised for ancillary or support functions. See **inhabited wall**.
point block	Another name for a multi-storey **tower-block**.
Post-Modernism	Generally, the philosophical and literary enquiry into and rejection of **Modernism**. Architecturally, the several design styles which accompanied it in the late 1960s to '90s.
promenade architecturale	A designed route through a building intended to aid appreciation of its spatial qualities. Epitomised in **Modernism** by the stair and ramp circulation system of Le Corbusier's Villa Savoye.

psuedo-isodomic	Masonry coursing of alternately wide and narrow courses.
Purism 1	A style of painting practiced by Le Corbusier and Amédée Ozenfant.
Purism 2	A **Functionalist** architecture developed and uniquely practised by Josef Chochol in the 1910s and '20s.
Regionalism	Architecture specific to a region or nation with identifiable regional or national characteristics. See **Critical Regionalism**.
Scottish Baronial	An architecture style of the middle decades of the 19th century based on the castellated architecture of the 12th to 17th centuries. Sometimes shown as Scots or Scotch Baronial.
Secession	Art and architecture movements in late 19th and early 20th century Europe which rejected the formalism of subject and technique favoured by the art academies.
shared activity space	An area in a dwelling which is intended to accommodate various different uses that occur at different times throughout the day or that can be managed and timetabled to do so.
sma burgh	(Scots) The smaller Scottish historic town such as Stirling, Haddington, Cupar Angus, Dunkeld, Stromness and so forth.
slab block	A long horizontal multi-storey block, generally not higher than 8 storeys. See also *zielenbau*.
-style	A range of columns: Distyle: two columns, may be in antis; Tetrastyle: four columns; Hexastyle: six columns; Octastyle: eight columns; Eannastyle: nine columns and so on.
Suprematism	An art form initiated and almost uniquely practised in the 1910s and early '20s by Kasimir Malevich.
Symbolism	Art movement of the late 19th century which used a language of mythic, magical or private symbols and oblique inference to express mystical concepts and emotional or mental states. Cf. the early paintings and panels of Margaret MacDonald Mackintosh and Charles Rennie Mackintosh.
tenement	A block of flats. In Scotland it does not have the negative associations which is attached to it in some other cultures.

trabeation	A structure which employs flat beams to span openings.
tower-block	a multi-storey residential block of limited floor plan area generally ten stories and over
Viennese Secession	The particular form that academic secession took in Vienna. Most closely associated with Gustav Klimt, Carl Moll, Josef Hoffmann and others.
ur-architecture	Any ancient architecture of a particularly massive, even superficially primitive aspect, usually applied to Assyrian or pre-Columbian architectures. Any architecture exhibiting such characteristics.
Usonia	Frank Lloyd Wright's name for the USA and which – Usonian – he applied to his domestic architecture from the 1930s onwards.
Ville radieuse	Effectively, the shining city. Le Corbusier's conception of a city of **tower blocks** housing tens of thousands.
Wagnerschule	Architectural design based on the late 19th and early 20th-century teachings of Otto Wagner.
white box	A generic term to cover the, usually white and flat-roofed Modernist houses of the 1920s and '30s.
white cube	The featureless, white-painted gallery space especially favoured for the display of Modern Art in the late 20th century.
Wiener Werkstätte	An organisation which encouraged, regulated and promoted Modern art, architecture and product design in Vienna in the 1910s to '30s. Closely associated with the **Viennese Secession** and the *Klimt-gruppe*.
zeitgeist	Generally explained as the 'spirit of the age', although it is usually that which is determined by those who write the histories rather than that which is necessarily experienced by society at large.
zielenbau	Long, 6 to 10-storey slab blocks usually organised in echelon across a site. See also **slab block**.

Bibliography

Acemoglu, Daron, and James A Richardson, *Why Nations Fail: The Origins of Power, Prosperity and Poverty* (London, 2012)
Adam, Peter, *Eileen Gray: Her Life and Work* (London, 2019)
Adams, Annmarie, 'Peter Collins: A Study in Parallax', *Journal of Architectural Education*, ACSA, Vol. 59, No. 2, October 2005
Aldiss, Brian, *Science Fiction Art: The Fantasies of SF* (London, 1975)
Alison, Archibald, *Essays on the Nature and Principles of Taste* (4th ed) (Edinburgh, 1815)
Allan, John, and Duncan Macmillan, *The Museum of Scotland: Benson + Forsyth* (London, 2000)
Allen, C Bruce, *Cottage Building or, Hints for improving the Dwellings of the Labouring Classes* (London, 1849–50)
Andreson, Henrick O, and Frederic Bedoire, *Stockholm: Architectural Townscape* (Stockholm, 1988)
Architectural Heritage Society for Scotland, *Architectural Heritage III: The Age of Mackintosh* (Edinburgh, 1992)
Ardrey, Adam, *Finding Arthur: The Origins of the Once and Future King* (London, 2013)
Audsley, W&G, *Cottage, Lodge and Villa Architecture* (London, 1862)
Bachelard, Gaston (trans Maria Jolas), *The Poetics of Space* (Boston, 1994)
Bain, George, *Celtic Art: The Methods of Construction* (London, 1951)
Baldwin, James, *Nobody Knows My Name* (London, 1969)
Balfour, Alan, *Berlin: the Politics of Order, 1737–1989* (New York, 1990)
Banham, Reyner, *Theory and Design in the First Machine Age* (London, 1960)
Banham, Mary, and Bevis Hillier, *A Tonic to the Nation: the Festival of Britain 1951* (London, 1976)
Barley, Nick (ed), *Homes for the Future* (London, 1999)
— Morag Bain and Oliver Lowenstein, *Architecture in Scotland 2006–2008: Building Biographies* (Glasgow, 2008)
Bartolucci, Marisa, *living large in small spaces* (London and New York, 2004)
Baudrillard, Jean (trans James Benedict), *The System of Objects* (New York, 1996)
Baxter, J Neil (ed), *St Peters & St Pauls Architectural Competition: Record of Entries* (Edinburgh, 1985)
Bell, Bryan, *Good Deeds, Good Design: Community Service through Architecture* (New York, 2004)
Bell, Victoria Ballard, and Patrick Rand (eds), *Materials for Architectural Design* (London, 2006)
Benedikt, Michael, *For an Architecture of Reality* (New York, 1987)
Benjamin, Andrew (ed), *The Lyotard Reader* (reprint) (Oxford, 1993)

Berger, Francisco, Luís Bissau Pereira and Michel Toussaint (eds), *Guia de Arquitectura Lisboa 94* (Lisbon, 1994)
Berger, John (Tom Overton, ed), *Portraits: John Berger on Artists* (London and New York, 2017)
Berkeley, Ellen Perry, and Matilda McQuaid (eds), *Architecture: A Place for Women* (Washington, 1989)
Berlage, Hendrik Petrus (trans Iain Boyd White and Wim De Wit), *Thoughts on Style 1886–1909* (Santa Monica CA, 1996)
Berman, Marshall, *All That Is Solid Melts Into Air: The Experience Of Modernity* (New York, 1983)
Bernstein, JM, *The Fate of Art: Aesthetic Alienation from Kant to Derrida to Adorno* (Cambridge, 1993)
Beveridge, Craig, and Ronald Turnbull, *The Eclipse of Scottish Culture: Inferiorism and the Intellectuals* (Edinburgh, 1989)
Bilcliffe, Roger, *Charles Rennie Mackintosh: The Complete Furniture, Furniture Drawings and Interior Designs* (2nd ed) (Guildford and London, 1980)
Billings, Robert William, *The Baronial and Ecclesiastical Antiquities of Scotland*, (4 vols) (Vol. 1) (Edinburgh, 1847–52)
Bishop, Jeff, *Milton Keynes: The Best of Both Worlds?* (Bristol, 1986)
Blackie & Son, *Villa and Cottage Architecture: Select examples of country and suburban residences recently erected; with a full descriptive notice of each building* (London, 1868)
Blanc, Hippolyte, 'Scottish Ecclesiastical Architecture in the Fourteenth and Fifteenth Centuries', *The Builder*, vol. LXXIV, March 1898
Blau, Eve, and Nancy J Troy (eds), *Architecture and Cubism* (Cambridge MA, 1997)
Bloomer, Ken C, and Charles W Moore, *Body, Memory and Architecture* (London, 1979)
Blundell Jones, Peter, *Architecture and Ritual: How Buildings Shape Society* (London, 2016)
Boardman, Philip, *The Worlds of Patrick Geddes: Biologist, Town Planner, Re-educator, Peace-Warrior* (London, 1978)
Bond, Gavin, *Fascist Scotland* (Edinburgh, 2013)
Bonnar, Thomas, *Biographical Sketch of George Meikle Kemp* (Edinburgh, 1892)
Borchardt-Hume, Achim (ed), *Malevich* (London, 2014)
Borden, Iain, Joe Kerr, and Jane Rendell with Alice Pivaro (eds), *The Unknown City: Contesting Architecture and Social Space* (Cambridge MA, 2001)
Borsi, Franco, and Ezio Godoli, *Vienna 1900* (London, 1986)
Bořutová, Dana, Anna Zajková and Matuš Dulla (eds), *Dušan Jurkovič* (Bratislava, 1993)
Bregant, Michal, Lenka Bydžovská, Vojtěch Lahoda, Zdeněk Lukeš, Karel Srp, and Rostislav Švácha, *Kubistická Praha* (Prague, 1995)
Brennan-Inglis, Janet, *Scotland's Castles: Rescued, Rebuilt and Reoccupied* (Stroud, 2014)
Brett, Lionel, *The Things We See – No. 2: Houses* (West Drayton, 1947)

Broadie, Alexander, *The Tradition of Scottish Philosophy* (Edinburgh, 1990)
Brownell, Blaine (ed), *Transmaterial: A Catalog of Materials that Define Our Physical Environment* (New York, 2006)
Brownlee, David B, and David G De Long, *Louis I Kahn: In the Realm of Architecture* (London, 1997)
Brumfield, William Craft, *A History of Russian Architecture* (Cambridge, 1993)
Buchan, James, *Capital of the Mind: How Edinburgh Changed the World* (London, 2003)
Buchanan, William (ed), *Mackintosh's Masterwork: The Glasgow School of Art* (Glasgow, 1989)
Buijs, Steef, Wendy Tam and Devisari Tuna (eds), *Megacities: Exploring a Sustainable Future* (Rotterdam, 2010)
Burgin, Victor, *In/different Spaces: Places and Memory in Visual Culture* (Berkeley, 1996)
Burnet, Sir John, Tait and Lorne, *The Information Book of Sir John Burnet, Tait and Lorne* (London, 1934)
Cahn, Stephen M (ed), *Classics of Western Philosophy* (Indianapolis, 1977)
Calder, Alan, *James McLaren: Arts & Crafts Pioneer* (Donnington, 2003)
Callinicos, Alex, *Against Postmodernism: A Marxist Critique* (Cambridge, 1989)
Campbell, Ian, 'A Romanesque Revival and the Early Renaissance in Scotland c.1380–1513', *Journal of the Society of Architectural Historians*, Vol. 54, No. 3, September 1995
Čapek, Karel (trans Paul Selver), *Letters from England* (London, 1926)
Československá Obchodní Banka, *Na Poříčí 24* (Prague, 1994)
Chadwick, Whitney, *Women, Art and Society* (London, 2007)
Chant, Colin, and David Goodman (eds), *Pre-Industrial Cities and Technology* (London, 1995)
Cheape, Hugh, 'Were but the white billow silver...' in *The Scottish Book Collector*, Vol. 3, No. 5, February/March 1992
Checkland, Olive and Stanley, *Industry and Ethos: Scotland 1832–1914* (Edinburgh, 1989)
Chochol, Josef, 'K funkci architektonikého článku (On the function of the architectonic element)', *Styl* v, 1913
— 'What we are aiming at', *Musaion II*, 1921
Collins, Bruce, and Keith Robbins (eds), *British Culture and Economic Decline* (London, 1990)
Collins, Peter, *Changing Ideals in Modern Architecture* (London, 1965)
Colquhoun, Alan, *Modernity and the Classical Tradition* (Cambridge MA, 1989)
— *Collected Essays in Architectural Criticism* (London, 2009)
Constant, Caroline, *Eileen Gray* (London, 2007)
Conzen, MRG, *Alnwick, Northumberland: A Study in Town Plan Analysis* (London, 1960)
Cook, John W, and Heinrich Klotz, *Conversations with Architects* (London, 1973)

Cooke, Catherine, 'Chernikhov: Fantasy and Construction', *Architectural Design* 54, 9/10, 1984
Cooper, Jackie (ed), *Mackintosh Architecture* (London, 1984)
Cooper, Malcolm, Ranald MacInnes, Deborah Mays, Dawn McDowell, and Miles Oglethorpe, *Scotland: Building for the Future: Essays on the Architecture of the Post-war Era* (Edinburgh, undated, ca. 2010)
Correa, Charles, *Housing and Urbanisation* (London, 2000)
County Council of Essex, *A Design Guide for Residential Areas* (reprint) (Chelmsford, 1975)
Craig, Maurice, 'James Fergusson' in John Summerson (ed), *Concerning Architecture: Essays on Architectural Writers and Writing Presented to Nikolaus Pevsner* (London, 1968)
Crawford, Robert, *On Glasgow and Edinburgh* (Cambridge MA, 2013)
Crinson, Mark, and Jules Lubbock, *Architecture, Art or Profession? Three Hundred Years of Architectural Education* (Manchester, 1994)
Crowley, David, *National Style and Nation-state* (Manchester and New York, 1992)
Cullen, Gordon, *Townscape* (London, 1961)
Curl, James Stephens, *Victorian Architecture* (Newton Abbot, 1990)
Curtis, William J R, *Modern Architecture Since 1900* (2nd ed) (Oxford, 1987)
Daiches, David, Peter Jones and Jean Jones, *A Hotbed of Genius: The Scottish Enlightenment 1730–1790* (Edinburgh, 1986)
Daily Express, These Tremendous Years, 1919–1938 (London, 1938)
Dakin, Anthony, Miles Glendinning and Aonghus MacKechnie (eds), *Scotland's Castle Culture* (Edinburgh, 2011)
Darbyshire, J Denis and Ian Darbyshire, *Political Systems of the World* (Oxford, 1996)
Diani, Marco, and Catherine Ingraham (eds), *Restructuring Architectural Theory* (Evanston, 1989)
Dent, Anthony H, and Leslie Sherr, *Material Innovation: Architecture* (London, 2014)
de Botton, Alain, *The Architecture of Happiness* (London, 2006)
de Eccher, Andrea, and Giulia Del Zotto, *Venezia e il Veneto: L'opera di Carlo Scarpa* (Milan, 1999)
de Graaf, Reiner, *Four Walls and a Roof: The Complex Nature of a Simple Profession* (Cambridge MA, 2017)
de Haan, Hilde, and Ids Haagsma, *The House Erasmus Built: A Profile of Architecture in the Netherlands* (Haarlem, 1995)
de Maré, Eric, *New Ways of Building* (London, 1948)
Donat, John (ed), *World Architecture One* (London, 1964)
Dormer, Peter, *The Meanings of Modern Design: Towards the Twenty-first Century* (London, 1991)
Dorward, David, *Scotland's Place-names* (Edinburgh, 1995)
dos Santos, José, *Alvaro Siza: Works and Projects 1954–1992* (Barcelona, 1993)

Drabble, Margaret, *A Writers' Britain: Landscape in Literature* (London, 1979)
— *The Radiant Way* (London, 1987)
Düchting, Hajo, *Wassily Kandinsky* (Köln, 1991)
Duff, S Grant, *Europe and the Czechs* (Harmondsworth, 1938)
Dyckhoff, Tom, *The Age of Spectacle: Adventures in Architecture and the 21st Century City* (London, 2017)
Ede, Siân (ed), *Strange and Charmed* (London, 2000)
Edwards, Brian, *Basil Spence, 1907–1976* (Edinburgh, 1995)
Ekelund, Hilding (trans Edward Birse), *Architecture in Finland* (Helsinki, 1932)
Emmerson, Roger, *Winners & Losers: Scotland and the Architectural Competition* (Edinburgh, 1991)
— and Daniela Karasová, Petr Krajčí and Radomíra Sedláková, *Prague 1891–1941* (Edinburgh, 1994)
— 'The Emperor's New Clothes: Pastiche and Reproduction', *Architectural Heritage VI* (Edinburgh, 1996)
— '(P/T)owerplay: A reading of national authority in architecture', *292:Essays in Visual Culture* (Edinburgh, 2000)
— and Mary Tilmouth, *Matt Steele Architect: A Biography* (Edinburgh, 2010)
— 'Circumnavigating the Globe: RW Forsyth's, Princes Street, and its meanings', *The Book of the Old Edinburgh Club*, New Series, Vol. 16 (Edinburgh, 2020)
Empire Exhibition, *Official Guide* (Glasgow, 1938)
Fawcett, Chris, *The New Japanese House: Ritual and Anti-ritual Patterns of Dwelling* (London, 1980)
Fawcett, Richard, *The Architectural History of Scotland: Scottish Architecture from the Accession of the Stewarts to the Reformation* (Edinburgh, 1994)
Ferguson, Niall, *Empire: How Britain Made the Modern World* (London, 2004)
— *Civilisation: The West and the Rest* (London, 2011)
— *The Square and the Tower: Networks, Hierarchies and the Struggle for Global Power* (London, 2017)
Ferguson, William, *The Identity of the Scottish Nation* (Edinburgh, 1998)
Fergusson, James, *An historical inquiry into the true principles of beauty in art, more especially with reference to architecture* (London, 1849)
— *History of Architecture in All Countries from the Earliest Times to the Present Day* (2 vols) Vol. 1 (New York, 1867)
— and Robert Kerr, *History of Modern Styles of Architecture* (3rd ed) (London, 1891)
Fest, Joachim (trans Ewald Osers and Alexandra Dring), *Speer: The Final Verdict* (London, 2002)
Fiddes, Valerie, and Alastair Rowan (eds), *Mr David Bryce* (Edinburgh, 1976)
Fiedler, Jeannine, and Peter Feierabend (eds), *Bauhaus* (Cologne, 2000)
Focillon, Henri, *The Life of Forms in Art* (New York, 1992)
Forster, EM, *Howard's End* (Harmondsworth, 1976)
Forty, Adrian, *Words and Buildings: A Vocabulary of Modern Architecture* (London, 2004)

Foster, Hal (ed), *The Anti-Aesthetic Essays on Post-Modern Culture* (Port Townsend, WA, 1983)
— *The Art-Architecture Complex* (London, 2013)
Foucault, Michel (Paul Rabinow, ed), *The Foucault Reader* (reprint) (Harmondsworth, 1991)
— *The Order of Things* (reprint) (London, 1997)
Fox, Kate, *Watching the English: The Hidden Rules of English Behaviour* (London, 2004)
Frampton, Kenneth, and Yukio Futagawa, *Modern Architecture 1851–1919 and 1920–1945* (2 vols) (New York, 1983)
— *Studies in Tectonic Culture: The Poetics of Construction in Nineteenth and Twentieth Century Architecture* (Cambridge MA, 1995)
— and David Larkin, *American Masterworks: The Twentieth Century House* (New York, 1995)
— *Labour, Work and Architecture: Collected Essays on Architecture and Design* (London, 2002)
— *Modern Architecture: a Critical History* (4th ed) (London, 2007)
— *A Genealogy of Modern Architecture* (Zurich, 2015)
Francastel, Pierre (trans Randall Cherry), *Art & Technology in the Nineteenth and Twentieth Centuries* (New York, 2003)
Fraser, Derek, *The Buildings of Europe: Berlin* (Manchester, 1996)
Freeman Fox Associates and Colin Buchanan & Partners, *The Recommended Plan* (Edinburgh, 1972)
Frew, John, and David Jones (eds), *Scotland and Europe: Architecture and Design 1850–1940* (St Andrews, 1991)
Friedman, Mildred (ed), *De Stijl: 1917–1931, Visions of Utopia* (Oxford, 1982)
Fromonet, Francoise, *Glenn Murcutt: Works and Project* (London, 1995)
Frueh, Joanna, *Erotic Faculties* (Berkeley, 1996)
Fry, Edward F, *Cubism* (London, 1966)
Fry, Maxwell, *Fine Building* (London, 1944)
Fry, Michael, *The Scottish Empire* (Phantassie and Edinburgh, 2002)
Gablik, Suzi, *Has Modernism Failed?* (New York, 1985)
— *The Re-enchantment of Art* (New York, 1991)
Garnham, Trevor, *Melsetter House, William Richard Lethaby* (London, 1993)
Gebhard, David, and Patricia Gebhard (eds), *Purcell & Elmslie: Prairie Progressive Architects* (Salt Lake City, 2006)
Ghirardo, Diane, *Architecture after Modernism* (London, 1996)
Giedion, Sigfried, *Space, Time and Architecture* (London, 1947), (5th ed) (Cambridge 1967)
— *Architecture, You and Me* (Cambridge MA, 1958)
Gifford, John, *The Buildings of Scotland: Fife* (London, 1999)
Gillespie, Neil, and Laura Kinnaird (eds), *Stravaigers* (Edinburgh, 2015)
Glancey, Jonathan, *C20th architecture: The Structures that Shaped the Twentieth Century* (London, 2000)

Glendinning, Miles, and Stephan Muthesius, *Tower Block: Public Housing in England, Wales, Scotland and Northern Ireland* (New Haven, 1994)
— Ranald MacInnes and Aonghus MacKechnie, *A History of Scottish Architecture: From the Renaissance to the Present Day* (Edinburgh, 1996)
— (ed), *Rebuilding Scotland: The Post-war Vision 1945–1975* (East Linton, 1997)
— and David Page, *Clone City: Crisis and Renewal in Contemporary Scottish Architecture* (Edinburgh, 1999)
— *The Architecture of Scottish Government: From Kingship to Parliamentary Democracy* (Dundee, 2004)
— *Modern Architect: The Life and Times of Robert Matthew* (London, 2008)
— and Aonghus MacKechnie, *Scotch Baronial: Architecture and National Identity in Scotland* (London, 2021)
Gloag, John (ed), *Design in Modern Life* (London, 1934)
Golynets, Sergei, *Ivan Bilibin* (Leningrad, 1981)
Gombrich, EH, *The Sense of Order* (Oxford, 1979)
Gomme, Andor, and David Walker, *Architecture of Glasgow* (London, 1968)
Gooding, Mel, *National and University Library, Ljubljana, Jože Plečnik* (London, 1997)
Gordon, George (ed), *Perspectives of the Scottish City* (Aberdeen, 1985)
Gössel, Peter (ed), *Julius Schulman: Architecture and Photography* (Köln, 1998)
Gowan, James, *Style and Configuration* (London, 1994)
Greater London Council, *An Introduction to Housing Layout* (London, 1978)
Greenberg, Clement, *Art and Culture* (London, 1973)
Greene, Herb, *Mind and Image: An Essay on Art and Architecture* (London, 1976)
Groenendijk, Paul, Piet Vollard and Han van Dijk, *Guide to Modern Architecture in the Netherlands* (Rotterdam, 1987)
Gropius, Walter, *The Scope of Total Architecture* (London, 1956)
Hall, Peter, *Cities of Tomorrow* (3rd ed) (Oxford, 2002)
Hampson, Frank, *Dan Dare, Pilot of the Future in the Man from Nowhere* (Henrick-Ido-Ambacht, 1979)
Harries, Karsten, *The Ethical Function of Architecture* (Cambridge MA, 1998)
Harwood, Elain, and Alan Powers (eds), *Houses: Regional Practice and Local Character* (London, 2015)
Hausen, Marika, Kirmo Mikkola, Anna-Lisa Amberg, and Tytti Valton (eds), *Eliel Saarinen, Projects, 1896–1923* (Cambridge MA, 1990)
Hawthorne, Chris, writer/director, *That Far Corner: Frank Lloyd Wright in Los Angeles*, KCETOnline: LaBella Films, 2018
Hejduk, John, *Práce* (Praha, 1991)
Herbenová, Olga, Mílena Lamarová and Vlasta Čiháková-Noshiro, *Czechoslovakia: Cubism* (Tokyo, 1984)
Herman, Arthur, *The Scottish Enlightenment: The Scots' Invention of the Modern World* (London, 2002)

Herschdorfer, Nathalie, and Lada Ustätter (eds), *Le Corbusier and the Power of Photography* (London, 2012)
Hiort, Esbjørn, *Exhibition of Danish Architecture Today* (Copenhagen, 1950)
Hitchcock, Henry-Russell, *Architecture: Nineteenth and Twentieth Centuries* (Harmondsworth, 1963)
— and Philip Johnson, *The International Style* (rev. ed) (New York, 1966)
— *Modern Architecture* (reprint) (New York, 1970)
Hobsbawm, Eric, *Age of Extremes: The Short Twentieth Century 1914–1991* (London, 1994)
— *Nations and Nationalism Since 1780: Programme, Myth, Reality* (2nd ed) (Cambridge, 1997)
— *Fractured Times: Culture and Society in the Twentieth Century* (London, 2014)
Hofman, Vlastislav, 'Nový princip v architektuře (A new principle in architecture)', *Styl*, Vol. 5, 1913
Horsman, Mathew, and Andrew Marshall, *After the Nation-State: Citizens, Tribalism and the New World Disorder* (London, 1994)
Howard, Deborah, *The Architectural History of Scotland: Scottish Architecture from the Reformation to the Restoration, 1560–1660* (Edinburgh, 1995)
Howard, Jeremy, *Art Nouveau: International and National Styles in Europe* (Manchester, 1996)
Howarth, TEB, *Prospect & Reality: Great Britain 1945–1955* (London, 1985)
Hubbard, William, *Complicity and Convention* (Cambridge MA, 1981)
Hurst, Michael, *States, Countries, Provinces* (Bourne End, 1986)
Ilonen, Arvi, *Helsinki, Espoo, Kauniainen, Vantaa: An Architectural Guide* (Helsinki, 1997)
Ingels, Bjarke, *Yes is More: An Archicomic on Architectural Evolution* (Copenhagen, 2009)
Isaacs, Reginald, *Gropius: An Illustrated Biography of the Creator of the Bauhaus* (Boston, 1991)
Jackson, Neil, *Japan and the West: An Architectural Dialogue* (London, 2019)
Jacobs, Jane, *The Death and Life of Great American Cities: The Failure of Town Planning* (Harmondsworth, 1964)
Janák, Pavel, 'Od moderní architektury k architekuře (From modern architecture to architecture)', *Styl*, Vol. 2, 1910
Jarman, David, *Fields of Vision: New Ideas in Rural House Design* (Edinburgh, 1993)
Jarvis, Alan, *The Things We See: Indoors and Out* (Harmondsworth, 1946)
Jencks, Charles, *Modern Movements in Architecture* (New York, 1973)
— *The Language of Post-Modern Architecture* (rev. ed) (London, 1978)
— *Le Corbusier and the Tragic View of Architecture* (rev. ed) (Harmondsworth, 1987)
— *The New Paradigm in Architecture: The Language of Post-Modernism* (Newhaven CT, 2002)
Joedicke, Jürgen, *A History of Modern Architecture* (London, 1961)

Jones, Peter Blundell, *Architecture and Ritual: How Buildings Shape Society* (London, 2016)
Jurkovič, Dušan, et al, *Slovak Peasant Art and Melodies* (London, 1911)
Kallas, Hillar, and Sylvie Nickels (eds), *Finland, Creation and Construction* (London, 1968)
Kallir, Jane, *Viennese Design and the Wiener Werkstätte* (London, 1986)
Kandinsky, Wassily, and Franz Marc, (Klaus Lankheit, ed), *The Blau Reiter Almanac* (reprint) (London, 1974)
Kant, Immanuel, 'Prolegomena to Any Future Metaphysics', 1783, in Steven M Cahn (ed), *Classics of Western Philosophy* (3rd ed) (Indianapolis, 1977)
— (trans and ed, Marcus Weigelt), *Critique of Pure Reason* (London, 2007)
Kaplan, E Ann (ed), *Post-Modernism and its Discontents* (London, 1988)
Kent, Neil, *The Soul of the North: A Social, Architectural and Cultural History of the Nordic Countries* (London, 2000)
Kern, Stephen, *The Culture of Time and Space 1880–1918* (Cambridge MA, 1983)
Kimura Hiroaki, 'Charles Rennie Mackintosh', *Process*, No. 50, August 1984
Kinchin, Perilla and Juliet Kinchin with J Neil Baxter, *Glasgow's Great Exhibitions: 1888, 1901, 1911, 1938, 1988* (Bicester, n.d., ca. 1988)
Kivinen, Paula, Pekka Korvenmaa, and Esa Piironen (eds), *Lars Sonck, 1870–1956, Architect* (Helsinki, n.d.)
Kleihues, Josef P, and Heinrich Klotz (eds), *The International Building Exhibition Berlin, 1987: Examples of a New Architecture* (London, 1987)
Kostof, Spiro, *A History of Architecture: Settings and Rituals* (New York and Oxford, 1995)
Kramer, Hilton, *The Triumph of Modernism: The Art World 1987–2005* (New York, 2013)
Krastiņš, Jānis (ed), *DOCOMOMO, National Register, Latvia* (Riga, 1998)
Kraukle, Daina, *Latvian Design* (Riga, 2006)
Krell, David Farrell (ed), *Martin Heidegger: Basic Writings* (London, 1978)
Kroyanker, David, 'Phases in the Orientalism of Modern Jerusalem Architecture', *Architecture of Israel*, No. 1, January 1988
Kubišta, Bohumil, 'Předpoklady slohu (Preconditions of style)', *Přehled*, x2, 6.x.1911
Kubler, George, *The Shape of Time* (New Haven CT, 1962)
Kultermann, Udo, *New Architecture in the World* (London, 1966)
Kurokawa Kisho, *Intercultural Architecture* (London, 1991)
Landau, Royston, *New Directions in British Architecture* (London, 1968)
Langmead, Donald, *Willem Marinus Dudok, A Dutch Modernist: A Bio-Bibliography* (Westport CT, 1996)
Latek, Irena (ed), *Peter Collins and the Critical History of Modern Architecture* (Montréal, 2003)
Le Corbusier (trans Frederick Etchells), *Towards a New Architecture* (London, 1946)
— (trans Ivan Žaknić), *The Journey to the East* (Cambridge MA, 1987)

Leśnikowski, Wojciech (ed), *East European Modernism: Architecture in Czechoslovakia, Hungary and Poland between the Wars* (London, 1996)
Lethaby, WR, *Architecture, Mysticism and Myth* (London, 1891)
— *Architecture* (London, 1911)
Levin, Janna, *Black Hole Blues, and Other Songs from Outer Space* (London, 2016)
Long, Philip, and Jane Thomas, *Basil Spence Architect* (Edinburgh, 2007)
Lootsma, Bart, *Superdutch: New Architecture in the Netherlands* (London, 2000)
Lyall, Sutherland, *The State of British Architecture* (London, 1980)
Lynch, Kevin, *The Image of the City* (Cambridge MA, 1960)
Lynch, Michael, *Scotland: A New History* (London, 1992)
McAra, Duncan, *Sir James Gowans: Romantic Rationalist* (Edinburgh, 1975)
McArthur, Alexander, and H Kingsley Long, *No Mean City* (London, 1943)
McCarter, Robert (ed), *On and By Frank Lloyd Wright: A Primer of Architectural Principles* (London, 2005)
MacCarthy, Fiona, *Walter Gropius: Visionary Founder of the Bauhaus* (London, 2020)
McCrone, David, *Understanding Scotland: The Sociology of a Stateless Nation* (London, 1992)
MacDiarmid, Hugh, *Aesthetics in Scotland* (Edinburgh, 1984)
McFadzean, Ronald, *The Life and Work of Alexander Thomson* (London, 1979)
MacGibbon, David, and Thomas Ross, *The Castellated and Domestic Architecture of Scotland from the Twelfth to the Eighteenth Century* (5 vols) (Edinburgh, 1887)
McKay, WB, *Building Construction* (3 vols) (London, 1938)
MacKay-Lyons, Brian, *Brian MacKay-Lyons: Selected Projects 1986–1997* (Halifax NS, 1998)
McKean, Charles, *Edinburgh: an Illustrated Architectural Guide* (Edinburgh, 1984)
— *The Scottish Thirties* (Edinburgh, 1987)
— *The Making of the Museum of Scotland* (Edinburgh, 2000)
McKinstry, Sam, *Rowand Anderson: 'The Premier Architect of Scotland'* (Edinburgh, 1991)
MacLeod, Robert, *Style and Society: Architectural Ideology in Britain 1835–1914* (London, 1971)
— *Charles Rennie Mackintosh: Architect and Artist* (London, 1983)
MacRae, EJ, *The Heritage of Greater Edinburgh* (Edinburgh, 1947)
Mactaggart & Mickel, *The Book of the Broom Estate, Whitecraigs* (Glasgow, n.d., ca. 1935)
Macpherson, James, *Fragments of Ancient Poetry* (Edinburgh, 1760)
McWilliam, Colin, *Scottish Townscape* (London, 1975)
Madge, John, *Tomorrow's Houses: New Building Method, Structures and Materials* (London, 1946)
Mallgrave, Harry Francis, *Gottfried Semper, Architect of the Nineteenth Century* (New Haven CT, 1996)

Mang, Karl and Eva, *Viennese Architecture 1860–1930 in Drawings* (London, 1979)
Mansell, HL, and J Veitch (eds), *William Hamilton: Lectures of Metaphysics and Logic* (2 vols) (Edinburgh, 1859 and 1860)
Markus, Thomas A (ed), *Order and Space in Society* (Edinburgh, 1982)
Martin, David, *The Glasgow School of Painting* (London, 1897)
Masák, Miroslav, Rostislav Švácha and Jindřich Vybíral, *The Trade Fair Palace in Prague* (Prague, 1995)
Masheck, Joseph, *Building-Art: Modern Architecture Under Cultural Construction* (Cambridge, 1993)
— *Adolf Loos: The Art of Architecture* (London, 2013)
Maudlin, Daniel, *The Highland House Transformed: Architecture and Identity on the Edge of Britain, 1700–1850* (Dundee, 2009)
Mellor, Roy, *Geography of the USSR* (London, 1965)
Millais, Malcolm, *Exploding the Myths of Modern Architecture* (London, 2009)
Mills, Edward D, *Architects' Detail Sheets* (London, 1952)
Ministry of Housing and Local Government, *Homes for Today & Tomorrow* (London, 1961)
Ministry of Works, *Post-war Building Studies No. 1: House Construction* (London, 1944)
Mitchell, William J, *City of Bits: Space, Place and the Infobahn* (Cambridge MA, 1997)
Moffat, Alexander, and David Riach, *Arts of Independence* (Edinburgh, 2014)
Moffat, Alistair, *Remembering Charles Rennie Mackintosh* (Lanark, 1989)
Morris, Eleanor, *James Morris: Architect and Landscape Architect, 1931–2006* (Edinburgh, 2007)
Morrison, Rev. Wm (Norman MacRae, ed), *Highland Second-Sight with Prophecies of Coinneach Odhar and the Seer of Petty* (Dingwall, 1910)
Murphy, Richard, *Ten Years of Practice* (Edinburgh, 2001)
Muthesius, Herman (trans Janet Seligman and Stewart Spencer), *The English House: Volume 1 Development* (London, 2007) (orig. Berlin, 1906)
Naismith, Robert, *The Buildings of the Scottish Countryside* (London, 1985)
Newton, SJ, *The Politics and Psychoanalysis of Primitivism* (London, 1996)
Nicholson, Peter, *The Principles of Architecture* (London, 1809)
Nikula, Riitta, *Armas Lindgren, 1874–1929, Architect* (Helsinki, 1988)
— *Architecture and Landscape: The Building of Finland* (Helsinki, 1993)
Noever, Peter, *The End of Architecture? Documents and Manifestos* (Munich, 1993)
Norberg-Schulz, Christian, *Intentions in Architecture* (London, 1966)
— *Principles of Modern Architecture* (London, 2001)
Normand, Charles, *A Parallel of Orders of Architecture* (Paris, 1891) (reprint) (London, 1929)
Normand, Tom, *The Modern Scot: Modernism and Nationalism in Scotland 1928–1955* (London, 2000)

Nuttgens, Patrick, *Reginald Fairlie 1883–1952: A Scottish Architect* (Edinburgh, 1959)
— (ed), *Mackintosh and His Contemporaries* (London, 1988)
O'Doherty, Brian, *Inside the White Cube: The Ideology of the Gallery Space* (Berkeley, 1999)
O'Donnell, Raymond, *James Salmon 1873–1924* (Edinburgh, 2003)
Osmond, John, *The Divided Kingdom* (London, 1988)
Owens, Craig (Scott Bryson, Barbara Kruger, Lynne Tillman and Jane Weinstock, eds), *Beyond Recognition: Representation, Power, and Culture* (Berkeley, 1992)
Paavilainen, Simo (ed), *Nordic Classicism 1910–1930* (Helsinki, 1982)
Pallasmaa, Juhani, *The Eyes of the Skin: Architecture of the Senses* (London, 1996)
— *The Thinking Hand: Existential and Embodied Wisdom in Architecture* (Chichester, 2009)
Papadakis, Dr Andreas C (ed), *British Architecture* (London, 1982)
Paxman, Jeremy, *The English: A Portrait of a People* (London, 2007)
Payne, Peter, *The Hydro: Study of the Development of the Major Hydroelectric Schemes Undertaken by the North of Scotland Hydroelectric Board* (Aberdeen, 1988)
Pearson, Paul David, *Alvar Aalto and the International Style* (London, 1989)
Peckham, Robert Shannan (ed), *Rethinking Heritage: Cultures and Politics in Europe* (London, 2003)
Pevsner, Nikolaus, *Pioneers of Modern Design* (Harmondsworth, 1966)
— and JM Richards, *The Anti-Rationalists* (London, 1973)
Phillips, R Randall, *The £1000 House* (London, 1928)
— *Houses for Moderate Means* (London, 1936)
Piddington, Justine, Simon Nicol, Helen Garrett and Matthew Custard, *The Housing Stock of the United Kingdom* (Watford, 2020)
Plummer, Henry, *Nordic Light: Modern Scandinavian Architecture* (London, 2012)
Polišenský, JV, *History of Czechoslovakia in Outline* (Prague, 1991)
Porphyrios, Demetri (ed), 'Building and Rational Architecture' in *Architectural Design*, Vol. 54, No. 5/6, 1984
— (ed), 'Leon Krier: Houses, Palaces, Cities' in *Architectural Design*, Vol. 54, No. 7/8, 1984
— *Sources of Modern Eclecticism* (London, 1982)
Quantrill, Malcolm, *Plain Modern: The Architecture of Bryan Mackay-Lyons* (New York, 2005)
Ravetz, Alison, *Model Estate: Planned Housing at Quarry Hill, Leeds* (London, 1974)
— *The Government of Space: Town Planning in Modern Society* (London, 1986)
Read, Herbert, *A Concise History of Modern Sculpture* (London, 1964)
Reade, Arthur, *Finland and the Finns* (London, 1915)

Reiach, Alan, and Robert Hurd, *Building Scotland: A Cautionary Guide* (Glasgow, n.d., ca. 1944)
Rhowbotham, Kevin, *Form to Programme* (London, 1995)
Richards, JM (ed), *New Buildings in the Commonwealth* (London, 1961)
— 'Architectural Criticism in the Nineteen-Thirties', in John Summerson (ed), *Concerning Architecture: Essays on Architectural Writers and Writing Presented to Nikolaus Pevsner* (London, 1968)
— *800 Years of Finnish Architecture* (Newton Abbot, 1978)
— *The Castles on the Ground: The Anatomy of Suburbia* (London, 2011) (reprint of 1973 edition: originally published 1946)
Riedl, Dušan (trans Tony Long, Ota Brídl and Irma Charvátová), *The Villa of the Tugendhats Created by Ludwig Mies van der Rohe in Brno* (Brno, 1997)
Ringbom, Sixten, *Stone, Style and Truth* (Helsinki, 1987)
Ripellino, Angelo Maria, *Magic Prague* (London, 1994)
Robb, Steven, 'Ebenezer MacRae and Interwar Housing in Edinburgh', in RJ Morris (ed), *The Book of the Old Edinburgh Club*, New Series, Vol. 13, 2017
Roberts, JM, *A History of Europe* (Oxford, 1996)
Robertson, Pamela (ed), *Charles Rennie Mackintosh: The Architectural Papers* (Cambridge MA, 1990)
Rock, Joe, *Thomas Hamilton Architect 1784–1858* (Edinburgh, 1984)
Rodger, Johnny, *The Hero Building: An Architecture of Scottish National Identity* (Farnham, 2015)
— (ed), *Gillespie, Kidd & Coia: Architecture 1956–1987* (Glasgow, 2007)
Rodger, Richard, *Housing the People: the Colonies of Edinburgh* (Edinburgh, 1999)
Rosenburg, Lou, with John Rosser, *Scotland's Homes Fit for Heroes: Garden City Influences on the Development of Scottish Working Class Housing 1900–1939* (Edinburgh, 2016)
Rossi, Aldo (trans Lawrence Vermuti), *The Architecture of the City* (Cambridge MA, 1984)
Rowe, Colin, *The Architecture of Good Intentions: Towards a Possible Retrospective* (London, 1994)
— (Alexander Caragonne, ed), *As I Was Saying: Recollections and Miscellaneous Essays* (3 vols) (Cambridge MA, 1996)
Royal Incorporation of Architects in Scotland, *RIAS Review of Scottish Architecture* (Macclesfield, 1992)
Ruskin, John, *Stones of Venice* (3 vols) (London, 1851–3)
— *Lectures on Architecture and Painting Delivered at Edinburgh, November 1853* (London, 1854)
— *Sesame and Lilies* (Orpington, 1893)
— *The Seven Lamps of Architecture* (London, 1907)
Russell, Frank (ed), *Art Nouveau Architecture* (London, 1979)
Rychlík, Jan, Thomas D. Marzik and Miroslav Bielik (eds), *R. W. Seton-Watson, Documents / Dokumenty 1906–1951*, Vol. 1 (Praha and Martin, 1995)

Saarinen, Eliel, *The Search for Form in Art and Architecture* (reprint) (New York, 1985)
Safran, Yehuda, and Wilfried Wang (trans Wilfried Wang, Rosamund Diamond and Robert Godsill), *The Architecture of Adolf Loos* (London, 1987)
Sarnitz, August, *RM Schindler, Architect, 1887–1953* (New York, 1988)
— *Adolf Loos, 1870–1933: Architect, Cultural Critic, Dandy* (Köln, 2003)
Sayers, Dorothy L, *Murder Must Advertise* (London, 1963)
Schama, Simon, *Landscape and Memory* (London, 1995)
Schirer, William L, *The Rise and Fall of the Third Reich* (London, 1973)
Scott, A MacCallum, *Suomi, the Land of the Finns* (London, 1926)
Scott, Geoffrey, *The Architecture of Humanism: A Study in the History of Taste* (2nd ed) (London, 1924)
Scottish Housing Advisory Committee, *Planning Our New Homes* (Edinburgh, 1944)
Scruton, Roger, *The Classical Vernacular: Architectural Principles in an Age of Nihilism* (Manchester, 1994)
Scully Jr., Vincent, *Modern Architecture: The Architecture of Democracy* (London, 1961)
Sedláková, Radomíra, *Prague: An Architectural Guide* (Venice, 1997)
— and Pavel Frič, *20 Století České Architektury* (Praha, 2006)
Semper, Gottfried (trans Harry Francis Mallgrave and Wolfgang Hermann), *The Four Elements of Architecture and Other Writings* (Cambridge, 1988)
— *Style* (Los Angeles, 2004)
Service, Alastair, *Edwardian Architecture* (London, 1977)
Sestoft, Jorgen, and Jorgen Heguer Christiansen, *Guide to Danish Architecture 1: 1000–1960* (Copenhagen, 1991)
Sharp, Dennis (ed), *Connell Ward & Lucas* (London, 1994)
Sinclair, Fiona, *Scotstyle: 150 Years of Scottish Architecture* (Edinburgh, 1984)
— and Neil Baxter (eds), *Scotstyle: 100 Years of Scottish Architecture (1916–2015)* (Edinburgh, 2016)
Šlachta, Štefan, *Moderná Architektúra na Slovensku 20. A 30. Roky* (Piešťany, 1991)
Smith, AD, *The Ethnic Origins of Nations* (Oxford, 1986)
Smith, George Gregory, *Scottish Literature: Character and Influences* (London, 1919)
Spaeth, David, *Mies van der Rohe* (London, 1985)
Spence, Rory, 'Lars Sonck' in *Architectural Review*, Vol. CLXXI, No. 1020, February 1982
Spuybroek, Lars, *The Sympathy of Things: Ruskin and the Ecology of Design* (2nd ed) (London, 2016)
Stamp, Gavin, 'Mackintosh, Burnet and Modernity', in *Architectural Heritage III: The Age of Mackintosh* (Edinburgh, 1992)
— and Sam McKinstry (eds), *'Greek' Thomson* (Edinburgh, 1994)
— *Alexander Thomson: The Unknown Genius* (London, 1999)
— (ed), *The Light of Beauty and Truth: The Lectures of Alexander 'Greek'*

Thomson Architect 1817–1875 (Glasgow, 1999)
Staňková, Jaroslava, Jiří Štursa, and Svatopluk Voděra, *Pražská architektura* (Praha, 1991)
Steele, James (ed), *Architectural Monographs No. 29, Eric Owen Moss* (London, 1993)
— *The Complete Architecture of Balkrishna Doshi: Rethinking Modernism for the Developing World* (London, 1998)
Stichting de Beurs van Berlage, *Soviet Architecture 1917–1987* (Amsterdam, 1989)
Sudjic, Deyan, Peter Cook and Jonathan Meades, *English Extremists: The Architecture of Campbell, Zogolovitch, Wilkinson and Gough* (London, 1988)
— *The 100 Mile City* (London, 1992)
— 'Identity in the City', in Steef Buijs, Wendy Tam, Devisari Tunas (eds), *Megacities: Exploring a Sustainable Future* (Rotterdam, 2010)
Sullivan, Louis, *Kindergarten Chats and Other Writings* (reprint) (New York, 1975)
Summerson, John (ed), *Concerning Architecture: Essays on Architectural Writers and Writing Presented to Nikolaus Pevsner* (London, 1968)
Švácha, Rostislav, *The Architecture of New Prague, 1895–1945* (Cambridge MA, 1995)
Tafuri, Manfredo, and Francesco dal Co, *Contemporary Architecture* (Milan, 1976)
Teichová, Alice, *The Czechoslovak Economy, 1918–1980* (London, 1988)
Thackara, John (ed), *Design after Modernism* (London, 1988)
Tonge, John, *The Arts of Scotland* (London, 1938)
Towndrow, FE, *Architecture in the Balance* (London, 1933)
— (ed), *Replanning Britain: The Oxford Conference of the Town and Country Planning Association, Spring, 1941* (London, 1941)
Tubbs, Ralph, *The Englishman Builds* (Harmondsworth, 1945)
Ungers, Oswald Matthias, *Morphologie: City Metaphor* (Köln, 1982)
Vale, Lawrence J, *Architecture, Power, and National Identity* (New Haven CT, 1992)
van Doesburg, Theo (trans Charlotte I Loeb and Arthur L Loeb), *On European Architecture: Complete Essays from Het Bouwbedrijf 1924–1931* (Basel, 1990)
Venturi, Robert, *Complexity and Contradiction* (New York, 1966)
Vergo, Peter, *Art in Vienna, 1898–1918* (2nd ed) (Oxford, 1981)
Vidler, Anthony, *The Architectural Uncanny* (London, 1992)
— *Warped Space: Art, Architecture and Anxiety in Modern Culture* (Cambridge MA, 2000)
— (ed), *Architecture between Spectacle and Use* (New Haven MA, 2008)
von Vegesack, Alexander (ed), *Czech Cubism* (London, 1992)
Walker, David M, *St Andrew's House: An Edinburgh Controversy 1912–1939* (Edinburgh, 1989)
Walker, Frank Arneil, 'National Romanticism and the Architecture of the City',

in George Gordon (ed), *Perspectives of the Scottish City* (Aberdeen, 1985)
— 'The Significance of the Folk House', in John Frew and David Jones (eds), *Scotland and Europe: Architecture and Design 1850–1940* (St Andrews, 1991)
Weber, Nicholas Fox, *Le Corbusier: A Life* (New York, 2008)
Wedebrunn, Ola (ed), *Modern Movement Scandinavia: Vision and Reality* (Copenhagen, Helsinki, Reykjavik, Oslo, Stockholm, 1998)
Welter, Volker M, *Biopolis: Patrick Geddes and the City of Life* (Cambridge MA, 2002)
Weston, Richard, *Alvar Aalto* (London, 1995)
— *Richard Murphy: Ten Years of Practice* (Edinburgh, 2001)
Wigley, Mark, *The Architecture of Deconstruction: Derrida's Haunt* (Cambridge MA, 1995)
Williams, Bernard, *Moral Luck* (Cambridge, 1981)
Wilkinson, Tom, *Bricks and Mortals* (London, 2014)
Wilson, Peter, *New Timber Architecture in Scotland,* (Edinburgh, 2007)
— *The Modern Timber House in the UK: New Paradigms and Technologies* (Edinburgh, 2017)
Wolfe, Tom, *From Our House to Bauhaus* (London, 1982)
Woolf, Stuart (ed), *Nationalism in Europe 1815 to the Present: A Reader* (London, 1996)
Worringer, Wilhelm (trans Michael Bullock), *Abstraction and Empathy: A Contribution to the Psychology of Style* (Chicago, 1997) (originally published in German as *Abstraktion und Einfühlung*, 1908)
Wright, Frank Lloyd, *Drawings and Plans of Frank Lloyd Wright: The Early Years (1893–1909)* (New York, 1983) (edited reprint of *Ausgeführte Bauten und Entwürfe von Frank Lloyd Wright*, Berlin, 1910)
— *The Natural House* (New York, 1954)
— *An Autobiography* (London, 1977)
Xianging, Li, *Contemporary Architecture in China: Towards a Critical Pragmatism* (Mulgrave, 2018)
Yamada, Chisaburoh F (ed), *Dialogue in Art: Japan and the West* (London, 1976)
Yorke, FRS, *The Modern House* (6th ed) (London, 1948)
Young, Andrew McLaren, *Charles Rennie Mackintosh (1868–1928): Architecture, Design and Painting* (Edinburgh, 1968)
Young, GM (ed), *Country and Town: A Summary of the Scott and Uthwatt Reports* (Harmondsworth, 1943)
Young, Michael, Peter Wilmott and Judith Stacey, *Family and Kinship in East London* (London, 1957)
Zevi, Bruno, *The Modern Language of Architecture* (New York, 1994) (paperback reprint of 1978 ed.)
— *Erich Mendelsohn* (New York and London, 1985)
Žižek, Slavoj, *The Parallax View* (Cambridge MA, 2006)
Zumthor, Peter, *Thinking Architecture* (Baden, 1998)
— *Peter Zumthor Works: Buildings and Projects 1979–1997* (Baden, 1998)

Endnotes

Introduction

1. 'The Broons' is a weekly comic strip concerning the doings of three generations of a large family living in a typical Scottish urban tenement. It has appeared in *The Sunday Post* since 1936 and is something of a Scottish cultural touchstone.
2. From the Czech word *robota* meaning indentured labour or slave.
3. Karel Čapek (trans Paul Selver), *Letters from England* (London, 1926), p.100. The title of this book, *Land of Stone*, is taken from Čapek's account of his travels in Scotland.
4. As related to me several years later by the Planning Case Officer from Newcastle upon Tyne City Council.
5. 'Granny-tops' are perforated rotating galvanised metal drums attached to the clay pots on the flues. By rotating in the wind they induce or enhance the Venturi effect which draws air and consequently smoke up the chimney while also negating 'blow-back', the opposite effect which drives smoke down the chimney and back into the room.
6. James Fergusson, *History of Architecture in All Countries from the Earliest Times to the Present Day* (vol. 2) (New York, 1867), pp.201–2.
7. Roger Emmerson, 'A Garden of Delights: Some preliminary notes on a developing theory of Scottish architecture', *Prospect*, no.28, Summer 1986, p.10.
8. Miles Glendinning, Ranald MacInnes & Aonghus MacKechnie, *A History of Scottish Architecture: From the Renaissance to the Present Day* (Edinburgh, 1993), p.497.
9. Nikolaus Pevsner provided a clue in his *Pioneers of Modern Design*, suggesting a link between Dutch and Scottish architecture. In a consciously post-Modern construct (see Chapter 6), the 'Scottish Brick Houses' were developed from an amalgam of 16th-century – not Mackintosh – motives and 1920s Dutch brick detailing garnered from studies made of the tenements in the Berlage-planned Amsterdam-sud. Mackintosh is the unfailing default reference for Scottish commentators when dealing with something new or different.
10. Joanna Frueh, *Erotic Faculties* (Berkeley, 1996), p.20.
11. Peter Collins, *Changing Ideals in Modern Architecture* (London, 1965), p.16.
12. Marshall Berman, *All That Is Solid Melts Into Air: The Experience of Modernity* (London, 1999), p.171.
13. Nikolaus Pevsner, *Pioneers of Modern Design* (Harmondsworth, 1966), p.18. The most recent of the new literature he listed in the bibliography was *Collins's Changing Ideals*, which should perhaps have given him pause for reflection.
14. FE Towndrow, *Architecture in the Balance* (London, 1933), flyleaf.
15. Matthew Horsman & Andrew Marshall, *After the Nation-state* (London, 1994), p.177.
16. Niall Ferguson, *The Square and the Tower: Networks, Hierarchies and the Struggle for Global Power* (London, 2017), p.296.
17. Michael Fry, *The Scottish Empire* (Phantassie and Edinburgh, 2002), p.vii.
18. James Baldwin, *Nobody Knows My Name* (London, 1969), p.3.
19. Tom Wolfe, *From Our House to Bauhaus* (London, 1982), or Malcolm Millais, *Exploding the Myths of Modern Architecture* (London, 2009).
20. Robert Shannon Peckham, 'The Politics of Heritage and Public Culture', in Robert Shannon Peckham (ed), *Rethinking Heritage: Culture and Politics in Europe* (London, 2003), p.2.
21. 'The English Question' survey 2018 conducted by YouGov, results analysed by Dr Kevin Cunningham & Dr Ian Warren of @ElectoralData. Info at: yougov.co.uk/topics//politics/articles-reports/2018/06/18/young-people-are-less-proud-being-english-than-their-elders, retrieved 6 November 2019.

Chapter 1

1. Gaston Bachelard (trans Maria Jolas), *The Poetics of Space* (Boston, 1994), p.65.
2. Whitney Chadwick, *Women, Art and Society* (4th ed) (London, 2007), p.468.
3. Alexander Moffat & David Riach, *Arts of Independence* (Edinburgh, 2014), p.11.
4. Slavoj Žižek, *The Parallax View* (Cambridge MA, 2006), p.377.
5. Craig Owens (Scott Bryson, Barbara Kruger, Lynne Tillman & Jane Weinstock, eds) *Beyond Recognition: Representation, Power, and Culture* (Berkeley, 1992), p.287.
6. Ibid., p.91.
7. For example, the Dress Act 1746, not re-pealed till 1783, banning the wearing of the tartan kilt and plaid in Scotland, the Slovakian Language Law of 2009 or the banning of the teaching of Magyar in the Hungarian

8. minority region of south-west Zakarpattia Oblast, Ukraine on 8 September 2017. There is considerable tit-for-tat language legislation in Central Europe between the Magyar and Slav languages with intended cultural consequences.
8. The border between Portugal and Spain dates from 1143, but was not complete in its present location until 1297.
9. One of the many actionable couplets from a poem by English poet and journalist James Michie (1927–2007), published in the *Spectator* magazine in 2004 under the editorship of Boris Johnson (UK Prime Minister 2019–2022). In full, it reads:

The Scotch – what a verminous race!
Canny, pushy, chippy, they're all over the place,
Battening off us with fake bonhomie;
Polluting our stock, undermining our economy.
Down with sandy hair and knobbly knees!
Suppress the tartan dwarves and the Wee Frees!
Ban the kilt, the skean-dhu and the sporran
As provocatively, offensively foreign.
It's time Hadrian's Wall was refortified
To pen them in a ghetto on the other side.
I would go further. The nation
Deserves not merely isolation
But comprehensive extermination.
We must not flinch from a solution.
(I await legal prosecution.)

Along with crude racial stereotyping there is 'ghetto', 'polluting our [English] stock', 'extermination', and 'solution'; the Holocaust inferences are unmissable. The wonder is that, despite Michie's justifiable expectation, not he, his editor Johnson nor the *Spectator* were ever prosecuted. Now deleted from the *Spectator* website, although not forgotten.
10. Deyan Sudjic, *The Hundred Mile City* (London, 1992), p.143.
11. Victor Burgin, *In/Different Spaces: Places and Memory in Visual Culture* (Berkeley, 1996), p.155.
12. John Berger (Tom Overton, ed), *Portraits: John Berger on Artists* (London and New York, 2017), pp.123–4.
13. Simon Schama, *Landscape & Memory* (London, 1995), p.7.
14. Colin Chant, 'Introduction', in Colin Chant & David Goodman (eds), *Pre-industrial Cities & Technology* (London, 1999), p.viii.
15. Schama, *Landscape*, p.13.
16. Volker M Welter, *Biopolis: Patrick Geddes and the City of Life* (Cambridge MA, 2002), p.62.
17. Ibid., p.63.
18. Pierre Francastel (trans Randall Cherry), *Art & Technology in the Nineteenth and Twentieth Centuries* (New York, 2003), p.275.
19. John Ruskin, *The Seven Lamps of Architecture* (London, 1907), pp.181–2.
20. Berger, *Portraits*, p.89.
21. Robert Naismith, *The Buildings of the Scottish Countryside* (London, 1989), pp.74, 102.
22. Daniel Maudlin, *The Highland House Transformed: Architecture and Identity on the Edge of Britain, 1700–1850* (Dundee, 2009), p.1.
23. Arnold Pacey, 'Five Chinese Cities before 1840', in Chant & Goodman, *Pre-industrial*, p.306 and Figure 8.26, p.307.
24. Yang Seng Toong & N Utaberta, 'Heritage Buildings Conservation Issues of Shophouses in Kuala Lumpur Chinatown', *Applied Mechanics and Materials*, vol.747, March 2015, pp.60–3. Info at: scientific.net/AMM.747.60, retrieved 4 July 2020. This was a live issue when I worked with Malaysian students on a shophouse project at the School of Architecture, Edinburgh College of Art in 1998.
25. Françoise Fromonet, *Glenn Murcutt: Works and Projects* (London, 1995), p.25.
26. Victoria Ballard Bell & Paul Rand (eds), *Materials for Architectural Design* (London, 2006), p.10.
27. Gail Peter Borden in Andrew H Dent & Leslie Sherr (eds), *Material Innovation: Architecture* (London, 2014), p.15.
28. Niall Ferguson, *Civilization: The West and the Rest* (London, 2011), p.xxvi.
29. Chadwick, *Women*, p.467.
30. George Gregory Smith, *Scottish Literature, Character and Influences* (London, 1919), p.4.
31. Chambers English Dictionary (Edinburgh, Cambridge, New York & Melbourne, 1988), p.1492.
32. Smith, *Literature*, p.5.
33. Žižek, *Parallax*, p.8.
34. Smith, *Literature*, p.19.
35. Le Corbusier (trans Frederick Etchells), *Towards a New Architecture* (reprint) (London & New York, 1963), p.202.
36. Žižek, *Parallax*, p.20.
37. Richard Faber, quoted in Jeremy Paxman, *The English: A Portrait of a People* (London, 2007), p.49.
38. Žižek, *Parallax*, p.377.
39. Richard Weston, *Alvar Aalto* (London, 1995), p.16.
40. The WHO's 2013 *Status Report on Alcohol and Health in 35 European Countries* established that Finland had 40–49.9 annual deaths per 100,000 related directly to cirrhosis, cancer

and accidents arising from alcohol consumption. No comparable current figures were found, although claims of improvement have been made by the Finnish government. UK statistics 2015 show that for the UK as a whole, the figure is between 20 and 29.9, with Scotland at the top end of that range.
41. Fromonet, *Murcutt*, p.15.
42. Chisaburoh Yamada (ed), *Dialogue in Art: Japan and the West* (London, 1976), p.287.
43. David McCrone, *Understanding Scotland: The Sociology of a Stateless Nation* (London, 1992), p.18.
44. Ibid., pp.177–184.
45. Burgin, *In/different*, pp.22–3.
46. Maudlin, *Highland House*, pp.92–126.
47. Author of the 1920 science-fiction play *RUR: Rossum's Universal Robots*. 'Rossum' from 'rozum', Czech for 'reason' or 'understanding', used here as a personal name.
48. Čapek, *Letters*, p.99.
49. Radomirá Sedláková & Dagmar Šefčiková, from the National Gallery and National Technical Museum of Prague, respectively, in Scotland in 1992 to discuss the organisation and content of the exhibition *Prague 1891–1941*, which was held at the City Art Centre, Edinburgh, October 1994 to January 1995.
50. In conversation with me regarding several illustrations of 17th to 19th century architecture which I tabled during a discussion about traditional Scottish architecture held at 54 Marchmont Crescent, Edinburgh, 30 March 1989.
51. Arthur Herman, *The Scots' Invention of the Modern World* (London, 2002), p.vii.
52. Ibid., p.349.
53. Olive & Sydney Checkland, *Industry and Ethos: Scotland 1832–1914* (2nd ed) (Edinburgh, 1989), p.161.
54. Demetri Porphyrios (ed), 'Building and Rational Architecture', *Architectural Design*, 54, 5/6, 1984, pp.35–40, and Demetri Porphyrios (ed), 'Leon Krier: Houses, Palaces, Cities', *Architectural Design*, 54, 7/8, 1984, pp.20–128.
55. Henry Russell Hitchcock, *Architecture: Nineteenth and Twentieth Centuries* (Harmondsworth, 1963), p.63.
56. Ibid., p.72.
57. Collins, *Ideals*, p.95.
58. Stamp taught at the Mackintosh School of Architecture, Glasgow, in the late 1990s and, for a while, lived at 1 Moray Place, Glasgow, Thomson's former home.
59. Gavin Stamp, *Alexander Thomson: The Unknown Genius* (London, 1999), p.164.
60. Rudolph Schindler, 'Modern Architecture', in August Sarnitz, *RM Schindler, Architect, 1887–1953* (New York, 1988), p.57.
61. At the time of the Glasgow Group's (Charles Rennie Mackintosh, Margaret MacDonald Mackintosh, John McNair & Frances MacDonald McNair) presence at the VIIIth Viennese Secession Exhibition of 1900, Schindler would have been 13 years old. Arguably, his father, being a Viennese craftsman in metal and wood, could have taken him to see the exhibits. By the time Schindler began his architectural training in 1906, the Glasgow Group was a declining force on the European scene.
62. David B Brownlee & David G De Long, *Louis I Kahn: In the Realm of Architecture* (London, 1997), p.96.
63. Gavin Stamp, 'Mackintosh, Burnet and Modernity', in *Architectural Heritage III: The Age of Mackintosh* (Edinburgh, 1992), p.17.
64. Stamp, *Unknown Genius*, p.15.
65. Mary Miller, 'The Ice Man Melteth', in *The Scotsman Weekend: Festival Preview*, Saturday, 13 August 1994, p.7.
66. Hermann Muthesius (trans Janet Seligman & Stewart Spencer), *The English House: Volume 1 Development* (London, 2007) (orig, published Germany, 1904), footnote, pp.80–1.
67. GM Young (ed.), *Country and Town: A Summation of the Scott and Uthwatt Reports* (Harmondsworth, 1943), pp.19–20.
68. Paxman, *The English*, p.161.
69. Margaret Drabble, *A Writer's Britain: Landscape in Literature* (London, 1979), p.229.
70. Young, *Country and Town*, p.56.
71. Craig Beveridge & Ronald Turnbull, *The Eclipse of Scottish Culture: Inferiorism and the Intellectuals* (Edinburgh, 1989), p.25.
72. Hugh MacDiarmid, *Aesthetics in Scotland* (Edinburgh, 1984), p.21.
73. Eric Hobsbawm, *Nations and Nationalism since 1780: Programme, Myth, Reality* (2nd ed) (Cambridge, 1997), p.36.
74. Ibid., p.37.
75. Hobsbawn, *Nations*, p.90.
76. Drabble, *Writers*, p.174.
77. Smith, *Literature*, p.44.
78. Ibid., p.171.
79. Smith, *Literature*, p.43.
80. MacDiarmid, *Aesthetics*, p.92.
81. Ibid., pp.92–3.
82. Ibid., p.93.
83. Margaret Drabble, *The Radiant Way* (London, 1987), p.396.
84. McCrone, *Understanding*, p.3.
85. Deyan Sudjic, 'Identity in the City', in Steef Buijs, Wendy Tam, Devisari Tunis (eds), *Megacities: Exploring a*

Sustainable Future (Rotterdam, 2010), p.184.
86. James Gowan, *Style and Configuration* (London, 1994), p.8.
87. Neil Gillespie, 'Graubünden: a reflection', in Neil Gillespie & Laura Kinnaird (eds), *Stravaigers* (Edinburgh, 2015), p.51.
88. Historic Environment Scotland, Ref. no. LB22380, 1 June 1979, Category A.
89. Henri Focillon, *The Life of Forms in Art* (New York, 1992), p.144.
90. Ibid., p.152.
91. Ibid., p.144.
92. Milena Lamarová in Alexander von Vegesack (ed.), *Czech Cubism* (London, 1992), p.74.
93. Focillon, *Forms in Art*, p.154.
94. Peter Zumthor, *Thinking Architecture* (Baden, 1998), p.36.
95. Vladimir Lenin, *Our Foreign and Domestic Position and Party Tasks*, Report on the Work of the Council of People's Commissars, approved at the 8th Congress of Soviets, 22 December 1920.
96. Focillon, *Forms in Art*, p.46.
97. Michel Foucault, *The Order of Things* (rep.) (London, 1992), p.132.
98. Focillon, *Forms in Art*, pp.40–41.
99. Joseph Masheck, *Building-Art: Modern architecture in cultural construction* (Cambridge, 1993), p.173.
100. Ibid., p.174.
101. This and the succeeding sections are distilled from two extended unpublished essays on Czechoslovakian and Finnish national architectures.
102. David Dorward, *Scotland's Place-names*, (Edinburgh, 1995), p.5.
103. In office for two terms, 1946–1950 and 1950–6.
104. Quoted in Mikko Juva, 'A thousand years of Finland', in Hillar Kallas & Sylvie Nickels (eds), *Finland, Creation and Construction* (London, 1968), p.17.
105. Anthony Upton, 'Finnish Nationalism', in Hurst (ed), *States*, p.149.
106. Roy E H Mellor, *Geography of the USSR* (London, 1965), p.80.
107. Britain's concerns were, at home, the first Jacobite uprisings of 1715 and 1719; abroad, the war with Spain that commenced 1718. For Sweden, Karl XII's adventuring was to be his undoing in his death at Fredriksten in 1718 on an expedition against Norway.
108. James Macpherson, *Fragments of Ancient Poetry* (Edinburgh, 1760).
109. Hugh Cheape, 'Were but the white billow silver... Ossian and Macpherson', *The Scottish Book Collector*, vol.3, no.3, February–March 1992, p.22.
110. Smith, *Literature*, p.170. Smith references Hugh Blair (1718–1800), Scottish rhetorician; Madame Germaine de Stael (1766–1817), political theorist and host of a literary salon; Friedrich Gottlieb Klopstock (1724–1803), poet; Johan Heinrich Voss (1751–1826), translator of Homer; Johan Gottlieb Herder (1744–1803), philosopher.
111. A MacCallum Scott, *Suomi, the Land of the Finns* (London, 1926), p.95.
112. Arthur Reade, *Finland and the Finns* (London, 1915), pp.113–132. Reade's book, part travelogue, part pro-Finnish pamphlet, contains a chapter on the *Kalevala*.
113. Žižek, *Parallax*, p.153. Žižek includes an extract of the WF Kirby translation, which is worth reciting if only for the very incantatory or 'parallax' atmosphere it creates.
114. Reade, *Finland and the Finns*, p.28.
115. Upton in *States*, p.155.
116. Since 1961, the Gallen-Kallela Museo.
117. Hilding Ekelund (trans Edward Birse), *Architecture in Finland* (Helsinki, 1932), p.xxxix.
118. Riitta Nikula, *Armas Lindgren, 1874–1929, Architect* (Helsinki, 1988), p.149.
119. Paula Kivinen, Pekka Korvenmaa, Esa Piironen (eds), *Lars Sonck, 1870–1956, Architect* (Helsinki, undated), p.63. At the time, Glasgow Corporation ran one of the few municipal telephone companies in Britain. There may be some reciprocal architectural connections here, as I suggest in Roger Emmerson & Mary Tilmouth, *Matt Steele Architect: A Biography* (Edinburgh, 2010), pp.15–17 and 37–40.
120. A small watercolour of Edinburgh Castle by Saarinen is in the Saarinen collection in the National Architecture Museum, Helsinki. Cat. no.: Saarinen 98/145.
121. Nikula, *Lindgren*, p.149.
122. Kivinen et al, *Sonck*, p.9.
123. Marika Hausen, Kirmo Mikkola, Anna-Lisa Amberg, Tytti Valton (eds), *Eliel Saarinen, Projects, 1896–1923* (Cambridge, MA, 1990), p.13.
124. Nikula, *Landscape*, p.95.
125. Sixten Ringbom, *Stone, Style and Truth* (Helsinki, 1987), p.41. I acknowledge individual quotations in the text, but Ringbom's work forms a constant underpinning to my own observations.
126. Ibid., p.42.
127. Eliel Saarinen, *The Search for Form in Art and Architecture*, rep. (New York, 1985), p.ix.
128. Nikula, *Landscape*, p.96.
129. Quoted in Kivinen et al, *Sonck*, p.47.
130. Ibid., p.61.
131. MacCallum Scott, *Suomi*, pp.61–2.
132. Ibid., pp.64–5.

133. Kallas & Nickels, *Finland*, pp.33–4.
134. Swedish architect Ferdinand Boberg's (1860–1946) work showed knowledge of contemporary American architecture and was couched in simple formats such as the Energy Authority Main Station, Stockholm, 1892, with its Sullivanesque arched doorway of lightbulb frieze, cable reel roundels and radiant lamp finials which came to the attention of Finnish architects at the 1897 Stockholm Exhibition of recent Swedish architecture and resulted in a rash of Boberg doorways in the work of Finnish architects.
135. Despite the fact that only Lindgren of the three had any direct experience of such investigatory work, all were acquainted with it through the publications of their friends Blomstedt and Suckdorf.
136. His son, Hans Hendrick Sebastian Gripenberg, studied naval architecture at Glasgow University 1904–5.
137. Nikula, *Lindgren*, p.153.
138. Ibid., p.153.
139. Following the break-up of the partnership, Lindgren continued with the Museum on his own, and his classicising tendencies and the changing architectural climate produced some odd late interventions such as the gate to the inner courtyard, a northern version of a Renaissance fantasy such as one might encounter at the Paláccio da Pena, Sintra, Portugal.
140. Paul David Pearson, *Alvar Aalto and the International Style* (London, 1989), pp.12–13.
141. Ekelund, *Architecture in Finland*, p.xl.
142. Given the changing status of the country identified as Czechoslovakia and its constituents, and the changing status of its imperial ruler, it is important to clarify terminology here. In respect to the Austro-Hungarian Empire I have used that term to signify the empire following the *Ausgleich* of 1867 and its clear division into spheres of Austrian and Hungarian rule; prior to that date, the description 'Habsburg Empire' has been used. In respect to Czechoslovakia and the terms Czech and Slovak I have used them thus: in any reference to the joint country or culture prior to 1918 I have used the terms Czecho-Slovakia and Czecho-Slovak, references post-1918 are to Czechoslovakia and Czechoslovak; occasionally I have employed the terms Czechia or Czech where I believe the preponderance of material relates to Bohemia and Moravia. Similarly, if I believe the material to be substantially Slovakian I have so described it. Likewise, post the 'Velvet Divorce' of 1993, I have referred to the independent nations as the Czech Republic and Slovakia. Certain descriptions such as Czech Cubism, as standard art-world terminology, I have left untouched. Authors I have quoted have not necessarily followed the niceties of this prescription. See also Jan Rychlík, Thomas D. Marzik & Miroslav Bielik (eds), *R. W. Seton-Watson, Documents / Dokumenty 1906–1951*, vol.1, (Praha and Martin, 1995), p.12. Since 2016, Czechia has come into use as the officially-preferred name for the Czech Republic.
143. Czech and Slovak are Slavic languages with the same generic relationship to each other as Danish to Swedish or Scots to English, and culture, especially in the Moravian-Slovakian border lands, the Slovacko, has common roots.
144. Rychlík et. al, *Seton-Watson*, p.21. Seton-Watson's interests and agitation in the nascent nations of Europe included Romania, Yugoslavia, Poland and Finland in addition to Czechoslovakia, pp.198–9. I was visiting Brno at the date of the 1997 Devolution Referendum. My Czech hosts were horrified that Seton-Watson's 'model' union was set on the path of break-up, as they saw it. The 'Velvet Divorce' from Slovakia of 1993 was still troubling to many.
145. Petr Krajčí, 'From the General Jubilee Exhibition to the President's residence', in Roger Emmerson, Daniela Karasová, Petr Krajčí & Radomíra Sedláková, *Prague 1891–1941* (Edinburgh, 1994), p.7.
146. Alice Teichová, *The Czechoslovak Economy, 1918–1980* (London, 1988), p.3.
147. Ibid. p.17.
148. Michal Bregant et al, *Kubistická Praha*, Prague: Odeon, 1995, pp.142–3.
149. Jaroslava Staňková, Jiří Štursa, Svatopluk Voděra, *Pražská architektura* (Prague, 1991), p.290.
150. Radomíra Sedláková, 'Prague architecture between the two world wars', in Emmerson et al, *Prague 1891–1941*, p.20.
151. Herbert Read, *A Concise History of Modern Sculpture*, London: Thames and Hudson, 1964, p.54.
152. Rostislav Švácha, *The Architecture of New Prague, 1895–1945* (Cambridge MA, 1995), p.45.
153. Slovakian proscriptions on the use of the Hungarian language by Slovakia's 560,000 Hungarian minority are merely another round of a century-old cultural conflict. See *The Prague Post*, 22–8 November 1995, p.6.
154. The empire described itself as Imperial and Royal – Kaiserlich und Koeniglich – which gave rise to the shorthand

155. form, K.u.K. then 'Ka-Ka', used eschatologically to mean 'shit'.
Peter Vergo, *Art in Vienna, 1898–1918* (2nd ed) (Oxford, 1981), p.10.
156. These works now form the basis of the 20th-century French and Czech Cubist collections of the National Gallery in Prague and are housed at the Veletržní palác.
157. Irena Žantovská Murray, 'The burden of cubism: the French imprint on Czech architecture 1910–1914', in Eve Blau & Nancy J Troy (eds), *Architecture and Cubism* (Cambridge, MA, 1997), pp.41–57 provides a detailed account of these transactions.
158. Edward F Fry, *Cubism* (London, 1966), p.111.
159. Vlasta Čiháková-Noshiro, 'Quotation of the painting and the sculpture in the Czech Cubist architecture', in Olga Herbenová, Mílena Lamarová and Vlasta Čiháková-Noshiro, *Czechoslovakia: Cubism* (Tokyo, 1984), p.23.
160. Petr Wittlich, 'The road to Cubism', in *Czech Cubism*, p.28.
161. Vladimír Šlapeta, 'Cubism in architecture', in ibid., p.37.
162. Pavel Janák, 'Od moderní architektury k architekuře' (From modern architecture to architecture), *Styl*, vol.2, 1910, pp.105–9. Newly translated, as are all the Cubist texts by Janák, Kubišta, Hofman and Chochol, by Radomíra Sedláková, to whom my profound thanks are due.
163. Ibid., pp.105–9.
164. Ibid., pp.105–9.
165. Bohumil Kubišta, 'Předpoklady slohu' (Preconditions of style), *Přehled*, x2, 6.x.1911, pp.37–8.
166. Ibid., pp.37–8.
167. Vlastislav Hofman, 'Nový princip v architektuře' (A new principle in architecture), *Styl*, vol.5, 1913, pp.13–4.
168. Ibid., pp.13–4.
169. Ibid., pp.13–4.
170. Not to be confused with the Purism of Amédée Ozenfant and Le Corbusier.
171. Josef Chochol, 'K funkci architektonikého článku"(On the function of the architectonic element), *Styl* vol.2, 1913, pp.94–4.
172. Kubišta, 'Předpoklady slohu', in *Přehled*, pp.37–8.
173. David Cottington, 'The Maison Cubiste', in Blau & Troy, *Architecture and Cubism*, pp.17–34, notes Duchamp-Villon's contribution as an example of a 'provincial classicism' which had an 'equivocal character'.
174. Jan Sokol quoted in Šlapeta, 'Cubism in architecture', in *Czech Cubism*, p.39.
175. Serbs, Bosnians, Croatians and Slovenes.
176. S. Grant Duff, *Europe and the Czechs* (Harmondsworth, 1938), p.44.
177. Rychlík et al, *Seton-Watson*, p.252.
178. Seton Watson, *Documents*, p.83.
179. Grant Duff, *The Czechs*, p.54.
180. Borsi & Godoli, *Vienna 1900*, p.173, ill.184.
181. Drawing exhibited in the permanent Cubist exhibition at the dům U Černé Matky Boží, Ovocný trh, Prague.
182. Československá Obchodní Banka, *Na Poříčí 24* (Prague, 1994), p.7.
183. Michal Bregant, Lenka Bydžovská, Vojtěch Lahoda, Zdeněk Lukeš, Karel Srp, & Rostislav Švácha, *Kubistická Praha* (Prague, 1995), p.99.
184. Ibid., p.58.
185. Quoted by Vladimír Šlapeta in *Czech Cubism*, p.51.
186. Radomíra Sedláková, *Prague: an architectural guide* (Venice, 1997), p.105.
187. Karel Teige, 'Le Corbusier in Prague', in Miroslav Masák, Rostislav Švácha & Jindřich Vybíral (eds), *The Trade Fair Palace in Prague* (Prague, 1995), p.41.
188. Roger Emmerson, 'Acts of forgetting, acts of remembering', in *Prague*, p.6.

Chapter 2

1. James Fergusson & Robert Kerr, *History of Modern Styles of Architecture* (3rd ed) (London, 1891), p.xii.
2. Robert MacLeod, *Style and Society: Architectural Ideology in Britain 1835–1914* (London, 1971), p.68.
3. Collins, *Ideals*, p.132.
4. Ibid., p.142.
5. Tom Dyckhoff, *The Age of Spectacle: Adventures in Architecture and the 21st Century City* (London, 2017), p.220.
6. Ute Poerschke, 'Architecture as a Mathematical Function: Reflections on Gottfried Semper', Pennsylvania State University, n.d. Info at: link.springer.com/content/pdf/10.1007/s00004-011-0101-5.pdf, retrieved 23 July 2019.
7. Gottfried Semper, *Style* (Los Angeles, 2004), p.109.
8. Such is the fecundity of contemporary material and product development that a nine-digit classification system was devised in 2004 by the Constructions Specification Institute as referenced in Blaine Brownell (ed), *Transmaterial: A Catalog of Materials that Define Our Physical Environment* (New York, 2006), pp.7–13.
9. Semper, *Style*, p.109.
10. Gottfried Semper (trans Harry Francis Mallgrave & Wolfgang Hermann), *The Four Elements of Architecture and other writing* (Cambridge, 1989), p.267.
11. Harry Francis Mallgrave, *Gottfried Semper: Architect of the Nineteenth*

12. Century (New Haven, 1996), p.274.
12. Ibid., p.268.
13. John Ruskin, *The Stones of Venice* (3 vols.) (London, 1851–3).
14. Ruskin, *Seven Lamps*, pp.197–8.
15. William Burn designed the ashlar, Gothic elevations, 1829–33.
16. Fergusson, *Modern Styles*, p.xiii.
17. Augustus Northmore Welby Pugin and Charles Barry's (1795–1860) Houses of Parliament, Westminster, 1840–76 is frequently cited as the major influence on Stiedl Imre's (1839–1902) design for symmetricised neo-Gothic Hungarian Parliament, 1885–1904.
18. For example, Hippolyte Jean Blanc, 'Scottish Ecclesiastical Architecture in the Fourteenth and Fifteenth Centuries', in *The Builder*, vol.LXXIV, March 1898, pp.272–81.
19. James Stephens Curl, *Victorian Architecture* (Newton Abbot, 1990), p.30.
20. MacLeod, *Style*, p.84.
21. Francastel, *Art and Technology*, p.95.
22. John Ruskin, *Sesame and Lilies* (London, 1893), p.153.
23. John Ruskin, *Lectures on Architecture and Painting Delivered at Edinburgh November 1853* (London, 1854), p.76.
24. Ibid., p.6. and Fig. 1.
25. Robert William Billings, *The Baronial and Ecclesiastical Antiquities of Scotland* (4 vols.) (Edinburgh, 1847–52).
26. 'Harling', Scots term for rendering with lime and small stones or simply lime and sand. From 'harl', Scots to drag roughly over a surface.
27. Billings, *Baronial*, p.6.
28. *The Edinburgh Guardian*, November 19, 1853.
29. Ruskin, *Edinburgh Lectures*, Lecture 1, Plate III, fig.6.
30. Wilhelm Worringer (trans Michael Bullock), *Abstraction and Empathy: A Contribution to the Psychology of Style* (Chicago, 1997) (first published in 1908 in German as *Abstraktion und Einfühlung*), p.4.
31. Ibid., p.4.
32. Gavin Stamp (ed) *The Light of Truth and Beauty: The Lectures of Alexander 'Greek' Thomson 1817–1875* (Glasgow, 1999), p.111. This is from Lecture I of Thomson's Haldane Lecture series, 'Art and Architecture: A Course of Four Lectures, No.I. Introductory', given at the Haldane Institute Glasgow in the Spring of 1874.
33. McLeod, *Style*, p.85. McLeod's prescription, made in 1971, regarding the continuity of Classicism in Scotland is largely unchallenged today, although it was based on aesthetic distinctions and a superficial assessment of the Scottish psyche. McLeod said that it was slightly easier to [reject the Gothic revival] in Scotland [because] there was a stronger reformation tradition which tended to shy away from anything implicitly catholic in its associations.
This ignores the considerable involvement of the Church of England in the Gothic Revival. He went on:
There was a proud consciousness of the classical contribution of 18th-century Scots such as William Chambers and the Adam father and sons. Such unique, indigenous tradition as there was had a strong infusion of French Renaissance influence, and the artistic and cultural connections with France and the Low Countries persisted. It could perhaps be argued that there was in the national character a greater attachment to the rational and to intellectual discipline than to the empirical and emotive.
34. Ronald McFadzean, *The Life and Works of Alexander Thomson* (London, 1979), p.262.
35. Nicholson is the grandfather of Thomson's wife.
36. Steven M Cahn, 'Immanuel Kant', in Steven M Cahn (ed), *Classics of Western Philosophy* (3rd ed) (Indianapolis, 1977), p.931.
37. Immanuel Kant, 'Prolegomena to Any Future Metaphysics', in ibid., p.982.
38. Ibid., footnote.38, p.982.
39. Bill Hare, *Scottish Artists in an Age of Radical Change: 1945 to the 21st Century* (Edinburgh, 2019), p.52.
40. JM Bernstein, *The Fate of Art: Aesthetic Alienation from Kant to Derrida to Adorno* (Cambridge, 1993), p.1.
41. Archibald Alison, *Essays on the Nature and Principles of Taste* (Edinburgh, 1815), p.118.
42. Ibid., p.121.
43. Ibid., p.138.
44. Ibid., p.142.
45. Ibid., p.153.
46. Ibid., p.156.
47. Ibid., p.156.
48. Ibid., p.195.
49. Ibid., p.441.
50. Reprinted in 1899, 1900, 1901, 1908 and 1909 (and, revealing its continuing influence, in 2000 and 2008).
51. Billings, *Baronial*, vol.1, p.1.
52. Ibid., p.5.
53. Ibid., p.3 above.
54. Ibid., p.3 below.
55. Glendinning et al, *History*, p.276.
56. Billings, *Baronial*, vol.1, p.2.
57. Muthesius, *English House*, pp. 993–4.
58. Lynch, *Scotland*, p.359.
59. N Ferguson, *Empire*, p.40.
60. Lynch, *Scotland*, pp.357–8.
61. Ibid., p.354.
62. Ibid., p.355.

63. Alan Calder, *James McLaren: Arts & Crafts Pioneer* (Donnington, 2008), p.12. Taken from Browne's Pugin Travelling Studentship Report of 1878.
64. Ian Campbell, 'A Romanesque Revival and the Early Renaissance in Scotland c.1380–1513', *Journal of the Society of Architectural Historians*, 54:3, September 1995, p.303
65. William Ferguson, *The Identity of the Scottish Nation: An Historic Quest* (Edinburgh, 1998), pp.15–6.
66. Ibid., p.9.
67. Campbell, *Romanesque*, p.312.
68. Fawcett, Richard, *The Architectural History of Scotland: Scottish Architecture from the Accession of the Stewarts to the Reformation* (Edinburgh, 1994), p.xvii.
69. Mark Baines, 'Exploring the Wall: the Urban Façades of Alexander Thomson', in Gavin Stamp & Sam McKinstry (eds), *'Greek' Thomson* (Edinburgh, 1999), pp.115–33.
70. Maurice Craig, 'James Fergusson', in John Summerson (ed), *Concerning Architecture: Essays on Architectural Writers and Writing Presented to Nikolaus Pevsner* (London, 1968), p.145.
71. Stamp, *Light*, pp.25–39.
72. James Fergusson, *An historical inquiry into the true principles of beauty in art, more especially with reference to architecture* (London, 1849), ill.12, p.249 and description, p.250: among the temples of the period still existing in Egypt, by far the most perfect and complete is that of Edfou.
73. Stamp, *Light*, p.31.
74. Ibid. p.33.
75. Ibid., p.32.
76. Ibid., p.34.
77. Worringer, *Abstraction*, p.79.
78. Ibid., p.82.
79. Stamp, *Light*, p.27.
80. Ibid., p.144.
81. Kant in Cahn, *Classics*, p.981.
82. HL Mansell & J Veitch (eds), *William Hamilton: Lectures of Metaphysics and Logic* (2 vols.) (Edinburgh, 1859 & 1860).
83. Beveridge & Turnbull, *Eclipse*, p.111.
84. Mansell & Veitch, *Hamilton*, p.203.
85. Listed on the Alexander Thomson Society website at The Lost Library, retrieved 23 May 2019.
86. Thomson and his then partner Baird married the Nicholson sisters in 1847, while in an odd parallelism, some fifty years later, Mackintosh and his colleague McNair married the MacDonald sisters.
87. P Nicholson, *The Principles of Architecture* (3 vols.) (London, 1809), p.107.
88. David M Walker, 'The Development of Thomson's Style: The Scottish Background', in Stamp & McKinstry, *Greek*, p.27. Fig.3.4 illustrates a design by Michael Angelo Nicholson from the Nicholsons' *New Practical Builder* of 1825 that embodies some of the motives that Thomson would more fully develop.
89. Ibid., p.v.
90. Fergusson, *True Principles*, pp.342–58.
91. Ibid., p.516.
92. Ibid., p.94.
93. Joe Rock, *Thomas Hamilton Architect 1784–1858* (Edinburgh, 1984), pp.40–7.
94. Ibid., cover. *Perspective* by David Roberts.
95. Ibid., p.73.
96. Stamp, *Light*, p.72.
97. Ibid., p.55. From the lecture 'The unsuitableness of Gothic Architecture to Modern Circumstances'. Thomson repeated a version of this in Haldane Lecture IV (ibid., p.168). Thomson may have got this from his grandfather-in-law Peter Nicholson, 'Propositions respecting the Mechanical Power of the wedge', *Philosophical Magazine*, 1798, pp.316–9.
98. Ibid., p.34.
99. Ibid., p.37.
100. Ibid., p.114, from Lecture I.
101. Ibid., p.170, Lecture IV.
102. Ibid., p.125, from Lecture II.
103. Ibid., pp.41–8.
104. C Bruce Allen, Architect, *Cottage Building or, Hints for Improving the Dwellings of the Labouring Classes* (London, 1849), pp.35–7. Several versions of a 'rat-trap' bond (recently revived in India by Laurie Baker (1917–2007) for the same economic, climatic and vermin-resistant reasons) are shown. The cavity wall comprising two leaves of brickwork connected by galvanised metal wall ties appears in some building construction textbooks from the 1890s onwards, though not in Jaggard & Drury's *Architectural Building Construction* of 1916, not even in its subsequent editions up to 1950. Allen's book was in the Philosophical Society collection, available to Thomson.
105. Stamp, *Light*, p.57.
106. Pamela Robertson, 'Mackintosh and Italy', in Pamela Robertson (ed), *Charles Rennie Mackintosh: The Architectural Papers* (Cambridge MA, 1990), pp.86–7, n.6.
107. Kenneth Frampton & David Larkin, *American Masterworks: the Twentieth Century House* (New York, 1995), p.38.
108. When I visited the house in 1988, it was still in use as a convent. The dining room was made into a chapel and the altar stood in the sideboard recess lit from the skylight above as if it were in a Baroque church.
109. Dismantled stone-by-stone, transported

110. by Trans-Siberian Railway and rebuilt two hours north of Tokyo, Japan in 1987 by the Asian film star Tsugawa Masahiko and renamed Lockheart Castle. Info at: scotsman.com/whats-on/arts-and-entertainment/man-who-moved-scottish-mansion-japan-840218 and canmore.org.uk/site/200121/milton-lockhart-house, both retrieved 20 November 2020.
110. Blackie & Son, *Villa and Cottage Architecture: select examples of country and suburban residences recently erected; with a full descriptive notice of each building* (London, 1868).
111. Lecture given to the Alexander Thomson Society, 6 April 2018, at the St Vincent Street UP Church, entitled 'Respecting The Past, Creating The Future'.
112. W Audsley & G Audsley, *Cottage, Lodge and Villa Architecture* (London, 1862), pp.4–9.
113. Neil Jackson, email from Jackson to Emmerson, 1 March 2021.
114. David M Breiner, *Bowling Green Offices Building*, New York City: Landmarks Preservation Commission Report, September 1995, Designation List 266, LP-1927, p.3.
115. Duncan is best-known for his Wolcott Hotel, 1902–4, and Grant's Tomb (based on the Mausoleum at Halicarnassus), 1897, both New York.
116. Some 15 Audsley drawings are held uncatalogued and undigitised in the Audsley Collection at the Stuart Weitzman School of Design, University of Pennsylvania from which these references were taken. My special thanks to Archivist Heather Isbell Schumacher for her invaluable help in this connection. Reference email correspondence Schumacher/Emmerson between 5 and 21 April 2021.
117. Stamp, *Unknown Genius*, p.14.
118. Stamp, *Light*, p.71.
119. Ibid., p.58.
120. Duncan McAra, *Sir James Gowans: Romantic Rationalist* (Edinburgh, 1975), p.1.
121. Ibid., p.25.
122. Gowans also worked in conventional ashlar construction but with the 2ft module either implicit as at Castle Terrace, 1866–70, or partially expressed as at Blacket Place, 1860–1, both Edinburgh.
123. Such a stone would weigh 30kg, which is comparable with the present-day HSE-approved lifting load limit for one tradesperson of 25kg. By way of contrast, a conventional ashlar block would weigh ca. 90kg.
124. McAra, *Gowans*, p.24.
125. McCrone, *Understanding*, p.10.
126. David Walker, 'Mackintosh on Architecture', in Robertson, *Papers*, p.153.
127. The Pre-Raphaelite Brotherhood [sic] was formed in 1848.
128. Muthesius, *English House, Volume 1*, p.77.
129. Frank Arneil Walker, 'The Significance of the Folk House', in John Frew & David Jones (eds), *Scotland and Europe: Architecture and Design 1850–1940* (St Andrews, 1991), p.55.
130. Collins, *Ideals*, p.122.
131. Annmarie Adams, 'Peter Collins: A Study in Parallax', *Journal of Architectural Education*, ACSA, vol.59, no.2, October 2005. Info at: mcgill.ca/architecture/files/architecture/2005petercollinspdf, retrieved 7 June 2018.
132. Rudolph Schindler, 'Care of the Body', *Los Angeles Times*, 18 April 1926, in Sarnitz, *Schindler*, p.46.
133. Collins, *Ideals*, p.178.
134. Walker, in Frew & Jones, *Scotland and Europe*, p.54.
135. Miles Glendinning & Aonghus MacKechnie, *Scotch Baronial: Architecture and National Identity in Scotland* (London & New York, 2021), p.200.

Chapter 3

1. Paul Groenendijk, Piet Vollard & Han van Dijk, *Guide to Modern Architecture in the Netherlands* (Rotterdam, 1987), p.14.
2. Hendrik Petrus Berlage (trans Iain Boyd White & Wim De Wit), 'Thoughts on Style in Architecture' (1905), in *Thoughts on Style 1886–1909* (Santa Monica CA, 1996), p.143.
3. Burgin, *In/different*, p.4.
4. Berlage, 'Architecture's Place in Modern Aesthetics' (1886), in *Thoughts*, p.96.
5. Iain Boyd White, 'Introduction', in ibid., pp.44–5.
6. Berlage, 'Art and Society' (1909), in ibid., p.292.
7. Berlage, 'Thoughts on Style in Architecture' (1905), in ibid., pp.150–1.
8. Ibid., pp.137–40.
9. Muthesius, *English House*. Scottish architects and designers take up nearly 20 per cent of the section 'B, the development of the modern English house under younger architects'.
10. Ibid., pp.76–7.
11. Ibid., p.81.
12. Collins, *Ideals*, p.101.
13. Muthesius, *English House*, p.177.
14. Ibid., p.76.
15. Ibid., p.209.
16. Yehuda Safran, Wilfried Wang & Michael Budny, *The Architecture of Adolf Loos* (2nd ed) (London, 1987), p.97.
17. Safran et al, *Loos*, p.97.
18. Joseph Masheck, *Adolf Loos: The Art of Architecture* (London, 2013), p.74.
19. Quoted in Jeannine Fiedler & Peter

20. Feierabend, *Bauhaus* (Cologne, 2002), p.271.
21. Herman, *Enlightenment*, p.271.
22. Loos, 'Cultural Degeneration', in Safran et al, *Loos*, p.98.
23. *Das Andere: Ein Blatt Zur Einfuehrung Abendlaender Kultur In Oesterreich* (*The Other: A Magazine for the Introduction of Occidental Culture to Austria*) was the title of his self-published magazine, which ran for two issues in 1903.
24. Loos, 'Vernacular Art', in ibid., p.110.
25. Ibid., p.110.
26. Loos, 'Cultural Degeneration', in ibid., p.98.
27. Masheck, *Loos*, p.53.
28. Dietmar Steiner, 'The Strength of the Old Masters: Adolf Loos and Antiquity', in ibid., p.23.
29. Loos, 'Vernacular Art', in Safran et al, *Loos*, p.113.
30. Ibid., p.113.
31. Ibid., p.112.
32. Berlage, *Thoughts*, p.96.
33. Loos, 'Architecture', in Safran et al, *Loos*, p.108.
34. Loos, 'Ornament and Crime', in ibid., p.102.
35. Ruskin, *Seven Lamps*, pp.189–90.
36. Loos, 'Culture', in Safran et al, *Loos*, p.97.
37. Muthesius, *English House*, p.77.
38. Adam Ardrey, *Finding Arthur: The Origins of the Once and Future King* (London, 2013).
39. EM Forster, *Howard's End* (London, 1976), p.262.
40. Hobsbawm, *Nations*, p.108.
41. JRR Tolkien, *The Lord of the Rings* (London, 1954–5).
42. Brennan-Inglis, *Scotland's Castle*, p.51, writes,
On a simple count of castles restored from a ruinous state between 1800 and 1945, the majority of rebuilding was carried out between 1887 and 1920, i.e., the 30 years or so after publication [of MacGibbon & Ross].
43. MacGibbon & Ross, *Castellated and Domestic*, p.v.
44. Ibid., p.v.
45. Ibid., pp.v and vi.
46. Ibid., p.vii.
47. Ibid., p.viii.
48. Ibid., p.234, Fig.192, sections and p.236, Fig.194, external form.
49. Ibid., p.238, Fig.196, plans and sections, p.242, Fig.196, external form.
50. Ibid., p.201, showing attached 'modern' (18th century) house.
51. Ibid., p.345, Fig.296, external view; p.346, Fig.297, plans; p.348, Fig.299, section; p.349, Fig.300, section.
52. Ibid., p.359.
53. Robertson, 'Seemliness', in *Papers*, 1902, p.220.
54. Ibid., p.221.
55. Allen, *Cottage Building*, p.1.
56. Nicholson, *Principles*, p.38.
57. Richard Rodger, *Housing the People: the Colonies of Edinburgh* (Edinburgh, 1999).
58. Ibid., pp.57–8.
59. Perilla & Juliet Kinchin with J Neil Baxter, *Glasgow's Great Exhibitions: 1888, 1901, 1911, 1938, 1988* (Bicester, ca. 1988), p.17.
60. Borsi & Godoli, *Vienna*, p.105.
61. Niall Ferguson, *Empire: How Britain Made the Modern World* (London, 2004), pp.221–2.
62. Eric Hobsbawm, *Fractured Times: Culture and Society in the Twentieth Century* (London, 2014), p.118.
63. Kinchin & Kinchin, *Great Exhibitions*, p.56.
64. Glendinning et al, *History*, pp.333–84. While I take exception to several of their contentions, I am indebted to their scholarship and have shamelessly plundered their useful taxonomy to pursue three notions of my own: the theoretical and political subtext to Scottish architecture; the derivation of the abstract components of Scottish architecture; and the significance of the 'appropriate' material in Scottish architecture.
65. Ibid., p.340.
66. F Walker, 'National Romanticism', in George Gordon (ed), *Perspectives of the Scottish City* (Aberdeen, 1985), p.152.
67. McWilliam, *Scottish Townscape*, p.156.
68. Robertson, *Papers*, Charles Rennie Mackintosh, lecture on 'Seemliness', 1902, p.223.
69. I do not pretend to have more than scratched the surface of the Mackintosh bibliography.
70. Alistair Moffat, *Remembering Charles Rennie Mackintosh* (Lanark, 1989), p.125. Letter from Mackintosh to his wife, 17 May 1927.
71. Calder, *McLaren*, Appendix A. Calder references McLaren's paper, 'of the Practice of Modern Architecture', published in the Architectural Association Notes IV (1889), pp.56–8, observing that Mackintosh seemed to have adapted part of that paper.
72. Frank Arneil Walker, 'Scottish Baronial Architecture', in Robertson, *Papers*, no.37, p.47.
73. Moffat, *Remembering*, p.40. Letter from Mackintosh to Herman Muthesius, 5 January 1903.
74. James Macaulay, in Robertson, *Papers*, p.127.
75. David Walker, in ibid., p.153.
76. Ibid., p.210. From Mackintosh's lecture 'Architecture' of 1893.
77. Ibid., p.52. From Mackintosh's lecture 'Scotch Baronial Architecture' of 1891.
78. Robert MacLeod, *Charles Rennie*

78. *Mackintosh: Architect and Artist* (London, 1983), p.90.
78. Kenneth Frampton, *Modern Architecture: A Critical History* (London, 2007), p.77.
79. MacLeod, *Mackintosh*, p.87.
80. Dictionary of Scottish Architects, entries for John Keppie and Charles Rennie Mackintosh.
81. Pevsner, *Pioneers*, p.175.
82. Ibid., p.171.
83. MacLeod, *Mackintosh*, p.7.
84. Ibid., pp. 135–44.
85. Ibid., p.149.
86. Vergo, *Art in Vienna*, p.179.
87. *Katalog der Internationalen Kunstschau Wien 1909* (Wien, 1909), p.48.
88. Vergo, *Art in Vienna*, p.202.
89. Mackintosh adopted JD Sedding's (1838–91) aphorism 'There is hope in honest error, none in the icy perfections of the mere stylist' as his personal motto.
90. Jane Kallir, *Viennese Design and the Wiener Werkstätte* (London, 1986), p.56.
91. Roger Bilcliffe, *Charles Rennie Mackintosh: The Complete Furniture, Furniture Drawings and Interior Designs* (2nd ed) (Guildford & London, 1980), pp.9–10.
92. Peter Vergo, *Vienna 1900: Vienna, Scotland and the European Avant-Garde* (Edinburgh, 1983), pp.31–2.
93. Kallir, *Viennese Design*, pp.68–71.
94. Masheck, *Loos*, pp.193–5.
95. Adolf Sarnitz, *Adolf Loos 1870–1933: Architect, Cultural Critic, Dandy* (Köln, 2003), p.80.
96. Kimura Hiroaki, 'Charles Rennie Mackintosh', *Process*, 50, August 1984, p.50.
97. Kallir, *Wiener Werkstätte*, p.126, ill.173.
98. Bilcliffe, *Mackintosh Furniture*, p.19.
99. Borsi & Godoli, *Vienna*, p.258. See also p.269, ill.326, the Women's Room at the Café Heinrich-Hof, Vienna.
100. Ibid., p.104, ill.118.
101. HS Goodhart-Rendell, *Architectural Review*, 53, January 1923, p.31.
102. Moffat, *Remembering*, p.100. WJ Bassett-Lowke, *A memoire*, 1939.
103. Moffat, *Remembering*, p.93. In a letter to Moffat, Philip Mairet (Ashbee's assistant and Geddes' biographer) recalled sharing a room with Mackintosh, who was working on the Indian designs at the time.
I was working at the wall lecture diagrams for Patrick Geddes, and Mackintosh was doing some plans, also, as I understood, for Geddes. Were these the drawings of something Geddes wanted to take back to India with him, I wonder? I remember nothing clearly, except that the work seemed as if inspired by Japan (like the work of Frank Lloyd Wright. The elevation of a building with a kind of pergola reminded of the work of Wright, whose work was already known in the office of CR Ashbee where I had worked). I knew enough to be impressed by the originality of Mackintosh's conception and the skill of his draughtsmanship. His personality, unfortunately, did not make a very congenial impression on me – but this was chiefly because his aura was suffused with the alcoholic potations to which he was addicted. About this I was perhaps rather puritanical. But on the other hand, we got on friendlily enough, and I attributed his evident intemperance to the trials and tribulations he had just been through.
104. Welter, *Biopolis*, pp.128–9, Table 5.1.
105. Philip Boardman, *The Worlds of Patrick Geddes: Biologist, Town Planner, Re-educator, Peace-warrior* (London, 1978), p.253.
106. Ibid., p.256.
107. Welter, *Biopolis*, p.23.
108. Glendinning et al, *History*, p.349.
109. With the onset of WWI, Schultz changed his name to become Robert S Weir.
110. Welter, *Biopolis*, p.19.
111. Comparable, perhaps, to what has recently been dubbed the 'Anthropocene' to designate a new age post-1945 when the detonation of the atom bomb at Hiroshima and Nagasaki was deemed to have ended the Holocene, if not potentially the human race.
112. Welter, *Biopolis*, p.18, quoting Geddes.
113. Ibid., p.15.
114. Ibid., p.18.
115. Ibid., p.18.
116. Checklands, *Ethos*, p.172.
117. Ibid., p.174.
118. Ibid., p.175.
119. Ibid., p.178.
120. Michael Fry, *Scottish Empire*, p.273.
121. Harold James, 'German Experience and British Cultural Exceptionalism', in Bruce Collins & Keith Robbins (eds), *British Culture and Economic Decline* (London, 1990), p.92.
122. Lynch, *Scotland*, p.422.
123. Ibid., p.425.
124. Stamp, *Light*, p.39.
125. Stamp, 'Burnet', in Nuttgens, *Contemporaries*, p.17.
126. Andor Gomme & David Walker, *Architecture of Glasgow* (London 1968), pp.204–5.
127. The Athenaeum tower bears a generic similarity to that of Allegheny Courthouse and Jail, Pennsylvania, 1883, by Henry Hobson Richardson, whose work was widely published in Britain in the closing decades of the 19th century. Charles Follen McKim, who preceded Burnet at the École de Beaux-Arts, and his subsequent partner, Stanford White (1853–1906), were Richardson's apprentices from 1870–2. There may be nothing more to this than proximity.
128. Macleod, *Style*, p.123.

129. Daniel Hudson Burnham, with his partner John Wellborn Root (1840–91), designed several early skyscrapers: the Rookery, Chicago, 1886; the Reliance, Chicago, 1890–5; Marshall Field, Chicago, 1891 and the Monadnock, Chicago, 1891. Following Root's death, Burnham completed the World's Colombian Exhibition, Chicago, 1893 and the Flat Iron Building, New York, 1901.
130. Stamp, 'Burnet', in Nuttgens, *Contemporaries*, p.13.
131. Louis H Sullivan, *Kindergarten Chats and other writings* (New York, 1978) (reprint of 1918 ed), pp.132–3.
132. Ibid., p.131.
133. The 'white city' motif resurfaced in *America the Beautiful*, first published as a national song in 1910, which describes America as a 'wilderness' [sic] ripe for occupation 'from sea to shining sea' with 'alabaster cities'.
134. Ibid., p.65.
135. Ibid., p.180.
136. Frank Lloyd Wright, *An Autobiography* (London, 1977), p.119.
137. David Gebhard (Patricia Gebhard, ed), *Purcell & Elmslie: Prairie Progressive Architects* (Layton, 2006), pp.28–45; Robert Winder, 'George Grant Elmslie and the Crucible of Creation'. Info at: www.youtube.com/watch?v=icbyUqPM3yE, 24 April 2020, and Richard L Kronick, 'George Elmslie: In the Shadow of Louis Sullivan'. Info at: www.youtube.com/watch?v=B8deg1ex40, 7 December 2020, both retrieved 25 August 2021. Also email from Emmerson to Kronick, 7 September 2021 and Kronick to Emmerson, 8 September 2021.
138. Frank Lloyd Wright, *The Natural House* (New York, 1954), p.21.
139. Not until the Indian Citizenship Act of 1924 were Native Americans given full legal rights, though that did not immediately resolve their societal status.
140. Patrick Pinnell, 'Academic Tradition and Individual Talent', in Robert McCarter (ed), *On and By Frank Lloyd Wright: A Primer of Architectural Principles* (London, 2005), pp.21–3.
141. Wright, *The Natural House*, p.35.
142. Kenneth Frampton, 'The Text-Tile Tectonic', in McCarter, *Wright*, p.187.
143. The Homestead Act of 1862 opened up South Dakota to settlement where a 160-acre (65ha) plot could be had for $18 (ca. $500 or $3 an acre today). In Scotland, it is difficult to come to terms with how recent is this American history of the settler occupation of native and/or virgin territory. For example, Alexander Thomson's three great churches bracket the above date 1857–67.
144. Masheck, *Loos*, 'Loosian vernacular', pp.33–61, takes as comparative reference of Bishop Berkeley's 'Whitehall', Middletown, Rhode Island, altered 1739–30, which demonstrates a fair degree of sophistication in its planning and the subtle asymmetry of the front elevation; a seemingly local convention.
145. Wright, *Natural House*, p.37.
146. Dakotan sod houses were often built into the dirt banks from which the sods had been cut for the construction of their front and partial side walls. Certainly horizontal, but not as conceived by Wright.
147. Wright, *An Autobiography*, p.198.
148. Ibid., p.254.

Chapter 4

1. The Daily Express, *These Tremendous Years: 1919–1938* (London, 1938), pp.66–70.
2. Stephen Kern, *The Culture of Time and Space 1880–1918* (Cambridge MA, 1983), p.14.
3. Emmerson & Tilmouth, *Steele*, pp.15–7.
4. N Ferguson, *Empire*, p.323.
5. Lynch, *Scotland*, p.424.
6. McKean, *Thirties*, p.15.
7. Gavin Bond, *Fascist Scotland* (Edinburgh, 2013), p.11.
8. Ibid., p.31.
9. Lynch, *Scotland*, p.422. There are no certified figures for Scottish war dead; these are upper and lower estimates.
10. Ibid., p.423.
11. Ibid., p.423.
12. Alexander McArthur & H Kingsley Long, *No Mean City* (11th imp) (London, 1943), p.vi.
13. Lynch, *Scotland*, p.324.
14. MacDiarmid, *Aesthetics*, p.76.
15. Lynch, *Scotland*, p.440.
16. Ibid., p.438.
17. Sergio Polano, 'De Stijl / Architecture = Nieuwe Beelding', in Mildred Friedman (ed), *De Stijl: 1917–1931, Visions of Utopia* (Oxford, 1982), p.87.
18. Ibid., p.90.
19. Ibid., p.96, ills. 58–60 and caption.
20. Ibid., pp.100 and 104, figs.63 and 64.
21. Wright, *Entwurfe*, pl.xlv.
22. Ibid., p.30, fig.15.
23. Achim Borchardt-Hume (ed) *Malevich* (London, 2014), pp.176–8, figs.160, 161, 162.
24. Friedman, *De Stijl*, pp.102 and 30, fig.14.
25. Ibid., p.128, fig.88.
26. Ibid., p.105.
27. Christina Lodder, *Russian Constructivism* (New Haven CT &

28. *Theo van Doesburg: on European Architecture* (trans Charlotte I Loeb & Arthur L Loeb) (Basel, 1990), p.107.
29. Ibid., p.109.
30. Ibid., p.115.
31. Ibid., p.115.
32. Le Corbusier, *Towards*, p.210.
33. Panel housing. The prefabricated concrete panel construction systems for mass housing that sprang up throughout Czechoslovakia in the immediate post-WWII period. It has to be said, however, that space standards in these apartments are considerably better than the minimum envisaged by the Modernists. I have stayed in such apartments in two peripheral estates in Prague and one in Hradec Králové.
34. Corbusier, *Towards*, p.10.
35. Ibid., pp.114–5.
36. Decades later, Alvar Aalto warned architects to 'photograph your building before the client takes possession'.
37. Rudolf Schindler, 'Space Architecture', from *Dune Forum* (Oceano CA, February 1934), pp.44–6, in Sarnitz, *Schindler*, pp.50–1.
38. Rudolf Schindler, 'Notes: Modern Architecture', unpublished, September 1944, in ibid., p.57.
39. Le Corbusier, *The Journey to the East* (trans Ivan Žaknić) (Cambridge MA, 1987).
40. Nicholas Fox Weber, *Le Corbusier: A Life* (New York, 2008), p.318.
41. Ibid., p.318.
42. Bachelard, *Poetics*, p.63.
43. Weber, *Le Corbusier*, p.318.
44. Christian Norberg-Schulz, *Principles of Modern Architecture* (London, 2000), p.89.
45. Neil Jackson, *Japan and the West: An Architectural Dialogue* (London, 2019), pp.304–5.
46. Tim Benton, 'Le Corbusier and the vernacular plain'. Info at: archivio.archiphoto.it/2011/01/25/tim-benton_le-corbusier-and-the-vernacular-plain/, retrieved 9 October 2020.
47. Weber, *Le Corbusier*, p.286.
48. Peter Adam, *Eileen Gray: Her Life and Work* (London, 2019), p.216.
49. Caroline Constant, *Eileen Gray* (London, 2007), p.190.
50. Tom Wilkinson, *Bricks & Mortals* (London, 2014), p.269.
51. Le Corbusier's other works in existing buildings were the Beistegui apartment 1930 – essentially an interior and roof terrace – and the Villa Church, Ville d'Avray, 1927, a series of pavilions linked to an existing neo-classical main house (all since destroyed).
52. Near the entrance is an ambiguous line drawing of what could be read as a seated man voyeuristically viewing two women engaged in a sex act.
53. Constant, *Gray*, pp.122–5.
54. Peter Davidson, 'Democratic Classicism', in Gillespie & Kinnaird, *Stravaigers*, p.21.
55. Karen A Franck, 'A Feminist Approach to Architecture', in Ellen Perry Berkeley & Matilda McQuaid (eds), *Architecture: A Place For Women* (Washington, 1989), p.201.
56. *Die Gläserne Kette*, the Glass Chain was a chain letter initiated by Bruno Taut (1880–1938) and exchanged between Expressionist architects, among whom were Bruno Taut and his brother Max (1884–1967), the Luckhardt brothers Wassili (1889–1972) and Hans (1890–1954), Hermann Finsterlin (1887–1973) and Hans Scharoun (1893–1972) (while Gropius was associated with the group, he did not contribute publicly to the chain letter, preferring to exchange correspondence directly with Taut). Most of the group, with the signal exception of Scharoun, were to abandon an overt Expressionism by the late 1920s or earlier.
57. Reginald Isaacs, *Gropius: an Illustrated Biography of the Creator of the Bauhaus* (Boston, 1991), p.65.
58. Walter Gropius, *The Scope of Total Architecture* (London, 1956) (based on writings and practice 1925–53), p.109.
59. Ibid., p.16.
60. Fiona MacCarthy, *Walter Gropius: Visionary Founder of the Bauhaus* (London, 2020), p.483.
61. Gropius, *Scope*, p.98.
62. Kate Fox, *Watching the English: The Hidden Rules of English Behaviour* (London, 2004), p.12.
63. Peter Hall, *Cities of Tomorrow* (3rd ed) (Oxford, 2002), p.246.
64. Bachelard, *Poetics*, p.47–8.
65. Gropius, *Scope*, p.113.
66. Bachelard, *Poetics*, p.26–7. Bachelard's reference to verticality derives from his requirement that a 'home' have an attic and a cellar.
67. Burgin, *In/different*, p.26.
68. Ibid., p.43.
69. Collins, *Ideals*, p.231.
70. Ibid., pp.94–5.
71. Janna Levin, *Black Hole Blues, and Other Songs from Outer Space* (London, 2016), p.79.
72. Robert McCarter, 'The Integrated Ideal', in McCarter, *Wright*, pp.21–3.
73. Chris Hawthorne, writer/director, *That Far Corner: Frank Lloyd Wright in Los Angeles*, KCETOnline: LaBella Films, 2018. Info at: www.youtube.com/watch?v+3juSckHif9o, retrieved 4 April 2019.
74. Michael Curtiz, director, *Female*, Warner Brothers, 1933.
75. William Castle, director, *House on*

76. *Haunted Hill*, Allied Artists, 1958.
76. John Schlesinger, director, *The Day of the Locust*, Paramount, 1974.
77. Ridley Scott, director, *Blade Runner*, Warner Brothers, 1982.
78. David Benioff, DB Weiss, *Game of Thrones*, HBO Entertainment, 2011–9, adapted from George RR Martin, *A Song of Ice and Fire*.
79. Frampton, 'The Text-Tile Tectonic', in MacCarter, *Wright*, p.184.
80. Rudolf Schindler, letter to Philip Johnson, 9 March 1932, Sarnitz, *Schindler*, p.209.
81. Iain Chambers, 'Architecture, Amnesia and the Emergent Archaic', in Iain Borden, Joe Kerr, Jane Rendell with Alicia Pivaro (eds), *The Unknown City: Contesting Architecture and Social Space* (Cambridge MA, 2001), p.414.
82. Ibid., p.415.
83. Henry-Russell Hitchcock, Philip Johnson & Alfred Barr, *Modern Architecture: International Exhibition* (catalogue) (New York, 1932), pp.29–178. Architects listed: Wright, Gropius, Le Corbusier, JJP Oud, Mies, Raymond Hood, Howe & Lescaze, Richard Neutra, the Bowman Brothers. Info at: www.moma.org/documents/moma_catalogue_2044_300061855.pdf, retrieved 5 October 2021.
84. Ibid., p.183.
85. Henry-Russell Hitchcock & Philip Johnson, *The International Style* (revised ed) (New York, 1966).
86. Ibid., p.241.
87. Ibid., p.242.
88. Juhani Pallasmaa, 'Tradition and modernity', *Architectural Review*, CLXXXIII, 1095, May 1988, p.34.
89. Hitchcock, *19th and 20th*, p.viii.
90. Hitchcock, *International*, p.19.
91. Ibid., p.239.
92. Henry-Russell Hitchcock, *Modern Architecture* (reprint) (New York, 1970).
93. Ibid., p.64.
94. Ibid., p.99.
95. Ibid., p.27.
96. Ibid., p.147.
97. Ibid., p.92.
98. Bachelard, *Poetics*, p.68.
99. Such removal already customary in Britain with the publication of the Tudor-Walters Report of 1915.
100. The issue of the kitchen in the *existenzminimum* dwelling was further compounded by the unrealistic expectations of its designers of the availability and affordability of 'white goods' to the working class family in the 1930s. Moreover, 'white goods' were intended to feature in the 'emancipation' of the housewife from domestic drudgery and isolation, thus rendering the Modernist experiment all the more palatable.
101. Hobsbawm, *Extremes*, p.181.
102. Ibid., p.185.
103. Lynch, *Scotland*, p.440.
104. Hitchcock et al, *International Exhibition*, p.24.
105. Donald Langmead, *Willem Marinus Dudok, A Dutch Modernist: A Bio-Bibliography* (Westport CT, 1996), pp.61–107.
106. McKean, *Thirties*, p.31.
107. MacCarthy, *Gropius*, p.332.
108. MacDiarmid, *Aesthetics*, pp. 34–5.
109. We find, among others, John James Burnet in New York in 1896 and 1908; Thomas Tait (1882–1954) in France, Holland, Belgium and Italy in 1904–5; T Craigie Marwick (1878–1965) in France and Belgium pre-1910; James Shearer in Germany in 1912 and in New York and Pittsburgh in 1925; Jack Coia (1898–1981) in Italy in 1924; Margaret Brodie in France in 1926 and at the British Academy in Rome in 1929; T Waller Marwick (1903–1971) in the USA and Canada for ten weeks in 1928 and in Spain and France for two months in 1930; Kininmonth's client, Dr King, in Germany to see the works of Behrens, Gropius and Taut in 1930; David Harvey (1908–75) in Amsterdam for a month in 1931; Launcelot Ross (1885–1956) for four weeks in France in 1931; Basil Spence (1907–76) at the Weissenhof, Stuttgart, 1934, and the Paris Exhibition, 1937; Philip McManus (1907–?) in Holland researching Duiker and Dudok in 1935; Alan Reiach (1910–92) in France, Germany, Scandinavia, USA and USSR between 1935 and 1936, including time at Wright's Taliesin East; and James Ebenezer MacRae (1881–1951) in Rotterdam, Amsterdam, Berlin, Hamburg, Frankfurt, Prague, Vienna and Paris in 1935 as part of an official housing research project. There was also extended work experience, such as Tait's in New York, 1905–14, Francis Lorne's (1889–1963) in New York, Montreal and Toronto, 1914–30, and Waller Marwick's in London, 1928–31.
110. John Gloag, 'Who knows what the public wants?', in John Gloag (ed), *Design in Modern Life* (London, 1934), p.17.
111. Ibid., pp.19–20.
112. FRS Yorke, *The Modern House* (6th ed) (London, 1948) (first published 1934), p.6.
113. Randal Phillips, *The £1000 House* (London, 1928), p.5.
114. Randal Phillips, *Houses for Moderate Means* (London, 1936), p.5.
115. Ibid., p.9.
116. Charles McKean, *The Scottish Thirties* (Edinburgh, 1987), p.56, footnote 136. McKean claims 150 such houses

for Scotland against 780 for the rest of Britain and infers a favourable comparative arithmetic measure of Scottish/British Modernist achievement pro rata; 1:5 for the number of houses as against 1:11 for population.
117. Ibid., p.43.
118. Ibid., p.180.
119. Glendinning et al, *History*, p.385.
120. Ibid., p.386.
121. Tom Normand, *The Modern Scot: Modernism and Nationalism in Scottish Art, 1928–1955* (Aldershot, 2000), p.2.
122. Ibid., p.5.
123. John Butt, 'The Changing Character of Urban Employment 1901–1981', in Gordon, *Perspectives*, p.212.
124. Glendinning et al, *History*, pp.422–4.
125. Normand, *Modern Scot*, p.42.
126. John Tonge, *The Arts of Scotland* (London, 1938), p.100.
127. Ibid., p.33.
128. A recent survey of Nordic culture, Neil Kent's *The Soul of the North: A Social, Architectural and Cultural History of the Nordic Countries, 1700–1940* (London, 2000), is dourly Calvinistic.
129. Christopher Grieve's recent adoption of the non-de-plume is apostrophised by Tonge.
130. Tonge, *Arts*, pp.16–7.
131. Ibid., p.103.
132. Ibid., p.104.
133. Ibid., p.127.
134. Worringer, *Abstraction*, p.129.
135. MacDiarmid, *Aesthetics*, p.42.
136. Ibid., p.57.
137. Beveridge & Turnbull, *Eclipse*, p.91.
138. Ibid., p.93.
139. Ibid., p.102.
140. Mark Wigley, *The Architecture of Deconstruction: Derrida's Haunt* (Cambridge MA, 1995), p.163.
141. Lou Rosenburg with John Rosser, *Scotland's Homes Fit for Heroes: Garden City Influences on the Development of Scottish Working Class Housing 1900–1939* (Edinburgh, 2016), pp.182–218.
142. Steven Robb, 'Ebenezer MacRae and Interwar Housing in Edinburgh', in *The Book of the Old Edinburgh Club: The Journal for Edinburgh History*, New Series, vol.13, 2017, pp.43–77.
143. For example: the Rietveld-Schröder House, 1924, Utrecht, Gerrit Rietveld; the Masters House, Dessau, 1925, Walter Gropius; the Lovell Beach House, Newport, 1926, Rudolph Schindler; the Villa Savoye, Poissy, 1928–31, Le Corbusier; the Tugendhat House, Brno, 1928–30, Mies van der Rohe; the Jacobs House, Madison, 1936, Frank Lloyd Wright; the Villa Mairea, Noormarku, 1938, Alvar Aalto, etc.
144. Glendinning et al, *History*, p.404.
145. Ibid., p.182.
146. Henrik O Andersson & Fredric Bedoire, *Stockholm: Architecture and Townscape* (Stockholm, 1988), pp.306–7.
147. Phillips, *Moderate Means*, pp.98–9.
148. Bruno Zevi, *Erich Mendelsohn* (New York & London, 1985), p.128.
149. Phillips, *Moderate Means*, pp.32–3; McKean, *Thirties*, p.149. A Stewart Thomson has a brief entry in the Dictionary of Scottish Architects giving the same address as he does in Philips, which implies they are the same individual.
150. McKean, *Thirties*, pp.175–6.
151. Even Burnet Tait and Lorne struggled to an extent and occupied themselves by producing and publishing the *Architect's Handbook*.
152. Langmead, *Dudok*, pp.22–3.
153. Noted by Hugh Mottram in his proposer's statement attached to Shearer's Fellowship application to the RIBA.
154. 'Extension of the Dunfermline Central Library', *The Architects' Journal*, 25 April 1923, p.723.
155. Alastair Service, *Edwardian Architecture* (London, 1977), pp. 128–39.
156. James Shearer, letter to his wife. Held in the Shearer Collection at RCAHMS. Letter in two parts, this part headed Pittsburgh Athletic Association, Pittsburgh, postmarked Grand Central Station, 11 Feb 1925, 9.30am.
157. Marcus Johnstone, senior partner in Shearer & Annand, interview with me at 11 Maygate, Dunfermline, on 14 September 1984.
158. Designers of the Thomas Jefferson Building (formerly the Library of Congress Building), Washington DC, 1890–7.
159. Henry Hobson Richardson, 1838–86. The Thomas Crane Memorial Library, Quincy, Massachusetts, 1880–2 comes to mind as a generic model.
160. John Gifford, *The Buildings of Scotland, Fife* (London, 1999), p.123.
161. Other colleges completed under this scheme were Bottisham and Linton, both 1937, by SE Urwin (1892–1968), County Architect, in a Dudok Modern, and Impington, 1939, by Maxwell Fry and Walter Gropius.
162. Letter to me from Andrew Saint, 15 June 1990, 5 rue des Pontonniers, Strasbourg, France.
163. Letter to me from Andrew Saint, 4 July 1990, 20 Raven Shaw Street, London NW6.
164. 'Sawston Village College, Cambridgeshire', *The Architect and Building News*, 14 November 1930, pp.651–4.
165. Peter MacDonald, technician with Shearer in the mid-1930s, interview with me at 1 Broughton Market, Edinburgh, 24 April 1986.

166. Marcus Johnston, assistant and subsequently partner with Shearer 1940s to '90s, interview with me at 11 Maygate, Dunfermline, 14 September 1984.
167. This was a common problem for Scots architects bold enough to use a flat roof. Steele encountered similar: see Emmerson & Tilmouth, *Steele*, p.73.
168. Interview, William Dey with Neil Baxter, 18 December 1985. I am indebted to Neil Baxter for a copy of his transcript. Dey had petitioned Robert Matthew to get him out of the army in Egypt in WWII and it was through Matthew's influence that Dey went to work with Shearer.
169. 'Dunfermline Corporation Fire Station', *The Architect and Building News*, 1 May 1939, pp.123–5.
170. Johnstone interview.
171. Intriguingly, following his flight from Nazi Germany in 1933, Mendelsohn lectured at the School of Architecture, Edinburgh College of Art in late 1933 and left behind, as a gift, a perspective rendering in blue pencil on tracing paper of his Kemperplatz skyscraper project of 1922; still in the College collection in 1995 when I saw it.
172. James Shearer, 'A Visit to Willem Marinus Dudok', *RIAS Quarterly*, no.89, August 1952, pp.52–5.
173. Ibid, p.54.
174. Peter Payne, *The Hydro: Study of the Development of the Major Hydroelectric Schemes Undertaken by the North of Scotland Hydroelectric Board* (Aberdeen, 1988), p.144.
175. Langmead, *Dudok*, pp.20–1.
176. Glendinning et al, *History*, p.394.
177. David M Walker, *St Andrew's House: An Edinburgh Controversy 1912–39* (Edinburgh, 1989).
178. McKean, *Thirties*, p.14.
179. Walker, *St Andrew's*, p.34.
180. Ibid., p.93.
181. McKean, 'The Nordic Virus', in Frew & Jones, *Scotland and Europe*, p.89.
182. Johnny Rodger, 'Towards the MacMillan and Metzstein Year', in Johnny Rodger (ed), *Gillespie, Kidd & Coia: Architecture, 1956–87* (Glasgow, 2007), p.12.
183. McKean, *Thirties*, p.104.
184. Rodger, *Gillespie, Kidd & Coia*, p.15.
185. McKean, 'Virus', in Frew & Jones, *Scotland and Europe*, p.93.
186. *Empire Exhibition: Official Guide* (Glasgow, 1938), p.72.
187. Neil Baxter, '1938', in Kinchin & Kinchin, *Great Exhibitions*, p.156.

Chapter 5

1. Lynch, *Scotland*, p.437.
2. TEB Howarth, *Prospect & Reality: Great Britain 1945–1955* (London, 1985), p.115.
3. There is considerable dispute about the annual GERS numbers, which the British government maintains show the correct relationship of monies raised in Scotland to those disbursed there. The matter appears to hinge around those parts of taxable income generated in Scotland – such as oil and whisky – but which are taxed as originated in London, in effect, a top-slicing of the Scottish economy that artificially reduces its tax base. Additionally, limits imposed on which taxes and to what extent they can be raised in Scotland directly are thought to limit options for local solutions to Scotland's long-term structural economic and poverty problems. What had been queried in Scotland for decades began latterly to impact on English regions, prompting the 2019 Tory government to conceive of 'levelling-up'; still, at the time of writing, little more than a slogan.
4. Daron Acemoglu and James A Robinson, *Why Nations Fail: The Origins of Power, Prosperity and Poverty* (London, 2012), pp.79–83.
5. Info at: www.twtd.c.uk/wiki/Scottish_Covenant, retrieved 5 September 2019.
6. N Ferguson, *Empire*, p.354.
7. Ibid., p.356.
8. Howarth, *Prospect*, p.123.
9. The final repayment to the USA and Canada made on 29 December 2006.
10. FE Towndrow (ed), *Replanning Britain* (London, 1941).
11. Alison Ravetz, *The Government of Space: Town Planning in Modern Society* (London, 1986), p.45.
12. Towndrow, *Replanning*, p.109.
13. Ibid., p.162.
14. Ibid., p.31.
15. Ibid., p.32.
16. Ebenezer MacRae, *The Heritage of Greater Edinburgh* (Edinburgh, 1947).
17. Alan Reiach & Robert Hurd, *Building Scotland, Past and Future: A Cautionary Guide* (Glasgow, n.d.), unpaginated. Various dates are given for publication: McKean proposed 1940, Glendinning et al 1941–4 and McWilliam 1948. Tom Johnstone's foreword referred to 'free people… who have paid such a high price for their freedom', which tends to rule out the book having been published in the dark days of 1940 to 1943.
18. Including an image of the Victorian working class tenements adjacent to the coal-fired electricity generating station in Kings Road, Portobello, Edinburgh, in which I was raised as a child.
19. Jarvis, later appointed Director of the Canadian National Gallery, 1955–9, produced *The Things We See* as a 13-

20. Alan Jarvis, *The Things We See – Indoors and Outdoors* (Harmondsworth, 1946).
21. Ibid., pp.29–31.
22. Lionel Brett, *The Things We See – Houses* (West Drayton, 1947), end cover.
23. Jarvis, *Indoors and Outdoors*, end cover.
24. Brett, *Houses*, p.6.
25. Ibid., pp.42–3.
26. Ibid., p.5.
27. Ibid., pp.38–41.
28. Ibid., p.62.
29. Ralph Tubbs, *The Englishman Builds* (Harmondsworth, 1945), p.34.
30. Ibid., p.74.
31. Maxwell Fry, *Fine Building* (London, 1944), pp.83–114.
32. Ibid., p.64.
33. Ibid., p.62.
34. Ibid., fig.17b, p. 125.
35. Judy Garland in *The Wizard of Oz*, MGM, 1939, dir. Victor Fleming, from the book by Frank L Baum.
36. Fry, *Fine Building*, p.122.
37. Ibid., p.2.
38. JM Richards, *The Castles on the Ground: The Anatomy of Suburbia* (London, 2011), (first published 1946, reissued with introduction 1973) (reprint), p.15.
39. Ibid., p.65.
40. MacTaggart & Mickel Limited, *The Book of Broom Estate, Whitecraigs* (Glasgow, n.d., prob. 1937).
41. WB McKay, *Building Construction*, 3 vols. (2nd ed) (London, 1938).
42. Eric de Maré (ed), *New Ways of Building* (2nd ed, revised and enlarged 1951) (London, 1948), p.13.
43. Ibid., p.15.
44. Madge subsequently became a noted expert in the design of prisons.
45. John Madge (ed), *Tomorrow's Houses: New Building Methods, Structures and Materials* (London, 1946), p.12.
46. Ibid., p.15.
47. Sir John, Burnet, Tait & Lorne, *The Information Book of Sir John Burnet Tait and Lorne* (London, 1934).
48. Edward D Mills (ed), *Architects' Detail Sheets* (London, 1952).
49. Interdepartmental Committee Appointed by the Minister of Health, the Secretary of State for Scotland & the Minister of Works, *Post-War Building Studies No. 1: House Construction* (London, 1944), clause 217, p.46.
50. Ibid., clause 302, p.56.
51. Ibid., clause 349, p.64.
52. Ibid., clause 552, p.90.
53. Ibid., p.138.
54. Ibid., p.139.
55. The Scottish Housing Advisory Committee, *Planning Our New Homes* (Edinburgh, 1944).
56. Ibid., Appendix 3, Questionnaire to HM Forces and Industry, pp.xix–xxxi.
57. Ibid., p.13.
58. Ibid., p.96. This is roughly twice the area of the Frankfurt Kitchen (see above). Mann was not seduced by the functional perfection of the kitchen on offer and knew that it had a role beyond basic housework. The maverick Schindler, proposing a more integrated kitchen, observed that 'simplified cooking will become part of a group play, instead of being the deadly routine for a lonely slave.' Schindler, 'Care of the Body' in *Los Angeles Times*, 2 May 1926, in Sarnitz, *Schindler*, p.46.
59. Glendinning et al, *History*, p.428, and Gropius. *Scope*, Fig.39 and Fig.40-a,b,c,d. Realised at Alton Estate, Roehampton in 1958 some years after Matthew left the LCC, although not, as far as I am aware, in Scotland, where point blocks and isolated slabs were the thing. Zielenbau-type slab blocks became an LCC, subsequently GLC, preference; I worked on two, 1969–70.
60. Michael Young, Peter Willmott & Judith Stacey, *Family and Kinship in East London* (London, 1957, reprinted 1983 and 2007). At a somewhat more populist level, architects could have read Richard Hoggart's *The Uses of Literacy* (London, 1957) for insight into working-class culture.
61. Erica Masters (dir), *Glasgow Today and Tomorrow*, Moviegram Films for the Planning Department of the Corporation of the City of Glasgow, 1949. NLS, Moving Image Archive, ref. 3158. Available at movingimage.nls.uk/film/3158, retrieved 10 March 2019.
62. Mary Banham & Bevis Hillier (eds), *A Tonic To The Nation: the Festival of Britain 1951* (London, 1976), p.48, p.xii.
63. Reyner Banham, 'The Style: "Flimsy... Effeminate"?', in ibid., p.190.
64. Ibid., p.193.
65. Frank Hampson, *Dan Dare, Pilot of the Future in The Man from Nowhere* (Hendrik-Ido-Ambact, 1979), vol.1., frontispiece.
66. Brian Aldiss, *Science Fiction Art: The Fantasies of SF* (London, 1975), p.100.
67. Ibid., p.60.
68. Ibid., p.45.
69. See Eva Rudberg, 'Building the Welfare of the Folkhemmet 1940–60', in Claes Caldeby, Jöran Lindvall & Wilfried Wang

(eds), *20th-Century Architecture: Sweden* (Munich and New York, 1998), pp.111–41. Rudberg notes the seminal article 'Function and Arabesque' of 1948 by the English architect Michael Ventris (1922–56) (best-known for deciphering the Linear B script), who had spent time in Sweden, in bringing Folkhemmet production to the attention of British architects.
70. Some 70 per cent of architects' work in this period was government funded directly or indirectly – through local authorities, health boards, development corporations and universities – and 70 per cent of employment was either with those agencies or in the architectural practices that were commissioned by them.
71. JM Richards, 'Failure of the New Towns', in *Architectural Review*, vol.114, no.679, July 1953, pp.31.
72. Ibid., p.29.
73. Ibid., p.32.
74. Lionel Brett, 'New Towns', *Architectural Review*, vol.114, no.680, August 1953, p.119.
75. Colin Ward, 'Why the British Don't Talk About New Towns Anymore', in *Reading and Design of the Physical Environment*, no.3 (Urbino, 1993), p.38.
76. Ministry of Housing and Local Government, *Homes for Today and Tomorrow* (London, 1961), p.iv.
77. Ibid., p.47, clause 211.
78. Ibid., pp.63–71, Appendix 2.
79. Ibid., p.50, para. 19.
80. Ibid., p.9, clause 30.
81. Info Department of Business, Energy and Industrial Strategy, 30 July 2020. Info at: www.gov.uk/government/statistical-data-sets/historical-coal-data-production, retrieved 6 February 2021.
82. MHLG, *Homes*, p.35, tables.
83. Ibid., p.2, clause 7.
84. Ibid., p.10, clause 32.
85. Jean Baudrillard (trans James Benedict), *The System of Objects* (New York, 1996), p.150.
86. Michael Young, 'Kinship and Family in East London', MAN, vol.54 (September 1954), p.138. Info at: jstor.org/stable/2785380?seq+1#metadata_info_tab_contents, retrieved 30 December 2021.
87. MHLG, *Homes*, p.9, clause 28.
88. Ibid., p.25, clause 106.
89. 'Christopher Wren', *New Builder*, October 1989.
90. Howarth, *Prospect*, p.238.
91. Both were employed by London County Council, Matthew as County Architect, and, with Peter Moro, they were the designers of the Royal Festival Hall as part of the 1951 Festival of Britain. Matthew became Professor of Architecture at Edinburgh University. Miles Glendinning, *Modern Architect: The Life and Times of Robert Matthew*, London: RIBA, 2008, p.226.
92. Mark Crinson & Jules Lubbock, *Architecture, Art or Profession? Three Hundred Years of Architectural Education in Britain* (Manchester, 1994), p.131.
93. Ibid., p.138.
94. Glendinning, *Modern Architect*, pp.313–5.
95. Crinson & Lubbock, *Art or Profession*, pp.1–2.
96. Siegfrid Giedion, *Space, Time and Architecture* (5th ed) (London, 1947; Cambridge MA, 1967), p.30.
97. Ibid., p.5.
98. Ibid., p.5.
99. Ibid., p.12.
100. Ibid., p.22.
101. Ibid., p.xxxvi.
102. Ibid., p.xxxvii.
103. Francastel, *Forms*, p.242.
104. Christian Norberg-Schulz, *Intentions in Architecture* (Oslo, 1963), p.18.
105. Gropius, *Scope*, p.96.
106. Norberg-Schulz, *Intentions*, p.206.
107. Hall, *Cities*, p.207.
108. Collins, *Ideals*, p.171.
109. Hall, *Cities*, p.113.
110. Norberg-Schulz, *Intentions*, p.15.
111. Norberg-Schulz briefly engaged with the concept of 'poles', although he did not develop it further or raise the matter of antinomy in an equally undeveloped footnote mention of Kant on p.196.
112. Ibid., p.18.
113. Ibid., p.89.
114. Ibid., p.91.
115. Collins, *Ideals*, p.298.
116. Sir John Summerson, unpublished paper (read on his behalf by John Richards [1931–2003]) given at the *Thirties Symposium*, Edinburgh College of Art, 12–13 October 1984.
117. Berman, *Solid*, p.346.
118. Colin Rowe, *The Architecture of Good Intentions: Towards a Possible Retrospective* (London, 1994), p.29.
119. Colin Rowe (Alexander Caragonne, ed), *As I Was Saying: Recollections and Miscellaneous Essays* (3 vols.) (Cambridge MA, 1996), p.279.
120. Anthony Vidler, *The Architectural Uncanny* (London, 1992), p.182.
121. Reyner Banham, *Theory and Design in the First Machine Age* (London, 1960), p.47.
122. Kevin Lynch, *The Image of the City* (Cambridge MA, 1960).
123. Jane Jacobs, *The Death and Life of Great American Cities: The Failure of Town Planning* (Harmondsworth, 1964), p.284.
124. Conzen was a delegate at the 1941 Town Planning conference.

125. MRG Conzen, *Alnwick, Northumberland: A Study in Town-plan Analysis* (London, 1960), revised and reprinted 1969.
126. Lynch, *Scotland*, pp.442–3.
127. NTS Records, letter of invitation dated 4 December 1952.
128. Ibid., Minute of Meeting, 15 July 1958, item 72, amendment of earlier Minute of Meeting 9 January 1958, item 70, which gave 'ill-health' as Shearer's reason for resignation. Sailors' Walk was restored by Wheeler & Sproson sometime between 1954 and 1959, though it is not clear whether even in 1959 it was harled, although it has been subsequently. It is presently on the HES Buildings at Risk Register, ref. 4863, though not perilously so.
129. Ibid., Minute of Meeting, 27 October 1955, item 20.
130. Ibid., Minute of Meeting, 23 April 1956, item 42.
131. Ibid., Minute of Meeting, 9 January 1958, item 67.
132. Ibid., Minute of Meeting, 15 July 1958, item 75.
133. This is as the result of the University's acquiescence to a petition signed by 1,700 students decrying David Hume's customary racism, not unusual for his time.
134. Jānis Krastiņš (ed), DOCOMOMO, *National Register Latvia* (Riga, 1998).
135. Ola Wedebrunn (ed), *Modern Movement Scandinavia: Vision and Reality* (Copenhagen, Helsinki, Reykjavik, Oslo, Stockholm, 1998).
136. MacDiarmid, *Aesthetics*, p.95.
137. Glendinning et al, *History*, p.469.
138. Tange Kenzō, 'Kurashiki City Hall', in John Donat (ed), *World Architecture One* (London, 1964), p.14.
139. Kurokawa Noriaki (Kisho), 'Metabolism: The Pursuit of Open Form', in ibid., p.11. For the early part of his career, Kurokawa was recorded as Noriaki; subsequently he was known as Kisho.
140. Nathalie Herschdorfer & Lada Ustätter (eds), *Le Corbusier and the Power of Photography* (London, 2012).
141. Jackson, *Japan and the West*, p.358.
142. Rowe, *As I Was Saying*, p.9.
143. Peter Gössel (ed), *Julius Shulman: Architecture and its Photography* (Köln, 1998), p.15.
144. Ibid., p.16.
145. Beatriz Colomina, 'Media as Modern Architecture', in Anthony Vidler (ed), *Architecture: Between Spectacle and Use* (New Haven MA, 2008), p.66.
146. Richard Murphy, *Ten Years of Practice* (Edinburgh, 2001), p.292.
147. Brian O'Doherty, *Inside the White Cube: The Ideology of the Gallery Space* (expanded ed) (Berkeley CA, 1986), p.23.
148. Collins, *Ideals*, p.262.
149. JM Richards, 'Criticism in the Thirties', in Summerson (ed), *Concerning Architecture*, p.254.
150. Ibid., p.255.
151. Rowe, *Good Intentions*, p.16.
152. Glendinning, *Modern Architect*, p.5.
153. Vincent Scully, 'Introduction', in Brownlee & De Long, *Kahn*, p.9.
154. Working with three separate developer clients based in West Yorkshire between 2007 and 2015 in the restaurant, hotel and start-up business sectors, I was struck how their business models, based on their 1990s English experience, did not translate to Scotland. The reasons were: one, site acquisition where the SDA had long since snapped up and developed the more viable former industrial sites, leaving only those requiring substantial land reclamation; two, the quality of development and aesthetic achievement required by Scottish authorities being greater than their English counterparts, which pushed up development costs; three, the higher cost of building in Scotland due to distance from national suppliers and historically higher square metre costs; four, adjacency to earlier quality SDA developments requiring the developer acting as landlord to seek out tenants of an equivalent higher quality in markets they had no experience accessing, or need to do so, in England. Ambitious development programmes by these clients of between 5 and 20 units a year dropped to between 1 and 3 a year as the costs of development became clear.

Chapter 6

1. Peter Eisenman (b. 1932), Michael Graves (1934–2015), Charles Gwathmey (1938–2009), John Hejduk (1929–2000) & Richard Meier (b.1934).
2. Hitchcock, *Nineteenth and Twentieth Centuries*, pp.531–2.
3. Hitchcock & Johnson, *The International Style*, p.532.
4. Hitchcock, *Nineteenth and Twentieth Centuries*, p.531.
5. Ibid., p.535.
6. Ibid., p.554.
7. Nikolaus Pevsner & JM Richards, *The Anti-Rationalists* (London, 1973).
8. Ibid., p.1.
9. Ibid., p.4.
10. Curtis, *Modern Architecture*, p.21.
11. Jeremy Howard, *Art Nouveau: International and National Styles in Europe* (Manchester, 1996), p.7.
12. Rowe, *Intentions*, p.11, 47.
13. David Crowley, *National Style and*

14. *Nation-state* (Manchester and New York, 1992), p.133.
14. Jacques Gubler, 'Switzerland, the temperate presence of Art Nouveau', in Frank Russell, (ed), *Art Nouveau Architecture* (London, 1979), p.160.
15. Spiro Kostof, *A History of Architecture: Settings and Rituals* (New York and Oxford, 1995), preface.
16. Ibid., p.717.
17. Paul Schultze-Naumberg (1869–1949) represented such intellectual basis which the totalitarian construct of national architecture was capable of offering, beyond Albert Speer's (1905–81) specious 'theory of the value of ruins'. Although less well-known than Troost or Speer, Schultze-Naumberg was of wider cultural significance in the early years of the Third Reich, less for his architecture than for his numerous polemical racist and anti-Semitic writings such as *Kunst und Rasse*, 1928; membership of the Nazi Party from 1930; and in the creation and membership of the *Kampfbund deutscher Architekten und Ingenieure*, the KDAI, 1931–4, an incomplete attempt to establish a professional institute for the accreditation of architects and engineers controlled by the NSDAP (the Nazi Party).
18. Frampton, *Critical History*, p.217.
19. Jencks, *Modern Movements*, p.48.
20. Weber, *Le Corbusier*, p.323.
21. William JR Curtis, *Modern Architecture since 1900* (2nd ed) (Oxford, 1987), p.211.
22. Ibid., p.212.
23. Ibid., p.221.
24. Ibid., p.214.
25. EH Gombrich, *The Sense of Order* (Oxford, 1979), pp.212–3.
26. Peter Blundell Jones, *Architecture and Ritual: How Buildings Shape Society* (London, 2016), p.115.
27. SJ Newton, *The Politics and Psychoanalysis of Primitivism* (London, 1996), p.34.
28. Vincent Scully Jr., *Modern Architecture: the Architecture of Democracy* (London, 1961), p.14.
29. Hitchcock, *International*, p.241.
30. Eric Hobsbawm, *The Age of Extremes: the Short Twentieth Century 1914–1991* (London, 1994), p.185.
31. Fest, *Speer*, p.78.
32. David Farrell Krell (ed), *Martin Heidegger: Basic Writings* (London, 1978), p.345.
33. Ibid., p.351–2.
34. 'Stay', in *Chambers English Dictionary* (Edinburgh, 1988), p.1437, and 'stey', in *The Chambers Concise Scots Dictionary* (Edinburgh, 1996), p.670.
35. Krell, *Heidegger*, p.358.
36. Bachelard, *Poetics*, p.4.
37. Karsten Harries, *The Ethical Function of Architecture* (Cambridge, Mass, 1998), p.202.
38. Jean Baudrillard, *The System of Objects* (London, 1996), p.16.
39. Ibid., p.17.
40. Collins, *Ideals*, p.26.
41. Bernstein, *Fate of Art*, p.263.
42. Etienne Gilson, 'Foreword to 1964 Edition', in Bachelard, *Poetics*, p.xxxvii.
43. Ibid., p.78.
44. Jackson, *Japan and the West*, p.74.
45. Noboru Kawazoe, 'Tradition and Innovation in Japanese Architecture', in Yamada (ed), *Dialogue in Art*, p.268.
46. Jackson, *Japan and the West*, p.56.
47. Chris Fawcett, *The New Japanese House: Ritual and Anti-ritual Patterns of Dwelling* (London, 1980), p.9.
48. Jackson, *Japan and the West*, p.70.
49. Sarnitz, *Loos*, pp.19–20.
50. Fawcett, *The New Japanese House*, p.172.
51. Harries, *Ethical*, p.144.
52. Jencks, *Modern Movements*, p.11.
53. Kurokawa Kisho, *Intercultural Architecture* (London, 1991), p.160.
54. Dorothy L Sayers, *Murder Must Advertise* (reprint) (London, 1963), p.136.
55. John W Cook & Heinrich Klotz, *Conversations with Architects* (London, 1973), p.251.
56. Berman, *Solid*, p.137.
57. Television advertisement for 'Flora' margarine featuring the Scots actor, Richard Wilson, current in early 1998. Wilson did indeed grow up in Greenock, further adding to the self-referential, inter-textual and thoroughly post-Modern construction of the advertisement.
58. Peter Dormer, *The Meanings of Modern Design* (London, 1991), p.13.
59. Ibid., p.17.
60. Richard Demarco, degree seminar, School of Architecture, Edinburgh College of Art, 29 January 1998.
61. Charles Jencks, *Modern Movements in Architecture* (New York, 1973).
62. Ibid., p.320.
63. Ibid., p.320.
64. Ibid., p.323.
65. Bruno Zevi, *The Modern Language of Architecture* (paperback ed of the 1978 publication) (New York, 1994), p.6, footnote.
66. Ibid., pp.62–3.
67. Ibid., p.72.
68. Ibid., p.67.
69. Roger Scruton, *The Classical Vernacular: Architectural Principles in an Age of Nihilism* (Manchester, 1994), p.11.
70. Zevi, *Modern Language*, p.45.
71. Jencks, *Modern Movements*, p.187.
72. Kurokawa, *Intercultural*, p.161.

73. Roger Emmerson, 'Circumnavigating the Globe', *The Book of the Old Edinburgh Club*, New Series, no.16, 2020, pp.9–10.
74. Charles Jencks, *The Language of Post-Modern Architecture* (6th ed) (London, 1991), p.124.
75. Kenneth Frampton, 'Place-form and cultural identity', in John Thackara (ed), *Design after Modernism* (London, 1988), pp.55–6.
76. cf. Giedion's 'new regionalism'.
77. Kenneth Frampton, 'Towards a Critical Regionalism: Six Points for an Architecture of Resistance', in Hal Foster (ed), *The Anti-Aesthetic Essays on Post-Modern Culture* (Port Townsend WA, 1983), pp.16–30.
78. Alan Colquhoun, 'Regionalism and Technology', (first published in Casabella 491, May 1983) in *Collected Essays in Architectural Criticism* (London, 2009), pp. 228–9.
79. Zumthor, *Thinking*, pp.16–7.
80. Juhani Pallasmaa, *The Thinking Hand: Existential and Embodied Wisdom in Architecture* (Chichester, 2009), p.113.
81. Owens, *Beyond Recognition*, p.91.
82. Sutherland Lyall, *The State of British Architecture* (London, 1980), p.3.
83. Zevi, *Modern Language*, p.68.
84. 'Lyall, *State*, p.14.
85. Ibid., p.70.
86. Gordon Cullen, *Townscape* (London, 1961).
87. Dr Andreas Papadakis (ed), *British Architecture* (London, 1982).
88. Richard Reid, 'Learning from the Vernacular', in ibid., pp.20–1.
89. Richard Reid & Ralph Lerner, 'The Vasone Villa, São Paulo, Brazil', in ibid., p.207.
90. Ibid., p.208.
91. Refer to compilations such as *The Architect's Eye: American architectural drawings from 1799–1978* (New York, 1979) edited by Deborah Nevins & Robert Stern, *British Architecture* (London and New York, 1982) edited by Dr Andreas Papadakis or *The International Building Exhibition Berlin, 1987: Examples of a New Architecture* (London, 1987) edited by Josef Kleihues & Heinrich Klotz.
92. Peter Davey, 'Delight', *Architectural Review*, August 1997, vol.CCII, no.1206, p.90.
93. Boito is possibly best known for his influential 'Prima Carta del Restauro' or the Charter of Restoration of 1883:

    1. The differentiation of style between new and old parts of a building.

    2. The differentiation in building materials between the new and the old.

    3. Suppression of mouldings and decorative elements in new fabric placed in a historical building.

    4. Exhibition in a nearby place of any material parts of a historical building that were removed during the process of restoration.

    5. Inscription of the date (or a conventional symbol) on new fabric in a historical building.

    6. Descriptive epigraph of the restoration work done attached to the monument.

    7. Registration and description with photographs of the different phases of restoration. This register should remain in the monument or in a nearby public place. This requirement may be substituted by publication of this material.

    8 Visual notoriety of the restoration work done.
94. Bruno Tobia, 'Urban Space and Monuments in the "Nationalisation of the Masses": The Italian Case', in Stuart Woolf (ed), *Nationalism in Europe 1815 to the Present: A reader* (London, 1996), pp.171–2.
95. Ibid., pp.173.
96. Jonathan Glancey, *C20th Architecture: the Structures that Shaped the Twentieth Century* (London, 2000).
97. Ibid., p.6.
98. Alison Ravetz, *Model Estate: Planned Housing at Quarry Hill, Leeds* (London, 1974), republished as a Routledge Revival, 2013.
99. Adam Curtis, *The Great British Housing Disaster*, BBC, 1984. Info at: www.youtube.com/results?search_
100. Malcolm Cooper, Ranald MacInnes, Deborah Mays, Dawn McDowell & Miles Oglethorpe, *Scotland: Building for the Future: Essays on the Architecture of the Post-war Era* (Edinburgh, undated, ca. 2010), p.4.
101. To put the matter of failures in context, the first large-scale panel system housing in Britain was erected at Quarry Hill, Leeds, 1934–41 (demolished 1976), by City Architect RAH Livett (1890–1959). It was constructed from a hybrid system of steel framing, concrete panels and steel tie rods designed by the French industrialist Eugene Mopin in 1930 for a housing project at Drancy, Paris where the annual rainfall is approximately 278mm compared to Leeds' 595mm. Damp penetration was the principal cause of building fabric deterioration. It was as a resident of Quarry Hill that Alison Ravetz began her significant career as planner and critic. Moreover, there was a Scottish connection which had its own tale to tell. Livett was assisted between 1936 and 1938 by the Scot George Clark Robb (1903–80) who, in a long public authority career, worked with EJ MacRae at Edinburgh, 1927–36, possibly assisting him on his multi-storey study (catalogued in the Edinburgh Room at the Central Library, but missing); at

Oxford, 1938–41, in Garden City mode; at Lanarkshire, 1941–3; at Stirlingshire, 1943–5; at Aberdeenshire, 1945–8; as planner for the Highland Region of the Department of Health for Scotland; and, post-1948, in various senior planning and architectural roles at the Scottish Office. Peripatetic 'backroom boys' like Robb, never remaining in post quite long enough see the consequences of their decision-making, had significant influence because they sat on the relevant committees and compiled policy. Robb even seemed to have designed a house, unbuilt, for Hugh MacDiarmid ca. 1935, although MacDiarmid had nothing to say about it in Aesthetics in Scotland.

102. M Pacione, 'Renewal, Redevelopment and Rehabilitation in Scottish Cities 1945–1981', in Gordon (ed), *Perspectives*, p.281, Table 1.
103. Andrew Noble, 'Urbane Silence: Scottish Writing and the Nineteenth-Century City', in Gordon (ed), *Perspectives*, p.89.
104. McWilliam, *Scottish Townscape*, pp.149–51.
105. Glendinning et al, History, p.476.
106. Neal J Mongold, *Community Architecture: Myth And Reality*, unpublished Masters dissertation, mit, Cambridge, MA, 1988, p.3. Info at: dspace.mit.edu/bitstream/handle/1721.1/789/18551870-MIT.df?sequence+2, retrieved 4 May 2019
107. Ravetz, *Space*, p.88.
108. Michael R Glass, 'Peter Shapely, The Skeffington Report: People and Planning, 1969, New York: Routledge, 2014', in *The AAG Review of Books*, 5:1, 26–7, 17 January 2017. Info at: www.tandonline.com/toc/rrob20/5/1, retrieved 18 December 2020.
109. Neither ever quite surpassed in Scottish folk-memory even by the equally entertaining and poignant comedy of high-rise living *Still Game*, Ford Kiernan & Greg Hemphill, BBC Scotland, 2002–19.
110. Refer to literary works such as Alan Sharp's incomplete Greenock trilogy, *A Green Tree in Gedde* and *The Wind Shifts*, Alasdair Gray's *Lanark* and James Kelman's *How Late It Was*; also Jeff Torrington's *Swing Hammer, Swing* and Irvine Welsh's *Trainspotting* together with Peter May's Western Isles novels. Crime fiction likewise has an identifiable Scottish urban quality such as is evident in the novels of William McIlvanney, Denise Mina, Ian Rankin, Val McDermid, Quintin Jardine among others; also Christopher Brookmyre and Douglas Lindsay's less classifiable works.
111. Freeman Fox Associates with Colin Buchanan and Partners, *Edinburgh: The Recommended Plan* (Edinburgh, 1972), p.141, para.653.
112. Ibid., p.142, para.659.
113. Ibid., p.143, para.665.
114. Ibid., p.143, para.663.
115. Goldberg's Department store (J&F Johnston and Partners, 1960, in a derivative Festival of Britain mode, demolished 1996 and replaced on the same site by social housing) was set sufficiently well back from existing street frontages to facilitate the construction of part of this roundabout, the need for which originated in the earlier Abercrombie plan for the city, and was of a scale to complement the termination of the urban motorway.
116. In 1975, along with a co-operative of other South Side residents, I wrote, illustrated and edited *The South Side News*, a community newspaper and anti-roads platform. The paper's lasting consequence is the Meadows Festival, conceived by several of the SSN editorial board.
117. Freeman Fox, *Recommended Plan*, p.141, para.654.
118. The Labour MP for Whitehaven and Under-Secretary of State for Energy in the Callaghan government, John Cunningham's late and approved amendment to the referendum legislation required that the 'Yes' vote must represent at least 40% of the total of registered voters not those who actually voted. This was a complete departure from standard and accepted British electoral practice and has never been revisited. Of those voting a majority were for a devolved parliament, 51.62 per cent for, 48.38 per cent against, on a 63.72 per cent turn out.
119. Miles Glendinning, *The Architecture of Scottish Government: From Kingship to Democracy* (Dundee, 2004), pp.317–9 and ills. 5.2 and 5.3 on p.318.
120. Royal Incorporation of Architects in Scotland, *RIAS Review of Scottish Architecture*, 1992 (Macclesfield, 1992), p.3.
121. Roger Emmerson, *Winners & Losers: Scotland and the architectural competition* (Edinburgh, 1991), p.35.
122. Mary Arnold-Forster in telephone conversation with me, 22 June 2021.
123. The report in *The Architect's Journal*, 11 May 1988, p.19, was a typical response. I was one of the 'architectural brothers', having designed the Broom Milk Bar for Mactaggart & Mickel and the Scottish Milk Marketing Board.
124. Aldo Rossi (trans Lawrence Vernuti), *The Architecture of the City* (Cambridge MA, 1984).
125. Demetri Porphyrios, *Sources of Modern Eclecticism* (London, 1982).
126. Oswald Mathias Ungers, *Morphologie: City Metaphors* (Köln, 1982).
127. Emmerson, *Winners*, pp.38-9.
128. J Neil Baxter (ed), *St Peters & St Pauls:*

Architectural Competition, Record of Entries (Edinburgh, 1985): Stephen, p.14; Appleton, p.15; Patience & Highmore, p.16; Watson, p.17; Design Detail Group, p.19; Douglas, p.20; Smoor, p.74; Webster, p.78; Cochrane McGregor, p.30; Brackenbury, p.35; Clelland, p.30; Murphy, p.37; Gillespie, p.40; MacRae, p.47; Gillespie, Kidd & Coia, p.41; McLachlan, p.55, Gasson, p.40.
129. Patrick Nuttgens, 'Epilogue', in Nuttgens, Mackintosh, p.156.
130. Stamp, 'Mackintosh, Burnet and Modernity', in Architectural Heritage Society of Scotland, Architectural Heritage III: The Age of Mackintosh (Edinburgh, 1992), p.11.
131. Andrew MacMillan, 'Mackintosh in Context', in ibid., p.31.
132. David M Walker, 'Mackintosh's Scottish Antecedents', in ibid., p.38.
133. Mark Baines, 'Themes and Variations', in Rodger (ed) Gillespie, Kidd and Coia, pp.48–69.
134. Ibid., p.51.
135. Ibid., p.59.
136. Gordon Benson, 'Sources, Ideas and Lessons', in ibid., p.30.
137. Mark Baines in ibid., p.59.
138. Ibid., p.64.
139. Ibid., p.51.
140. Deyan Sudjic, Peter Cook & Jonathan Meades, English Extremists: The Architecture of Campbell Zogolovitch Wilkinson Gough (London, 1988).
141. Dampness exacerbated by the fact that at 643mm, Glasgow's annual rainfall is 3 times that of the Tracoba system's place of origin and initial use.
142. Scottish Government, Planning Advice Note 83: Master planning (Edinburgh: Scottish Government, 16 September 2008), p.40.
143. Charles McKean, Edinburgh: an Illustrated Architectural Guide (2nd ed) (Edinburgh, 1986), p.100.
144. Peter Davey, 'National Treasure House', Architectural Review, April 1999, vol. ccv, no.1226, pp.54–63.
145. John Allan, 'Museum of Memory', Architecture Today, no.100, July 1999, pp.28–45.
146. Patrick Hodgkinson, ibid., pp.28–45.
147. Paul Clarke, ibid., pp.28–45. This is almost a paraphrase of Heidegger's 'building thinking dwelling'.
148. Neave Brown, ibid., pp.28–45.
149. Bernstein, The Fate of Art, p.3.
150. Charles McKean, The Making of the Museum of Scotland (Edinburgh, 2000), p.xii.
151. Ibid., p.40.
152. Richard Weston, Richard Murphy: Ten Years of Practice (Edinburgh, 2001), p.12.
153. Richard Murphy, Carlo Scarpa and Castelvecchio (London, 1990) and Carlo Scarpa and Castelvecchio Revisited (Edinburgh, 2017).
154. These architects include Wayland Tunley (1937–2012), David Grindley (n.d.), Andrew Scott (n.d.) and Adrian Morrow (n.d.), who had worked at mkdc in the 1970s and early 1980s, and subsequently and variously in several private practices – Wayland Tunley Trevor Denton; Denton Scott; Grindley Denton; Grindley Architects and Adrian Morrow Architects – or went into teaching – Denton (briefly) and Scott (permanently).
155. Info at: catalogue.mkcdc.org.uk/content/catalogue_item/adrian-morrow-collection, grindleyarchitects.co.uk, and www.livingarchive.org.uk/content/catalogue_item/the-peoples-history-of-milton-keyne/oral-history, all retrieved 23 August 2020.
156. Penny Lewis 'Elder and Cannon', in Urban Realm, 11 February 2005. Info at: www.urbanrealm.com/features/archive/2005/2, retrieved 14.01.2021.

Chapter 7

1. Rev. Wm. Morrison (Norman MacRae, ed), Highland Second-Sight with Prophecies of Coinneach Odhar and the Seer of Petty (Dingwall, 1910), p.1.
2. In fact, 'nothing happened' because people worked very hard behind the scenes to ensure the issue was fixed; info at: https://time.com/5752129/y2k-bug-history/.
3. Info at: evangelicalfocus.com/Europe/2514/Church-attendance-in-Scotland-falls-from-12-7-in-fifteen-years, retrieved 20 November 2020.
4. Sir Colin St John Wilson, 'Foreword', in Benson + Forsyth, Museum of Scotland (London, 1999), p.4.
5. Annemarie Adams, 'Peter Collins: A Study in Parallax', in Irena Latek (ed) Peter Collins and the Critical History of Modern Architecture (Montréal, 2003), pp.30–43 and Journal of Architectural Education, ACSA, 2005, p.29, quoting Peter Collins. Info at: www.mcgill.ca/architecture/files/architecture/2005/petercollins.pdf, retrieved 21 April 2018.
6. Charles Jencks, The New Paradigm in Architecture (New Haven, 2002).
7. William Gibson, Neuromancer (New York, 1984).
8. William J Mitchell, City of Bits: Space, Place and the Infobahn (Cambridge MA, 1996), p.172.

9. Thomas Rid, *The Rise of the Machines: The Lost History of Cybernetics* (London, 2017).
10. Jonathan Taplin, *Move Fast and Break Things: How Facebook, Google and Amazon Cornered Culture and Undermined Democracy* (New York, 2017).
11. Mitchell, *City of Bits*, p.167.
12. Antonio Canova (1757–1822) drew tight rectilinear grids in red chalk over his full-size maquettes with every grid-line intersection marked with a pin fixing those points in Cartesian space so that accurate copies could be made. Scottish neo-classical sculptor Sandy Stoddart employs a similar reproductive technique on clay models later to be cast in bronze.
13. Zevi, *Modern Language*, p.13.
14. Ibid., p.70.
15. Foster, *Art-Architecture*, p.84.
16. Winner of the European Museum of the Year, 2013.
17. Juhani Pallasmaa, *The Eyes of the Skin: Architecture and the Senses* (London, 1996), p.20.
18. Foster, *Art-Architecture*, p.129.
19. Collins, *Ideals*, p.226.
20. In the words of the local authority, it currently faces problems with its structure, exterior, and operational systems that repairs alone cannot address. To protect and preserve this major public investment, the City has initiated a $195 million project to reconstruct the Portland Building by the end of 2020. Info at: www.portlandoregon.gov/omf/66129, retrieved 18 December 2021.
21. Mike Davis, 'Urban Renaissance and the Spirit of Post-Modernism', in E Ann Kaplan (ed), *Post-Modernism and its Discontents* (London, 1988), p.82.
22. Vidler, *Uncanny*, p.190.
23. Info at: whotel.com-edinburgh.com, retrieved 13 October 2021.
24. Reiner de Graaf, *Four Walls and a Roof: The Complex Nature of a Simple Profession* (Cambridge MA, 2017), p.72.
25. Dyckhoff, *Spectacle*, p.338.
26. Vidler, *Warped Space*, p.235.
27. Ibid., p.242.
28. Peter Noever, *The End of Architecture? Documents and Manifestos* (Munich, 1993), p.9.
29. Lebbeus Woods, 'Freespace and the Tyranny of Types', in ibid., p.89.
30. James Steele (ed), *Architectural Monographs No. 29, Eric Owen Moss* (London, 1993), p.9.
31. Zevi, *Modern Language*, p.57.
32. Žižek, *The Parallax View*, p.332.
33. Steele, *Owen Moss*, p.10.
34. Dezeen reports that residents at the Embassy Gardens development in southwest London claim its controversial Sky Pool is too cold to be used in winter, despite heating costs of £450 a day. Info at: www.dezeen.com/2021/12/15/sky-pool-cold-weather-heating-costs, retrieved 18 December 2021.
35. Carol Willis, *Form Follows Finance* (New York, 1995).
36. Vidler, *Uncanny*, p.9.
37. Info at: en.wikipedia.org/wiki/Taipei_101, retrieved 11 May 2018.
38. Info at: www.dezeen.com/2009/08/25/astana-national-library-by-big, retrieved 11 May 2018.
39. Info at: www.bing.com/
40. Now renamed, without irony, 'Ithra' (enrichment).
41. Info at: www.archdaily.com/878775/king-abdulaziz-centre-for-world-culture-snohetta, retrieved 11 May 2018.
42. Foster, *Art-Architecture*, p.x.
43. Berman, *Solid*, p.346.
44. Alain de Botton, *The Architecture of Happiness* (London, 2006), pp.218–28.
45. Ibid., p.228.
46. See: Yamada, *Dialogue in Art*; Jackson, *Japan and the West*.
47. De Botton, *Happiness*, p.229.
48. Ibid., p.230.
49. Ibid., p.234.
50. Marisa Bartolucci, *living large in small spaces* (London and New York, 2003), p.12.
51. Ruth Slavid, *Micro: Very Small Architecture* (London, 2009), p.12.
52. Lars Spuybroek, *The Sympathy of Things: Ruskin and the Ecology of Design* (2nd ed) (London, 2016), p.67.
53. Ibid., p.xviii.
54. Ibid., p.13.
55. Ibid., p.22.
56. Ibid., p.255.
57. Focillon, *The Life of Forms*, p.50.
58. John Lennon, 'Imagine' on *Imagine*, Apple Records, released September 1971.
59. Zumthor, *Thinking Architecture*, p.26.
60. Sudjic, *100-Mile*, p.207.
61. Bachelard, *Poetics*, p.61.
62. It's worth noting how Wells's phonemes, like Tolkien's later, are constructed to signify to English-speakers social and behavioural dualities such as good/bad, privileged/underprivileged, in/out.
63. Suzi Gablik, *The Reenchantment of Art* (London, 1991), p.179.
64. Foster, *Art-Architecture*, p.82.

65. Zumthor, *Thinking Architecture*, p.10.
66. Ibid., p.18.
67. Charles Jencks, Modern Movements in Architecture (New York, 1973), p.323.
68. Ibid., p.36.
69. Essy Baniassad, 'Introduction', in Brian Carter (ed), *Brian MacKay-Lyons: Selected Projects 1986–1997* (Halifax, 1998), p.5.
70. 'Plain Modern' is Quantrill's term – Malcolm Quantrill, *Plain Modern: The Architecture of Brian MacKay-Lyons* (New York, 2005) – although it seems perverse in describing an architecture of intricacy, complexity and richness. I suppose Quantrill uses 'plain' to denote a modesty of approach.
71. Ibid., p.31.
72. Zumthor, *Thinking Architecture*, p.13.
73. Miles Glendinning & David Page, *Clone City: Crisis and Renewal in Contemporary Scottish Architecture* (Edinburgh, 1999), p.x.
74. See Introduction.
75. Glendinning & Page, *Clone City*, pp.7–8.
76. Ibid., p.51.
77. Ibid., p.25.
78. Antoine Grumbach, 'Cities – a perpetual incompleteness', unpublished paper given at the *Second Jerusalem Symposium on Heritage*, 13–18 March 1994. Grumbach is architect for House 16A at Tegeler Hafen and the corner block at Lützostasse and Kluckstrasse, both 1985, IBA, Berlin.
79. Roger Emmerson, 'The Emperor's New Clothes: Pastiche and Reproduction', *Architectural Heritage VI* (Edinburgh, 1996), p.88.
80. K Lynch, *Image.*, p.117.
81. Ibid., p.119.
82. Glendinning & Page, *Clone City*, pp.157–8.
83. See the endpapers and Fig. 2.4 in Alan Balfour, *Berlin: The Politics of Order, 1737–1989* (New York, 1990) which illustrate the original open-core perimeter block planning of the 1737 south-western extension of the city.
84. Glendinning & Page, *Clone City*, p.64.
85. Ibid., p.66.
86. Ibid., p.78.
87. Ibid., p.140.
88. Isaacs, *Gropius*, p.65.
89. Mitchell, *City of Bits*, p.166.
90. Glendinning & Page, *Clone City*, p.155.
91. Ibid., p.157.
92. Ibid., pp.222–3.
93. George Kerevan, 'City to City, Coast to Coast', in *ARCA*, no.2, August 1999, p.61.
94. Adrian Welch, report on Homes for the Future in *e-architecture*, 28 September 2013. Info at: www.glasgowarchitecture.co.uk/homes-for-the-future-glasgow, retrieved 17 July 2020.
95. Derek Fraser, *Berlin: The Buildings of Europe* (Manchester, 1996), pp.80–1.
96. Ibid., pp.64–5.
97. Ibid., p.93.
98. Derek Fraser, email from Fraser to Emmerson, 12 November 2021.
99. Fraser, *Berlin*, p.95.
100. Ibid., pp.60–1.
101. Glendinning, *Architecture of Scottish Government*, p.362.
102. High Pearman, 'Ecosse: It's a Miralles', in *The Sunday Times*, 23 May 2004. Info at: www.thetimes.co.uk/article/ecosse-its-a-miralles-wcv296gf2qv, retrieved 23 November 2020.
103. Neil Gillespie, 'The Scottish Parliament', *AJ*, 30 September 2004. A word perhaps needs saying about the 'white land'. It refers to the paleness of granite, the whiteness of snow and ice, the bark of the birch, the sands at Luskentyre, Na h'Eilean Siar, the haar from the North Sea etc, and only that.
104. Glendinning & MacKechnie, *Scotch Baronial*, p.251.
105. Ibid., pp.251–2.
106. Riss was born to Jewish parents in Vienna and studied at the Wiener Technische Hochschule and, at some point, the Bauhaus where he got to know Paul Klee and Oskar Kokoschka. He worked with Fritz Judtman (1899–1968) from 1924–34, largely on health and colliery projects. He escaped to England via Prague in 1938 and went to work for Jack Pritchard (1899–1992), developer of the Lawn Road Flats, where Riss also lived. In consultation with Penguin Books he designed the 'Gull' and the 'Donkey' book and magazine holders for Pritchard's Isokon furnishing company. He was interned in 1939, but was soon released on appeal and served in the Royal Engineers in WWII. After working for Furneaux-Jordan in London he joined the National Coal Board Scottish Division as Chief Production Architect in 1947, a position he held to his death in 1964. Info at the Dictionary of Scottish Architects and Wikipedia, retrieved 20 August 2020.
107. Published as Scotland's contribution to the 1984 Festival of Architecture, celebrating 150 years of the Royal Institute of British Architects.
108. Neil Baxter & Fiona Sinclair (eds), *Scotstyle: 100 Years of Scottish Architecture (1916–2015)* (Edinburgh, 2016), p.3. Four hundred public

109. 'nominations' were recorded, although it was unclear either how many of those were from architects, or quite how the final ten were selected and ranked.
109. A crude concrete bothy at Loch Inver self-built by the virtually unknown David Scott and lived in by him for one night only.
110. Peter Wilson, *The Modern Timber House in the UK: New Paradigms and Technologies* (Edinburgh, 2017), pp.163–4.
111. Alan Dickson, Rural Design, email from Dickson to Emmerson, 3 November 2020.
112. Andrew Brown, Brown and Brown, email from Brown to Emmerson, 10 March 2021.
113. Mary Arnold-Foster, 'Highlanders Have Long Travelled', in Nick Barley, *Architecture*, p.153.
114. Neil Gillespie, Reiach and Hall, email from Gillespie to Emmerson, 2 December 2020.
115. Nicola Hall, Lee Boyd, email from Hall to Emmerson, 4 May 2021.
116. Jude Barber, Collective Architecture, email from Barber to Emmerson, 18 May 2021.
117. Roy Milne, formerly MD of Michael Laird Architects, email from Milne to Emmerson, 3 February 2021.
118. Andy Summers, Architecture Fringe, email from Summers to Emmerson, 16 May 2021.
119. Chris Dobson, 3DReid, email from Dobson to Emmerson, 7 March 2021.
120. Gordon Ferrier, 3DReid, email from Ferrier to Emmerson, 1 March 2021.
121. Mary Arnold-Forster, telephone conversation with Emmerson, 22 June 2021.
122. Gillespie, 2 December 2020.
123. Hall, 4 May 2021.
124. Richard Murphy in conversation with Emmerson at 2B Hart Street, Edinburgh, 26 February 2022.
125. Chambers, *English Dictionary*, p.888.
126. Barber, 18 May 2021.
127. Gillespie, 2 December 2020.
128. Hall, 4 May 2021.
129. Dobson, 7 March 2021.
130. Brown, 10 March 2021.
131. Dickson, 3 November 2020.
132. Arnold-Forster, 22 June 2021.
133. This compares poorly with the specific building detail and explication of historic and architectural merit supplied by the Landmarks Preservation Commission for an equivalent statutory certification of the Bowling Green Office Building, New York (see Chapter 2: An architecture for the age, endnote 112).
134. Cables Wynd House, listed A, 30 January 2017, ref. LB52403.
135. A recent demonstration project led by the Edinburgh World Heritage Trust at the Basil Spence Canongate flats, Edinburgh, of similar vintage and concrete construction, although with less complicated cavity brick external walls to those of Cables Wynd House, racked up costs of between £64,000 and £93,000 per flat to resolve the environmental issues, putting such remedial works beyond most household budgets or available loan facilities. The works never quite resolved the issue of cold-bridging.
136. Roger Emmerson, 'DOCOMOMO and the Modern Movement', ARCA Six, 2002, pp.64–5.
137. Glendinning (ed), *Rebuilding Scotland: The Post-war Vision 1945–1975* (East Linton, 1997).
138. Cooper et al, *Scotland: Building for the Future*.
139. Ibid., p.2.
140. Ibid., p.98.
141. A brief survey of contemporary titles on Scottish architecture revealed the following incomplete list, presented chronologically:

Robert Clow (ed), *Restoring Scotland's Castles* (Glasgow: 2000).

MacGibbon & Ross, *The Castellated and Domestic Architecture of Scotland* (2000), reprint.

Charles McKean, *The Scottish Chateau: The Country House of Renaissance Scotland* (Stroud, 2001).

Richard Fawcett, *The Conservation of Architectural Ancient Monuments in Scotland: Guidance on Principles* (Edinburgh, 2001).

Hugh Montgomery-Massingberd & Christopher Simon Sykes, *Great Houses of Scotland* (New York, 2001).

Margaret HB Sanderson, *A Kindly Place? Living in Sixteenth-Century Scotland* (East Lothian, 2002).

Ian Gow, *Scotland's Lost Houses* (London, 2006).

Martin Coventry, *The Castles of Scotland* (4th ed) (Edinburgh, 2006).

Geoffrey Stell, *Castle Tioram: A Statement of Cultural Significance* (Edinburgh, 2006).

MacGibbon & Ross, *The Castellated and Domestic Architecture of Scotland* (2008), reprint.

Tina Glenapp Rosenberg, *Castle: A Scottish Intrigue* (New York, 2009).

Michael Brown & Adam Hook, *Scottish Baronial Castle: 1250–1450* (Oxford, 2009).

Brian C Mack, *Scotland: Castles and Clans: The*

Legends (Estes Park CO, 2010).

Richard Dargie, *Scottish Castles and Fortifications* (Doulting, 2011).

Richard Fawcett & Allen Rutherford, *Renewed Life for Scottish Castles* (York, 2011).

Audrey Dakin, Miles Glendinning & Aonghus MacKechnie (eds), *Scotland's Castle Culture* (Edinburgh, 2011).

Michael C Davis, *The Scottish Castle Restoration Debate 1990–2012* (Ochiltree, 2013).

Janet Brennan-Inglis, *Scotland's Castles: Rescued, Rebuilt and Reoccupied* (Stroud, 2014).

Johnny Rodger, *The Hero Building: An Architecture of Scottish National Identity* (Farnham, 2015).

David Cook, *Scottish Castles* (London, 2019).

Miles Glendinning & Aonghus MacKechnie, *Scotch Baronial: Architecture and National Identity in Scotland* (London, 2019).

142. Janet Brennan-Inglis, *Scotland's Castles: Rescued, Rebuilt and Reoccupied* (Stroud, 2014), p.13.
143. Ibid., p.54.
144. Ibid., pp.188–90.
145. Ian Begg, 'Castles in the Modern Age', in Dakin et al (eds), *Castle Culture*, p.311.
146. Rodger, *The Hero Building*, p.215.
147. Glendinning & MacKechnie, *Baronial*, p.252.
148. Immanuel Kant (trans & ed Marcus Weigelt), *Critique of Pure Reason* (London, 2007), p.388.
149. Cahn, *Western Philosophy*, pp.981–2, or in detail in Kant, *Critique*, pp.391–419.
150. Glendinning et al, *History*, p.410.
151. Hall, 4 May 2021.
152. Hugh Metcalf, 'Shettleston HA by Elder and Cannon', *OnOffice*, 19 January 2011. Info at: www.onofficemagazine.com/architecture/shettleston-ha-by-elder-and-cannon, retrieved 28 October 2021.
153. Info at: www.elder-cannon.co.uk/copy-of-tollcross-ha, retrieved 28 October 2021.
154. Info at: www.elder-cannon.co.uk/sandiefield, retrieved 28 October 2021.
155. Murphy, *Ten Years of Practice*, p.136.
156. Murphy, *Ten Years of Practice*, p.136.
157. Ibid., p.136.
158. Info at: www.dropbox.com/s/4t8yf7lh1blaf5w/Maggies.pdf?dl=0, retrieved 29 October 2021.
159. Peter Wilson, *The Modern Timber House in the UK: New Paradigms and Technologies* (Edinburgh, 2017).

Index of people, places and associations

Key

Demolished (dem.)
Attributed (attrib.)
Illustrations are referenced in italics (*86*)
Endnote references are shown as en106

A

Aalto, Alvar 38, 76, *76*, 337
    Säynätsalo Town Hall 393
    Turun Sanomat Building, Turku 76
Abercrombie, Professor Sir Patrick 244, 259
Acemoglu, Daron, and James A Morrison 241
ACM/IEEE Computer Society 290
Adam, Peter 196
Adam, Robert 21, 22, 106, 219-20, 247
Adams, Annemarie 130
Aitchison, George 107
Aitken, George Shaw
    Lady Stair's House, Edinburgh 171-2
Albert, Prince Consort 106, 108, 150
Alexander Thomson Society 280, 329
Alfred, Lord Tennyson
    Idylls of the King 144
    Lady of Shallot 144
Alison, Archibald 24, 100, 100-4
Alison & Hutchison
    Cables Wynd House, Leith, Edinburgh 383-4, en133, *383*
Allen, C Bruce 150
Allen, John 338
Allen, William 260
'An Clachan' 239
Anderson, John 221
Anderson, Sir Robert Rowand 57, 145, 146, 156, 159, 222
    Allermuir 156
Anderson, Rowand, Kininmonth & Paul
    Pollock Halls of Residence, Edinburgh 258
    Scottish Provident Association (dem.), St Andrew's Square, Edinburgh 281
Anderson, Wardrop & Browne 162
Appleton Partnership 329
Apollinaire, Guillaume 82
Araki Nobuyoshi, 360
Aramco 249
ARCHImedia (see also Roger Emmerson)
    Scottish Brick Houses, the 16-7 *17*
    McKean House extension, Edinburgh 335, *336*

'Architects for Independence' 347-8
Architecture Fringe 379
Architecture of soubriquet
    Armadillo, Cheese-grater, Dog Turd, Gherkin, Pink Pay Phone, Razor, Shard, Walkie-Talkie 351
    Bird's nest 352
    Walnut Whip 353
Architectural Association London 214,
Architectural Heritage Society of Scotland 280
Architectural Institute of Scotland 106
Ardrey, Adam 144
Arnold, Matthew 54
Arnold-Forster, Mary 327, 377, 381, 382
    NEDD, Nedd, Highland 396, 398
    Raasay Hall, Raasay 398, *398*
Art Workers Guild 162
Arup, Ove, & Partners 348, 350
Ash, Marinell 44
Ashbee, Charles Robert 165, 166, 167
Ashpitel, Arthur 107
Ashton, Henry 107
Asplund, Gunnar
    Stockholm Public Library 297
Association for the Vindication of Scottish Rights 108
Atkinson, William 104
Audsley, George Ashdown and William James 123-5
    92 Bold Street, Liverpool 123, *124*
    Bowling Green Offices, New York NY 123-4, 231, *124*
    Layton Art Gallery, Milwaukee WI (dem.) 123
    Liverpool Union Bank, Bold Street, Liverpool 123
    New West End Synagogue, London 123
    New York City Hall Competition (not premiated) 124
    Princes Road Synagogue, Liverpool 123
    Racquet Club, Toxteth, Liverpool (dem.) 123
    Scottish Equitable, Castle Street, Liverpool 123
    17 Seel Street, Liverpool (attrib.) 123
Australia
    Adelaide, Thomson copy 123
    First People 34, 35
    Parliament competition 177

B

Bachelard, Gaston 31, 194, 202, 203, 211-2, 301, 360, 389, 390

Badovici, Jean 196
Baillie-Scott, Hugh 162-3, 362
Blackwell, Bowness, Cumbria 161
Baines, Mark 109, 118, 331
Baird II, John 114, 122
Baird, John Logie 47
Baird Premier, John 107
Baldwin, James 23
Baltard, Victor 203
Bakema, Jaap 258
Banham, Reyner 209, 257, 258, 274, 313, 345
Baniassad, Essy 365
Barber, Jude 379, 381, 382
Barley, Nick 270
Barnsdall, Aline 204
Barrow, Clive 226
Barry, Sir Charles 107
Bassett-Lowke, Wenman Joseph 168, 170
Baťa Shoe Company 199
Baudrillard, Jean 247, 300, 360
Bauhaus, Dessau 167
    Zielenbau 256
Baumgarten, Lothar 32
Bayer, Herbert 295
Baxter, Clark & Paul
    Housing in Peterhead and Fraserburgh 336
Beardsley, Aubrey 163
Beck, Louis White 221
Begg, Ian 311, 387
    Scandic Crown Hotel, Edinburgh 310, 311
Behrens, Peter 75, 166, 170
    AEG Turbine Factory, Berlin 317
    New Ways, Northampton 170
Belgioioisi, Peressutti & Rogers 252, 288
Bell, Victoria Ballard and Paul Rand 39
Bennetts Associates 379
Benson, Gordon and Alan Forsyth
    Museum of Scotland, Edinburgh 26, 337-40, 337
Benthall, Michael 187
Benton, Tim 198
Berger, John 34-5, 37
Berlage, Hendrik Petrus 25, 79, 134-6, 140, 142, 177, 180, 191, 225
    Amsterdam Stock Exchange 136
    Beethovenhuis 296
    Gemeentemuseum, Den Haag 136, 238
Berman, Marshall 20, 273, 305, 358
Berry, Wendell 14
Beveridge, Craig, and Ronald Turnbull 44, 53, 113, 221
Bilcliffe, Roger 166, 169
Billings, RW 24, 25, 97, 104-7, 145, 149, 159, 222
Binney, Marcus 374
Blackie Family 121, 162

Blanc, Hippolyte Jean 146
Blanchard-Bethune, Louise 197
Blankett, Hugo 66
Bliss, Sir Arthur 187
Blomstedt, Yrjö 67
Blomstedt, Paul 76
Blore, Edward 104
Blundell Jones, Peter 298
Boardman, Philip 171
Boberg, Ferdinand 71
Bobrikov, General 74
Bobrinsky, Count 74
Bodley, George Frederick 1621
Boeing 737 Max 308
Boito, Camillo 316
Bonaparte, Napoleon, 64
Bond, Gavin 186
Borden, Gail Peter and Andrew H Dent 39
Born & Chermayeff 252
Borsi, Franco, and Ezio Godoli 154
Bosnia, Bosnia-Herzogovina
    War 22, 23
Botta, Mario 290, 311
Boulez, Pierre, 51
Bow, Andy, and Graeme Robertson 329
Brackenbury, Michael 329
Braque, Georges 80, 82
Brennan-Inglis 386
Brett, Lionel (Lord Esher) 247, 259, 260
Breuer, Marcel 252
Brick
    Scottish Brick Houses, the 16-17
    transport of 37
Britain
    Britain Can Make It 256
    British Commonwealth 37, 242-3
    British Empire Exhibition 184
    British Leyland, Bathgate 291
    British Steel, Ravenscraig 291
    Festival of Britain 26, 256-8
    Welfare State 26
Brodie, Margaret 197, 215 en109, 239
    Women of Empire Pavilion, Glasgow Empire Exhibition 239
Brown, Andrew
    Brown & Brown 378, 380, 382
Brown, Neave 338
    Alexandra Road Estate, London 338
Browne, Sir George Washington 108
Broons, The 322
Bruce, Sir George 46
Bruce, Robert 256, 259
Brunelleschi, Filippo 109
Bryant, Ray, and Peter Mason
    Burrell Collection, Pollok, Glasgow

(unpremiated entry) 326
Bryce, AD 240
Bryce, David 98, 107, 145, 146, 158, 159
    Balfour Castle, Shapinsay, Orkney 98, *98*
    Carradale 381
Bryce, John 46
Bryggman, Erik 76
Buchan, John, MP 232
Buchanan, Colin, & Partners with Freeman Fox 322-4
Budapest Arts & Crafts Exhibition 1902 154
Bull, Reina Mary 258
Burges, William 145
Burgin, Victor 33-4, 44, 134, 203
Burke, Edmund 100
Burke, Ian, and Hugh Martin
    St James Centre, Edinburgh 322
Burn, William 98, 104, 145, 159
    Milton Lockhart 121
    St Giles' Cathedral, Edinburgh 95
Burnet, John (senior) 175
Burnet, Sir John James 129, 175-8, 225, 237, 385
Burnet, John, & Son
    Albany Chambers, Glasgow 176
    Athenaeum, Glasgow 175
    Atlantic Chambers, Glasgow 176
    Black's Warehouse, Glasgow 176
    Campbelltown Library and Museum 177
    Civil Service and Professional Association, Edinburgh 176
    Glasgow Stock Exchange 176
    King Edward VII Galleries, British Museum, London 177
    Kodak Building, Kingsway, London 177
    McGeoch's (dem.) Glasgow 177
    RW Forsyth's, Edinburgh 176-7, *177*
    Selfridges, Oxford Street, London 177
    Wallace Scott Tailoring Institute, 177, 278
    Waterloo Chambers, Glasgow 176
Burnet, Sir John, & Partners
    Adelaide House 230, *231*, 278
    Daily Telegraph Building, London 232
    St Andrew's House, Edinburgh 232, *233*, 341
    Silver End, Braintree, Essex 232
Burnet, Tait & Lorne
    Hawkhead Hospital, Paisley 235
    Royal Masonic Hospital, London 232
    Tait's Tower, Glasgow Empire Exhibition 235, *235*
    The Information Book of Sir John Burnet, Tait and Lorne 252
Burnham, Daniel 177
Burns, Robert 54
Burra, Edward

Gorbals Glasgow 187
Buredi (Burrell Company and City of Edinburgh Council) 336
Burrell, Andrew, and Andrew Doolan as Kantel:
    East Crosscauseway, Edinburgh 336
    Forrest Hill, Edinburgh 336
    Ingram Square, Glasgow 336
    St Bernard's Row, Edinburgh 336
Burrell Company 336
Butt, John 218
Byron, Lord 57

C

Calatrava, Santiago 357
Calthrop & Mars
    Angle Park Terrace, Edinburgh 335
    Thomson's Court, Grassmarket, Edinburgh 335
Cambridge School of Architecture 328
Campaign for a Scottish Assembly, The 328
Campbell, Alexander Buchanan
    Dollan Baths, East Kilbride 374
Campbell, Ian 97, 108-9, 157, 234-5
Campbell, John Archibald 129, 175
Campbell, Wilkinson, Zogolovitch & Gough (CWZG)
    Crown Street, Glasgow, masterplan 334
Cannon, Dick 342
    (Elder & Cannon q.v.)
Čapek, Karel 15, 45-6,
Capper, Henbest 129
    James Court, Edinburgh 171
Carlyle, Thomas, 47
Carnegie Dunfermline Trust (CDT) 171
Carnegie United Kingdom Trust (CUKT) 226
Carnegie, Mrs Andrew (Louise Whitfield) 226
Carr, David
    Kirkcaldy Town House 279, *279*
Carrick, James
    Cragburn Pavilion, Gourock 235
    Rothesay Pavilion 235, *234*
Carruthers-Ballantyne Robert
    Lamburn, Old Edinburgh Road, Inverness 224
Castrén, Matthias 65
Césaire, Aimé 23-24
Chadwick, Whitney 31-2, 40
Chambers, Iain 208
Chamberlain, Neville, PM 239
Chant, Colin 35
Charles, Prince of Wales 37
Charles Rennie Mackintosh Society 280
Cheape, Hugh 64
Checkland, Olive and Sydney 47, 173
Chermayeff, Serge 235, 253

Chernikhov, Iakov 291
China 23
    Chenggong 363
    Great Wall of, 33
    Lanzhou 363
    Nanhui 363
    oppression of minorities 23
    Pudong 363
    Shenzen 317
    shop-house (*tong lau*) 38
    Yingkou 363
Chochol, Josef 82, 85, 86
    Apartments, Neklanova ulice, Prague 86, *80*, 236
    Triplex, Rašinkovo nábřeži, Prague 86
    Villa, Libušinkovo ulice, Prague 86
Čihàkovà-Noshiro, Vlasta 82, 83
City Architect, The, Edinburgh 335
Civic Amenities Act 1967 320
Clarke, Paul 338
Clelland, Doug 329
    Centre for the Deaf, Friedrichstrasse, Berlin (with Peter Wilson) 328
Coats, Welles
    Isokon Flats, Hampstead, London 199-200
Cochrane McGregor Partnership 329
Cockburn Association 276, 280
Cocker, Philip, & Partners
    Jamaica Street megastructure Edinburgh (unbuilt) 322
    Link Housing Association, east Central Scotland 280-1
Coia, Jack 385
    (Gillespie, Kidd & Coia)
    St Bride's Church, East Kilbride 395
    St Patrick's Church, Greenock 234
    St Peter in Chains, Ardrossan 234
    St Lawrence's Church Greenock 234
Collins, Peter 19, 26, 48, 91-2, 130, 131, 137, 203, 209, 272-1, 287, 300, 313, 348, 352, 364
Colomina, Beatriz 286
Colquhoun, Alan 312
Congrès Internationaux d'Architecture Moderne (CIAM)
    CIAM 1928 La Sarraz 134
    CIAM 1933 Athens (Athens Charter) 209
    CIAM 1951 Hoddesdon 258
    CIAM 8 1956 Team X 259
Cook, William and Jeanne Cook (Jeanne Moallic) 192
Cooper, Malcolm, et al 320, 384-5
Coop Himmelb(l)au
    (Wolf Prix and Helmut Swiczinsky) 290, 355
Constant, Caroline 196-7
Conzen, MRG 275

Corby 244
Council of Industrial Design (COID) 246-7
Cousin, David 362
Craig, Maurice 110
Craigie, JH 121
Craigievar/Mackintosh/Corbusier-Bauhaus trajectory 163, 164, 182, 217, 237
Cranston, Catherine Miss 162
Cret, Paul Philippe
    Federal Reserve, Washington DC 294
Crichton-Stuart, John, 3rd Marquess of Bute 145
Crinson, Mark, and Jules Lubbock 265
Crowley, David 293
Cullen, Gordon 315
Cuneo, Terence 257
Cunningham, John, MP
    1979 Devolution Referendum 327
Curl, James Stephens 96
Curtis, William 292-3, 295-6
Curtis, Adam 318
Czechoslovakia 17,
    Czech Legions 72-4
    Hradec Králové 81
    nation 13, 18, 50
    Prague 46
        Art Nouveau 155
        Malá Strana 46
        Nové Město 46
        Vltava 46
        Southern Bohemia 46
        Wallachia 77
Czeschka, Carl Otto 169

D

Daifu Motoyuki 360
Daily Express 184
Darbourne, John, and Geoffrey Darke
    Lillington Gardens, Pimlico, London 314
    Marquess Road, Islington, London 314
D'Aronco, Raimundo
    1902 Turin International Exhibition 153-4, *153*
Davey, Peter 315-7, 337
Davidson Family 162
Davidson, Peter 198
Davis, David Stratton
    Inch Housing, Edinburgh 256, *257*
Davis, Mike 353
de Beistegui, Charles 195
de Botton, Alain 358-9
de Carlo, Giancarlo 260
de Chirico, Giorgio 259
Delaunay, Sonia 40
de Graaf, Reiner 354-5

de Groot, Jan Hessel 136
de Klerk, Michel
    Het Schip, Amsterdam 163-4
de Klerk & Kramer
    De Dageraad Amsterdam 163-4, *164*
Demarco, Richard 308
de Maré, Eric 250-1
de Maria, Mario
    Tre Oci, Venice *316*
Dempster, JA
    Cardowan Pithead Baths 235
Denby, Elizabeth 214, 248
Denmark 17, 18
Denton, Professor Trevor 342
    Denton Scott 342 en154
    Grindley Denton Architects 342 en 154
    Wayland Tunley Trevor Denton Architects 342 en 154
Derain, Andre 82
Derrida, Jacques 25, 222, 224
Design Detail Group 329
Dey, William 228
DFDS 43
Dickson, Alan 378, 382
    (see also Rural Design)
Disney Corporation 362
Dixon, Jeremy, and Ed Jones 329
Dobson, Chris 379, 380, 382
Donald, James 231
Dormer, Peter 306
Douglas, Jonathan 329
Drabble, Margaret 52, 54-5
Dresser, Dr Christopher 167, 301
Driba, Dzintars, and Gūnars Lūsis-Grīnbergs
    Riga Ghetto and Latvian Holocaust Museum (formerly the Occupation Museum) 357
Dualchas
    Ionad Hiort Visitor Centre, Uig (unbuilt) 398
    Raasay Community Hall 398
Duchamp-Villon, Raymond
    Maison Cubiste, Paris 85
Dudley Report 1940 264
Dudok, Willem Marinus 25, 213, 225, 229-30, 236
    De Bijenkorf, Rotterdam 235
    Hilversum Town Hall 227, 229
    own house, De Wikke, Hilversum 229-30
Duff, Sheila Grant 86, 87
Dunbar, Evelyn 40
Duncan, John 64
Duncan, John Hemenway
    New York City Hall 124
Duncan's of Edinburgh 354
Dunn, HH
    Sawston Village College, Cambridgeshire 226
Dyce, William 144

Dyckhoff, Tom 92, 355

E

Eco, Umberto 311
Egypt
    Temple at Edfu 110, *110*
Ednie, John 154
Ehn, Karl
    Karl Marx Hof, Vienna 142-3
Einzig, Richard 285
Eisler, Otto
    Pair of houses Lipová ulice, Brno 90
Eisenman, Peter 290 en2
Ekelund, Hilding 66, 75-6
Elder & Cannon 342, 372, 376, 390
    Church of the Holy Name, Mansewood, Glasgow 342
    Crown Street, Glasgow 371
    Glasgow City Mission 391
    Ingram Square, Glasgow 336, *336*
    Lanark Street, Glasgow 371
    National Bank of Pakistan, Glasgow 342
    St Aloysius College Junior School, Glasgow 342
    Sandiefield, New Gorbals, Glasgow 391, *392*
    Shettleston Housing Association offices, Glasgow 390, *191*
    Tollcross Housing Association Offices, Glasgow 391
Eliot, TS 40-1
Elliot, Walter, MP 240
Elmslie, George Grant 180
    (see also Purcell and Elmslie)
Emberton, Joseph
    British Railways Pavilion, Glasgow Empire Exhibition 239
Emergency Hospital Service 240
Emerson, Ralph Waldo 178
Emin, Tracey 40
Emmerson, Roger
    (with Sandy Stoddart) Scottish Parliament, Royal High School 326
    (with Waring & Netts) The 'Scottish Flats', Gosforth 15 *15*
    (see also ARCHImedia)
England
    Alnwick 276
    Berwick on Tweed 33
    Brighton population 56
    Bristol population 56
    Constituent nation 27-8
    Hadrian's Wall 33
    Hoddesdon, Hertfordshire 258
    London

British Empire Exhibition 1924 184-5
Dome of Discovery 248
Empire Exhibition 1859 152
Empire Exhibition 1899 152
Empire Exhibition 1911 152
Festival of Britain 1951 258-9
Festival Hall 259
Franco-British Exhibition 1908 152
Great Exhibition 1851 152
Grenfell Court 306
Ideal Home Exhibition, Olympia 249
Imperial Austrian Exhibition 1906 152
Japanese-British Exhibition 1910 152
Ronan Point 320
Skylon 259
County Council (LCC) 267
Sheffield population 56
Erasmus 31
Errázuriz, Eugenia 194
(see also Le Corbusier)
Erskine, Ralph 259
Eaglestone, Milton Keynes 314
European Economic Community (EEC) 325
European Regional Development Fund (ERDF) 325
European Union (EU) 325
'Accession states' 325
Ewing, Winifred, MP, Hamilton 325
Exner, Hilde 169

F

Farrell, Terry 329
Fawcett, Chris 303-4
Fawcett, Richard 97, 109, 157
Feininger, Lyonel
The Cathedral of Socialism 199
Feininger, T Lux 139
Ferguson, Niall 23, 107-8, 185, 242
Fergusson, James 16, 27, 91, 94-5, 114-5, 146, 159
Ferrier, Gordon 380-1
Fest, Joachim 298
Finland 43
Helsinki Art Nouveau 155
Kalevala 65
Karelia 65
Literature Society 65
nation 13, 18
National Museum 73-4
National Theatre 63
SAD 43
Saturday Club 65
Fleming, Alexander 47
Focillon, Henri 59, 60, 61, 219, 361
Forster, EM 145

Förstner, Leopold 169
Forsyth, RW 174
Foster, Hal 351-2, 361
Foster, Norman, Associates 342, 343
SECC, Glasgow 354
Foucault, Michel 33, 61
Fowke, Captain Francis
Royal Museum of Scotland, Edinburgh 29, 30
Fox, Kate 202
Frame, Adam
41-5 Mill Street, Alloa 122-3
Frampton, Kenneth 21, 26, 120-1, 160, 206, 294, 311-2, 361
Francastel, Pierre 36, 96, 269
France
baguettes 43
berets 43
Gauloises 43
Paris 46
Eiffel Tower 43, 185
Salon d'Automne 85
Franck, Karen 198
Fraser, Derek 371-2
Fraser, Malcolm 342
Storytelling Centre, Edinburgh 335, 395
Frederick, Lord Leighton 167
Freed, Arthur 45
Fromonet, Francoise 39
Frosterus, Sigurd 75
Frueh, Joanna 19, 24, 178
Fry, Maxwell 23, 174
Kensal House, London (with Elizabeth Denby) 248, 254
Fry, Michael 23, 174
Fuchs, Bohuslav and Oldřich Tyl
Veletržní palác, Holešovice, Prague 89, 90
Fuller, Richard Buckminster 345

G

Gablik, Suzi 363
Galizia, Fede 40
Gallen-Kalela, Akseli 66
Galloway, Mike 372
Gandy, Joseph 215
Gardner-Medwin, Robert
Sighthill Health Centre, Edinburgh 258
Gasson, Barry 329
Burrell Collection, Pollok, Glasgow (with Meunier and Andreson) 326, 327, 382
Gau, Franz Christian 115
Gaudí, Antonio 292
Gebhard, David & Patricia 180
Geddes, Alastair 172
Geddes, Sir Patrick 25, 36, 171-3

Dunfermline *A Study of Parks, Gardens And Culture-Institutes* 171
Hebrew University, Jerusalem 173, 296
Temple of Geography, Edinburgh 173
University of Central India, Indore 173
Gehry, Frank 350, 355, 361
　The Dancing House, Prague (with Vlado Milunić) 348, *349*
　Guggenheim Art Museum, Bilbao 348
Gesellius, Herman 68
Gesellius, Lindgren and Saarinen
　Apartments Hämeenkatu, Helsinki 70
　Doctor's House, Fabianinkatu, Helsinki 71
　Eol Apartments, Katajanokka, Helsinki 71
　Finnish Pavilion, Paris 71, *71*,153
　House for Count Bobrinsky 74
　Hvittorp, Kikkonummi 72
　Hvitträsk, Kikkonummi 72, *72*
　Library, Turku 70
　National Museum 73-4, *73*
　Sports Palace, Helsinki 70
　Olofsborg Apartments, Katajanokka, Helsinki 71, 72
　Pohjola Fire Insurance Building, Helsinki 70-1, *71*
　K Selim's Villa, Espoo 72
　Suur-Merijoki Farm, Vipuri 72
General Assembly, The, of the Church of Scotland 346-7
Gentileschi, Artemisia 40
George IV 108
George V 184
George, David Lloyd 162
Germany 25
　Berlin
　　East and west 33
　　Friedrichstadt 48
　　IBA (*Internationale Bauaustellung*) 330
　bratwurst 43
　Celle, Rathenow, Karlsruhe, Kassel 208
　Düsseldorf population 56
　engineering precision 43
　humour, lack of a sense of 43
　knickerbockers 43
　Limes Germanicus 33
　Werkbund 140
Gibberd, Sir Frederick
　Lansbury Estate, Poplar, London 258
Giedion, Siegfrid 19, 209, 258, 266-9, 313
Giedion, Sert and Leger 298
Gillespie, Neil 57-8, 329, 374-5, 378-9, 381, 382
Gillespie, Kidd & Coia 329
　St Bride's Church, East Kilbride 382
　St Paul's, Glenrothes 281, 282, 340, 377
　St Peter in Chains Church, Ardrossan 234, *234*

St Peters College, Cardross 252, 377
Robinson College, Cambridge 332-3, *332*
Round Riding Sheltered Housing, Dumbarton 281
Gilly, Friedrich 115
　Pfielerhalle 118
Gilson, Etienne 301
Glancey, Jonathan 317
Glass, Michael R 321
Gleave, Joseph
　Columbus Memorial Lighthouse, Dominican Republic 278, 296
Gleizes, Albert 82
Glendinning, Miles 125, 288
　The Cumbernauld Conservation Society 317
Glendinning, Miles, and David Page (q.v.) 366-70
Glendinning, Miles, and Ranald MacKechnie 375, 376, 387
Glendinning, Miles, et al 132, 156, 217, 218, 220, 224, 283, 320-1, 327, 384, 385, 389
Gloag, John 214-5
Gočár, Josef 82, 190
　Mánes Hall, Vodičkova, Prague 86
　Legiobanka, Prague 87-89, *88*
　Spa Bohdaneč, Pardubice 86
　U černé Matky Boží, Prague 86
Goldsworthy, Andy 35
Gombrich, EH 296
Gomme, Andor 175
Goodheart-Rendell, HS 170
Gordon, Esme 240
Gordon, John 122
Gordon, John Graham, and David Bennett Dobson 122
　53 Pentland Terrace, Edinburgh 113
Gössel, Peter 285-6
Gowans, Sir James 125-9
　Castle Terrace, Edinburgh 127, *128*
　Edinburgh Exhibition 1886 150
　Lammerburn, Napier Road, Edinburgh 127, *127*
　Rockville, Napier Road Edinburgh (dem.) 128
Gowan, James 24, 57, 385
Grahame-Thomson, Leslie 276
　Reid Memorial Church, Edinburgh 222
Grassi, Giorgio
　Urban villa, Tiergarten, Berlin 372
Graves, Michael 290 en2
　Humana Building, Louisville 353
　Portland Building, Oregon 353
Gray, Eileen 196-8
　E.1027, Roquebrune-Cap-Martin 197
　Lou Perou, Chapelle-Ste-Anne 196
　Tempe a Pailla, Castellar 196, *197*
　Zervos House, La Goulotte 196

Gray, Sophy 197
Greece
    Athens
        Choragic Monument of Thrasyllos 111, *111*, 114, 120
        Choragic Monument of Lysicrates 120
Greene, Herb 311
Gregotti, Vittorio 325
Gripenberg, Sebastian 73
Gropius, Walter 25, 198-204, 209, 269, 295, 313, 368, 369-70
    Chicago Tribune Tower 199, 235
    Graduate School of Design, Harvard 265
    own house, Lincoln Massachusetts 201, *201*
    Masters' Houses, Bauhaus, Dessau 211
    Monument to the March Dead, Weimar (dem.) 199
    Sommerfeld House, Berlin 168, 198, 199
    Törten Siedlung, Dessau 200, *200*
    Total Theatre project 170
    Wohnberge 199
Groves-Raines, Nick, and Michael Spens
    Moncrieff Terrace, Edinburgh 334-5, *335*
Grumbach, Antoine
    Urban villa, Tegeler Hafen, Berlin 372
Gubler, Jacques 294
Guedes, Amancio d'Alpoim 311
Guimard, Hector 153
Gutfreund, Otto 82
Gwathmey, Charles 290 en2
Gwilt, Joseph 114

H

Hadden, Thomas 162
Hadid, Zaha 350
    Bergisel Ski Jump, Innsbruck 348
    Riverside Museum, Glasgow 351, *351*
Haesler, Otto
    Housing at Celle, Rathenow, Karlsruhe and Kassel, Germany 208
Hall, Eric, & Partners
    Housing and shops, Gracemount Road, Edinburgh 281
Hall, Nicola 379, 381, 382, 389
Hall, Peter 202, 271
Hamilton, Thomas
    Arthur Lodge, Edinburgh 116
    Falcon Hall, Edinburgh (dem.) 116
    Royal High School, Edinburgh 116, 340
    Scottish Academy and National Gallery of Scotland, Mound, Edinburgh (unbuilt) 116
Hamilton, William Stirling 113
Hampson, Frank 258
Hardie, Keir 185

Hare, Bill 101
Häring, Hugo 295
Harries, Karsten 299-300, 304, 389
Harris, E Vincent
    Ministry of Defence, Whitehall, London 294
Harvey, David
    St Cuthbert's Showroom, Edinburgh (with Philip McManus) 224
Hawthorne, Chris
    That Far Corner: Frank Lloyd Wright in Los Angeles 205
Heidegger, Martin 298-9, 390
Hejduk, John 290 en2
    Urban villa, Tegeler Hafen, Berlin 372
Heliopolis (Port Tewfik) 232
Helpmann, Robert 187
Henderson, Graham 276
Herman, Arthur 46-7, 140
Hertzberger, Herman 334
    Haarlemmer Houtuinen, Amsterdam 372
    Lindenstrasse, Berlin 371
    Markgrafenstrasse, Berlin 371
Hertzog & De Meuron
    Olympic Stadium, Beijing (with Li Xinggang) 358
Hitchcock, Henry-Russell 19, 25, 48, 50-1, 125, 181, 204, 207-9, 213, 266, 291-2, 343, 368
Historic Environment Scotland (HES) 383
Hitler, Adolf 298, 299, 300
HM Office of Works
    Sherriff Court (now High Court), Edinburgh 238, 294
Hobsbawm, Eric 53-4, 145, 155, 213, 297
Hodgkinson, Patrick 338
    Brunswick Centre, London 338
Hoffmann, Josef 99, 154, 160, 165, 166-8, 169, 177, 274, 292, 296
    Eight Villas, Hohe Warte, Vienna 165
    Grosser Hof, Vienna 165
    Henneberg House, Vienna 167
    Hochstetter House, Vienna 166
    Palais Stoclet, Brussels 166, *166*
    Primavesi Country House, Kouty, Czechia 166
    Purkersdorf Sanatorium, Austria 166
    Villa Ast, Vienna 166, 167
    Villa Skywa-Primavesi, Vienna 166
    Weltfriedenshaus, Vienna 298
Hofman, Vlastislav 82, 84-5, 136
Hogg, James 55
Holl, Stephen 355
Hollein, Hans
    Urban villa, Tiergarten, Berlin 372
Hope, John C
    Holyrood masterplan 335
Horsman, Matthew and Andrew Marshall 22

Horta, Victor 177
Howard, Ebenezer 243
Howard, Jeremy 293
Howarth, TEB 242
Howarth, Thomas 20-1
HRI Architects
    Biomass Centre, Fort William (unbuilt) 398
    Brachla Harbour, Loch Ness (unbuilt) 398
Hughes, Professor T Harold
    Chemistry Building, Glasgow University 238
    Reading Room, Glasgow University 238
Hungary
    personal names 27
Hurd, Robert 218, 235, 245-6, 276
    (as Neil & Hurd)
    Ravelston Flats, Edinburgh 280
Hutcheson, Jim (Benson + Forsyth) 337-8
Hypostyle Architects 336

I

Incorporation of Architects in Scotland 156
India 37
    Ocean 43
Ingels, Bjarke 345
    (BIG)
    National Library, Astana, Kazakhstan 357-8
Ingres, Jean-Auguste-Dominique 64
International Committee for the Documentation
    And Conservation of Buildings, Sites and
    Neighbourhoods of the Modern Movement
    (DOCOMOMO)
    DOCOMOMO Denmark 278
    DOCOMOMO Finland 278
    DOCOMOMO Iceland 278
    DOCOMOMO Latvia 278
    DOCOMOMO Norway 278
    DOCOMOMO Scotland List 278, 376-7
    DOCOMOMO Sweden 278
International Style 207
    Exhibition, MOMA, New York 207
Irvine Development Corporation
    Housing, Girdle Toll, Irvine 281
Isaacs, Reginald 199
Ishimoto Yasuhiro 285
Israel
    Israel-Gaza Strip Barrier 33
    Nation 17, 18
Italy
    Genoa 46
    Naples 46

J

Jacobs, Jane 274

Jackson, Neil 301, 302, 303
Jahrhundertwerken 198
Janák, Pavel 79, 82, 83-4, 86, 190
    Crematorium, Pardubice 88
    palác Adria, Jungmannova, Prague 79, 89
Japan
    bullet train 43
    Katsura Palace 43, 285
    Kimono 43
    personal names 27
    tea ceremony 43
Jarvis, Alan 246
Jencks, Charles 26, 295, 304, 306-8, 309, 310-1, 349, 364
    Cells of Life, Jupiter Artland, Edinburgh 310
    The Garden of Cosmic Speculation, Dumfriesshire 310
    Landform, Scottish National Gallery of Modern Art 310
    Star of Caledonia (project) (with Cecil Balmond), Gretna 310
    Thematic House, London 310
Jensen-Klint, Peter and Kaare Klint
    Grundtvig's Church, Copenhagen 299
Jerdan, James 156
Jestico & Whiles
    W Hotel, Edinburgh 354, *354*
Johansson, Anders 43
Johnson, Boris 33 en9
Johnson, Philip 181, 204, 266, 295, 345
    AT&T Building, New York 353
    Glass House, New Canaan, USA 302
Johnson, Marcus 227-8
Johnson, Samuel 44
Johnson-Marshall, Percy 265
Johnston, Tom, MP 240
Johnstone, Ninian 214
Jones, Owen 114
Jones, Patrick Lloyd 185
Jones, Peter Blundell 296
Jordan, R Furneaux
    Glass and steel reimagining of Princes Street, Edinburgh 239
    Timber Pavilion, Glasgow Empire Exhibition 239
Jung, Bertel 67
Jurkovič, Dušan 77, 79
    Private house, Trenčianske Teplice 78

K

Kahlo, Frieda 40
Kahn, Louis I 15, 49-50, 120, 281, 290, 340
    Esherick House, Philadelphia PA 50
    Korman House, Fort Washington PA 50

Richards Medical Institute, Pennsylvania PA 50
Kallio, Oiva 72
Kallir, Jane 166, 169
Kant, Immanuel 26, 41, 42, 100-1, 113, 220, 328, 388, 390
Karfík, Vladimír, and František Gahura
    Hostels, Zlín, Czechoslovakia 199
Karasová, Daniela 46 en49
Kawauchi Rinko 360
Kawazoe Noburo 302
Keatinge-Clay, Paffard
    Burrell Collection, Pollok, Glasgow (honourable mention) 326
Kelly, Gene 45
Kengo Kuma
    V&A, Dundee 354
Keppie, John 129, 163
Keppie & Mackintosh 163
Kerevan, George 370
Kerr, Robert 48
Kimura Hiroaki 168
Kinchin, Perilla, and Juliet 155
King, Dr 215 en109
King, Jessie M 153, 155
King, Thomas Starr 35
Kininmonth, William
    Lane House, Edinburgh 222, 278, 223
Kininmonth & Spence
    Broughton Place, Broughton 224-5, 225
    Lismhor, Edinburgh 222
Kinross, John 156
Kissinger, Henry 23
Kikutake Kiyonori
    Izumotaishi-Chonoya, Japan 284
Kivinen, Paula 69
Klimt, Gustav 165
Klimt-gruppe 165
Klint, Peter Jensen, and Kaare Klint
    Grundtvig's Church, Copenhagen 297, 297, 317
Knott, Ralph
    County Hall, London 257
Knox and Hutton
    5-9 S St Andrews St, Edinburgh 122
Kohn Brothers 167
Kokoschka, Oskar 165
Koolhaas, Rem 346
    as OMA (Office for Metropolitan Architecture) Central China Television Building, Beijing (with Arups) 352
Kostof, Spiro 294
Kotěra, Jan
    Peterka House, Prague 78
    Urbanek House, Prague 78-9
Krajči, Petr 77

Kramář, Dr Vincenc 82
Krell, David Farrell 298
Krier, Leon 48, 328
    Poundbury, Dorsetshire 324
Kronick, Richard L 180
Kubišta, Bohumil 82, 84, 85, 142
Kučerová-Záveská, Hana 198
Kurokawa Noriaki (Kisho) 283-4, 304-5, 309
    Pavilions at Kodomo-No-Kuni, Japan 284
Kysela, Ludvík 82

L

Lallerstedt, Erik
    Technical High School (Royal Institute of Technology), Stockholm 211, 297
Lamarová, Milena 60
Langmead, Donald 214, 225
Lapidus, Morris 345
La Roche, Raoul 192
Latvia 17
    nation 13, 18
    Riga Art Nouveau 155
Lauder, Sir Harry 45
Laugier, Marc-Antoine
    Primitive Hut 396
Law, Graham 50, 125
Layard, Sir Austen Henry 115
League of Nations competition 177
Le Corbusier 25, 42, 89, 101, 134, 163, 191-6, 198, 209, 248, 252, 258, 285, 290, 295, 313, 337
    Chandigarh, India 259
    Church of Saint-Pierre, Firminy 332
    Cité de Refuge, Paris 195
    Le Sextant, Royan 195
    Maison Jaoul, Neuilly-sur-Seine 195
    Pilgrimage Chapel, Ronchamp 333
    Unité d'habitation, Marseille 252
    Villa l'Artaude (Maison de Mandrot), near Toulon 194
    Villa Errázuriz, Chile 194
    Villa Savoye, Poissy 192, *193*
    ville radieuse 256
    Wiessenhofsiedlung, Stuttgart 211
Led Zeppelin 290
Lee Boyd 342
    Pitt Street, Edinburgh 381
Lee, CY, & Partners
    Taipei 100, Taiwan 357
Lefebvre, Henri 203
Leiper, William 157
    Templeton's Carpet Factory, Glasgow 177
Lenin, Vladimir 60
Lennon, John 361
Lenormant, Charles 115

Lescaze, William
    Vanderbilt House, Connecticut 222
Lethaby, William Richard 21, 134, 157, 159, 170
    Melsetter, Hoy, Orkney 157, *157*
Levin, Janna 204
Lewerentz, Sigurd 395
Lewis, Brian
    The Yellow Submarine 258
Lewis, Penny 342
Libeskind, Daniel 350
    Jewish Museum, Berlin 348, 357
Limes Germanicus 33
Lindberg, Hugo 66
Lindgren, Armas 66, 67, 68
    (see also Gesellius, Lindgren and Saarinen)
Lindahl, Karl, with Valter Thomé
    Otava Publishing Building, Helsinki 72
    Poli Students Union, Helsinki 72
Lindqvist, Selim 72
Lindsay, Ian 276
Line City, Neon, Saudi Arabia 353
Lipton, Thomas 174
Lissitsky, El 189
Livett, RAH
    Quarry Hill, Leeds (dem.) 384
Llewellyn-Davies, Richard, Professor Lord 267
Löffler, Berthold 165, 169
Lon, Wivi 198
Lönnrot, Elias, 65
Loos, Adolf 25, 49, 134, 136, 138-44, 171, 191, 212, 303
    Goldman & Salatsch, Vienna 167, 171
    Muller House, Prague *139*
    Khuner Country Villa, Kreuzberg 167
    Project for a Settlement with Seven Metre Long Gardens, Vienna 167
    Spanner House, Grumpoldskirchen 167
Lord Cockburn 281
Lorimer, James 146
Lorimer, Robert 49, 138, 156, 159, 162, 229, 385
    Formakin Castle 157
    Scottish National War Memorial, Edinburgh Castle 222
Lorne, Francis 215 en109
    (see also Burnet Tait and Lorne)
Lubetkin, Berthold
    Peterlee New Town 259
    Spa Green Estate, Finsbury, London 259
Luckhardt, Wassili 295
Lurçat, André 134
Lutyens, Sir Edwin
    Viceroy's House, New Delhi 294
Lyall, Sutherland 313-4
Lynch, Kevin 274, 367
Lynch, Michael 3107, 174, 185, 187, 213, 240-1, 275
Lyotard, Jean-François 339

M

MacArthur, Alexander, and H Kingsley Long 187
McAslan, John 379
MacAulay, James 159
MacAra, Duncan 126-7
MacBeth, Ann 155
McCarter, Robert 204-5
McCrone, David 44, 56, 307
MacDiarmid, Hugh 25, 53, 54-5, 186, 218, 219, 220-1, 281
MacDonald, Margo, MP, Glasgow Govan 327
MacDonald, Ramsay, MP 185
McFadzean, Ronald 125, 329
MacGibbon, David, and Thomas Ross 25, 51, 146-50, 156, 159, 222
Machoň, Ladislav 79
MacIntyre, Alasdair 47, 221
MacKay-Lyons, Brian 38, 312, 365
McKean, Charles 186, 216-7, 220, 224, 233, 235, 238, 339, 385
MacKenzie, Alexander 276
MacKenzie, Alexander Marshall
    Northern Assurance, Aberdeen 67
    Marischal College, Aberdeen 67
McKeown Alexander (subsequently jm architects)
    Lanark Street, Glasgow 371
McKim, Charles Follen 176
Mackintosh, Charles Rennie 17, 20, 21, 22, 25, 49, 50, 57, 99, 134, 137, 141, 159-70, 225, 228, 246, 292, 339, 385
    Artist's Cottage 167
    Basket of Flowers 169
    Chelsea Studios, London, project 170
    Daily Record, Renfield Street 330, 332
    Das Haus Eines Kunstsfreundes 160-2, *161*, 170
    Derngate, Northampton 168, *168*, 170
    Edinburgh International Festival Exhibition 1968 20-1
    Glasgow International Exhibition 1901:
        Stand for Francis Smith 154
        Stand for Glasgow School of Art 154
        Stand for Pettigrew and Stephens 154
        Stand for Rae Brothers 154
    Glasgow School of Art 160, 220, 235, 237, 330, 340
    Hill House, Helensburgh 160
    Margaret Morris Theatre project 170
    Mossyde, Kilmacolm 157
    Scotland Street School 160, 330
    Scottish Room, Turin International

Exhibition 1902 153, *154*
Shops and offices project, India 170-1
Willow Tea Rooms, Glasgow 160, 169
Windyhill, Kilmacolm 157
Mackintosh, Margaret MacDonald 153, 170
McKissack, James
    Cosmo Cinema, Glasgow 235
Mackovecz, Imre 311
MacLachlan, Ewan and Fiona 329, 335
MacLaren, John Marjoribanks 49, 159, 162
    Fortingall, Glen Lyon 157, *156*
    Stirling High School extension 157
MacLeod, Robert 91, 97, 100, 164-5
McManus, Philip 224
    (see also David Harvey)
MacMillan, Andy 57, 125, 329
    (see also Gillespie Kidd and Coia)
MacNair, Frances MacDonald 153
MacNair, James Herbert 141, 153
MacPherson, James 64-5
MacRae, James Ebenezer 222, 245
MacRae, Ken 329
    Stratford Street, Maryhill, Glasgow (with McGurn, Logan, Duncan & Opfer) 329, 333-4, *333*
MacTaggart & Mickel
    Broom Estate, Glasgow 250
MacWilliam, Colin 58, 157-8, 277
Madge, John 251-2
Maelmura of Othain 109
Mahoney, Marion 197-8
Malaysia
    Kuala Lumpur 38
    shop-house (*tong lau*) 38 en14
Malevich, Kazimir
    Architectons *Alpha*, *Zeta* and *Gota 2a* 189
Mallet-Stevens, Rob 192
    Tourist Pavilion, Art Deco Exhibition, Paris 235
Mann, Councillor Mrs Jean 243-4, 254, 259
Margold, Joseph Emmanuel 169
Marie Antoinette
    L'Hameau de la Reine, Versailles 194
Marin, Louis 33
Markelius, Sven
    Villa Nockeby, Stockholm 223
Marshall, Ian
    Burgess Terrace, Edinburgh 281
Martin, John 116
Martin, Sir Leslie 265
Martin, Hugh, & Partners
    Princes Square, Buchanan Street, Glasgow 377
Marwick, T Craigie 205 en109
Marwick, T Waller 25, 385
    National Bank of Scotland (dem.), George Street, Edinburgh 235-8, *236*
    St Cuthbert's Store, Edinburgh 278
Marx, Groucho 377
Masaryk, Tomáš 76
Masheck, Joseph 61, 138, 141, 167
Mather, Rick
    Lanark Street, Glasgow 371-2
Matthew, Robert 255, 259, 265, 276, 368
Matthew, Robert, Johnson Marshall and Partners (RMJM) 27, 259
    David Hume Tower (40 George Square) University of Edinburgh 277
    Hillingdon Civic Centre, London 314
    Lanark Street, Glasgow 371
    Pathfoot Building, University of Stirling 377
    Royal Commonwealth Pool, Edinburgh 377
    William Robertson and Adam Ferguson Buildings, University of Edinburgh 277
Maudlin, Daniel 38
Maxwell, James Clerk 47
May, Ernst 212
Mayne, Thom 355
Mears, Sir Frank 172, 276
    Hebrew University, Mount Scopus, Jerusalem 298
    Housing and Coronation Clock Tower, Penicuik 258
    Scottish Office project, Calton Hill, Edinburgh (with Charles Carus-Wilson) 296
'Medicis of Maryhill, The' 320
Meier, Richard 290
Mellor, Roy 63
Melnikov, Constantin 291
Mendelsohn, Erich 25, 222, 229
    De La Warr Pavilion, Bexhill-on-Sea (with Serge Chermayeff) 235
    Houses, Charlottenburg, Berlin 223
    own house, Rupenhorn, Berlin 211
Mercereau, Alexandre 82
Meredith, Amaza Lee 198
Merrylees, Andrew
    National Library of Scotland extension, Causewayside, Edinburgh 333
Metzinger, Jean 82
Metzstein, Isi 57, 331
Meyer, Alfred 168
Meyer, Hannes 134
MGM
    Brigadoon 44-5
Michie, James 33 en9, 42
Middle East 36, 37
Miller, James 151, 154
Milne, Roy 379-80, 382
Miller, Mary 51
Milton Keynes Development Corporation (MKDC)

Neath Hill Housing and Health Centre 342
Stantonbury Campus 342
Miralles, Enric and Benedetta Tagliabue (EMBT)
(with RMJM) Scottish Parliament, Edinburgh 26, 27, 344, 373-6, 374
Mitchell, Sydney 156
Mitchell, Sydney, and Henbest Capper
Ramsay Garden, Edinburgh 171
Mitchell, William J 349-50, 370
Ministry of Housing and Local Government (MHLG) 255 en55
Planning our new homes 255-7
Ministry of Works (MOW) 252
Moffat, Sandy 32
Moffat, William Lambie
Patriot Hall, Edinburgh 151
Rosemount Buildings, Edinburgh 151
Moll, Carl 165
Moneo, Raphael 342, 343
Mongold, Neal J 321
Moore, Ruble & Yudell
Tegeler Hafen, Berlin 371
Mopin, Eugene 334 en141
Morgan, Julia 197
Moriyama Daido 360
Morris, Henry 226
Morris, Margaret 170
Morris, Sir Parker
'Homes for tomorrow', Parker Morris Report 261-5
Morris & Steedman 396
Avisfield, Cramond, Edinburgh 377
Morris, Talwin 153
Morris, William 107, 144-5, 156
Defence of Guenevere 144
Queen Guenevere 144
The Well at the World's End 145
Morris & Co 162
Moser, Koloman 'Kolo' 165, 167, 169, 177
Moss, Eric Owen 356-7
Munkenbeck & Marshall 376
Münzbyer, Bedřich
Industrial Palace, Prague 77
Murcutt, Glenn 38, 39, 43
Murdock, George Peter 202
Murphy, Richard 286, 341-2, 376, 381
Dunfermline Library and Galleries 393-5, 394
Inverewe Gardens architectural competition (winner) (unbuilt) 329
Murray, Allan, Architects (AMA Studio) 392-3
Calton Square, Edinburgh 393
Lochside View, Edinburgh 393
St James Quarter, Edinburgh 393
Mussolini, Benito 186
Muthesius, Herman 25, 49, 51, 106, 134, 136-8, 222

Myanmar
oppression of minorities 23

N

Naismith, Robert
corrugated iron 37-8, 38
Nakamura Hiroshi
(with NAP) Ribbon Chapel, Hiroshima 354
Napoleon III 64
NASA 362
National Art Survey 57
National Library of Scotland (NLS)
Moving Image Archive 256
National Health Service (NHS) 240
National Trust for Scotland (NTS)
Architectural and Artistic Advisory Committee (AAAC) 275-7
National Union of Civil and Public Servants 326
Nénot, Paul
Palace of Nations, Geneva 233
Netherland
Amsterdam 46
Delft 46
Leeuwarden
Art and Architecture Festival 1990 46
Neutra, Richard 207-8
Newbery, Fra 277
Newcastle upon Tyne
Gosforth 15
Hadrian's Wall 33
Nicolas II, Tsar 68
Nicoll Russell Studio
Dundee Repertory Theatre 343
Grianan Building, Dundee Technology Park 343
Palace Green Housing, Berwick-on-Tweed 343
Scrymgeour's Corner, Crieff 343-4, 343
TSB, St Andrews 343
White Top Youth Day-Care Centre, Dundee 344
Nicolson, Peter 24, 100, 114, 151
Nicolson, Michael Angelo 115
Nikula, Riitta 68
Norberg-Schulz, Christian 26, 195, 269-72
NORD 376
Normand, Tom 217, 218
NORR
Dalmunach Distillery Carron, Morayshire 398
Northern Ireland
Constituent nation 27-8
Brexit protocol 23
Good Friday Agreement 23
Peace Wall 33

471

'The Troubles' 290
'Ulster Plantation'
North Korea 296
North Sea oil 324-5
    Forties Field 324
    Indefatigable Field 324
    Leman Field 324
    Viking Field 324
    West Sole Field 324
North of Scotland Hydro-Electric Board (NSHEB) 240
Novotný, Otakar
    Štenc Publishing House, Prague 79
Nur-Maler 165
Nuttgens, Patrick 330
Nyström, Alexander 66
Nyström, Gustav 66, 67, 68

O

O'Doherty, Brian 286-7
O'Keefe, Georgia 40
Olbrich, Josef Maria 154, 166, 167
Osborn, Sir Frederick J 245
Ossian, Tales of 137
Ostberg, Ragnar
    City Hall, Stockholm 211, 291, 297
Outram, John
    Burrell Collection, Pollok, Glasgow
    (unpremiated entry) 326
Owens, Craig 32-3, 239, 313
Ozenfant, Amédée 192

P

Paasikivi, President PK 62-3
Pacione, M 318
Page \ Park 342, 376
    Crown Street, Glasgow 371
    Lanark Street, Glasgow 370-3
    The Lighthouse, Glasgow 396
    Spens Building, Fettes College, Edinburgh 396
Palestine 23
Pallasmaa, Juhani 313
Papadakis, Andreas 314-5
Paris
    Art Deco Exhibition 1925 239
    Eiffel Tower 185
    International Exhibition 1900 71
Parker, Barry 244
    (with Raymond Unwin):
    Letchworth 244
    Welwyn 244
Parr, James, and Partners
    Commercial Street, Perth 336, 336
Parry, Eric 123, 327

23 Saville Row, London 123
One Eagle Place, London 123
Paterson, Alexander Nisbet 129
Paterson, John L
    Two Hundred Summers in the City
    Exhibition 1966 322
Patience & Highmore 329
Patkau, John and Patricia 38, 312
Paxman, Jeremy 52
Paxton, Joseph 92
Pearman, Hugh 374
Peche, Dagobert 169
Pelli, Cesar
    Petronas Towers, Kuala Lumpur 317
Petit, Rev. JL 130
Pevsner, Nikolaus 20, 25, 163-4, 209, 237, 266, 292-3, 313
Phillips, Randal 215
Piano, Renzo 361
Picasso, Pablo 80
Pick, Frank 214
Pietilä, Reima 76
Pinnel, Patrick 181
Pinós, Carme 356
Piper, John 332
Piranesi, Giovanni Baptista 340
Pirie, John Bridgford 48, 66-7, 71, 122
    Queen's Cross Church, Aberdeen 122, 67
    53 Queen's Road, Aberdeen 49, 122
Planeix, Antoine 192
Playfair, James
    Cairness House, Buchan 340
Playfair, William Henry 107
Plečnik, Jože
    Slovenska akropola and *Katedrala svobode*, Ljubljana 296
Poelzig, Hans 75
    Haus das Freundschaft, Istanbul 296
Polano, Sergio 188
Pope-Hennessy, John 55
Porphyrios, Demetri 328
Portoghesi, Paolo
    Urban villa, Tegeler Hafen, Berlin 372
Portugal 17, 18
Powers, Harriet 40
Prague
    Art Nouveau
Prince Philip, Duke of Edinburgh 217
Proclaimers, The
    Letter from America 242
Prutscher, Otto 169
    Women's Drawing Room, Museum of Art and Industry, Vienna 1696
    Women's Room, Café Heinrich-Hof, Vienna 170

Pugin, AWN 36, 96, 107, 156
Purcell, William Gray 180
Purcell & Elmslie
    Merchant Bank, Winona,Minnesota 180
    Old Second National Bank, Aurora, Illinois 180

Q

Quantrill, Malcolm 365

R

Raeburn, Sir Henry
    The Skating Minister 375
Ravetz, Alison 318, 321
Raymond, Antonin
    House, Karuizawa, Japan 195
Read, Herbert (Sir) 80-1, 83, 214
Reade, Arthur 65 en112, 66 en116
Reiach, Alan 245, 259, 276,277, 376
    Building Scotland (with Robert Hurd) 245-6, 246
    Appleton Tower, University of Edinburgh 277
Reiach & Hall
    Clapperfield, Edinburgh 281
    Community Health Centre, East Kilbride 392
    Community Health Centre, Wishaw 392
    10 George Street, Edinburgh (altered) 396
    Maggie's Centre, Monklands, Airdrie 395, *395*
    Pier Arts Centre, Stromness 397, 398
    Saltire Square, Granton, Edinburgh 392, *392*
    Yeaman Place, Edinburgh 335
Reid, Richard, and Ralph Lerner
    Vasone Villa (project) São Paulo, Brazil 315
Revell, Viljo 76
    Toronto City Hall 348
Riach, Alan 32
Rhind, David 107
Rhowbotham, Kevin, 345
Richards, JM 209, 249-50, 259, 259-60, 287-8, 314
Richardson, Henry Hobson 49,71, 226
Richardson, John 194
Rietveld, Gerrit
    Child's Chair 189
    Rietveld-Schröder House, Utrecht 188, *189*, 285
    Sideboard 189
Ringbom, Sixten 48
Riss, Egon 376, en104
Ritchie, Ian
    Lanark Street, Glasgow 371
Robb, George Clark 334 en101
    House for Hugh MacDiarmid (project) 334 en101

Roberts, David 107, 116-7
Robertson, Brian
    Little Lindisfarne, Hawick, Scottish Borders 398
Robertson, John Murray
    India Buildings, Dundee 122
    Victoria Buildings, Dundee 122
Robertson, Pamela 120
Rochead, John T
    City of Glasgow Bank 122
    Wallace Monument, Stirling 122
Roche Dinkeloo
    Cummins Engine Factory, Darlington 382
Rodger, Johnny 234, 237, 387
Rodger, Richard 151-2
Roller, Alfred 169
Rootes Group, Linwood 289
Ross, Launcelot 239
Ross, William, MP 299
Rossi, Aldo 290, 328
    Teatro del Mundo, Venice 329
    Urban villa, Tiergarten, Berlin 372
Rowe, Colin 209, 273, 288, 293
Rowell, Clunie, with Douglas Niven and Gerard Connolly
    St John Ogilvie, Irvine 333
Rowse, EAA 241
Rowse, Herbert
    United Kingdom Pavilion, Glasgow Empire Exhibition 39
    Liverpool Concert Hall 239
Royal Commission for the Architectural and Historical Monuments of Scotland (RCAHMS) 317, 383
Royal Incorporation of Architects in Scotland (RIAS)
    Architectural competitions 328
    Prospect List 2005 376-7
    RIAS List 1984 376-7
    RIAS List 2016 376-7
Royal Institute of British Architects (RIBA)
    Oxford Conference 1958 265-6
Royal Navy 262
Roxburgh, Graham 170
Rural Design (see also Alan Dickson)
    Bogbain Mill, Dingwall 398
    Hen House, Fiscavaig, Skye 398
    Invisible House, Colbost, Skye 398
    R House various sites in Skye 397-8
    Turf House, Kendram, Skye 398
Ruskin, John 24, 36-7, 92, 94-100, 143, 146, 156, 178, 360
Russell, Gordon 214
Russia
    invasion of Ukraine 22, 23
Runciman, Alexander 64

S

Saarinen, Eliel 66, 67-8, 74
  (see also Gesellius, Lindgren and Saarinen)
  Chicago Tribune Tower competition 75
  Cranbrook College, Michigan, USA 75
  Helsinki Railway Station 74-5, 74
  Kalevala House, Helsinki 296
Sacconi, Giuseppe
  Vittoria Emanuele II, Rome 316
Saint, Andrew 226-7
Salmon, James 49, 385
  Lion Chambers, Glasgow 170, 278
Saltire Society 277
Sarnitz, August 167
Savoye, Pierre and Eugénie 192
  (see also Le Corbusier)
Sayers, Dorothy L 305
Scandinavia
  joke 43
Scarpa, Carlo 332, 337, 340, 341
  Banca Popolare di Verona 341, 395
  Fondazione Querini Stampalia, Venice 341
  Gipsoteca Canoviana, Possagno 393
  Museo Castelvecchio, Verona 341
  Tomba Brion e Santuario, San Vito d'Altivole 341, *341*
Schama, Simon 35
Schauman, Eugene 74
Schindler, Rudolf 49, 131, 192-3, 207, 242 en100
  Schindler-Chase House, Los Angeles, California 207, *207*
Schinkel, Karl Friedrich 50, 51, 64, 114, 116, 125
  Gardener's House, Potsdam 116, *116*
  Schauspielhaus, Gendarmenmarkt, Berlin 116
Schinkel/Thomson/Sullivan/Wright trajectory 164, 182
Schröder-Schräder, Truss 188
  (see also Gerrit Rietveld)
Schulz, Antonin
  Bohemian Museum, Prague 78
Schulz, Robert Weir 172
Schultze-Naumburg, Paul 295
Schütte-Lihotzky, Margarete 212, *212*
Scota, daughter of Pharaoh 109
Scotland
  Aberdeen 48
    Marischal College 66
    Northern Assurance 66
    St Machar's Cathedral 66
  Aberdeenshire
    Baronial clone 314
  Antonine's Wall 33
  bagpipes 51
  blackhouse 38

Borthwick Castle, Midlothian 148
Brigadoon 44-5
Caerlaverock Castle, Dumfriesshire 148
Camlongan Castle, Dumfriesshire 148
Cardoness Castle, Kirkcudbright 148
Castle Blair, Blair Atholl, Pitlochry 148
Castle Fraser, Inverurie 148
Castle Menzies, Aberfeldy 148
clachan 38, 45
Clearances 45
constituent nation 27-8
Coupar Angus 322
Craigievar Castle, Alford 148 *50, 148*
Crathes Castles, Banchory 148, 160, *148*
Crichton Castle, Midlothian 148, 395
Culross Palace 46
Department for Health 252
Devolution Referendum 1997 16
Dundee 322
  city plan 48
Dunfermline
  Abbey, Abbot Pitcairn's Tombstone 226
  Council Architects Department, Carnegie Library Extension 382
East Kilbride 256, 259
Edinburgh 48
  Architectural Association 145
    Sketchbooks 25, 145, 149, 222
  Buccleuch Street 317
  Calton Hill 325
  Central Library 108
  Charlotte Square 325
  city plan 48
  College of Art 17, 272
    School of Applied Arts 156
    School of Architecture 16, 214, 342, 379
  compared to Prague, Paris Genoa, Naples 46
  Cooperative Building Company 151-2
    Stockbridge Colonies 151
  Craigmillar Castle 96
  Dundee Street 326
  Exhibition 1886 150, 152
  Elm Row 325
  Fountainbridge 326
  Georgian Society 271
  Gillespie Crescent 122
  Haymarket 326
  Holyrood, Abbey 96
  John Knox's House 99, *99*
  Lamb's House, Leith 139, *139*
  Marchmont and Warrender flats 46
  Museum of Scotland 26
  New Town 364, 376

INDEX

Conservation Committee 32
Old Town 161, 364
Philosophical Society, Queen Street 97
Queensberry House 369
Queen's Park 325
Royal Scottish Museum 29
St Andrew's House 26
St Giles' Cathedral 94
St Mary's Episcopal Cathedral 29
Scottish Parliament 27
Southside 325
Tollcross 326
Western Approach 317
Eilean Donan Castle 45
Elgin town centre 281
Elphinstone Tower, Ormiston 147
Enlightenment 46-7
Esk Valley 323
Floors Castle, Kelso 106
Glasgow 48
   city plan 48
   City of Architecture 1999 57
   Crown Street Regeneration 372
   dunlins 370
   Empire Exhibition 26, 239-40
   European City of Culture 1991 320 365
   1988 327-8
   'Glasgow School' 274
   Great Storm, winter of 1968 26, 318
   Lanark Street 351
   Homes for the Future 271
   Hutcheson E 334
   'Ideal Hut Show' 360
   International Exhibition 1888 152-3
   International Exhibition 1901 150
   population 57
   Architectural Society 113, 118
   Institute of Architects 145
      Sketchbooks 25, 145, 149, 157, 222
   Mackintosh School of Architecture 330
   School of Art 163
   School Board 163
Haddington, East Lothian 256
Hermit's Castle, Achmelvich 377
Hopetoun House, South Queensferry 106
Inverary
   town plan 48
Jacobite Rebellion 16
Kirkcaldy
   Sailors Walk 276, 277
Linlithgow Palace 148
Melrose
   Abbey 104
Muchalls Castle, Kincardineshire 148

New Towns
   Cumbernauld
      Development Corporation, Housing, Seafar 281, 283
   East Kilbride
   Glenrothes 256, 259
   Irvine
Perth 48, 326
'room and kitchen' 319-20, *319*
Roslin Chapel, Midlothian 98
Southern Uplands 33
Thurso
   town plan 48
Scott, A MacCallum 64, 69-70
Scott Brown, Denise 305-6
Scott, Geoffrey 51-2
Scott, Sir George Gilbert 162
   St Mary's Cathedral, Edinburgh 29, *30*
Scott, Sir Giles Gilbert
   Liverpool Anglican Cathedral 162
Scott Morton 156, 162
Scott, Sir Walter 45, 54, 104, 137, 210
Scott and Uthwatt Reports 51-3
Scottish Council of Industry 240
Scottish Constitutional Convention 326
Scottish Covenant Association 242
Scottish Development Agency (SDA) 289
Scottish Development Department (SDD) 289
Scottish Enterprise 289
Scottish Georgian Society 280
Scottish Government
   PAN83 334
Scottish Housing Advisory Committee (SHAC) 252
   Sub-committee on Housing Design 254
Scottish Special Housing Association (SSHA) 240
Scottish Professional Football League (SPFL) 376
Scruton, Roger 308
Scully, Vincent 289
Sedláková, Radomira 46 en49, 79-80 en150
Selfridge, Harry Gordon 177
Sellars, James
   Milton Street School, Glasgow 122
   New Club, Glasgow 122
   St Andrews Halls, Glasgow 122
Semper, Gottfried 24, 92-4, 136, 158, 179, 182, 395
   Caribbean Hut 396
Sert, Josef Lluís 258
   Law and Administration Building, Boston University 277
Seton-Watson, RW (Scotus Viator) 57, 76, 86
Shand, P Morton 330
Shankland Cox
   Housing, Hillingdon, London 314
Shaw, Richard Norman 130, 149, 162
Shearer & Annand 5.33

475

Shearer, Donald
    (see also Elder & Cannon) 390
Shearer, James 25, 187, 225-30, 236, 276, 385
    Carnegie Birthplace Memorial, Dunfermline 222, 226
    Carnegie Library Extension, Dunfermline 225-6, 227, 278
    Clackmannan County Plan 228
    Dunfermline Fire Station 227-8, 228
    Fasnakyle Generating Station 230
    Sawston Village College, Cambridgeshire 225
Shearer, Moira 187
Shekhtel, Fyodor 155
Sheppard, Sir Richard 265
Shore, Peter, MP 265
SHS Burridge
    Tigh Beag, Nethybridge, Cairngorm National Park 398
Shulman, Julius 285, 286
Silsbee, Josef 180
Simister Monaghan 342
Simpson, John William, and Edmund Milner Allen
    Kelvingrove Art Gallery and Museum, Glasgow 152-3
Sinclair, Dr Colin 239
Sirén, Johan Sigrid
    Finnish Parliament, Helsinki 75
Siza de Viera, Alvaro 312
Skeffington Report 321
Skirving, Alexander
    Langside Church, Glasgow 122
Šlapeta, Vladimír 82-3
Slavid, Ruth 360
Smirke, Sir Robert 107
Smith, George Gregory 25, 26, 41-2, 54, 328, 390
Smithmeyer & Pelz
    Carnegie Library, Allegheny 226
Smithson, Alison & Peter 259
Smithson, Robert 35
Smoor, France 329
Snøhetta
    King Abdulaziz Centre for World Culture, Dharan, Saudi Arabia 358
Society for the Protection of Ancient Buildings (SPAB) 276
Soleri, Paolo 311
Sonck, Lars 66, 67
    St Michael's Church, Turku 67, 69
    St John's Church, Tampere 69 69
South America 32, 37
Spain
    Civil War 57
Spence, Sir Basil 276
    Housing at Dunbar 258
    Housing at Newhaven, Edinburgh 258
    House and surgery, Ormiston 382
Spence, Sir Basil, Glover & Ferguson
    79-121 Canongate, Edinburgh 281, 281
    Library, University of Edinburgh 277, 278
    Sussex University, Halls of Residence 281
Spuybroek, Lars 360-2
    Son-O-House, Son en Breughel, Netherlands 361-2
    (as NOX) World Trade Centre, New York (unpremiated entry) 361
Stadtkronen 296
Stamp, Gavin 48, 50-1, 125, 164, 175, 177-8, 329
Stark, James 258
Steele, Matt
    Hippodrome Cinema, Bo'ness 58-9, 58, 278
Steiner, Dietmar 141
Stenbäck, Josef 67
Stephen, James
St Anthony of Padua, Kirriemuir 328
    St Peters and St Pauls, Rosyth architectural competition (winner) (unbuilt) 328
Stern, Robert
    Celebration, Florida, USA 317
    Urban villa, Tegeler Hafen 372, 373
Stevenson, John James 162
Stoller, Ezra 285
Strengell, Gustav 75
Strnad, Oskar 212
Stuart, James and Nicholas Revett 114
Sucksdorf, Victor 67
Sudjic, Deyan 33, 56-7, 362
Sullivan, Louis 49, 99, 134, 177, 178-80, 345
    Auditorium Building, Chicago (with Dankmar Adler) 180
    Guaranty Building, Buffalo, New York 180
    Carrie Eliza Getty Tomb, Chicago 179
    Carson, Pirie, Scott (Schlesinger & Mayer), Chicago 180
    National Farmers' Bank, Owatonna, Minnesota 179
    Transportation Museum, Columbian World's Exhibition, Chicago 153, 179
    Wainwright Building, St Louis, Missouri 180, 179
Sultan Abdulhamid II 153
Summers, Andy 379, 380, 382
Summerson, Sir John 214, 216,228, 272
Švácha, Rostislav 81
Sweden 17, 18
Switzerland 17, 18

T

Tait, Gordon 239
Tait, Thomas 25, 213-4, 230-3, 385

(see also Burnet and Tait, Burnet, Tait and Lorne)
Tange Kenzō 43-4, 258, 283
   Kurashiki Town Hall, Japan 277, 284
   National Gymnasia, Tokyo, Japan 284
Tarjanne, Onni
   National Theatre, Helsinki 75
Taut, Bruno
   Berlin housing 382
Tayler, Herbert and Davis Green 247
Taylor, EA 154
Team Ten 259
Telescope, James Webb 34
Tengbom, Ivar 177
   Högalids Church, Stockholm, 211, 297
Terragni, Giuseppe 290
   Casa del Fascio, Como 296
   Danteum 296
Terry, Quinlan 311
Tessenow, Heinrich 294
Thomson, Alexander 21, 22, 24, 48, 50, 51, 100, 109-23, 125-6, 158, 171, 231, 232, 236, 329, 340
   Buck's Head Building, Glasgow 120
   Caledonia Road UP Church, Glasgow (partially destroyed) 329
   Chalmers Memorial Free Church, Glasgow (dem.) 120
   Egyptian Halls, Glasgow 118, *119*
   Gordon Street, Glasgow 121
   Holmwood, Glasgow 120, *121*
   Moray Place, Glasgow 48, 118
   47-49 Oakfield Avenue, Glasgow *115*, 116
   Queen's Park UP Church, Glasgow (destroyed) 125
   St Vincent Street UP Church, Glasgow 125
   South Kensington Competition (unbuilt) 116-7, *117*
Thomson, J Taylor 329
Thomson, Stuart
   House, Hornchurch, Essex 224
Thomson, William (Lord Kelvin) 47
Thonet Brothers 167
Tigerman, Stanley
   Urban villa, Tegeler Hafen, Berlin 372
Tite, Sir William 107
Tobia, Bruno 316
Tolkien, JRR 145
Tonge, John 25, 218-9, 385, 390
Toorop, Jan 163
Town and Country Planning Association
   Oxford Conference 1941 243-5
   Regions 245
   Town and Country Planning Act 1947 255
Towndrow, FE 21, 243-5

Traquair, Phoebe 155, 162
   Murals, St Mary's Choir School, Edinburgh 370
Traquair, Ramsay
   First Church of Christ Scientist, Edinburgh 157
Tubbs, Ralph 247
   Dome of Discovery, Festival of Britain 247-8, 257
Tutankhamun's Tomb, Egypt 231
Tzara, Tristan 192
Twentieth Century Society (C20) 230

U

Ungers, Otto Matthias 259, 328
   Lützowplatz, Berlin 371
Ungless & Latimer 335
United Kingdom
   constituent nations 27-8
University of Edinburgh
   George Square 276
   School of the Built Environment 265
Upton, Anthony 63, 65-6
USA
   Big Sur, California 45
   Civil War 35
   Hollywood 45
   Mexican Border Wall 33
   New York
      Harlem 187
      'New York Five, The' 290
   Yosemite National Park 35, 45
Ushida Findlay
   Lanark Street 371
Utzon, Jørn
   Sydney Opera House (with Ove Arup & Partners) 348

V

van der Rohe, Ludwig Mies 25, 125, 163, 295, 313, 345
   Farnsworth House, Plano, USA 302
   Rhiel House, Potsdam 167
   Tugendhat House, Brno 285
van de Velde, Henri 75
van Dijk, Hans 134
van Doesburg, Theo 188-91, 361
   House, Meudon-Val-Fleury, Paris 188
van Eyck, Aldo 259
van't Hoff, Robert 189
   Henny House, Utrecht 189
   Stepped Column 189
Venturi, Robert 20, 269, 342, 345

Vanna Venturi House, Philadelphia 269, 270
Vergo, Peter 165, 166
Vesely, Dalibor 327
Victoria 106, 108
Victorian Society, The 280
Vidler, Anthony 273, 353, 355-6, 357
Vienna
    Architectural Conference 1992 355-6
    Kunstschau 1909 165
    Wiener Werkstätte 25, 169
von Essen, Werner 73
von Klenze, Leo 115
Voysey, CFA 168
    The Orchard 317

W

Wagner, Otto 49, 79, 83, 165, 167, 177
    Wagnerschule 274
Wales
    constituent nation 27-8
    Offa's Dyke 33
    slate 37
Walker, David M 159, 175, 232-3, 331
Walker, Frank 130, 131, 157, 159, 220
Walker, James Campbell
    Dunfermline Municipal Chambers 122
    Carnegie Library, Dunfermline 122, 225
    Hawick Municipal Chambers 122
Walton, George Henry 49, 154
    Glasgow International Exhibition 1901
        Stand for T & R Annan 154
        Stand for Wylie and Lochhead 154
Wann McLaren
    'Holyrood 2000' charette 335
Ward, Colin 260
Wardrop & Reid
    5 & & Abbot Street, Dunfermline 394
Ware, Ritva 68
Wärndorfer, Fritz 167
Warners, Philip Anne
    Atlanta Building, Amsterdam 233
Watkins, Carleton 35
Watkins, Dudley D 322
Watson, James, Associates 329
Watt, James 140
Watts & Co 162
Webb, Philip 149, 167
    Arisaig House, Beasdale 107
Webb, Sam 318
Weber, Nicholas Fox 194, 196
Webster, Robin 329
Wiener Werkstätte 25, 274
Welch, Adrian 371
Wells, HG 52

Eloi 363
Morlocks 211, 363
Welter, Volker M 36, 172-3
Wemyss, Charles 16-7
Wemyss, Lord 276
Weston, Richard 43, 340
Wheeler & Sproson
    Flat blocks, Dysart 281
    Sailor's Walk, Kirkcaldy 276
Whytock & Reid 156, 162
Wiecherinck, Dries 46
Williams, Sir Owen
    Daily Express Building, Glasgow 224, 278
Wilkinson, Tom 197
Willis, Carol 345, 357
Wilson, Patrick
    Chalmers Buildings, Edinburgh 151
    Pilrig Model Buildings, Edinburgh 151
Wilson, Peter 373, 397-8
    ARCA Magazine 377-8
Wilson, Robert
    Outlook Tower, Edinburgh 172
Wilson Sisters 155
Wittlich, Petr 83
Witzmann, Carl 169
    Kosmak House, Vienna 170
Womersley, Peter 396
    Bernat Klein Studio, Galashiels 377
    Edenside Group Practice, Kelso 281-2, 282, 340
Woods, Lebbeus 356
Wordsworth, William 54
World
    Covid-19 pandemic 22
Worringer, Wilhelm 25, 100, 112, 219, 220
Wren, Sir Christopher
    Royal Observatory, Greenwich 185
Wren Rutherford ASL (subsequently Austin, Smith-Lord)
    Lanark Street, Glasgow 371
Wright, Frank Lloyd 25, 38, 50, 51, 99, 120, 125, 134, 180, 181-3, 204-7, 209, 225, 231, 295, 313, 345, 395
    Block House project, Chandler, Arizona 206
    Dana House, Springfield, Illinois 189
    Ennis-Brown House, Los Angeles, California 205, *205*
    E-Z Polish Factory, Chicago, Illinois 177
    First Jacobs House, Madison, Wisconsin 206, 207
    Freeman House, Los Angeles, California 206
    Gale House, Oak Park, Chicago, Illinois 189
    Hollyhock House, Hollywood, California 182
    Imperial Hotel, Tokyo, Japan 136, 168

La Miniatura, Los Angeles 204
Oak Park Studio, Chicago, Illinois 182
Ocatillo Desert Camp, Chandler, Arizona 205-6
Richard L Jones House, Tulsa, Oklahoma 206
Solomon R Guggenheim Museum, New York 348
Storer House, Los Angeles, California 120
Taliesin II, Scottsdale, Arizona 205
Wasmuth Edition 180
Willey House, Minneapolis, Minnesota 206

WT Architects
The Mill, Southside Steading, Scottish Borders 398

Wylie, Shanks & Underwood
Stow College of Building and Printing, Glasgow 377

Y

Yorke, FRS 215, 259
(see also YRM 259)
Young, William
Glasgow Municipal Chambers 124
Young, Michael 264
Young, Wilmott & Stacey 255, 261, 264

Z

Zasche, Josef 79
Zevi, Bruno 26, 308, 350, 356,
Žižek, Slavoj 26, 32, 41, 42, 65, 356, 388, 390
Zumthor, Peter 38, 57-8, 60, 312-3, 362, 364, 364-5
Therme Vals, Switzerland 382

Luath Press Limited

committed to publishing well written books worth reading

LUATH PRESS takes its name from Robert Burns, whose little collie Luath (*Gael.*, swift or nimble) tripped up Jean Armour at a wedding and gave him the chance to speak to the woman who was to be his wife and the abiding love of his life. Burns called one of the 'Twa Dogs' Luath after Cuchullin's hunting dog in Ossian's *Fingal*. Luath Press was established in 1981 in the heart of Burns country, and is now based a few steps up the road from Burns' first lodgings on Edinburgh's Royal Mile. Luath offers you distinctive writing with a hint of unexpected pleasures.

Most bookshops in the UK, the US, Canada, Australia, New Zealand and parts of Europe, either carry our books in stock or can order them for you. To order direct from us, please send a £sterling cheque, postal order, international money order or your credit card details (number, address of cardholder and expiry date) to us at the address below. Please add post and packing as follows: UK – £1.00 per delivery address; overseas surface mail – £2.50 per delivery address; overseas airmail – £3.50 for the first book to each delivery address, plus £1.00 for each additional book by airmail to the same address. If your order is a gift, we will happily enclose your card or message at no extra charge.

Luath Press Limited
543/2 Castlehill
The Royal Mile
Edinburgh EH1 2ND
Scotland
Telephone: 0131 225 4326 (24 hours)
Fax: 0131 225 4324
email: sales@luath.co.uk
Website: www.luath.co.uk